EXIL-STUDIEN
EINE INTERDISZIPLINÄRE BUCHREIHE
EXILE STUDIES
AN INTERDISCIPLINARY SERIES

BAND/VOL. 7

Edited by
ALEXANDER STEPHAN

PETER LANG
Oxford • Bern • Berlin • Bruxelles • Frankfurt am Main • New York • Wien

Tibor Frank

Double Exile

Migrations of Jewish-Hungarian Professionals through Germany to the United States, 1919–1945

PETER LANG
Oxford · Bern · Berlin · Bruxelles · Frankfurt am Main · New York · Wien

Bibliographic information published by Die Deutsche Bibliothek
Die Deutsche Bibliothek lists this publication in the Deutsche Nationalbibliografie;
detailed bibliographic data is available on the Internet
at ‹http://dnb.ddb.de›.

A catalogue record for this book is available from The British Library.

Library of Congress Cataloging-in-Publication Data:

Frank, Tibor.
Double exile : migrations of Jewish-Hungarian professionals through
Germany to the United States, 1919-1945 / Tibor Frank.
p. cm. -- (Exile studies ; 7)
Includes bibliographical references and index.
ISBN 978-3-03911-331-6 (alk. paper)
1. Refugees, Jewish--United States--Social conditions--20th century.
2. Jews, Hungarian--United States--Social conditions--20th century. 3.
Professional employees--United States--Social conditions--20th century.
4. Refugees, Jewish--Germany--Social conditions--20th century. 5.
Jews, Hungarian--Germany--Social conditions--20th century. 6.
Professional employees--Germany--Social conditions--20th century. 7.
Jews--Hungary--Social conditions--20th century. 8. Professional
employees--Hungary--Social conditions--20th century. 9. Jews,
Hungarian--Germany--Migrations. 10. Jews--Hungary--Migrations. I.
Title.
E184.36.S65F736 2009
305.892'4073--dc22
                                            2009002738

ISSN 1072-0626
ISBN 978-3-03911-331-6

© Peter Lang AG, European Academic Publishers, Bern 2009
Hochfeldstrasse 32, Postfach 746, CH-3000 Bern 9, Switzerland
info@peterlang.com, www.peterlang.com, www.peterlang.net

All rights reserved.
All parts of this publication are protected by copyright.
Any utilisation outside the strict limits of the copyright law, without
the permission of the publisher, is forbidden and liable to prosecution.
This applies in particular to reproductions, translations, microfilming,
and storage and processing in electronic retrieval systems.

Printed in Germany

Contents

List of Illustrations	7
Acknowledgments	9
Preface	13
I The Social Construction of Hungarian Genius	21
1. The Secret of Survival: An Introduction	21
2. The Chemistry of Fin-de-Siècle Budapest	33
3. Schooling	55
II The Hungarian Trauma, 1918–1920	79
1. Watershed 1919: Social Tension and Intellectual Exodus	79
2. Leaving Hungary	98
3. The Escape of Hungarian Modernism	104
III Berlin Junction	121
1. Hungary and the German Cultural Tradition	121
2. The Human Geography of Interwar Migrations	129
3. From Budapest to Berlin	131
4. The *Amerikanisierung* of Berlin	142
5. 'The Babel of the World'	148
6. Temptations and Pressures	151
7. Other Options in Europe	159
IV Hungary and Selective Immigration to the U.S.	167
1. From Quota Laws to Private Bills	167
2. New York: City of Immigrants	204

V	"Incipit Hitler:" Double Expulsion, Double Trauma	243
1.	Ever Ready to Go: The Multiple Exiles of Leo Szilard	243
2.	The Copernican Turn of Michael Polanyi	264
3.	Networking, Cohorting, Bonding: American Patterns	270
4.	Rescue Operations: Institutional	278

VI	Problem Solving and the U.S. War Effort	351
1.	The Heuristic Tradition: George Pólya	351
2.	Heuristics Applied: Theodore von Kármán	367
3.	Faith in Progress: John von Neumann	382
4.	The Manhattan Project and Leo Szilard	401

VII Conclusion 431

Appendix
Select List of Notable Hungarian-American Émigrés, 1919–1945 439

Bibliography 455

Index 485

List of Illustrations

The author is grateful to the Photographic Collection of the Hungarian National Museum (HNM) and school, as well as private collections in Budapest for permission to reproduce photos in their custody.

Figure 1	Budapest, 1930s (a) (HNM)	35
Figure 2	Budapest, 1930s (b) (HNM)	37
Figure 3	*Mintagimnázium* [Model High School], Budapest (Archive of the ELTE Trefort Ágoston Practice School)	61
Figure 4	Physics classroom, *Mintagimnázium*, Budapest (Archive of the ELTE Trefort Ágoston Practice School)	62
Figure 5	Design of the Lutheran *Gimnázium* [High School] in the *Fasor* [Esplanade] 1905 (School History Collection, Lutheran *Gimnázium* in the *Fasor*, Budapest)	65
Figure 6	Nobel Laureate Eugene Wigner in his Princeton study with a picture of László Rátz on the wall (School History Collection, Lutheran *Gimnázium* in the *Fasor*, Budapest)	67
Figure 7	Graduating Jewish Students of the Lutheran *Gimnázium* in the *Fasor*, 1933 (School History Collection, Lutheran *Gimnázium* in the *Fasor*, Budapest)	120
Figure 8	Berlin, *Unter den Linden*, 1920s (HNM)	128

Figure 9	Paul Abraham, composer, 1950s (HNM)	139
Figure 10	Fritz Reiner, conductor, 1920s (HNM)	144
Figure 11	New York, 1933 (Photo John Albók) (HNM—with the kind permission of Ms. Ilona Albók Vitarius)	206
Figure 12	Béla Bartók, composer, 1938 (HNM)	209
Figure 13	Peter Flesch, research dermatologist, on *Medical Science*, 1958	210
Figure 14	Demonstration against the Horthy Regime, New York, 1919 (HNM)	229
Figure 15	Inauguration of the Kossuth Memorial, New York, 1928 (HNM)	233
Figure 16	Jolán Gross-Bettelheim, Slum (Hungarian *Látványtár* Art Foundation and Collection, Budapest)	235
Figure 17	Ferenc Molnár, playwright, 1925 (HNM) (Custody of Ferenc Molnár's family, with the kind permission of Mr. Ádám Horváth)	237
Figure 18	Theodore von Kármán, aerospace scientist, on U.S. and Hungarian stamps, 1992	368
Figure 19	John von Neumann, mathematician, on Hungarian stamp (1992)	400
Figure 20	Leo Szilard, nuclear scientist, 1960s (HNM)	410
Figure 21	Edward Teller visiting the Lutheran *Gimnázium*, 1991 (School History Collection, Lutheran *Gimnázium* in the *Fasor*, Budapest)	413
Figure 22	Emil Lengyel, *America's Role in World Affairs* (Hungarian edition, 1947)	446
Figure 23	Eva Zeisel, designer, 2000s (on the cover of Lucie Young's biography, 2003)	452

Acknowledgments

Research for this book was done in a wide variety of archives and libraries, mainly in the United States. My scattered material was found mainly in the following collections, where archivists and librarians gave me tremendous help through my many years of preparation: The American Philosophical Society Library, Philadelphia, PA; California Institute of Technology, Robert A. Millikan Memorial Library, Institute Archives, Pasadena, CA; Cecil H. Green Library and University Archives, Stanford University Libraries, Stanford, CA; Columbia University Libraries [Avery Library, Butler Library, Rare Book and Manuscript Library, The Bakhmeteff Archive of Russian and East European History and Culture, Oral History Collection], New York, NY; The Hoover Institution on War, Revolution and Peace, Library and Archives, Stanford University, Stanford, CA; The Harvard University Library [The Houghton Library, The Widener Library, Harvard Theatre Collection], Cambridge, MA; The Joseph Regenstein Library, Department of Special Collections, The University of Chicago Library, Chicago, IL; The Library of Congress [Rare Book and Special Collections, The Law Library, The Congressional Research Services], Washington, DC; The Margaret Herrick Library of the Academy of Motion Picture Arts and Sciences and Academy Foundation, Beverly Hills, CA; Mugar Memorial Library, Boston University, Boston, MA; National Archives and Records Administration, Washington, DC; The New York Public Library, Central Research Library, Rare Books and Manuscripts Collection, New York, NY; The Pierpont Morgan Library, New York, NY; The Rockefeller Archive Center, Sleepy Hallow, NY; UCLA Film and Television Archive, Los Angeles, CA; University of California, Berkeley, Main Library, Berkeley, CA; University of California, Los Angeles (UCLA), University Research Library, Los Angeles, CA; University of California, San Diego Central University Library, Mandeville Department of Special Collections, La Jolla, CA;

University of California, Santa Barbara Library and Special Collections, Santa Barbara, CA; University of Pennsylvania, University Archives, Philadelphia, PA; The Woodrow Wilson International Center for Scholars, Washington, DC; Yale School of Music, Oral History Collection; New Haven, CT; Haus-, Hof- und Staatsarchiv, Wien, Austria; Archiv der Max-Planck-Gesellschaft, Berlin-Dahlem, Germany; Politisches Archiv des Auswärtigen Amtes, Berlin, Germany; Geheimes Staatsarchiv Preußischer Kulturbesitz, Berlin-Dahlem; Landesarchiv Berlin; Universitätsarchiv der Humboldt-Universität zu Berlin; Universitätsarchiv der Universität der Künste, Berlin; Magyar Országos Levéltár [Hungarian National Archives], Budapest; Magyar Tudományos Akadémia Könyvtára [Library of the Hungarian Academy of Sciences], Budapest; Országos Széchényi Könyvtár [National Széchényi Library], Budapest; Petőfi Irodalmi Múzeum [Petőfi Museum of Literature], Budapest.

The book is based also on personal information that came down to me through my grandmother, Marianne Flesch, and her friends such as Mrs. Frederick Antal née Dr. Ilona Waldbauer, Mrs. Árpád Dános, Dr. Károly Goldziher, Dr. Endre Makkai, Professor Antal Molnár, Mrs. Lajos Szőllősy, who knew most of the people presented and discussed here. My parents' companionship with Imre Csécsy and his wife as well as my own early friendship with the poet Ákos Dutka was of considerable help also.

Several agencies and institutions supported my work with grants and scholarships. I am indebted to the following for their support: Institute for Hungarian Studies, Budapest; Fulbright Scholarship, Council for International Exchange of Scholars [CIES], Washington, DC; University of California, Santa Barbara and particularly its Department of History and the Interdisciplinary Humanities Center; Santa Barbara, CA; Woodrow Wilson International Center for Scholars, Washington, DC; American Philosophical Society, Philadelphia, PA; Rockefeller Foundation, Bellagio, Italy; The Salzburg Seminar in American Studies, Salzburg, Austria; Pro Renovanda Cultura Hungariae; Budapest; The Soros Foundation/Hungary, Budapest; Hungarian Ministry of Culture and Education; Kellner Foundation, New York, NY; *Humboldt Forschungspreis* (Research Award of the Alexander von Humboldt-Stiftung), Bonn, Germany; Max-

Acknowledgments

Planck-Institut für Wissenschaftsgeschichte, Berlin-Dahlem; as well as the John Templeton Foundation and Princeton University.

The author also wishes to express his gratitude to the following individuals for all the scholarly advice, practical help, or technical assistance provided: Professor Gerald L. Alexanderson (University of Santa Clara, Santa Clara, CA), Professor Bernard Bailyn (Harvard University, Cambridge, MA), +Professor George Barany (University of Denver, Denver, CO), Professor Frank Baron (University of Kansas and Max Kade Center for German-American Studies), +Anne Bodenheimer (Fulbright Program, Los Angeles, CA), Sylvia Y. Curtis (UCSB Library, Santa Barbara, CA), Susan Forbes-Martin (Committee on Immigration Reform, Washington, DC), Randi Glick (UCSB Interdisciplinary Humanities Center, Santa Barbara, CA), Judith R. Goodstein (California Institute of Technology, Pasadena, CA), Professor Paul Hernadi (UCSB Interdisciplinary Humanities Center, Santa Barbara, CA), Paula Hurwitz (California Institute of Technology, Pasadena, CA), Gabor Kalman (Los Angeles, CA), Dr. Andrew C. Klay (Washington, DC), Dr. Erwin Levold (Rockefeller Archive Center, Sleepy Hollow, NY), Professor Albert S. Lindemann (UCSB, Santa Barbara, CA), Professor Barbara Lindemann (SBCC, Santa Barbara, CA), Georgene B. Lovecky (Fulbright Program, Washington, DC), Professor John Moore (UCSB, Santa Barbara, CA—Eötvös Loránd University, Department of American Studies), Richard Popp (Joseph Regenstein Library, University of Chicago, Chicago, IL), Dr. Andrew Recsei (Santa Barbara, CA), Robert Schrott (Congressional Research Service, Library of Congress, Washington, DC), +Andrew Sekey (UCSB, Santa Barbara, CA), +Professor Wilbur Shepperson (University of Nevada, Reno), Professor Neil Smelser (UC Berkeley, Berkeley, CA), Professor John M. Spalek (University at Albany, SUNY), Mr. and Mrs. Marcel Stein (New York, NY), +Professor Peter F. Sugar (University of Washington, Seattle, WA), Barbara Thomas (Washington, DC), Gary Venzente (Joseph Regenstein Library, University of Chicago, Chicago, IL), Professor Harriet A. Zuckerman (Columbia University, New York, NY); Gianna Celli (Rockefeller Center, Bellagio, Italy), Dr. Marion Kazemi (Archiv der Max-Planck-Gesellschaft, Berlin-Dahlem, Germany), Professor Berndt Ostendorf (Universität München),

Rüdiger vom Bruch (Humboldt Universität, Berlin), Professor Jürgen Renn (MPIWG, Berlin-Dahlem), Pasquale Pesce (Rockefeller Center, Bellagio); +Professor Gyula Juhász (Országos Széchényi Könyvtár, Budapest), +János Kerekes (Budapest), Gábor Palló (MTA Filozófiai Intézet, Budapest).

I am especially grateful to Professors Thomas Bender (New York University, New York, NY), Enikő Bollobás (Eötvös Loránd University, Budapest), István Deák (Columbia University, New York, NY), Nándor Dreisziger (Royal Military College of Canada, Kingston, Ontario, Canada), István Hargittai (Budapest University of Technology and Economics, Budapest), Dieter Hoffmann (MPIWG—Humboldt Universität, Berlin), Katherine Newman (Princeton University, Princeton, NJ), Werner Sollors (Harvard University, Cambridge, MA), Roger H. Stuewer (University of Minnesota, Minneapolis, MN), as well as Vera Bánki (Budapest), Dr. Mark Saul (John Templeton Foundation, West Conshohocken, PA), and my wife Zsuzsa F. Várkonyi for reading and commenting on the various drafts of my manuscript, or parts of it. Their invaluable support largely contributed to making my text more coherent and enabled me to express my thoughts more clearly and precisely. My book benefited from their comments and I am most grateful for their time and advice. I am particularly indebted to Ms Patricia F. Howell (Leucadia, CA) for her unfailing efforts to improve the language of this book.

Preface

Intellectual fermentation in Hungary, particularly in fin-de-siècle Budapest, brought about, and was created by, a uniquely gifted generation. Changes in the structure and organization of Hungarian society, along with the distinguishing features of Hungarian assimilation, helped to nurture a typically Hungarian, and more specifically Budapest, talent. These patterns of assimilation in pre-World War I Austria-Hungary and Hungary, as well as in the United States, share a number of remarkable similarities.

This book discusses many impulses influencing a generation of Hungarian emigrants, mostly Jewish, presenting them by way of *prosopography*, a vision of a group rather than just a series of personal biographies. Several of these émigré Hungarians were not Jewish, but the overall nature of emigration from Hungary in the interwar period was Jewish. In an effort to identify the conditions of "Hungarian genius," one may claim the following propositions.

By the late 19th century, feudal privilege was on the decline in Hungary, with hereditary prerogatives challenged, and occupational status gradually evolving as a source of prestige. This was a particularly welcome opportunity for the transformation of a variety of marginal ethnic, social, and religious groups that had never had access to hereditary privilege; and this social change encouraged the infusion of Jews into the world of learning–in exchange, as it were, for their growing willingness to assimilate into the Hungarian nation. The fact that the state wished to increase the number of people self-identified as *Magyars* in this multiethnic country opened doors that were closed elsewhere, at least for a time. Previously excluded groups would flood into these professional domains and make a mark for themselves.

The rapidly developing economy of the Austro-Hungarian Monarchy fostered a premium on the development of technology, mathematics, medicine, science, and finance, whereas, conservative control was often exercised over the humanities and the arts, now viewed as more political.

The newly established (1873) capital city of Budapest played an outstanding role in generating this new, modern culture and spreading an innovative spirit in and out of the country. Budapest developed as a center of culture and learning, and by the beginning of the 20th century, a special social and intellectual chemistry there resulted in unusually creative and productive thinking, with mathematics and music as the best examples of this unique constellation of events I would call "Budapest chemistry."

Because of the traditionally elitist nature of Hungarian (and Central European) education, universities could absorb only a fragment of the available research talent, and some of this talent found its place teaching in high schools. Moreover, as the very definition of the teaching occupation included original research, gifted students of the best schools encountered brilliant researchers at a much earlier age than in the U.S. or, sometimes, even in Western Europe.

Intellectual, artistic, and musical talent acquired high prestige. A cultural premium on the idea of competitive knowledge poured into education. Practices like student competitions and specialized journals for high school students, designed to surface outstanding talent, led to a celebration of gifted students, providing a different kind of prestige than occupational status alone. A cultural emphasis on modernism paved the way to an increasing internationalization, mainly in the best schools of fin-de-siècle Budapest, which prized experimentation, inductive reasoning, pattern-breaking innovation, less formal relations between teacher and student, and personalized education.

Culture transfer, mostly from Germany, helped shape Hungarian arts and sciences at the highest level of European education. The influence of the German school system, of German art, music, and science, directly benefited Hungary and had a major impact on teaching, learning, and research. Much of the result was once again exported by eminent exiles—from Hungary back to Germany, and then from Germany to the United States.

The period of 1918–20 marked the end of the Austro-Hungarian Monarchy and historical Hungary within it, creating a vastly different period in national history, and with some of the best minds, most of them Jewish-Hungarian mathematicians, scientists, and musicians, compelled to leave the country. Despite profoundly different political conditions that followed, some of the great traditions of education, particularly science and mathematics education, have survived until today.

The social and legal interplay of Jewish–Gentile relations—such as religious conversion, mixed marriages, forced and voluntary *Magyarization* and ennoblement—became prevalent by World War I. Post-World War I social dynamics coalesced to condition a significant intellectual and professional emigration from Hungary. It was in this post-War social upheaval, and particularly in the Hungarian "Soviet revolution" of 1919, that professional and intellectual emigration became rooted; moreover, intellectual emigration came to be seen as one possible solution to the problems of Hungary's upwardly mobile and suddenly overgrown Jewish middle and, particularly, upper-middle classes, the Jewish-Hungarian economic and social élite.

Most persons leaving Hungary in 1919 and the early 1920s were directly involved in running one of the revolutions of 1918–19, particularly the Bolshevik-type Republic of Councils (*Tanácsköztársaság*) of 1919, and/or were, as a consequence, threatened by the ensuing anti-Semitism unleashed in the wake of that disastrous political and social experiment. It is sadly ironic that most Hungarian Jews who felt endangered after 1919 were in fact more Hungarian than Jewish, representing mostly an assimilated, Magyarized, typically non-religious middle or upper-middle class which had profoundly contributed to the socio-economic development and, indeed, the modernization of Hungary. Their exodus was a tremendous loss for the country just as it became a welcome gain for the other countries they chose to settle in.

For the intellectually gifted Hungarians, often of Jewish origin, who started their migration toward other European countries and the United States after the political changes of 1918–20, the typical choice was to move to one of the German-speaking countries. Austria and Germany were most commonly chosen, but many went to Czechoslovakia or even

Switzerland, which boasted of prestigious German universities. Berlin was certainly not the only, though a typical destination, and a powerful symbol of interwar migration centers. After what often proved to be the first step in a chain- or step-migration, most Hungarian émigrés found they had to leave those countries upon the rise of Hitler as Chancellor of Germany and continue on their way, in most cases, to the United States. This was not the only pattern, though this double migration emerged as the most typical one.

Professional migration was a European phenomenon after World War I, not restricted to Hungary alone. The War was followed by immense social convulsions that drove astonishing numbers of people into all directions. Russian and Ukrainian refugees escaped Bolshevism; Poles were relocated into reemerging Poland; Hungarians escaped from newly established (or aggrandized) Czechoslovakia, Romania, and Yugoslavia and tried to find some place in a new Hungary.[1] Outward movements from Hungary in the 1920s were part of this emerging general pattern, and cannot be defined as emigrations proper. Many people went on substantial and extended study tours of varied length—just as others did before World War I. Contrary to general belief, migrations were not limited to Jews suffering from the political and educational consequences of the counterrevolutionary White Terror in Hungary, a reaction to both revolutions of 1918–19. Yet Jewish migrations were a definitive pattern of the 1920s, when the "Numerus Clausus" law of XXV:1920 excluded many of them from college.

A significant, though smaller, group of non-Jews also left Hungary at the same time. Motivated by anti-liberal politics, poverty, or curiosity, gentiles with dramatically mixed convictions hit the road and tried their luck in Paris, Berlin, or Hollywood.

In an effort to increase their chances of getting into the United States, many Hungarians left the successor states of the former Austro-Hungarian Monarchy self-identified as "Romanians," "Czechoslovaks," or "Yugoslavs"

---

[1] G. Barraclough (ed.), *The Times Atlas of World History* (Maplewood NJ: Hammond, rev. ed. 1984, repr.1988), 265.

as U.S. Quota Laws enabled very few Hungarians to enter the United States. Nevertheless, most migrants were directed to centers in Europe, and most of all, to Germany. German centers of culture, education, and research represented the pre-eminent opportunity for young Hungarians searching for patterns and norms of modernization.

Research on the history of intellectual migrations from Europe, a broad and complex international field, was based initially on eye-witness accounts which served as primary sources, rather than scholarly literature.[2] Even Laura Fermi's classic study on *Illustrious Immigrants*,[3] focusing on the intellectual migration from Europe between 1930 and 1941, falls into that category. Research proper brought its first results in the late 1960s and early 1970s. Soon after Fermi's pioneering venture, Donald Fleming and Bernard Bailyn significantly extended the period of investigation through a series of related articles in their *The Intellectual Migration—Europe and America, 1930–1960*.[4] From the beginning, it was German-Jewish emigration that was best researched, a pattern that was partly reinforced by H. Stuart Hughes' *The Sea Change—The Migration of Social Thought, 1930–1965*, an excellent survey of the movement of European thinkers and thinking before and after World War II.[5] By the end of the 1970s, the first guide to the archival sources relating to German-American emigration during the Third Reich was compiled.[6] The 1980s

---

[2] Norman Bentwich, *The Refugees from Germany, April 1933 to December 1935* (Allen and Unwin, 1936); Norman Bentwich, *The Rescue and Achievement of Refugee Scholars: The Story of Displaced Scholars and Scientists 1933–1952* (The Hague: Martinus Nijhoff, 1953).

[3] Laura Fermi, *Illustrious Immigrants. The Intellectual Migration from Europe 1930–41* (Chicago—London: University of Chicago Press, 1968).

[4] Donald Fleming, Bernard Baylin (eds.), *The Intellectual Migration. Europe and America, 1930–1960* (Cambridge, MA: The Belknap Press of Harvard University Press, 1969).

[5] H. Stuart Hughes, *The Sea Change. The Migration of Social Thought, 1930–1965* (New York: McGraw-Hill, 1975).

[6] John M. Spalek, *Guide to the Archival Materials of the German-speaking Emigration to the United States after 1933* (Charlottesville: University Press of Virginia, 1978), xxv, 1133 p.

produced the much-needed biographical encyclopedia, which paved the way for further fact-based, quantitative research.[7] Soon the results of this research became available in a variety of German, English, and French publications focusing on German, German-Jewish, and other Central European emigration in the Nazi era.[8] The primary foci of the research of the 1980s were the émigré scientists and artists fleeing Hitler, with a growing interest in U.S. immigration policies during the Nazi persecution of the Jews of Europe.[9]

In contemporary statistics and journalism, most refugees from Germany were hurriedly lumped together as "Germans" or "German-Jews" without their actual birthplace, land of origin, mother tongue or national background being considered as they were forced to leave Germany. This unfortunate tradition has tended to survive in the otherwise rich and impressive historical literature on the subject. The great and unsolved problem for further research on refugees from Hitler's Germany remained how to distinguish the non-German, including the Hungarian, elements: people, problems, and cases in this complex area. This is important not only for Hungarian research but may result in a more realistic assessment of what we should, and what we should not, consider "German science" or "German scholarship" in the interwar period.

Laura Fermi was probably the first to notice the significant difference between German refugee scientists and Hungarians forced to leave

---

7   H. A. Strauss, W. Röder (eds.), *International Biographical Dictionary of Central European Emigrés 1933–1945* (München-New York-London-Paris: K.G. Saur, 1983), Vols. I–II/1–2+III, xciv, 1316 p.

8   P. Kröner (ed.), *Vor fünfzig Jahren. Die Emigration deutschsprachiger Wissenschaftler 1933–1939* (Münster: Gesellschaft für Wissenschaftsgeschichte, 1983); J. C. Jackman, C. M. Borden (eds.), *The Muses Flee Hitler. Cultural Transfer and Adaptation 1930–1945* (Washington, DC: Smithsonian, 1983); R.E. Rider, "Alarm and Opportunity: Emigration of Mathematicians and Physicists to Britain and the United States, 1933–1945," *Historical Studies in the Physical Sciences*, 15, Part I (1984), 107–176; J.-M. Palmier, *Weimar en Exil. Le destin de l'émigration intellectuelle allemande antinazie en Europe et aux Etats-Unis* (Paris: Payot, 1987), Tomes 1–2, 533, 486 p.

9   Richard Breitman and Alan M. Kraut, *American Refugee Policy and European Jewry, 1933–1945* (Bloomington and Indianapolis: Indiana University Press, 1987).

Germany. Her *Illustrious Immigrants* included a few pages on what she termed the "Hungarian mystery," referring to the unprecedented number of especially talented Hungarians in the interwar period.[10] The systematic, predominantly biographical treatment of the subject was begun by Lee Congdon in his eminent *Exile and Social Thought*, which surveyed some of the most brilliant careers of Hungarians in Austria and Germany between 1919 and 1933.[11] A contribution on the achievement of the great Hungarian-born scientists of this century, mostly biographical in nature, came from fellow-physicist George Marx.[12] In a recent book, István Hargittai assessed the achievement of five of the most notable Hungarian-born scientists who contributed to the U.S. war effort.[13]

Throughout the book I endeavoured to use primarily the material of my own, extensive archival research done in over 40 U.S. archives, and a dozen Hungarian, German, and Austrian collections. My biographical sketches are also based on the personal papers of my heroes, more detailed where there is an abundance of material, sketchy where I found little or nothing in terms of archival sources. My approach is social historical rather than biographical: wherever I present particular people I do it to show what they brought from Hungary to Germany and then on to the New World, or directly from Budapest to the U.S. I tried to integrate my own findings, often published first in articles over the years, with the ever growing literature on the subject, listed in my bibliography.

10　Laura Fermi, *op. cit.*, 53–59.
11　Lee Congdon, *Exile and Social Thought. Hungarian Intellectuals in Germany and Austria 1919–1933* (Princeton N.J.: Princeton University Press, 1991).
12　George Marx, *The Voice of the Martians*, 2nd ed. (Budapest: Akadémiai Kiadó, 1997).
13　István Hargittai, *The Martians of Science: Five Physicists Who Changed the Twentieth Century* (New York: Oxford University Press, 2006).

I The Social Construction of Hungarian Genius

1 The Secret of Survival: An Introduction

Problem Solving in Hungarian History

For all the centuries of political failure, Hungarians at the individual level have evidently thrived, developing an art of survival and a readiness to restart their lives against all odds. They have endured in those "Lands Between," to use the telling phrase of the British historian Alan Palmer,[1] at the meeting point of North with South and West with East, at the confluence of some of the largest and most powerful empires in world history. The Roman, Ottoman, Russian, Holy Roman, Habsburg, Napoleonic French, Nazi German, and Soviet empires all stretched as far as Hungary and at some time laid claim to part or all of her territory, treating it as war booty, a border area, a *cordon sanitaire,* or a defensive line.

The Hungarians were never able to ward off such powerful empires for long, yet they were always able to perpetuate themselves as an indigenous culture and as a nation, even if they were at times merely a virtual entity. Located in a region that has an almost in-built geopolitical menace as a honey-pot for hungry neighbors, Hungary and the Hungarians have proved to be predestined losers, perhaps, yet shrewd survivors all the same.

As a result, Hungarians typically tend to suppose that their country's story is one of failure. They were beaten by many enemies, failed in repeated revolutions and wars of independence, and were on the losing side in both World Wars. The country was overrun by Mongols in the 13th

---

[1] Alan Palmer, *The Lands Between: A History of East-Central Europe since the Congress of Vienna* (New York: Macmillan, 1970).

century, by Ottoman Turks in the 16th, by Germans and Soviet Russians in the 20th, and in between, Hungary spent nearly half its entire history under foreign domination as part of the Habsburg Empire. When it finally regained sovereignty in 1920, after almost 400 years, it was at the price of losing over two-thirds of its historical territory and some three and a half million kinsmen, roughly one third of the total number of ethnic *Magyars* in the region. Many national political leaders died in exile, including Prince Ferenc II Rákóczi, Governor-President Lajos Kossuth, President Count Mihály Károlyi, Regent Admiral Miklós Horthy, and the Communist dictators Béla Kun and Mátyás Rákosi. A distressingly long list of the country's best minds were also "lost" to the (mostly Western) world, including many of the fourteen Nobel laureates of (sometimes arguably) Hungarian origin—among them, Georg von Békésy,[2] János Harsányi, George de Hevesy, György Oláh, Albert Szent-Györgyi, and Eugene Wigner—as well as composers Franz Liszt, Béla Bartók, and Ernő (Ernst von) Dohnányi; Albert Szirmai, Paul Abraham; conductors Fritz Reiner, George Szell, Eugene Ormandy, Sir Georg Solti, Antal Doráti, Ferenc Fricsay, István Kertész, Eugen Szenkár, Georges Sebastian; internationally acclaimed violinists from the school of Jenő Hubay such as Joseph Szigeti, Stefi Geyer, Ferenc (Franz von) Vecsey, Emil Telmányi, Ede Zathureczky, and Yelly d'Aranyi; scientists Leo Szilard, Edward Teller, Theodore von Kármán, Michael Polanyi; mathematicians John von Neumann, George Pólya, John Kemény; film directors and producers Sir Alexander Korda, Michael Curtiz, and Joe Pasternak;[3] photographers Brassaï (Gyula Halász), Robert Capa, and André Kertész; artists/designers Laszlo Moholy-Nagy and Marcel Breuer; social scientists and scholars such as Karl Mannheim, Charles de Tolnay, Frederic Antal, Otto Gombosi, Arthur Koestler, and Karl Polanyi, and a host of others. The Communists of them, such as pioneering film-theoretician Béla Balázs *(Der sichtbare Mensch,* 1924) and the philosopher Georg Lukács went to the Soviet Union, and returned to Hungary after World War II. Among

---

[2] The spelling of Hungarian names follows contemporary usage in Hungary and, later, abroad.

[3] Film director George Cukor was born in the U.S.

the notable returnees to Budapest there were also others such as Ernő Kállai and, much later, Arnold Hauser. Avant-garde artists who made their reputation in Germany, such as Sándor Bortnyik, Lajos Kassák, Hugo Scheiber, and Béla Kádár returned to their native Hungary before Hitler took over, many in the 1920s.[4] Only a few visual artists stayed outside the country and left later for the United States.

Yet is it right to regard Hungary's history as one of abysmal failure only? The outcome is a national mentality that is split between a sense of inferiority and an exaggerated sense of self-worth; insecurity and self-pity on the one hand, overconfidence and an inflated national ego on the other—both extremes equally justified and unsound in their hyperbole.

The Hungarian background, schooling, and social connections largely contributed to the foreign successes of these easily assimilating achievers. Émigré Hungarians transplanted a set of values and patterns of thinking that were viewed as unique outside Hungary, and particularly in the United States—in Hungary, however, those were shared by a broad social layer, the emerging Hungarian middle class. With fascination, foreign contemporaries tried to understand the hidden dimensions of what they labelled the "Hungarian mystery."[5] This book offers possible social, political, psychological, educational, and economic explanations for some of the special distinguishing features of the Hungarian, in fact often Jewish-Hungarian, mind, in and out of Hungary.

The early years of the 20th century conditioned social and cultural change, while the immediate post-World War I scene provoked emigration

---

[4] S. A. Mansbach, "Revolutionary Engagements: The Hungarian Avant-Garde," in: S. A. Mansbach, ed., *Standing in the Tempest. Painters of the Hungarian Avant-Garde, 1908–1930* (Santa Barbara, CA: Santa Barbara Museum of Art—Cambridge, MA—London: MIT Press, 1991), pp. 74–83, 90–91, see esp. the impressive list of repatriating artists and critics on p. 75.

[5] Laura Fermi, *Illustrious Immigrants. The Intellectual Migration from Europe 1930–41* (Chicago—London: The University of Chicago Press, 1968), pp. 53–59; Stefan L. Wolff, "Das ungarische Phänomen—ein Fallbeispiel zur Emigrationsforschung," *Deutsches Museum Wissenschaftliches Jahrbuch 1991* (München: Deutsches Museum, 1992), pp. 228–245.

from Hungary. It is from this period of upheaval, and particularly from the protracted turning point of 1918–1920, including the territorially and socially disastrous Treaty of Trianon (1920) that social and political change in Hungary can be best understood and reinterpreted, particularly in terms of the problems of Hungary's middle class, which for many years was more German and Jewish than Hungarian.

Their leaving Hungary should not be viewed exclusively in terms of a final *emigration* but in most cases either as a temporary effort or a link in a process of step migration. At this point, staying out of Hungary permanently was rarely considered. To understand the nature of this step migration, Berlin (and other German cities) must be recognized as the single most important point(s) of transfer. Germany was already a favorite of Hungarian intellectuals well before World War I. It was logical, prior to the takeover of Adolf Hitler, that Berlin functioned as a Hungarian cultural center in exile. The German capital also gave many Hungarians a foretaste of America and modernism. The Americanization of Berlin is viewed as an important dimension of trans-Atlantic migrations and knowledge transfer, for the German period that often preceded emigration to America acted as a bridge between the two cultures.

Irrespective of their nationality, the rise of Hitler and the Nazi party forced all leftist, liberal, and Jewish intellectuals to leave Berlin and, subsequently, most of Europe. Thoroughly Germanized by that point, most Hungarians left for the U.S. as part of the huge German exile group. These German-Hungarian refugees were highly visible and superbly qualified; they were generally to be well received in the United States serving important U.S. interests in technological development, modernization, and later, in the war effort. The relatively easy ("non-quota") admission of this group was in marked contrast to the restrictionist spirit of the Quota Laws, the National Origins provisions, as well as the social psychological impact of the great depression, which heightened U.S. xenophobia and anti-Semitism. By admitting the useful few, United States immigration policies adhered to the principle and practice of the Quota Laws, but also went a step further in the selection process, preferring mental over physical abilities.

Central European immigrants in the interwar period (1918–1939) transplanted some essential elements of modernism and problem-solving, as well as the general values of classical European heritage. The American success of Hungarian immigrants of this period may partly be attributed to the specific intellectual qualities they brought from Budapest. Driven away on "racial" grounds, this impressive group of émigré intellectuals from post-Versailles Germany and, also, from post-Trianon Hungary were given a moderately warm welcome once they demonstrably contributed to the educational and cultural standards of their host country.

It is important to note that the earlier experience of this group with assimilation in Hungary seems to have contributed to the success of their Americanization. Several émigré professionals and their families underwent repeated assimilation in quick succession; they often became double exiles, resulting in double or multiple identities and loyalties.

The Lands Between: The Setting

International political events in the 1860s forced Austria to regroup and abandon the monolithic structure of the Habsburg Empire, firmly centered on Vienna, for the Austro-Hungarian ("Dual") Monarchy. The political Compromise or Settlement *(Ausgleich)* negotiated by Austria and Hungary in 1867 secured the political supremacy of the German and the Magyar element in the Habsburg Monarchy and created unparalleled economic opportunities for Hungary, opening up a "golden age" of rapid economic and social advance and sharing Great Power status that is still often looked upon by both Austrians and Hungarians with nostalgia and fondness. According to its Gross National Product, the Austro-Hungarian Monarchy was a stable fifth power in Europe in the period between 1830 and 1913, behind only Russia, Germany, Britain, and France. After the

Treaty of Trianon, partitioned Hungary's per capita GNP dropped to number 16 in Europe.[6]

The total population of Hungary rose from 13,663,691 in 1869 to 18,264,533 in 1910. Only 54.5% of the total population in 1910 were ethnic Magyars. The census of 1920 found only 7.89 million people in the Hungary of the Treaty of Trianon, with a mere 2.4% representing all the national minorities. By 1930, the overall population was 8.68 million, which by 1941 had reached 9.32 million. The number of Jews in 1869 was 542,257 (4%), while in 1910 the number rose to 911,227 (5%), and remained around 5% in the interwar era.[7]

While Hungary continued to be the breadbasket of Central Europe, that half-century of prosperity, with no internal war, gave her a modern industrial base, up-to-date communications, and a thriving international commerce and banking sector. In 1873, the hitherto separate municipalities of Buda, Old Buda, and Pest were unified as a newly inaugurated capital city of Budapest, vying with Vienna in ambition and splendor. By the turn of the century, that Hungarian metropolis was the very symbol of the era with its magnificent avenues and boulevards, its imposing public buildings, its subway (the first in continental Europe), its glittering opera house, theaters, museums, thermal baths, hotels and great parks. This was also a highly productive period for the sciences, humanities and arts. The

---

6   Paul Bairoch, "Europe's Gross National Product 1800–1975." *Journal of European Economic History*, Vol. 5, No. 2, 1976, p. 281. Quoted by Iván T. Berend, *Európa gazdasága a 19. században* [European Ecomony in the 19th Century] (Budapest: Gondolat, 1987), p. 661, as well as by Ignác Romsics, *Hungary in the Twentieth Century* (Budapest: Corvina—Osiris, 1999), p. 144. Cf. Iván T. Berend and György Ránki, *Economic Development in East-Central Europe in the 19th and 20th Centuries* (New York—London: Columbia University Press, 1974), pp. 16–27.

7   Péter Hanák, Magyarország társadalma a századforduló idején [Society in Fin-de-Siècle Hungary], in Péter Hanák, ed., *Magyarország története 1890–1918* [A History of Hungary, 1890–1918] (2nd ed., Budapest: Akadémiai Kiadó, 1983), pp. 405, 414, 420; Iván T. Berend, A magyar társadalom a két világháború között [Interwar Hungarian Society] in György Ránki, ed., *Magyarország története 1918–1919, 1919–1945* [A History of Hungary, 1918–1919, 1919–1945] (Budapest: Akadémiai Kiadó, 1976), pp. 765, 767, 768.

University of Budapest and its prestigious faculty was blossoming; Franz Liszt had founded the Music Academy that bears his name to this day; new medical clinics approached the highest standards in Europe; and these high level achievements were sustained by the general excellence of the country's secondary schooling.

Defeat in World War I ended all pretensions Hungary had to at least half of a Great Power status. Hungary's wartime misfortune, the ensuing revolution of 1918, and particularly that of 1919, the subsequent foreign occupation were partly attributed to the country's Jewish population which was scapegoated to take a huge share of the blame for the catastrophe. As in Austria and Germany, the Jews were often perceived as a monolithic, alien, leftist, disruptive group in society. Though a gross travesty, it gained credence from the fact that the overwhelming majority of the leaders of the 1919 Commune, the "republic of councils," a short-lived offshoot of Lenin's Bolshevik Revolution of 1917, were of Jewish descent.

The Peace Treaty of Trianon provided the final blow in 1920 to a most promising and thriving period of cultural development. Grand Trianon, the bigger of the two small *châteaux* in the park of the great palace of Versailles where Hungary signed a humiliating peace treaty with the Allies on June 4, 1920, became synonymous with defeat, disgrace, and despair—and the single most important event in modern Hungarian history. The territorial and population concessions dictated by the treaty turned Hungary overnight into an independent, but small, landlocked, and vulnerable state, with a full-blown small-country complex.

In the poisonous atmosphere engendered by being on the losing side in the war and seeing the country stripped of so much of its historical lands, the new régime that installed itself under Admiral Miklós Horthy in the fall of 1919 produced the continent's first anti-Semitic legislation of that century, the 1920 quota system which compared the number of Hungarian Jews to the overall population of Hungary and allowed only a limited number of students to be of Jewish origin in higher education. This new system was particularly painful for Hungarian Jews as they were disproportionately represented in the "free" professions, comprising more than 50% of private medical doctors, lawyers, journalists, merchants, and businessmen. By contrast, there were relatively few Jews among officials working for the state of Hungary or for municipal authorities, or among teachers and professors.[8] Though the system lapsed, for a while, by the end of the decade, it was a powerful spur for many bright young Hungarian intellectuals of Jewish background to leave the country and complete their education or seek employment elsewhere. Many would have preferred to emigrate to the United States, but as mentioned above, entry there was restricted by the introduction of the quota system, starting with the emergency immigration restriction law of 1921, and finalized by the even more restrictive national origins scheme of the Reed-Johnson Act of 1924, under which only 869 persons from Hungary could be admitted annually, later reduced to a mere 473.

Hungary thereby lost large numbers of budding natural scientists, physicians, engineers, architects, musicians, artists, film-makers, sociologists, and authors, who would go on to make distinguished names for themselves in the West. That was compounded by further rounds of increasingly drastic anti-Jewish legislation in 1938–41, modeled on that introduced in Nazi Germany.

The still predominantly elitist and highly conservative school system, largely feudal in its politics, managed, despite the loss of some of the very brightest students, to maintain such high academic standards that several Hungarian universities held their place, continuing to produce a stream of graduates who went on to demonstrate excellence in diverse fields, the positive effects of which were still evident after World War II.

The history of Hungary in the interwar period and during World War II can best be understood as a quest to regain the lost territories. That quest led the country to support and enter the War on the side of Hitler's Germany, albeit as a somewhat "unwilling satellite,"[9] though the support included contributing to the Holocaust by ordering the ghettoization of

---

8   Katalin N. Szegvári, *Numerus clausus rendelkezések az ellenforradalmi Magyarországon* [Numerus clausus provisions in counter-revolutionary Hungary] (Budapest: Akadémiai Kiadó, 1988), pp. 52–53.
9   The term was borrowed from U. S. Minister John F. Montgomery's memoir on *Hungary: The Unwilling Satellite,* published in 1947. For many Hungarians, Hungary

its large Jewish population and carrying out the deportation of the great bulk of that community to perish in Hitler's gas chambers.

Hungary managed to avoid active involvement in the War until 1941, but was then caught on the horns of the dilemma of whether to fear most the Nazis or the Soviets. In truth, the die had been cast long before, given the long tradition of pro-German orientation, including alliance during World War I and the adverse experience of the country's experiment with Bolshevism in 1919. Disastrously, an entire Hungarian army was committed to Hitler's invasion of Russia. It is a measure of the reluctance of Hungary's support, however, that Hitler, in an effort to keep Hungary on his side, deemed it necessary to order an army of occupation into the country in March 1944. With Germany deciding to make a stand in Hungary against the advancing Red Army by the end of that year, the outcome was virtually inevitable. World War II saw the demise of a productive and rich culture. Having ousted the Germans, the Soviet Union sponsored a fledgling but aggressive local Communist Party under Mátyás Rákosi, which rapidly proceeded seizing full control over the now nominally democratic Hungary. By 1947–1948, the country had effectively lost whatever slight independence it possessed and was absorbed into the Soviet bloc.

Hungarian Creativity

Hungarian creativity is embedded in a complex tradition. Two aspects should be emphasized: the almost constant entanglement with internal and international conflicts, wars, and revolutions, and the long coexistence with German culture and civilization. Often in a cross-fertilizing way, both left a lasting imprint on the Hungarian mind, its means for solving problems, creating new ideas, and organizing thoughts.

---

always seemed like an "unwilling satellite," whether coerced by the Ottoman Turks, the Habsburgs, the Nazis, or the Soviets.

The standard joke about Hungarians is that they are the ones who can enter a revolving door behind you, but leave ahead of you. A backhanded compliment, but if there is such a thing as national character, then this can be taken as a sign of respect for a certain shrewdness, ingenuity, originality, and an uncommon approach to problem-solving.

The social history of the Hungarian cast of mind—indeed the way of thinking across much of East-Central Europe—is deeply rooted in war and conflict, abetted by a foe of an entirely different nature: poverty. Naturally well-endowed as Hungary is, most of its inhabitants throughout the ages have faced hardship, and often outright privation, which by 1920 called for considerable resourcefulness just to survive. Strategies had to be developed to obtain a bare minimum of food, clothing, shelter, and protection. A keen sense of the unpredictability of the future engendered in many a certain cynical, ironic, flippant, devil-may-care attitude. Equally, many were prone to feelings of pessimism, hopelessness, disillusionment, as reflected in the appallingly high suicide rates of the region. Lamentation over the nation's lost glory permeates Hungarian poetry, painting, opera, indeed the words of the national anthem itself, as penned by the early 19th century poet Ferenc Kölcsey (1790–1838):[10] although there is always a sense that individual courage may count, the nation as a whole is doomed.

By the late 19th century, the Hungarian school-system contributed to problem solving. A potent factor in that record of achievement lay in the manner that secondary schooling was reorganized after the Compromise of 1867. Soon after, the German model of the theory and practice of

---

[10] "Castle once, now heap of stones;
Fled are all its graces,
Death-cries, rattles, sighs and groans
Occupy their places.
Ah but liberty disdains
Veins that death must vanquish,
Red-eyed orphans in their chains
Weeping where they languish."
(Translated by George Szirtes)

teacher training was introduced in Hungary. This laid the ground for ensuring that the best Hungarian schools consistently had access to first-class teaching resources capable of encouraging students to standards of attainment that compare favorably with many of the higher tier colleges in the United States today. On the German model, the high school, or *Gymnasium*, placed heavy emphasis on the Classics, Hungarian language and literature, and universal culture, without neglecting mathematics and the natural sciences. These were unashamedly elitist institutions, with a student intake drawn typically from a rather narrow upper-middle section of Hungary's then relatively conservative, even feudalistic society. However, they attracted a teaching staff of a very high caliber; many recognized scholars in their own fields, as reflected in their subsequent membership of the Hungarian Academy of Sciences and appointment to university professorships. As a result, the country's top schools, such as the Lutheran high school in Pest or the *Mintagimnázium* (The "Model") of the University of Budapest, succeeded for several decades in cultivating an astonishingly consistent succession of brilliant young minds, of whom Theodore von Kármán, John von Neumann, Edward Teller, prospective Nobel Laureate Eugene Wigner were a few of the more prominent.

The German influence during this era penetrated so widely that, in many ways, Hungary was often considered an outpost of German culture, whose icons—from writers Goethe and Schiller, philosophers Kant and Schopenhauer, composers Beethoven, Brahms and Wagner, painters Kaulbach and Piloty, to scientists Gauss, Haeckel, and Brehm—were held in unparalleled esteem. Even news of the wider world outside the German universe reached Hungarian aristocratic libraries, coffeehouses and salons refracted through the medium of the German language and its cultural paradigms.

Of course, there was also animosity to innovation: conservatism prevailed in much of the Austro-Hungarian Monarchy. Although Hungary was in many ways an ideal creative spawning ground, some of its achievements were made in the face of official Austrian and Hungarian disapproval. For the greater part of the 19th century the national tradition was conservative and its mentality hostile to innovation, with its authoritarian insistence on strict and often antiquated rules and standards, established patterns of thinking, and unalterable methods. The general ambiance favored preserving the *status quo* rather than supporting new ideas. Accordingly, the ruling conservative forces of the pre-1867 period ignored or spurned many reform-minded Hungarians, which more often than not led to exile, the lunatic asylum, or suicide. This contradiction between conservatism and renewal was evident in a plethora of different occupations and life styles.

After the Austro-Hungarian Compromise of 1867, however, Franz Joseph I, Emperor of Austria (1848–1916), and Apostolic King of Hungary (1867–1916), presided over a tide of change during the half century of his "dual" Monarchy. Innovative spirits flourished in many walks of life; large industrial firms sprang up, and in their search for competitive edge, founded product-oriented experimental laboratories in fields as diverse as telephony, lighting, pharmaceuticals, armaments, and electric locomotion. Later generations were to look back on these as the "good old days" of peace and prosperity.

At the same time, widely different luminaries of the Austro-Hungarian Monarchy such as the poet Endre Ady, the psychoanalyst Sigmund Freud, the author Franz Kafka, the statesman Lajos Kossuth, and the writer Robert Musil were, in very different ways, all highly critical of the Habsburg Empire and exposed its troubled nature. In many ways, as the poet Endre Ady said, official Hungary was a "cemetery of souls," where new ideas were doomed to failure. Unfortunately, the country was unable to sustain either full employment or a bare modicum of social services. Between the 1880s and World War I, one and a half to two million people (Magyars and, mostly, non-Magyars) left Hungary, mainly for the United States, as part of an unparalleled international migration. Their exodus, in some ways a natural and recurrent historical pattern, was essentially economic: a search for better wages by, in many cases, illiterate, uneducated peasants that would enable them to remit part of their pay to their families back home or, having "made it", return with whatever earnings they had accumulated. Indeed, the majority of these masses are more properly considered "birds of passage," rather than true "emigrants" in the sense that many of them never intended to become American citizens and longed to return to their native land. However, with the collapse of the Monarchy and Hungary's subsequent dismemberment and dire economic plight leaving nothing to which they might return, many were forced to remain in their new lands.

The economic advance that occurred under the Austro-Hungarian Monarchy, however, did spur the development of the Hungarian language, furnishing it with a technical vocabulary that served as a continued vehicle for professional communication and understanding—again reflecting the willingness of the culture to adapt itself to the modern world. This was particularly notable at the universities, where Hungarian gradually displaced German as the main language of instruction.

2 The Chemistry of Fin-de-Siècle Budapest

The importance of the Hungarian genius as embodied by the internationally recognized émigré scientists, musicians and filmmakers of the first half of the twentieth century[11] has stimulated several attempts to define its exact nature. Though these distinguished individuals belonged to a special and select group, they were nonetheless the products of turn-of-the-century Hungarian society.

---

11   Laura Fermi, *Illustrious Immigrants, op. cit.*, pp. 53–59; Paul Ignotus, "The Hungary of Michael Polanyi," in *The Logic of Personal Knowledge. Essays Presented to Michael Polanyi on His Seventieth Birthday* 11 March 1961 (Glencoe, IL: The Free Press, 1961), pp. 3–12; Mario D. Fenyo, *Literature and Political Change: Budapest, 1908–1918*, Transactions of the American Philosophical Society, Vol. 77, Part 6, 1987; John Lukacs, *Budapest 1900. A Historical Portrait of a City and Its Culture* (New York: Weidenfeld & Nicolson, 1988); Lee Congdon, *Exile and Social Thought. Hungarian Intellectuals in Germany and Austria 1919–1933* (Princeton, N. J.: Princeton University Press, 1991); William O. McCagg, Jr., *Jewish Nobles and Geniuses in Modern Hungary* (Boulder CO: East European Monographs, 1972, repr. 1986).

The Making of a Capital City

Soon after the creation of the Austro-Hungarian Monarchy (1867) and the unification of Buda, Pest, and Óbuda into the representative and impressive Hungarian capital city of Budapest (1873), a new, complex and modern, Hungarian intellectual élite emerged. Centered in the city of Budapest, this modernizing group came partly from the decaying landed gentry of feudal origins and partly from intellectually aspiring members of the assimilating (predominantly German and Jewish) middle class. While creating metropolitan Budapest in the intellectual sense, they constituted themselves as a group through what proved to be a completely new and unique social and psychological experience.

Before the unification of Buda, Pest, and Óbuda, the population of Pest-Buda was 269,293 (1869). Between 1890 and 1910, the population grew from 492,227 to 880,371, with additional growth in the suburbs (from 61,289 to 217,360).[12] By 1930, the city had 1 million people, and by 1941, it reached 1,2 million. In the meantime, the suburbs grew from 311,000 in 1920 to 560,000 in 1940.[13]

Several economic and social factors contributed to the emergence of this gifted and creative professional group at the time of the rise and fall of the Austro-Hungarian Monarchy (1867–1918). In a country where the long decay of feudalism had become visible and the political and social system based on huge landed estates had come under sharp attack, the beginnings of a new, capitalist society stimulated work in science, technology and the arts. The transformation of the Habsburg Monarchy and the creation of a "Hungarian Empire" contributed to an economic prosperity that brought about a building and transportation boom, the advancement of technology, and the appearance of a sophisticated financial system.

---

12   Károly Vörös, ed., *Budapest története a márciusi forradalomtól az őszirózsás forradalomig* [The History of Budapest from the March Revolution to the Frost Flower Revolution] (Budapest: Akadémiai Kiadó, 1978), pp. 185, 577.
13   Miklós Horváth, ed., *Budapest története a forradalmak korától a felszabadulásig* [The History of Budapest from the Revolutions to the Liberation] (Budapest: Akadémiai Kiadó, 1980), p. 418.

Figure 1. Budapest, 1930s (a) (HNM).

The rise of a new urban middle class affected the school system. Around 1900, there was a creative spirit in the air throughout Europe, permeating literature, music, the arts, and sciences. In Hungary, the poet Endre Ady, the editors of the new literary journal *Nyugat* (West) (1908), the composers Béla Bartók and Zoltán Kodály, the artistic group The Eight, philosophers such as Georg Lukács and Karl Mannheim, art historians such as Charles de Tolnay, Arnold Hauser, Lajos Fülep, and Frederick Antal, offered a new and stimulating agenda for artistic and social discourse. This creative atmosphere set the tone for a generation that included the many celebrated scientists born in the early years of the new century.

From assimilated Jewish-Hungarian upper middle-class families, Theodore von Kármán, John von Neumann, Leo Szilard, Eugene Wigner, and Edward Teller were born into this challenging intellectual atmosphere of Budapest, which bred provocative questions and pioneering answers. Paradoxically, the approaching decline of the Austro-Hungarian Monarchy seemed to have generated unusual sensitivity and creativity.[14] In many ways, the political and social decline of the monarchy created a special opportunity for Hungarian Jewry, which had grown and flourished throughout the fifty years of the Monarchy. The result was a professionally defined middle class, instead of a feudally-defined one in Hungary. Whereas the first generations of assimilating middle class Hungarian Jews concentrated on amassing material wealth, subsequent generations

---

14 László Mátrai, *Alapját vesztett felépítmény* [Superstructure Without Base] (Budapest: Magvető, 1976); Kristóf Nyíri, *A Monarchia szellemi életéről* [The Intellectual Life of the (Austro-Hungarian) Monarchy] (Budapest: Gondolat, 1980); J. C. Nyíri, *Am Rande Europas. Studien zur österreichisch-ungarischen Philosophiegeschichte* (Wien: Böhlau, 1988); Péter Hanák, *The Garden and the Workshop. Essays on the Cultural History of Vienna and Budapest* (Princeton, NJ: Princeton University Press, 1998); Károly Vörös, ed., *Budapest története* [The History of Budapest], Vol. IV (Budapest: Akadémiai Kiadó, 1978), pp. 321–723; John Lukacs, *Budapest 1900, op. cit.;* Mary Gluck, *Georg Lukács and his Generation 1900–1918* (Cambridge, MA and London: Harvard UP, 1985); István Hargittai, *The Martians of Science: Five Physicists Who Changed the Twentieth Century* (New York: Oxford University Press, 2006), pp. 3–31.

The Social Construction of Hungarian Genius 37

Figure 2. Budapest, 1930s (b) (HNM).

were destined to focus their activities on accumulating knowledge.[15] Their often-strong financial background enabled them to concentrate exclusively on their studies and eventually join the various scholarly or scientific groupings such as the *Társadalomtudományi Társaság* [Society for the Social Sciences], the *Galilei Kör* [Galileo Circle], or the journal *Huszadik Század* [Twentieth Century] where the critical social issues were often debated with a highly politicized focus. These circumstances provided a good schooling for this generation of prospective émigré intellectuals.

The period that ended with World War I saw a relatively peaceful cooperation and often-true friendship between Jew and Gentile in Hungary. What historian Raphael Patai described as "the love affair [...] between the Jews and Hungary"[16] often resulted in intermarriages and other forms of close social ties and networking. For those opposing the influx of Jews into Hungary, however, Budapest seemed a special, "un-Hungarian" case, out of line with Hungarian tradition. The popular conservative author Ferenc Herczeg expressed this sentiment in a straightforward manner when he spoke about "foreign elements in [the] chemistry" of Budapest.[17]

Assimilation was the by-word of the period: religious conversion, the dropping of German, Slavic, and particularly Jewish family names,

---

15 William O. McCagg, Jr., *op. cit.*
16 Raphael Patai, *The Vanished Worlds of Jewry* (New York: Macmillan, 1980), p. 68; cf. Nobuaki Terao, "Oscar Jászi and the Magyar-Jewish Alliance" (1997); Tibor Frank, ed., *Honszeretet és felekezeti hűség: Wahrmann Mór 1831–1892* [Patriotism and Religious Loyalty: Mór Wahrmann 1831–1892] (Budapest: Argumentum, 2005), English edition forthcoming as Tibor Frank, ed., *The Jew as Hungarian Patriot: Mór Wahrmann 1831–1892* (Oxford: The Littman Library of Jewish Civilization, 2012).
17 Zoltán Horváth, *Magyar századforduló. A második reformnemzedék története 1896–1914* [Hungarian fin-de-siècle. A history of the second reform generation]. (Budapest: 1961, 2nd ed. Budapest: Gondolat, 1974), pp. 205–6; quoted by John Lukács, *op. cit.*, p. 202.

The Social Construction of Hungarian Genius

and ennoblement were all standard practice.[18] The tortuous process of Jewish assimilation in Budapest was (often ironically) documented by the Hungarian novels of the period such as *Az éhes város* (The Hungry City, 1900) and *Az aruvimi erdő titka* (The Secret of the Aruvim Forest, 1917) by Ferenc Molnár, *Budapest* (1901) by Tamás Kóbor, *A nap lovagja* (The Knight of the Day, 1902) by Sándor Bródy, and *Andor és András* (Andrian and Andrew, 1903) by Ferenc Herczeg.[19] Nevertheless, the full social history of Magyarization at all levels is yet to be fully researched and written. The capital city of Hungary played the role of a Hungarian melting pot through the four decades preceding World War I. It attracted a vast number of migrant workers, professionals, and intellectuals from all quarters of the kingdom of Hungary and beyond. It became an energized meeting ground for a multitude of ethnic and religious groups with varying social norms, modes of behavior and mental patterns. The mixing and clashing, fusion and friction, of such diverse values and codes of behavior created an unparalleled outburst of creativity, a veritable explosion of productive energies. In this exciting and excited ambiance, a spirit of intellectual competitiveness was born, which favored originality, novelty and experimentalism. Budapest expected and produced excellence and became deeply interested in the secret of genius. For many of those who were later to be known both nationally and internationally as geniuses, Budapest seems to have been the natural place to have been born.

---

18   Cf. József Gerő, ed., *A királyi könyvek. Az I. Ferenc József és IV. Károly által 1867-től 1918-ig adományozott nemességek, főnemességek, előnevek és címerek jegyzéke* [Royal Books. A List of Persons Who Received Noble and Aristocratic Ranks, Titles, and Coats of Arms by (Kings) Ferenc József I and Károly IV between 1867 and 1918] (Budapest, 1940).
19   Cf. Marianna Birnbaum, "Budapest in the Literature of the Fin-de-Siècle," in György Ránki and Attila Pók, eds., *Hungary and European Civilization,* Indiana Studies on Hungary, 3 (Budapest: Akadémiai Kiadó, 1989), pp. 331–342.

Fathers and Sons: Family Background

The emergence of those splendidly gifted generations in turn-of-the-century Hungary should be explained not only in terms of economic opportunity and political expediency, but also in terms of social need and psychological disposition.

Just as in most of Europe, middle class and upper-middle class Hungarian families, particularly Jewish-Hungarian ones in the late nineteenth and early twentieth centuries, were based on the dominant role of fathers, with mothers relegated to the role of preserving the German trinity of *Kinder, Küche, Kirche* (children, kitchen, church). Most families were supported by the single income of the father who reigned supreme in his family. More often than not, fathers had the final word in serious matters such as the education of the children as well as decisions about their marriages and jobs. Indeed, fathers loomed so large in middle class Jewish-Hungarian as well as Austrian families that one of the most significant issues to be resolved for young people was their relationship to their fathers. Sigmund Freud's concept of the dominating father figure was experienced in most middle class families, especially among Jews. The problem was conceptualized by Freud's notion of the "father complex." In his 1899 *Die Traumdeutung* [The Interpretation of Dreams], Freud observed that

> even in our middle class families, fathers are, as a rule, inclined to refuse their sons' independence and the means necessary to secure it, and thus to foster the growth of the germ of hostility which is inherent in their relation. A physician will often be in a position to notice how a son's grief at the loss of his father cannot suppress his satisfaction at having at length won his freedom. In our society today fathers are apt to cling desperately to what is left of a now sadly antiquated *potestas patris familias* and an author who, like Ibsen, brings the immemorial struggle between fathers and sons into prominence in his writings, may be certain of producing his effect.[20]

20 Sigmund Freud, *The Interpretation of Dreams* (Translated by James Strachey) (New York: Avon Books, 1965), p. 290. One could easily add several other literary examples to Freud's reference to Ibsen, from German, Austrian, and Hungarian literature.

As Claudio Magris added in his *The Habsburg Myth*, the source of Freud's general assumption is not only a basic rule of psychology, but it is also recognized today as an imprint of the particular Austrian social and family structure based on the dominating figure of the father. The crumbling, patriarchal institution of the family, Magris concluded, reflected the hierarchical order of the Habsburg system.[21]

From our own sample, a case in point is Edward Teller, who remembered his father to have drummed it into him that because of the anti-Semitism of the political restoration after 1919, "he, as a Jew, had to excel just to keep abreast; that because of it he would have one day to emigrate to a country where conditions were more favorable for minorities; and that from anti-Semitism a sure escape was science, an international discipline."[22] Though he had shown a precocious gift for mathematics, Edward Teller studied chemical engineering and took a degree in that subject, mainly because his father, a lawyer, thought his son ought to study a practical subject.[23] Many fathers at the time thought that chemistry would be the appropriate subject to secure a safe future for their sons.[24] Similarly, noted psychologist Géza Révész was forced by his father to study law instead of psychology, in which he was interested from very early on.[25] Like Max Teller, the father of Révész was convinced that his son would make a better living with a "useful" degree. It was only after

---

[21] Claudio Magris, *Il mito absburgico nella letteratura austriaca moderna* (Torino: Einaudi, 1963), *A Habsburg-mítosz az osztrák irodalomban* (Budapest: Európa, 1988), p. 91.

[22] Edward Teller and Alan Brown, *The Legacy of Hiroshima* (Garden City: Doubleday, 1961); *Life,* Dec. 13, 1963. p. 89. Cf. William O. McCagg, Jr., *Jewish Nobles, op. cit.,* p. 164.

[23] C. P., "Edward Teller" (Bio-bibliography), Archive for the History of Quantum Physics, American Philosophical Society Library, Philadelphia, PA; J. R. Shetley and Clay Blair Jr., *The Hydrogene Bomb* (New York, 1954), p. 41.

[24] Cf. Gábor Palló, *Zsenialitás és korszellem. Világhírű magyar tudósok* [Genius and *Zeitgeist.* World Famous Hungarian Scientists] (Budapest: Áron, 2004), pp. 161–166.

[25] Judit Gál Csillag, "Bevezető tanulmány" [Introduction], in Géza Révész, *Tanulmányok* [Studies] (Budapest: Gondolat, 1985), p. 9.

completing law school in 1902 that young Révész was able to pursue his real interest and study experimental psychology with G. E. Mueller in Göttingen, Germany.

Even at a late age, Theodore von Kármán maintained regular, almost daily contact with his father, who gave his son, by then a professor at a respectable German university, instructions on all issues of life. Kármán Sr. remained a decisive influence in the life of his son until the elder's death in 1915. Von Kármán kept his father's letters framed in his study during his long years at Caltech in Pasadena, California in the 1930s and 1940s.[26] Freud's words should also be recalled when we realize that the death of Mihály Pollacsek, the father of Michael and Karl Polanyi, was such a loss to his children that they exchanged letters to commemorate the event each year until the very end of their lives, over half a century later.[27]

Toward Assimilation

It is informative to look at some of the crucial issues of change in Hungary (and Austria-Hungary). Assimilation, and particularly Jewish assimilation, seemed one of the most important gateways of opportunity in the country. In order to strengthen the national identity in a rather disparate, diversified society, Magyarization proved a guiding principle of building the Hungarian nation, itself traditionally a composite mixture of ethnic, religious, and language groups of all sorts.

In a country that provided an almost unparalleled measure of religious tolerance before World War I, assimilation often included language shift, name change, ennoblement, mixed marriage, and religious conversion.

---

26   Tibor Frank, "Kármán Mór levelei Kármán Tódorhoz," [Mór Kármán to Theodore von Kármán: Correspondence], *Pedagógiai Szemle,* in press; Mór Kármán to Theodore von Kármán, Correspondence 1912–14., Theodore von Kármán Papers, 141.10, 141.11, 141.12, 141.14, 142.1, California Institute of Technology Archives, Pasadena, CA.
27   Ilona Duczynska, "Polányi Károly (1886–1964)," [Karl Polanyi, 1886–1964], *Századok,* Vol. 105, No. 1, 1971, p. 91.

This was particularly the case in Budapest, a city referred to by the contemporary poet Endre Ady as "made by Jews for us."[28] The change from German or Yiddish into Hungarian, from Jewish into Hungarian families, from Judaism to Roman Catholicism or various forms of Protestantism, served the purpose of integration into Hungarian society, yet these various forms of assimilation often created a sense of spiritual vacuum, an aura of lost identity, a religious no man's land.

Assimilation, along with its various manifestations, reflected the measure of psychological insecurity, social uneasiness, and inner unrest of generations of Jews in Budapest as well as elsewhere in the Austro-Hungarian Monarchy and even beyond.[29] This issue has been discussed by a growing and increasingly interesting literature on Jewish insecurity.[30] Ironically, the insecurity of the assimilated Jew was particularly noticeable, revealing a tradition abandoned in converted individuals and families, and a set of values yet to be conquered. The price of assimilation for religious converts was the loss of roots, social and psychological; its reward was promotion and social recognition. In the increasingly secularizing world of fin-de-siècle Budapest, it often seemed a reasonable bargain to exchange socially undesirable traditions for the psychological and commercial benefits of a seemingly secure position in gentile Hungarian society.

---

28   Endre Ady, "Korrobori," in Ady Endre *publicisztikai írásai* [The Journalism of Endre Ady] Vol. III (Budapest: Szépirodalmi Könyvkiadó, 1977), p. 520.
29   William O. McCagg Jr., *A History of Habsburg Jews, 1670–1918* (Bloomington and Indianapolis: Indiana University Press, 1989). Cf. Elzbieta Ettinger, *Hannah Arendt/Martin Heidegger* (New Haven, CT: Yale UP, 1995), quoted by Alan Ryan, "Dangerous Liaison," *The New York Review of Books,* January 11, 1996, p. 24.
30   Sander L. Gilman, *Jewish Self-Hatred: Anti-Semitism and the Hidden Language of the Jews* (Baltimore—London: The Johns Hopkins University Press, 1986), pp. 22–67, 139–308; Viktor Karády, *Zsidóság Európában a modern korban* [Jewry in Modern Europe] (Budapest: Új Mandátum, 2000), pp. 125–284; William O. McCagg Jr., *A History of Habsburg Jews, 1670–1918, op. cit.,* pp. 47–158; Raphael Patai, *The Jews of Hungary: History, Culture, Psychology* (Detroit: Wayne State University Press, 1996), pp. 230–441; Jacob Katz, *From Prejudice to Destruction: Anti-Semitism, 1700–1933* (Cambridge, MA—London, England: Harvard University Press, 1980), pp. 203–209, 221–242.

For the converts of the World War I era and the immediate postwar years, these benefits were short-lived. Nevertheless, assimilation into Hungarian society provided the Jewish middle class with a set of experiences that prepared them for successful immigration and naturalization in the United States. Their success in the U.S. was conditioned by having already experienced comparable change in Hungary and the Austro-Hungarian Empire. They were prepared for the typical problems of émigrés/immigrants, having already experienced multiple values, double identities, and a sense of living, as it were, in between different societies.

The single most remarkable characteristic of assimilation in Hungary around the turn of the century (and a measure of its success) was Magyarization. The abandonment of the German language for Hungarian was rapid: the number of Jewish speakers of German dropped from 43 percent in 1880 to 21.8 percent by 1910, and the percentage of Magyar speakers in Hungary reached 75.6 percent.[31] To some degree, name change, already a frequent phenomenon in Hungary by the 1840s, was also part of this movement. Changes in family name often were from Hebrew to German under Joseph II, then from German to Hungarian in the 19th century, and again, among émigrés and exiles, from Hungarian to American.

Historian Peter Gay briefly noted the widespread practice of changing Jewish-sounding names in late nineteenth-century Germany. His German examples (Abramsohn to Otto Brahm, Goldmann to Max Reinhardt, Davidsohn to Jakob van Hoddis, Julius Levi into Julius Rodenberg) resemble the corresponding practice in Hungary where Magyarization of Jewish-sounding German names became increasingly customary through the nineteenth century.[32] The Hungarianization of names became a real movement in the 1880s–1890s: in the two decades preceding World War I, name changes amounted to 2,000–3,000 annually. An estimated 66,000

---

31   William O. McCagg Jr., *A History of Habsburg Jews, 1670–1918*, op. cit., p. 190.
32   Peter Gay, *Freud, Jews and Other Germans. Masters and Victims in Modernist Culture* (Oxford: Oxford University Press, 1979), p. 98, n.12.

people of Jewish origin chose a new, Hungarian name between 1848 and 1917.[33] Szilard, Polanyi, Kármán are all Hungarianized family names.

Another avenue of assimilation was mixed marriage. The politically right-wing statistician Alajos Kovács estimated the number of Jewish-gentile intermarriages between the mid-nineteenth century and World War II as 50,000.[34]

The boldest, and least likely, step toward gentile Hungarian society was ennoblement. The late William O. McCagg provided a detailed survey of Jewish nobles around the turn of the century.[35] Ennoblement gave the Jewish upper middle-class a chance to integrate into Hungarian high society, i.e. into the nobility or, eventually, the even higher echelons of aristocracy. Von Kármán and von Neumann were born into such families.

Religious Conversion

More than perhaps any other change, religious conversion from Judaism to Christianity marked the deepest level of assimilation. Religious conversion seems an indication of a certain type of mental pattern that enabled and prepared some of the émigré intellectuals and professionals to adapt to the challenges of life outside Hungary.

It would be misleading to suggest that conversions in the Jewish upper class started at the turn of the century. The history of apostasy

33 Alajos Kovács quoted by Miklós Mester, "Magyar nevet minden magyarnak!" [A Hungarian Name for Every Hungarian!] Parts I–II, *Nemzeti Figyelő*, December 31, 1939, p. 3. and January 6, 1940, p. 3.
34 Kovács considered this a fairly small number, altogether some 0.7% of the Jewish population in the territory of partitioned Hungary. Cf. Alajos Kovács, "Adatok a zsidók bevándorlására és kikeresztelkedésére vonatkozólag" [Facts Concerning the Immigration and Religious Conversion of Jews], MS, For Count Pál Teleki, April 24, 1939, Központi Statisztikai Hivatal Könyvtára, V B 935. Cf. the theoretical considerations of Victor Karády, "Vers une théorie des mariages inter-confessionnels: Le cas de la nuptialité hongroise sous l'Ancien régime," *Actes de la recherche en sciences sociales*, nr. 57–58, 1985.
35 William O. McCagg, *Jewish Nobles and Geniuses*, op. cit.

goes back to biblical times, and has been known as emancipation, or as assimilation where it became a movement in some European countries. The nineteenth century produced a long list of significant individuals who converted, including French actress Sarah Bernhardt, British statesman Benjamin Disraeli, German poet Heinrich Heine, Hungarian-German violinist Joseph Joachim, the father of the political economist Karl Marx, and the composer Felix Mendelssohn Bartholdy.[36] Because of its importance as a social phenomenon, conversion was discussed in this period in a number of novels, short stories and dramas, both in Europe and the United States, including *Die Jüdinnen* and *Arnold Beer* by Max Brod; *Israël, Après moi, L'Assaut,* and *Le Secret* by Henry Bernstein; *Der Weg ins Freie* by Arthur Schnitzler; *Dr Kohn* by Max Nordau; *Az új keresztény* [The New Christian] and *A túlsó parton* [On the Other Bank] by Péter Ujvári, *Quelques Juifs* by André Spiré.[37]

Conversion to Christianity was a familiar form of assimilation in Germany, where Jews played a strong role in the "free" professions. "The exodus was not massive," historian Peter Gay noted: one source estimated the number of converts in the nineteenth century at around 22,000. Anti-Semitism, however, produced repeated waves of conversion. Half of Germany's Jewish academics and most of the Jewish journalists and editors were, in fact, converts. Conversion was, as Peter Gay points out, the "one way to ease ascent on the academic ladder:"[38] when the Jewish medievalist Harry Bresslau complained to Leopold von Ranke that his religion blocked his career, he was advised to be baptized. Until the 1870s, conversion was essentially the only way to leave Judaism. It was only after 1876 that Prussian legislation made it possible for Jews to leave their faith without adopting another one, a turning point that facilitated escape

---

36 R[ezső] S[eltmann], "Aposztázia és kitérés a zsidóságból [Apostasy and Jewish Conversion]," in *Magyar Zsidó Lexikon* (Budapest: Magyar Zsidó Lexikon, 1929), p. 54–57.
37 R[ezső] S[eltmann], "Asszimiláció [Assimilation]," in *Magyar Zsidó Lexikon* (Budapest: Magyar Zsidó Lexikon, 1929), p. 63–65.
38 Peter Gay, *Freud Jews and Other Germans. Masters and Victims in Modernist Culture* (Oxford: Oxford University Press, 1979), p. 116.

from Jewish identity.[39] It was not enough, however, to convert and baptize one's children:

> Normally it took several generations, several intermarriages, possibly a change of name and of residence before the past of the new Christian faded into invisibility. Jews generally despised their baptized brethren as renegades, Christians despised them as opportunists. Convert, seeking to win by moving from one camp to another, lost in both. [...][40]

> Everyone understood—everyone, philo-Semite and anti-Semite alike—that even those former Jews who had repudiated Judaism by religious conversion to Christianity, or legal disaffiliation from the Jewish community, were still somehow Jews: it never occurred to treat radicals like Karl Marx or the conservative legal theoretician Friedrich Julius Stahl as non-Jews. Berlin was full of Jewish agnostics, Jewish atheists, Jewish Catholics, and Jewish Lutherans. Indeed, these non-Jewish Jews were, if anything, more conspicuous than those who held, no matter how tepidly, to their ancient label, for they labored under the added reproach of cowardice, social climbing, secret service in a world-wide conspiracy—in a word, self-seeking mimicry. By the nature of things, these non-Jewish Jews were among the most prominent figures on the Berlin intellectual landscape.[41]

The number of conversions in Hungary was relatively small before 1910: in the twenty years between 1890 and 1910, only 5,046 chose religious conversion. Although the tendency was relatively new and limited, contemporary urban authors such as Ferenc Molnár referred to it as a typical Budapest phenomenon and used it as a major theme as early as 1900.[42] It took the great political upheavals such as the revolutions following World War I to make religious conversion into a mass movement.[43]

---

39 Peter Gay, *Freud, Jews and Other Germans, op. cit.*, pp. 96–98, quote p. 97, cf. Carl Cohen, "The Road to Conversion," LBI Year Book, Vol. VI, 1961, pp. 259–269.
40 Peter Gay, *Freud, Jews and Other Germans, op. cit.*, p. 98.
41 Peter Gay, *Freud, Jews and Other Germans, op. cit.*, pp. 174–175.
42 Ferenc Molnár, *Az éhes város* [The Hungry City] (1st ed. 1900; Budapest: Pesti Szalon, 1993; ed. György Bodnár), pp. 6–7, 13–14, 165–166.
43 P[éter] U[jvári], "Áttérés" [Conversion], in *Magyar Zsidó Lexikon* (Budapest: Magyar Zsidó Lexikon, 1929), p. 65.

Historian William O. McCagg, Jr. observed that "in 1919 and 1920 there was a massive wave of conversions out of Judaism among wealthy families. Contingent on this was a great deal of name changing and deliberate expunging of the past[...]"[44] Between 1919 and 1924, 11,688 Jewish persons (6,624 men and 5,064 women) were baptized. In 1919 alone, the number increased by 7,146.[45]

From our own sample, Leo Szilard made the decision to get himself baptized in the Calvinist church of Hungary on July 24, 1919 (i.e., just before the fall of the Soviet system), at the age of twenty-one.[46] Michael Polanyi was baptized into the Catholic Church on October 18, 1919 (i.e., well into the times of the White Terror), but it is unclear whether this represented his faith or was a practical step to facilitate his employment in Karlsruhe, Germany, where he was to emigrate shortly.[47] The choice of the date during the last days of 1919 is noteworthy and follows the pattern suggested by McCagg. In Hungary, members of the Jewish intellectual élite could claim substantial rewards in terms of career opportunities and advancement for converting. Thus, some had already started converting earlier in the nineteenth century or at least had had their children baptized. George Pólya was baptized a Roman Catholic weeks after his birth

---

44 William O. McCagg, Jr., *Jewish Nobles, op. cit.*, p. 240.
45 Zs[igmond] T[ieder], "Magyarországi zsidóság statisztikája" [The Statistics of Hungarian Jewry], in *Magyar Zsidó Lexikon* (Budapest: Magyar Zsidó Lexikon, 1929), p. 554. Cf. Alajos Kovács, *A zsidóság térfoglalása Magyarországon (Budapest, 1922).*
46 Kivonat a budapesti VI–VII. ker. fasori református egyház keresztelési anyakönyvéből [Extract from the Baptismal Registry of the Calvinist Church at he Fasor, Budapest, VI–VII District] II. kötet, 14. lap, Budapest, July 24, 1919. Leo Szilard Papers, Box 1, Folder 11, Mandeville Special Collections Library, University of California, San Diego, La Jolla, CA.
47 [Author Not Indicated,] "Polanyi Biography," Draft of Chapter One, Summer 1979, MS, George Polya Papers, SC 337, 86–036, Box 1, Folder 1, Department of Special Collections and University Archives, Stanford University Libraries, Stanford, CA.

in January 1888, in Budapest, and the baptismal records show his parents as Roman Catholic as well.[48]

Mass conversion became a serious proposition only as late as 1917: in a book on Jewish-Hungarian social problems, law professor Péter Ágoston suggested that total assimilation and mass conversion should be the correct attitude to solve the problems of growing anti-Semitism in Hungary.[49] As a reaction to Ágoston's proposition, the social science journal *Huszadik Század* (Twentieth Century) addressed some 150 leading intellectuals and public figures in spring 1917, focusing public attention on the Jewish question in Hungary.[50] But the Jewish leader Ferenc Mezey considered conversion cowardice; for such people would be looked upon as opportunists and conversion would not exempt them from racism.[51] Mass conversions had a modernizing effect within the Jewish community itself in that they forced Jewish leaders to introduce a more liberal, worldly fraction, one hospitable to new ideas: a Neology section in addition to the Orthodox majority. Psychologically, it was easier to convert from Judaism to Christianity for those whose families had earlier changed from Orthodox to Neological theology (roughly the equivalent of "Reform" Judaism in the U.S.).[52]

---

48   Kereszt-levél [Baptismal Record], Kivonat a budapest-terézvárosi római katholikus plébánia, Kereszteltek Anyakönyvéből, Vol. XXXIV, p. 6, January 9, 1888. I am grateful to Professor Gerald Alexanderson of the University of Santa Clara for showing me this document as well as his collection of Pólya documents that were to be transferred to the George Polya Papers, Department of Special Collections and University Archives, Stanford University Libraries, Stanford, CA.—It is interesting to note that the godfather of George Pólya was Count Mihály Károlyi's uncle, Count Sándor Károlyi, one of the great feudal landowners of Hungary.
49   Péter Ágoston, *A zsidók útja* [The Way of the Jews] (Nagyvárad: 1917).
50   Partially republished by Péter Hanák, ed., *Zsidókérdés, asszimiláció, antiszemitizmus. Tanulmányok a zsidókérdésről a huszadik századi Magyarországon* [Jewish Question, Assimilation, Anti-Semitism. Studies on the Jewish Question in Twentieth Century Hungary] (Budapest: Gondolat, 1984), pp. 13–115.
51   Péter Hanák, ed., *Zsidókérdés, op. cit.*, pp. 32–33.
52   William O. McCagg, Jr., "Jewish Conversion in Hungary," in Todd Endelmann, ed., *Jewish Apostasy in the Modern World* (New York: Holmes and Meier, 1987), pp. 142–164; George Barany, "'Magyar Jew or Jewish Magyar?' Reflections on

Conversions continued during the interwar period, even among immigrant Jewish-Hungarian-Americans. An interesting case was that of John von Neumann, who converted to Catholicism after his father's death in 1929, "for the sake of convenience, not conviction," as his brother Nicholas remembered in 1987.[53] Von Neumann was baptized again in Trenton, New Jersey, in April 1935, at the age of thirty-two, perhaps as an added effort to provide security for his family. In his last illness, while being attended by a Benedictine monk, various legends spread about yet another conversion and baptism.

The Act of Creation

One of the best examples of the chemistry of Budapest, the contribution of immigrants (predominantly Austrians, Germans, and Jews) to

---

the Question of Assimilation" in Bela Vago and George L. Mosse, eds., *Jews and Non-Jews in Eastern Europe 1918–1945* (Jerusalem: Keter, 1974), pp. 51–98; Péter Hanák, "Problems of Jewish Assimilation in Austria-Hungary in the Nineteenth and Twentieth Centuries," in P. Thane et al., eds., *The Power of the Past* (Cambridge: Cambridge University Press, 1984), pp. 235–250; Péter Hanák, "Stages and Types of National Assimilation in Hungary in the 19th Century" (MS, Budapest, 1983); Péter Hanák, "Polgárosodás és asszimiláció Magyarországon a XIX. században," [Embourgeoisement and Assimilation in 19th Century Hungary] *Történelmi Szemle*, Vol. XVII, 1974, pp. 513–536; Lajos Venetianer, *A magyar zsidóság története. Különös tekintettel gazdasági és művelődési fejlődésére a XIX. században* (Budapest: Fővárosi Nyomda Rt, 1922, new ed. Budapest: Könyvértékesítő Vállalat, 1986) pp. 147–173. Cf. Marsha L. Rozenblit, *The Jews of Vienna: Assimilation and Identity, 1867–1914* (Albany: SUNY, 1983); Gyula Farkas, *Az assimiláció kora a magyar irodalomban* [The Age of Assimilation in Hungarian Literature] (Budapest: Franklin, n.d.). For a stimulating contribution to this discussion see Nobuaki Terao, "Oscar Jászi and the Magyar-Jewish Alliance" (offprint, 1997).

53 Certificate of Baptism, Saint Mary's Cathedral, Trenton, NJ, April 11, 1935. John von Neumann Papers, Box 7, "Birth, Divorce, Other official documents," The Library of Congress, Washington, DC, Rare Books and Special Collections; Nicholas A. Vonneumann, *John von Neumann as Seen by his Brother* (Meadowbrook, PA, 1987), p. 17.

the success of Hungarian culture comes from the field of music. Here we see how the Hungarian version of the melting pot worked, especially in Budapest, showing the imprint of great German masters on their sometimes even greater Hungarian students, the transformation of cosmopolitan, European taste into the Hungarian vernacular, as well as the merging of the European traditions of musical high culture with the ancient folk legacy of Hungary. Music performed in the concert halls or often home made, played an important social and psychological role in the life of the middle class in an era when there was no gramophone, tape recorder or CD-player to produce it. Home produced music contributed to and helped sustain several layers of urban society.

Most Hungarian musicians received their professional education at the Music Academy of Budapest, founded by Franz Liszt in 1875. Liszt made a concerted effort to link his native Hungary with the more advanced, western part of Europe. He is remembered today primarily as a composer and a piano virtuoso and less for his organizational achievements in the international field of music, from which Hungary benefited perhaps most of all. After the Austro-Hungarian Compromise of 1867, Liszt, more at home in Weimar, Germany, and Rome, Italy, than anywhere in his native Hungary, settled in what was Pest, then a small, German-speaking provincial city connected to Buda by a single bridge. He stayed there from 1868 through the mid-1870s and his presence contributed to the spiritual growth of the city that became Budapest. He handpicked the first professors of musicology, violin, and cello, among others, and founded a musical tradition equal to the very best in Europe. He had both the reputation and the authority to attract the best people, Hungarians and foreigners, who came to the new Music Academy at his invitation. Professor Jenő Hubay gave up a promising career in Brussels, where he worked with the great violinist Eugene Ysaÿe, to return to Budapest and found what was to become a great school of violin at the Music Academy, where he remained for the rest of his life. Professor David Popper, originally from Prague and arguably the greatest cellist before Pablo Casals, came from a distinguished position as concertmaster in Vienna to teach and perform in Budapest. With Hubay, he formed a unique string quartet to present classical and contemporary chamber music by Johannes Brahms,

Antonín Dvořak, Josef Suk, Karl Goldmark, and others. Professor Hans Koessler came from his native Bavaria and became the teacher of subsequent generations of Hungarian composers. Though he was conservative in his own music and a follower of Brahms, he allowed his students a great measure of freedom to write their own, modern music. They included Béla Bartók, Zoltán Kodály, Ernő (Ernst von) Dohnányi, Leo Weiner, Imre (Emerich) Kálmán, Gershwin-editor Albert Szirmai, and several other well-known composers.[54]

However, none of these examples of late-19th century "modernism" should cause us to believe that Budapest did indeed become a center of modern music. Liszt himself was modern, the Music Academy much less so. As Bartók added in his inaugural address at the Hungarian Academy of Sciences in 1936, "[t]he compositions of Liszt exerted a greater fertilizing effect on the next generation than those of Wagner."[55] Liszt's Music Academy, however, set out to preserve classical values and nurtured conservative and cosmopolitan tastes; contemporary music was not appreciated, although it is difficult to argue that the musical public of the Hungarian capital was not at all responsive to the new voice of the twentieth century. Up to the end of the 19th century, however, the ideal was the late romanticism of Johannes Brahms, who often came to the Hungarian capital from nearby Vienna and some of his works were first performed by the Hubay-Popper Quartet and fine pianists like Vilma Adler-Goldstein in Budapest.

It was in the decade immediately preceding World War I that, in a delicate interplay with music, most modernist trends swept across the country in literature, the arts, philosophy, and the social and physical sciences. This incentive produced a renaissance of Hungarian national culture and the birth of modernism. It symbolically started with the

---

54   Tibor Frank, "Liszt, Brahms, Mahler," in György Ránki and Attila Pók, eds., *Hungary and European Civilization,* Indiana Studies on Hungary, 3 (Budapest: Akadémiai Kiadó, 1989), pp. 346–347.
55   Béla Bartók, "Liszt-problémák," [Liszt-Problems] *Nyugat* 29/3 (March 1936), pp. 24–28, quoted by Andor C. Klay, "Bartók on Liszt," *Journal of the American Liszt Society,* 1987, pp. 26–30.

poetry of Endre Ady (1877–1919), whose *Új versek* [New Poems] made a veritable literary revolution in 1906, and with the poetry anthology *A holnap* [Tomorrow] (1908–1909), with Ady, Mihály Babits, Béla Balázs, and Gyula Juhász among the most prominent names represented. The movement came into full speed with the launching of the (mainly) literary periodical *Nyugat* [West] in 1908, which was to become the dominating organ of the modernists through World War II and which published vintage modern poetry and prose by authors like, again, Endre Ady and Mihály Babits, as well as Margit Kaffka, Frigyes Karinthy, Dezső Kosztolányi, Zsigmond Móricz, Árpád Tóth, and a host of others.

The literary pioneers had their counterparts in almost every other field. The art group *Nyolcak* [The Eight], with Károly Kernstok, Róbert Berény, Béla Czóbel, and other excellent artists, was as important to this new generation as Béla Bartók and Zoltán Kodály were in music. Hungarian modernism was present in almost every field, and usually ahead of many European countries. The very best left Hungary early, first temporarily, most either during or right after the revolutions of 1918–1919. Many migrants kept returning to Hungary for visits before their decision to leave became final.

The immediate pre-World War I period nurtured a gifted and ambitious generation with politically liberal and sometimes leftist views intent on changing the outdated social and political system of the country.[56] Most who left Hungary after World War I were members, students or followers of this generation.

The lists are impressive by themselves and speak highly of the ability of many of the professors in Budapest to give not only a thorough musical training but also a good sense of how to understand the contemporary world. For the post-World War I generation of Hungarian musicians, Béla Bartók and Zoltán Kodály were the great examples admired and emulated. As Eugene Ormandy pointed out in a 1937 article for *The Hungarian Quarterly,* it was because of those two

---

56   John Lukacs, *op. cit.,* pp. 140–141.

that Hungary has emerged as a musical entity. This Hungarian music of the twentieth century is intensely nationalistic and, while nationalistic art is of necessity limited and destined to a comparatively short life, paradoxically enough the worlds of these two composers in the very intensity of their nationalism transcend[ed] nationalistic bounds.[57]

Ormandy added, "[i]n the dramatic inevitability of Bartók, we have a composer who might be compared to Beethoven [...] Breaking away from the over-refined, essentially cerebral and decadent music of the post-Romantic period, Bartók has injected new life blood into his music. It has a savagery and yet withal a youthful vitality that makes it of universal importance."[58] Bartók and Kodály revived "the racial idiom of Magyar music," Ormandy acknowledged, "to portray the distinct individuality of Hungarian music."[59]

The modernism of the music and ideas of Bartók and Kodály, their philosophy and lifestyle, integrity and puritanism, served in many ways as a model for their students at the Music Academy. Ormandy, along with Fritz Reiner and George Szell, was the first to present the music of Bartók to audiences outside Hungary. These conductors remained deeply committed to modern music throughout their career. Though mainly performing a classical repertoire, Eugene Ormandy had a real interest in contemporary music such as Gustav Mahler, Richard Strauss, Dimitri Shostakovich, and Dimitri Kabalevsky, whom he frequently introduced with the Philadelphia Orchestra.[60] Antal Dorati, besides being a composer himself, performed the work of many of his contemporaries like Paul Hindemith, as did Fritz Reiner who played Stravinsky, William Schuman, Zoltán Kodály, and Leo Weiner, and George Szell who also delighted in

---

57 Eugene Ormándy, "Modern Hungarian Music," *The Hungarian Quarterly* III, No. I, Spring 1937, p. 165.
58 *Ibid.*, pp. 165–167.
59 *Ibid.*, p. 167.
60 See Ormandy's correspondence with Princess Irina Sergeevna Volkonskaia, the daughter of Sergei Rachmaninov, 1955–1968; Columbia University, Butler Library, Rare Book and Manuscript Library.

performing Mahler, Hindemith, and Kodály, as well as Leoš Janáček, Jean Sibelius, Sergei Prokofiev, Sir William Walton, and Lukas Foss.

3 Schooling

Importing the Gymnasium

The outstanding success of education, and mathematics education in particular, underlines the significance of the Hungarian school system from the turn of the century until World War II. The secret of Hungary's émigré geniuses is partly the secret of Hungarian high schools before World War II and the result of a systematic effort in Hungary to develop an educational system along German lines. The Hungarian *gimnázium* was modeled upon the German *Gymnasium* and this was a studied effort on behalf of the new Hungarian government established after the Austro-Hungarian Compromise of 1867.[61]

The architect of this admirable knowledge transfer was Mór Kármán (1843–1915), one of Hungary's most renowned educational experts, a pedagogical reformer and the father of Theodore von Kármán. Kármán Sr. came from a distinguished Jewish-Hungarian background, studying philosophy and classical philology at the University of Vienna and receiving his Ph.D. in Budapest in 1866. In 1869, the able young educational philosopher was commissioned by Minister of Religion and Education Baron József Eötvös (1813–1871) to Leipzig, Saxony (in Germany), to study pedagogy and the modern theory and methods of training high school teachers, under the philosopher Professor Tuiscon Ziller (1817–

---

61 There were three types of *gimnázium* in Hungary: the regular *gimnázium* [high school] spanned over 6 years, the *algimnázium* [lower high school] 4 years, the *fögimnázium* [main or full high school] 8 years.

1882), founder of the pedagogical seminar at Leipzig.[62] Upon returning from Germany in 1872, Eötvös's immediate successor, Tivadar Pauler, helped him introduce the German system in Hungary and found the Institute for Teacher Training at the University of [Buda]Pest, as well as the "Practicing High School," or Model*gimnázium,* for prospective teachers, thus profoundly influencing Hungarian education in a German spirit and tradition.[63] Mór Kármán himself became director of the school, which all four of his sons, including Theodore, attended.

Becoming Hungary's foremost expert on education, Mór Kármán was elevated to the Hungarian nobility in 1907,[64] and became a full professor at Budapest University in 1909. He belonged to the assimilated Jewish upper-middle class of Hungary, and married into a well-connected family through which he was distantly related to the titled Jewish aristocracy of Hungary.[65] Mór Kármán felt himself close to Hungarian culture, and studied Hungarian literature.[66]

---

62 Baron József Eötvös, Minister of Religion and Education to Mór Kleinmann, Buda, July 20, 1869. No. 12039, Theodore von Kármán Papers, 142.10, California Institute of Technology Archives, Pasadena, CA.

63 Baron József Eötvös to Mór Kleinmann, Buda, July 20, 1869, *loc. cit.*; Untitled memoirs of Theodore von Kármán in his File 141.6, pp. 1–2. Cf. István Sőtér, *Eötvös József* [József Eötvös] (2. ed., Budapest: Akadémiai Kiadó, 1967); Miklós Mann, *Trefort Ágoston élete és működése* [The Life and Work of Ágoston Trefort] (Budapest: Akadémiai Kiadó, 1982).

64 Mór Kármán had some responsibility for planning the education of one of the Habsburg Archdukes and he received his title partly for this reason. Cf. William O. McCagg, Jr., *Jewish Nobles and Geniuses in Modern Hungary,* Boulder, CO, East European Monographs, 1972, repr. 1986. s, p. 209, note 46—it was this title that Theodore von Kármán used in a Germanized form.

65 Theodore von Kármán, Untitled note on Mór Kármán, Theodore von Kármán Papers, 141.6. Dr József Gerő, ed., *A Királyi Könyvek* [Royal Books] (Budapest, 1940), p. 100; William O. McCagg, Jr., *Jewish Nobles, op. cit.,* pp. 209; Péter Újváry, ed., *Magyar Zsidó Lexikon* (Budapest, 1929), pp. 453–454.

66 Mór Kármán, "Az Ember Tragédiája. Elemző tanulmány" (*Budapesti Szemle,* No. 346, 1905).—It is interesting to note that the Tragedy of Man was also a source of inspiration for other émigré scientists, such as Leo Szilárd.

Some of the high schools developed under Kármán's oversight were connected in various ways with the University of Budapest. Graduating university students were expected to do their practice teaching in "model" high schools. High school teachers themselves were expected to do original research and be published regularly, both in- and outside of Hungary. The most eminent teachers were invited to give university courses; some even became professors and were elected members of the Hungarian Academy of Sciences. The faculty of the best high schools in Budapest enjoyed a privileged position and high social prestige.

Most high school students came from the sheltered and privileged social background of a narrowly constructed middle class. For many years, these schools were all-male domains: the first *gimnázium* for girls was not opened in Austria until in 1892 and 1896 in Hungary. For socially aspiring Jewish students in particular, these schools acted as social equalizers, a much sought-after opportunity to integrate, emancipate, and assimilate into the emerging Hungarian "gentlemanly" middle class. Upon reaching the age of eighteen, the state-controlled, uniform system of Hungarian final examinations brought high school studies to a demanding, challenging conclusion, and catapulted young men into the Hungarian élite.[67]

The choice by many Jewish students (or their parents) to attend various Christian denomination high schools in the early twentieth century was related to the phenomenon of religious conversion. Though these schools were of exceptionally high quality,[68] sending children of Jewish origin to them expressed a willingness to assimilate. The Lutheran high school at Városligeti Fasor in Pest was a case in point, with dozens of extremely capable Jewish boys among the students every year. Notable examples were John von Neumann and Eugene P. Wigner. Teachers in these schools excelled in their field, as well as in the art of teaching, and

---

67 Viktor Karády, "A középiskolai elitképzés első történelmi funkcióváltása (1867–1910)," In: Viktor Karády, *Iskolarendszer és felekezeti egyenlőtlenségek Magyarországon (1867–1945). Történeti-szociológiai tanulmányok* [School system and denominational inequalities in Hungary 1867–1945. Historical-sociological studies] (Budapest: Replika Kör, 1997), pp. 169–194.

68 John Lukács, *op. cit.,* pp. 142–146.

several were recognized members of the scientific and scholarly community of Hungary.[69]

Defined by the act 1924:XI, high schools in Hungary were of three kinds: the *gimnázium*, the *reálgimnázium,* and the *reáliskola*. The *gimnázium* provided an all-round humanistic education, based primarily on studies in Latin and Greek language and literature. The *reálgimnázium* added modern languages and literatures to Latin, while the *reáliskola* gave a careful introduction to arithmetic and natural sciences and focused on modern languages alone.

As mentioned before, the *gimnázium* was an élitist school for the select few. In Budapest, there were 38 high schools with around 16,000 students in 1914–15, 46 high schools with 21,356 students in 1929–30, and 81 high schools with 32,111 students in 1942–43. In 1929–30, there were only 7 *gimnázium*s with 3,482 boys and another 7 with 2,907 girls, 14 *reálgimnázium*s with 8,167 students, and 7 *lycée* type schools for girls with 3,262 students. Altogether, 3,250 students attended the 7 *reál*schools. Even in 1941–42, there were only 26 *gimnázium*s for boys and 7 for girls, with 10 *lycée*s, while the other 24 schools were industrial, agricultural, commercial, and business in nature.[70]

In 1929–30, the number of Jewish students in the *gimnázium*s was 1,022 (out of the 2,806 who actually graduated), and in the *reálgimnázium*s there were 1,956 (out of 7,806 graduates). Altogether, 3,408 boys and 2,122 girls were Jewish out of the total of 14,142 boys and 6,384 girls who completed high school of some sort. By 1941–42, the number of Jews who attended *gimnázium*s was 3,742 (out of 21,369), altogether

---

69   László Kovács, *Mikola Sándor* [Sándor Mikola] (2nd ed., Budapest: Országos Pedagógiai Könyvtár és Múzeum, 1995).

70   Miklós Horváth, ed., *op. cit.,* p. 480; Lajos I. Illyefalvi, *Budapest Székesfőváros Statisztikai és Közigazgatási Évkönyve* [Yearbook of Statistics and Public Administration for the Capital City of Budapest], Vol. XIX, 1931 (Budapest: Budapest Székesfőváros Statisztikai Hivatala, 1931), pp. 426–427; Lajos Illyefalvy, ed., *Budapest Székesfőváros Statisztikai Évkönyve* [Yearbook of Statistics for the Capital City of Budapest] Vol. XXXI, 1943 (Budapest: Budapest Székesfőváros Statisztikai Hivatala, 1943), pp. 346–347.

totaling 4,365 Jewish students from an overall high school student body of 30,730.[71] The figures demonstrate the impact of emigration, conversion, and anti-Semitic legislation.

The Mintagimnázium

The *Mintagimnázium* [model high school], founded and first directed by Mór Kármán, was best described by his son Theodore von Kármán, himself a student of this school.

> The Minta, or Model Gymnasium, was the gem of my father's educational theories. It was designed to be directed by a professor at the University but to maintain an independent status. It became the model for all Hungarian high schools and today is quite famous in Hungary, though little known in the West. Recently, however, its high standing over the years was noted by a writer for the London *Observer*, who called the Minta a "nursery for the elite," and compared it with such schools as Eton for Conservative M.P.'s and [the Institut] Le Rosey [in Switzerland] for ex-kings and socialites. The Minta graduated two of Britain's top economists, Dr. Thomas Balogh of Balliol College (a son of one of my cousins) and Nicholas Kaldor of King's, Cambridge. ...[72]

As in all the *gimnázium* throughout Hungary, Latin was of paramount importance. Until the end of 1844, Latin was the state language of Hungary and educated people were all expected to read and write classical Latin. The study of Latin was also viewed as being useful for training the mind, strengthening the memory, and introducing the student to a complex system: Latin grammar.

> For me the Minta was a great educational experience. My father was a great believer in teaching everything—Latin, math, and history—by showing its connection

---

71 Lajos I. Illyefalvi, ed., *op. cit.*, pp. 426–427; Lajos Illyefalvy, ed., *op. cit.*, pp. 346–347.
72 Theodore von Kármán with Lee Edson, *The Wind and Beyond: Theodore von Kármán, Pioneer in Aviation and Pathfinder in Space* (Boston—Toronto: Little, Brown and Co., 1967), pp. 20–21.

with everyday living. In our beginning Latin class, for instance, I remember that we did not start with rules of grammar. Instead we were told to walk around the city and copy the Latin inscriptions on statues, churches, and museums. There were many of these to be found, since Latin was the official language in Hungary until 1848.[73] When we had collected the phrases and brought them to class, the teacher asked us which words we already knew. We usually could recognize a few words among the phrases. If we didn't, we looked them up. Then he asked us if we recognized the same word in different forms. Why were the forms different? Because they showed different relationships to other words in the inscription. We continued in this way until we understood each phrase and why it was placed on the monument. As a result of this practice, we all accumulated a Latin vocabulary which we retained and we deduced some fundamental rules for inflection of the Latin word. We also learned something of Hungary's past.[74]

Theodore von Kármán remembered fondly his Mathematics classes which also were based on inductive methods and related to practical life. (Another future celebrity from Budapest, Edward Teller, thought very differently of these classes and complained bitterly of the school as well as of his experiences with mathematics teaching.)[75] Von Kármán drew an important parallel between his classes in Latin and in Mathematics, the two cornerstones of Hungarian education in the *gimnázium*.

Mathematics, which I now studied eagerly, was taught in terms of everyday statistics and it had a fascination for me all over again. For instance, we looked up the figures on the production of wheat in Hungary for several years. We set up tables and then drew graphs, so we could observe the changes and locate the maximum and the minimum wheat production. In the diagrams we searched for correlations, and we learned about "the rate of change," which brought us to the edge of the calculus. We thus learned in a practical way that there was a relationship between quantities that varied, and, as with Latin, we learned at the same time something of the changing social and economic forces in the country.

---

73   In fact until the end of 1844 only.
74   Theodore von Kármán with Lee Edson, *The Wind and Beyond, op. cit.*, p. 20.
75   István Hargittai, *op. cit.*, pp. 14–15.

Figure 3. *Mintagimnázium* [Model High School], Budapest.
(Archive of the ELTE Trefort Ágoston Practice School)

Figure 4. Physics classroom, *Mintagimnázium*, Budapest. (Archive of the ELTE Trefort Ágoston Practice School)

> At no time did we memorize rules from the book. Instead we sought to develop them ourselves. I think this is a good system of education, for in my opinion how one learns the elements of reasoning in primary school will determine his later capacity for intellectual pursuits. In my case the Minta gave me a thorough grounding in inductive reasoning, that is, deriving general rules from specific examples—an approach that remained with me throughout my life.[76]

Mór Kármán was also a pioneer in initiating "practice teaching" in his school, regularly inviting graduating university students from various disciplines to acquire practical experiences for their future careers as high school teachers.

> In addition to introducing what were then novel methods of teaching, my father also started at the Minta the system of practice teaching by university graduate students. Some educators opposed this plan: it would expose us to inexperienced teachers, the *koca* (sows) as we high school students ungraciously called them. My father, on the other hand, firmly maintained that students would find it an advantage to learn as early as possible to distinguish between good and bad teaching.

The *Minta* school also provided a more democratic model, regarding especially teacher-student relations, which in most Hungarian and Austrian schools were traditionally rigidly formal and inpersonal.

> The Minta was the first school in Hungary to put an end to the stiff relationship between the teacher and the pupil which existed in the Empire [the Austro-Hungarian Monarchy] at the time. In the corridors of the Minta the teachers moved constantly among the pupils. Contrary to the practice in other high schools, students could talk to the teachers outside of classes and could discuss matters not strictly concerning school. The charter of the Minta declared in writing for the first time in Hungary that a teacher might go so far as to shake hands with a pupil in the event of their meeting outside class.[77]

---

76 *Ibid.*, pp. 21–22.
77 *Ibid.*, pp. 20–22.

The Lutheran Gimnázium

John von Neumann and Eugene Wigner attended the Lutheran *Gimnázium* in Budapest, became two of its top students and in turn made it internationally recognized.[78]

The origins of the Lutheran *gimnázium* of Pest go back to the late 18th century.[79] The earliest motor behind the school was Lajos Schedius (1768–1847), the enlightened, Göttingen-educated professor of philosophy at the University of Pest whose anonymously published *Die Schule der evangelischen Gemeinde A. C. in Pesth* (1816) emphasized the public nature of schools, and the importance of quality training of teachers, and spoke against the practice of mere recitation, calling instead for the emotional development of students. Much of the philosophy behind Lutheran education in Hungary came from the Swiss educator Johann Heinrich Pestalozzi (1746–1827).[80]

Lutheran schools mushroomed in the country; there were some twenty of them outside the city of Pest. The Pest school was so popular that it had to move to a new building in 1864 and then again in 1904. Erected in the *Városligeti fasor*, the elegant and fashionable esplanade that runs parallel to Budapest's prominent avenue, Andrássy út, the new building was one of the most up-to-date schools in contemporary Hungary. Designed by architecture professor Samu Pecz, the building was fully equipped with electricity and steam heating, 18 large class rooms, 14 cabinets for teachers and classroom demonstration material, dark rooms for experiments with light, film projection and photography, a six-room library, a five-room apartment for the director, a specially paved gym, and a huge community room for celebrations. By the beginning of the

---

[78] Krisztina Dobos, István Gazda, László Kovács, *A fasori csoda* [Miracle in the Fasor] (Budapest: Országos Pedagógiai Könyvtár és Múzeum, 2002), pp. 66–109; Norman Macrae, *John von Neumann* (New York: Pantheon Books, 1992), pp. 61–84.

[79] Victor Karády, "Juifs et luthériens dans le système scolaire hongrois." *Actes de la recherche en sciences sociales*, Vol. 69, 1987, pp. 95–110.

[80] Krisztina Dobos, István Gazda, László Kovács, *A fasori csoda, op. cit.*, pp. 8–9.

Figure 5. Design of the Lutheran *Gimnázium* [High School] in the *Fasor* [Esplanade] 1905. (School History Collection, Lutheran *Gimnázium* in the *Fasor*, Budapest)

century, there were 12,000 volumes in the library, which subscribed to some 20-30 foreign journals, half of them in German and English. As of 1901-1902, the supervisor of the library was no less a person than Sándor Mikola, the celebrated teacher of physics and prospective director of the school.[81]

The Lutheran Church of Hungary was convinced, however, that it was not the material equipment but the quality of the faculty that defined education. "Good teacher = good school" as the almost mathematical equation suggested in the school's 1922-1923 yearbook. Members of the faculty were near the level of university professors, with fourteen having graduated from the Eötvös Collegium, a Budapest version of the *École Normale Supérieure* in Paris, founded by Loránd Eötvös in 1895 to commemorate his father, Baron József Eötvös.[82]

Many of the best teachers had also studied in Germany, among them Károly Bőhm, Gedeon Pecz, János Loisch, Aurél Bászel, Sándor Dietze, Rudolf Weber, and Róbert Fröhlich, who studied with Theodor Mommsen. Several of the teachers went on to become university professors, such as Dezső Kerecsényi, who later taught Hungarian literature in the University of Debrecen, botanist Sándor Sárkány at the University of Budapest, mathematician Ágoston Schultz at the Technical University of Budapest; and the mathematician and physicist János Renner, who became the director of the Institute of Geophysics in Budapest. About two-thirds of the teachers in the *Fasor* regularly published in the most important (typically Hungarian) journals of their own field.[83]

---

81 *Ibid.*, pp. 10-13.
82 The case of the Collegium clearly demonstrated that Hungary's new intellectual élite was rooted not only in the middle- and uppermiddle-class of Budapest but also in the provinces, thus producing at least two, often competing factions. The Collegium provided a framework for the training of an élite, with its pool of young people coming mainly from the Hungarian countryside. Cf. Victor Karády, "Le Collège Eötvös et l'École Normale Supérieure vers 1900. Note comparatiste sur la formation d'intellectuels professionnels," in: Béla Köpeczi, Jacques Le Goff, eds., *Intellectuels français, intellectuels hongrois – XIIIe–XXe siècles*. Paris-Budapest, 1986.
83 Krisztina Dobos, István Gazda, László Kovács, *A fasori csoda, op. cit.*, pp. 13-18.

Figure 6. Nobel Laureate Eugene Wigner in his Princeton study with a picture
of László Rátz on the wall.
(School History Collection, Lutheran *Gimnázium* in the *Fasor*, Budapest)

Two important members of the faculty who had a major impact on John von Neumann were the mathematician László Rátz and the physicist Sándor Mikola. It is enlightening to assess the source of their impact.

A member of the *Fasor* faculty for 35 years, László Rátz (1863–1930) studied in the Lutheran *lycée* of Sopron, and the universities of Budapest, Berlin and Strassbourg. He treated all of his students equally and made them love his subject by demonstrating how best they could approach it at their own particular level. This highly individualized treatment brought the subject closer to students, irrespective of the nature of their own individual talent. He documented the practical aspects of mathematics and made its usefulness come alive. As editor of *Középiskolai Mathematikai Lapok* [High School Papers in Mathematics], he turned the school into a national center of mathematics teaching and made problem-solving into a national mathematics education program. He published the material of the first ten volumes in his *Mathematikai gyakorlókönyv* [Problem Book for Mathematics] in two parts (algebra and geometry), which became one of the basic textbooks of mathematical problem-solving worldwide. Many outstanding Hungarian mathematicians and scientists received their basic training in mathematics, and particularly mathematical problem-solving, through the work of László Rátz. As an acknowledgment of his role in modernizing mathematics education in 1909, he became the Hungarian member of the international committee for mathematics education and attended the congresses of Milan, Cambridge, and Paris. He was at his best when discovering, acknowledging, and nurturing talent and making his difficult subject generally well-liked and appreciated.[84]

As a teacher of mathematics, Rátz was a pioneer in introducing the elements of infinitesimal calculus and made the concept of the *function* a central aspect of his teaching. He published his new educational ideas along with colleague Sándor Mikola in 1910 under the title *Az infinitezimális számítások elemei a középiskolában* [Elements of infinitesimal calculus in the high school][85] which they later published in a new, improved

---

84   For the biography of Rácz see Krisztina Dobos, István Gazda, László Kovács, *A fasori csoda, op. cit.,* pp. 27–45.
85   Budapest: Franklin, 1910.

edition as *A függvények és az infinitezimális számítások elemei* [Elements of function and infinitesimal calculus][86]

Like his friend László Rátz, Sándor Mikola (1871–1945) was also a student of the Lutheran *lycée* of Sopron and of the University of Budapest where he studied with the Eötvös-student János Renner and met Loránd Eötvös himself. He became a teacher at the Lutheran *gimnázium* in 1897 and remained a member of the faculty until his retirement in 1935. He was director of the school between 1928 and 1935, and co-editor, with Lipót Fejér, of *Mathematikai és Fizikai Lapok* [Papers in Mathematics and Physics].[87] Mikola was an active experimental physicist whose studies on electricity were rewarded with a membership of the Hungarian Academy of Sciences in 1923. He was an enthusiastic teacher and educator, who loved his work as well as his students. He thrived when free to choose his working methods and put into application exact scientific terms such as the notion of development, the use of analogies and the creation of models.[88] For him, the notions of physics were born and developed rather than merely existing in a physical form: physical reality is the result of a process and not an existing set of facts. The teaching of physics started with either qualitative or virtual experiments, which helped students to develop their notions of physics. Mikola was enthusiastic about the inductive and heuristic method, which he believed was especially created for physics.[89]

> By applying appropriate questions the teacher tries to direct the thinking of his students to the subject, to help the subconscious experiences and making their instinctive mechanical notions conscious, to turn the direction of their thinking toward selecting the important, to develop their ability to observe and analyze, to enlighten the development of abstract physical notions and keep their interest in the subject by inspiring the necessary stimuli constantly awake...[90]

---

86 2nd ed. Budapest: Franklin, 1914.
87 For a biography of Mikola see László Kovács, *Mikola Sándor, op. cit.,* especially pp. 5–7; Krisztina Dobos, István Gazda, László Kovács, *A fasori csoda, op. cit.,* pp. 46–65.
88 László Kovács, *Mikola Sándor, op. cit.,* p. 21.
89 *Ibid.,* pp. 22–24.
90 Quoted by László Kovács, *Mikola Sándor, op. cit.,* p. 25.

He developed his principles of physics over the writing of several books such as *A physikai alapfogalmak kialakulása* [The development of the basic terms of physics] (1911), *A fizika gondolatvilága* [The Mind of Physics] (1933) and *A fizikai megismerés alapjai* [The Basics of Physical Cognition] (1941), which brought him full membership of the Hungarian Academy of Sciences by 1942.[91]

The Formative Years of Mathematics Education

When asked about the reasons for the development of so many excellent mathematicians in Hungary emerging at the turn of the century and after, George Pólya answered, "[a] general reason is that mathematics is the cheapest science." This was, indeed, important in a relatively underdeveloped country. As to specific reasons, Pólya listed the *Középiskolai Mathematikai Lapok* [High School Papers in Mathematics], the Eötvös Competition, and the personality of the mathematician Lipót Fejér.[92]

The key personality in late 19th century Hungarian science and mathematics was Baron Loránd Eötvös (1848–1919). Son of the author, philosopher, and statesman Baron József Eötvös, young Loránd was not only a major physicist in his own right, but also one of the truly great organizers of Hungarian science. Two subsequent ministers of education, his father József Eötvös as well as his uncle, Ágoston Trefort, who continued József Eötvös's work as Minister of Religion and Education, influenced him. It is important to notice, though for a very limited time, that Loránd Eötvös himself became Minister of Education (1894), in addition to his distinguished service as President of the Hungarian Academy of Sciences (1889–1905).

---

91   László Kovács, *Mikola Sándor, op. cit.*, p. 57.
92   G. Pólya, "Leopold Fejér," *Journal of the London Mathematical Society*, Vol. 36., 1961, p. 501; Ágnes Árvai Wieschenberg, "Identification and Development of the Mathematically Talented—The Hungarian Experience." Ph.D. Dissertation, The Graduate School of Arts and Sciences, Columbia University, 1984, pp. 86–87.

With his German (Heidelberg, Königsberg) educational background and inspiration, Eötvös created a small, private Mathematics Circle in Budapest, in the fall of 1885, to build an informal network among university professors and high school teachers and their best students.[93] As of 1891, this circle continued as the *Mathematikai és Physikai Társulat* [Society of Mathematics and Physics] with some 300 members. Loránd Eötvös served as the first president of the *Társulat*, which launched *Mathematikai és Physikai Lapok* [Mathematical and Physical Papers]. In his inaugural address, Eötvös expressed his hope that they "will do great service to the general cultural development of the country, because undoubtedly, the success of teaching in both higher and secondary schools depends above all on the scientific preparation of the teachers."[94] The special emphasis on the training of mathematics and physics teachers and on the achievement of the secondary school student in Hungary can thus be traced back to Loránd Eötvös.

When Loránd Eötvös became Minister of Education in 1894, this event was looked upon as the beginning of great scientific opportunity in Hungary. The time was ripe to launch a new, practical and successful Hungary in the realm of sciences. With the so-called *millennium* celebrations underway in 1896 to commemorate the 1000 years of the state of Hungary, these were times to impress the world with Hungary's achievements. Accordingly, Continental Europe's first subway system and largest Parliament were built in Budapest, along with a host of public buildings, theaters, museums, and universities, all as tributes to Hungary's architectural and building skills, innovative spirit in engineering, and entrepreneurial excellence.

As students were expected to compete in regular national interschool competitions in mathematics and science, the *Mathematikai és Physikai Társulat* honored Eötvös by launching an annual mathematics and physics competition "in order to discover those who are exceptional

---

93 Eötvös also surrounded himself with a circle of fellow Hungarian physicists in Heidelberg, see Gyula Radnai, *op. cit.*, p. 349.
94 Loránd Eötvös, "Szaktársainkhoz" [To our colleagues], *Mathematikai és Physikai Lapok*, Vol. 1, 1892, p. 1. Quoted by Ágnes Árvai Wischenberg, *op. cit.*, p. 23.

in these fields."[95] Appropriately named the Eötvös Competition, a first and a second prize were awarded to the best secondary school graduates. Results were reported directly to the Ministry of Education, along with their teachers' names, and also were published in the *Mathematikai és Physikai Lapok*.

To support preparations for future competitions, 1894 also saw the inauguration of *Középiskolai Mathematikai Lapok* [High School Papers in Mathematics], edited by Dániel Arany, an outstanding high school mathematics teacher from the Western Hungarian city of Győr. László Rátz, the future teacher of mathematics of John von Neumann and Eugene Wigner, continued Arany's editorial work, between 1896 and 1914. The problems to be solved crossed a variety of fields such as algebra, calculus, combinatorics, geometry, number theory, and trigonometry, and the problems always required creative thinking. Pride, rather than money was the reward of the best students.

The organizational structure of these competitions, along with the related new publications, provided a well-structured and carefully regulated framework of preparation for future professional challenges these students would face.

The idea of awards and competitions was not restricted to Budapest and the Eötvös Prize alone. For example, upon the death of the reputable high school mathematics teacher Adolf Prilisauer (1859–1913), his city of Kaposvár in Western Hungary along with his former teaching colleagues, established a prize for the best student in mathematics.[96]

---

95 "Értesítő a Mathematikai és Physikai Társulat választmányának f. é. Június hó 22-ikén tartott üléséről." [Minutes of the June 22 meeting of the Mathematical and Physical Society], *Mathematikai és Physikai Lapok* 3, 1894, 197–198, quoted by Ágnes Árvai Wischenberg, *op. cit.,* p. 26.
96 Gyula Kovács-Sebestény and Károly Pongrácz, "Felhívás." [Appeal] Kaposvár, June 1913. *A kaposvári Magyar Királyi Állami Főgimnázium Emlékkönyve 1812–1912* [Centenary Memorial of the Hungarian Royal State High School at Kaposvár] (Kaposvár: Szabó Lipót Könyvsajtója, 1913), pp. 177–178.

The *Középiskolai Matematikai és Fizikai Lapok* [Highschool Papers in Mathematics and Physics], the *Eötvös Loránd fizikai verseny* [Eötvös Loránd Competition in Physics] and the *Arany Dániel országos matematika verseny* [Arany Dániel National Competition in Mathematics] have survived until today and maintain the living tradition of a world-class mathematics education based on early training, competitive spirit, and the recognition of talent.

Fascination with Genius

In and out of the school system, mental processes and the concept and structure of cognition received increasing attention in fin-de-siècle Central Europe. Hungary's new generation was intrigued by the phenomena of scientific discovery and problem-solving. Contemporary Europe was fascinated, indeed, thrilled by genius, and the subject seemed particularly relevant in Germany and the Austro-Hungarian Monarchy, well before World War I. Italian psychiatrist Cesare Lombroso's landmark study on genius and insanity [*Genio e follia*, 1864] was translated into German in 1887, his *L'uomo di genio in rapporto alla psichiatria* (1889) in 1890. Hermann Türck published a highly successful study on genius in 1896 in Berlin, Albert Reibmayer described talent and genius in Munich in 1908 in two volumes, and Wilhelm Ostwald studied the biology of genius in Leipzig in 1910. Ernst Kretschmer published his Marburg university lectures on genius in 1929, shortly after the appearance of W. Lange-Eichbaum's volume on genius and madness.[97]

---

97 Cesare Lombroso, *Genie und Irrsin* (Übersetzt von A. Courth; Leipzig: Reclam, 1887); Hermann Türck, *Der geniale Mensch* (7. Aufl., Berlin: Dümmlers, 1910); Dr. Albert Reibmayr, *Die Entwicklungsgeschichte des Talentes und Genies,* Vols. I–II (München: J. F. Lehmanns, 1908); Wilhelm Ostwald, *Grosse Männer* (Leipzig: Akademische Verlagsgesellschaft m.b.H., 1910); W. Lange-Eichbaum, *Genie, Irrsinn und Ruhm* (München: Ernst Reinhardt, 1928); Ernst Kretschmer, *Geniale Menschen* (2. Aufl. Berlin: Julius Springer, 1931); W. Lange-Eichbaum, *Das Genie-Problem* (München: Ernst Reinhardt, 1931).

Research in Germany obviously influenced, or at least coincided with, Lewis M. Terman's Stanford studies on genius. Both the German and the American studies on intelligence were based largely on the French Binet-Simon intelligence test, which was adapted for the needs of several countries (for example, the Stanford-Binet Scale developed by Terman in the United States, as well as the tests by Bobertag in Germany, Jaederholm in Sweden, and Mátyás Éltes in Hungary). Considerable interest was shown in the subject in contemporary Hungary, as indicated by Henriette von Szirmay-Pulszky's study of genius and insanity among Hungarian intellectuals[98] as well as József Somogyi's book on talent and eugenics.[99] Psychologist Géza Révész studied talent and genius throughout his career, culminating in his 1952 book *Talent und Genie*.[100]

To be sure, Central Europe was dazzled and perplexed by the secrets of the mind and its workings, and the processes of understanding/knowing, intuition/perception, intelligence/intellect came to be recognized as central issues in the sciences and humanities of German-speaking Europe. In 1935, Karl Duncker of the University of Berlin provided a summary of the psychology of productive thinking.[101] To those trained by the German literature on the subject, including several generations of Hungarian scientists and scholars, the plethora of work done on productive thinking in German provided copious introductions to the theory of knowledge, the biology of talent, and the philosophy of problem-solving. Much of

98 H. von Szirmay-Pulszky, *Genie und Irrsinn im Ungarischen Geistesleben* (München: Ernst Reinhardt, 1935).
99 Dr. József Somogyi, *Tehetség és eugenika. A tehetség biológiai, pszichológiai és szociológiai vizsgálata* [Talent and Eugenics. The Biological, Psychological, and Sociological Study of Talent] (Budapest: Eggenberger, 1934).
100 Géza Révész, "Das frühzeitige Auftreten der Begabung und ihre Erkennung," *Zeitschrift für angewandte Psychologie*, Band 15 (Leipzig: Lippert & Co., 1921); Géza Révész, *The Psychology of a Musical Prodigy* (London: Kegan, 1925); Géza Révész, *Das Schöpferisch-persönliche und das Kollektive in ihrem kulturhistorischen Zusammenhang* (Tübingen: Mohr, 1933); Géza Révész, *Talent und Genie. Grundzüge einer Begabungspsychologie (Bern: Francke, 1952).*
101 Dr. Karl Duncker, *Zur Psychologie des produktiven Denkens* (Berlin: Julius Springer, 1935).

the interest in the theory of knowledge and of knowing was generated in Vienna, where philosophers such as Professors Ernst Mach and Ludwig Boltzmann contributed significantly to the development of a scientific interpretation of the workings of the mind. Mach's main concern was the relationship between everyday thinking and scientific reasoning.[102] Franz Brentano and his students Kasimir Twardowski and Christian von Ehrenfels were active in the field of phenomenology and knowledge and played an important role in the philosophical study of language.[103] From Vienna these new ideas and trends spread quickly to Budapest.

Mach's work had considerable influence on contemporary European philosophers and scientists such as the English Sir Oliver Lodge and Karl Pearson, the Russian A. Bogdanov, and the Austrian Friedrich Adler, assassin of Austrian Prime Minister Count Karl von Stürgkh. These works became a target of vicious critical attack by V. I. Lenin in his defense of Marxism in 1908 for "the old absurdity of philosophical subjective idealism."[104] It is remarkable how anti-Marxist, non-Marxist, pseudo-Marxist scholarship, and particularly Ernst Mach's work, influenced the philosophical tradition in central Europe, including Germany, Austria and Hungary.[105] Apart from the actual content of Mach's studies, their philosophical and political implications were also relevant in the region, making a lasting impact on liberal thinkers who endeavored to maintain an anti-totalitarian stance in an age of political and doctrinal dictator-

---

102 Ernst Mach, *Erkenntnis und Irrtum. Skizzen zur Psychologie der Forschung* (2nd ed. Leipzig: Barth, 1906), p. XI.
103 Peter Weibel, "Das Goldene Quadrupel: Physik, Philosophie, Erkenntnistheorie, Sprachkritik. Die Schwelle des 20. Jahrhunderts: Wissenschaftliche Weltauffassung in Wien um 1900," in: *Wien um 1900. Kunst und Kultur* (Wien-München: Christian Brandstätter, 1985), 407–418; J. C. Nyíri, "Ehrenfels und Masaryk: Überlegungen an der Peripherie der Geschichte," in: *Am Rande Europas, op. cit.,* pp. 40–67.
104 V. I. Lenin, *Materialism and Empirio-Criticism. Critical Comments on a Reactionary Philosophy* (1st ed. 1908; London: Lawrence and Wishart, 1950), p. 93.
105 Péter Hanák, "Ernst Mach und die Position des Phänomenalismus in der Wissenschaftsgeschichte," in *Europa um 1900* in Fritz Klein, Hg., Texte eines Kolloquiums [Association Internationale d'Histoire Contemporaine de l'Europe] (Berlin: Akademie Verlag, 1989), pp. 265–282.

ships. Albert Einstein extensively used Mach's epistemology and physics, including "Mach's Principle," in his theory of general relativity.[106]

The anti-Marxian roots of liberal thought contributed to the complete estrangement of Hungarian émigré scientists and scholars such as Michael Polanyi and Oscar Jászi after the Soviet takeover of 1945 and made their already existing, pre-War anti-Soviet attitudes definitive. Apart from directly political reasons, this framework may be helpful in understanding the seemingly unconditional support given to the U.S. military and to NATO during the Cold War period by scientists such as John von Neumann, Theodore von Kármán, Karl Mannheim, and, most notably, Edward Teller. The philosophical underpinnings of the anti-totalitarian politics of Hungary's émigré professionals can thus be traced to the traditional idealistic approach to science in Central Europe and the corresponding *Weltanschauung*, a legacy emanating from the philosopher George Berkeley through Albert Einstein.

The notion of a new type of learning, utilizing problem solving and the heuristic method came to be proposed by European immigrant scientists and mathematicians, several of them Hungarians. By the end of World War I, young Karl Mannheim had already written his doctoral dissertation in Budapest on the structural analysis of the theory of knowledge. The dissertation became well known after being published in German in 1922 as *Die Strukturanalyse der Erkenntnistheorie* [The Structural Analysis of Cognition Theory]. Mannheim drew heavily on the work of the Hungarian philosopher Béla Zalai, who, though largely forgotten today, was instrumental in presenting the question of systematization as

---

106 *The Encyclopaedia Britannica* (Chicago: Encyclopaedia Britannica, 1990), Vol. 7, p. 631; cf. Albert Einstein, "Principles of Research," Address before the Physical Society in Berlin, 1918; "Geometry and Experience," Lecture before the Prussian Academy of Sciences, January 27, 1921; "On the Theory of Relativity," Lecture at King's College in London, 1921; "Physics and Reality," *The Journal of the Franklin Institute*, Vol. 221, No. 3, March 1936, republished in Albert Einstein, *Ideas and Opinions* (New York: Bonanza Books, 1954), pp. 227, 239, 248, 303.

The Social Construction of Hungarian Genius

a central issue in Hungarian philosophy. In 1918, Mannheim referred to a 1911 article by Zalai on the problem of philosophical systematization.[107]

In a related field, heuristics was described as "tactics of problem solving," and "an interdisciplinary no man's land which could be claimed by scientists and philosophers, logicians and psychologists, educationalists and computer experts."[108] Fascination with the subject among émigré Hungarians is probably best demonstrated by three important books by the author Arthur Koestler. Sharing the background of many of the Hungarian scientists in exile, Koestler was intrigued by the "act of creation" for a long time after World War II *(Insight and Outlook, 1949; The Sleepwalkers, 1959; The Act of Creation, 1964)*. While working on these books, Koestler regularly consulted some of his illustrious Hungarian friends in England, such as Nobel Laureate Dennis Gabor or Michael Polanyi, and Koestler once went to Stanford specifically to discuss the matter with Hungarian-American mathematician George Pólya.[109] The

---

107 Karl Mannheim, *Die Strukturanalyse der Erkenntnistheorie*, Kant-Studien, Ergänzungshefte, No. 57, Berlin: Reuther & Reichard, 1922. (Hungarian original: *Az ismeretelmélet szerkezeti elemzése*, Budapest: Athenaeum, 1918); Béla Zalai, "A filozófiai rendszerezés problémái," [The Problem of Philosophical Systematization], *A Szellem*, 1911, No. 2, pp. 159–186; Vilmos Szilasi, *A tudati rendszerezés elméletéről. Bevezetés* [On the Theory of Systematization of the Mind. An Introduction] A Magyar Filozófiai Társaság Könyvtára, Vol. II (Budapest: Franklin, 1919) Cf. Otto Beöthy, "Zalai Béla (1882–1915). Egy pálya emlékezete," [Béla Zalai (1882–1915). The Memory of a Life], in: Endre Kiss and Kristóf János Nyíri, eds., *A magyar filozófiai gondolkodás a századelőn* [Hungarian Philosophy at the Turn of the Century] (Budapest: Kossuth, 1977), pp. 228–231.
108 George Polya, "Methodology or Heuristics, Strategy or Tactics?" *Archives de Philosophie*, Tome 34, Cahier 4, Octobre-Décembre 1971, pp. 623–629, quote p. 624.
109 Arthur Koestler, *Insight and Outlook: An Inquiry into the Common Foundations of Science, Art and Social Ethics* (New York: Macmillan, 1949); *The Sleepwalkers: A History of Man's Changing Vision of the Universe* (New York: Grosset & Dunlap, 1959); *The Act of Creation* (New York: Macmillan, 1964). Cf. M[enachen] M. Schiffer, "George Polya, 1887–1985," George Pólya Papers, SC 337, 87–034, Box 1, Department of Special Collections and University Archives, Stanford University Libraries, Stanford, CA; cf. Arthur Koestler, *The Act of Creation, op. cit.* p. 23;

tradition of heuristics is deeply European, with roots in antiquity (Euclid, Pappus, and Proclus) and with forerunners such as Descartes and Leibniz. Heuristic thinking reached the Habsburg empire early in the nineteenth century when it became part of Bernard Bolzano's philosophy: his four-volume *Wissenschaftslehre* [Theory of Science] (1837) already contained an extensive chapter on *Erfindungskunst* [The Art of Discovery], meaning heuristics. Through the questionable services of his disciple Robert Zimmermann, who possibly plagiarized much of Bolzano's original book and published many of his master's ideas under his own name in a popular and widespread textbook called *Philosophische Propädeutik* [Philosophical Propedeutics] (1853), these ideas reached a wide audience, and *Erfindungskunst* became an integral part of the philosophical canon of the Habsburg monarchy just before the great generation of scientists and scholars was about to be born.[110]

Béla Hidegkuti, "Arthur Koestler and Michael Polanyi: Two Hungarian Minds in Partnership in Britain," *Polanyiana*, Vol. 4, No. 4, Winter 1995, pp. 1–81.

110 Eduard Winter, Hg., *Robert Zimmermanns Philosophische Propädeutik und die Vorlagen aus der Wissenschaftslehre Bernard Bolzanos. Eine Dokumentation zur Geschichte des Denkens und der Erziehung in der Donaumonarchie* (Wien: Böhlau Verlag, 1975), pp. 7–36. Cf. Bernard Bolzanos *Wissenschaftslehre*: Versuch einer ausführlichen und grösstentheils neuen Darstellung der Logik mit steter Rücksicht auf deren bisherige Bearbeiter (Sulzbach: J. E. v. Seidel, 1837).

II The Hungarian Trauma, 1918–1920

1 Watershed 1919: Social Tension and Intellectual Exodus

Hungary was particularly hard hit by the consequences of World War I, not only from her association with Germany and thus being irredeemably on the losing side, but the lost war also released long simmering social tensions and energies that facilitated the outbreak of subsequent revolutions. In addition, the country had to accept the humiliating peace treaty of Trianon, the symbol and consequence of the military success of the Entente powers. Tragically, the treaty paved the way for Hungary's involvement in World War II. Though much of this is textbook history, a review of some of the crucial points of Hungarian history in the years 1918–1920 can serve as a background to the devastating intellectual exodus that followed postwar events.[1]

World War I, the "Great War," was immediately followed by the "Frost Flower (Aster) Revolution" (October 31, 1918), which preceded the German armistice. Headed by Count Mihály Károlyi, a magnate and one of the few steady opponents of the War from its beginning, the 1918 revolution was geared toward a liberal transformation of Hungary from a largely feudal to a bourgeois-democratic system with well-known radicals and liberals, including scholars and social scientists, in the government. The liberal-democratic, occasionally leftist élite, and the radical elements in early twentieth-century Hungarian politics, academia, literature and the arts, may have felt for a brief period of time that their long fight for the

---

1   For a brief introduction to the period see Tibor Hajdú and Zsuzsa L. Nagy, "Revolution, Counterrevolution, Consolidation," in: Peter Sugar, Péter Hanák, and Tibor Frank, eds., *A History of Hungary* (Bloomington–Indianapolis: Indiana University Press, 1990), pp. 295–318.

modernization of the country against the repressive régimes of pre-World War I Hungary had finally come to a successful and promising climax. Prime minister-turned-president in the newly proclaimed Republic of Hungary, Count Károlyi promoted a much-overdue land reform and addressed major social problems. He failed, however, to handle the rapidly deteriorating international as well as domestic political and economic situation and half-heartedly handed over power to the Communists, whom his government quite stubbornly and effectively oppressed until their takeover on March 21, 1919.

The short-lived Hungarian "Republic of Councils" (in Hungarian: *Tanácsköztársaság*) was a translation of the "soviets" and was largely imported from Soviet Russia by former Hungarian prisoners of war, who had spent years in Russian POW camps during World War I where they had been indoctrinated with the ideas and ideals of Communism. It seemed that the "Soviet" Republic of Hungary tried to realize the dreams of the Bolsheviks: its leader, Béla Kun, as well as some of his associates were in constant, sometimes even personal touch with Lenin himself. The leaders of 1919 outdid those of 1918 in terms of radicalism, social engineering and imported visionary utopianism and were often completely detached from the realities of post-World War I Hungary. Theirs was a major social experiment turned into total disaster. Initially popular among certain groups of workers, poor people in general, and some intellectuals, the system succeeded in alienating not only the middle class but even the peasantry, and ended up after 133 days with no social backing whatsoever. Its only visible success was a nationally popular effort to retake former Hungarian territories that by 1919 had become dominated by the Czechs and its willingness to fight for Transylvania, occupied by Romania, which had used the political vacuum to move well into the heart of Hungary. By early August 1919, the Soviet experiment was over, and Béla Kun's régime had to go.[2]

---

[2] On the first year of the (mainly Communist) Hungarian emigration see György Borsányi, "Az emigráció első éve" [The first year of emigration], *Valóság*, 1977/12, pp. 36–49.

Many of the leaders in both revolutions, but particularly of the 1919 Republic of Councils, came from a Jewish background. About two-thirds of the "people's commissars" (as ministers of the government were then called) and their deputies were Jews. Jewish presence was particularly noted in the police forces and in the cultural ministry. To appreciate and understand 1919, we must set it against the background of Jewish-Hungarian social history.

By the end of the nineteenth century, in little over two generations, Hungary had absorbed a vast influx of several hundred thousand Jewish immigrants from Russian and Austrian Poland. Hungary was a country whose Hungarian citizens were not necessarily all native speakers of the Magyar tongue. Yet, the new refugees were for the most part little tolerated and even despised by the happier few who had arrived earlier, between the mid-eighteenth and the mid-nineteenth century, either from Moravia or other westernized territories of the Habsburg Monarchy. Many of these earlier arrivals had quickly assimilated to the Hungarian traditions, learned the Hungarian language, appreciated the dominant Hungarian culture, and become devoted to the national/nationalist sentiment that swept across the country during much of the nineteenth century. They played an important role in building the new Hungary of the Austro-Hungarian Monarchy (1867–1918), its economy, its professional class, its culture and knowledge. They had quickly entered politics, even parliament and the government. Just like their equivalents in Vienna, they received titles from the emperor-king Franz Joseph I, entered the ranks of the lower nobility, and for some, even the titled ranks of high aristocracy. They produced and owned much of the new wealth and exercised considerable influence and even political clout by the time the "newcomers" from Galicia or Russia were moving into the country. It was almost inevitable that the two groups would find each other offensive, and their conflicts contributed to the end of their "love-affair."[3]

---

3 Raphael Patai, *The Vanished Worlds of Jewry*, p. 68. For some brief but very succinct comments see Hugh Seton-Watson, *Nations and States. An Enquiry into the Origins of Nations and the Politics of Nationalism* (London: Methuen, 1977), pp. 389–390, 394, 426.

After the takeover of Admiral Miklós Horthy's White Army in August 1919 and a succession of extremely right-wing governments, "Jew" and "Communist" became almost synonymous. As Hugh Seton-Watson remarked, "[t]he identification of 'the Jews' with 'godless revolution' and 'atheistic socialism,' characteristic of the Russian political class from 1881 to 1917, was now also largely accepted by the corresponding class in Hungary."[4] Bolshevism was considered "a purely Jewish product," as sociologist Oscar Jászi described it in his reminiscences. Jews were punished for the Commune as a group.[5] Until Horthy was proclaimed regent of Hungary on March 1, 1920, the country lived under the constant threat of extremist, sometimes paramilitary commandos, who tortured and killed almost anyone, Jew or non-Jew, who was said or thought to have been associated in any way with the Béla Kun government. Intellectual leaders lost their jobs as a matter of course. Jewish students were repeatedly beaten. In Prague and Brünn (today Brno), many Hungarians "indeed almost Hungarian colonies, of some 100–200 people" according to New York engineer Marcel Stein's memory, "left Hungary not as Communists but as Jews."[6] The year 1920 saw the introduction of the Numerus Clausus Act: for anyone who was Jewish, starting a career was becoming nearly impossible. There were few ways to survive politically, economically, and intellectually; the safest solution was, indeed, to flee the country.[7]

On top of this turmoil, the devastating peace treaty of Trianon effectively transferred the larger part of the former kingdom of Hungary to newly created or aggrandizing neighboring "nation-states" (in actual fact multi-ethnic, multinational countries) such as Czechoslovakia,

---

4   Hugh Seton-Watson, *op. cit.*, p. 399.
5   Oscar Jászi, *Revolution and Counter-Revolution in Hungary* (New York: Howard Fertig, 1969), pp. 122–124, quote p. 123.
6   Interview with Marcel Stein at Columbia University, New York City, November 29, 1989.
7   The first major introduction to the territory of Hungarian intellectual emigration after World War I is Lee Congdon's *Exile and Social Thought. Hungarian Intellectuals in Germany and Austria, 1919–1933* (Princeton, N.J.: Princeton University Press, 1991), an important book.

Romania, and the "Kingdom of Serbs, Croats, and Slovenes" (later, as of 1929, Yugoslavia). The Hungarians of those multiethnic territories immediately began experiencing many difficulties. Once again, Hungarian intellectuals or would-be intellectuals of those regions had very little choice but to leave.

Budapest became frustrated, angry, and dangerous. Leaders and members of the Radical Party felt particularly bitter and lost.[8] One of those was a former cabinet minister under Count Károlyi and one of his few personal friends, the anti-Bolshevik radical Oscar Jászi[9] (1875–1957). A versatile and original social scientist/politician, "Minister Entrusted with the Preparation of the Right of Self-Determination for Nationalities Living in Hungary" in late 1918, he became a professor at Oberlin College, Ohio, from the 1920s until his death, and author of the widely read *The Dissolution of the Habsburg Monarchy*. Jászi's Hungarian friends included some of the best liberal and radical minds of early twentieth-century Hungary, most of whom gathered in the *Társadalomtudományi Társaság* [Society for Social Sciences], and published in its journal *Huszadik Század* [Twentieth Century], which was introduced by no less a patron than Herbert Spencer. The spectacular galaxy that surrounded them and who made their reputations abroad included art historians Frederick Antal, Arnold Hauser, and Charles de Tolnay, film theoretician and poet Béla Balázs, philosopher Georg Lukács, sociologist Karl Mannheim, economic historian Karl Polányi and his brother, the physical chemist turned philosopher Michael Polanyi.

---

8   On the differences between Radicals and Socialists see Imre Csécsy, "Radikalizmus és szociálizmus," (Radicalism and Socialism) in: *Radikalizmus és demokrácia* [Radicalism and Democracy]: *Csécsy Imre válogatott írásai* [The Select Writings of Imre Csécsy] (Szeged, 1988), pp. 47–49.
9   Péter Hanák, *Jászi Oszkár dunai patriotizmusa* [Oscar Jászi's Danubian Patriotism] (Budapest: Magvető, 1985); see also Hugh Seton-Watson, *op. cit.*, pp 166–167. Cf. Tibor Hajdu, *Az 1918-as magyarországi polgári demokratikus forradalom* [The Hungarian Bourgeois Democratic Revolution in 1918] (Budapest: Kossuth Könyvkiadó, 1968); György Litván, *A Twentieth-Century Prophet: Oscar Jászi 1875–1957* (Budapest: Central European University Press, 2005).

Jászi's first marriage is a good example of some of the social patterns of Hungarian Jewry. The gifted author and artist Anna Lesznai (1885–1966) came from a distinguished, gentrified, upper-middle class Jewish-Hungarian family. Her grandfather was a celebrated doctor in northeastern Hungary, who distinguished himself in the fight against the cholera epidemic of 1831 and could even boast of a personal relationship with Hungary's great 19th century national leader Lajos Kossuth. Lesznai's father, Geyza Moscowitz de Zemplén, was a rich landowner who gave important support to Count Gyula Andrássy, the first Hungarian prime minister in the newly transformed monarchy (1867–1871) and later, more importantly, Austro-Hungarian minister of foreign affairs (1871–1878). Moscowitz received a title and was the only Jewish member of the discriminating aristocratic *Nemzeti Casino* [National Club].[10] Anna Lesznai changed her name and took one from the family estate at Körtvélyes (today Hrušov in Slovakia) where she grew up.

Jászi's own reminiscences indicate his detesting equally both "Bolshevism" and the "White Terror," a stance typically shared by the radicals of Hungary.[11] He soon came to the conclusion that "the mechanical State Communism of the Marxists cannot be a higher stage of development, as it would completely absorb the freedom and self-direction of the individual."[12] Jászi provided the first scholarly and penetrating "critical estimate of the proletarian dictatorship" and demonstrated, in his own words, "the economic and moral bankruptcy of the Soviet Republic."[13] He abhorred the raging of the White Terror, which he described as "one of the darkest pages of Hungarian history," and condemned the new régime just as uncompromisingly for "the complete suppression of popular liberties."[14]

10 For the family background see Anna Lesznai, *Kezdetben volt a kert* [First There Was the Garden] (Budapest: Szépirodalmi Könyvkiadó, 1966), Vols. I–II.
11 Oscar Jászi, *op. cit.*, Chapter IX.
12 *Ibid.*, p. 113.
13 *Ibid.*, p. 153.
14 *Ibid.*, pp 160, 177.

The Hungarian Trauma, 1918–1920

The letters Jászi received from family and friends during his 1919–1920 Vienna exile reveal much of the anguish, distress, and misery of the post-revolutionary period. Father Sándor Giesswein's letter to him reflected the Budapest mood in the fall of 1919: "With us the atmosphere is like in the middle of July 1914—were we not at the outset of Winter we would again hear the voice subdued in so many bosoms: Long live the war!—This is what the Hungarian needs."[15]

The successful author and playwright Lajos Biró received similar news in Florence from his friends in Hungary: "Letters from home keep telling me that everybody reckons with the opportunity of a new war by next Spring. The war is unimaginable, impossible, madness; but in Hungary, so it seems, it is the unimaginable that always happens."[16] Jászi's brother-in-law, Professor József Madzsar added:

> [...] the distant future is dark. The air is unbelievably poisoned, it feels as if in a room filled with carbon dioxide, one must get out of here, anywhere, otherwise it gets suffocating. Please write to me whether there is something toward Yugoslavia or whether or not something can be done in Czechoslovakia. There are serious negotiations here with the British and there is some chance toward Australia, the very best prepare themselves, it will be good company.[17]

Others also placed their hopes on newly-established Czechoslovakia. Lajos Biró, however, had a number of questions: "What do the Czechs say? How do they envisage the future? How does Masaryk envisage it?"[18] On

---

15 Sándor Giesswein to Oscar Jászi, Budapest, November 24, 1919, Columbia University, Butler Library, Rare Book and Manuscript Library, Oscar Jászi Papers, Box 5. [Original in Hungarian.]—Sándor Giesswein (1856–1923) was co-founder of the Christian Socialist movement in Hungary, and a courageous and outspoken Member of Parliament.

16 Lajos Biró to Oscar Jászi, Firenze, December 25, 1919, Oscar Jászi Papers, Box 5. [Original in Hungarian]

17 József Madzsar to Oscar Jászi, Budapest, November 6, 1919, Oscar Jászi Papers, Box 5. [Original in Hungarian.]—József Madzsar (1876–1940) was a versatile doctor and social activist, editor and author who moved from a Radical background toward the Communist Party in later life.

18 Lajos Biró to Oscar Jászi, Firenze, December 25, 1919, *loc. cit.*

another occasion Biró, with some bitterness and mockery, felt he had a bad choice in front of him when it came to Czechoslovakia: "If news about Horthy turns out to be true and he resorts to conscription and attacks the Czechs, then–then one can only shoot oneself in desperation over the fate of Hungary or else... he can volunteer to join Horthy's army."[19]

"To live here in [Buda]Pest today is very obnoxious, the uncertainty, that on anybody's petty accusations or charges you could get into prison, how nauseating," the influential avant-garde artist Károly Kernstok thought.[20] The air was filled with fear. "Dénes Nagy resigned from the secretaryship of the Free School, *he is afraid as are most people*, he is anxious to keep his job in the [ministry of] Public Food Supply,"[21] an admirer of Jászi, Ambró Czakó, informed him at the time. "I was also hit by clericalism, I lost my job (in the pedagogical institute)," he went on,

> although the faculty nominated me three times in the first place, it was the secretary of the Calvinist department of the Christ[ian] Soc[ialist] Party who got the job[...] It is a great pity, that the element which supported us in the progressive cause is— cowardly. [...][The socialist editor] Béla Somogyi[22] was right when he said to me the other day: It is very bad that however outstanding a man Jászi is, there is no one behind him, as there is no radical bourgeoisie, only cowardly Jews. Though this is not true that way, but it does contain some truth [...] The Hungarians are indeed angry at the Jews, the clericals for Bolshevism, we on the other hand for their recent spineless behavior.[23]

This was a pointed reference, indeed, to the lack of courage or simply unwillingness of Jewish intellectuals to rally against the White Terror in the fall and winter of 1919–1920 and stand up against the "White" army of Admiral Miklós Horthy. Madzsar made the point in a different way:

---

19   Lajos Biró to Oscar Jászi, Firenze, December 4, 1919, Oscar Jászi Papers, Box 5.
20   Károly Kernstok to Oscar Jászi, Budapest, October 27, 1919, Oscar Jászi Papers, Box 5.
21   Ambró Czakó to Oscar Jászi, Budapest, November 28, 1919, Oscar Jászi Papers, Box 5. [Emphasis added.]
22   Béla Somogyi (1868–1920) editor of the Socialist daily *Népszava*, killed by an extremist military commando for his open criticism of the white terror.
23   Ambró Czakó to Oscar Jászi, Budapest, November 28, 1919, *loc. cit.*

"Should you return, you will find all the valuable people of the former Radical Party around you, the Gentiles without exception [...] the Jews are much more cowardly."[24] Anything but an anti-Semite, Jászi came quickly to the conclusion that "on the whole, the atmosphere of the Socialist parties is poisoned, made terribly Jewish through a grocery store spirit. This should be cured in some way, as in the Church through the Reformation, since this current Social Democracy is unable to prepare the future."[25]

The Freemasons of Hungary were also Jewish to a considerable extent and Czakó blamed them as well for inaction, remarking: "Balassa e.g. (for whom I have otherwise high regard!) has no courage to summon the . ˙ . -s and the Symbolic Grand Lodge did not make a single step toward foreign lodges, particularly toward the French Grand Orient to support the Hungarian progressives."[26] Others were also giving up hope about Freemasons, and the liberal daily *Világ* came under heavy criticism for its failing tenacity to represent basic liberal values and its lack of moral strength. Early in December 1919, Lajos Biró received firsthand information on Hungarian Freemasonry and the daily *Világ* when the art historian Arnold Hauser[27] arrived in Florence from Budapest. "I was most embarrassed and upset when he spoke to me about the tone of Világ," Biró wrote. "He cannot exactly quote the articles but he says, Világ disavows even the revolution of October [1918]. If this be the case, it's most deplorable. The white terror does not last for ever, and how does Világ want to do politics later if it denies everything three times before the cock will crow?"[28] *Világ* made a lot of its former friends and readers

---

24 József Madzsar to Oscar Jászi, Budapest, November 6, 1919, *loc. cit.*
25 Oscar Jászi to Mihály Károlyi, Wien, Austria, September 21, 1919, Boston University, Mugar Memorial Library, Special Collections, Károlyi Papers, Box 2, Folder 4/II/3. Throughout I have used the original Károlyi and Jászi correspondence in U.S. libraries, checking it against *Károlyi Mihály levelezése*, Vols. I–III (Budapest: Akadémiai Kiadó, 1978 [ed. György Litván], 1990, 1991 [ed. Tibor Hajdu].
26 *Ibid.*
27 Arnold Hauser (1892–1978), internationally recognized sociologist of art, author of critically acclaimed *The Social History of Art*.
28 Lajos Biró to Oscar Jászi, Florence, December 4, 1919, *loc. cit.*—Biblical reference at the end of the passage from John 13:36.

deeply unhappy. "A number of people come to me who are dissatisfied with Világ and Co, they would want a little more serious, combating approach,"[29] József Madzsar reported to Jászi.

The dangerous and often demoralizing ambience increasingly made people think about leaving the country. As mentioned above, emigration for Hungarians was not a novel idea: some one and a half to two million people had left the country between 1880 and 1914 for the United States. Few of these early emigrants were intellectuals, however. By 1919 the situation had changed. "How different is the air that [authors in Hungary] breathe since 1918 in contrast to what they had breathed before 1918...," author and critic Ignotus noted. "The air, just as wine or sulfur dioxide, influences man's mind as it considers things, man's eyes as they look at things, and man's judgment as it measures things."[30] "Today it is good for any honest man to have a passport," as Mrs. Madzsar summarized the case in a late 1919 letter to her brother Oscar in Vienna.

Many didn't wait to get a real one and forged documents: "There are any number of people now trying to leave the country for various purposes with false passports," U.S. General Harry Hill Bandholtz of the Inter-Allied Military Commission in Budapest reported in early January 1920 to the American Mission in Vienna.[31] A character in author Gyula Illyés's novel, *Hunok Párisban* (Huns in Paris) remarked in a conversation in Paris in the early 1920s: "Soon there will be no one left in Hungary!"[32] A lot of people had little else in mind but emigration. Leading Communists had no other option. Some people had mixed feelings about it, others seemed quite terrified:

29 József Madzsar to Oscar Jászi, Budapest, November 6, 1919, *loc. cit.*
30 Ignotus, "A Hatvany regényéről" [On Hatvany's novel], in *Ignotus válogatott írásai* [Selected Writings by Ignotus] (Budapest: Szépirodalmi Könyvkiadó, 1969), p. 266.
31 Gen. Harry Hill Bandholtz to Albert Halstead of the American Mission, Vienna, Austria, Budapest, January 3, 1920. Memoranda to American Commission to Negotiate Peace, 1919–1920. Louis Szathmáry Private Collection, Chicago, IL, consulted on March 27, 1990.
32 Gyula Illyés, *Hunok Párisban* [Huns in Paris] 3rd. ed. (Budapest: Szépirodalmi Könyvkiadó, 1961, Vol.I.) p. 102.

Józsi [Madzsar] is strongly concerned with the idea of emigration, which can only be understood by those who went through all this, from March [1919] till now. But particularly the last four months. I did not believe that there could be anything which I detested more than Communism. [...] Though I don't deny, I would suffer very much from leaving Hungary.[33]

Madzsar had the same feelings: "Alkó [Jászi's sister Alice] is very nervous, she is terribly excited about my thinking of emigration, it is only yesterday that has value for her, and she can only look forward to tomorrow terrified. And yet, this is going to be the end of it."[34] The idea of emigration soon obsessed Madzsar entirely. This became his only dream. "There is one hope to keep me alive, perhaps one could emigrate. This is the only thing I can think of, and I start next spring if there is just the tiniest opportunity to make a living somewhere else."[35]

Some of those involved in the revolutions, like the author Lajos Biró, had already become émigrés and found themselves on their way toward some unknown destination. Biró (1880–1948), an acclaimed novelist, playwright, and journalist went on to success in Hollywood as a script writer on several films directed by fellow Hungarian [Sir] Alexander Korda (1893–1956). Yet, gloomy and forlorn in 1919, Biró settled temporarily in Florence, Italy, and derived moral strength from Jászi's friendship, to whom he wrote at the end of December:

> I am full of doubt and wavering, even my health was in terrible shape until very recently. I had unhappy and aimless weeks and in these deaf weeks I am sometimes inclined to commit moral suicide. In soul only, of course; one mentally breaks with everything that is dear to him and says this hopeless race, man, should be damned: he does not deserve anything else but what in fact happens to him.[36]

---

33   Alice Madzsar to Oscar Jászi, [Budapest], n.d. [Most probably November 1919], Oscar Jászi Papers, Box 5.
34   József Madzsar to Oscar Jászi, Budapest, November 6, 1919, *loc. cit.*
35   József Madzsar to Oscar Jászi, [Budapest], November 19, [1919], Oscar Jászi Papers, Box 5.
36   Lajos Biró to Oscar Jászi, Firenze, December 25, 1919, *loc. cit.*

Biró was contemplating going to the United States to work for Hungarian papers and discussed his plans with Jászi, who already had harbored similar ideas. Biró was successful and, unlike most Hungarian authors, was well known even outside Hungary, yet he felt uncertain about leaving Italy. "One or two of my plays will be soon shown and one or two of my novels published. Perhaps they also show one of my plays in London; if I happened to have success that would at any rate facilitate my American trip. By any means I want to spend half a year there and want to learn English well enough to write for papers in English."[37] He kept himself open to both options: "I do believe that it will be possible to return home in the spring [of 1920]. Yet it would be good to keep the way open toward the West."[38]

Biró was optimistic about Jászi's emigration plans, noting:

> What you wrote about American plans is entirely convincing to me. That *English*-speaking America would give you as much as you modestly need or even a lot more is quite clear to me. My doubts concern *Hungarian* America. But I might be wrong even there. I think that the New York reporters would welcome me already on the ship, will write a lot of nonsense, in some sensationalist fashion, on what I may have to say; and this great reception will perhaps impress our good Hungarians to an extent that even they would behave like a man.[39]

Even the liberals of Hungary could not emotionally accept what had happened to the country and her borders in the treaty of Trianon (1920). Lajos Biró's assessment of the political situation of partitioned Hungary was not just a personal one: it was, indeed, a statement for very nearly his entire generation. "I am very biased against the Czechs," Biró admitted,

> particularly because they are the finest of our enemies (and because their expansion is the most absurd). I think if I was in charge of Hungarian politics I would compromise with everybody but them. Here I would want the whole: retaking complete Upper Hungary, from the Morava to the Tisza [Rivers]. I don't know

---

37 Ibid.
38 Lajos Biró to Oscar Jászi, Firenze, December 4, 1919, *loc. cit.*
39 Ibid.

the situation well enough but I have the feeling that Hungarian irredentism will very soon make life miserable for the Czech state and that the Slovak part will tear away from the Czechs sooner than we thought. Then we can make good friends with the Czechs.[40]

Biró's vision proved to be prophetic in some ways, and as was fairly typical among assimilated Jewish-Hungarian intellectuals at the turn of the century, he proved to be very much a Hungarian nationalist when deliberating the partition of former Hungarian territories and their possible return to Hungary.

To me, I confess, any tool served well that would unite the dissected parts with Hungary. I feel personal anger and pain whenever I think for example of the Czechs receiving the Ruthenland. I really think any tool is good that would explode this region out from the Czech state. I believe in general that Hungarian nationalism will now receive the ethical justification which she so far totally lacked; nations subjugated and robbed have not only the right but also the duty to be nationalist. We must see whether or not the League of Nations will be an instrument to render justice to the peoples robbed. If yes, it's good. If not: then all other tools are justified. First everything must be taken back from the Czechs that they themselves took away, as this will be the easiest. Then from the Serbs. Finally from the Romanians.[41]

Nonetheless, Biró felt pessimistic about the prospects of returning to Hungary and thought, oddly but not atypically, that his Jewishness compelled him to demonstrate his Hungarian patriotism by way of making himself financially independent of Hungary.

I have settled for a long, long stay abroad. I hope I will be able to live here or elsewhere and make a living. I have a burning desire to make my personal economy completely independent from any financial source at home: I want to prove to myself that my painful love toward Hungary and the Hungarians is independent from what the Hungarian book-market can give me, just because I do not happen to be an engineer or a doctor but an author.—Sometimes I think that this feeling is a Jewish feeling, Ady might not even have such an idea. All

---

40   Lajos Biró to Oscar Jászi, Firenze, November 24, 1919, Oscar Jászi Papers, Box 5.
41   *Ibid.*

the worse for me. To be a Hungarian is quite a problem. To be a Hungarian Jew is doubly so. To be a Hungarian Jewish author: this is the piling of pains by way of [Heinrich] Heine.[42]

In virtual exile since before the Republic of Councils, which he detested, Jászi did not feel optimistic. In letters to Mihály Károlyi in the early Fall of 1919, he spelled this out clearly. "The situation is undoubtedly dark," he wrote from Prague. "Vienna is swirling again and rough. The whole of Europe is like a mortally operated man sick in fever, and poor Hungary, as Návay added, received a cadaverous poisoning."[43] Jászi's sister, Mrs. Alice Madzsar, made her brother particularly distressed by telling him that the "white" régime was not at all attacking Communists only.

> In the University, [political] reaction is raging mostly in the school of medicine, led by Grand Master [Árpád] Bókai [Bókay]. [...] The party started in the university faculty by first putting together a kangaroo-court with Bókai, [János] Bársony and I do not remember the third; the 4 professors of Jewish origin, Leo [Liebermann], [Rezső] Bálint, [Emil] Grósz, and [Adolf] Onody [Onodi] were "interrogated" as defendants. [Baron Sándor] Korányi was spared with a view to the merits of his father. They voted after the interrogation and declared that the people in question are rehabilitated with flying colors except for Onodi against whom the process will continue [...].
>
> According to the blacklist compiled by [Professor Ernő] Jendrassik's senior assistant Csika, the Adjunct Professorship[44] was taken from Józsi [József Madzsar], Lajos [Dienes], Pali Liebermann, Tibor Péterfi, [Miksa] Goldzieher, Jenő Pólya, [Sándor] Barron [Báron], Károly Engel and 54 people lost their job in the University. Among the Adjunct Professors as you can see there is not one Communist.[45]

---

42 Lajos Biró to Oscar Jászi, Firenze, November 24, 1919, *loc. cit.*
43 Oscar Jászi to Mihály Károlyi, Praha, October 15, 1919, Boston University, Mugar Memorial Library, Special Collections, Károlyi Papers, Box 2, Folder 4/ II/3.
44 Equivalent to a German *Privatdozentur*.
45 Alice Madzsar to Oscar Jászi, [Budapest], n.d. [end of 1919?]—Several of the doctors mentioned here left Hungary at some point before World War II, e.g. Miksa Goldzieher for the U.S., Károly Engel for Australia, Tibor Péterfi for Czechoslovakia and Germany. Liebermann committed suicide in 1938.

The Hungarian Trauma, 1918–1920

Madzsar himself wrote Jászi to this same effect about the purges in early September 1919, adding that "their crime is mainly that they are Jews. They took my Adjunct Professorship without any hearing, and also from Pólya, Péterfi, Lajos Dienes, Goldzieher, Károly Engel and Pali Liebermann, as you can see, none of them is a Bolshevik, but this is now good excuse to persecute all modern people."[46] A little later Madzsar repeated the phrase as if he found the point, "*All modern people are persecuted,* this company created a terrible atmosphere."[47] No wonder that Jewish intellectuals in the fall of 1919 were intimidated to a degree that they seemed or, in fact, became "cowards."[48]

Alice Madzsar had hardly more encouraging news from other parts of the University of Budapest, "though the situation is perhaps milder than in the Medical School," she believed. "As I hear, [Manó] Beke, [Bernát] Alexander, [Géza] Révész, [Lipót] Fehér [Fejér] have to go.[49] On the suggestion of [Lajos] Lóci [Lóczy] the Hungarian Academy of Sciences declared that Jews can no longer be members."[50] Jászi received no better news from other intellectual quarters.

> Action was taken in the [Municipal] Library against Józsi [József Madzsar], [Soma] Braun, Laci [László] Dienes, [Béla] Kőhalmi, Blanka Pikler. [...] Poor Blanka, she was detained for 2 weeks, *she, who just like us, despised these Communists*. But at least she was not beaten. Terrible things go on in the police, in the Transdanubian area, everywhere. But you certainly know about these from the papers in Vienna.[51]

The painter Károly Kernstok was even more succinct about the paradox of people with an anti-Communist record now going to the "white" prisons of Admiral Horthy's army.

---

46 József Madzsar to Oscar Jászi, [Budapest], September 3, 1919, Columbia University, Butler Library, Rare Book and Manuscript Library, Oscar Jászi Papers, Box 5.
47 *Ibid.*–Emphasis added.
48 For a general survey of anti-Semitism in the medical profession in the 1920s see Mária M. Kovács, "A Numerus Clausus a húszas években" [The Numerus Clausus in the 1920s], *Budapesti Negyed*, 1995/8, pp. 137–158.
49 Eminent professors of the School of Philosophy, of Jewish origin.
50 Alice Madzsar to Oscar Jászi, [Budapest], n.d. [end of 1919?]
51 *Ibid.*—Emphasis added.

You know it was bad in the prison from the dirty worn out trousers to the prisoner-cap and the linen which saw the dream of prisoners, and from the rebuke, the kicking to the clearing of the table- [illegible word] we had a number of other pleasures like this, pour compléter la biographie.—Yet damn it, during the whole time I reproved the Commune, to peasant and gentleman and to Béla Kun. But you know the Hungarian country gentleman who was reddest of them all, who remained and served the Bolsheviks, just as he did Károlyi, Tisza; this is how that country bumpkin wanted to deserve some praise.[52]

And yet in the crestfallen mood of the fall of 1919, after the fall of Béla Kun but before the consolidation of the Horthy régime, those at home hoped to get out while the émigrés hoped to get back. When Biró tried to help his friend Jászi find his way to the United States, Biró was desperate: "My heart is heavy when I write this letter. What misery and what sadness this is."[53] And in four weeks, on Christmas Day, he added: "Sometimes I am tortured by unbearable homesickness."[54] The misery of the exiles was not mitigated by some countries wishing to see the aliens out of their land and denying them jobs or other forms of livelihood: "Here in Switzerland distrust of the 'Usländers' [foreigners][55] is just raging, so that a foreigner can hardly get here to some income, in addition, those after this will hardly be allowed in at all. [...] your tendency is certainly right: emigrate."[56]

The old animosities and personal, often petty, biases among the Hungarian radicals were exacerbated and even transferred into the emigration. The Jászi circle for instance, partly at least because of its own mixed Jewish/gentile, upper-class background, never liked the Polányis,[57]

---

52   Károly Kernstok to Oscar Jászi, Budapest, October 27, 1919, *loc. cit.* The same idea emerges in Jászi's *Revolution and Counter-Revolution in Hungary, op. cit.,* p. 173.
53   Lajos Biró to Oscar Jászi, Firenze, November 27, 1919, *loc. cit.*
54   Lajos Biró to Oscar Jászi, December 25, 1919, *loc. cit.*
55   Swiss-German for "foreigner."
56   Károly Méray-Horváth, Davos-Platz, Switzerland, December 9, 1919, Oscar Jászi Papers, Box 5.
57   Cf. Női Líceum. Magyar nők tudományos továbbképző tanfolyama, 1912–1913, 1913–1914 ("Értesítő" and "Munkaterv"), [Budapest, 1913]. Ilona Duczynska and Zoltán Horváth, "Polányi Károly és a Galilei-Kör" [Károly Polányi and the

and this type of division damaged the chances of concentrated radical-liberal political action. The Polányi family is one of the most outstanding in modern Hungarian cultural history. Its members built a remarkable and modern intellectual tradition. Of Jewish-Lithuanian background, Cecilia Polányi, the mother of Michael and Karl and soon a widow, was the focus of a popular, largely Jewish intellectual circle. She was also an enthusiastic follower of Émile Jacques-Dalcroze and set up an "institute of eurhythmics" to teach the representation of musical rhythms in movement in Budapest. She wrote for liberal German papers in Budapest (*Pester Lloyd, Neues Pester Journal*), Vienna (*Neues Wiener Journal*), and Berlin (*Berliner Börsen-Courier* and the *Berliner Montagspost*). More importantly, she was one of the earliest feminists of Hungary who between 1912 and 1914, established and maintained her own private "women's college," called Női Líceum, which she interpreted as an open university for Hungarian women. Its faculty included some of the best scholars, social scientists and artists of the day, whose list reflected the intellectual scope and horizon of the Polányi circle before World War I. The student list demonstrated the social background of Mrs. Polányi's school, representing mostly rich, upper-middle class, Jewish Budapest.

Family interests were truly encyclopedic. One of "Mother Cecile's" sons, Mihály (Michael) Polányi (1891–1976), was the distinguished physical chemist turned philosopher, author of *Personal Knowledge*, first in Germany, later in Britain. His brother Károly (Karl) (1886–1964), cofounder of the radical pre-World War I Galilei Club in Budapest, became a pioneering economic historian/anthropologist in the United States (*The Great Transformation*, 1944; *Dahomey and the Slave Trade*, 1966); his wife Ilona Duczynska (1897–1978) was also a leading figure in the radical movements of the early twentieth century. Michael's son, John C. Polanyi (b. 1929, and living in Canada), received the Nobel Prize

---

Galileo Circle], *Századok* 1971/1, pp. 89–104; and Lee Congdon, "Karl Polányi in Hungary, 1900–19," *Journal of Contemporary History*, 11, No. 1 (1976), pp. 167–183; Hans Zeisel, "Karl Polanyi," in David L. Sills, ed., *International Encyclopedia of the Social Sciences*, Vol. 12 ([New York:] The Macmillan Co & The Free Press, 1968), pp. 172–174.

in Chemistry in 1986. Several other members of the family were equally interesting and active.

Nonetheless, regardless of the Polányis' outstanding record, Alice Jászi-Madzsar was particularly hostile to Károly (Karl) Polányi and his followers, and warned her brother against possible cooperation with Károly in the United States which he seemed to have considered at that point. Károly Polányi was attacked even in the most liberal circles though, as Alice Jászi-Madzsar added, "[o]f course they themselves do not mean Károly himself, but the many chaos-minded, ill-mannered Jews who made up his entourage [...]"[58]

József Madzsar joined his wife in attacking Jászi's plans to cooperate politically with Karl Polányi in the United States.

> (1) It is unfortunate that the American plan is common knowledge, you still don't know the Polányis; (2) You couldn't have worse company in America than Karli; (3) All the plans of our friends concerning the future end with the ceterum censeo:[59] but without the Polányis! Those who would go for you into the fire make a proviso that the P[olányi] dynasty must not enter the club. There isn't a single Gentile among us (including myself) who would be once again willing to do any common work with any of the Polányis [...] [D]on't alienate your best allies by exposing yourself again with a member of the P[olányi] dynasty. One cannot undertake this burden after their participation in the [Communist] dictatorship, not to speak about the damage done by their participation in the Radical Party.[60]

This was more than just personal animosity against Karl Polányi, this was a dedicated attempt to draw the line between the radicals and the Communists, between the two revolutions of 1918 and 1919, and make the radical-liberal position clearer, devoid of the extremities of both left and right. This included the avoidance of people discredited during what

---

58   Alice Madzsar to Oscar Jászi, [Budapest], n. d. Oscar Jászi Papers, Box 5.—János Hock (1859–1936), author, orator and Member of Parliament, left Hungary after the declaration of the Republic of Councils.
59   "I keep telling you ...," from the speeches of the Elder Cato (234–149 B.C.) who often repeated it in his outbursts against Carthage.
60   József Madzsar to Oscar Jászi, Budapest, December 28, 1919, Oscar Jászi Papers, Box 5.

was commonly called the Commune. It became a running theme among radicals and liberals, and distancing themselves from the memory of 1919 was rapidly becoming an integral part of the new progressive-liberal agenda. A friend wrote to Jászi on the necessary changes during the fall of 1919:

> They plan to reopen the Free School but the list of speakers is not good in my mind: mostly people who played a role during the Commune. [...] In general, my feeling is that the world, the public sentiment, has changed very considerably, those who supported Hungarian progress up to now are disturbed; on the one hand they have a certain animosity against the progressive direction, on the other hand they do not like the contemporary state of affairs either. This mood makes a new, adapted method necessary. The old, excellent, aggressive, critical voice, dating back to some two years ago, is today out of place.[61]

It was certainly not the White Terror that created the "Jewish question" in 1919; it was already there, deeply embedded in early twentieth-century Hungarian society. There were, of course, biases of all sorts. The Polányi circle, typically, would deal only with Jews and was often convinced that everybody of importance was, could, or should be Jewish. This often damaged their links with potential non-Jewish political allies. As a friend put it in mid-1921 writing to Michael and his family: "There is a new tenant in your apartment [in Germany], I don't know whether or not you know him, Sanyi [Sándor] Pap, a boy from Pozsony [today Bratislava in Slovakia], and he is not even Jewish. He has never been. None of his relatives have ever been. I don't believe the whole story; there is no such person in the world."[62]

---

61 Jenő [Gönczi] to Oscar Jászi, [Budapest], n. d., Oscar Jászi Papers, Box 5. I am indebted to the late György Litván for identifying Gönczi as the author of this letter.
62 Gyuri [?] to Michael Polányi and family, Wildbad, Germany, June 12, 1921, Michael Polányi Papers, Box 1, Folder 14, University of Chicago, Joseph Regenstein Library, Special Collections.—The perception of Jewish intellectual ubiquity was not quite a delusion or self-deception. The professional élite in Hungary had very frequently intermarried with Jewish families and the Gentile author Lajos Zilahy provided an unusual and unexpected explanation, in his unpublished autobiography: "Christian intellectuals met with rigid, almost hostile reactions from

2 Leaving Hungary

Whatever their faith, the drive to leave Hungary was preeminent and urgent for thousands. Contemporary observers commented on the "crisis of the university degree," which was widely discussed in Hungarian public life, in parliament, at social gatherings, as well as at student meetings. Though the *Numerus Clausus* of 1920 created a particularly severe situation for young Jewish professionals, the crisis had a dramatic impact on most of the young students in Trianon-Hungary.[63] Social critics in the late 1920s pointed to "such an astonishing measure of intellectual degradation that the bells should be tolled in the whole country."[64] Emigration seemed to be a serious option for every college graduate throughout the 1920s. Jews, of course, found they could not place realistic hopes on having a Hungarian higher education and a Hungarian career. Foreign universities and other institutions promised a good education and perhaps also a job. Good people freshly out of the excellent secondary schools started to gravitate toward German or Czechoslovak universities. Several of the latter also taught in German, and the Hungarian middle class of the Austro-Hungarian monarchy, Jew and Gentile alike, spoke German

---

their families and relatives. This is the explanation of the fact that some seventy percent of them–beginning with Jokai, the greatest novelist in the last century up to the youngest generation in literature, the composers Bela Bartok and Zoltan Kodaly [sic], prominent actors and painters–married Jewish girls, not for money, but for the warmer understanding of the Jewish soul for their professions." Lajos Zilahy, Autobiography, Boston University, Mugar Memorial Library, Lajos Zilahy Papers, Box 9, Folder 5. [English original.]–Mixed marriages in fact have remained a basic pattern in Hungarian middle-class and upper-middle-class society and have added to its creativity and intellectual intensity. Cf. John Lukacs, *Budapest 1900. A Historical Portrait of a City and Its Culture* (New York: Weidenfeld & Nicolson, 1988), pp. 189–190.

63 Dezső Fügedi Pap, "Belső gyarmatosítás vagy kivándorlás," *Új élet*. Nemzetpolitikai Szemle, 1927, Vol. II, Nos. 5–6. p. 175.—Pap cites pathetic details about the lifestyle of Hungary's ca. 10,000 students, most of whom were deprived of even the most essential conditions and many were hungry and sick.

64 Dezső Fügedi Pap, *op. cit.*, pp. 175, 180–182.

well. They brought it from home, learned it at school, occasionally in the army or during holidays in Austria, and it now became their passport to some of the best universities of Europe. The papers of almost every major Hungarian scientist or scholar include requests for letters of recommendation to attend fine German institutions. Already in Germany, Michael Polányi and Theodore von Kármán were in constant contact with each other and with some of their best colleagues in Hungary and abroad, and paved the way for many young talents who were unable or unwilling to stay in their native Hungary. This is partly how interwar Hungarian émigrés started "cohorting" or "networking," and gradually built up a sizeable, interrelated community in exile.[65] The network of exiles often continued earlier patterns of friendship in Hungary.

Curiously enough, Vienna was not particularly inviting. With his mother in Budapest and his adored brother Michael in Karlsruhe, Karl Polányi's discomfort in Vienna was typical. Though he was recognized as an economist of some standing and soon became editor of *Der österreichische Volkswirt,* he complained bitterly about the ambiance of the city. "The spiritual Vienna is such disappointment, which is deserved to be experienced by those only who imagine the spirit to be bound to a source of income."[66]

Germany seemed much more challenging than Austria. With its sophistication and excellence, it was the dreamland for many who sought a respectable degree or a fine job. Young Leo Szilard was somewhat compromised under the Republic of Councils as a politically active student, and found the Horthy régime, in the words of William Lanouette, "thoroughly distasteful, and dangerous. [...] He thought he was in physical danger by staying because of his activities under the Béla Kun government [...] [He] was [...] afraid to come back. He stayed in Berlin."[67] At first Szilard

---

65 Mihály Freund to Michael Polányi, [Budapest], May 4, 1920; Imre Bródy to Michael Polányi, Göttingen, March 24, 1922; both in the Michael Polányi Papers, Box 17.
66 Karl Polányi to Michael Polányi, Vienna, April 24, 1920, Michael Polányi Papers, Box 17, Folder 2. [Original in German]
67 William Lanouette on His Leo Szilárd Biography. Gábor Palló in Conversation with William Lanouette, *The New Hungarian Quarterly,* XXIX, No. 111 (Autumn

wanted "to continue [his] engineering studies in Berlin. The attraction of physics, however, proved to be too great. Einstein, Planck, von Laue, Schroedinger, Nernst, Haber, and Franck were at that time all assembled in Berlin and attended a journal club in physics which was also open to students. I switched to physics and obtained a Doctor's degree in physics at the University of Berlin under von Laue in 1922."[68]

Already in Karlsruhe, Germany, and on his way toward a career in physical chemistry, Michael Polányi was searching for a good job. He turned for help to the celebrated Hungarian-born professor of aerodynamics in Aachen, Theodore von Kármán, seeking advice as to his future. Von Kármán himself came from the distinguished, early assimilated Jewish-Hungarian professional family of Mór Kármán. Theodore went to study and work in Germany as early as 1908 and acquired his *Habilitation* there. By the end of World War I, he already had a high reputation when, after a brief interlude in Hungary and some largely inaccurate accusations that he was a Communist, he quickly returned to Aachen in the fall of 1919.[69]

    1988), pp. 164–165. A missing link: Szilard received a certificate from Professor Lipót Fejér dated December 14, 1919, testifying that he won a second prize in a student competition in 1916, and he presented this document to a notary public in Berlin-Charlottenburg on January 3, 1920. This is how we know, almost exactly, when he left Hungary. Cf. *Beglaubigte Abschrift*, signed by the Notary Public Pakscher, Charlottenburg, January 3, 1920, Leo Szilard Papers, Mandeville Special Collections Library, University of California, San Diego, Geisel Library, La Jolla, California, MSS 32, Box 1, Folder 12.

68 Leo Szilard, Curriculum Vitae (Including List of Publications), August 1956, updated June 23, 1959, Leo Szilard Papers, MSS 32, Box 1, Folder 2. Albert Einstein, Fritz Haber, Max von Laue, Walther Nernst, and Max Planck were Nobel Laureates, while Erwin Schrödinger and James Franck were prospective Nobel Laureates.

69 For the 1919 incident in Hungary see Theodore von Kármán with Lee Edson, *The Wind and Beyond: Theodore von Kármán*, Chapter 11: "Revolution in Hungary," (Boston-Toronto: Little, Brown & Co, 1967), pp. 90–95; Gábor Palló, "Egy tudománytörténeti szindrómáról—Kármán Tódor pályafutása alapján" [On a History of Science Syndrome–Based on the Career of Theodore von Kármán], *Valóság*, Vol. XXV, No. 6, 1982, p. 26.

Young Michael Polányi's questions to von Kármán about a job in Germany were answered politely but with caution.

> The mood at the universities is for the moment most unsuitable for foreigners though this may change in some years, also, an individual case should never be dealt with by the general principles [...] To get an assistantship is in my mind not very difficult and I am happily prepared to eventually intervene on your behalf, as far as my acquaintance with chemists and physical chemists reaches. I ask you therefore to let me know if you hear about any vacancy and I will immediately write in your interest to the gentlemen concerned.[70]

Polányi's Budapest University colleague and friend, George de Hevesy (1885–1966), chose Copenhagen. The prospective Nobel Laureate (Chemistry, 1943), who also came from a wealthy upper-middle class Jewish family, was subjected to a humiliating experience just after the Republic of Councils came to an end.[71] De Hevesy received his associate professorship (the actual title was "Extraordinary Professor") from the Károlyi revolution and his full professorship from the Commune. He had a special task to perform: with Theodore von Kármán in his short-lived, though influential job in the ministry of education as head of the department of higher education, de Hevesy tried to obtain enough money to equip the Institute of Physics at the University of Budapest with important new technology and materials that would also serve other departments. Allegations were made that he used his friendship with von Kármán to prepare the Institute of Physics for Kármán and the department of physical chemistry for himself. He was accused of having been a member of the university faculty council during the Commune and to have received his professorship from its government. He was dismissed and was even denied the right to teach at the University of Budapest.

---

70   Theodore von Kármán to Michael Polányi, Aachen, March 17, 1920, Michael Polányi Papers, Box 17.
71   The history of the "trial" of De Hevesy in late October 1919 was reconstructed by Gábor Palló, "Egy boszorkányper története. Miért távozott el Hevesy György Magyarországról?" [The History of a Kangaroo Court: Why Georg de Hevesy Left Hungary?] *Valóság* XXVIII (1985), No. 7, pp. 77–89.

In an important letter written to Niels Bohr in the middle of his "trial," de Hevesy bitterly complained that "politics entered also the University [...] hardly anybody who is a jew [sic] or a radical, or is suspected to be a radical, could retain his post [...] The prevalent moral and material decay will I fear for longtime prevent anykind of successfull scientific life in Hungary." Hevesy left Hungary in March 1920.[72]

Others tried their luck in the German universities of Prague or Brünn [Brno] in newly created Czechoslovakia, where good technical and regular universities were available and the language of instruction was German. Many Hungarians had been natives of Pozsony or the Slovak parts of former greater Hungary and spoke German as their mother tongue. Standards were high and the students were still close to home. In an interview given in late 1989 in Columbia University in New York City, former Hungarian engineering student Marcel Stein vividly remembered the heated and dangerous atmosphere of late 1919 and early 1920 in Budapest. Though many moved to Berlin-Charlottenburg, or Karlsruhe in Germany or, like the distinguished engineer László Forgó, toward Zürich, Switzerland, Marcel Stein remembered that many émigrés returned to Hungary later.[73] Though their actual number is unknown, the returnees were lured back to Hungary chiefly because of their sense of linguistic isolation, their keenly felt separation from family and friends, and, most of all, the gradually consolidating situation of Hungary in the mid-1920s.

Still some of the best scientists, engineers, scholars, artists, musicians, and professionals of all sorts, continued to leave Hungary in large numbers in 1920 and later.[74] For many, there was real danger in staying as they had

---

72 George Hevesy to Niels Bohr, Budapest, October 25, 1919, Bohr Scientific Correspondence, Archive for History of Quantum Physics, Office of the History of Science and Technology, University of California, Berkeley. [English original.]

73 Marcel Stein in conversation with the present author, November 29, 1989, Columbia University, New York City. In 1990–91 I was granted several very valuable interviews by Andrew A. Recsei (1902–2002), a distinguished chemist in Santa Barbara, CA, another former Hungarian student who also studied once in Brno (Brünn) in exactly the same period of time.

74 For the earliest and consequently incomplete list of important people who left Hungary in, or right after, 1919–1920, see Oscar Jászi, *op. cit.*, pp. 173–174.

actively promoted the Commune of 1919, such as the future Hollywood star Béla Lugosi, remembered primarily for his role in *Dracula,* who left for the U.S. in 1921, and film director Mihály Kertész, who became the successful and productive Michael Curtiz of *Casablanca, Yankee Doodle Dandy,* and *White Christmas.* For those who were actually members of the Communist government at some level, like the philosopher Georg Lukács and the author and future film theorist Béla Balázs and many others, there was simply no choice but to leave.

Hungary became more civilized and less dangerous in the latter part of the 1920s under the government of Count István Bethlen (prime minister between 1921 and 1931), and some of the heated issues of 1919–1920 subsided by the end of the decade. The radical-liberal agenda no longer had a wide appeal, losing many of its champions who chose exile, and meeting with a measure of disregard under the régime of Regent Adm. Miklós Horthy. It became apparent to most people how difficult it had become, in the suddenly and drastically changed international and national, political and social conditions of the immediate post-World War I period, to uphold Western ideas and ideals. Even the liberal agenda, which looked back almost a century in Hungarian history, and which embraced formerly immigrant Jews as well as the ideals of modernization through much of the nineteenth century, was in many ways closed off. Interwar Hungary became a thoroughly conservative, nationalist, and emphatically "Christian" country, as it was defined by the ruling élite. Though uncertain whether to leave their native Hungary, many radicals and liberals, despite their ambivalence, resolved their dilemma by necessity alone: there was no choice left to them but emigration.

3 The Escape of Hungarian Modernism

The unparalleled artistic, cultural, and intellectual upheaval in the final decades of the Austro-Hungarian Monarchy has been amply treated by a growing literature, in and out of Austria and Hungary.[75] Much of what we call "the modernist movement" in European music, literature, the arts, social thought, philosophy, and psychology was started in the fertile, sensual and decaying intellectual climate of turn-of-the-century Vienna and Budapest. There was a certain playfulness and experimentalism in the air, the creative élite became attracted to novelty and invention, intellectual challenge and a call for change.

Less has been written about the link between the spiritual and artistic upsurge in what the Austrian author Stefan Zweig called the "World of Yesterday" and the subsequent post-World War I exodus of the Austro-Hungarian intellectual élite. The revolutionary movement in the arts and thought of pre-War Vienna and Budapest was radically transformed after the collapse and dissolution of the Monarchy in 1918–1920. The modernist movement suddenly lost momentum and was transformed into a more professional and more conservative tradition. It was also gradually relocated to other countries such as Austria, Czechoslovakia, Germany, Soviet Russia, Great Britain, and ultimately, the United States. In the following

---

[75] Stefan Zweig, *The World of Yesterday. An Autobiography* (1943, repr. Lincoln: University of Nebraska Press, 1964); W. M. Johnston, *The Austrian Mind. An Intellectual and Social History, 1848–1938* (Berkeley: University of California Press, 1972); Allan Janik & Stephen Toulmin, *Wittgenstein's Vienna* (New York: Simon & Schuster, 1973); László Mátrai, *Alapját vesztett felépítmény* [Superstructure Without Base] (Budapest: Magvető, 1976); Carl E. Schorske, *Fin-de-Siècle Vienna. Politics and Culture* (New York: Knopf, 1980); Kristóf Nyíri, *A Monarchia szellemi életéről. Filozófiatörténeti tanulmányok* [The Intellectual Life of the Monarchy. Studies in the History of Philosophy] (Budapest: Gondolat, 1980); J. C. Nyíri, *Am Rande Europas. Studien zur österreichisch-ungarischen Philosophiegeschichte* (Wien: Böhlau, 1988); *Wien um 1900. Kunst und Kultur* (Wien-München: Brandstätter, 1985); John Lukacs, *Budapest 1900. A Historical Portrait of a City and Its Culture* (New York: Weidenfeld & Nicolson, 1988); Péter Hanák, *The Garden and the Workshop: Essays in the Cultural History of Vienna and Budapest* (Princeton: Princeton University Press, 1998).

I will show some of the characteristic patterns of this migration of intellectual and artistic experimentalism and innovative spirit, illustrated here by two creative Hungarians who contributed to U.S. culture and civilization in a major way, Joseph Szigeti and Laszlo Moholy-Nagy.

Pioneer in Programming: Joseph Szigeti

Budapest was a center for the discovery of talented young people like Rafael Kubelik, Franz von Vecsey, Isadora Duncan, and somewhat earlier, Gustav Mahler, Arthur Nikisch[76] and Hans Richter. The man who did most for modern music among the Hungarian musicians was probably the violinist Joseph Szigeti (1892–1973). This Jewish-Hungarian virtuoso was perhaps the most celebrated and well-known student of Jenő Hubay and he carried the Hubay tradition literally all around the world. All his life he was conscious of the continuity of the Brahms tradition, both in Vienna and Budapest, which he had received from his Budapest professor Hubay. The example of Szigeti is relevant in demonstrating the strong links between the old Music Academy tradition and the musical philosophy of the post-World War I generation.

In an effort to describe the tradition of the European chamber music tradition as well as his own roots, Szigeti wrote,

> [...] I felt that these notes might interest the listener of our days who has been to a great extent deprived of the real "habitat" of chamber music: the small Hall and—better still—the music room in which the congenial few gather around the players in rapt concentration. I was in my late teens when I turned pages at a rehearsal of the d minor Sonata. Leopold Godowsky and [my master] Jenő Hubay [rehearsed it] in preparation for their concert in Budapest, some twenty years after [Brahms had brought the pencil manuscript of his work to my master Hubay for] this Vienna "try-out." [...] One has reason to feel grateful for having been born at a time when these sonatas were still a comparative rarity, when [their performances presupposed mature players and] they had not yet become class room "material" and grateful "vehicles" for debut recitals. There were at the time a dozen-or-so

---

76 For his autobiography see Joseph Szigeti, *With Strings Attached. Reminiscences and Reflections* (New York: Knopf, 1947; 2nd ed. 1967), pp. 28–30.

recordings from which the student could choose his "model;" [...] As the rare live performances he heard were mostly by mature interpreters and took place in halls of modest proportions (world famous performers like Ysaÿe, Sarasate, d'Albert, Busoni played in Vienna's Bösendorfer Saal, in the old Paris Salle Pleyel in the rue Rochechouart seating barely 4 or 500, in the small "Royal" Hall in Budapest), the intimate chamber-music characteristics of these sonatas were brought home to him [...] Hubay told me at the time how much these fine points meant to Brahms, how literally he took his marking[s]...[77]

Szigeti mastered nearly the entire classical violin repertoire, and yet he became one of the few leading soloists in the world who was attracted to contemporary music. He even began to play the solo sonatas by Bach at the instigation of Milán Füst, a modernist poet who was his Budapest friend in their young days and became one of the leading spirits of the modernist movement in Hungarian literature and aesthetics.[78] For Szigeti, the living tradition of late 19th century music in Budapest and Vienna also implied the inclusion of contemporary music. This became evident from the beginning, as Otto Eckermann carefully observed as early as 1922, stating, "Mr Szigeti is one of the few violinists who always brings novelties [...], and he commissioned me to look for appropriate new works."[79] Szigeti was always eager to learn new things and to understand music from the composers' point of view. "If we concede—as I am inclined to do—an important role to this auto-suggestive faculty in our work, what better schooling in it than commerce with new works and their composers?"[80]

At 80, he was awarded the George Washington Award of the American Hungarian Studies Foundation for identifying "himself with

---

77 Joseph Szigeti, "Jacket Notes for a Columbia Brahms Sonata Album," Circa 1955?, In Szigeti's handwriting, Boston University, Mugar Memorial Library, Joseph Szigeti Papers. Deleted parts appear in brackets.
78 "Joseph Szigeti, Pioneer in Violin Programming," Unfinished MS, Joseph Szigeti Papers, Box 1, Folder 4, p.2.
79 Otto Eckermann to Kurt Atterberg, June 24, 1922, quoted in Kurt Atterberg to Joseph Szigeti, Stockholm, July 28, 1958, Joseph Szigeti Papers, Box 1, Folder 4. [English translation of a German translation by Kurt Atterberg.]
80 "Joseph Szigeti, Pioneer in Violin Programming," *op. cit.* p. 43.

The Hungarian Trauma, 1918–1920

the new, untried and progressive," giving of himself "unstintingly so that a significant new voice in music might be heard."[81] More contemporary composers of all nationalities dedicated their work to Szigeti, or were commissioned by him, than perhaps any other contemporary soloist. He readily lent the power of his charisma to Hungarians such as Béla Bartók, Pál Kadosa, Antal Molnár, Americans like George Templeton Strong, Russians such as Nikita Magaloff and Sergei Prokofiev, the Armenian Aram Khachaturian, Irishmen like Sir Hamilton Harty, Englishmen like Alan Rawsthorne, the Italian Alfredo Casella, the Jewish-Lithuanian Joseph Achron, the Swiss Ernest Bloch, and the Polish Alexander Tansman, often at an early stage in their careers when his support was especially beneficial. He considered it important to keep a whole series of contemporary music on his program, such as work by the Polish Karol Szymanowski, the French Albert Roussel and Darius Milhaud, the Roumanian Filip Lazar, the Russian Igor Stravinsky, the Italians Ferruccio Busoni and Ildebrando Pizzetti, as well as the Englishmen Sir Edward Elgar and Sir Arnold Bax,[82] and, later, the American David Diamond, Charles Cadman, and Henry Cowell.[83] He also worked in close collaboration with both Paul Hindemith and Igor Stravinsky. In this respect, Szigeti resembled Hungarian-American conductor Fritz Reiner who had a similar reputation for playing a lot of new Hungarian music such as that of Béla Bartók, Ernst von Dohnányi and Leo Weiner.[84] In what was probably early 1922, Szigeti played Dohnányi's *Violin Concerto* with the Berlin Philharmonic Orchestra conducted by Reiner.[85]

---

81 Diploma of the George Washington Award, April 19, 1972, Joseph Szigeti Papers, Box 4, Folder 3.
82 Szigeti assisted by Nikita de Magaloff. Programme for June 13, 1935, Queen's Hall, London. Inside: A Few Contemporary Works from Szigeti's Repertoire. Joseph Szigeti Papers, Box 2, Folder 1. See also V. Bazykin to Herbert Barrett, November 12, 1943, on Aram Khachaturian, Joseph Szigeti Papers, Box 1, Folder 3. Szigeti added to Bazykin's signature in pencil: "in the meanwhile, he became Ambassador."
83 Joseph Szigeti Memorial Exhibition, Joseph Szigeti Papers, Box 6, Folder 2.
84 Philip Hart, *Fritz Reiner. A Biography* (Evanston, IL: Northwestern University Press, 1994), pp. 23, 195, 225. Cf. Rollin R. Potter, "Fritz Reiner: Conductor, Teacher. Musical Innovator" (Ph.D. Thesis, Northwestern University, 1980).
85 Philip Hart, *Fritz Reiner. A Biography*, op. cit., p. 23.

There was a great deal of the Liszt tradition continuing in these gestures. Szigeti often invited composers to appear in recital with him performing their own work "thus creating a little oasis in a recital program where the composer and not the reproducing artist is the center of interest."[86] In the 1950s, he repeated a number of series entitled "20th Century Cycles" in several U.S. universities and music centers,[87] which he recalled as a "pleasure evening series of eleven contemporary master-pieces, entitled 'Sonatas of the 20th Century.' I gave this series about fifteen times on different campuses in America and also in Zurich and over the Italian Radio in 1959. I recorded it for the Swedish Radio."[88] In cases where he could not promote a contemporary work himself, he did everything in his power to make other artists interested, for example, in the case of Gian Francesco Malipiero's *Concerto for Violin and Orchestra,* which he showed "to my friend, Maestro George Szell," as well as to Leopold Stokowski in New York and Henri Barraud at the Radio Diffusion Française in Paris.[89] By carrying the tradition of an active interest in the contemporary, Szigeti made an example to his entire generation throughout a long and productive life. As Manoug Parikian saluted him in *The Royal Academy of Music Magazine* on his 80th birthday in 1972,

> All this would seem commonplace in these days of over-consciousness of contemporary music; in the 1920s and 1930s, in the midst of virtuoso-type recitals and endless repetitions of the same five or six concertos it was a brave crusade. His deep knowledge and understanding of the spirit of Bach, Mozart and Beethoven was as important as his search for new music.[90]

---

86 "Joseph Szigeti, Pioneer in Violin Programming," *op. cit.* p. 5.
87 Joseph Szigeti to Ralph Vaughan Williams, April 10, 1957, Joseph Szigeti Papers, Box 1, Folder 4.
88 Joseph Szigeti to Michael Kennedy, Baugy s/Clarens, February 11, 1965, Joseph Szigeti Papers, Box 1, Folder 4.
89 Carisch S. p. A., Milano, to Joseph Szigeti, Milano, January 14, 1958, and Joseph Szigeti to Carisch S. p. A., Palos Verdes Estates, CA, January 25, 1958, Joseph Szigeti Papers, Box 1, Folder 4.
90 Manoug Parikian, "A birthday tribute to Joseph Szigeti," *The Royal Academy of Music Magazine,* [1972], Joseph Szigeti Papers.

In the U.S., Szigeti's delayed popularity has been attributed to the slow growth of intellectual sophistication in American audiences. His was a long and tedious journey toward making contemporary music recognized there. His pioneering efforts in front of select audiences of metropolitan music halls, enterprising campus groups, and on élitist radio programs, were often unnoticed or not remembered. He was often criticized for his programming. "Playing the Roussel Sonata No. 2, once lost Szigeti a prospective manager who heard him perform at Carnegie Hall. Modern composers do not sell programs, Szigeti was promptly informed. Recalling this incident Szigeti wrote, 'needless to say I was entreated once again to mend my already notoriously incorrigible ways of programming.'"[91] Yet, his pioneering efforts led to breakthroughs even in the U.S. where his philosophy of musical programming came through triumphantly: when playing the world premiere of the Bloch *Concerto* in Cleveland in 1938; Bartók's *Contrasts* with Benny Goodman and the composer in Carnegie Hall in 1939; Prokofiev's *Sonata in D*, op. 94 in Boston in 1944 and his *F minor*, op. 80 in San Francisco in 1946; and the U.S. premier of Prokofiev's *Concerto in D* and the Ravel *Sonata*.[92]

For Béla Bartók, a contemporary composer self-exiled in the U.S., Szigeti did more than perhaps anybody else between 1940 and 1945. Their friendship started in the 1920s, and they toured together in Berlin in 1930. Szigeti used his connections to make Bartók's music available and popular to audiences in the U.S. He appeared with Bartók in recitals at the Library of Congress and played with the newly-arrived Hungarian composer in 1940 at Carnegie Hall. He was in touch with leading U.S. conductors such as Leopold Stokowski and tried to get Bartók's American composition performed. Szigeti was one of the loyal supporters of Bartók during his last illness and tactfully helped the poor, though proud, composer receive help from wealthy patrons like Mrs. Elizabeth Sprague Coolidge in 1943. He was ready to be at Bartók's disposal to the very last when the terminally ill composer requested his help to interest conductors in his third Piano

---

91 "Joseph Szigeti, Pioneer in Violin Programming," *op. cit.* p. 5.
92 *Ibid.*, pp. 6–7.

Concerto, the last he composed.[93] After Bartók's death, Szigeti served as one of the trustees on the board of the Bartók Archives in New York.[94]

Joseph Szigeti lived most of his adult life abroad, though he visited Hungary regularly to the end of his life, except for a gap after World War II. Throughout, Szigeti maintained excellent relations with Hungarian musicians and helped a number of them start their own careers. He was glad to be associated with Hungarian causes, and, along with Arthur Koestler and Nobel Laureate Albert Szent-Györgyi, was acknowledged by honorary membership in the Association of Hungarian Authors in Foreign Countries, located in London, right after the revolution of 1956.[95] He was instrumental in launching the career of cellist Janos Starker at the Indiana University School of Music.[96] Newcomers from post-1945 Hungary such as pianist-conductor Tamás Vásáry were glad to register their homage to the *maître*.[97]

Szigeti found it important to publish his autobiography in Hungarian, thinking that "this new Hungarian intelligentsia should get to know me a little."[98] He asked Hungarian-American diplomat Andor C. Klay how he felt about it and Klay's answer was most enthusiastic:

> I have found that they know about you to a degree which is surprising in the light of your long absence from Hungary and their long years of isolation from the West. I recall examples from Camp Kilmer when I visited there in order to select some refugees to form a delegation which could be presented to the President

---

93 *Ibid.;* Agatha Fassett, *The Naked Face of Genius: Bela Bartok's American Years* (Boston: Houghton Mifflin, 1958); Agatha Fassett, *Bela Bartok—The American Years* (New York: Dover Publications, 1970).
94 Victor Bator to Joseph Szigeti, New York City, February 18, 1963, Joseph Szigeti Papers, Box 1, Folder 4.
95 Joseph Szigeti to Magyar Irók Szövetsége, Céligny (Geneva), November 17, 1958, Joseph Szigeti Papers, Box 1, Folder 4.
96 Joseph Szigeti to Wilfred C. Bain, Palos Verdes Estates, CA, January 22, 1958, Joseph Szigeti Papers, Box 1, Folder 4.
97 Tamás Vásáry to Joseph Szigeti, Chardonne, October 26, 1960, Joseph Szigeti Papers, Box 1, Folder 4.
98 Andor [C.] Klay to Joseph Szigeti, American Embassy, Belgrade, March 3, 1960, Joseph Szigeti Papers, Box 1, Folder 4.

and the Secretary. I raised various questions, ranging from the political to the cultural, in order to gauge their range of knowledgeability. Your name was repeatedly mentioned.[99]

Szigeti always tried to include Hungarian pieces in his U.S. programs and even his most popular ones such as the People's Symphony Concerts on CBS, included a Scène de la Csárda by his master Jenő Hubay, Rhapsody in C by Ernst von Dohnányi and a piece by Bartók played with the composer.[100]

"New Vision:" Laszlo Moholy-Nagy

Comparable in many ways to the achievement of Szigeti in the performing arts was the *New Vision* of László Moholy-Nagy (1895–1946), a dramatic testimony to the significance and range of the modernist contribution in the visual arts from Hungary. Coming from the same generation of Jewish Hungarians, Moholy-Nagy was probably the most versatile of the Hungarian artists, being an architect, photographer, designer, prolific author, and filmmaker.[101] Along with fellow-Hungarian Marcel Breuer, he was a founding member of the *Bauhaus* school, first in Germany and later, in 1937, in Chicago. Moholy became a pioneer in diverse fields such as non-figurative geometric art, kinetic sculpture, typographical design, as well as in photography. *Bauhaus* founder and lifelong friend Walter Gropius characterized Moholy-Nagy's abstract art, his "new vision," in musical terms at the opening of the Moholy-Nagy Exhibition at "London Galleries," in 1936, providing one of the most lucid and rational explanations of abstract art ever given.

---

99 Andor [C.] Klay to Joseph Szigeti, American Embassy, Belgrade, March 3, 1960, *loc. cit.*
100 Columbia Concerts Corporation of CBS to Joseph Szigeti, New York, December 31, 1940, Joseph Szigeti Papers, Box 1, Folder 3.
101 Moholy-Nagy's films, lesser known today, included *Berlin Still Life* (1926), *Marseille vieux port* (1929), *Lightplay: Black, White, Gray* (1930), *Gypsies* (1932).

> You know that musical work, a composition, consists, just like painting, of form and content. But its form is only in part a product of the composer, for in order to make his musical ideas comprehensible to any third person, he is obliged to make use of counterpoint which is nothing more than a conventional agreement to divide the world of sound into certain intervals according to fixed laws. These laws of counterpoint, of harmony, vary among different peoples and in different centuries, but the changes are very slow [...] In earlier days the optical arts also had firm rules, a counterpoint regulating the use of space. The academies for art which had the task of keeping up and developing these rules, lost them—and art decayed. Here the abstract painters of our day took up the threads and used their creative powers to conquer a new statutory law of space. This new counterpoint of space, a new vision, is the core of their achievement.[102]

Gropius described Moholy-Nagy's entire work as

> a mighty battle to prepare the way for a new vision, in that he attempts to extend the boundaries of painting and to increase the intensity of light in the picture by the use of new technical means, thus approximating nearer to nature. Moholy has observed and registered light with the eye of the camera and the film camera, from the perspective of the frog and the bird, has tried to master impressions of space and thus developed in his paintings a new conception of space.[103]

Moholy-Nagy was a most intense and insightful observer of the "modern" world of the 1920s and 1930s. Like the best of his generation, he went far into the visual exploration of form, construction, spacial relationships, and light effects.[104] "We might call the scope of his contribution "Leonardian," so versatile and colorful has it been," said Walter Gropius in eulogizing him at his Chicago funeral in 1946.[105] "His greatest effort as an artist was devoted to the conquest of pictorial space, and

---

102 Walter Gropius, "Speech for the Opening of the Moholy-Nagy Exhibition at 'London Galleries,'" December 31, 1936, Walter Gropius Papers, Harvard University Libraries, The Houghton Library, bMS Ger 208 (5).
103 Gropius, "Speech," December 31, 1936, *op. cit.*
104 Eleanor Margaret Hight, "Moholy-Nagy: The Photography and the 'New Vision' in Weimar Germany," Harvard University Ph.D. Thesis, 1986, p. 238.
105 Walter Gropius, "Eulogy for Ladislaus Moholy-Nagy," Chicago, November 1946, Walter Gropius Papers, bMS Ger 208 (86).

The Hungarian Trauma, 1918–1920

he commanded his genius to venture into all realms of science and art to unriddle the phenomena of space. In painting, sculpture and architecture, in theater and industrial design, in photography and film, in advertising and typography, he constantly strove to interpret space in its relationship to time, that is motion in space."[106]

What Gropius attempted to explain particularly was the source of Moholy-Nagy's modernism, the basis of his deep and enthusiastic interest in anything new.

> Constantly developing new ideas, he managed to keep himself in a stage of unbiased curiosity from where a fresh point of view could originate. With a shrewd sense of observation he investigated everything that came his way, taking nothing for granted, but using his acute sense for the organic. [...] Here I believe was the source of his priceless quality as an educator, namely his never ceasing power to stimulate and to carry away the other fellow with his own enthusiasm. What better can true education achieve than setting the student's mind in motion by that contagious magic?[107]

Just as many other contemporary artists of the early 20th century represented varied brands of modernism, Moholy was described as a technical pioneer "who was fascinated and stirred by the dynamic pace of the machine age. His élan vital thrived on the tempo and the motorized rhythm of big-city life."[108] He deeply believed in the new unity of art and technology.[109] The big European and American metropoles exerted an unmistakably "modern" influence and left a lasting imprint on his whole generation. An important aspect of Moholy's life was the big city, the continuous mechanization of the world and human life with it. For him, modern man's structure was mechanical, "the synthesis of all his functional mechanisms."[110] "Man is unique in the insatiability of his

---

106 Gropius, "Eulogy," *op. cit.*
107 *Ibid.*
108 Eberhard Roters, *Painters of the Bauhaus* (New York—Washington: Praeger, 1969), p. 165.
109 Eberhard Roters, *op. cit.*, pp. 164–165.
110 Laszlo Moholy-Nagy, *Malerei, Photographie, Film* (München, 1925) p. 23, quoted by Eberhard Roters, *op. cit.*, p. 165.

functional mechanisms, which hungrily absorb every new impression and never cease to crave for more. This is one reason for the continuing need for the creation of new forms," as he explained in *Malerei, Photographie, Film*.[111] As an artistic expression of his functionalist artistic philosophy, Moholy-Nagy experimented with what he called the "space modulator," a pioneering optical-kinetic sculpture pointing towards a new art form. Others of his ideas contributed to new branches of knowledge such as cybernetics and semantics.

Experimentation was fundamental throughout Moholy's life, starting with his participation in the *Ma* group in Budapest, and his cooperation with Lajos Kassák. But it was in Germany, in the early Bauhaus period, that his experimenting blossomed and young Moholy became particularly productive.

A primary example is his discovery of creative photography as a new artistic discipline. He became convinced that photography came to replace painting in representing reality. In his painting, he was striving for "organized order." In his photography he proved to be a superb master of new techniques, but his photographs became artistically significant through "his completely novel and individual manner of looking at familiar things—the use of bold foreshortening, unusual angles, and superimposed light-dark structures, such as the shadow of a net or a fence."[112] His growing reputation made movie director Sir Alexander Korda request that he do the special effects for his *The Shape of Things to Come*, based on a novel by H. G. Wells.

His experimental photography gave fresh impetus to advertising techniques. To this end, he renewed the art and technology of typography in order to create a new form for communicating messages. He argued that "printing processes had not undergone a significant change, either technically or aesthetically, since Gutenberg's time, and that the printed image should be made lively and interesting and should be brought up to date to make it worthy of the twentieth century."[113] Here again, his

---

111 Moholy-Nagy, *Malerei*, quoted by Roters, *op. cit.*, p. 165.
112 Eberhard Roters, *op. cit.*, p. 171.
113 *Ibid.*, p. 172.

innovative spirit was preoccupied with modern technology and the use of machines.

> Opportunities for innovations in typography are constantly developing, based on the growth of photography, film, zincographic and galvanoplastic techniques. The invention and improvement of photogravure, photographic typesetting machines, the birth of neon advertising, the experience of optical continuity provided by the cinema, the simultaneity of sensory experiences—all these developments open the way for an entirely new standard of optical typographic excellence; in fact, they demand it.[114]

Though Moholy-Nagy in his American years continued to do the experimental art of his German Bauhaus period and gradually became a very influential teacher of its ideas, like Szigeti, he had a long fight for recognition in the United States. The idea to invite him came from his mentor Walter Gropius, then Chairman of the Department of Architecture at Harvard, who had worked out details with the people in Chicago. For Moholy, this sounded like intellectual salvation, as in London he had bitterly complained that "from a spiritual point of view one can reach here nothing or only the minimum and that every stimulus and every excitement is missing."[115] He was anxious to get back and work in a school just as in the old days of the Bauhaus. Now the chances were good for being able to develop an American version of the Bauhaus in Chicago and Moholy eagerly answered, "for plan highly interested [—] please send more details."[116]

His friend Walter Gropius, then 60, was optimistic about the U. S. environment.[117] He called America a "pleasant continent," and gave details

---

114 Laszlo Moholy-Nagy, "Zeitgemässe Typographie—Ziele, Praxis, Kritik," in *Offset, Buch und Werbekunst*, No. 7 (Leipzig: [Bauhaus,] 1926). Quoted by Eberhard Roters, *op. cit.*, p. 173.
115 Laszlo Moholy-Nagy to Walter and Ise Gropius, London, May 28, 1937, Walter Gropius Papers, bMS Ger 208 (1221).—Keeping with the Bauhaus tradition, Moholy did not capitalize in his correspondence.
116 *Ibid.*
117 Walter Gropius to Laszlo Moholy-Nagy, [Cambridge, MA,] June 1, 1937, Walter Gropius Papers, bMS Ger 208 (1221).

about the Chicago plans which were based on the money of department store millionaire Marshall Field and located in one of his buildings. One of the crucial points of Moholy-Nagy's candidacy was his strong relationship with British and German industry, and firms like Simpson and International Textile, and people such as Julian Huxley provided references.[118]

After what he labelled "*diesem enervierenden kleinkram hier*" [these enervating odds and ends], Moholy was eager to leave Britain and relocate, as it were, the Bauhaus spirit in Chicago. "Everything calls here for a better design in industry," said Gropius underlining the nature of the new job he helped to find for Moholy.[119] He planned four classes in industrial art, in metal, wood, "typo-photo-film (commercial graphic)," and textile. Gropius suggested that he would "be given free hand to develop the thing in a direction as you like fit."[120] He also thought Moholy could put together his faculty as he pleased, and the opportunity to start from scratch seemed to have particular advantages.

Moholy put enormous energies into what became "the new bauhaus—American School of Design, founded by the Association of Arts and Industries." First he had to fight for the very name *bauhaus* itself, for he thought that since the Americans had adapted *weltanschauung,* they might as well use the term *bauhaus* as well.[121] Immediately, he wanted to become part of the Bauhaus exhibition of the Museum of Modern Art at Rockefeller Center in New York.[122] He also intended to continue the old Bauhaus book series, particularly as the Nazi takeover had closed the

118 Walter Gropius to Laszlo Moholy-Nagy, [Cambridge, MA,] June 10, 1937, Walter Gropius Papers, bMS Ger 208 (1221).
119 Laszlo Moholy-Nagy to Walter and Ise Gropius, London, June 13, 1937, Walter Gropius Papers, bMS Ger 208 (1221).
120 Walter Gropius to Laszlo Moholy-Nagy, [Cambridge, MA,] June 10, 1937, *loc. cit.*
121 Laszlo Moholy-Nagy to Ise and Walter Gropius, Chicago, July 31, 1937, Walter Gropius Papers, bMS Ger 208 (1221).
122 Laszlo Moholy-Nagy to Ise and Walter Gropius, July 24, 1937; Laszlo Moholy-Nagy to Alfred H. Barr, Chicago, September 15, 1937, [English original], Walter Gropius Papers, bMS Ger 208 (1221).

German market for Bauhaus publications.[123] He shared, however, the opinion of Gropius who saw great potential in bringing over the Bauhaus to the U.S., but considered it essential to adapt its methods to the country and to the character of its people.[124]

The new bauhaus was finally opened in Chicago on October 18, 1937.[125] Moholy was pleased with his first experiences which he found interesting, particularly as he had earlier considered the Americans not clever enough; soon he had to realize how mistaken he had been. "Their intellectual standard, the quick copying of the facts is fascinating. Only their capacity of experiences must be enlarged, I think. They eat knowledge really with the spoon, with large, real, round soup spoons."[126] He persuaded some of the best available people to join his faculty, including Archipenko for modeling, David Dushkin for music, the journalist Howard Vincent O'Brien to lecture on "the meaning of culture," as well as three professors of the University of Chicago, Charles W. Morris to teach "intellectual integration," Ralph W. Girard for life sciences, and Carl Eckart for physical sciences. "Kepes will arrive, with all the gods' help, in the middle of November," he added to the list.[127]

The first school year was academically successful. At its end, however, they experienced financial difficulties to an extent that Moholy-Nagy was advised by the Association of Arts and Industries to tell his faculty that if they were offered other positions "they should take them because the Association's financial position made it probable that we would not open next semester."[128] Moholy-Nagy felt especially bitter about experi-

---

123 Laszlo Moholy-Nagy to Alfred H. Barr, Chicago, September 15, 1937, *loc. cit.*
124 Walter Gropius to [?] Krüger, [Cambridge, MA,] [October, 1937], Walter Gropius Papers, bMS Ger 208 (1221).
125 Laszlo Moholy-Nagy to Walter Gropius, Chicago, October 20, 1937, Walter Gropius Papers, bMS Ger 208 (1221). [English original].
126 Laszlo Moholy-Nagy to Ise and Walter Gropius, Chicago, August 12, 1937, Walter Gropius Papers, bMS Ger 208 (1221).
127 Laszlo Moholy-Nagy to Walter Gropius, Chicago, October 20, 1937, *loc. cit.*
128 Laszlo Moholy-Nagy to The Executive Committee, Association of Arts & Industries, Chicago, August 16, 1938, Walter Gropius Papers, bMS Ger 208 (1221). [English original].

encing a typical émigré situation: "After I and my teachers were asked by the Association of Arts and Industries to come to this country and after we have shown every possible amount of good will, the reason why she [Miss Stahle of the Association] could not raise money for the school was the resentment against foreigners in this country."[129] The school started to disintegrate: teachers were dismissed, equipment became less and less available. Moholy felt he had to look for other sponsors and get out of the Association. Gropius called the story "the first case of Chicago gangsterism that we experienced in actual fact," and tried to use his prestige to help.[130] Moholy thought "America was always a country of pioneers and there is no doubt my next time will be a justification of this term."[131] He felt compelled to fight for survival. "Now sometimes I think why is to fight? As stranger in a foreign country! But I found such a great enthusiasm everywhere I go for the Bauhaus that I think it would be a pity to drop it. Also the last year I felt that I grew really, more and quicker than in the past 5 years all together."[132] Oddly enough, he felt at home and wrote most of his letters, even the ones to Gropius, increasingly in English.

At Christmas 1938, the situation was still unchanged and Moholy's wife Sybill complained bitterly to Mr. and Mrs. Gropius, "*Es ist immer und immer die alte schmutzige Geschichte mit ihnen* [...] [It is always and always the old dirty story with them...]"[133] Moholy himself wrote a long letter to *The New York Times* and gave a detailed story of their humiliation. Soon he was able to gather enough support to open the school again, under a new name, School of Design, at a new address, starting February 22, 1939. The "Sponsors' Committee" included distinguished

---

129   *Ibid.*
130   Walter Gropius to Laszlo Moholy-Nagy, [Cambridge, MA,] August 19, 1938, Walter Gropius Papers, bMS Ger 208 (1221).
131   Laszlo Moholy-Nagy to Walter Gropius, Chicago, August 19, 1938, Walter Gropius Papers, bMS Ger 208 (1221). [English original].
132   Laszlo Moholy-Nagy to Walter Gropius, [Chicago?] November 15, 1938, Walter Gropius Papers, bMS Ger 208 (1221) [English original].
133   Sybill Moholy-Nagy to Ise and Walter Gropius, Chicago, December 24, 1938, Walter Gropius Papers, bMS Ger 208 (1221).

The Hungarian Trauma, 1918–1920

names such as Alfred H. Barr, Jr., Walter Gropius, and Julian Huxley. He was able to offer a summer course in 1940 and a series of evening lectures in 1939–1940. By Christmas 1939, the storm was over, and Moholy confidently reported to Gropius, "Indeed the school looks fine. We have much more and better machines and equipment than we had on Prairie Avenue and as good luck, my public lecture on "The New Vision and Photography" drew about two hundred and twenty people and was very well received."[134] He was also able to secure a grant of $10,000 from the Carnegie Foundation and another $7,500 somewhat later, which were major triumphs.[135] He planned to invite Stravinsky to lecture and perform at the School. By March 1, 1942, the School had 120 students "which is absolutely wonderful as it is 20% more than last semester and so many art schools and colleges have lost rather than gained students."[136]

The School was blossoming when leukemia claimed Moholy's life in 1946.[137] Robert J. Wolff commented on the book by Sybill Moholy-Nagy on her husband, "Laszlo Moholy-Nagy will perhaps be best remembered as the man who not only helped to formulate one of the most vital manifestos of our time, but who, unlike many of his brilliant Bauhaus colleagues, had the power and the faith to fight to the point of death for the social implementation of the brave young words of the original Bauhaus documents."[138]

---

134 Laszlo Moholy-Nagy to Walter Gropius, Chicago, December 21, 1939, Walter Gropius Papers, bMS Ger 208 (1221).
135 Laszlo Moholy-Nagy to Charles W. Morris, Chicago, February 8, 1940, Laszlo Moholy-Nagy to Ise and Walter Gropius, Chicago, August 13, 1941, Walter Gropius Papers, bMS Ger 208 (1221).
136 Laszlo Moholy-Nagy to Mr. and Mrs. Walter Gropius, Chicago, March 9, 1942, Walter Gropius Papers, bMS Ger 208 (1221).
137 Moholy's last available report on the school is dated September 27, 1943, and is most optimistic. Walter Gropius Papers, bMS Ger 208 (1221).
138 Robert J. Wolff on Sybill Moholy-Nagy, *Moholy-Nagy: Experiment in Totality* (New York: Harper & Bros., 1950).

Figure 7. Graduating Jewish Students of the Lutheran *Gimnázium* in the *Fasor*, 1933 (School History Collection, Lutheran *Gimnázium* in the *Fasor*, Budapest)

III Berlin Junction

1 Hungary and the German Cultural Tradition

For those trying to escape Hungary after World War I and the revolutions, the German-speaking countries appeared the most obvious destination. The German influence in the Austro-Hungarian Monarchy was particularly strong in the education system, in the musical tradition, and in the arts and sciences. Members of the Austro-Hungarian middle classes spoke German well, and countries like Austria, Germany, and newly-established Czechoslovakia were close to Hungary, not only in geographic, but also in cultural terms. Weimar Germany and parts of German-speaking Czechoslovakia were also liberal and democratic in spirit and politics. In addition, like the former Austro-Hungarian Monarchy, Germany and to some extent, Czechoslovakia, represented a multi-centered world: each of the "gracious capitals of Germany's lesser princes,"[1] as István Deák put it, could boast of an opera, a symphony, a university, a theater, a museum, a library, an archive, with an appreciative and inspiring public which invited and welcomed international talent. Young musicians graduating from the *Hochschule für Musik* in Berlin could be reasonably sure that their diploma concerts would be attended by the music directors and conductors of most of the German operas across the country, poised to offer them a job in one of the many cultural centers of the *Reich*.[2] Berlin and other cities of Weimar Germany shared many of the cultural values and

---

[1] István Deák, *Weimar Germany's Left-Wing Intellectuals. A Political History of the Weltbühne and Its Circle* (Berkeley—Los Angeles: University of California Press, 1968), p. 13.

[2] Information from Budapest Opera conductor János Kerekes, August 1994. Cf. Antal Doráti, *Notes of Seven Decades* (London: Hodder and Stoughton, 1979), pp. 90–125.

traditions which young Hungarian scholars, scientists, musicians, visual artists, film makers and authors were accustomed to, providing an attractive setting and an intellectual environment comparable to the one that perished with pre-War Austria-Hungary, or was left behind, particularly that of Budapest.[3] The vibrant, yet tolerant spirit of pre-Nazi Germany, and particularly the atmosphere of an increasingly Americanized Berlin, gave them a foretaste of the United States and some of her big cities.

Both as a language and as a culture, German was a natural for Hungarians in the immediate post-World War I era. The *lingua franca* of the Habsburg Empire and of the Austro-Hungarian Monarchy, German was used at home, taught at school, spoken on the street and needed in the army.[4] This was more than a century-old tradition: the links between Hungary and the Austrian and German cultures went back to the 17th and the 18th centuries. The average "Hungarian" middle class person was typically German or Jewish by origin, and it was German culture and civilization that connected Hungary and the Austro-Hungarian Monarchy with Europe and the rest of the World. Middle class living rooms in Austria, Hungary, Bohemia, Galicia, and Croatia typically boasted of the complete work of Goethe and Schiller, the poetry of Heine and Lenau, the plays of Grillparzer and Schnitzler.[5]

Not only were German literature and German translations read throughout these areas: German permeated the language of the entire culture. When Baron József Eötvös, a reputable man of letters and Minister of Education, visited his daughter in a castle in Eastern Hungary, he noted: "What contrasts! I cross Szeged and Makó, then visit my daughter to find Kaulbach on the wall, Goethe on the bookshelf and Beethoven on

---

3   See Chapter II, note 75.
4   István Deák, *Beyond Nationalism: A Social and Political History of the Habsburg Officer Corps, 1848–1918* (New York–Oxford: Oxford University Press, 1990), pp. 83, 89, 99–102.
5   Cf. Gyula Illyés, *Magyarok. Naplójegyzetek*, 3rd ed. (Budapest: Nyugat, n.d. [1938]), Vol. II, p. 239.

the piano."⁶ Scores of *Das wohltemperierte Klavier* by Johann Sebastian Bach, *Gigues* and *Sarabandes* by Georg Friedrich Händel, the sonatas of Joseph Haydn, Wolfgang Amadeus Mozart, and Ludwig van Beethoven, the *Variations sérieuses* by Felix Mendelssohn, the popular songs of Franz Schubert or Robert Schumann, piano quintets of Johannes Brahms, and the brilliant transcriptions of Franz Liszt—these were the works which adorned the living room, or, in higher places, the music room.

Throughout the entire Austro-Hungarian Monarchy and beyond, Hungarians looked to import from Germany its modern theories and modern practices. Two examples from the beginning and the end of the period are characteristic. For generations of Hungarian lawmakers, the German school provided the finest example in Europe. When young Bertalan Szemere, a future prime minister of Hungary, went to study "what was best in each country, [he] tried to consider schools in Germany, the public life in France, and prisons in Britain [...]."⁷

As mentioned earlier, after almost two years under Professor Liller in Leipzig, Mór Kármán returned to Hungary and founded, in 1872, both the Institute for Teacher Training at the University of [Buda]Pest as well as the closely related Student Teaching High School or *Mintagimnázium* for prospective teachers, thus profoundly influencing Hungarian education in a German spirit and tradition.⁸ Likewise, in December 1918, Cecilia Polányi, the mother of Michael and Karl Polanyi and future grandmother of Nobel Laureate John C. Polanyi, intended to study the curricula and methods of German institutions in the field of "practical social work" and planned to go to Berlin, Frankfurt am Main, Mannheim, Hannover, Düsseldorf,

---

6   István Sőtér, *Eötvös József* [József Eötvös] 2nd rev. ed. (Budapest: Akadémiai Kiadó, 1967), p. 314.
7   Journal entry from Berlin, October 31, 1836. Cf. Bertalan Szemere, *Utazás külföldön* [Travel Abroad] (Budapest: Helikon, 1983), p. 59.
8   Baron József Eötvös to Mór Kleinmann, Buda, July 20, 1869, #12039, Theodore von Kármán Papers, California Institute of Technology Archives, File 142.10, Pasadena, CA; Untitled memoirs of Theodore von Kármán of his father, File 141.6, pp. 1–2. Cf. István Sőtér, *Eötvös József, op. cit.,* Miklós Mann, *Trefort Ágoston élete és működése* [The Life and Work of Ágoston Trefort] (Budapest: Akadémiai Kiadó, 1982).

Cologne, Augsburg, Munich, Heidelberg, Königsberg, and a host of other places where the various *Soziale Frauenschulen, Frauenakademie, Frauenseminare* were the very best in Europe.[9]

The effort to study and imitate what was German was, of course, natural. German was then the international language of science and literature: in the first eighteen years of the Nobel prize, between 1901 and 1918, there were seven German Nobel Laureates in Chemistry, six in Physics, four in Medicine (one Austro-Hungarian), and four in Literature.[10] Scholars and scientists read the *Beiträge*, the *Mitteilungen*, or the *Jahrbücher* of their special field of research or practice, published at some respectable German university town such as Giessen, Jena, or Greifswald. The grand tour of a young intellectual, artist, or professional, would unmistakably lead the budding scholar to Göttingen, Heidelberg, and, increasingly, Berlin. Artists typically went to Munich to study with Piloty.[11]

The illustrious faculty of the newly-founded Music Academy of Budapest, typically taught young Hungarians such as Béla Bartók or Zoltán Kodály through German.[12] When German composer Johannes Brahms performed his works in Pest (later Budapest), he recognized that the best music critics wrote in the German papers, the head of the leading chamber group was German-Hungarian Jenő Hubay (formerly Huber), the cellist of the quartet was the Prague-born David Popper, the second violinist was the Viennese Victor Ritter von Herzfeld, and that the viola player was an Austrian of peasant origin, József Waldbauer. German was

9   Cecilia Polányi to the Minister of Religion and Public Education, Budapest, December 11, 1918 and enclosures. (Hungarian and German) Michael Polanyi Papers, Box 20, Folder 1, Department of Special Collections, University of Chicago Library, Chicago, IL.
10 *The World Almanac and Book of Facts 2008* (New York: World Almanac Books, 2008), pp. 246–248.
11 Károly Lyka, *Magyar művészélet Münchenben* [Hungarian Artist-Life in Munich] (2nd ed., Budapest: Corvina, 1982); László Balogh, *Die ungarische Facette der Münchner Schule* (Mainburg: Pinsker-Verlag, 1988).
12 Tibor Frank, "Liszt, Brahms, Mahler: Music in Late 19th Century Budapest," in György Ránki, ed., *Hungary and European Civilization,* Indiana University Studies on Hungary, Vol. 3 (Budapest: Akadémiai Kiadó, 1989), *op. cit.,* p. 346.

the language in which Professor Hans Koessler taught composition and Xavér Ferenc Szabó taught orchestration. When Brahms visited the music shop Rózsavölgyi & Co's downtown Budapest, he was received by the German-speaking Herr Siebreich, who gave him the recently-published Hungarian folk pieces that formed the basis of Brahms' four-handed *Ungarische Tänze* [Hungarian Dances]. There was no reason for the strongly *Gesamtdeutsch-* [All-German-] oriented Brahms to doubt the "deep German embeddedness" of Hungarian culture. This is why his Hungarian pieces were composed as though they represented a particular, Eastern branch of German music: they jump about, as it were, in a pair of German trousers, the *mádjárosch Hopsassa*, as musicology professor Antal Molnár put it remembering his early years in Budapest.[13]

Ironically, it was the Moravian-Jewish Gustav Mahler who, as Director of the Royal Hungarian Opera between 1888 and 1891, was one of the first to demand that singers use the Hungarian language instead of the generally-accepted German,[14] though Mahler himself, as well as several other celebrated conductors in Budapest such as Hans Richter and Arthur Nikisch, only spoke German. The Hungarian middle classes often read local papers published in German that were available throughout the Monarchy until its dissolution and even beyond. Founded in 1854, the authoritative *Pester Lloyd* of Budapest, for example, continued as one of the most appreciated and well-read papers of the Budapest middle class until almost the end of World War II (1944). German in language but committed to Hungarian culture,[15] this part of the press helped bridge the gap between the two cultures. In much of the 18th and 19th centuries,

---

13 Antal Molnár, *Eretnek gondolatok a muzsikáról* [Heretic Thoughts on Music] (Budapest: Gondolat, 1976), pp. 27–28; quoted by Tibor Frank, "Liszt, Brahms, Mahler," p. 351. Cf. Károly Goldmark, *Emlékek életemből* [Memories of My Life] (Budapest: Zeneműkiadó, 1980), pp. 74–83.
14 Tibor Gedeon-Miklós Máthé, *Gustav Mahler* (Budapest: Zeneműkiadó, 1965), pp. 103–105; Gustav Mahler, *Briefe, 1879–1911* (Berlin–Wien–Leipzig: Zsolnay, 1924), pp. 115–116.
15 József Kiss, "Petőfi in der deutschsprachigen Presse Ungarns vor der Märzrevolution," in *Studien zur Geschichte der deutsch-ungarischen literarischen Beziehungen* (Berlin, 1969), pp. 275–297.

German novels and poetry, written and published in Hungary, were as integral to *Gesamtdeutsch* [Greater-German] literature as anything written in Königsberg or Prague.[16] The Jewish population of the Empire/Monarchy, and particularly its educated urban middle class, embraced German first and foremost as a new common language and contributed to making the Austrian realm a part, and not just an outskirt, of German civilization.[17] Moreover, for socially aspiring Jewish families, German was the language of education and upward mobility.

Yet, with all this infusion of German blood into Hungarian musical life and education, Budapest in the early 1900s still did not seem comparable to Berlin. Young and gifted Ernő (Ernst von) Dohnányi considered the *Hochschule für Musik* in Berlin a much greater challenge. "To choose Budapest instead of Berlin would have been such a sacrifice on my part which, considering my youth, the fatherland cannot demand and, considering my art, I cannot make," he wrote to the Director of the Budapest Music Academy around 1905. "Berlin is unquestionably the center of the musical world today. Budapest, we must admit, does not play even a small role in the world of music. Even if it is true that the *Hochschule of Berlin* is simply the center of a clique, that clique is enormous and has played a role for decades whereas the musical world doesn't even notice whether or not I take a dominating position in Budapest."[18] Dohnányi stayed in Berlin until World War I and, using his Germanized name Ernst von Dohnányi, became one of the internation-

---

16 László Tarnói, *Parallelen, Kontakte und Kontraste. Die deutsche Lyrik um 1800 und ihre Beziehungen zur ungarischen Dichtung in den ersten Jahrzehnten des 19. Jahrhunderts* (Budapest: ELTE Germanisztikai Intézet, 1998), pp. 203–322; Ulrik R. Monsberger, *A hazai német naptárirodalom története 1821-ig* [A History of German Calendar Literature in Hungary to 1821] (Budapest, 1931).

17 György Szalai, "A hazai zsidóság magyarosodása 1849-ig," [The Magyarization of the Hungarian Jewry to 1849], *Világosság* 15 (1974), pp. 216–223; Róza Osztern, *Zsidó újságírók és szépírók a magyarországi német nyelvű időszaki sajtóban, a "Pester Lloyd" megalapításáig, 1854-ig* [Jewish Journalists and Authors in the German Periodical Press of Hungary, up to the Foundation of the Pester Lloyd in 1854] (Budapest, 1930).

18 Bálint Vázsonyi, *Dohnányi Ernő* (Budapest: Zeneműkiadó, 1971), pp. 67–68.

ally most attractive professors of the *Hochschule für Musik*. Promising pianists from Hungary such as Ervin Nyiregyházi, Imre Stefániai, and Marianne Adler of Budapest, and even international students such as Swedish composer Franz Berwald's granddaughter Astrid Berwald of Stockholm, came to study with him in pre-War Berlin.[19]

Not only musicians went to Berlin. The city in the early pre-War era proved to be an irresistible magnet for the new Hungarian intellectual and professional classes. Many of the young Hungarians who frequented Berlin around the turn of the century were Jewish. The Jewish-Hungarian middle class felt at home in imperial Germany and sent their sons and daughters there to study. After completing their courses in Budapest before World War I, Hungary's up-and-coming mathematicians saw Göttingen and Berlin as the most important places to study. As a very young man, the celebrated Lipót Fejér spent the academic year 1899–1900 in Berlin where he attended the famous seminar of Hermann Amandus Schwarz. In 1902–1903, he studied in Göttingen and in subsequent years returned to both universities.[20] A gifted student of Fejér, Gábor Szegő also followed his path and went to study in pre-War Berlin, Göttingen and Vienna, and later became professor of mathematics at Stanford.[21]

Men of letters also followed in numbers. The poet and future film theoretician Béla Balázs went to study with Georg Simmel in 1906, and dedicated his doctoral dissertation *Az öntudatról* [On Self Consciousness], later renamed *Halálesztétika* [The Aesthetics of Death], to his German master.[22] The heroine of Balázs's first literary work, *Doktor Szélpál Margit*, spent three years in Berlin as a student, a typical pattern in pre-War

---

19 Bálint Vázsonyi, *Dohnányi Ernő, op. cit.*, p. 83, and personal information of the present author from Marianne Flesch (1890–1966).
20 Gábor Szegő, "Leopold Fejér: In Memoriam, 1880–1959," *Bulletin of the American Mathematical Society*, Vol. 66, No. 5 (September 1960), pp. 346–347.
21 [Gábor Szegő] "Lebenslauf." Gábor Szegő Papers, SC 323, Boxes 85–036. Department of Special Collections and University Archives, Stanford University Libraries, Stanford, CA.
22 Herbert Bauer, *Az öntudatról* [=Béla Balázs, *Halálesztétika*] (Budapest: Deutsch Zsigmond, n.d.).

Figure 8. Berlin, Unter den Linden, 1920s (HNM).

German-Hungarian relations.[23] Critic, author, and patron Baron Lajos Hatvany studied classics with the prestigious Ulrich von Wilamowitz-Moellendorff in Berlin—an experience which he came to denounce in his sarcastic *Die Wissenschaft des nicht Wissenswerten [appr. The Science of what is Not Worth Knowing]*, first published in Leipzig, Germany.[24] His second book, *Ich und die Bücher [I and the Books]*, was published simultaneously in both German and Hungarian in 1910.[25] Others who went included important businessmen such as stock exchange wizard Alfred Manovill who, well before the War, joined the Berlin bank Mendelssohn & Co. at the age of 24 and acted as the honorary president of the *Berliner Ungarn-Vereins* [Association of Hungarians in Berlin] through the advent of Hitler.[26]

2 The Human Geography of Interwar Migrations

After the political changes of 1918–20, small groups of intellectually gifted Hungarians started to migrate toward a variety of European countries and the United States. After what often proved to be the first step in a chain- or step-migration, most of the Hungarian émigrés found they had to leave the German-speaking countries upon the rise of Hitler as chancellor of Germany and they continued on their way, in most cases

---

23 Béla Balázs, *Doktor Szélpál Margit* [Dr. Margaret Szélpál] (Budapest: Nyugat, 1909), p. 10.
24 Ludwig Hatvany, *Die Wissenschaft des nicht Wissenswerten* (Leipzig: Julius Zeitler, 1908; 2. Auflage, München: Georg Müller: 1914); Hungarian translation: *A tudni-nem-érdemes dolgok tudománya*, transl. by Klára Szőllősy (Budapest: Gondolat Kiadó, 1968).
25 Ludwig Hatvany, *Ich und die Bücher* (Selbstvorwürfe des Kritikers) (Berlin: Paul Cassirer, 1910); in Hungarian: Lajos Hatvany, *Én és a könyvek* (Budapest: Nyugat, 1910).
26 "Alfred Manovill 50 Jahre." (German) Manuscript of a newspaper article in the Michael Polanyi Papers, Box 20, Folder 2.

to the United States. This pattern was certainly not the only one, though it was by far the most typical.

Professional migration as a European phenomenon after World War I was certainly not restricted to Hungary alone. The immense social convulsions that followed the war drove astonishing numbers of people in all directions. Russian and Ukrainian refugees fled Bolshevism, Poles were relocated in reemerging Poland, Hungarians escaped from newly established Czechoslovakia, Romania and Yugoslavia.[27] Outward movements from Hungary in the 1920s were part of this emerging general pattern and cannot be clearly defined as *emigrations* proper. Most people simply went on substantial and extended study tours of varied length, just as others did before World War I. Contrary to general belief, migrations were not limited to Jews suffering from the political and educational consequences of the White Terror in Hungary. Yet, Jewish migrations were a definitive pattern of the 1920s when the *numerus clausus* law kept many of them out of university. The result of these migrations was the vulnerability of statelessness, or at least mental statelessness, the troubled existence of living long years without citizenship in a world built on nationality.[28]

Gentile Hungarians also left their country in considerable numbers in this era, for a variety of reasons. In subsequent years many of them returned to Hungary. Their list included the likes of authors Gyula Illyés, Lajos Kassák, and Sándor Márai, visual artists Aurél Bernáth, Sándor Bortnyik, Béni and Noémi Ferenczy, Károly Kernstok, singers Anne Roselle (Anna Gyenge), Rosette (Piroska) Anday, Koloman von Pataky, actors/actresses Vilma Bánky, Ilona Hajmássy, Béla Lugosi, Lya de Putti, organist/composer Dezső Antalffy-Zsiross, composer Béla Bartók, and Nobel Laureate Albert Szent-Györgyi. Motivated by politics, poverty, curiosity, or longing for an international career, people of dramatically opposed convictions hit the road and tried their luck in Paris, Berlin, or Hollywood.

---

27 Geoffrey Barraclough, ed., *The Times Atlas of World History* (Maplewood NJ: Hammond, rev. ed. 1984, repr. 1988), p. 265.
28 Linda K. Kerber, "Toward a History of Statelessness in America," *American Quarterly*, Volume 57, Number 3, September 2005, pp. 727–749.

Many Hungarians left the successor states of the former Austro-Hungarian Empire, labeled as "Romanians," "Czechoslovaks," or "Yugoslavs." Because of the Quota Laws, however, very few Hungarians headed toward the United States: migrations were directed toward European centers, in the first place to Germany.

3 From Budapest to Berlin

Networking, bonding, cohorting, using available contacts, and relying on people already established abroad was among the most natural methods used to secure a place in a new environment, particularly in Germany. A lot of people needed help and this induced a veritable "chain reaction" of migrations.

Unfortunately, most Hungarians who made their way toward Germany did not easily find ideal places for their studies or for their ambitions. It was somewhat easier to succeed before the War, though when Theodore von Kármán completed his *Habilitation* in Germany in 1908 he was emphatically warned that no one could guarantee he would ever get a university chair. "But I received a call after a waiting time which would have been considered short even for Germans."[29] Prospective Berlin professors expected introductions for students. Typically, mathematics student Gábor Szegő in 1914 asked for a letter for Professor E. Landau from his Budapest colleague Lipót Fejér, who had spent years in Germany.[30] The search for education or academic posts in Germany became a lot more difficult during the war. When in 1916 Michael Polanyi inquired about his own prospects for a *Habilitation* under Professor G.

---

29 Theodore von Kármán to Michael Polanyi, Aachen, March 17, 1920, (German), Michael Polanyi Papers, Box 17.
30 Leopold Fejér to E. Landau, Budapest, May 23, 1914 (German), Gábor Szegő Papers, SC 323, Boxes 85–036.

Bredig at the Institute for Physical Chemistry and Electrical Chemistry of the University of Karlsruhe, he was politely turned down.

> We are compelled, now after the War [had started] more than ever before, to take into account the public opinion which urges us to fill in the available places for Dozenten by citizens of the Reich as much as possible. Even though we like to treat the citizens of our Allies the same way as our own, you must have seen in my Institute that the situation was pushed so strongly in favor of them, that as of now, and more than ever before, I must see to attracting more Imperial Germans.[31]

A year later, Polanyi tried Munich and turned to Professor K. Fajans in what was then the Chemical Laboratory of the Bavarian State. Though his request was well received there and an offer was made to become an assistant to Dr. Fajans, Polanyi's German plans did not materialize until after the War.[32]

After World War I ended, the prospects for Hungarians in beaten Germany were even worse. Well established in Germany after receiving his Ph.D. in Göttingen in 1908, Theodore von Kármán, professor at the University of Aachen, helped a number of Hungarians start their careers in Germany, readily sponsoring friends of his family, often under the most adverse circumstances.[33] He described the 1920 situation in chilling terms to Michael Polanyi, who was still trying to decide about his future as a scientist and get his *Habilitation* or a job. An assistant to George de Hevesy during the Hungarian commune, Polanyi left Budapest at the end of 1919 and went to Karlsruhe where he had studied chemistry from 1913–1914.[34] Initially, the prospects seemed discouraging. "The mood in the universities vis-à-vis foreigners is momentarily very bad but it may change in a few years [...] The inflation conditions are very unpleasant

---

31 G. Bredig to Michael Polanyi, Karlsruhe, February 12, 1917 (German), Michael Polanyi Papers, Box 1, Folder 5.
32 K. Fajans to Michael Polanyi, München, June 26 and October 5, 1918. (German) Michael Polanyi Papers, Box 1, Folder 5.
33 Cf. e.g. the case of the son of his brother's friend Michael Becz, see Elemér Kármán to Theodore von Kármán, Budapest, May 9, 1920 (German), Theodore von Kármán Papers, File 139.1.
34 *Ibid.*

today and it is much more difficult to wait for a job."[35] Several years later, in 1923, American visiting scholar Eric R. Jette described the German university scene in remarkably similar terms: "Conditions in the universities were very bad, of course, in all places. The same story was heard everywhere, no money, no new professors or docents but laboratories filled with students who had almost nothing to live on. Yet the research goes on and the students still keep at their books."[36]

Hungarians, however, were difficult to turn down. Networking, using available contacts and relying on people already established in Germany, was one of the most natural methods used to secure a place somewhere in Germany. Michael Polanyi turned to von Kármán for help. In turn, the future engineering professor Mihály Freund asked for Polanyi's assistance for a young relative, Tibor Bányai, who had just finished high school in Budapest and wanted to become an engineer at the University of Karlsruhe, where Polanyi had been active for some time. More importantly, in 1922 Polanyi paved the way for Leo Szilard who tried to get an assistant's job at the Institute of Physical Chemistry at the University of Frankfurt am Main. The degree he had just received in Berlin under Max von Laue was the best letter of recommendation he could possibly present. Yet, under the circumstances, he still needed Polanyi's letter to Frankfurt professor Richard Lorenz which called him a "wonderfully smart man."[37]

---

35 *Ibid.*
36 Eric R. Jette to Michael Polanyi, Up[p]sala, February 10, 1923, Michael Polanyi Papers, Box 1, Folder 19.
37 Michael Polanyi to B. Lorenz, October 16, 1922 (German), Michael Polanyi Papers, Box 1, Folder 18.

After the War ended, the prospects for Hungarians in defeated Germany got even worse. From 1920 on, von Kármán increased his assistance to Hungarians, readily sponsoring friends of his family, often under the most adverse circumstances.[38] Of all the Hungarian scientists, von Kármán proved to be the most active and successful contact person.

His German and subsequent American correspondence provides a wealth of information on half a century of Hungarian networking. A typical letter from his German period was sent in 1924, by a Hungarian friend in Vienna, asking for his assistance for Hungarian chemical engineering student Pál Acél to continue his studies "in Germany, preferably under you."[39] Correspondence on these matters sometimes had to be clandestine: in dangerous years such as 1920, such mail was better sent to Vienna, rather than Budapest, and picked up there personally.[40]

Students continued in their attempts to get to Germany for many reasons, one of them being the commitment of the German professors to their gifted students and the time and interest they allotted to young people. A brief stay in Berlin promised to be significant, as in the case of young John von Neumann. From Budapest, Professor Lipót Fejér asked fellow Berlin mathematician Gábor Szegő in early 1922: "What does little Johnny Neumann do? Please let me know what impact you notice so far of his Berlin stay."[41] In a 1929 interview Michael Polanyi, since early 1923 a *habilitierter* Berlin professor himself,[42] proudly yet sadly described the essential difference between the contemporary Hungarian and German

---

38 Cf. e.g. the case of the son of his brother's friend Michael Becz, see Elemér Kármán to Theodore von Kármán, Budapest, May 9, 1920 (German), Theodore von Kármán Papers, File 139.1.
39 Elemér Székely to Theodore von Kármán, Wien, April 29, 1924 (Hungarian), Theodore von Kármán Papers, File 29.14.
40 Mihály Freund to Michael Polanyi, May 4, 1920 (Hungarian), Michael Polanyi Papers, Box 17.
41 Gabor Szegő Papers, SC 323, Boxes 85–036, Department of Special Collections and University Archives, Stanford University Libraries, Stanford, CA.
42 Obersekretär Breuder [?], Technische Hochschule zu Berlin, to Michael Polanyi, Charlottenburg, November 8, 1923. (German) Michael Polanyi Papers, Box 1, Folder 20.

educational scenes declaring that "professors in Germany grab with avid interest the hand of any student considered to be gifted. They are like the art-collector whose utmost passion is to discover talent. This is part of the profession of a university professor."[43] It is important to note that his generation shared essentially the same experience later in U.S. universities: for *émigré* scholars and scientists, the welcoming atmosphere of German universities was happily rediscovered in the United States.

One of the outstanding qualities of the post-World War I German environment was tolerance—political, religious, professional and artistic. People, professions, ideas, and art ridiculed at home in Hungary were welcome in the open atmosphere of Weimar Germany. Béla Bartók's pioneering ballet *A csodálatos mandarin* [The Miraculous Mandarin], unaccepted and persecuted in Hungary, found a sympathetic audience in Cologne where Hungarian-born Eugen Szenkár performed it for the first time in 1926.[44] Working for the Collegium Hungaricum in Berlin from 1927 for almost a decade, Dezső Keresztury noticed that anti-Semitism among the Hungarian students was kept under control in the Weimar period. Jewish-Hungarian students declared their faith in Hungary as their "accepting, raising mother who, though she became a stepmother now due to circumstances, we should tolerate this as we know she will take us under her wings again."[45] Moving to Germany was not only a question of survival in terms of studies, jobs, and promotions: it also meant an opportunity to resume one's original professional activities or intellectual direction. It was not merely the acquisition of a new address: it led to the reconstruction of spiritual (and often bodily) health, the realization of the self, a restoration of the mind.

43 "Polányi Mihály Nádas Sándorhoz," *Pesti Futár*, 1929, pp. 37–38.; repr. in: *Polanyiana*, I/1, 1991, p. 26.
44 József Ujfalussy, *Béla Bartók* (Budapest: Corvina, 1971), pp. 237–240; György Kroó, *A Guide to Bartók* (Budapest: Corvina, 1974), pp. 97–105. The ballet was not tolerated even in Cologne, where the conservative mayor of the city, Konrad Adenauer stopped the production.
45 Dezső Keresztury, *Emlékezéseim. Szülőföldeim* (Budapest: Argumentum, 1993), p. 176.

A case in point is psychoanalyst Michael Balint, who decided to leave Budapest for what was then a typical combination of political and professional reasons. "It was very difficult—it was 1920 then—and it was the worst period of the Horthy Régime, very anti-Semitic and anti-liberal and so on," he declared in a Columbia University oral history interview toward the end of his life. "So it was with my interests in analysis [...] It was almost impossible to get any [position] at the university, so I started to work as a biochemist and bacteriologist [...] However, I did not think that anything could be done in Budapest. So I decided to leave Budapest and try something in Germany."[46] Balint went to Berlin as a chemist. He used the introduction of his friend and former colleague Michael Polanyi to get a job at the AGFA laboratories there.[47] "So we departed to Berlin, where I got a small job as a research chemist, with permission that I work for a Ph.D. degree."[48] Most Hungarian psychoanalysts ended up in the U.S.[49]

Physicist Imre Bródy also complained of the situation in Hungary when trying to get to Germany. "You know very well," he wrote to Michael Polanyi in Berlin, "as you did what you did for that very reason, what it means to me to be able to get out of here, so that I could work, getting out of here, where scientific work, at least for me, is both physically and psychologically equally impossible. Your encouragement and active support, I believe, made successful work possible."[50] Derailed in his scientific

46 Michael Balint interview; Columbia University Oral History Project, Columbia University Libraries, New York, NY. Balint authored *Primary Love and Psycho-Analytic Technique* (New York: Liveright, 1953); *The Doctor, His Patient and the Illness* (London: Pitman, 1957); [with Enid Balint], *Psychotherapeutic Techniques in Medicine* (London: Tavistock, 1961); *The Basic Fault. Therapeutic Aspects of Regression* (London: Tavistock, 1968).
47 Michael Polanyi to Dr. John Eggert, [Berlin,] May 16, 1922, Michael Polanyi Papers, Box 1, Folder 18.
48 Michael Balint interview, Columbia Oral History Project, *loc. cit.*
49 Judit Mészáros, "The Tragic Success of European Psychoanalysis: 'The Budapest School,'" *Int. Forum Psychoanal.* 7, 1998, pp. 207–214.
50 Imre Bródy to Michael Polanyi, August 26, 1920. (Hungarian) Michael Polanyi Papers, Box 1, Folder 10.

activities in physical chemistry, Bródy intended to devote his energies to the theory of relativity.[51] "For the moment I find Berlin the most appropriate place to go to," he added, though scientists Max Born and James Franck had helped him get a job at the University of Göttingen which he accepted.[52] In a letter written to Albert Einstein, Polanyi also supported physicist Imre Bródy in 1922, asking him to write to the leaders of Robert Millikan's newly founded institute in Pasadena, CA so that Bródy could get a job as an assistant.[53] Bródy was one of the few notable émigré scientists to return to Hungary and fall victim to Nazism there.

Joining prewar Hungarian groups and friends in Germany, new Hungarians came by the hundreds to Berlin in the 1920s. They found what increasingly amounted to a Hungarian community, with bass Oszkár Kálmán singing in the Staatsoper and tenor Pál Fehér in the Städtische Oper, and a host of Hungarian singers including Gitta Alpár, Rózsi Bársony, Oszkár Dénes, and Tibor Halmai featuring in Paul Abraham's popular operetta *Ball im Savoy*. It was after the Nazi takeover, that Maestro Fritz Busch presented Verdi's *Ballo in maschera* in the Städtische Oper with the non-Jewish Hungarian soprano Mária Németh and tenor Koloman von Pataky. The accompanist Árpád Sándor was an organic part of the musical life of the city.[54] Hungarians assembled in four different circles that alternately organized the annual Hungarian ball, helped introduce the new Berlitz method for studying German, and socialized around the Collegium Hungaricum of Berlin, which attracted influential people like the Prussian minister of science, culture, and education Karl Heinrich

---

51   *Ibid.*
52   *Ibid.;* Max Born to Michael Polanyi, September 26, 1921 (German); Imre Bródy to Michael Polanyi, Göttingen, March 24, 1922 (Hungarian) Michael Polanyi Papers, Box 1, Folder 15.
53   Michael Polanyi to Albert Einstein, March 14, 1922. (German) Michael Polanyi Papers, Box 1, Folder 17.
54   Information obtained from Budapest Opera conductor János Kerekes, August 1994.

Becker, physicists such as Max Planck and Albert Einstein, and linguist Willy Bang-Kaup.[55]

Berlin was certainly not the only destination. Mathematician Gábor Szegő was happy to accept a full professorship at Königsberg in 1926, chemist Ferenc Kőrösy went to study at Karlsruhe in 1923, philosopher Karl Mannheim settled in Heidelberg where he had studied before World War I[56] (and became a professor of sociology 1930 at the university of Frankfurt am Main until escaping to Britain). Mathematician Otto Szász gave up a position at the University of Frankfurt am Main in 1933 to leave for the U.S., where he taught mostly in Cincinnati.[57]

Hungarian filmmakers formed an integral part of the German film industry after World War I. German film established its independence from foreign influence at the same time and film production was supported by massive government aid: the UFA (Universum-Film Aktien Gesellschaft) was founded in 1917 and remained the dominant force of the film industry until the end of World War II. The 1920s was known as the golden age of the German cinema. A large number of Hungarians served their film apprenticeship at the UFA studios in Berlin-Babelsberg. As they did not all work there continuously until Hitler emerged, they did not all leave Germany as a group after 1933. Directors Michael Curtiz (Mihály Kertész), Joseph Pasternak, and Charles Vidor, actors Peter Lorre, Bela Lugosi, Paul Lukas (Pál Lukács), S. Z. Sakall, Victor Varconi

---

55 Dezső Keresztury, "Berlin tetői alatt (Részletek visszaemlékezéseimből)" [Under the roofs of Berlin: From my memoirs], *Magyar Nemzet*, March 27, 1993.
56 Éva Gábor, "Mannheim in Hungary and in Weimar Germany," *The Newsletter of the International Society for the Sociology of Knowledge*, Vol. 9, Nos. 1–2 (August 1983), pp. 7–14; Lee Congdon, "Karl Mannheim as Philosopher," *Journal of European Studies*, Vol. 7, Part I, No. 25 (March 1977), pp. 1–18.
57 Michael Polanyi to G. Bredig, Berlin June 23, 1923 (German) Michael Polanyi Papers, Box 1, Folder 20; Brian Longhurst, *Karl Mannheim and the Contemporary Sociology of Knowledge* (New York: St. Martin's Press, 1989), p. 5; Gabor Szegő, "Otto Szász," *Bulletin of the American Mathematical Society*, Vol. 60, No. 3, May 1954, pp. 261.

Figure 9. Paul Abraham, composer, 1950s (HNM).

left Germany for the United States, some of them well before the Nazis came to power, as they had found Hollywood's offers more attractive.[58]

At one point toward the end of the 1920s, the Hungarian government began to realize the significance to Hungarian culture of the continuous outward flow of émigré professionals. Count Kuno Klebelsberg, minister of religion and education between 1922 and 1931, visited some of the key German universities, trying to invite the promising Hungarian scientists back to Hungary. Mrs. Szegő, wife of the mathematician Gábor Szegő, described the conversation, where Count Klebelsberg was confronted with the long list of successful Jewish-Hungarian mathematicians and scientists in Germany:

> When Klebi [Klebelsberg] celebrated some time ago in Göttingen, the mathematician Courant who sat next to him at the dinner table tried to impress him by listing a number of Hungarian though non-Aryan scientists (such as [Lipót] Fejér, [George] Polya, Misi [Michael Polanyi], [John von] Neumann, [Theodore von] Kármán, Gábor [Szegő]). [Max] Born seconded. Klebi said that Misi had received an invitation to return to Budapest. [...] Tammann [also at the table that night] remarked that he doubted whether Misi would accept the invitation, and give up his position in Germany. Klebi responded with the by now classical adage: *Wenn Vaterland ruft, kommt Ungar!* [When the Fatherland calls, the Hungarian comes!][59]

Mrs. Szegő added with a measure of cynicism, "*Si non è vero, è ben trovato.*" [If it's not true, it's well invented].

Returning to Budapest, the minister published a prominent article on the first page of the popular daily *Pesti Napló*. In the title of his article, Count Klebelsberg used a reference to the poet Endre Ady's famous line from 1906, which referred to modernization in Hungary. For the minister, the great national problem in 1929 was to "preserve the genuine features of the nation while at the same time raising [Hungary up] to a completely European level and learning from the nations that surround

---

58 Ephraim Katz, *The Film Encyclopedia*, op. cit., pp. 476–7, 665, 1181, 1187, 1194; 293–4, 741–2.
59 Mrs. Gábor Szegő to Mrs. Michael Polanyi, K[önigs]berg, May 15, 1929 (Hungarian), Michael Polanyi Papers.

us."[60] He suggested the importance of maintaining the strong Hungarian national character in literature and the humanities but argued differently in regard to the field of medicine, economics and the technical and natural sciences: "Chauvinism and particularism would take a cruel revenge there," he said, "for them we must open the gates widely [...] May a lot of people come in, a great many of them, as many as possibly can, with the new inventions of new times, new methods of production, and, first and foremost, with new energies."[61] The minister wrote the article as an open invitation to all Hungarian professionals currently in other countries in an effort to induce a return migration in the key professions. For him this was not a novel idea: as a young associate to then Prime Minister Kálmán Széll, Klebelsberg was instrumental in 1902–1903 in establishing the guidelines of the "American project" of the Hungarian government, which endeavored to take care of, and eventually bring back home, ethnic Hungarians who left for the United States.[62]

Klebelsberg's article stirred the Hungarian émigré community in Germany. At one point or another, many of them had difficulties finding jobs and the call of the Hungarian government sounded good. Michael Polanyi showed his copy of *Pesti Napló* to his Berlin friends. Prospective Nobel Laureate Eugene Wigner and Leo Szilard actually signed it as if

---

60   Count Kuno Klebelsberg, "Szabad-e Dévénynél betörnöm új időknek új dalaival?" [May I break in at Dévény with the new songs of new times?] *Pesti Napló*, May 5, 1929.
61   Ibid.
62   It is characteristic how Kuno Klebelsberg differentiated between ethnic vs. non-ethnic Hungarians in 1902, respectively between representatives of national subjects vs. natural sciences 1929. Kuno Klebelsberg, "Exposé," Budapest, July 29, 1902; prime minister Kálmán Széll to foreign minister Count Agenor Goluchowsky, Budapest, March 6, 1903, published by Albert Tezla, ed. *The Hazardous Quest. Hungarian Immigrants in the United States 1895–1920. A Documentary* (Budapest: Corvina, 1993), pp. 486–492.—For the "American project" of the Hungarian Government see Ilona Kovács, *Az amerikai közkönyvtárak magyar gyűjteményeinek szerepe az asszimiláció és az identitás megőrzésének kettős folyamatában 1890–1940* [The role of the Hungarian collections of American public libraries in the dual process of assimilation and identity preservation] (Budapest: Országos Széchényi Könyvtár, 1997), pp. 41–60.

acknowledging the message—but they decided to stay in Germany. A day after the article appeared, the minister was interviewed about the actual intentions of the government. Klebelsberg became suddenly cautious and backpedaled when confronted with questions about returning professors, suggesting that this was in fact up to the Hungarian universities. Some scientists did return, however, and the most notable among them, later Nobel Laureate Albert Szent-Györgyi, concluded a successful period of research in Groningen (Holland), Cambridge (England) and the Mayo Clinic at Rochester, Minnesota, and returned to Hungary in 1928, apparently at the instigation of Klebelsberg.[63] Others, such as the celebrated Hungarian-American conductor Fritz Reiner of Cincinnati, also toyed with the plan of returning to Hungary, where he was apparently invited to become music director of the Budapest Opera. Reiner's conditions, however, were so demanding that the appointment never materialized.[64]

4 The *Amerikanisierung* of Berlin

While visiting Berlin, the young Henry Adams found very little of interest in 1858–1859 and noted that "the German university and German law were failures; German society, in an American sense, did not exist, or if it existed, never showed itself to an American." Adams also spoke about

---

63 Szent-Györgyi mistakenly remembers 1932 as the date of his return upon which he accepted the chair of Medical Chemistry at the University of Szeged, Hungary. Cf. Albert Szent-Györgyi, "Prefatory Chapter—Lost in the Twentieth Century," *Annual Review of Biochemistry*, Vol. 32, 1963, Repr., p. 8.

64 Béla Bartók discussed this plan with the conductor who wanted membership in the Upper House of Hungarian Parliament, an effort that Bartók discouraged. Cf. Béla Bartók to Fritz Reiner, Budapest, October 29, 1928, published by János Demény ed. *Bartók Béla levelei* [Letters of Béla Bartók] (Budapest: Művelt Nép Könyvkiadó, 1951), p. 109; K[ároly] K[ristóf], "Reiner Frigyes,", in *Magyar Zsidó Lexikon* (Budapest: Magyar Zsidó Lexikon, 1929), p. 788.

the "total failure of German education."[65] For German cultural critics such as Julius Langbehn, Paul de Lagarde, and Moeller van den Bruck, Berlin a mere couple of decades later had taken on an American flavor that seemed to be evil itself. "Spiritually and politically, the provinces should be maneuvered and marshaled against the capital," exclaimed Julius Langbehn in his diatribe against Berlin.[66] It was he who thought that the ancient spirit of the Prussian garrison town had been corrupted by the poison of commerce and materialism, which he identified with the *Amerikanisierung* (Americanization) of Germany. Langbehn bitterly resented "the crude cult of money which," he insisted, "was also a North American trait, which takes over more and more in today's Berlin; a German and honorable spirit should definitely stand up against it. Coins of money are mostly dirty. For the Germans of today, they should be the tool and not the purpose."[67] Langbehn's was a typical voice crying out against the big new cities across the continent of Europe as well as in the United States. His tract appeared approximately at the same time as the Rev. Josiah Strong's *Our Country*, which described the American city as one of the great perils of his day.[68] In time, however, Langbehn

---

65 *The Education of Henry Adams. An Autobiography* (Boston and New York: Houghton Mifflin, 1918), p. 80. Cf. Kurt Albert Mayer, "Some German Chapters of Henry Adams's Education: "Berlin (1858–1859), Heine, and Goethe," *AAA— Arbeiten aus Anglistik und Amerikanistik*, Vol. 19, No. 1 (Tübingen: Narr, 1994), pp. 3–25; Kurt Albert Mayer, "Henry Adams: 'And I've Retouched My Austria,'" Francke Verlag, 1996.

66 Julius Langbehn, *Rembrandt als Erzieher*, 33. ed. (Leipzig: Hirschfeld, 1891), p. 133. Quoted by Fritz Stern, *The Politics of Cultural Dispair. A Study in the Rise of the Germanic Ideology* (Berkeley—Los Angeles: University of California Press, 1974), p. 131.

67 Julius Langbehn, *Rembrandt als Erzieher*, 49. ed. (Leipzig: Hirschfeld, 1909), p. 320. 12. ed.: "...der rohe Geldkultus ist auch ein nordamerikanischer Zug, welcher in dem jetzigen Berlin mehr und mehr überhand nimmt; ...." 49. ed.: "...der rohe Geldkultus ist ein nordamerikanischer und zugleich — jüdischer Zug, welcher in dem jetzigen Berlin mehr und mehr überhand nimmt; ..."

68 Josiah Strong, *Our Country. Its Possible Future and Its Present Crisis*. Ed. by Jurgen Herbst (Cambridge, MA: Belknap Press of Harvard University Press, 1963), pp. 171–186.

Figure 10. Fritz Reiner, conductor, 1920s (HNM).

identified "the crude cult of money" not only with North America but also as "a Jewish trait," an assertion he added to subsequent editions of his phenomenally popular book.[69]

Conservatives in imperial Germany were particularly concerned with the Americanization of their country, the coming of a mass society with its materialism, mechanization, and idolized riches. The first to use the term in a speech in 1877 was Emil du Bois-Reymond, who warned of "*Amerikanisierung* in terms of the growing overweight of technology."[70] Du Bois-Reymond made frequent references to the threat of Americanization for Europe, her intellectual life as well as for her economy. By the turn of the century the term was so widely used and considered such a pernicious threat in Germany that Paul Dehn spoke of the potential dangers of an "Americanization of the Earth" in a paper published in 1904: "What is Americanization? In the economic sense Americanization means the modernization of the methods of industry, commerce, and agriculture as well as in all areas of practical life. In a broader sense, socially and politically considered, Americanization means the [uncontrolled], exclusive, and [inconsiderate] drive for possession, riches and influence [...]"[71]

For contemporaries with knowledge of both German and American culture, post-World War I Berlin was the city most thoroughly Americanized. The *Diary* of Lord D'Abernon, British ambassador to Berlin in the early 1920s, is full of references to the American features of Berlin and Germany and to the affinity of Germans to American style and methods. "The similarity of Berlin to an American city has impressed

---

69   See note #67.
70   Emil du Bois-Reymond, "Kulturgeschichte und Naturwissenschaft," in *Reden*, Vol. l, p. 280, see also pp. 281, 283. Quoted by Otto Basler, "Amerikanismus. Geschichte des Schlagwortes," *Deutsche Rundschau*, Vol. CCXXIV (July-August-September 1930), p. 144.
71   Paul Dehn, "Die Amerikanisierung der Erde," in *Weltwirtschaftliche Neubildungen* (1904), p. 238. Quoted by Otto Basler, *op. cit.*, p. 144. Cf. Frank Becker und Elke Reinhardt-Becker, Hg., *Mythos USA. "Amerikanisierung" in Deutschland seit 1900* (Frankfurt a. M.: Campus Verlag, 2006).

many travelers," the ambassador noted in an "Introductory Survey" to his *Diary*.[72] He observed a mutual impact: "The methods of American trade and finance are derived from Germany rather than from England, being based in the main on the traditions of Frankfurt and Hamburg,"[73] concluding "the close sympathy and instinctive understanding between Americans and Germans is difficult to analyze and explain. The German accepts an American argument far more readily than that of a European. [...] The American he at once finds practical and convincing."[74] Many contemporaries agreed with the British diplomat, who considered Berlin not really German at all but an American city planted in Germany and temporarily dominating it. For them, Berlin was perceived as essentially non-German and foreign. In D'Abernon's view, "Berlin, with its broad regular streets and squares at fixed intervals, with an entire absence both of the picturesque and the squalid, is much more like an American than a European city."[75] Toward the end of his term in Berlin, the British diplomat drew a comparison between American and German ambitions and success in 1926:

> A parallel is sometimes drawn in this respect between America and Germany. Both appear to me animated with similar ambitions and to measure success almost exclusively by wealth. [...] The Germans will adapt themselves to American industrial methods much more easily than the English will. In business, there is a temperamental affinity between them.[76]

The American industrialist Henry Ford was very popular in Germany and his 1922 *My Life and Work* was published almost instantly in a German translation that sold 200,000 copies. F. W. Taylor's book *Scientific Management* was equally popular, both as a slogan and as a practical way to deal with the economy. Moreover, there were all the American-type

---

72 *An Ambassador of Peace. Lord D'Abernon's Diary* (London: Hodder and Stoughton, 1929), Vol. I, p. 18.
73 Lord D'Abernon, *op. cit.*, Vol. I, p. 18.
74 *Ibid.*, p. 19.
75 Lord D'Abernon, *op. cit.*, Vol. II, p. 102.
76 Lord D'Abernon, *op. cit.*, Vol. III (1930), p. 245.

high rises, jazz bands, Black American musicians, and the entire American entertainment industry to dazzle the German mind and mold the German way of life according to American patterns. Josephine Baker, Fred Astaire, Greta Garbo, Jeanette MacDonald and Nelson Eddy were just as popular with the German audience as they were in the U.S.[77]

Berlin's open-mindedness to contemporary music was also to some extent an American feature: in the mid-1920s the various opera companies of the city presented Alban Berg's *Wozzeck,* Igor Stravinsky's *Oedipus Rex,* Paul Hindemith's *Cardillac,* Kurt Weill's *The Threepenny Opera,* Arnold Schoenberg's *Die Glückliche Hand,* and several of the new operas by Richard Strauss under the baton of some of the most celebrated conductors of operatic history such as Wilhelm Furtwängler, Erich Kleiber, Otto Klemperer, Bruno Walter. It was in the Gesellschaft der Musikfreunde zu Berlin that Swiss-American composer Ernest Bloch's *Amerika* was first performed in the 1930–1931 season, almost exactly at the same time when Dr. Charlotte Weidler lectured on *Amerikanische Kunst* in the Lessing-Hochschule in a Berlin series on modern art.[78]

For international émigrés Berlin was a center which attracted them from the many peripheries of Europe. Berlin's attraction to anything new and, often, American, became one of the fundamental experiences of this émigré generation of Europeans which a few years later would flee the rise of Nazism and leave Hitler's Germany for the United States. German author Thomas Mann pointedly commented on the Americanization of Europe in 1929, but also suggested that it went hand in hand with "the cultural and artistic Europeanization of America."[79]

---

77 Lajos Kerekes, *A weimari köztársaság* [The Weimar Republic] (Budapest: Kossuth, 1985), p. 206.
78 *Gesellschaft der Musikfreunde zu Berlin e. V.,* Programme Saison 1930–31, Michael Polanyi Papers, Box 45, Folder 2; *Lessing-Hochschule, Vorlesungen Frühjahr 1931,* Michael Polanyi Papers, Box 45, Folder 8.
79 László Ormos, "Thomas Mann plaudert," *Pester Lloyd,* December 18, 1929, published by Antal Mádl und Judit Győri, Hg., *Thomas Mann und Ungarn. Essays, Dokumente, Bibliographie* (Budapest: Akadémiai Kiadó, 1977), p. 342.

5 The Babel of the World

That "American" meant "modern" and Berlin was "American" in that sense became most evident in Weimar Germany after World War I. With most German cities turning conservative, Berlin became progressive, its attractions making it truly the cultural capital of Germany.[80] "Berlin harbored those who elsewhere might have been subjected to ridicule or prosecution," wrote historian István Deák, and added:

> Comintern agents, Dadaist poets, expressionist painters, anarchist philosophers, *Sexualwissenschaftler,* vegetarian and Esperantist prophets of a new humanity, *Schnorrer* ("freeloaders" — artists of coffeehouse indolence), courtesans, homosexuals, drug addicts, naked dancers and apostles of nudist self-liberation, black marketeers, embezzlers, and professional criminals flourished in a city which was hungry for the new, the sensational, and the extreme. Moreover, Berlin became the cultural center of Central and Eastern Europe as well. Those who now dictated public taste and morals, who enlightened, entertained, or corrupted their

---

80 There is a substantial and growing literature on Weimar Germany and its culture which I do not intend to fully present here. Some of the most important titles are *The Weimar Republic: A Historical Bibliography* (Santa Barbara, CA: ABC-CLIO Information Services, 1984); Peter Gay, *Weimar Culture: The Outsider as Insider* (New York: Harper and Row, 1968, 1970; Harmondsworth, Middlesex: Penguin, 1974); Gerhard Schulz, Hg., *Ploetz Weimarer Republik. Eine Nation im Umbruch* (Freiburg-Würzburg: Ploetz, 1987); Walter Mönch, *Weimar. Gesellschaft—Politik—Kultur in der Ersten Deutschen Republik* (Frankfurt a. M.—Bern—New York—Paris: Peter Lang, 1988); J. W. Hiden, *The Weimar Republic* (London: Longman, 1974); Frank Grube—Gerhard Richter, Hg., *Die Weimarer Republik* (Hamburg: Hoffmann und Campe, 1983); John Willett, *The Weimar Years. A Culture Cut Short* (London: Thames and Hudson, n.d.); Michael Stark, Hg., *Deutsche Intellektuelle 1910–1933. Aufrufe, Pamphlete, Betrachtungen* (Heidelberg: Lambert Schneider, 1984); Henry Pachter, *Weimar Etudes* (New York: Columbia University Press, 1982); Stephan Waetzoldt—Verena Haas, Hg., *Tendenzen der zwanziger Jahre* (Berlin: Dietrich Reiner Verlag, 1977); Eric D. Weitz, *Weimar Germany: Promise and Tragedy* (Princeton—Oxford: Princeton University Press, 2007); Rainer Metzger—Christian Brandstätter, *Berlin: The Twentieth* (New York: Abrams, 2007).

customers were not only Germans but [also] Russian refugees from the Red and Hungarian refugees from the White terror, voluntary exiles from what was now a withering and poverty-stricken Vienna, Balkan revolutionaries, and Jewish victims of Ukrainian pogroms.[81]

Deák noted some of these famous "Berliners:" "the Hungarian Marxist philosopher György [Georg] Lukács, the Austrian theater director Max Reinhardt, the Prague journalist Egon Erwin Kisch, the phenomenal operetta singer from Budapest Gitta Alpár, and the Polish embezzlers Leo and Willy Sklarek."[82]

Henry Adams' 1858 Berlin as the "poor, keen-witted, provincial town" quickly changed after the unification of Germany and the nation needed a large national political capital city to govern the new Reich. Just like Budapest after the Austro-Hungarian Compromise or St. Petersburg under Peter the Great, the new, cosmopolitan and culturally important Berlin was created largely by political exigencies. Big newspaper and many new theaters helped the city become preeminent by invigorating its cultural life and making it, by the beginning of the new century, "an important gathering place for artists who casually defied Imperial and bourgeois cultural standards, and cultivated everything that was artistically modern."[83] Though Berlin was not charming and easy-going like Vienna, it was also less traditional, less conceited and welcomed experimental art and artists, science and scientists. Richard Strauss made his reputation there, and even Italian pianist-composer Ferruccio Busoni moved from Italy to Berlin.[84] The city had the ill fame of being a crazy place and the *Berliner* made fun of themselves, citing a little verse in the local dialect:

81 István Deák, *Weimar Germany, op. cit.*, pp. 13–15.
82 *Ibid.*, pp. 13–15.
83 *Ibid.*, p. 14.
84 Bálint Vázsonyi, *Dohnányi Ernő, op. cit.*, p. 69; William Manchester, *The Last Lion*, p. 57.

> Du bist verrückt, mein Kind,
> Du mußt nach Berlin,
> Wo die Verrückten sind,
> Da jehörst de hin.[85]

> You are crazy, my child,
> You must go to Berlin,
> That's where the crazy are,
> That's where you belong.

In the 1920s, in what turned out to be a brief but shining moment, a splendid cultural life emerged. Berlin became the European center for film and theater, photography and literature, opera and the performing arts, architecture and the social sciences. Conductor Bruno Walter remembered this creative splendor, suggesting that it seemed "as if all the eminent artistic forces were shining forth once more, imparting to the last festive symposium of the minds a many-hued brilliance before the night of barbarism closed in."[86] "Berlin aroused powerful emotions in everyone—'delighted most, terrified some, but left no one indifferent,'" commented the biographer of piano virtuoso Vladimir Horowitz.[87] Berlin was the center of Germany's cultural upheaval, "a magnet for every aspiring composer, writer, actor, and performing musician."[88] The playwright Carl Zuckmeyer remembered it as a city that "gobbled up talents and human energies with unexampled appetite." He added, "One spoke of Berlin as one speaks of a highly desirable woman whose coldness, coquettishness is widely known. She was called arrogant, snobbish, parvenu, uncultivated, common, but she was the center of everyone's fantasies."[89] Cosmopolitan Berlin supported nearly 120 newspapers, while 40 theaters, some 200 chamber groups, and more than 600 choruses gave performances in 20 concert halls and innumerable churches. "Ten or fifteen years earlier, Paris had been the undisputed queen of Europe [...] But Berlin with its sensitive restlessness and unerring instinct for quality, had emerged after the

---

85 Annemarie Lange, *Berlin in der Weimarer Republik* (Berlin: Dietz 1987), p. 596.
86 Bruno Walter, *Theme and Variations; An Autobiography (1946)*. Quoted by Peter Gay, *Weimar Culture, op. cit.*, p. 130.
87 Glenn Plaskin, *Horowitz. A Biography of Vladimir Horowitz* (New York: William Morrow and Co., 1983), p. 70.
88 Glenn Plaskin, *Horowitz, op. cit.*, p. 69.
89 Carl Zuckmeyer, quoted by Glenn Plaskin, *Horowitz, op. cit.*, p. 69.

First World War as Paris' rival [...]"⁹⁰ Such was the attractiveness of life in Berlin, that housing was in great demand and hard to obtain. Michael Polanyi and mathematician Gábor Szegő each had to wait for several years to get a decent apartment.[91]

This modernism and obsession with innovation also produced a lot of trouble. "Material problems, lodging miseries, an introduction to life's sad chapter called 'wie man Professor wird,' etc. would easily explain, even in your young age, your passing depression," said Lipót Fejér, trying to cheer up his student Gábor Szegő, who was on his way to becoming a professor of mathematics in Berlin.[92] Michael Polanyi in 1920 complained about the *Unerfreulichkeit* [unpleasantness] of the city, which his Karlsruhe friend Alfred Reis described to him as a "serious jungle."[93] Berlin also changed in terms of social behavior, sexual ethics and the moral code. Austro-German author Stefan Zweig, one of the most significant and popular figures of modern German literature, remembered Berlin in the 1920s as a crazy, highly eroticized whirlwind, "the Babylon of the world."

6 Temptations and Pressures

The attachment Germany held for Hungarian immigrants was tested by possibilities in other countries in the pre-Nazi period. The first test of immigrant loyalty in Germany came in 1923–24 when inflation and unemployment suddenly destabilized the economic and social situation of most newcomers. Some Hungarian émigrés, particularly those who

---

90 Glenn Plaskin, *Horowitz, op. cit.,* p. 69–70.
91 Michael Polanyi to the *Wohnungsamt* in Berlin, Berlin, June 18, 1923. (German) Michael Polanyi Papers, Box 1, Folder 20.
92 Lipót Fejér to Gábor Szegő, Budapest April 27, 1922. (Hungarian and partly German) Gábor Szegő Papers, SC 323, Boxes 85–036.
93 Alfred Reis to Michael Polanyi, Karlsruhe, October 14, 1920. (German) Michael Polanyi Papers, Box 1, Folder 11.

essentially failed, or felt themselves to have failed in Germany, were lured back to Hungary in hope of greater personal stability. Frightened by the rampant inflation that swept across Germany in 1923, several newcomers gave up their good German jobs only to become quickly disillusioned in Budapest. Imre Pártos was employed as a leading engineer at the Cologne firm Heinrich Butzer, but decided to return to Hungary when the German currency dramatically collapsed in the late Fall of 1923. But within a year and a half, it had become evident that he had made a big mistake. As Pártos complained to Professor von Kármán,

> Life is very sad here in Budapest, unemployment grows almost by the hour, people are naturally sad, the city is desolate in the evenings, and the Winter will be unbearable unless conditions get better in a month or two. The famous good old spirit is gone and few companies may survive these critical times in good health.[94]

Pártos added, "The local situation is best shown by the case of our mutual friend Tibor Szivessy who [...] accepted a job in Saloniki, [...] but so many Hungarian engineers emigrated there that the salaries became so low that one can hardly survive from them."[95] At this point, engineer Pártos desperately tried to get back to Germany to find a decent job there, and was eventually supported by Professor von Kármán.

Among the Hungarian psychoanalysts in Germany, Sándor Radó (1890–1972) studied in pre-War Berlin where he settled in 1922. He left for the U.S. in 1931 and rose to a measure of prominence as the leader of a psychoanalytic training and research program at Columbia University. A heretic of psychoanalysis, Radó rejected the central psychoanalytic concept of the unconscious, providing a bridge between the psychological, the psychodynamic, and the physical world of brain science.[96]

Several psychologists went to, and returned from, Germany after a few years. Lajos Kardos (1899–1985) studied with Karl Bühler in Vienna

---

94 Imre Pártos to Theodore von Kármán, Budapest, June 27, 1925 (Hungarian), Theodore von Kármán Papers, File 22.26,
95 *Ibid.*
96 Paul Roazen and Bluma Swerdloff, *Heresy: Sandor Rado and the Psychoanalytic Movement* (Northvale, NJ: Jason Aronson, 1995).

and published his first major articles in Germany.[97] A Rockefeller grant took him to Columbia University in 1930–31,[98] in 1934, however, he returned to Hungary, where, much later, he became a leading figure in psychology. A fellow Hungarian followed a different path. Michael Balint (Mihály Bálint, 1896–1970) became dissatisfied with his Berlin experiences and returned from Germany in 1924. Though he admired the Berlin psychoanalytical clinic in its heydays under Karl Abraham and Ernst Simmel, with colleagues such as Max Eitingen, Franz Alexander (himself a Hungarian by birth), Melanie Klein, Helene Deutsch, Mary Chadwick and others, "We had enough of Berlin. I had my Ph.D. by that time," Balint remembered the mid-1920s. But he soon discovered that times were also hard in Budapest. "We were very squashed in the University, with the Horthy Regime and anti-Semitism, and analysis was a very left wing thing. All sorts of troubles."[99] Balint left again and went to the U.S. for a year in 1926. In 1930 he opened his own clinic in Budapest, associated with the Hungarian Psychoanalytical Society, and consciously modeled after the Berlin clinic he had known so well. It lasted for eight years only: when the Germans occupied Austria, Balint "thought that was the time to go. I didn't want to be caught up in it. So I tried to move all sorts of things, and eventually we got permission to come to England."[100] Balint made his career in Britain, becoming, in 1968, president of the British Psychoanalytical Society.

Though many Hungarian painters were lured to Germany, most of them had little success there and returned in desperation to Hungary through the 1920s. The long list of returnee artists thus differs from almost all other professional groups:

---

97 Ludwig Kardos, *Die "Konstanz" phänomenaler Dingmomente* (Jena, 1929); *Ding und Schatten* (Leipzig, 1934); *Versuch einer mathematischen Analyse von Gesetzen des Farbensehens* (Leipzig, 1935).
98 Ludwig Kardos, *Ding und Schatten. Eine experimentelle Untersuchung über die Grundlagen des Farbensehens* (Leipzig, 1934).
99 Michael Balint interview, Columbia Oral History Project, *loc. cit.*
100 *Ibid.*

Róbert Berény
Aurél Bernáth
Dezső Bokros Birman
Sándor Bortnyik
Miklós Braun
Béla Czóbel
Noémi Ferenczy

Vilmos Huszár
Béla Kádár
Károly Kernstok
János Máttis-Teutsch
József Nemes-Lampérth
László Péri
Lajos Tihanyi

Hugo Scheiber was the last of this group to return, in 1934.

Few of these artists were versatile and experimental enough to enter into the European artistic mainstream of the 1920s, though some such as László Moholy-Nagy and László Péri, exhibited their work with the best-known contemporary avant-garde visual artists, such as Archipenko, El Lissitzky, Gabo, Malevich, Puni and Tatlin.[101] Discovered by Herwarth Walden, Moholy-Nagy and Péri entered the Berlin art scene with uncommon vigor and success through the famous modernist gallery *Der Sturm*.[102] As discussed above, Moholy-Nagy joined Walter Gropius and became co-founder of the *Bauhaus*. Along with architect Marcel Breuer, he ultimately moved to the U.S., becoming one of the few Hungarian visual artists to make a lasting international reputation.[103] His success as well as

---

[101] Artist and author Aurél Bernáth gave a vivid and poetic description of these Berlin years in his autobiography, *Kor és pálya* [Times and Life], Vol. II, *Utak Pannóniából* [Journeys from Pannonia] (Budapest: Szépirodalmi Könyvkiadó, 1960), pp. 351–383. Cf. Nóra Aradi, "Berlin-Budapest," in Klaus Kändler, Helga Karolewski, Ilse Siebert, Hg., *Berlin Bewegnungen: Ausländerische Künstler in Berlin 1918 bis 1933* (Berlin: Dietz Verlag, 1987), pp. 219–234. See also the excellent bibliography in: S. A. Mansbach, "Revolutionary Engagements: The Hungarian Avant-Garde," in: S. A. Mansbach, ed., *Standing in the Tempest. Painters of the Hungarian Avant-Garde 1908–1930* (Santa Barbara Museum of Art, Santa Barbara, CA–The MIT Press, Cambridge, MA/London, England, 1991), pp. 213–227.

[102] Georg Brühl, *Herwarth Walden und "Der Sturm"* (Köln: DuMont Buchverlag, 1983).

[103] Krisztina Passuth, "Hungarian Art Outside Hungary: Berlin in the 1920s," in Tibor Frank, ed., Culture and Society in Early 20th-Century Hungary, *Hungarian Studies*, Vol. 9, Nos. 1–2 (1994), pp. 127–138; Hubertus Gaßner, Hg., *WechselWirkungen. Ungarische Avantgarde in der Weimarer Republik* (Marburg: Jonas Verlag, 1986).

Péri's, and the growing fame of brilliant and powerful Hungarian photographers such as Brassaï, Robert Capa, György Kepes and André Kertész, rests on their having introduced radically new techniques such as collage, assemblage and photomontage, as well as experimental approaches to space and time, making their talents imperative in the burgeoning business of advertising.

Completely different was the case of those scientists who were a success in Germany and had already developed an international reputation. These personages were repeatedly tempted to return to Hungary, both by private businesses as well as by the government, nevertheless they felt secure enough to say no to both. A remarkable example was Michael Polanyi, the distinguished physical chemist in Berlin.

Polanyi considered a job in the research department of Hungary's internationally recognized Egyesült Izzólámpa és Villamossági Rt. [United Lightbulb and Electric Co.], then under the direction of Professor Ignác Pfeiffer. Returning in early 1923 from a business trip in The Netherlands, Pfeiffer stopped in Berlin in an attempt to persuade Polanyi to take a job in the company's Budapest-based chemical, physical and metallographical laboratory which is "quite well equipped by our circumstances."[104] Polanyi declined the invitation, but offered to work for the Budapest company in his Berlin laboratory.[105]

Those who did not feel entirely comfortable in Germany, but did not want to go home either, attempted to get jobs in the U.S. This was particularly true in the early 1920s when living conditions in Germany were deplorable and the future seemed bleak. Beginners with little reputation had a rough time. Physicist Imre Bródy asked several people in 1922 to intervene on his behalf, and though Professor Paul S. Epstein of

---

104 Ignác Pfeifer to Michael Polanyi, Ujpest (outside Budapest), February 6, 1923 (Hungarian), Michael Polanyi Papers, Box 1, Folder 19.
105 Ignác Pfeifer to Michael Polanyi, Ujpest (outside Budapest), April 9, 1923 (Hungarian); Michael Polanyi to Ignác Pfeifer, [Berlin,] April 14, 1923 (German); Ignác Pfeifer to Michael Polanyi, Ujpest (outside Budapest), May 15, 1923 (German); Michael Polanyi to Ignác Pfeifer, [Berlin,] May 28 and June 22, 1923 (German); Michael Polanyi Papers, Box 1, Folder 19.

the California Institute of Technology thought that there may be some hope elsewhere in the U.S., he was negative as to Caltech itself. "Foreign citizenship is not a problem there, but the language and my bad ears may be," Bródy commented. Early in 1924, mathematician Gábor Szegő also had doubts as to his future in Germany and seriously considered an offer from the United States. He sought advice from his mentor, Budapest professor Lipót Fejér who, characteristically, thought much more highly of Germany than of the U.S. His reactions reflected the typical opinion of German and U.S. universities in the European scientific community at this time:

> You should only ponder about the American job if the offer is indeed very very good, if you are not supposed to be further promoted but the very best and safest is ready right away. ... But even in this case it must be considered a hundred times. At the same time, vis-à-vis the current conditions, it cannot be dismissed a limine [=offhand].[106]

A few months later, when Szegő refused the American job, Fejér sighed with relief: "I am happy that you did not go to America. I talked to Mises about you in Innsbruck and he said that, with the safety of human foresight, you will succeed in Germany in terms of a job nicely and in time. ... I believe you may feel safe."[107] Indeed, Szegő became an *außerordentlicher Professor* in early 1925 in Berlin and a full professor at Königsberg in 1926 where he taught until the Nazi takeover.[108]

The misjudgment of the German situation in late 1932, early 1933 was not unique: as late as January 1933, the operetta *Ball im Savoy* by Hungarian Berliner Paul Abraham's was played with enormous success in Berlin and sung by Hungarian stars Gitta Alpár and Rózsi Bársony – a

---

106 Lipót Fejér to Gábor Szegő, Budapest March 6, 1924 (Hungarian), Gábor Szegő Papers.
107 Lipót Fejér to Gábor Szegő, Budapest November 26, 1924 (Hungarian), Gábor Szegő Papers.
108 Gábor Szegő, "Lebenslauf" [1925?] and "Personnel Security Questionnaire" [1950?], Gábor Szegő Papers, SC 323, Boxes 85–036.

composer and two singers who, within a matter of a few weeks, had no place in Hitler's officially anti-Semitic Germany.[109]

The short novels of British author Christopher Isherwood (*Mr. Norris Changes Trains*, 1935, *Goodbye to Berlin*, 1939), as well as films like *Cabaret*, *Mephisto*, and *Julia* have chronicled the breathtaking immediacy of change from Weimar to Nazi Germany. Though some members of the Hungarian community attempted to survive by answering the question "Arisch oder nicht-Arisch?" [Aryan or non-Aryan?] on Nazi questionnaires by answering, "Ungarisch, evangelisch" [Hungarian, Lutheran],[110] Berlin was no longer safe, with the ever-present swastika on the red Nazi banner, marching SA troops, NSDAP party-rallies, book-burnings and mushrooming new anti-Semitic slogans and regulations. More and more frequently, demonstrators appeared on the streets singing *Sturm- und Kampflieder* against "alien Jews" making many in the Hungarian community of Berlin alarmed and frightened:

> Deutschland erwache aus deinem bösen Traum, gib fremden
> Juden in deinem Reich nicht Raum!
> Wir wollen kämpfen für dein Auferstehn,
> Arisches Blut soll nicht untergeh'n![111]

In English:

> Wake up Germany from your bad dream,
> Don't give shelter to alien Jews in your realm,
> We want to fight for your resurrection,
> Aryan blood should not disappear.

---

109 Personal memories of Mrs. Éva Kerekes, August 1994.
110 The author's interview with conductor-composer János Kerekes, 1992.
111 Paul Hochmuth, *Sturm- und Kampflieder-Buch* (Berlin—Schöneberg: Verlag Deutsche Kultur-Macht, 1933), No. 29. Michael Polanyi Papers, Box 46, Folder 11.

In another song, paratroopers turned to the Führer:

> Adolf Hitler, unserm Führer, reichen wir die Hand,
> Brüder auf zum letzten Kampfe für das Varterland.

> To Adolf Hitler, our Führer, we give our hand,
> Brothers ho, to the last battle for the fatherland.

The refrain was enthusiastically repeated:

> Fort mit Juden und Verrätern. Freiheit oder Tod.
> Adolf Hitler schwör'n wir Treue. Treue bis zum Tod.[112]

> Away with Jews and traitors. Liberty or Death.
> We swear allegiance to Adolf Hitler. Allegiance unto Death.

Some Hungarians, such as Michael Polanyi, collected Nazi propaganda material and Jewish immigration statistics such as those claiming that of 404,000 Jews in Prussia in 1925, some 76,000 were foreigners—and therefore recognized the Nazi perspective which held this as entirely unacceptable.[113] The same sources also suggested that there was a "Jewish overalienization in the scientific and artistic professions in Berlin."[114]

Yet, living the sheltered life of a Berlin University professor, Polanyi, along with many other refugee foreigners as well as Germans, was both unprepared and unwilling to realize the dangers of an eventual Nazi dictatorship. He received ample warning: already by the Summer of 1932, friends had urged him to give up his naiveté as to the chances of preserving the political situation in Germany. "If we lift our leg we must put it

---

112   *Ibid.*, No. 1.
113   "Deutschlands Kampf für die abendländische Kultur," Berlin, n.d. [1933?] p. 5.
114   *Ibid.*, p. 12.

down somewhere, forwards or backwards, right or left!"[115] – he was urged by a friend of the family.

Jewish-Hungarian members of German scientific organizations typically severed their links after the Nazi takeover. Von Kármán left Germany well before Hitler's *Machtergreifung* and his settling at Caltech was a consequence of developments inherent in his research area, and not of political or racial persecution. Nevertheless, when the Nazis came to power, he completely turned against Germany where he spent some 25 years. John von Neumann left the Deutsche Mathematiker-Vereinigung in 1935 shortly after his *Mathematische Grundlagen der Quantenmechanik* [The Mathematical Foundations of Quantum Mechanics] was published in Berlin.[116] Others followed suit.

7 Other Options in Europe

Emigration from Germany to various European countries and into the United States started immediately. The outward flow of eminent German-Jewish professionals resulted in one of the greatest intellectual migrations in world history and in one of the most tragic losses the German mind had ever suffered. But was it really the "German mind" alone that suffered from the Nazi take-over?

In contemporary statistics and journalism, most refugees were hurriedly lumped together as "Germans" or "German-Jews" without considering the birthplace, the actual land of origin, the mother tongue or national background of the people who were forced to leave Germany and this

---

115 "Márti" to Michael Polanyi, Stary Smokovec, Czechoslovakia, July 30, 1932, (Hungarian) Michael Polanyi Papers, Box 2, Folder 8.
116 John von Neumann to W. Blaschke, Princeton, January 28, 1935 (German), John von Neumann Papers, 1933–37, Box 4, Library of Congress, Washington, DC. Cf. Johann von Neumann, *Mathematische Grundlagen der Quantenmechanik* (Berlin: Julius Springer, 1932).

unfortunate tradition has survived in the otherwise rich and impressive historical literature on the subject.[117] The great and hitherto unsolved problem for research on Hungarian and other non-German refugees from Hitler's Germany is to distinguish the specifically Hungarian (or other non-German) elements: people, problems, and cases in this complex area. This is not only important for Hungarian research but may result in a more realistic assessment of what we usually consider "German science" or "German scholarship" in the interwar period.

After Adolf Hitler was sworn in as Chancellor of Germany, it took very little time for even the most optimistic or naïve Jewish-Hungarians in Germany to realize the terrifying urgency of escaping the country. They had several options: the most natural was to return to Hungary where the right-wing régime of Regent Miklós Horthy (1920–44) and Prime Minister Gyula Gömbös (1932–36) was friendly towards the new

---

117 John M. Spalek, *Guide to the Archival Materials of the German-speaking Emigration to the United States after 1933* (Charlottesville: University Press of Virginia, 1978), xxv, 1133 p.; Herbert A. Strauss and Werner Röder, eds., *International Biographical Dictionary of Central European Emigrés 1933–1945* (München—New York—London—Paris: K. G. Saur, 1983), Vols. I–II/1–2+III, xciv, 1316 p.; Peter Kröner, ed., *Vor fünfzig Jahren. Die Emigration deutschsprachiger Wissenschaftler 1933–1939* (Münster, 1983); Jean-Michel Palmier, *Weimar en Exil. Le destin de l'émigration intellectuelle allemande antinazie en Europe et aux États-Unis* (Paris: Payot, 1988) Tomes 1–2, 533, 486 p.; Laura Fermi, *Illustrious Immigrants. The Intellectual Migration from Europe 1930–41* (Chicago & London: University of Chicago Press, 1968); Jarrell C. Jackman and Carla M. Borden, eds., *The Muses Flee Hitler. Cultural Transfer and Adaptation 1930–1945* (Washington, DC: Smithsonian, 1983); Harriet Zuckerman, *Scientific Elite: Nobel Laureates in the United States* (New York: Free Press, 1977), xv, 335 p.; Richard Breitman and Alan M. Kraut, *American Refugee Policy and European Jewry, 1933–1945* (Bloomington and Indianapolis: Indiana University Press, 1987); Norman Bentwich, *The Refugees from Germany, April 1933 to December 1935* (Allen and Unwin, 1936); Norman Bentwich, *The Rescue and Achievement of Refugee Scholars: The Story of Displaced Scholars and Scientists 1933–1952* (The Hague: Martinus Nijhoff, 1953); Robin E. Rider, "Alarm and Opportunity: Emigration of Mathematicians and Physicists to Britain and the United States, 1933–1945," *Historical Studies in the Physical Sciences*, Vol. 15, Part I (1984) pp. 107–176.

Germany but not yet adhering to its virulent anti-Semitism. Hungarian Jews enjoyed a decade of openly undiscriminating citizenship, from the late 1920s through the first anti-Semitic laws in 1938–39, and many who felt threatened in Germany returned right away to Budapest.

Another option was to leave for some other European country: many went to Czechoslovakia, France, the Netherlands, countries which provided temporary asylum with the coming of World War II. A sizable group felt unsafe anywhere on the Continent of Europe and headed immediately towards Britain or the United States. Let us consider now this last category.

Though Germany was certainly the most tempting and promising emigrant destination after World War I, Hungarian step-migration to the United States did not lead through Germany alone. Persecuted in or barred from their homeland, many young Hungarians, usually equipped with a good working knowledge of German (and German alone), moved to a number of other German-speaking countries.

Unlike Berlin, Vienna was disillusioned, uninspiring and lacking substance. Though many Hungarians lived there, they did not necessarily like it. The ambiance in the city was particularly bad after the revolutions of 1918–19. Karl Polanyi, who lived there for many years serving as the editor of the economic paper *Der österreichische Volkswirt*, compared it to a "salt desert, where not even through loneliness can one get rid of the aggressive atmosphere of barrenness."[118] He complained bitterly in a letter to his mother: "To live here in Vienna is just nonsensical: It is expensive (!!), bad (!!), dusty (!!) hot (!!) dull, desolate, nervekilling and rash. Everybody escapes Vienna [...]"[119]

---

118   Karl Polanyi to Michael Polanyi, Küb/Semmering, n.d. (Hungarian) Michael Polanyi Papers.
119   Karl Polanyi to Cecilia Polanyi, [Vienna,] April 24, 1920, (German) Michael Polanyi Papers, Box 17, Folder 2.

Karl Polanyi became increasingly anxious to leave and prepared to transfer his paper to Berlin.[120] "A hundred doubts, a thousand problems," a friend wrote to Michael Polanyi.

> This doubt and restlessness tortures everybody and as people exchange their Deutschmarks into [U.S.] dollars, their dollars into [Swiss] francs, their francs into [Russian] rubles, they change their beliefs accordingly. Revolutionaries, monarchists, republicans, terrorists, religious errants, etc., etc. The road is loud of the army of the erring and mistaking, their word makes the world loud.[121]

Many young people went to Czechoslovak universities. There were general and technical German universities both in Prague and in Brno; this, combined with the shared cultural heritage within the Austro-Hungarian Monarchy, as well as the budding democracy of the new country, proved very attractive. "There was an entire colony of Hungarian students in Brno," remembered engineer Marcel Stein in an interview granted in New York in 1989.

> I came from a Pozsony [Bratislava, Preßburg] family where the mother tongue was German. Most of us in Brno were not Communists, but members of the Jewish middle-class. For the holidays, students [like Mr. Stein] went to Pozsony rather than Budapest, but after graduation the majority returned to Hungary. Some of them continued their studies in Berlin-Charlottenburg and Karlsruhe in Germany, or, like the eminent engineer László Heller, in Zürich, Switzerland. Coming home to anti-Semitic Hungary was a real shock after the experiences in democratic Czechoslovakia.[122]

Though born in Nagyvárad (today Oradea, Romania), Kálmán Z. Istók was educated in Rim. Sobota (Czechoslovakia), and received his medical degree in 1934 at the German Charles University in Prague. He practiced medicine in Czechoslovakia until early 1945 when he left for

---

120 Karl Polanyi to Michael Polanyi, Vienna, October 7, 1925 (Hungarian) Michael Polanyi Papers, Box 17.
121 Unknown to Michael Polanyi, Vienna, March 11, 1920 (Hungarian) Michael Polanyi Papers, Box 1, Folder 7.
122 The author's interview with Marcel Stein, New York, Columbia University, November 29, 1989.

Austria to become a doctor at various Displaced Persons hospitals. He emigrated to the U.S. through the International Rescue Committee as well as the National Committee for Resettlement of Foreign Physicians in 1951.[123]

Several in the Hungarian community of Pozsony (today Bratislava, Slovakia) attempted to have their children educated in Germany. Some worked through Hungarian connections in Germany and later in the U.S., and sent these often very gifted students to German or American universities. This was the case of engineering professor Andrew Fejér, whose parents desperately tried to send him to study with Theodore von Kármán in Aachen in 1930; when that plan failed, young Fejér joined von Kármán as a graduate student at the California Institute of Technology in Pasadena in 1938.[124]

The Hungarian intellectual diaspora was huge and not confined to German-speaking Europe: it was scattered all over the Continent. The human geography of Hungarian intellectual migrations followed complex patterns. Mathematician György Pólya married his Swiss professor's daughter and settled in Switzerland during World War I. He became a citizen of Zürich in early 1918 and ultimately, in 1928, a full professor of the reputable *Eidgenössische Technische Hochschule* of that city. It was at the invitation of his friend and co-author Gábor Szegő, that he left Switzerland for Brown University shortly after the outbreak of World War II.[125]

Not even all of the eminent Hungarians who wished to go to Germany could go there. "There are enough physical chemists in Germany so it is

---

123 Dr. Kálmán Istók file, International Rescue Committee, Box 7, Archives of the Hoover Institution on War, Revolution and Peace, Stanford, CA.
124 Jenő Fejér to Theodore von Kármán, Bratislava, April 25, 1930, Ilus Fejér, Bratislava, May 20, 1936, Ilus Fejér, June 17, 1938 (Hungarian), Theodore von Kármán Papers, File 9.3.
125 Georg Pólya, "Bürgerrechts-Urkunde," March 7, 1918; Appointment to the Eidgenössische Technische Hochschule, February 24, 1928, George Pólya Papers, SC 337, Box 87–034:3, Department of Special Collections and University Archives, Stanford University Libraries, Stanford, CA.

hardly possible for me to get a job there. I don't even entertain such plans," prospective Nobel Laureate George de Hevesy (Chemistry 1943) wrote to Michael Polanyi in early 1920, as he settled in the institute of Nobel Laureate Niels Bohr in Copenhagen, Denmark.[126] Nevertheless, he maintained his scientific connections with Germany in subsequent years.[127] Life in post-War Copenhagen characteristically reminded Hevesy "of the good old times when there was a k.u.k. army and other nice institutions, and retired generals and others like them lived in Graz or Klagenfurt."[128]

On a sabbatical from the University of Budapest, psychologist Géza Révész left for Germany in 1920 and tried to settle in Göttingen, where he had studied from 1902–06. In search of a job, he also visited Heidelberg, Frankfurt, Rostock, Munich, and Berlin. When it became obvious that there was no chance for him in Germany, he accepted an invitation from the University of Amsterdam in the spring of 1921. In 1932, he became Head of the Psychological Laboratory in Amsterdam, and subsequently a naturalized Dutch citizen. Though several of his relations did go to the United States, Révész never wanted to leave Europe. Unlike his brother-in-law, the psychologist Franz Alexander, he considered the U.S. culture alien to him and his world. Thus, music and language psychologist Géza Révész became internationally acknowledged at the University of Amsterdam, where he was a full professor from 1939.[129]

---

126 George de Hevesy to Michael Polanyi, [Budapest,] January 27, 1920 (Hungarian), Michael Polanyi Papers, Box 1, Folder 6.
127 George de Hevesy to Theodore von Kármán, København, May 20, 1920 (Hungarian) Theodore von Kármán Papers, File 13.5.
128 "[…] ich hier im schönen Kopenhagen auf einer Weise lebe, wie einst, in den guten alten Zeiten, wo es eine k.u.k. Armee gab und andere schöne Einrichtungen, pensionierte Generäle und dgl. in Graz oder Klagenfurt lebten." George de Hevesy to Michael Polanyi, København, June 27, 1920 (German), Michael Polanyi Papers, Box 1, Folder 9.
129 Judit Csillag Gál, "Bevezető tanulmány [Introduction]," in Géza Révész, *Tanulmányok* [Studies] (Budapest: Gondolat, 1985), pp. 9–11. I am grateful to Ms. Judith Révész for the biographical details on her father, provided in an interview in Budapest, January 26, 1996.

Mathematician Marcel Riesz settled in Sweden, taught in Stockholm and in Lund until 1952 when he went to teach in the United States at Princeton, Stanford, the University of Maryland and the University of Indiana.[130]

Some Hungarians who were not in a position to leave the country chose a special form of intellectual migration, that of publishing their books and articles in Germany throughout the 1920s and the early 1930s. Some of the politically motivated books by historians Gyula Szekfű and Elemér Mályusz were first published in Germany.[131] Non-political books were also taken to German publishers, such as the one on Hungarian geniuses by psychologist H. von Szirmay-Pulszky.[132] Theodore's brother, Elemér von Kármán, an expert in correctional education, published his *Einführung in die Kriminalpaedagogik* [Introduction to Criminal Education] in München in 1923 and was immediately contracted by the Berlin publisher Carl Heymann to write another book with two eminent German scholars, on *Leitfaden für die Untersuchung verwahrloster und krimineller Kinder und Jugendlichen* [Guidelines for the study of orphaned and criminal children and young people].[133]

Similarly, important Hungarian singers such as Gitta Alpár, Piroska Anday, Mária Németh, and Koloman von Pataky were frequent guests of German and Austrian operas without actually leaving Hungary permanently. Authors such as Ferenc Molnár and Ignotus increasingly spent their time out of the country without it being considered an "emigration".

---

130 L. Gårding, "Marcel Riesz in Memoriam," *Acta Mathematica* 124 (1970), pp. I–XI; János Horváth, "Riesz Marcel matematikai munkássága I" [The Mathematical Work of Marcel Riesz], *Matematikai Lapok*, Vol. 26, No. 1–2 (1975), pp. 11–37.
131 Julius Szekfű, *Der Staat Ungarn. Eine Geschichtsstudie* (Stuttgart-Berlin: Deutsche Verlags-Anstalt, 1917); Elemér Mályusz, *Sturm auf Ungarn. Volkskommissäre und Genossen im Auslande* (München: Südost-Verlag Adolf Dresler, 1931).
132 H. von Szirmay-Pulszky, *Genie und Irrsinn im ungarischen Geistesleben* (München: Ernst Reinhardt, 1935).
133 Elemér Kármán to Theodore von Kármán, Budapest, June 14 and August 1, 1923 (Hungarian), Theodore von Kármán Papers, File 139.1.

Further research should illuminate how this kind of "overseas" publishing, musical activities, and lifestyles can be seen as important but hidden forms of intellectual migrations.

IV Hungary and Selective Immigration to the U.S.

1 From Quota Laws to Private Bills

World War I: Towards 100 Percent Americanism

It was World War I that brought the conflict between advocates and adversaries of unrestricted immigration to a climax. Loyalty became the byword, and large forces were mobilized to root out what was perceived as disloyalty. "Loyalist" citizens' groups introduced methods of what later became known as thought control: "opening mail, tapping telephones, and in general attempting to impose unity of opinion on their communities."[1] Immigrants were generally the victims, primarily German-Americans, Irish-Americans and Jews. Just as in Britain and Russia, public opinion in the U.S. turned vehemently against all things German and tried to curtail or even abandon the presence of German culture and its representatives.[2]

---

[1] Alan Brinkley, *The Unfinished Nation. A Concise History of the American People* (New York: McGraw-Hill, 1993), p. 618.

[2] For details about extreme manifestations of anti-German sentiment see John A. Hawgood, *The Tragedy of German America* (New York: Putnam, 1940); Frederick C. Luebke, *Bonds of Loyalty: German Americans and World War I* (De Kalb: Northern Illinois University Press, 1974); Phyllis Keller, *States of Belonging. German-American Intellectuals in the First World War* (Cambridge, MA and London: Harvard University Press, 1979); Julius Drachsler, *Democracy and Assimilation: The Blending of Immigrant Heritages in America* (New York: Macmillan, 1920), pp. 22–25; Maldwyn Allen Jones, *American Immigration* (Chicago and London: University of Chicago Press, 1960), pp. 270–271; Leonard Dinnerstein and David M. Reimers, *Ethnic Americans. A History of Immigration* (New York: HarperCollins, 3rd ed. 1988), p. 73; Alan Brinkley, *op. cit.*, pp. 619–619.

Even many who had been the proponents of German culture earlier made a volte-face. A student in Germany for five years and a former disciple of Wundt, Helmholtz, du Bois-Reymont and Carl Ludwig, with "an affinity for Germany and German philosophy,"[3] the great American experimental psychologist Granville Stanley Hall (1844–1924) came to suggest, towards the end of his life, that "there [was] something fundamentally wrong with the Teutonic soul."[4] The stereotype of "the armored, bloodthirsty Hun" became an anti-German slogan in the Anglo-American press, a popular epithet originally launched by Kaiser Wilhelm II who appealed to German soldiers to be hard as Huns. Germany became identified as "not just the guilty party but the enemy."[5] As Robert H. Wiebe quoted "a leader in the settlement movement," the war with Germany "brought the realization, with an intense feeling of shame and danger, that we [Americans] were a nation only in a very imperfect sense [...]," wrote a leader in the settlement movement, concluding that the nation was "stirred to a new sense of responsibility for a more coherent loyalty [...] a vital Americanism [...]."[6]

Immigrants from countries allied to Germany, on the other hand, did not share the fate of German-Americans, and many seemed to avoid the anti-alien sentiment inspired by the war effort.[7] Many of the "new" immigrants such as the Czechs, Slovaks, Poles, and Southern Slavs displayed a great deal of hatred towards the Central Powers including Germany and the Austro-Hungarian Monarchy and had a proven record of pro-American and pro-war sentiments.[8] Their leaders worked on reaching, directly or indirectly, the ear of President Wilson and on creating

---

3 R. Jackson Wilson, *In Quest of Community. Social Philosophy in the United States, 1860–1920* (London—Oxford—New York: Oxford University Press, 1970), pp. 114–143.
4 Alan Brinkley, *op. cit.*, p. 619
5 Robert H. Wiebe, *The Search for Order 1877–1920* (New York: Hill and Wang, 1967), pp. 264–265.
6 Robert H. Wiebe, *op. cit.*, p. 292.
7 Maldwyn Allen Jones, *op. cit.*, p. 272.
8 *Ibid.*

American public opinion favoring the break-up of the Austro-Hungarian Monarchy. Nonetheless, the influence on the U.S. government of such immigrant groups from the Monarchy remained very limited: the Poles alone were able to exert influence successfully, and it was only after this had been underway for several years that the U.S. President finally made his decision to break up the Austro-Hungarian Monarchy.[9]

Hungarians, however, were of divided loyalties, and several groups faced open hostilities. Though many Hungarian civil and middle class groups made statements of loyalty towards the United States in late 1917 and early 1918, Hungarian-American working class organizations and socialists opposed the war effort and thereby exposed themselves to attacks by nativists for their alleged disloyalty to the United States.[10] Even those Hungarian-Americans who demonstrated their loyalty towards the U.S. remained torn between their native land and their adopted country.

The strong American demand for "preparedness" during the neutrality years grew into a bitter hostility towards Germany, making immigration restriction and "Americanization" of the newcomers the rallying cry of "good Americans." Closing America's gates as far as possible evolved into a commitment during and immediately after World War I. The efforts of certain "Americanizers," who made public attacks on the use of foreign languages and strange customs, resulted ironically in an intensified ethnic consciousness. When Congress passed a literacy test in 1917 over the idealist veto of President Wilson, members of both Houses immediately called for more energetic measures of exclusion.[11]

Though the idea was favored for decades by large sections of both Houses of Congress, it was the post-War scare of a potentially overwhelming

---

9   Joseph P. O'Grady, "Introduction," in Joseph P. O'Grady, ed., *The Immigrant Influence on Wilson's Peace Policies* (University of Kentucky Press, 1967), pp. 1–29. Victor S. Mamatey, *The United States and East Central Europe, 1914–1918: A Study in Wilsonian Diplomacy and Propaganda* (1957), pp. 74, 117, 131.
10 Julianna Puskás, *Kivándorló magyarok az Egyesült Államokban 1880–1940* [Emigrating Hungarians in the United States 1880–1940] (Budapest: Akadémiai Kiadó, 1982), pp. 306–312.
11 Robert H. Wiebe, *op. cit.*, p. 288.

influx of immigrants from war-torn Europe which created a sufficient number of votes in both the Senate and the House of Representatives. World War I supplied the prompt for action, the culmination, the enabling event of a long campaign by immigration restrictionists.[12] While earlier support of restrictive measures was chiefly conditioned by economic, social and sanitary motives, the post-War shift of public opinion was fueled as well by negative reaction to wartime pro-German and pacifist propaganda and German-American resistance to conscription.[13] Both German and Irish Americans came under particularly vigorous attack. The War unleashed unparalleled amounts of xenophobia and America withdrew into isolationism.[14]

The closing of America's gates in 1921 was thus directly related to World War I and particularly to the conflict between the U.S. and Germany.

The War contributed to the radicalization of second and third generation immigrants in American politics. Richard Hofstadter rightly argued that many of them "had been moved for the first time to violent enthusiasms on one side or the other by the policies of Wilson, which had an intimate bearing on the fate of almost every European country."[15] Their pride and their family plans were affected by the Quota Law of 1921, their sense of security by the uprisings of the Ku Klux Klan and their leisure by Prohibition. "The ethnic conflict, heightened by the fight over Prohibition, became during an age of prosperity far more acute than any economic issue."[16] In Hofstadter's views, the ethnic/immigrant issue was crucial in shaping American domestic politics through the 1920s

---

12   Cf. John Higham, *Strangers in the Land: Patterns of American Nativism, 1860–1925* (New Brunswick, NJ: Rutgers University Press, 1955, repr. 1988).
13   Cf. Marion T. Bennett, *American Immigration Policies: A History* (Washington, DC: Public Affairs Press, 1962) and Edward P. Hutchinson, *Legislative History of American Immigration Policy, 1798–1965* (Philadelphia: University of Pennsylvania Press, 1981).
14   Leonard Dinnerstein and David M. Reimers, *op. cit.*, p. 73.
15   Richard Hofstadter, *The Age of Reform. From Bryan to F. D. R.* (New York: Vintage Books, 1955), p. 299.
16   Richard Hofstadter, *op. cit.*, p. 299.

and 1930s as it pulled the working class, "heavily immigrant, Catholic, and wet, and 'democratic' in its social bias,"[17] away from the Republican Party and moving it into the Democratic Party. Thus the election of F. D. Roosevelt was to a considerable extent determined by resentment toward the nativism and restrictionism of the early part of the century.

The Selective Principle

Based on data from the 1910 U.S. Census, the Act of May 19, 1921 established a quota limit of 3% of the number of people belonging to any nationality, thereby restricting immigration into the United States in a highly selective way. In addition, the Act provided that not more than 20% could be admitted in any one month.[18] The new law had very specific purposes: it aimed at severely restricting population movements from Eastern and Southern Europe and the Near East, and at allotting generous quotas to Great Britain, Germany and Scandinavia. In several cases, the countries of Northwestern Europe were given greater quotas than the pre-War immigration would have allowed. As a result, after a temporary set-back in 1922, Britain, Germany and the Scandinavian countries retained their pre-War immigration figures in 1923 and 1924, while Hungary, Austria, Italy, Greece, and Russia maintained merely a fraction of their earlier immigration figures. The statistics of the period are self-explanatory:[19]

---

17 Ibid., p. 301.
18 Jeremiah Jenks and W. Jett Lauck, *The Immigration Problem. A Study of American Immigration Conditions and Needs* (New York and London: Funk & Wagnalls, 1926), pp. 448–449.
19 Jeremiah Jenks and W. Jett Lauck, *op. cit.*, pp. 449–450.

IMMIGRANT ALIENS ADMITTED FROM CERTAIN COUNTRIES AND AREAS IN SPECIFIED FISCAL YEARS

Countries	1914	1921	1922	1923	1924
England, Scotland and Wales	48,729	51,142	25,153	45,759	59,490
Germany	35,734	6,803	17,931	48,277	75,091
Ireland	24,688	28,435	10,579	15,740	17,111
Norway, Sweden, and Denmark	29,391	22,854	14,625	34,184	35,577
Other northern and western Europe	25,591	29,317	11,149	12,469	16,077
Total	164,133	138,551	79,437	156,429	203,346
Austria	134,831	4,947	5,019	8,103	7,505
Hungary	143,321	7,702	5,756	5,914	5,806
Greece	35,832	28,502	3,457	3,333	4,871
Italy	283,738	222,260	40,319	46,674	56,246
Russia	255,660	6,398	17,143	17,507	12,649
Other southern and eastern Europe	40,876	244,004	65,254	69,960	73,916
Turkey in Asia	21,716	11,735	1,998	2,183	2,820
Total	915,974	525,548	138,946	153,674	163,813
British North America	86,139	72,317	46,810	117,011	200,690
Mexico	14,614	30,758	19,551	63,768	89,336
All other countries	37,620	38,054	24,812	32,037	49,711
Grand total	1,218,480	805,228	309,556	522,919	706,896

IMMIGRANT ALIENS ADMITTED BY PRINCIPAL RACES OR PEOPLES IN FISCAL YEARS SPECIFIED

Race or People	Number admitted			Per cent. of total		
	1923-24	1920-21	1913-14	1923-24	1920-21	1913-14
Northern and western Europe	393,342	206,995	253,855	55.7	25.7	20.8
Southern and eastern Europe and Turkey	192,599	537,144	921,160	27.2	66.7	75.6
Mexicans	87,648	29,603	13,089	12.4	3.7	1.1
All others	33,307	31,486	30,376	4.7	3.9	2.5
Total	706,896	805,228	1,218,480	100.0	100.0	100.0

Introducing the percentage plan into American legislation, the Act of 1921 was designed as an emergency measure that was considered temporary. Nonetheless, it was the direct outcome of long deliberations by the Immigration Commission. Senator William P. Dillingham, Chairman of the Commission, first suggested it officially, and the work was actually executed by the Commission's Secretary, former U.S. Commissioner General of Immigration, W. W. Husband.[20] Another temporary measure, the Johnson-Reed Immigration Act of 1924 employed similar techniques of computation but "put the clock back" in time and set a new 2% immigration quota against the U.S. Census of 1890, at which point only a small number of East and Southern Europeans had arrived. The result was dramatic: the total number allotted to Southern and Eastern Europe was reduced from 155,585 to 20,423. While continuing to ration U.S. immigration on a quota basis, the second Quota Law employed racial discrimination on an even larger scale. Whereas the total quota for Eastern and Southern Europe was cut by 87%, that for Northern and Western Europe was reduced by only 29%.[21] This large variance is understandable within the context of the continued, heated debates of the early 1920s, both in and out of Congress, which was conditioned by influential articles such as "The Immigration Peril," authored by the Italian-American lawyer Gino Speranza (and subsequently published in his 1925 book *Race or Nation*). Members of Congress were swayed also by the "scientific" pronouncements of the extreme eugenicist H. H. Laughlin, an advocate of sterilization of inmates.[22]

Critics of the quota laws continued to view them as temporary measures destined to meet what they perceived as the emergency situation of post-War America. In a 1925 book entitled *Selective Immigration*, Secretary

---

20 *Ibid.*, p. 463.
21 William S. Bernard, ed., *American Immigration Policy – A Reappraisal* (New York: Harper & Brothers, 1950), pp. 25–26.
22 William S. Bernard, ed., *op. cit.*, p. 23. Cf. Harry Hamilton Laughlin, *Immigration and Conquest. A Study of the United States as the Receiver of Old World Emigrants Who Became the Parents of Future-Born Americans* (New York, NY, 1939).

of Labor James J. Davis spoke of the "good stock" that new European governments want to retain, while letting go of others:

> And while they may not actively assist in the departure of the jobless weak, the unstable of mind and nerve, the easily discontented and the constitutionally inferior, they need not be expected to stand in the way of such people taking passage for other lands! An official of one of the new republics in Europe frankly stated that his country's only concern with American immigration was the hope to get rid of the "old men and rubbish."[23]

While upholding the principle of limiting the total number of immigrants, Davis called for strengthening "our selective tests" and for the upkeep of high standards "in terms of personal fitness and of personal character."[24] The Secretary of Labor, considering both quota acts emergency measures, called for an immigration policy "that will work now, and work down the years into the future. It must be a selective policy, aiming to admit to this Republic only the best, only the sound of all those peoples who will press to come across seas."[25]

The 1924 Act also provided that as of July 1927, the total quota should be 150,000 per annum and that each country should receive a yearly number "which bears the same ratio to 150,000 as the number of inhabitants in continental United States in 1920 having that national origin [...], but the minimum quota of any nationality shall be 100."[26]

The principle of the "national origins" of the American population, the result of decades of public discussion and the much-wanted ultimate "scientific basis" of future immigration policies, required several years of intensive statistical studies. It involved the Bureau of the Census and the American Council of Learned Societies and drew heavily from a 1909 publication of the Bureau of the Census, *A Century of Population Growth*, which relied chiefly on an evaluation of family names. The national origins

---

23 James J. Davis, *Selective Immigration* (St. Paul, Minnesota: Scott-Mitchell, 1925), p. 169.
24 James J. Davis, *op. cit.*, p. 173.
25 *Ibid.*, p. 179.
26 Jeremiah Jenks and W. Jett Lauck, *op. cit.*, p. 544.

system established once again new quotas which were markedly different from those based on the census of 1890, and the plan was adopted by Congress in 1924 with very little consideration or discussion.

Controversy did not break out until this provision went into effect in 1927.[27] The debate focused on the differential treatment of the various immigrant groups as introduced by the National Origins provision, and openly bared the question of their innate mental and physical qualities. This was the enactment of the pseudo-scientific theory of the inherent inferiority of the Eastern and Southern European nations which was drawn largely from the highly questionable results of new intelligence tests which had first been used in the U.S. Army. Eastern and Southern Europeans were largely Catholics and Jews, immigration restriction was quite Protestant. When referring to certain geographic areas, religious background was quite specifically meant.

A further aspect of the invalid underpinnings of this principle of National Origins was that its executors were unable to follow accurately the European border changes and population shifts after World War I, which drastically altered the ethnic composition of the new Europe.[28]

The execution of the quota laws and the issuance of visas was controlled by American consuls, who acted under instruction from the Department of State.[29] In concert with a practice which had grown out of World War I, the United States did not require that passports of foreigners be visaed until their country had entered the War. After the declaration of War, consuls were "further enjoined to scrutinize the applicants carefully before affixing the visas."[30] The executive order of July 26, 1917 required all aliens planning to enter into the United States to have a visa issued

---

27 Robert A. Divine, *American Immigration Policy, 1924–1952* (New Haven: Yale University Press, 1957), pp. 26–27.
28 William S. Bernard, ed., *op. cit.*, p. 28–29.
29 Second Acting Secretary of Labor W. W. Husband to John F. Carew, Member of Congress, June 4, 1926, The National Archives (NA), Washington, DC: RG 85, [55598/31]= 53827/14.
30 Graham H. Stuart, *American Diplomatic and Consular Practice* (New York: Appleton-Century-Crofts, 1952), p. 363.

by a U.S. consul, and an executive order and proclamation by President Wilson on August 8, 1918 regulated the whole system of passports and entrance into the country.

The consular service was consolidated in 1924, when the quota act arranged for scrutinization and selection of immigrants at their departure points, rather than permitting them to come to the U.S. and then having them sent back. U.S. consulates were made responsible for quota control by means of the visas issued. When the new system was first introduced, however, the immigration service was in total disarray. "With the passage of the immigration quota law, the office was in a quandary," remembered a former U.S. vice consul during the crucial year of 1924.

> No new visas had been granted for over six months. There was an ever increasing waiting list. No exact information could be given the applicants for visas and when finally definite word was received from Washington regarding quotas and procedure we had only the scantiest instructions on which to work. [...] The less doubtful and more urgent applicants were given their visas first. Even then, the next ship brought back nearly half of our applicants from Ellis Island, for during the period of the voyage across new provisions had been added to the regulations.[31]

Despite continued changes in regulations, consuls had such power that immigration cases did not come within the jurisdiction of the Immigration Service or the Department of Labor until immigrants actually arrived at a port of entry where their admissibility, under the general requirements of the immigration laws, was determined by officials of the Immigration Service.[32] The authority of the consuls' decision was such that not even the Department of Labor could subsequently change the status of immigrants from one class of visa to another (e.g. non-immigrant into non-quota) once they were visaed for a particular class.[33]

---

31   Graham H. Stuart, *op. cit.*, p. 365.
32   Second Acting Secretary of Labor W. W. Husband to Mrs. Julia Varga, February 2, 1926, NA: RG 85, [55598/31]= 53827/14. Cf. Acting Secretary of Labor Robe Carl White to John F. Carew, July 28, 1926, NA: RG 85, [55598/31]= 53827/14.
33   Second Acting Secretary of Labor W. W. Husband to W. Frank James, M. C., January 8, 1926, NA: RG 85, 55608/120.

Consuls had influence on the process of immigration in several other ways, too. In March 1925, the U.S. Consul General in Prague sent a detailed report to the Department of State on "Emigration from Czechoslovakia," surveying the years 1924–1925, which he called the period of the Restrictive Immigration Act. After some basic statistics, the consul went on to describe the "Habits and Customs of the People," an exercise in naïve cultural anthropology. Consul General C. S. Winans made the same type of observations for the State Department which the immigration inspectors of the pre-war period recorded for the Department of Labor. Some remarks of the U.S. consuls reflect on how the American image of Central Europe was shaped by the foreign service.

The U.S. Consul in Prague, C.S. Winans in his persuasive statements attributed Hungary's pre-World War I educational policies as being responsible for Slovak ignorance, poverty and emigration.

> The majority of the Slovaks and Ruthenians are rather dull and uneducated and, as a general rule, are slow to think and act, have been accustomed all their lives to little of worldy goods and are satisfied with less. This condition may be partly attributed to the lack of elementary schools in that section of former Austro-Hungary. [...] As a rule, these people do not have much initiative and ability to organize—quite to the contrary, they are more inclined to be led than to be leaders. Their idea of sanitation is nil and standard of living low. The rule rather than exception being that several persons occupy a small house which comprises one or two small rooms. During the Winter months most of the family life is confined to one room [...]
>
> Their food consists chiefly of potatoes, rye bread and soup. Their clothing is of the poorest quality and practically all the manfolks of Podkarpatská Rus wear home spun garments. [...]
>
> Emigrants from Bohemia, Moravia and Silesia are more educated and intelligent, and have more initiative and ability to organize. They are of ordinary stature, rugged build and healthy. In fact, generally speaking, the emigrants from Czechoslovakia are, with the exception of the Jewish element, producers and not consumers, and as such are not likely to become public charges through an aversion to work.[34]

---

34 Consul General C. S. Winans and Vice-Consul J. L. Calnan to the Department of State, March 13–24, 1925, NA: RG 85, 55452/223.

Consul Winans described the fundamental difference between pre-War and post-War emigration from Slovakia and Podkarpatská Rus. While previous emigrants left their homes with the intention to return as soon as they had acquired enough wealth, the emigrants of the 1920s sold everything to obtain sufficient funds to take their families to, and stay permanently in, the United States. Poverty is responsible for the unparalleled desire among practically everyone in Slovakia and Podkarpatská Rus to emigrate to the U.S.: there were 40 thousand applications for emigration passports on file in the Czechoslovak Ministry of Social Welfare. Prospective emigrants from the Slovak and Ruthene [i.e. Subcarpathian Ukrainian] areas represented approximately 80% of the total emigration.[35]

The Consul helped the State Department understand the new realities of Central Europe by describing how the prohibition of seasonal work in post-War Hungary's agriculture contributed to the pauperization of the Slovak and Ruthene peasantry. His remarks underlined the similarities between the pre-War migration patterns and the socio-economic functions of large geopolitical entities such as the Austro-Hungarian Monarchy and the United States.[36]

"the perfectly legitimate needs of American interests..."

The 1924 Act divided immigrants into the categories of quota immigrants and non-quota immigrants. The former could only be admitted within the quotas of their respective countries, while the latter could be admitted without any reference to the quota restrictions. By establishing the class of non-quota immigrants, Congress provided a special opportunity for reuniting families of U.S.

Most importantly, however, non-quota immigrants included well-trained professionals with special intellectual abilities, and prospective

---

35 Ibid.
36 Ibid.

professionals. Section 4 of the law stipulated that non-quota immigrants include

> (d) An immigrant who continuously for at least two years immediately preceding the time of his application for admission to the United States has been, and who seeks to enter the United States solely for the purpose of, carrying on the vocation of minister of any religious denomination, or professor of a college, academy, seminary, or university…; or

> (e) An immigrant who is a bona fide student at least 15 years of age and who seeks to enter the United States solely for the purpose of study at an accredited school, college, academy, seminary, or university […][37]

This was a direct response to the statistics of "new" immigrants wherein professionals represented a mere 0.3% of the total of approximately 5,000,000 people who had entered the country between 1899 and 1909.[38] In subsequent years, plans were made to amend the Immigration Laws, and Bill S. 3019 of 1928 significantly extended the selective principle by allowing 75% of the quota, rather than the previous (1924) 50%, to be subject to various preferences. The Department of Labor strongly favored the extension of the selective principle and put in a word for "those who are actually needed." Secretary Davis's comments for the Senate Immigration Committee made it clear that the Government tried to maneuver within the quota system by increasing the percentage of highly qualified people at the expense of average citizens of foreign birth.

> In the course of a year a good many cases arise in which some deserving American interest desires to bring in a chemist or an electrical or mechanical engineer to aid in improving processes already in use or, in some cases, in establishing new industries. Other cases arise in which educational institutions in the United States desire the services of an alien as a teacher or a professor and it so happens that such person, although fully qualified to fill the position involved, cannot meet the requirements of Section 4 of the Immigration Act of 1924 under which professors must have had two years experience immediately preceding their entry before they can qualify as nonquota immigrants. In all such cases […] there must be a compliance with the

---

37 Jeremiah Jenks and W. Jett Lauck, *op. cit.*, p. 538.
38 *Ibid.*, p. 32.

quota limit provisions, and as in most countries the quotas are pledged to previous applicants for two years or more, the perfectly legitimate needs of American interests are defeated.[39]

Soon the quota system turned counterproductive. Other government organizations reached conclusions similar to those of the Department of Labor, with even more expressive language being used by the U.S. Chamber of Commerce in early 1931. Its Immigration Committee called for a "method supplementing numerical restriction," "if we want greater selection and more flexibility in our immigration policy." The Chamber urged

> some practical selective provision in our immigration laws for the admissions of immigrants designated as scientists, inventors, technical experts and "key men"—persons with brains and ideas—who are deemed essential for the industrial, commercial, and economic development of our country, and who are needed both by American concerns and industries and also for new enterprises established here by foreigners and foreign capital.[40]

The Chamber of Commerce called for "Emergency Immigration Legislation" to make "the admission of immigrants with technical skills, capital, ideas, new machinery and new processes" possible in conjunction with the existing quota system.

It must be noted that even some members of the U.S. Senate were interested in the admission of "college teachers and professors," as a letter by New York Senator Robert F. Wagner to the Commissioner General of Immigration demonstrated in May 1929.[41] Similarly, Representative W.

---

39 Secretary of Labor James J. Davis to Hiram W. Johnson, Chairman, Senate Committee on Immigration, March 24, 1928, NA: RG 85, 55777/359C, p. 9.
40 "Emergency Immigration Legislation," Chamber of Commerce of the United States, Washington, DC, January 1931, pp. 10–11. NA: RG 85, 55639/617A.
41 Robert F. Wagner to the Commissioner General of Immigration [Harry E. Hull], U.S. Senate, May 10, 1929; Harry E. Hull to Robert F. Wagner, May 17, 1929. NA: RG 85, 55599/875.

Frank James intervened in 1926 for a Hungarian student who wished to matriculate at an American college.[42]

Hungary and the National Origins Principle

In the long period during which the Quota Laws defined emigration from Europe to the U.S., the citizens of Hungary were particularly affected. As is well known, Hungary was a major victim of the Quota Laws' limitation on the number of immigrants. This abrupt discontinuation of U.S. immigration hit Hungary most severely at the time of economic and social disaster created by the lost War, the revolutions and the Paris Peace Treaties. By depriving Hungarian society of a well-established outlet, the enactment of the Quota Laws and, in particular, their timing, made U.S. immigration legislation a disastrous impact on Hungarian history, comparable in many ways only to the disastrous impact of the Treaty of Trianon.

As one of the top contributors to U.S. population growth in pre-World War I Europe, Hungary sent approximately a hundred thousand people per annum for the decade before 1914 (with peaks of 193,400 in 1907 and 143,321 in 1914). The Act of 1921, based on the 1910 Census, provided Hungary with a meager quota of 5,747; the Act of 1924, based on the Census of 1890, significantly reduced it again to a paltry 473.[43]

Not that the virtual abolishment of U.S. immigration discouraged everybody in Hungary from applying. As of July 1, 1927, the demand against the Hungarian quota, as estimated by the State Department, was still 20,000.[44] It did not help very much the intended immigrants from

---

42 Second Acting Secretary of Labor W. W. Husband to W. Frank James, M. C., January 8, 1926, NA: RG 85, 55608/120.
43 Jeremiah Jenks and W. Jett Lauck, *op. cit.,* p. 455, 670, 672, 674. NB: The actual figures of those admitted varied somewhat between 1922–1924.
44 Edward R. Lewis, "National Origins and American Immigration. A Compilation of Source Material" (Chicago, IL: Immigration Restriction Association, [1928?]), p. 7–11, NA: RG 85, 55639/577A.

Hungary that the National Origins provision of the 1924 Act more than doubled their quota, bringing it to 1,181.[45] Yet, even this small increase was upsetting to certain groups of "old" immigrants, such as Scandinavian-Americans, who considered this detrimental to their interests and bitterly complained about it to Congress.[46] By the late 1920s, the Hungarian figure was reduced to 869.[47] This was such a small figure that in the six months from July through December 1928, when the registered number of U.S. visa applications from Hungary was only 3,802, it generated a waiting list of more than four years.[48] That "the quota for Hungary was exhausted in prospect for a number of years in the future" was a well-known fact in the late 1920s, both in Congress as well as throughout the U.S. government.[49]

Hungarians, many of them more desperate to leave in the 1920s than ever before, tried to use all remaining categories of the new laws to get into the U.S., first and foremost the preference sections. Half of the Hungarian quota was assigned to relatives, principally parents of U.S. citizens, and to persons skilled in agriculture.[50]

With so many incomplete Hungarian families in the U.S. after World War I, securing the entrance of relatives of former immigrants became a priority. In the session of 1926–1927, some twenty bills to amend the law

45 Immigration Quotas on the Basis of National Origin. Message from the President of the United States, February 27, 1928, Senate Document No. 65, 70th Congress, 1st Session; cf. Secretary of Labor James J. Davis to Hiram W. Johnson, Chairman, Senate Committee on Immigration, March 24, 1928, NA: RG 85, 55777/359C, p. 15.
46 The Scandinavian American Citizens' League, Troy, NY, "Is Immigration from Scandinavia and other Northern European Countries to be still further reduced by Congress?" Attached to the SACL's letter to Congressman James S. Parker, March 20, 1928, NA: RG 85, 55639/617A.
47 Department of State press releases, June 1931–May 1933, NA: RG 85, 55398/2F.
48 Acting Secretary of Agriculture R. N. Dunlap to Mississippi Governor Theodore G. Bilbo, September 23, 1929, NA: RG 85, 55777/359C.
49 Commissioner General of Immigration Harry E. Hull to Senator Robert F. Wagner, May 3, 1928, NA: RG 85, 55599/875.
50 Acting Secretary of Agriculture R. N. Dunlap to Mississippi Governor Theodore G. Bilbo, September 23, 1929, NA: RG 85, 55777/359C.

were introduced in Congress, typically to allow entrance for relatives.[51] Yet, the fact that so many Hungarians had family in the United States did not entitle relatives in Hungary "to exemption from the quota restrictions nor to preference in the issuance of a quota visa."[52] Would-be emigrants from Hungary were strictly advised to apply "for an immigration visa within the quota."[53]

Subsequent to September 22, 1922, marrying a U.S. citizen did not confer United States citizenship upon an alien woman and could not be interpreted as an exemption from the quota regulations. A Hungarian woman visiting the U.S. in 1928 was advised "to depart not later than the expiration of her authorized stay." A case from 1926 revealed that adoption after January 1, 1924 did not entitle a child to exemption from the quota either, nor to preference in the issuance of a quota visa.[54] However, in another case where a U.S. Senator intervened on behalf of a husband, a positive result was achieved.

A special feature of the 1924 Act was that it extended preference in the issuance of quota immigration visas to aliens skilled in agriculture. Citizens of what was still basically an agricultural country, many Hungarians tried to capitalize on this, only to be warned in each case that the law "does not entitle every person who has worked on a farm or every farmer to such preference, and the question would be decided by the consul to whom the aliens apply for the necessary visas."[55]

---

51   Edward R. Lewis, *op. cit.*, p. 19.
52   Acting Secretary of Labor W. W. Husband to Matthew Feitz, October 8, 1926, NA: RG 85, 53827/14.
53   Second Acting Secretary of Labor W. W. Husband to John F. Carew, Member of Congress, June 4, 1926, NA: RG 85, [55598/31]= 53827/14.
54   Acting Secretary Robe Carl White to W. Frank James, M. C., October 6, 1926, NA: RG 85, 55608/120. Recently, Linda K. Kerber addressed similar issues in her "Toward a History of Statelessness in America,"*American Quarterly*, Volume 57, Number 3, September 2005, pp. 727–749.
55   Second Acting Secretary of Labor W. W. Husband to John F. Carew, Member of Congress, June 4, 1926, NA: RG 85, [55598/31]= 53827/14. Cf. Second Acting Secretary of Labor W. W. Husband to Mrs. Julia Varga, February 2, 1926, NA: RG 85, [55598/31]= 53827/14.

National quotas were so rigid that they could not be suspended even if there were some legitimate American interests involved. The Governor of Mississippi tried to settle a large group of Hungarian farmers on agricultural lands in his state. Nonetheless, he was advised by Secretary of Labor James J. Davis "that while persons skilled in agriculture are accorded a preference in the issuance of immigration visas, such preference does not carry with it exemption from the quota limit or contract labor provision of the immigration laws."[56] In principle, the stringent quota provision overruled all other considerations.

Despite the fact that U.S. observers traveling to Hungary were keenly aware of the deplorable circumstances of post-World War I Hungarian professors and their universities, the extensive report from 1923 for the Rockefeller Foundation does not mention the possibility that those professors might be recruited for the United States.[57]

Critics of U.S. Immigration Policies

The history of U.S. immigration policy from the late 1920s was characterized by conflict between the need to maintain the framework of restrictive immigration laws while upholding the traditional American ideal of providing asylum from oppression. Instead of the extensive manpower requirements of the pre-World War I era, by 1921 the country was in need of only a select élite. The conflict between economic need and humanitarian ideals resulted in a new and ugly form of racial awareness, but often also in an emerging spirit of solidarity and humanitarianism both before and during the War.[58] Unfortunately, economic depression

---

56 Secretary of Labor James J. Davis to Mississippi Governor Theodore G. Bilbo, October 17, 1929, NA: RG 85, 55777/359C.
57 Dr. H. O. Eversole, "Medical Education in Hungary. Reports on the Medical Faculties at the Universities of Szeged, Pecs, and Debreczen, 1923," Rockefeller Foundation Archives, RG 1.1 Projects, Series 750A Hungary, Box 2, Folder 13.
58 Joyce C. Vialet, *A Brief History of U.S. Immigration Policy*, CRS Report for Congress, Washington, DC: Congressional Research Service, The Library of Congress, January 25, 1991, p. 12.

and the ensuing rebirth of racism made efforts to liberalize immigration legislation futile at a time when the nation might have saved so many people from persecution and certain death. President Herbert Hoover proved tragically mistaken when he declared in October 1932,

> [w]ith the growth of democracy in foreign countries, political persecution has largely ceased. There is no longer a necessity for the United States to provide an asylum for those persecuted because of conscience.[59]

Nonetheless, the U.S. admitted an estimated 250,000 refugees from Nazi Germany before entering the War in 1941.[60]

The emerging tension could be best observed and demonstrated in the national debate on the National Origins Provision of the Quota Law as well as the fact of growing anti-Semitism through the 1930s.

Opposition to the idea of National Origins could be divided into three groups. First there were those who were against all forms of immigration restriction and considered national origins as the front line of restriction defenses. These people demanded wholesale exceptions in favor of relatives. The second group consisted of people whose countries received a more generous quota under the 1890 foreign-born system than under National Origins, and who were losers under the new provision. The third group in opposition to National Origins, consisting mainly of later immigrants, who wanted to base quotas on the 1920 foreign born assessment in the hope that it would reflect more adequately on the recent social composition of the country.[61]

The following table shows the quotas on the three different systems referred to:[62]

The figures of the National Origins scheme were based on an elaborate study of the census of 1790, *A Century of Population Growth*, under-

---

59 Quoted by Robert A. Divine, *op. cit.*, p. 92.
60 Joyce C. Vialet, *op. cit.*, p. 13.
61 Edward R. Lewis, *op. cit.*, p. 5.
62 *Ibid.*, p. 7.

	1890 Foreign Born Basis*		National Origins Basis**		1920 Foreign Born Basis***	
		Percentage		Percentage		Percentage
NORTHWEST EUROPE:						
Belgium	512	.31	1,328	.86	778	.50
Denmark	2,789	1.69	1,234	.80	2,358	1.52
France	3,954	2.40	3,308	2.15	1,925	1.24
Germany	51,227	31.12	24,908	16.21	20,769	13.46
England, Scotland, Wales and North Ireland	34,007	20.65	65,894	42.89	16,957	10.99
Irish Free State	28,567	17.37	17,427	11.34	10,195	6.61
Netherlands	1,648	1.00	3,083	2.00	1,657	1.07
Norway	6,453	3.92	2,403	1.56	4,518	2.95
Sweden	9,561	5.80	3,399	2.21	7,769	5.03
Switzerland	2,081	1.26	1,614	1.05	1,473	.95
Other Northwest Europe	200	.12	200	.13	256	.16
TOTALS	140,999 =	85.6%	124,798 =	81.2%	68,655 =	44.5%
SOUTHEAST EUROPE:						
Austria	785	.47	1,639	1.06	5,556	3.60
Czecho-Slovakia	3,073	1.86	2,726	1.77	6,205	4.02
Finland	471	.28	568	.36	1,860	1.20
Greece	100	.06	312	.20	1,677	1.08
Hungary	473	.28	1,181	.76	4,602	2.99
Italy	3,845	2.33	5,989	3.89	20,024	12.97
Lithuania	344	.20	492	.32	1,504	.97
Poland	5,982	3.63	6,090	3.96	14,484	9.39
Portugal	503	.30	457	.29	1,295	.83
Rumania	603	.36	311	.20	1,104	.71
Russia	2,248	1.36	3,540	2.30	15,554	10.08
Yugo-Slavia	671	.40	739	.48	5,471	3.54
Other Southeast Europe	1,225	.74	1,385	.90	1,886	1.22
TOTALS	20,323 =	12.3%	25,429 =	16.5%	81,222 =	52.6%
ASIA:	1,624 =	.99%	1,758 =	1.14%	2,603 =	1.77%
AFRICA:	1,200 =	.72%	1,200 =	.78%	1,200 =	.78%
AUSTRALASIA:	521 =	.31%	500 =	.32%	536 =	.55%
GRAND TOTALS	164,667		153,685		154,216	

*Each country gets 2% of those born in that country counted in the 1890 census. These quotas, therefore, are based on 8,000,000 people in 1890.

**Based on the entire white population in 1920, native and foreign born alike, derived from the quota countries, 89,332,158 in all. Each country gets such proportion of 150,000 immigrants as it contributed to the total white population from quota countries, 89,332,158.

***Based on the foreign born counted in the 1920 census. These quotas, therefore, are based on 12,000,000 people in 1920.

taken by the U.S. Census Bureau in 1909.[63] Names, both first and last, found in this census, were classified by college-trained clerks and the classifications were later corrected by historian Marcus Hansen and geneologist Howard Barker, experts who worked in the Library of Congress and were appointed by the American Council of Learned Societies. As Joseph A. Hill, Assistant to the Director of the Census, explained, the main question for these experts was "whether a name was distinctively English or whether it was not distinctively English."[64] County histories and local records were used and a competent historian also consulted.

A storm broke when the report of the Quota Board was presented to Congress in January 1927. The inherent problem with National Origins was its distinctly un-American nature which critics found disuniting to American society and "deconstructing" of the American identity.

> It compels each and every one of us to ask ourselves the question, "What nationality am I?" Under this law none of us can ask ourselves the real and only question, "Am I an American?" no matter how far back we can trace our ancestry in the United States, it is a dissimilating, rather that an assimilating policy.[65]

German, Italian, Irish, and Scandinavian citizens and their organizations were quick to launch an avalanche of attacks on President Hoover insisting that he use his power against the National Origins clause and its consequences. Indirectly, attacks on National Origins were directed against Hungary, which, compared with other nations, would have benefited from it. Speaking for German-American interests, the Steuben Society of America pointed to the unreliabilty of names used as scholarly evidence.

---

63 For a full survey of the National Origins debate see Robert A. Divine, *op. cit.*, pp. 26–51, esp. 28–33.
64 Joseph A. Hill, Assistant to the Director of the Census, explaining the methods of the Quota Board to the House Immigration Committee on January 18, 1927, quoted by Edward R. Lewis, *op. cit.*, p. 7–11.
65 John W. McCormack, M.C. to President Herbert C. Hoover, March 8, 1929, NA: RG 85, 55639/577.

> Considering illiteracy prevalent in those early days, it is easy to vizualize the anglization [sic] of such names as Braun, Erhard, Fuchs, Hecht, Klein, into Brown, Earhart, Fox, Pike, Kline, Loewenstein into Livingston, the hosts of Schmitt or Schmidt into Smith, Lauer becomes Lawyer, Pfeffer becomes Pepper, and as a final instance, Pfannkuchen changes to Pancake. Graf and Schneider are metamorphosed into Lord and Taylor [...] The absurdity of fixing quotas even in part re such deductions is apparent.[66]

The United Irish-American Societies of New York spoke for all when denouncing the National Origins scheme "as an attempt on the part of propagandists to falsify American history and to subvert the old-time American theory that Europe, and not any particular nation of that continent, is the mother country of America."[67] Michigan critics of the provision formed their own Anti-National Origins Clause League which sent a long letter in protest to the *Detroit Times* on May 20, 1929. The letter considered the ever-changing allotments to any one nation the most vulnerable aspect of the provision. The President of the League used the changing figures of Hungary as good examples of the weakness and inconsistencies of the proposition.

> When the present method of determining quotas was enacted into law in 1924, estimates were furnished showing the numbers that would be allowed in under the National Origins method, and a committee of six experts put on the job to verify or correct them, and have the permanent allotments prepared before April 1, 1927. These estimates and two one year postponements gives us four columns of figures on this National Origins affair. Let us take a squint at them. For instance, Austria's estimate was 2,171. Three years later this body of experts found that 1,486 would be the permanent allotment. Working for another year they found that the honest-to-goodness permanent allotment was 1,639. Working for still another year they found that the honest-to-goodness cross-my-heart permanent allotment was 1,413. France's 1924 estimate, 1,772; 1927 allotment, 3,839; 1928, 3,308; 1929, 3,086. Hungary, 1,521, 967, 1,181, 869, but even in the very small allotments the variation

---

66   Chas. J. Wolfram, Secretary, National Council of the Steuben Society of America to President Herbert Hoover, New York, NY, March 16, 1929, NA: RG 85, 55639/577A.
67   James Reidy of the United Irish-American Societies of New York to the President, February 19, 1929, NA: RG 85, 55639/577.

in the figures is astonishing. For instance, Roumania shows 222, 516, 311, 295; Spain, 148, 674, 305, 252. And so it goes all the way through. Of the allotments accorded to the 28 countries above the 100 maximum, not one remains unchanged. And this appalling exhibition of mathematical jugglery you call "accurate and scientific." [...] You say we should have started in 1928 – would it have been fair to give Hungary 1,181 each year if it is true that the correct number is 869? Is it fair to the American people to force upon them this hodgepodge theory of quota fixing that can never be worked out in practice [...][68]

Though the House repeatedly passed postponement resolutions and the National Origins clause was almost defeated by 1929, racial nationalism was still strong enough to force Congress to retain the provision. Historian Robert A. Divine suggested that "the majority of the American people appeared to be unconcerned over how the quotas were distributed as long as the principle of restriction was maintained."[69] "The striking feature of the national origins debate," Divine continued, "was the wide agreement between the opposing sides on the basic principle of racial, or at least of cultural, nationalism."[70]

While it was possible for some to reprimand the United States for its narrow immigration policies in 1928,[71] once the Great Depression started, restrictive immigration became the slogan of the day. Immigration restriction at the time of the presidential election of 1928 was largely a bipartisan effort.[72] President Hoover repeatedly expressed his support of immigration restriction and was urged from all quarters to carry on his policies. The Commonwealth Club of California cabled their endorsement to the President and urged that "a further development of our machinery

---

68 Joseph Carey, President, The Anti-National Origins Clause League of Michigan, to the Editor, *Detroit Times,* Detroit, Mich., May 20, 1929, NA: RG 85, 55639/577.
69 Robert A. Divine, *op. cit.,* p. 49.
70 *Ibid.,* p. 50.
71 Isaac Jackson to President Calvin Coolidge, Boston, MA, April 30, 1928, NA: RG 85, 55639/617A.
72 Harry E. Hull, Commissioner of Immigration to Admiral H. O. Stickney, Republican Headquarters, October 9, 1928, NA: RG 85, 55639/617A.

for selection of desirable immigrants be sought."[73] The Patriotic Order Sons of America demanded drastic restriction in all spheres of immigration policy.[74]

The Great Depression mobilized an additional avalanche of anti-foreign sentiment and the same racial nationalism experienced at the time of Hoover's election was the general motive behind the rising tide of xenophobia and anti-Semitism in the 1930s. The Department of Immigration received the brunt of the criticism. "Low Irish, Italian Mafia, degenerate Spanish & Mexicans—as well as Negro immigrants, & other colored races, should all stop—& none ever eligible excepting a very few of the very highest standard," wrote R. Sayre & Co. to the Department at height of the Depression in 1930.[75] "The Country is overrun with immigrants and the people here cannot get work and the immigrants are coming in by the score [...] there are plenty of people here for the work," added "A Citizen" from New York City.[76] "Why not amend the 1924 Quota Law and stop immagration [sic] until every person in America has a position," J. J. Brown of Brooklyn, NY added.[77]

Unemployment was also a problem for artists, a former member of the Immigration Service told the Secretary of Labor. His remarks had a direct relevance to Hungarian musicians arriving by the dozens into the U.S. and, thanks to their superb musical education and expertise, were usually successful in obtaining good jobs with American symphonies.

> I happen to know a great deal about the lot of American artists abroad, how they are hounded and pounded upon by all sorts of sharks and relieved of their money

---

[73] William Fitch Cheney, President, and Earle A. Walcott, Executive Secretary, Commonwealth Club of California to President Herbert Hoover, December 24, 1929, NA: RG 85, 55639/617A.

[74] C. B. Helms, State Secretary, Patriotic Order Sons of America to President Herbert Hoover, Philadelphia, December 3, 1929, NA: RG 85, 55639/617A.

[75] R. Sayre & Co. to Department of Immigration, Chicago, May 12, 1930, NA: RG 85, 55639/617A.

[76] "A Citizen" to Department of Immigration, n. d. NA: RG 85, 55639/617A.

[77] J. J. Brown to Secretary of Labor James J. Davies, Brooklyn, NY, April 2, 1930, NA: RG 85, 55639/617A.

without giving anything in return; how they are made to pay for the privilege of singing, while the aliens are getting fabulous sums for singing in this country.

Now, as Secretary of Labor I think you ought to bring this to the attention of Congress. If any privileges [sic] are accorded to foreign singers or other artist, [sic] for heaven's sake let those provileges [sic] be withdrawn at once. I know of American artists who are literally starving in this country while aliens are waxing fat in this land only to take that money away to foreign lands.[78]

Musical America quoted the celebrated Ossip Gabrilowitsch, longtime conductor of the Detroit Symphony who said essentially the same: "The number of artists is steadily increasing, many of them coming from Europe. This growth is out of all proportion to the audiences."[79]

While it has been customary to describe the pre-War mood as completely anti-foreign, xenophobic, and restrictive in terms of immigration policies, others voiced their concern for those who would be deported as illegal aliens. "You and your friends or family have no more right to remain than those who are deported," the Commissioner General of Immigration was told in an anonymous letter which accompanied pictures of aliens leaving the country in October 1931. "No Uncle Sam sends such greetings but those aliens who are in positions now the high-falutin jealous clique who hate to give the other fellow a chance—lest his efforts excelled."[80]

However, the overwhelming majority of those who wrote to the government were restrictive in their philosophy, suggesting citizenship qualification, a system to catalogue people in the centrally controlled countries of Europe, or a return to the ideal of "good Americans," based on Protestant values of loyalty and patriotism, in response to fear about the overwhelming number of Catholics entering the country under the Quota Laws.[81]

---

78 Joseph Alvarez to the Secretary of Labor, New York City, April 1930, RG 85, 55639/617A.
79 *Musical America,* March 25, 1930, clipping; NA: RG 85, 55639/617A.
80 Anonymous to the Commissioner General of Immigration, October 1931, NA: RG 85, 55639/617A.
81 Franklin Armstrong to President Herbert Hoover, June 22, 1931, and Mrs. D. D. Wood to the Secretary of Labor, March 1931, NA: RG 85, 55639/617A.

In many ways, anti-Semitism used arguments identical with, or very similar to, those of the racist interest groups in the National Origins debate, particularly in regard to Germans. There was a remarkable interest in the pro-German quarters about Hitler's new Germany and the *Freunde des Neuen Deutschlands* and its paper *Deutscher Weckruf und Beobachter* made efforts to popularize Nazism as a legitimate response to "world-encircling Marxism."[82] Anti-Semitic attacks, however, were already pouring forth before Hitler rose to power: the Secretary of Labor received an angry warning in 1932 that the Jews "are getting out of Germany [...] preparing for their farther trip to the United States" and urged the Labor Department "to stop this filthy influx."[83] Such racism did not focus on the Jews alone. "To ban the immigrant" was not just the wish of one woman who wrote to the Secretary of Labor: "We all long for the day to come when we will arrive in New York to stay, and see something else than Polish Jews, stinking Italians, and communist Russians."[84]

Ironically, Anti-Semitic agitation became more energetic in the U.S. as the persecution of Jews took on serious proportions in Germany. "It isn't fair under any circumstances, to permit the great Jewish influence in the United States of America to control this situation to the detriment of the American born christian people" [sic] the Stephen Girard Council (Junior Order United American Mechanics) expressing their sentiments to President Franklin D. Roosevelt in December 1938. The National Council of the Daughters of America voiced their opposition to changing the established quotas in favor of political refugees from Austria and Germany.[85] In certain instances, fear of rivalry tinged the perception of Jewish professional immigration. One Eric R. Wilson, M.D., for example,

---

82   Local group New York commemorates December 12, 1934, with a grand festival in the Yorkville Casino, NA: RG 85, 55738/157.
83   Anonymous to Secretary of Labor William N. Doak, August 1932, NA: RG 85, 55639/617A.
84   Mrs. Henry Peeples to Secretary of Labor William N. Doak, Paris, November 17, 1931, NA: RG 85, 55639/617A.
85   Resolutions, Nancy Hanks Council, No. 114, Daughters of America, Flushing, NY, December 1938, NA: RG 85, 55789/979.

complained about German and Austrian Jewish doctors being admitted "and with a working agreement with the Bureau of Immigration given licenses to practice in some cases the credentials are not even checked."[86] Others made it clear that they were not against German Jews alone, but also against any German refugees as they were "nearly all communists and knowing them to be communists [...] our country cannot afford to invite them to stay here."[87]

The number and language of the letters directed to President Roosevelt at the turn of 1938–1939 against the admittance of Jewish refugees from Germany and Austria is indeed shocking. As one typical correspondent put it in January 1939,

> as a Christian and an American I must ask that you, who are likewise an American and a Christian to exercise a little concern for your own people first and worry about Russian, Roumanian, Polish and German Jews later on. I am deeply sympathetic of their plight. But I am far more gravely concerned about my own kind first.[88]

The message of "A Citizen" to the President in late November 1938 was loud and clear: "We hope Congress acts and stops Jews from coming over here."[89] Not even the terrible news of the *Kristallnacht* mellowed the minds of most people: most of those writing to the President at this juncture referred to the unemployment figures and called upon him to deal with domestic issues first.[90] "LET US MIND OUR OWN BUSINESS"

---

86 Eric R. Wilson to Bureau of Immigration, Los Angeles, February 28, 1939, NA: RG 85, 55789/979.
87 Members of Camp 254, P. O. of A. Camp to Franklin D. Roosevelt, December 9, 1938, NA: RG 85, 55789/979.
88 Walter J. Bott to President Franklin D. Roosevelt, January 22, 1939, NA: RG 85, 55789/979.
89 "A Citizen" to The President, New York City, November 23, 1938, NA: RG 85, 55789/979.
90 Marguerite Haag to President Franklin Delano Roosevelt, New York, November 20, 1938; Marion Wall to Franklin D. Roosevelt, November 20, 1938; Illegible to State Department, Elmhurst, L.I., NY, November 16, 1938; Mr. & Mrs. Sweeny, Chicago, IL, November 20, 1938; G. P. Winter to President Franklin D. Roosevelt, November 28, 1938; NA: RG 85, 55789/979. — For a broad survey of U.S. policy

cried out Helen F. Luth on November 18, 1938 and added, "[i]n times of economic stress, when our relief rolls are full, why add more to the already overburdened American citizen."[91]

The Curtain Falls:
The Admission of Hungarians in the Early War Years

Appreciating Hungary's neutrality at the beginning of World War II, the United States developed an attitude of tolerance toward Hungarian immigration in 1939–40.[92] This was abruptly changed, however, when Hungary joined the Tripartite Agreement on November 20, 1940 and János Pelényi, the Hungarian Minister in Washington, DC tendered his resignation and remained in the United States.[93] Pelényi's letters from November 1940 documented the dramatic change in the U.S. image of Hungary, a country now increasingly viewed as a satellite of Germany, albeit an unwilling satellite.[94]

As the War approached Hungary, Hungarian-Americans became increasing politicized and polarized. For a time, the shady figure of Tibor Eckhardt emerged, a close associate of Regent Miklós Horthy and a politi-

---

on the issue of Jewish refugees see Arthur D. Morse, *While 6 Million Died: A Chronicle of American Apathy* (New York: Ace, 1968). Morse failed to make the connection between the lack of American political support of Jewish refugees and anti-Semitic public opinion in the U.S.

91 Helen F. Luth to the President, Brooklyn, NY, November 18, 1938, NA: RG 85, 55789/979.
92 Thomas Sakmyster, *Hungary's Admiral on Horseback: Miklós Horthy, 1918–1944* (Boulder, CO: East European Monographs, 1994), pp. 237–267; see esp. p. 250.
93 János Pelényi to Rufus B. von KleinSmid, January 29, 1941, Theodore von Kármán Papers, File 22.36, California Institute of Technology, Robert A. Millikan Memorial Library, Institute Archives, Pasadena, CA.
94 János Pelényi to Prime Minister Count Pál Teleki, Washington, DC, November 28, 1940, János Pelényi to Count Miklós Bánffy, January 11, 1941, Janos Pelenyi Papers, Box 1, Archives of the Hoover Institution on War, Revolution and Peace, Stanford, CA. Cf. John F. Montgomery, *Hungary the Unwilling Satellite* (Devin-Adair, 1947, repr. Morristown, N.J.: Vista Books, 1993).

cal adventurer, who tried to dominate the political scene. Eckhardt was rumored to have been sent by the Hungarian political élite to work on the eventual formation of a government in exile,[95] but had little credibility with the majority of the Hungarian-American community who frequently cited his political past of 1919–1920 in the extreme right wing of Hungarian politics.[96] His critics included former Hungarian President Count Mihály Károlyi, who launched from his London exile vicious attacks on Eckhardt and his U.S. followers.[97] Several new action groups were formed and added to the dozens of already existing Hungarian-American organizations, with the *Amerikai Magyar Szövetség* (Federation of American Hungarians) representing the right-wing and the *Demokratikus Magyarok Amerikai Szövetsége* (American Federation of Democratic Hungarians) the left-wing or liberal immigrants. A host of public meetings, newspaper campaigns, and political rallies tried to win over the sympathies of the hundreds of thousands of Hungarian-Americans in the highly charged atmosphere of 1941.[98]

With the War threatening Hungary and the rest of Europe, the last wave of interwar Hungarian emigration began. Terrified and desperate, Jewish Hungarians tried to leave Continental Europe, as well as Britain, to come to the United States. The refugee problem became a major theme in the ongoing debate among Hungarian-Americans. A leader of the liberals, law professor and prospective post-War Hungarian minister

95 János Pelényi, "Secret Plan," *The Journal of Modern History,* Vol. XXXVI, No. 2, June 1964.
96 György Faludy, "Manhattan szigetén," [On Manhattan Island] [original source unknown]; "Pro and Con Mr. Eckhardt," *The Nation,* October 1940; Rusztem Vambery Papers, Box 8, Archives of the Hoover Institution on War, Revolution and Peace, Stanford, CA; Katalin Kádár Lynn, *Tibor Eckhardt: His American Years 1941–1972* (Boulder, CO: East European Monographs, distributed by Columbia University Press, 2007).
97 Count Mihály Károlyi to Emil Lengyel, London, November 25, 1942, Emil Lengyel Collection, Bakhmeteff Archives, Butler Library, Columbia University Library, New York, NY.
98 See clippings and posters in the Rusztem Vambery Papers, Box 8, Archives of the Hoover Institution on War, Revolution and Peace, Stanford, CA.

to Washington, DC, Rusztem Vámbéry (1872–1948) argued that the refugee-problem could only be solved by the elimination of the causes that force persecuted minorities either to perish or leave their country and suffer in an alien and unwelcoming environment.[99] This became a burning issue, and by the end of the year, when the United States entered the War, Vámbéry, himself a 1938 refugee in the U.S.,[100] launched the Free Hungary Movement, intended as a new group against what he saw as the semi-feudal military dictatorship of the Horthy régime.[101]

The Private Bills of 1939–1941

As Robert A. Divine pointed out, until 1930 it was Congress that formulated immigration policy, but by the end of the 1930s the dominance of the executive branch prevailed. Throughout the 1930s, immigration was discussed along three basically different lines: the public charge policy, the refugee problem, and the prevention of admission of subversive elements. These reflected the traditional conflict between idealists trying to help the oppressed of other nations (with Senator Wagner of New York as their chief advocate), and restrictionists who argued that "charity should begin at home."[102] A series of bills were introduced both to protect refugees, especially from Germany after 1933, and to keep out subversive aliens. Most of these bills died at various stages in the legislative process. The end of this period of immigration legislation came with the entry of the United States into the War in December 1941.

In the heated atmosphere of the early war years, the competition among would-be immigrants became even more fierce, almost lethal,

---

99 "Vámbéry Rusztem beszél a refugee-problémáról" [Rusztem Vámbéry on the Refugee Problem], *Igazság*, December 1, 1940 [?], Rusztem Vambery Papers, Box 7.
100 Abraham Flexner to Rusztem Vámbéry, May 7, 1938, Rusztem Vambery Papers, Box 1.
101 Rustem Vambery, "'Free Hungary' Movement in U.S.," *Voice of Freedom*, December 1941, Rusztem Vambery Papers, Box 3.
102 Robert A. Divine, *op. cit.*, pp. 100–101, 108.

without the principles of their selection always being clear, transparent, or germane. When the War broke out, it was estimated by members of the House Committee on Immigration and Naturalization that large numbers of people were "here temporarily and for one reason or another can not get out and are seeking legal admission,"[103] thousands in California alone. As it became more difficult and dangerous for temporary visitors in the United States to go home, or ask and wait for a regular quota number, Congress made it possible to appeal to the House Committee on Immigration and Naturalization. Representing both restrictionists and liberals, the Committee received hundreds of appeals, many of which came from people who were still considered able to "go out and come back in the regular way."[104] In those cases, however, where people could not be sent home, a private bill was considered by Congress which would circumvent the regular immigration process.

Political considerations were declared, if only for the record, and in this early part of the War, Hungary's quasi-belligerent nature, her half-hearted joining of the Tripartite Pact, her role as an "unwilling satellite" were clearly important issues. In January 1941, well before Hungary's actual entry into the War, the Chairman of the House Committee noted "that Hungary more or less declared war upon this country, whether it was done voluntarily or not," and the Chairman made it clear that he was forced to make this comment "because I do not want to be told on the Floor [of the House] that I have not gone into it and the Committee should have clarified the admission."[105]

---

103 "A Bill for the Relief of Tibor Hoffman and Magda Hoffman," House Report 3315, February 12, 1941, 77th Congress, 1st Session; Library of Congress: Law Library, RR (77) HIm-T.43, p. 6; Unpublished U.S. House of Representatives Committee Hearings, Committee on Immigration and Naturalization, 1941–1942.
104 "A Bill for the Relief of Tibor Hoffman and Magda Hoffman," *op. cit.,* p. 2.
105 "A Bill to record the lawful admission to the United States for permanent residence of Reverend Julius Paal," House Report 1374, January 3, 1941, 77th Congress, 1st Session, p. 2; Library of Congress: Law Library, RR (77) HIm-T.87, Unpublished U.S. House of Representatives Committee Hearings, Committee on Immigration and Naturalization, 1941–1942.

In early 1941, the Chair of the House Committee launched a vehement attack on the immigration bureaucracy for making the procedure so complicated. "Under the new regulations," he stated openly, "the Department [of State] has set up that it needs a Jesus to get by. They have got 4,000 questions and forms, and it would take eight lawyers, two from Philadelphia and two from New York and three from California [...]"[106] Without a private bill, unlawful aliens were subject to deportation. Private bills of this sort were numerous and were referred to the House Committee of Immigration and Naturalization. In various ways, these bills saved a number of Hungarians who had arrived into the country earlier without being properly authorized to stay, and many of whom had been ordered to be deported from the U.S. A separate bill was needed for every visitor-to-be-immigrant, and members of the House Committee themselves criticized the apparent lack of policy in a situation where there many thousands of cases were involved.[107] Some of these immigrants first arrived with a visitor's visa and later found a way to present their case to the House Committee. The Committee faced a relatively large crowd of "visitors of all nations who have come here as visitors and have been caught in this international situation."[108] The Committee evidently tried to shape some kind of policy towards these visitors, but ultimately failing to do so. Finances were always a consideration: if visitors could prove that they possessed enough money so they "would never become a public charge," their case was favorably reported to the House. Such was the case of businessman Ernest Ungar, who had a large discount clothing store in Budapest employing 250 clerks and who had also bought a large farm in New Jersey. He thus had sufficient proof that he was "a desirable alien to be admitted to this country."[109] Indeed, money often made aliens desirable.

---

106 Samuel Dickstein, M.C., Chair, "A Bill for the Relief of Tibor Hoffman and Magda Hoffman," *op. cit.*, p. 2.
107 "A Bill for the Relief of Tibor Hoffman and Magda Hoffman," *op. cit.*, pp. 11–13.
108 *Ibid.*, p. 12.
109 "A Bill for the Relief of Ernest Unger [sic]," House Report 7626, November 3, 1939, 76th Congress, 2d Session; Library of Congress: Law Library, RR (76) HIm-T.92,

Money alone did not do it, though. It is evident from the questions of the Committee members that in various cases they handled over the years 1939–1942, they were looking for the combination of financial stability, good character, young age, and some class. Table tennis champions Tibor and Magda Hoffman were made U.S. citizens on the merit of their star quality sportsmanship. The Hoffmans arrived in the U.S. in 1939, at the invitation of the United States Table Tennis Association and found themselves, as they told the House Committee on Immigration and Naturalization, "unable to return to their native country,"[110] probably because of their Jewish origins. Colonel George H. Foster, general counsel for the U.S. Table Tennis Association, testified to the Committee that the Hoffmans "are splendid people, have high ideals, and would be in our opinion worthy citizens of the United States."[111] Reminding his colleagues of a similar case, Mr. Kramer, a member of the House Committee, recalled another couple "whose property was all taken over and confiscated by Hitler because they were Jews, but," he added, "they are very high class people, people that I would welcome to get into this country [...]."[112] This was a revealing though thinly-veiled anti-Semitic statement that made a point about rich and high class Jews being wanted, and poor and low class Jews being unwanted. It is noteworthy that such a reference was made in Congress concerning a division within the Jewish community along class lines, and consequently differing attitudes toward Jews in terms of their social position. After a thorough cross-examination of their politics and their finances, the Hoffmans were placed in the nonpreference category of the Hungarian quota, deduction from which being the standard practice followed in all similar cases for several years.

The Paris representative of a Hungarian firm manufacturing electric lamps and radio tubes, engineer Ladislas Frank came to the U.S. in October 1939 and was unable to return to France after the German

p. 5; Unpublished U.S. House of Representatives Committee Hearings, Committee on Immigration and Naturalization, 1939–1941.
110 "A Bill for the Relief of Tibor Hoffman and Magda Hoffman," *op. cit.*, p. 1.
111 *Ibid.*, p. 5.
112 *Ibid.*, p. 7.

occupation. Frank was questioned by the Committee in painstaking detail as to the circumstances of his entry into the U.S. from France, in an effort to ascertain the genuineness and honesty of his original intentions of returning to Europe.[113] Adherence to the prescriptions of the quota system proved to be more a dominating factor than an applicant's experience and expertise, yet this case serves as an example of some attempts made by the Committee to show a measure of human understanding, yet often being torn between their official function to keep people out of the country and their personal inclinations to give support to those in trouble.

Signals or symbols of willingness to assimilate, such as having entered the U.S. armed forces or exerting some Americanizing influence in the local community by using the English language, were among the strongest recommendations for admission into the country. The Reverend Julius Paal [Gyula Paál] arrived in the country in 1937 as a student at the Princeton Theological Seminary. When the War broke out, he voluntarily offered his services to the U.S. Army. Previously he had written anti-Nazi articles for the Hungarian-American press and worked for the Evangelical Reform Church in Bethlehem, PA.[114] For members of the Committee the vital question was whether or not the Reverend Paal was trying to prolong his studies in the U.S. in an effort to stay indefinitely in the country or whether he had been a *bona fide* student for the five years between 1937 and 1941. The Committee turned favorably towards Paal's case when they learned that he had conducted his services in English (as he actually said, "in American"), which had had a beneficent effect on the local community. Representative Walter, who introduced the private bill on behalf of Reverend Paal, explained to the Committee why he had appreciated Paal's efforts:

---

113 "A Bill for the Relief of Ladislas Frank," House Report 4584, April 29, 1941, 77th Congress, 1st Session; Library of Congress: Law Library, RR (77) HIm-T.45, Unpublished U.S. House of Representatives Committee Hearings, Committee on Immigration and Naturalization, 1941–1942.
114 "A Bill to record the lawful admission to the United States for permanent residence of Reverend Julius Paal," *op. cit.*

I represent a district in which there are many races. Up to a few years ago on the very street in which this church is located with which Reverend Paal is connected, there are three churches, and on Sunday mornings the services were conducted in each of the three churches in three different languages [...] And during the last few years there has been a departure from that, and I think that Reverend Paal pioneered the way. [...] All of these churches are now conducting their services in English, and it has had a very good effect on the older people, who found it difficult to master the English language, but found it easy to go to church and have the sermons and the services conducted in their own language, so they had never bothered very greatly in learning the English language. There is a tremendous change now throughout that entire section of Pennsylvania.[115]

The Reverend Paal's admission was charged against the Hungarian quota by order of the Committee.

Investigating the 1941 case of builder Marcel Stark, the House Committee noted that in Canada there were 137 people waiting for a quota number. As the Hungarian quota was "behind," "closed," admission through individual bills was made possible if charged against the Hungarian quota, of course only "for the first year the said quota was available."[116]

Occasionally, in a case handled by the House Committee, the procedure was surprisingly quick and seemed a mere formality. Sometimes there was no indication as to the reason why someone immediately received a quota number through the direct intervention of the House Committee on Immigration and Naturalization. Temporarily admitted to the U.S., Otto Rudolf Nemeth, for example, was without further explanation and discussion "admitted and permitted to remain in the United States permanently as though he had in all respects complied with the immigration

---

115 *Ibid.*, p. 9.
116 "A Bill for the Relief of Marcel Stark," House Report 4181, March 25, 1941, 77th Congress, 1st Session; Library of Congress: Law Library, RR (77) HIm-T.24, p. 3 and titlepage; Unpublished U.S. House of Representatives Committee Hearings, Committee on Immigration and Naturalization, 1941–1942.

laws upon entry."[117] As he came from Austria, his admission was charged against the German quota.

In certain cases the House Committee acted as a court of appeal. The Department of Labor charged garage owner Charles Molnar with fraud, as it was accidentally discovered in 1936, at a crossing of the Canadian border, that he had entered the U.S. illegally in 1922. Nevertheless, the verification of his *bona fide* actions and his financial status was enough for the Committee to report favorably to the House: Molnar was admitted legally in 1936.[118]

Even this small sample of Hungarians admitted through the Congressional Commission of Immigration and Naturalization gives us a sense of U.S. immigration priorities at a time when international developments renewed restrictionist sentiments and produced an atmosphere in which aliens, once again, were looked upon with growing suspicion and fear. The image of the foreigner was tinged with threat and confusion when the security of the United States was jeopardized by international circumstances. Speaking for the Hungarian-American community before the House Committee of the Judiciary, critics spoke specifically of the disastrous consequences of this changing perception. Louis Perlman, representing the Hungarian Societies Central Committee in New York, an organization to which some 25 Hungarian societies belonged, declared on April 18, 1941:

> Up until comparatively recently in our history admission to the United States was practically at the will of the individual. It was on that fact that our Nation's development was based, and it was on that fact [...] that the prosperity of our country was also based.

---

[117] "A Bill for the Relief of Otto Rudolf Nemeth," House Report 390, January 3, 1941, 77th Congress, 1st Session; Library of Congress: Law Library, RR (77) HIm-T.21, titlepage; Unpublished U.S. House of Representatives Committee Hearings, Committee on Immigration and Naturalization, 1941–1942.

[118] "A Bill for the Relief of Charles Molnar," House Report 7749, January 8, 1940, 76th Congress, 3d Session; Library of Congress: Law Library, RR (76) HIm-T.94, Unpublished U.S. House of Representatives Committee Hearings, Committee on Immigration and Naturalization, 1939–1941.

Hungary and Selective Immigration to the U.S.

At this time a number of bills have been presented, quite possibly because of the conditions abroad. Certainly to the alien these conditions cannot be attributed, because for the most part these aliens who have come to the United Sates, whether they are here legally or not, have sought to escape those conditions, have sought asylum in the only country in the world where asylum was possible. But suddenly the entire picture is changed. We are determined to put the alien in a separate class apart from the body politic; to point him out as one who is not a citizen.[119]

In an attempt to defend aliens arriving without a proper visa, Perlman used some of the well-known liberal arguments for keeping the gates open amidst adverse circumstances:

Failure of citizenship may be an accident, due to chance, due to failure to come here properly; and I think an alien who comes to the United States without a visa illegally is to be commended for his feelings, is to be commended for his faith and his hope in this country, because that alien that has sought asylum in the United States, for the most part, is seeking relief from conditions over which he has no control, and over conditions oppressing to him in the country of his birth. Those aliens, I say, are to be commended, although they are criminals in the United States, because they know that for centuries this wonderful land of ours has been an asylum, a place where a man can seek his own place in the universe, without fear of religion, social standing, or economic beliefs.[120]

Though defending the bill under consideration, the Chair of the session commented favorably on the contribution of Hungarians to the United States. "I think we are wholly cognizant of the contribution citizens of your country, that is, the country for which you speak, have made;

---

[119] "Statement of Louis Perlman, representing the Hungarian Societies Central Committee, New York, NY" House Report 3, Supervision and Detention of Certain Aliens, Hearings before Subcommittee No. 2 of the Committee on the Judiciary, House of Representatives, 77th Congress, 1st Session, Serial No. 2, Part II (Washington: U.S. Government Printing Office, 1941), pp. 161–162; Library of Congress: Law Library, RR (77) H 929-7, Published Hearing, 77th Congress, Senate Library, Vol. 929, 1941.

[120] *Ibid.*

we appreciate the contribution which Hungarians have made time and again to the building of our American civilization [...]"[121]

Despite continually shifting U.S. immigration policies, intolerable political and social conditions exerted such an influence that many of Hungary's talented and ambitious people were forced to find creative ways of doing battle with these changing and uncertain policies for the sake of their personal survival. Despite the numerous difficulties associated with immigrating into the U.S. and recording exact figures, by the end of 1941, an estimated group of up to 12–15,000 Hungarian interwar immigrants could have claimed the U.S. as their home. In many cases, separation from the motherland resulted in painful consequences. Many others, however, found ways to overcome the hardships of their alienation from Hungarian culture and contributed to American society in numerous valuable and creative ways. Though often first received begrudgingly in the New Land, the American soil eventually proved fertile for thousands of Hungarian-Americans before World War II. Their contributions were ultimately acknowledged, and often deeply valued, by American society.

2 New York: City of Immigrants

New Identity in an Alien World

"'Everything is larger, wider, more powerful and vivacious here,' I thought when we walked through the streets of Manhattan. London, Paris, Berlin, each one had its special charm, but New York with its skyscrapers, with its millions of lights when evening came, made an overwhelming impression on us newcomers."[122] German author Marta Appel captured the typical immigrant's first impressions upon arrival in New York. German architect

---

121 *Ibid.*
122 Marta Appel, "The Sight of New York," unpublished manuscript in the Memoir Collection of the Leo Baeck Institute, New York, published by Mark M. Anderson,

Erich Mendelsohn was completely overwhelmed by his first experiences there in the mid-1920s: "Quick drive-in, turns, curves, space cataract, space battle, unending euphoria of victory."[123] For him, Manhattan represented the "harbor of the world, messenger of the new land, of freedom and of the unmeasurable wealth behind it, of the most adventurous exploitation, of the golddiggers and of world conquest."[124] This was what most Europeans felt upon arrival. They shared Edith Wharton's vision of "the huge menacing mass" of the city with its "soulless roar," "its devouring blaze of lights, the oppression of its congested traffic, congested houses, lives, minds..."[125] Erich Mendelsohn was impressed by the sudden growth of the City, "Driven by unforeseen accumulation of money, (and) exploded in an unparalleled short time from an immigrant harbor to the business center of the world."[126] For émigré Hertha Nathorff, the cheerful people in Central Park and the charm of the Park itself conveyed the sense of freedom. She described

> how beautiful the park is [...] It is bitter cold and the people we meet have red, friendly, laughing faces. Joyful, laughing people—how long have we not seen such a sight! [...] How fascinating this city is, how immense, how beautiful. Will the city give us work and food? Early tomorrow morning I will start looking. I want to earn a new homeland for myself.[127]

---

ed., *Hitler's Exiles. Personal Stories of the Flight from Nazi Germany to America* (New York: The New Press, 1998), p. 207.
123 Erich Mendelsohn, *Amerika. Bilderbuch eines Architekten* (Berlin: Rudolf Mosse Buchverlag, 1926), p. 21.
124 Erich Mendelsohn, *op. cit.*, p. 1.
125 Edith Wharton, "Autre temps...," "Pomegranate Seed," in *The New York Stories of Edith Wharton*, selected by Roxana Robinson (New York: New York Review Books, 2007), pp. 291, 404.
126 Erich Mendelsohn, *op.cit.*, p. VI.
127 Hertha Nathorff, "Arriving in New York," *Das Tagebuch der Hertha Nathorff*, German ed. by Wolfgang Benz (München: Oldenbourg Verlag, 1987), for an English version see Mark M. Anderson, ed., *op. cit.*, p. 216.

Figure 11. New York, 1933 (Photo John Albók)
(HNM—with the kind permission of Ms. Ilona Albók Vitarius).

She also quickly noticed

> How hectic life is in this country. There's not even enough time to admire all the beautiful things in this fascinating city. The technology, the tall buildings, the bridges, tunnels, subway—I'm constantly amazed, but where is the time to take it all in? To go to a museum or, a special treat, to a movie or a concert—who has the time and the money?[128]

It soon became evident that immigrants were left to themselves socially. Most immigrants wanted to become "a part of the American people," and they recognized that "without knowing the language we should always be strangers."[129] Accordingly, Nathorff remarked,

> [o]ur social circle here is composed almost entirely of immigrants, almost all of them people we knew earlier and who represent a piece of our homeland as we do to them. ... We remain faithful friends and try to give each other support. But the uncried tears can be heard in our voices when we speak about the old country.[130]

Most émigrés were confined in their own social circles. Even Thomas Mann complained upon arrival in New York in September 1938 that his English was "still too weak and poor"[131] and his social life was confined to the narrow circle of fellow German immigrants. He found the Americans quite empty and full of cliches, though he was full of appreciation and gratitude. "[...] in sociable concourse with the [Bruno] Franks, [Franz] Werfels, [Wilhelm] Dieterles, [Alfred] Neumanns—always the same faces, and if occasionally an American countenance appears, it is as a rule

---

128 Hertha Nathorff, *op. cit.*, p. 219.
129 Marta Appel, *op. cit.*, p. 208.
130 Hertha Nathorff, *op. cit.*, p. 220.
131 Save Czechoslovakia. Addresses delivered by Dorothy Thompson and Thomas Mann ... at the Save Czechoslovakia Meeting at Madison Square Garden, September 25, 1938. New York, Save Czechoslovakia Committee, [1938]. p. 7. Carnegie Endowment for International Peace, Columbia University, Rare Book and Manuscript Library, Committee to Aid Czechoslovakia, Box 288, Folder 5, 102514.

so strangely blank and amiably stereotyped that one has had enough for quite some time to come."[132]

By the same token, Béla Bartók surrounded himself with fellow Hungarians in New York. When he arrived in there he was readily received by (Jewish-) Hungarian friends such as dermatology professor István Rothman, Dr. Gyula Báron, Dr. Peter Flesch[133] and István Sichermann, mostly medical doctors.[134]

With great sensitivity and a sense of irony, Hannah Arendt described the quick identity changes immigrants were to go through in an effort to become part of their new home country.

> We were told to forget; and we forgot quicker than anybody ever could imagine. In a friendly way we were reminded that the new country would become a new home; and after four weeks in France or six weeks in America, we pretended to be Frenchmen or Americans. [...] After a single year optimists are convinced they speak English as well as their mother tongue; and after two years they swear solemnly that they speak English better than any other language [...].[135]

Arendt made fun of the overzealous German-Jewish immigrant who professed himself or herself to be the patriotic son or daughter of any country he/she was able or forced to enter.

> Mr. Cohn from Berlin who had always been a 150 percent German, a German superpatriot [...] in 1933 [...] found refuge in Prague and very quickly became a convinced Czech patriot—as true and as loyal a Czech patriot as he had been a German one. [...] About 1937 [...] Mr. Cohn [...] went to Vienna; to adjust oneself there a definite Austrian patriotism was required. The German invasion forced Mr.

---

132   Thomas Mann to Bruno Walter, Pacific Palisades, May 6, 1943. *Letters of Thomas Mann, 1889–1955*. Selected and translated by Richard and Clara Winston (Berkeley—Los Angeles: University of California Press, 1975), p. 315.
133   Peter Flesch (1915–1969) became an eminent research professor of dermatology at the University of Pennsylvania.
134   Peter Flesch to his parents in Budapest, November 25, 1941, received on October 19, 1946, author's collection.
135   Hannah Arendt, "We Refugees," *The Menorah Journal,* January 1943, repr. in Mark M. Anderson, ed., *op. cit.,* p. 254. On Arendt and her "statelessness" see Linda K. Kerber, "Toward a History of Statelessness in America,"*op. cit.,* pp. 727–749.

Figure 12. Béla Bartók, composer, 1938 (HNM).

Figure 13. Peter Flesch, research dermatologist, on *Medical Science*, 1958.

Cohn out of that country. He arrived in Paris [...] and [...] prepared his adjustment to the French nation by identifying himself with "our" ancestor Vercingetorix. [...] As long as Mr. Cohn can't make up his mind to be what he actually is, a Jew, nobody can foretell all the mad changes he will still have to go through.[136]

It is important to recognize that New York was a society of transients for more than half a century: in 1910, 40% of the City's residents were immigrants and until World War II, the City was "full of single men and women who had left their families in Europe or the American South [...]."[137] This also led to a relatively open gay life in several parts of the City such as the Bowery, Times Square and the waterfront.

Anti-Foreignism and Anti-Semitism in New York

Despite the heady climate of creativity, New York's existing dense foreign-born population and high unemployment rate, along with its heavy concentration of new refugees added to the city's serious social problems. In 1922, critic James L. Ford in the New York *Tribune* spoke of "an enormous element in its population [that] is of alien birth."[138] From quite early on, the Lower East Side became a particularly cosmopolitan community with almost every conceivable East European ethnic enclave in it, side by side.

Though many would have agreed with John Dos Passos, who in 1933 thought that "[...] this town's a hard nut to crack,"[139] newcomers of both Jewish and non-Jewish origin had a tendency to stay in New York City. Though different sources give slightly different and contradictory numbers, the tendency seems to have been stable. In April 1934, 1,086

---

136   Hannah Arendt, *op. cit.*, p. 259.
137   George Chauncey, *Gay New York: Gender, Urban Culture, and the Making of the Gay Male World 1890–1940* (BasicBooks, 1994), p. 11.
138   Quoted by Angela M. Blake, *How New York Became American, 1890–1924* (Baltimore: The Johns Hopkins University Press, 2006), p. 139.
139   John Dos Passos, *The Big Money*. In John Dos Passos, *U.S.A.* (New York: The Library of America, 1996), p. 818.

of the city's 2,378 new residents of German ethnicity remained in New York State. Of the total of 2,194 persons belonging to the "Hebrew race," coming from quotas of many countries including Germany, 1,338 remained in New York State, with the balance going to other states.[140]

In 1934, an estimated 1,000–1,500 refugees lived in Greater New York. "About 3,500 German emigrants have entered the country since July 1st, 1933. Since 1,500 would have normally entered as immigrants, it is estimated that 2,000 entered as a result of State Department action in letting down the bars to take care of the German situation. [...] at least 500 left New York City for other points, leaving a possible 1,500 still in New York City."[141] In July 1934, the Committee for Aid to Refugees and Emigrants Coming from Germany estimated the number of German refugees in New York City somewhere between 2,000 and 4,000. "150 have come to organized agencies."[142] By early February 1935 most of the 300 medical doctors admitted to the U.S., happened to be found largely in the State of New York.[143]

---

140 Cecilia Razovsky Davidson, "Report of Situation of German Refugees in the United States," April 18, 1934, Columbia University, Rare Book and Manuscript Library, Herbert H. Lehman Suite and Papers, James G. McDonald Papers, National Coordinating Committee, Cecilia Razovsky File, D356 H21.
141 Cecilia Razovsky, Minutes, Meeting of Executive Committee of National Coordinating Committee for Aid to Refugees and Emigrants Coming from Germany, New York, June 29, 1934, Columbia University, Rare Book and Manuscript Library, Herbert H. Lehman Suite and Papers, James G. McDonald Papers, National Coordinating Committee, Cecilia Razovsky File, D356 H21.
142 Minutes, Board Meeting, Committee for Aid to Refugees and Emigrants Coming from Germany, New York, July 23, 1934, Columbia University, Rare Book and Manuscript Library, Herbert H. Lehman Suite and Papers, James G. McDonald Papers, National Coordinating Committee, Cecilia Razovsky File, D356 H21.
143 Walter M. Kotschnig to Dr. Samuel Guy Inman, February 21, 1935, Columbia University, Rare Book and Manuscript Library, Herbert H. Lehman Suite and Papers, James G. McDonald Papers, Walter M. Kotschnig File, 1935—April 1936, D356 H20.

The agencies were at first optimistic about the situation.

> It is in New York City where large numbers are now living that the question of unemployment is likely to be a difficult one to solve. However, at a meeting called by a committee of German Jewish refugees recently it was stated that of the total number in New York City of which the group was aware one-third is being well cared for by its relative, another third brought with them sufficient funds to enable them to manage until they can find positions. About 36 newcomers are in need of immediate guidance and help to enable them to carry on. In view of the desperate unemployment situation here this is certainly a very hopeful record.[144]

In Spring 1934, it seemed that immigration was a gradual and manageable process. Interested social agencies were of the opinion that this process was successful because the tide of immigration had been coming in slowly and not in such vast numbers so as "to swamp the relatives and agencies interested in this problem."[145]

That Europeans were anxious to remain in New York was quite natural. The desire of the French group of the New School appointees "was prompted chiefly by the 'European atmosphere' which they find there; by the fact that most of their European refugee friends are in New York; and they consequently feel less 'expatriated' here than they think they would in any other part of the U.S."[146] There was also another reason for their willingness to stay: in New York scholars had opportunities to augment their rather meagre New School salary which they would not have elsewhere. "I had always thought these men *would* earn some money by writing articles for reviews; but I had not suspected that they would in some cases more than double their salaries by 'consultations.'"[147]

Soon, however, American institutions dealing with the refugee problem became worried about the number of Jewish professionals staying in

---

144 Cecilia Razovsky Davidson, "Report of Situation of German Refugees in the United States," April 18, 1934, *loc. cit.*
145 *Ibid.*
146 A[...] B[...] to T. B. Appleget, New York, October 24, 1941, Rockefeller Archive Center, Rockefeller Foundation Archives, RG 1.1, Series 200, Box 47, Folder 537.
147 A[...] B[...] to T. B. Appleget, New York, October 24, 1941, *loc. cit.*

New York. By the end of 1934, at a meeting of the Board of Directors of the National Coordinating Committee, it was

> reported that Prof. Chamberlain and Mr. Sulzberger together wrote a letter to cities throughout the country asking them to form local committees to assist refugees in their own cities and to take over some of the refugees from New York City. [...] Prof. Chamberlain felt that if Miss Razovsky could go in the field and take with her lists of refugees with data about them, he feels certain that some of the people from New York could be sent inland.[148]

It also became evident that "[...] New York is the only state which gives an endorsed license to practise in the state but does not give the applicant a right to expect any reciprocity from other states, the majority of the doctors have settled here and there has been some complaint from the American doctors."[149]

Jewish agencies were some of the first to realize the danger of a concentration of Jewish professionals in New York City. The *Hilfsverein der Juden in Deutschland E. V.* admitted in late 1935 that "it's not viable that all immigrant doctors remain concentrated in N.Y. We do our best to draw their attention to this fact and try to derail those interested from N.Y."[150]

As soon as they started to arrive in larger numbers, it was recognized that refugee Europeans became an increasingly serious challenge to the City. Jacob Billikopf of the National Coordinating Committee for Aid to Refugees reported of his difficulties in finding jobs for the refugees as early as 1937:

---

148 Cecilia Razovsky, Minutes of Meeting of Board of Directors of the National Coordinating Committee, New York, December 31, 1934, Columbia University, Rare Book and Manuscript Library, Herbert H. Lehman Suite and Papers, James G. McDonald Papers, National Coordinating Committee, Cecilia Razovsky File, D356 H21, p. 4.
149 Cecilia Razovsky, Minutes, *loc. cit.*, pp. 3–4.
150 Hilfsverein der Juden in Deutschland E. V. to the Emergency Committee In Aid of Deplaced [sic] Foreign Physicians, Berlin, November 21, 1935, Rockefeller Archive Center, Alfred E. Cohn Papers, RG 450 C661-U, Box 13, Folder 31.

> We have been cooperating [...] vigorously with the Employment Bureau of the Greater New York Committee, in finding jobs for people who do not wish to leave New York. In the case of at least half a dozen department stores, I have spoken personally to chief executives seeking their cooperation with the Employment Bureau. There are refugees in whose behalf we have spoken to perhaps a dozen persons and written any number of letters. When we find that applicant wishing to leave the City could not, for one reason or another, be recommended for out of town placement, we try, in cooperation with the Employment Bureau, to make suitable provision for him in New York.[151]

Later that same year, Jacob Billikopf complained that "[...] the Greater New York Committee [...] after all is called upon to bear the brunt of the problem."[152] "At least 25 or 30 individuals or families," he added, "for whom placements had been obtained, refused at the last moment, to leave the City."[153]

By the next year, signs of a "congestion of the refugees" were obvious. In August 1938, the Rockefeller Foundation found it mandatory that refugees be transferred from New York to elsewhere throughout the United States. This was recognized by the Jewish community in the U.S. as a major issue of concern. An invitation to a meeting on September 17, 1938 suggested that it will "represent an historical moment in the life of American Jewry...".[154]

> The Resettlement Division of the National Coordinating Committee has during the past three months reorganized its program and its organizational structure in order to make possible and easier, and in terms of number, a more significant transfer of refugees from the port of entry, New York City, to other sections and

---

151 Jacob Billikopf to Joseph P. Chamberlain, New York, May 6, 1937, attached to Jacob Billikopf to John Whyte, June 9, 1937, Rockefeller Archive Center, Alfred E. Cohn Papers, RG 450, C661-U, Box 2, Folder 7.
152 Jacob Billikopf, National Coordinating Committee, to William Rosenwald, New York City, December 1, 1937, Rockefeller Archive Center, Alfred E. Cohn Papers, RG 450, C661-U, Box 5, Folder 5.
153 Jacob Billikopf to Joseph P. Chamberlain, New York City, May 6, 1937, *loc. cit.*, Box 5, Folder 5.
154 William Rosenwald to Dr. Alfred Cohn, August 25, 1938, Rockefeller Archive Center, Alfred E. Cohn Papers, RG 450 C661-U, Box 13, Folder 35.

communities of the United States. During the past year a number of events occurred which have made us realize that the congestion of the refugees in New York City cannot be permitted to continue. It is absolutely necessary in the interests of the refugee and the good repute and security of American Jewry that this problem be handled on a sound and effective basis.[155]

The Rockefeller Foundation keenly felt the pressure of this congestion in New York City and in 1941 spoke out against the "high concentration of refugees in the metropolitan area."[156]

The deposed scholars who reach America from the terrorized lands of Europe have a tendency to remain in New York. That is usually the port of arrival, there they find other refugees with whom to talk over experiences, and the hospitality of the New School for Social Research and other New York institutions naturally attracts them. Some—specialists in economics, politics, engineering, and other techniques—have found opportunities in New York to pick up an occasional fee as consultants to corporations with business interests in the war zones, or as sources of information to writers on foreign affairs. The resultant of these influences has been a high concentration of refugees in the metropolitan area.[157]

The Emergency Committee in Aid of Deposed Scholars doubted in 1941 "if this concentration was a healthy condition."[158] They felt that a wider distribution was desirable, both for the refugees and for the country.

If these eminent persons who are Hitler's loss are in fact our gain, they ought to be shared. Institutions all over America ought to know about them and have the opportunity to make use of their services. Especially, if regard is to be given the future of these uprooted humans, there should be an effort to settle them as soon as possible in permanent positions.

155 Ibid.
156 Resettling the Refugee Scholars. Excerpt from Trustees' Confidential Monthly Report, October 1, 1941, Rockefeller Archive Center, Rockefeller Foundation Archives, RG 1.1, Series 200, Box 47, Folder 538.
157 Resettling the Refugee Scholars, *loc. cit.*
158 Ibid.

During the past year a $10,000 grant from the [Rockefeller] Foundation enabled the Committee to engage the full-time services of Dr. Laurens H. Seelye as executive officer. His special assignment has been to travel over the United States, visit colleges and universities, and feel out the opportunities that may exist for the placement of refugee scholars.[159]

By 1942, the National Committee for Resettlement of Foreign Physicians entered into a press campaign to stop current opinion from resenting the émigré physician. Early that year, *The New York Times* was full of articles about easing the rules for alien doctors, sometimes joined by similar articles in the *Philadelphia Bulletin* and the *Boston Herald*.[160]

The Rockefeller Foundation, however, still found it natural that refugee scholars concentrated

in urban centers near the Coasts. Most of the private institutions are in these areas, as well as most organizations aiding refugees. This concentration would seem to be likely since many of the state institutions would have difficulties in providing salaries from state funds. It is also true that people near the ports of entry hear more about the landings and the needs of aliens.[161]

Circulated around the Foundation was a memo that acknowledged and appreciated the fact that

the coastal institutions from New England to Washington have tried to place a reasonable number of aliens in their research programs when they could not do it in their teaching programs. These groups would be stranded if there were a blanket order to evacuate aliens within one hundred miles or so of the coast, since Harvard, Yale, Columbia, New York University, the New School, among the large institutions and smaller places like Haverford, Swarthmore, and Bryn Mawr, have been active in giving a chance to displaced scholars. A similar situation must prevail on

---

159 *Ibid.*
160 *The New York Times*, January 31, February 7 and 21, 1942, *Philadelphia Bulletin*, January 22, 1942, *Boston Herald*, January 25, 1942.
161 AB to RFE, February 26, 1942, Rockefeller Archive Center, Rockefeller Foundation Archives, RG 1.1, Series 200, Box 47, Folder 540.

the Pacific Coast, at Stanford and California, to say nothing of the Food Research Institute and the Hoover and Huntington Libraries.[162]

As time went by, the concentration of foreign-born professionals became a major social and political issue, keenly felt in both the City and the State of New York. By the end of 1943, it was feared that there will be "a preponderance of Jewish physicians" in the metropolitan area as well as in New York State. There was a real danger that the negative image of Jewish professional immigrants in New York City would spread all over the country. As a Report of the Executive Director to the Executive Committee of the National Refugee Service pointed out in mid-December 1943, there are "about 6,200 refugee physicians in the United States" and it was estimated that "over 4,000 of the group will be licensed in New York State. [...] Over two thousand will probably be in practice in New York City." As the report warned,

> Normally there were 7,300 Jewish physicians in New York City out of a total of 18,000. The licensing of refugees may thus increase the number of Jewish physicians in the city by 50 percent. After the war this proportion will be further increased because during the present emergency, due to wartime exigencies, many medical schools have relaxed their "quota" restrictions with regard to the admission of Jewish students.
>
> There is already a great deal of evidence to indicate the growing resentment among native American physicians, e.g., the New York County Medical Society is considering a plan for non-voting "Associate Membership" for all new members. (Since over 90 percent of the new members are emigre physicians, it is logical to assume that this measure is directed at them.)[163]

A 1943 report of the National Committee for Resettlement of Foreign Physicians spoke in grave terms of the danger of prejudice against émigré

---

162 AB to RFE, February 26, 1942, *loc. cit.*
163 Harry D. Biele, Report of the Executive Director to the Executive Committee, December 17, 1943, attached to a letter by Harry D. Biele, National Committee for Resettlement of Foreign Physicians, to Dr. Alfred Cohn, New York City, December 22, 1943, Rockefeller Archive Center, Alfred E. Cohn Papers, RG 450 C661-U, Box 13, Folder 41.

(meaning mostly Jewish) doctors, "the current wave of hostile propaganda and of activities antagonistic to refugee physicians." Harry D. Biele, Secretary of the National Committee added that "the Jewish community and American Jewish physicians have in some cases unfortunately given countenance and support." As a result, Biele pointed out, the Committee will continue to have an unusual measure of responsibility for refugee doctors even after their term of five years residence.[164]

Intellectual New York

German architect Erich Mendelsohn repeatedly spoke of the "wild growth" of the City and the country, and saw it as the "financial overlord of the world" yet spoke of its "worldly power combined with a poverty of the mind."[165] For him the Woolworth Building was a "romantic combination [...] great and grotesque at the same time. The tragic expression of today's America."[166]

By the late 1920s, New York artists continued to draw upon elements of, but no longer imitated, European modernism. Jazz Age New York art, however, "included only Americans of European descent," suggest cultural historians William B. Scott and Peter M. Rutkoff.[167] "New York is something which Europe is not," wrote Charles Demuth from Paris in 1921 to Alfred Stieglitz, "All the others, those who count, say that all the 'modern' is to us [sic] and of course, they are right. [...] Together we will add to the American Scene, more than has been added since the 60s and 70s—maybe more than they added."[168] In all spheres of art, New York

---

164 Harry D. Biele, Report of the Executive Director to the Executive Committee, December 17, 1943, *loc. cit.*
165 Erich Mendelsohn, *op. cit.*, pp. VI, 49–50, 30–31.
166 *Ibid.*, p. 32.
167 William B. Scott and Peter M. Rutkoff, *op. cit.*, p. 103.
168 Demuth to Stieglitz, November 28, 1921, Stieglitz Papers. Quoted by William B. Scott and Peter M. Rutkoff, *New York Modern: The Arts and the City* (Baltimore and London: The Johns Hopkins University Press, 1999), p. 112.

Modern made use of European traditions which it blended with the American idiom. For Erich Mendelsohn, "[w]hat we nowadays generally call 'typical American,' is actually a distorted image of the European mothercountries of America. From the left-over objects they have brought along, Americans have created wild symbols of the 'elevated civilisation,' made it 'gigantic' as Money Center or World Center, overdone into Grotesque, only to reach the point through a brave step, of creating 'the new, the upcoming.'"[169]

In the long decades from the 1920s through the 1960s, the City was drastically transformed and modernized by master builder Robert Moses who, in the words of Kenneth T. Jackson, "adapted New York City to the twentieth century."[170] The City not only welcomed modernism, it became synonymous with it. Thus, the artistic sensibilities of Europe, the struggle of New York's talented and displaced new citizens to reformulate their identity, and the energetic *zeitgeist* of the new American century, combined to mold New York City into the world's quintessential 20th century city.

As Thomas Bender clearly put it, the 1930s were "a political decade" that saw the "translation of New York City from province to international metropolis."[171] Literary modernism, and perhaps modernism as such, had to be imported from Europe: the *Partisan Review* in the 1930s proved to be "a provincial importer of European literary modernism."[172] In his Nobel Prize acceptance address of 1930, Sinclair Lewis, the first American author ever awarded with the Prize spoke of "the stuffiness of safe, sane, and incredibly dull provicialism" from which, he hoped,

---

169 Erich Mendelsohn, *op. cit.*, p. IX.
170 Kenneth T. Jackson, quoted by http://c250.columbia.edu/c250_celebrates/remarkable_columbians/robert_moses.html; Robert A. Caro, *The Power Broker: Robert Moses and the Fall of New York* (New York: Knopf, 1974); Kenneth T. Jackson and Hillary Ballon, eds., *Robert Moses and the Modern City: The Transformation of New York* (New York: W. W. Norton, 2007).
171 Thomas Bender, *New York Intellect: A History of Intellectual Life in New York City, from 1750 to the Beginning of Our Own Time* (New York: Alfred A. Knopf, 1987), p. 321.
172 Thomas Bender, *op. cit.*, p. 321.

"we are coming out."[173] "Political 'New York Intellectuals' represented a collaboration of WASPs[174] and upwardly mobile Eastern European Jews who united under the aegis of the cosmopolitan ideal, the art-oriented group (Uptown Bohemia) consisted of rich WASPs and wealthy German Jews, wrote social and cultural historian Thomas Bender.[175] The universities, such as the NYU, the New School and Columbia University (where Lionel Trilling taught modern literature) served as centers for teaching modernism.[176] New York was the place to assimilate the culture of Paris [...]"[177] The decade is justly considered by cultural historians as the era of cultural relativism,[178] cultural reorientation.[179]

Interwar American intellectual and, particularly, literary life mostly centered around New York, with paradoxical features such as alienation and consumerism, communal solidarity and self-expression, cosmopolitanism and parochialism.[180] The world of letters, concluded intellectual historian Lewis Perry, "suspended its belief in a unitary culture that required either the 'Americanization' or the exclusion of foreigners."[181] German Jews were joined by East European Jews after World War I, and dominated the literary scene of the City, paving the way to "modernism in art and left-liberal views in politics."[182] Also, many Southerners and Midwesterners returned to New York after a spell in Europe, as described by Malcolm Cowley in his *Exile's Return* (1934).[183] New York intellectuals,

---

173 Sinclair Lewis, "The American Fear of Literature," Nobel Address, December 10, 1930, in Daniel J. Boorstin, ed., *An American Primer* (New York: Mentor, 1968), p. 860.
174 WASP = White Anglo-Saxon Protestant.
175 Thomas Bender, *op. cit.*, p. 325.
176 *Ibid.*, pp. 330–2.
177 *Ibid.*, p. 335.
178 Lewis Perry, *Intellectual Life in America: A History* (Chicago and London: The University of Chicago Press, 1989), p. 319.
179 Thomas Bender, *op. cit.*, pp. 324, 328.
180 Lewis Perry, *op. cit.*, p. 330–334.
181 *Ibid.*, p. 334.
182 *Ibid.*, p. 335.
183 Lewis Perry, *op. cit.*, pp. 327–330, 334–336, 338–339.

particularly the WASPs were always joined by migrants from other parts of the country, such as the Midwest, New England and the South.

The intellectuals of New York City represented a mixture of European radicalism, Jewish orthodoxy, and a love-hate relationship with the Soviet type of socialism. The American Left was still hopeful of "changing the capitalist world by next day," a characteristic Communist slogan of the day. The intellectual mood of the 1930s was tinged by clashes between Stalinist and anti-Stalinist Marxists and socialists, as well as by the rise of an élite of social and literary critics who tried to look beyond the brand of social democracy that the New Deal offered.[184] In his *New York Intellect,* Thomas Bender spoke about the "two worlds of art and intellect"[185] and suggested that the new, interwar culture of the City was the result of modernism in the arts, liberal politics, and moral intensity.[186] For Bender, the expansive development schemes of New York Mayor Fiorello LaGuardia were "distinctively American and aggressively democratic."[187] For LaGuardia's generation, the Works Progress Administration (WPA)[188] of President Franklin D. Roosevelt was also the defining experience in the area of culture. *The WPA Guide to New York City* of 1939,[189] the Federal Writers' Project Guide to 1930s New York, testified to "that ceaseless change, the cycle of decay and renewal, the leapfrogging vagaries of fashion," "the striking extremes, the best and the worst of it."[190] As William H. Whyte put it in his introduction to the recent, new edition of the *WPA Guide,* "New York had always been the nation's cultural capital,"[191] though it expanded

---

184 Neil Jumonville, *Critical Crossings: The New York Intellectuals in Postwar America* (Berkeley—Los Angeles—Oxford: University of California, Press, 1991), pp. 1–48.
185 Thomas Bender, *op. cit.,* p. 324.
186 *Ibid.,* pp. 322–323.
187 *Ibid.,* p. 332.
188 *Ibid.,* p. 332.
189 *The WPA Guide to New York City* (New York: Random House, 1939, repr., with an introduction by William H. Whyte, New York: The New Press, 1992).
190 William H. Whyte in *The WPA Guide to New York City, op. cit.,* p. xxi.
191 *Ibid.,* p. xxi.

really after World War II, "with the high spirits and strengthened economy of victory."[192]

A significant part of New York Modern emerged from recently arriving European modernism. "Expatriation began to run in a new direction: instead of Americans taking off to Europe, Europeans were finding refuge here. The 'cosmopolitan culture' of America became a matter of intense, frequently articulated pride."[193] The artistic communities of the city became ethnically diverse as the city itself diversified in the interwar years. The public and artistic worlds affected each other. New York and New York Modern established their respective public identities between the two world wars.[194] In the New York of the 1940s, the children of typically poor immigrants got to college, often the free City College, and that made them upwardly mobile, entering not only the traditional professions but also the intellectual and artistic world of the City.[195] After World War I American artists made their almost "obligatory pilgrimage" to Paris. William Carlos Williams "visited the American expatriates on the Left Bank, who gathered at Sylvia Beach's Shakespeare and Company, drank tea with Gertrude Stein and Alice Toklas, conversed with James Joyce, heard Igor Stravinsky," only to find out that Paris was "dead, dead, dead" and that "the time drift favors America."[196] New York's up and coming composers such as Aaron Copland, Roy Harris, Walter Piston, and Virgil Thomson left for Paris after World War I to study with Nadia Boulanger at the newly established *Conservatoire Americain* in Fontainebleau. When they returned to New York they found themselves out of the musical establishment and decided to form their own organizations in an effort to modernize concert music in the City. They began composing modern American music incorporating both European

---

192   *Ibid.*, p. xxi.
193   Lewis Perry, *Intellectual Life in America: A History* (Chicago and London: The University of Chicago Press, 1989), pp. 335–336.
194   William B. Scott and Peter M. Rutkoff, *New York Modern: The Arts and the City* (Baltimore and London: The Johns Hopkins University Press, 1999), pp. xvii, xix.
195   Personal communication from Prof. Thomas Bender, May 3, 2008.
196   William B. Scott and Peter M. Rutkoff, *op. cit.*, p. 102.

modernism and the American folk heritage.[197] Soon, American visual artists also discovered New York and, building on elements of European modernism and American realism, they created the city "as the embodiment of all things modern."[198]

Visiting European artists saw the City in the mid-1920s as a place where "the whirlpool rebounds and crescends from a cry for wealth and power into a cry of victory over old Mother Europe and (over) the whole world."[199]

Hungarian Immigrants in the City: Jews and Gentiles

In this rapidly modernizing and increasingly intellectual city, most immigrants from Central Europe—German, Jewish, and Austro-Hungarian—continued to live their traditional lives and maintain a conservative lifestyle. We need to go back to the late 19th century to review population growth in the City.

To a significant extent Central-European immigrants contributed in the late 19th century to an odd, small town quality of the City's social composition. The great influx of "Italians, Russians, Rumanians, Hungarians, Slovaks, Greeks, Poles, and Turks" into the Lower East Side began in 1881.[200] German-speaking, mainly Jewish, immigrants were attracted to New York City's Washington Heights—Inwood area, particularly those who came from socially modest, religiously traditional, small town, Southern Germany. These groups came with conflicting German and Jewish identities, with those who settled in Washington Heights being proportionately more Jewish. Most of the settlement in this area of Northern Manhattan occurred during the peak of the Jewish flight from

---

197 *Ibid.*, p. 228.
198 *Ibid.*, p. 102.
199 Erich Mendelsohn, *op. cit.*, p. 28.
200 *The WPA Guide to New York City, op. cit.*, p. 109.

Nazi Germany, between 1937 and 1940.[201] Out of the 150,000 German-Jewish refugees from Nazi Germany, well over 20,000 people settled in Washington Heights making it the largest German-Jewish settlement in the world.[202] These German-Jewish immigrants communicated with each other nation wide, particularly through their German newspaper the *Aufbau* (Reconstruction). They maintained minimal relationships with non-German neighbors of their own generation, but their children, and particularly, grandchildren married Jewish men or women outside the German community, and increasingly outside of their faith. Upon leaving Nazi Germany, and especially after World War II, most of the German Jews lost their emotional connections with Germany and while maintaining their strong attachment to German culture, they increasingly identified themselves with America. Washington Heights stopped being essentially German Jewish after the first generation.[203]

From the late 19th century onwards, Hungarian-Americans also built up a visible presence in New York City, creating their own Hungarian-speaking environment, and a challenging ethnic network which in turn attracted newcomers from the Old Country as a special magnet. Newly-arrived Hungarians were attracted to a variety of "melting pots": recent immigrants were able to assimilate into the American nation as a whole, and also to the varied subgroups of their ethnic cohort, their coreligionists, and their professional groups.

"Little Hungary" started to emerge around 1890. The Hungarian community was small in the early 1900s as approximately 80% of immigrants from Hungary continued their journey on to other cities, as well as to mines, factories, and farms all over the country.[204] "[D]uring the three years ending June 30, 1903, only 19 per cent of the total were booked to

---

201 Steven Lowenstein, "Foreword," in: Gloria DeVidas Kirchheimer and Manfred Kirchheimer, *We Were So Beloved: An Autobiography of a German Jewish Community* (Pittsburgh: University of Pittsburgh Press, 1997), pp. ix–x.
202 Steven Lowenstein, "Foreword," op. cit., p. x.
203 *Ibid.*, pp. xi–xii.
204 Agnes Primes, "The Hungarians in New York; A study in immigrant cultural influences," M.A. Thesis, Columbia University, 1940, p. 24.

New York as compared with 36 per cent to Pennsylvania, 16 per cent to New Jersey and 15 per cent to Ohio," said Louis H. Pink in *Charities* in 1904.[205]

In the first half of the 20th century, New York was the biggest "Hungarian city" in the United States. Not only were there some 60–70,000 Hungarians in the greater metropolitan area, but a great number of Hungarians also lived in the neighboring cities of New Jersey, such as Trenton, Passaic, Perth Amboy, Newark, Bridgeport and New Brunswick. Cleveland, Ohio ranked second after New York, to be followed by Chicago.

Early in the century, most Hungarians in New York City settled in the Lower East Side of Manhattan, but rather than inhabiting large single blocks, they were dispersed throughout the area. In a pioneering 1904 article for *Charities*, Louis H. Pink defined the Hungarian area in the City by comparing it to the whole of Manhattan, "East Houston Street is the Broadway of the Hungarian Colony; Second Avenue is its Riverside Drive; Avenues A, B, and C are important centers of social and business activity."[206] There were some 50,000–60,000 Hungarians living in this area around 1904. According to the estimate of immigration inspector Marcus Braun, 75% of the Hungarian immigrants in the Lower East Side were Jewish.[207] Ilona Kovács provided a more detailed social geography of Manhattan Hungarians,[208] who were located primarily around the then-popular business area and cultural center of Houston Street, largely

---

205 Louis H. Pink, "The Magyar in New York," *Charities*, Vol. 13, No. 10, December 3, 1904, p. 262. Quoted by Agnes Primes, *op. cit.*, pp. 24–25.
206 Louis H. Pink, "The Magyar in New York," quoted by Agnes Primes, *op. cit.*, p. 25.
207 Agnes Primes, *op. cit.*, p. 25; cf. Tibor Frank, "'For the Information of the President': The US Government Surveillance of Austro-Hungarian Emigration (1891–1907)," *Hungarian Journal of English and American Studies*, Vol. 6, No. 2, Fall 2000, pp. 213–237, see esp. pp. 218–221.
208 Ilona Kovács, "New York magyarságának demográfiai átrendeződése a változó olvasói igény tükrében (1900–1940)" [Demographic trends of New York Hungarians as reflected in the circulation of libraries, 1900–1940], *Magyarságkutatás. A Magyarságkutató Intézet évkönyve* (Budapest, 1988), pp. 259–281.

between the 1st Street and the 10th Street around the First and Second Avenues, and they moved later along the same avenues further North toward Tomkins Square, and then to 55th and 72nd Street.[209] As Agnes Primes added in 1940, "at the present time... further up town Christians predominate."[210]

By the 1920s, Hungarians increasingly moved further North, into the Upper East Side, up to 60th Street and continuing on to 86th Street.[211] The "Magyar district," as Konrad Berkovici stated,

> [...] runs parallel with it [= the German quarter] of Second Avenue as its main street, from Ninth Street to Eighteenth and Nineteenth Streets, and then extending eastward, it sinks below the lower avenues A and B, and with few interruptions runs along in the same way to Sixtieth Street. There the Magyar district takes a jump of about ten or twelve blocks where the Czechoslovaks live. Skirting their territory, the Hungarian quarter continues from it to Eighty-sixth Street, always running parallel with the German district.[212]

209 Zoltán Biró, *Amerika. Magyarok a modern csodák világában* [America: Hungarians in the world of modern miracles] (Budapest: Novák, 1929), p. 99. Biró gave the strongly overdone estimate of 200,000 as the number of New York Hungarians.
210 Agnes Primes, *op. cit.,* p. 25.
211 "A magyarság mai elhelyezkedése," in: Sándor Incze, *Magyar album* [Hungarian Album] (Elmhurst, IL: American Hungarian Studies Foundation, 1956), p. 23; Zoltán Fejős, *A chicagói magyarok két nemzedéke 1890–1940* [Two Generations of Chicago Hungarians] (Budapest: Közép-Európa Intézet, 1993), p. 27–29; Géza Hoffmann, *Csonka munkásosztály. Az amerikai magyarság* [Rump working class. The Hungarian Americans] (Budapest: Magyar Közgazdasági Társaság, 1911), p. 374; Ilona Kovács, *Az amerikai közkönyvtárak magyar gyűjteményeinek szerepe az asszimiláció és az identitás megőrzésének kettős folyamatában 1890–1940* [The role of the Hungarian collections of American public libraries in the double process of assimilation and identity preservation 1890–1940] (Budapest: Országos Széchényi Könyvtár, 1997), pp. 65–67.
212 Konrad Bercovici, *Around the World in New York* (New York: Century Company, 1924), p. 346.

When life in Yorkville[213] became too expensive in the mid 1910s, Hungarians began to move to the Bronx, Astoria and Queens. In the 1920s, there were some 13,190 Hungarians in the Bronx whose mother tongue was Hungarian, more than half of whom were born in Hungary.

Population statistics tell us that the Hungarian-born group in New York rose from 16,857 in 1890 to a relatively stable 123,175 by 1920.[214] According to a 1910 statistics, most (70%) of the Hungarian immigrants were Jewish, 20% Catholic, and 10% Protestant.[215] Immigrant Hungarian Jews differed from other Jews in many ways and lived near fellow Hungarian immigrants of Gentile origins. Konrad Berkovici noted in the mid-1920s that

> There are a great number of Jews of Hungarian origin living in this city, and most of them live in the Hungarian district among their Christian brethren. The Hungarian Jews, though there are among them some who are strictly orthodox, are much more liberal than the Jews of other nations. There have been mixed marriages in Hungary for the last hundred years. Even the type of the Hungarian Jews is totally different from the type of any other Jews. Neither do they speak Yiddish, the language spoken by almost all the Jews except the Spanish ones. The Hungarian Jews here have their separate synagogues, not because their rites of worship are very different from the others, but because of their clannishness, and because of their feeling of superiority, by reason of the fact that they had political equality in Hungary long before the Jews of other countries where so privileged.[216]

As a result, émigré middle class Hungarians, particularly the distinguished scientists among them, demonstrated a particularly Hungarian brand of Jewishness or, much rather, the lack of it.[217]

---

213 Yorkville is a neighborhood in the Upper East Side of Manhattan in New York City.
214 Ira Rosenwaike, *Population History of New York City* (Siracuse: University Press, 1972), pp. 202–204.
215 Ira Rosenwaike, *op. cit.,* p. 123.
216 Konrad Bercovici, *op. cit.,* pp. 360–361.
217 István Hargittai, *The Martians of Science: Five Physicists Who Changed the Twentieth Century* (Oxford—New York: Oxford University Press, 2006), pp. 225–227.

Figure 14. Demonstration against the Horthy Regime, New York, 1919 (HNM).

As early as 1904, Louis H. Pink recognized quite a few professionals among new arrivals and the American-born second generation.[218] In the interwar years, the Hungarian middle class of New York developed its cultural life around its own churches, church and charitable organizations, benefit societies, youth circles, cafes, newspapers, literary societies, and the Hungarian Reference Library.

"Little Hungary" excelled in a few particular businesses such as pastry, tailoring, and fur. In the 1930s, there was an abundance of Hungarian restaurants in New York, estimated in 1940 at an almost unbelieveable number of more than four hundred. Hungarian laborers were employed in cigar, shoe, and wire factories, and gas works.

Though "Little Hungary" was definitely not intellectual and certainly not "modern," the Hungarian-American educational, scientific, and cultural life of the City profited from the activities of outstanding professionals, such as surgery professor Tibor de Cholnoky, a cancer specialist of Columbia University, the historian Arpad Kovacs at St. John's, political scientist Gabor de Bessenyei at Fordham, and law professor Francis Deak at Columbia. The bibliophile Charles Feleky built the Hungarian Reference Library, a rich collection of books relative to Hungary and Hungarians, written in English, since 1562.[219] A number of churches acted as Hungarian community centers for Hungarian-American congregations.[220]

Several Hungarian playwrights reached Broadway regularly, such as Ferenc Molnár (*Liliom, The Devil, The Guardsman, The Phantom Rival, The Swan*), Menyhért [Melchior] Lengyel and Lajos Biró (*The Czarina, The Dancer*), and Ernest Vajda (*Fata Morgana*).[221] On the whole, they mostly represented popular entertainment rather than serious literature. New York Hungarians loved to see movies featuring Hungarian

---

218 Agnes Primes, *op. cit.,* p. 26.
219 Kenneth Nyirady, *The History of the Feleky Collection and Its Acquisition by the Library of Congress* (Washington, DC: The Library of Congress, European Division, 1995).
220 Agnes Primes, *op. cit.,* pp. 91–93.
221 *Ibid.,* pp. 62–65.

Hollywood stars such as Vilma Bánky and Lya de Putti in the silent film era, and later Ilona Massey, Steffi Duna, Zita Johann, Bela Lugosi, and Paul Lukas, as well as Hungarian films with Hungarian performers produced in Hungary.[222]

Hungarian movies were shown on a daily basis in the Modern Playhouse at 3rd Avenue and 81st Street and some were even reviewed by major New York newspapers such as *The New York Times* and the *Daily News*.[223] Visual artists William Andrew ("Willy") Pogany, Alexander Finta, Isidore Konti, and Julio Kilenyi acquired national fame contributing to a series of New York buildings, parks, museum collections, and publications in very different genres.[224]

Of conductors of Hungarian origin, Erno [Ernő] Rapée (1891–1945) was the most closely associated with New York City. After graduating from the conservatory of Budapest, Rapée came to the United States in 1912. He was active in several New York theaters such as the Rialto, the Rivoli, the Capitol, and the Roxy and became especially famous as the head conductor of Roxy's *Radio City Music Hall* Symphonic Orchestra. Rapée successfully mixed light classical music with popular entertainment and became one of the most celebrated conductors of New York City.[225] Eugene Ormandy also started his phenomenal career in the music world of entertainment and film,[226] and conducted the Capitol Theatre Orchestra in the 1920s. Impressario Belle Schulhof justly wondered whether or not, with more professional PR activities, Rapée could have been built up into a serious conductor just as Ormandy was some time later—a typical problem for immigrant artists at the time. The bonds between American popular culture and consumerism had started to become strong.[227]

---

222   *Ibid.*, p. 66.
223   *Ibid.*, pp. 26, 66.
224   *Ibid.*, pp. 57–59.
225   Belle Schulhof, *Roundtrip Budapest/New York: The Experiences of an Impressario in the Music World* (New York–Atlanta–Los Angeles–Chicago: Vantage Press, 1987), p. 32.
226   Belle Schulhof, *op. cit.*, p. 32.
227   Lewis Perry, *Intellectual Life in America: A History*, *op. cit.*, p. 329.

In the same period, Sandor Harmati (1892–1936) acted as the conductor of the Women's String Orchestra in New York. New York boasted of excellent Hungarian singers such as mezzo soprano Margaret Matzenauer, Anna Roselle, Frederick Schorr (1888–1953) and Arnold Gabor (1880–1950), while noted Hungarian-American concert instrumentalists included violinist Joseph Szigeti, *Radio City Music Hall* organist Dezső Antalffy-Zsiross, pianists Ernő Balogh and Yolanda Mero, violinist Alexander Harsanyi, and cimbalom performer Ladislas Kun.[228]

In the interwar period, the population of the Lower East Side declined, dropping from "well over half a million in 1920 to less than a quarter million in 1938."[229] Still, during this period, connections between immigrant Hungarians and the old country remained strong. Its most memorable bond and symbol was the full-size statue of 1848–49 Hungarian freedom fighter Lajos Kossuth, erected in 1928 on Riverside Drive with some 500 visitors from the home country attending.

In addition to the complex enculturation issues these immigrants faced, there were also difficulties associated with the City itself. As *The WPA Guide to New York City* described it in 1939, "throughout most of the section the smothering heat of summer still drives East Siders to the windows and fire escapes of their ill-ventilated dwellings, to the docks along the river or to the crowded smelly streets, where half-naked children cool themselves in streams from fire hydrants. In winter, basement merchants sell coal and kindling in minute portions for the stoves of unheated cold-water flats."[230]

---

228 Agnes Primes, *op. cit.*, pp. 77–80.
229 *The WPA Guide to New York City, op. cit.*, p. 113.
230 *Ibid.*, p. 113.

Figure 15. Inauguration of the Kossuth Memorial, New York, 1928 (HNM).

Pains of Integration

Though the career of the average Hungarian-American was typically one of success, and Hungarian books of the United States provided examples of the Hungarian success stories in the U.S.,[231] several travelogues by Hungarians, increasingly on the eve of World War II, noticed the growing difficulties newcomers experienced while trying to integrate into American society. Refugees from Hungary found it increasingly hard to assimilate at an age when this was becoming problematic both physically and mentally. As the Hungarian-American impressario Belle Schulhof noted,

> We all like to think we control our own destinies, and to a certain degree we do, through the personal choices and decisions we make as we face new circumstances. But really, the control we have is quite limited, since the decisions we make are often responses to the larger, stronger currents of history that buffet us as we make our way through life.[232]

Mrs. Ferenc Völgyesi, wife of well-known Hungarian psychiatrist and hypnosis expert, joined her husband on a major trip to the United States in 1939. An assistant to her husband throughout his life, she shared many of his ideas and opinions. Her richly documented travelogue, *Ujra itthon*[233] [Back at Home] was probably the first in Hungary to discuss on a medical basis the problems of homesickness. Mrs. Völgyesi described homesickness as a serious disease and gave numerous interesting details on the sufferings of Hungarian-Americans in the immediate pre-war era.

> Homesickness is such a grave illness which those living in their native country cannot even imagine. In places densely populated by Hungarians, such as the allegedly cosmopolitan New York with its 200,000 Hungarians, and Cleveland,

---

231 "Mr. Tóth," in Zoltán Biró, *op. cit.*, pp. 123–132.
232 Belle Schulhof, *op. cit.*, p. 31.
233 Mrs. Ferenc Völgyesi, *Ujra itthon. Tanulmányút Amerika és Európa 17 államán keresztül a háború kitörésének izgalmai között* [Back Home: A study tour through 17 countries of America and Europe among the excitements of the outbreak of the war] (2nd ed. Budapest: Hornyánszky Viktor, 1939).

Figure 16. Jolán Gross-Bettelheim, Slum
(Hungarian *Látványtár* Art Foundation and Collection, Budapest).

Pittsburgh, Hollywood, etc., acquaintances always recognize who is seized by this epidemic, which in grave cases might develop into insanity. I have spoken to a Hungarian-American who cried out that if the political, travel, and financial situations do not improve enough to allow him to visit the old country, he would, he swore, commit suicide within a year."[234]

Mrs. Völgyesi described the immigrant as someone who would never entirely assimilate if he did not get out quite young. The immigrant would remain alien for decades and he/she would not be able to enjoy even some of the best lines of dialogue in movies there. First and foremost he/she would miss the family left behind, the many acquaintances, communication with the usual people and objects. "At home there were many acquaintances. The immigrant continues to look for faces in America to find some familiar acquaintances. He/she must be content with one or another American resembling someone at home. This involuntary habit of comparing can result only in mental illness or a psychological breakdown."[235]

One of the most interesting comments of Mrs. Völgyesi reflected on her husband's reference to "psychological vitamins," such as connections with the fatherland, memories of childhood and youth, as well as the natural habitat. Missing these "vitamins" may result in homesickness that might become lethal. Another of these psychological vitamins was, in Dr. Völgyesi's judgment, having "freedom." As a telling example of what homesickness may lead to, Mrs. Völgyesi recalled the story of an émigré German conductor in his 40s whose longing for his home country became so strong that he became a serious psychiatric case. Though he had terrible previous experiences in Germany and a wonderful job in a New York theater, he would have accepted even the worst job in his native country, just to be at home. It is only possible to transplant very young plants, Mrs. Völgyesi concluded. The situation is the same with problems of emigration. If a grown-up man and his family leave their home country, this could lead to psychological suicide. "I spoke to many

---

234 Mrs. Ferenc Völgyesi, *op. cit.*, p. 88.
235 *Ibid.*, pp. 88–89.

Figure 17. Ferenc Molnár, playwright, 1925 (HNM)
(Custody of Ferenc Molnár's family, with the kind permission of Mr. Ádám Horváth).

immigrants, not only during our recent trip but also in Europe, people who came for a visit or who wanted to stay 'at home' for good. In every case, I became convinced that men over 35–40, and women over 18–20, cannot get rooted in the new soil and fully assimilate to the new psychological environment."[236] She also mentioned national food as the ultimate connection to the fatherland.[237]

A few years later, the celebrated Hungarian playwright Ferenc Molnár (1878–1952), by then also a New York exile, went as far as to describe emigration as an illness. The émigré, he sadly noted,

> may not have noticed it himself, but others did observe his less and less controllable nerves, the huge quantities and low qualities of his complaints, the quick development of his critical faculty, the steady decline of his willingness to communicate with his compatriots, and his constantly vanishing ability to speak English as he subconsciously gave up his futile struggle with the foreign language.[238]

Molnár measured this illness with the growing number of sleeping pills an émigré is supposed to take and added,

> The chlorine-handled tapwater tastes more and more strange. The humidity in the air, the emissions of carbonic oxide and the smell of acrolein produced by cars are less and less enjoyable. Tobacco, coffee, and bread are incresingly alien. Discussions of interior policy, local jokes, comics are less and less to understand. News from home come more frequently and they are   worse and worse. To measure weights and length, to translate the thermometer gets increasinly complicated. One becomes more and more what he was, while everything around him turns more and more different from what it seemed.[239]

---

236 *Ibid.*, p. 90.
237 *Ibid.*, p. 90.
238 Ferenc Molnár, "New York-i gondolatok," [New York Thoughts], in Ferenc Molnár, *Szülőfalum, Pest* [Pest, My Native Village] (Budapest: Szépirodalmi Könyvkiadó, 1962), p. 584. For Molnár's American exile see Ágnes Széchenyi, "Ferenc Molnár and His New York Exile, 1940–1952", in John M. Spalek, *Deutschsprachige Exilliteratur*, Vol 7 (München: K. G. Saur, 2008), forthcoming.
239 Ferenc Molnár, *op. cit.*, p. 585.

The once superbly successful operetta composer Paul Abraham arrived from Berlin via Vienna, Paris, and Cuba in New York, right after World War II, as a grave psychiatric case.

A fellow Hungarian traveller, Géza Zsoldos, made similar observations in 1941–42. "In the old-country," he noted in his 1942 *Ez Amerika* [This is America]

> this crowd lived in so-called middle-class comfort, many with a fortune and now [...] they would have to start life again, perhaps at an age when human strength is waning and they can only find a place in a new field, in a multitude of quickly spinning people, at the expense of great bodily fatigue. There would never be a happy and contented person from among this group and he would be tortured by painful thoughts all the way until his death. The situation of American arrivals is essentially influenced by age and earlier lifestyle and the newcomer can never accept the sudden change that derailed his [...] once so carefully tended and driven car.[240]

Zsoldos surveyed the great achievements of American higher education in the interwar period and came to the conclusion that newcomers from Europe may no longer expect to experience a natural superiority over their counterparts in the U.S. Under the current circumstances, he added, "we may no longer be in a situation to write a sentimental novel on the 'newcomer' of World War II and on his swift career and enrichment."[241]

Zsoldos described what he saw as the essential differences between old immigrants and new. In a brief survey of the several difficulties waiting for the newcomers, he mentioned first the problem of English. Immigrant workers of former times, he suggested, were not excluded by their lack of English from the class of fellow wage earners. They could enter the jobmarket as physical workers in a mine or a factory. Contemporary migrants, however, due to their psychological and bodily features, are hardly able to do physical work and have to look for a career in some other field. There they would have to know at least some English to communicate in everyday life. "Nevertheless,

---

240 Géza Zsoldos, *Ez Amerika* [This is America] (Budapest, 1942), p. 231–2.
241 Géza Zsoldos, *op. cit.*, p. 232.

English is not a language that can be learned as easily as legend puts it in Europe. Its vast vocabulary, the many meanings of its words, the differences between the spoken and written forms, as well as having a great many dialects: all this requires the tough work of many years until full acquisition. If the newcomer belongs to an elderly group, he would never acquire American slang, particularly not that of the rapid-fire American."[242]

Zsoldos next mentioned the lack of some readily available opportunities for people who were earlier employed at a high managerial level in their native Hungary but would have to start all over again in the United States. "What could a 40 or 50 year old 'newcomer' do who was, just yesterday, a director in his old country but who today would have to restart at the lowest possible level in America. For him, America is anything but a dream, as there, due to the huge competition, the struggle for life is indeed tough, very tough."[243]

For Zsoldos, the third difficulty encountering newcomers is the threat of unemployment, and he mentions the growth of American nationalism as a fourth. Newcomers are required to produce their "first paper" which is considered a pledge to become an American citizen within five years.

In a quasi-sociological effort, the author of *Ez Amerika* adds a series of case studies from his own experience describing the typical problems of a handful of new arrivals. The people he quotes went to the United States in 1937–1939 from Hungary, Austria, and Germany and were hard hit by the combination of their evident lack of English and by having come from the medical profession in Europe, which made it hard to pursue this profession in the U.S. Without a working knowledge of English, a dentist from Austria (42) was forced to accept an unskilled job in a department store. An Austrian engineer (40) as well as a Hungarian merchant (25) and a doctor (32) were convinced that immigrants should not stay in New York as the chances for their getting jobs are much better inside the

---

242 *Ibid.*, p. 233.
243 *Ibid.*, p. 234.

country. A lawyer from Vienna (61) was quite hopeless after repeatedly unsuccessful attempts to get his law degree renewed. A business representative from Hungary (50) clearly stated that

> this country is for young men who quickly adapt themselves to the lifestyle here and are able to acquire the language. What takes two-three years for me is a matter of months for them. All my three sons speak perfect English and they even start searching for words in their mother tongue but substitute them with English. Two of them make money and the small family can live quietly on the income of the three of us.[244]

---

244 *Ibid.*, p. 240.

V "Incipit Hitler:"[1]
Double Expulsion, Double Trauma

1 Ever Ready to Go: The Multiple Exiles of Leo Szilard

The life and work of Leo Szilard (1898–1964) illustrates a characteristic form of emigration—double, or even multiple exiles—with their compounding destabilizing impact on career, lifestyle, and mental health. Szilard seemed to be continually in search of himself throughout his life, to travel where his mind led him, to chase the world. Szilard's life was one of continual change and intellectual unrest; it was a quest for role, influence, and identity. To understand Szilard in particular, we have to understand, first, that he was driven by events to numerous departures, escapes, and exiles, changing his religion, his language, his country of residence, and his scientific disciplines; second, that he was a man haunted by major moral dilemmas throughout his life, burdened by a sincere and grave sense of responsibility for the fate of the world; and, third, that Szilard experienced a terrible sense of *déjà vu*. His excessive sensitivity and constant alertness were products of his experiences as a young student in Budapest in 1919; consequently, the mature Szilard in the Berlin of 1933, and forever after, was always ready to move.

Szilard was a member of the distinguished group of Hungarian émigré scientists whose work became most closely associated with the atomic bomb.[2] A student of Max von Laue and close associate of Albert Einstein

---

[1] "Hitler coming," or "Enters Hitler." Stefan Zweig uses the phrase as a chapter heading in his autobiographical *The World of Yesterday*.
[2] Stefan L. Wolff, "Das ungarische Phänomen–ein Fallbeispiel zur Emigrationsforschung," *Deutsches Museum Wissenschaftliches Jahrbuch 1991* (München: Deutsches Museum, 1992), pp. 228–245.

in Berlin, Szilard probably was the most imaginative and original member of this outstanding group of scientists whose pervasive characteristics were imagination and originality.

Szilard's colleagues saw him as a genius. Eugene Rabinowitch remembered him as a "brilliant, paradoxical, arrogant, lonely man of ideas and sudden action"; Eugene Wigner asserted that he had met "no one with more imagination and originality, with more independence of thought and opinion [...]"[3] He was the ultimate problem solver, one who identified, posed, and solved problems of very different types, in a variety of fields. He seems to have faced the world with a certain playful readiness to attack an unending sequence of problems that he felt called upon to solve. He had a strong sense of urgency to find causes that he could identify with and apply his strong sense of mission. He cannot be located in any narrow intellectual field within the confines of some academic discipline; his field was the universe.

Budapest

Leo Szilard (1898–1964) was born in Budapest into a middle class family with some upper class aspirations and a great deal of common sense.[4] His father, a construction engineer, changed his original German-Jewish name Spitz to Szilárd in 1900 when his son was barely two years old. His

---

[3] Eugene Rabinowitch, "James Franck 1882–1964, Leo Szilard 1898–1964," *Bulletin of the Atomic Scientists* 20 (October 1964), 16–20; quote on 20; Eugene P. Wigner, "Leo Szilard 1898–1964," *Biographical Memoirs of the National Academy of Sciences* 40 (1969), 337–347; quote on 337.

[4] William Lanouette with Bela Silard, *Genius in the Shadows: A Biography of Leo Szilard* (New York: Charles Scribner's Sons, 1992), pp. 3–29; reviewed by Dick Teresi, Book Review Section, *The New York Times* (January 24, 1993); Gábor Palló, "William Lanouette on his Leo Szilárd Biography. Conversation with William Lanouette," *The New Hungarian Quarterly* 29, No. 111 (Autumn 1988), pp. 160–170; "A kívülálló: Szilárd Leó," *Fizikai Szemle*, No. 8 (1993), 335–341; Eugene P. Wigner, "Leo Szilard 1898–1964," *Biographical Memoirs of the National Academy of Sciences* 40 (1969), 337–347.

parents were freemasons; their Jewish faith was probably more a tradition than a doctrine. They helped their children study languages and all of European culture. In their beautiful home on Városligeti fasor in the most fashionable district of Pest, their son Leo experimented in physics and at age 10 read the difficult philosophical drama of Imre Madách, *Az ember tragédiája* [The Tragedy of Man], a dramatic 19th-century vision of human existence in poetic form, which provided the greatest source of intellectual inspiration in his childhood.[5] It had such a profound and lasting influence on him that after the atomic bomb was dropped, he spoke of it at length to *New York Post* interviewer Oliver Pilat. Szilard saw Madách's *Tragedy* as applicable to the atomic era, and described the story's relevance to the post-Hiroshima world.

> In that book the Devil shows Adam the history of mankind with the sun dying down. Only Eskimos are left and they worry chiefly because there are too many Eskimos and too few seals. The thought is that there remains a rather narrow margin of hope after you have made your prophecy and it is pessimistic. That is exactly the situation in regard to the atomic bomb. We must concentrate on that narrow margin of hope.[6]

Szilard was particularly successful in mathematics in high school (*Főreáliskola*) in Budapest's 6th District, studying under Ignácz Rados (1859–1944),[7] one of the best mathematics teachers of the period whose brother was the great mathematician Gusztáv Rados (1862–1942). Szilard

---

5 Lanouette, *Genius, op. cit.*, pp. 23–24. On the strong Hungarian identity of émigré scientists see István Hargittai, *The Martians of Science: Five Phyisicists Who Changed the Twentieth Century* (Oxford—New York: Oxford University Press, 2006), pp. 227–228.

6 "Leo Szilard," *Current Biography* (1947), 622; based upon *New York Post* (November 24, 1945), p. 7.

7 Leó Szilárd, "Reáliskolai Érettségi Bizonyítvány" [High School Final Certificate], Budapest, June 27, 1916; Leo Szilard Papers, Mandeville Special Collections Library, University of California, San Diego, Geisel Library, La Jolla, California, Box 1, Folder 9, MSS 32. Ignácz Rados, one of the school's most notable teachers, taught there between 1894–1920; see *Magyar Életrajzi Lexikon* [Hungarian Biographical Encyclopedia], Vol. II (Budapest: Akadémiai Kiadó, 1969), p. 466.

finished high school in 1916 by winning second prize in the prestigious national competition for physics students administered by the Hungarian Association for Mathematics and Physics.[8] He went on to study engineering at the Technical University of Budapest.[9]

Along with so many of his young Budapest contemporaries who shared the same social background,[10] Szilard joined the *Galilei Kör* [Galileo Circle], where he was influenced by radical currents in philosophy and politics.[11] He and his younger brother Béla (1900–1993) founded the Hungarian Association of Socialist Students, a small group which distributed a pamphlet he had written on tax and monetary reform, inflation, and related matters; otherwise he never got involved in student politics. He joined the army in World War I but never saw action. After the War he was initially enthusiastic about the Commune, but there is no evidence that he joined the Red Army or played any other active political role.[12]

---

8 Leopold (Lipót) Fejér, "Erklärung," Budapest, December 14, 1919; "Beglaubigte Abschrift," Berlin-Charlottenburg, January 3, 1920; Leo Szilard Papers, Box 1, Folder 12.

9 Ferenc Szabadváry, "Leo Szilard's Studies at the Palatine Joseph Technical University of Budapest," *Periodica Politechnica* (1987), pp. 187–190.

10 Tibor Frank, "Der Kult des Allwissens im Budapest des Fin-de-Siècle," in Frank Baron, David N. Smith, and Charles Reitz, ed., *Authority, Culture, and Communication: The Sociology of Ernest Manheim* (München: Synchron Verlag, 2004), pp. 89–116; Tibor Frank, "George Pólya and the Heuristic Tradition," *Polanyiana* 6, No. 2 (1997), 22–37; reprinted in *Revista Brasileira de História da Matemática* 4, No. 7 (Abril-Setembro 2004), pp. 19–36.

11 Márta Tömöry, *Uj vizeken járok. A Galilei Kör története* [Sailing Unchartered Waters. The History of the Galileo Circle] (Budapest: Gondolat, 1960); Kende Zsigmond, *A Galilei Kör megalakulása* [The Founding of the Galileo Circle] (Budapest: Akadémiai Kiadó, 1974). See also György Litván, "Jászi Oszkár, a magyar progresszió és a nemzet" [Oscar Jaszi, Hungarian Progressivism, and the Nation], in Endre Kiss and Kristóf János Nyíri, ed., *A magyar filozófiai gondolkodás a századelőn* [Hungarian Philosophical Thought in the Early 20th Century] (Budapest: Kossuth, 1977), p. 107.

12 Lanouette, *Genius, op. cit.*, pp. 45–50; Palló, "Lanouette," pp. 164–165; "A kívülálló: Szilárd Leó," p. 336; Wigner, "Szilard," *op. cit.*, pp. 337–338.

In an otherwise well-documented life, Szilard hardly ever mentions his experiences during the tumultuous year 1919. Yet that was a year of monumental importance in his life: within a few months, he left his native Hungary, his religion, his field of study, and to an ever-increasing extent, his language, starting to use German, and later English, instead of his mother tongue. Together these changes represented the first major turning point in his life, and perhaps the single most important one.

Military Service and Personal Identity

Leo Szilard's social situation and identity crisis after his military service in the *kaiserlich und königlich*, i.e. *k.u.k.* [Austro-Hungarian Imperial and Royal] Army resembled that of the officers portrayed in Austrian playwright Franz Theodor Csokor's *3. November 1918*. In this play a group of wounded officers talk about their national origins after they hear about the end of the War. Some are happy to embrace their specific national identities as the supranational *k.u.k.* identity of the Austro-Hungarian Army is about to be dissolved. But the highest ranking officer still identifies himself with this supranational Austro-Hungarian Army, while the Jewish reservist identifies himself with supranational Austria.[13] Szilard, after a year in the *k.u.k.* Army, must have felt much like the Jewish reservist. He became a volunteer in a reservist officer school in Budapest on September 27, 1917, and then a *Kadettaspirant* [officer cadet] in the Tyrol. His military career ended in a Budapest military hospital; he was discharged on November 17, 1918.[14]

Memories of World War I cropped up much later in Szilard's mind. In a "Letter to Stalin" in 1947, he recalled his Hungarian past to make a point about the growing threat of a new war and his deep concern about the steady deterioration of Soviet-American relations.

---

13 István Deák, *Beyond Nationalism: A Social and Political History of the Habsburg Officer Corps, 1848–1918* (New York and Oxford: Oxford University Press, 1990), p. 184.
14 Leo Szilard, "Biographical Table," Leo Szilard Papers, Box 2, Folder 9.

Situations of this general type are not without precedent in history; they occur also on occasion in the lives of individuals, and the story of one such occurrence made a very deep impression on me. In 1930, twelve years after the end of the First World War, I met a classmate of mine and we talked of what had happened to us since we had separated. He had been a lieutenant in the Austrian [Austro-Hungarian] Army, and in the last days of the war in the Carpathian Mountains he was in charge of a patrol. One morning they heard by way of rumor that an armistice had been concluded, but being cut off from communications they were unable to obtain confirmation. They rode out on patrol duty as usual, and as they emerged from the forest, they found themselves standing face to face with a Russian patrol in charge of an officer. The two officers grabbed their guns and, frozen in this position, the two patrols remained for uncounted seconds. Suddenly the Russian officer smiled and his hand went to his cap in salute. My friend returned the salute, and both patrols turned back their horses. "To this day," my friend said to me, "I regret that it was not I who saluted first."[15]

After his discharge from the army, Szilard continued his studies in engineering at the Technical University of Budapest and took his first major comprehensive examination on July 16, 1919.[16] The atmosphere at the university was heavily charged with social conflict, bitter animosity, and political infighting. The Galileo Circle had ceased to exist in the fall of 1918, leaving him without a support group of like-minded intellectuals. That he still was able to pursue and complete his engineering studies during the academic year 1918–1919, with its turmoil, increasing racial hatred, and political battles, speaks highly for his intellectual discipline. That momentous year was also his last year in Hungary, and on July 24, 1919, he converted from Judaism and was baptized into the Calvinist faith.[17] The date of his baptism reveals a sense of urgency: the Hungarian Soviet Republic would exist for just one more week, and the signs of an

15 Leo Szilard, "A Letter to Stalin," MS, November 10, 1947, Leo Szilard Papers, pp. 2–3; *Bull. Atom. Sci.* 3 (December 1947), 347–350, 353, 376; reprinted in Helen S. Hawkins, G. Allen Greb, and Gertrud Weiss Szilard, ed., *Toward a Livable World: Leo Szilard and the Crusade for Nuclear Arms Control* (Cambridge, MA and London: The MIT Press, 1987), pp. 26–34; quote on p. 27.
16 Szilard, "Biographical Table."
17 "Kivonat a budapesti VI-VII. ker. Fasori református egyház keresztelési anyakönyvéből [Extract from the Baptismal Registry of the Calvinist Church in

anti-Semitic wave of revenge for what was generally viewed as a Jewish takeover of the government were evident.

The Roots of Anxiety: Escape to Berlin

During the clouded months of late 1919, Szilard felt increasingly insecure as the White Terror reigned and threatened his future. In September, he and his brother Béla suffered a humiliating attack at the Technical University for being Jewish, and his recently acquired baptismal certificate, which he naïvely presented in self-defense, seemed to further inflame the anti-Semitic hatred of their attackers. Béla remembered that Leo was unable to obtain a visa after the establishment of the Commune but ultimately secured an official document, within 24 hours, from the Budapest police on December 11, 1919, testifying to his "political reliability,"[18] because his name "had not been entered into the books of the political police." He also acquired a written statement from the mathematician Lipót Fejér (1880–1959) on December 14 proving that he had won second prize in the student competition in physics under the auspices of the Mathematical and Physical Society. These documents allowed him to leave Budapest for Berlin within a few days at the end of 1919.

Just as the year 1919 was one of national identity crisis for Hungary, it also was one of personal identity crisis for Szilard and the root of major fears. The long and agonizing fall of 1919 left a lasting impression on his young mind and imprinted on it an acute awareness of history's dangerous turns. His various psychological complexes, such as his impulse to live always in hotels or rented rooms instead of setting up his own residence,[19]

---

the Fasor, Budapest, VI-VIIth District]," Vol. II (Budapest: July 24, 1919), p. 14; Leo Szilard Papers, Box 1, Folder 11. See also Lanouette, *Genius, op. cit.,* pp. 30–51.

18 Leo Szilard, "Petition to the Budapest Police, December 11, 1919," Leo Szilard Papers, Box 1, Folder 11; Palló, "Lanouette," *op. cit.,* pp. 164–165.

19 His hotels included the Imperial Hotel in London, the International House and King's Crown Hotel in New York City (opposite Columbia University), the Quadrangle Club in Chicago, the Webster Hotel and Dupont Plaza in Washington,

and his constant state of alert, allowing him to move quickly whenever necessary, probably have their roots in the terrible anguish he experienced in 1919. It is telling that he kept his most important belongings, particularly his papers, in two suitcases ready to be carried away at a moment's notice—as he did in Berlin in the beginning of March 1933, right after the *Reichstag* fire.[20] Like so many of his Hungarian contemporaries who were then living in Germany, he experienced a terrible sense of *déjà vu* of the Budapest of 1919, a disagreeable sense of familiarity with a threat that warranted steady vigilance and urgent response. It is perhaps not far off the mark to speak here of an *Angstneurose* [anxiety neurosis] in Sigmund Freud's sense, the symptoms of which Szilard experienced throughout his life.[21] The sudden outburst of anti-Semitism, the violence of a right-wing takeover, and the threatening atmosphere of vengeance were all well known to Szilard and his Hungarian contemporaries from their experiences in Budapest well over a decade before the Nazi takeover in Germany, and would remain in their minds for the rest of their lives. Szilard's excessive sensitivity and constant alertness were products of his experiences as a young student in Budapest in 1919; the mature Szilard in the Berlin of 1933, and forever after, was always ready to move. (The somewhat younger Jewish-Hungarian mathematician Paul Erdős (1913–1996), who lived a comparable life especially after World War II, offers an interesting parallel.)

DC; even the small cottage in which the Szilards lived during the last few months of his life in early 1964 in La Jolla, California, was connected to a motel; see Lanouette, *Genius, op. cit.,* pp. 136, 149, 163, 173, 230-231, 274–275, 321, 329, 383, 398, 430–432, 466–467.

20   Wolff, "Das ungarische Phänomen," *op. cit.,* p. 236; Lanouette, *Genius, op. cit.,* pp. 110, 115.

21   Sigm[und] Freud, "Über die Berechtigung, von der Neurasthenie einen bestimmten Symptomencomplex als 'Angstneurose' abzutrennen," *Neurologisches Centralblatt,* Band 14, Heft 2 (Leipzig: Verlag von Veit & Comp., 1895), pp. 50–66; reprinted in Sigmund Freud, *Gesammelte Werke,* 6. Auflage, Bd. I (Frankfurt a. M.: S. Fischer Verlag, 1991), pp. 315–342; translated in *The Standard Edition of the Complete Psychological Works of Sigmund Freud,* Vol. III (London: The Hogarth Press, 1999), pp. 90–115; on the translation of "Angst," see pp. 116–117.

German social historian Joachim Radkau's diagnosis of the age of *Nervosität* [nervousness] in Germany from Bismarck to Hitler also fits Hungary after World War I.[22] In a roundabout way, the rise of a distinct Hungarian school of psychology, with internationally recognized achievements in psychoanalysis, fate analysis, and stress, point to the psychological consequences of a society in turmoil.[23] Émigrés of Jewish origin, like Szilard, had additional reasons to be nervous.[24] One may venture to think that psychological impulses motivated his pioneering efforts to build the bomb against the threat of Hitler. His Hungarian-Jewish background, his upbringing and his long and permanent exile contributed to a troubled and difficult psyche. It is also true, however, that his psychological makeup equipped him with the skills to survive and the sensitivity to help anyone who needed his support, often in the face of adversity. After World War I and the Hungarian revolutions of 1918–1919, Szilard's life reveals a continuous interplay of politics and science, a drama in which he seems to have been too political for a scientist and too scientific for a politician.

22 Joachim Radkau, *Das Zeitalter der Nervosität: Deutschland zwischen Bismarck und Hitler* (München: Propyläen Taschenbuch, Econ Ullstein List, 2000), pp. 201, 534, 598, where Radkau rightly quotes Budapest hypnotist Ferenc Völgyesi's book, *Botschaft an die nervöse Welt! Nervosität, Hypnose, Selbstbeherrschung* (Zürich: Orell-Füssli, 1936); translated as *A Message to the Neurotic World* (London: Hutchinson, 1935), as a contribution to his own thesis on *Nervosität*. The international popularity of Völgyesi's book (it was published in at least four languages) demonstrated the timeliness and importance of this problem. Vögyesi was one of the most popular psychiatrists in Budapest for forty years; he had altogether well over 40,000 private patients; Mrs. Ferenc Völgyesi (who served as his assistant), personal communication, February 3, 1992.

23 Franz Alexander (1891–1964), Michael Bálint (1896–1970), Sándor Ferenczi (1873–1933), Imre Hermann (1889–1984), Hans Selye (1907–1982), and Leopold Szondi (1893–1986) were among the most widely known Hungarians in the history of 20th-century psychology; see Lívia Nemes und Gábor Berényi, Hg., *Die Budapester Schule der Psychoanalyse* (Budapest: Akadémiai Kiadó, 1999).

24 Radkau, *Zeitalter, op. cit.*, pp. 357–362; Lanouette, *Genius, op. cit.*, p. 466. Jonas Salk recalled after Szilard's death: "There was something driving Leo;" *ibid.*, p. 476.

Berlin, 1920–1933

By January 3, 1920, Szilard was in Berlin-Charlottenburg, where he presented his documents and continued his studies in engineering at the *Technische Hochschule* [Technical University] for two semesters, and then turned to science at the University of Berlin for an additional four semesters. He defended his doctoral dissertation in the summer of 1922.[25]

The University of Berlin offered great prospects for Szilard, now in his early twenties. In physics he could work with Nobel Laureates Max von Laue (1879–1960), Max Planck (1858–1947) and Albert Einstein (1879–1955), not to mention lesser figures.[26] Berlin physicists favored theory, yet also were deeply interested in experiment—an ideal combination for a man who was theoretically gifted and also was challenged by the exciting potential of modern technology. He showed a remarkable talent, in fact, for putting his theoretical knowledge to use in the form of patents, products and practical ideas.[27]

In his doctoral dissertation of 1922, Szilard showed that statistical fluctuations, which hitherto had been taken as proof of the reality of atoms, can be included within the framework of phenomenological thermodynamics without making any reference to atoms. He arrived at his results in a characteristic way. He remembered much later that he had spent several agonizing months working hard on a problem in thermodynamics and had come to believe that he had no chance at solving it.

---

25 Leo Szilard, "Lebenslauf," *Habilitationsschrift*, University of Berlin, March 15, 1926; Universitätsarchiv, Philosophische Fakultät, Humboldt-Universität zu Berlin, Nr. 1242, Blatt 120, Fiche 3/16.
26 Hubert Laitko, "Zentrum, Magistrale und Fluchtpunkt. Der Wissenschaftsstandort Berlin im 20. Jahrhundert," in Rüdiger vom Bruch und Eckart Henning, Hg., *Wissenschaftsfördernde Institutionen im Deutschland des 20. Jahrhunderts* [Dahlemer Archivgespräche 5] (Berlin: Archiv zur Geschichte der Max-Planck-Gesellschaft, 1999), pp. 11–39. See also Tibor Frank, "Station Berlin: Ungarische Wissenschaftler und Künstler in Deutschland 1919–1933," *IMIS-Beiträge,* Institut für Migrationsforschung und Interkulturelle Studien, Universität Osnabrück, 10/1999, pp. 7–38.
27 Wolff, "Das ungarische Phänomen," *op. cit.,* p. 238.

He then took a vacation for a month, determined just to loaf, but while relaxing, an unrelated idea in statistical mechanics occurred to him and he solved the problem before the end of his vacation. Einstein, much of whose past work had been based upon the analysis of statistical fluctuations, did not believe Szilard's solution until Szilard showed him how he arrived at it. Von Laue also was skeptical about Szilard's solution when Szilard handed him his manuscript, but the next day von Laue telephoned the young man, saying that his work had been accepted as a doctoral thesis.[28] Von Laue praised Szilard's dissertation as an "independent" and "major achievement," primarily for his pioneering use of Einstein's analysis of energy fluctuations, and judged it to be outstanding (*Eximium*). His dissertation was published three years later.[29]

After receiving his degree, Szilard first carried out experimental work in the Kaiser Wilhelm Institute for *Faserstoff-Chemie* [Fiber Chemistry] and then, in 1924, received a stipend from the Kaiser Wilhelm Institute for Physics. At the end of that year he became an assistant in the Institute for Theoretical Physics at the University of Berlin,[30] working under von Laue, investigating the relationship between entropy and information, soon conceiving ideas that would form part of modern information theory. He completed his *Habilitationsschrift* (a second thesis leading to a higher university degree) in 1925 although it was not published until 1929.[31] Von

---

28 Szilard mentions this in a letter to Richard Gehman, April 8, 1952; Leo Szilard Papers, Box 8, Folder 27; see also Friedrich Herneck, *Max von Laue* (Leipzig: Teubner, 1979), p. 47.
29 Leo Szilard, "Über die Ausdehnung der phänomenologischen Thermodynamik auf die Schwankungserscheinungen," *Zeitschrift für Physik* 32 (1925), 753–788; reprinted in Bernard T. Feld and Gertrud Weiss Szilard, ed. *The Collected Works of Leo Szilard: Scientific Papers* (Cambridge, MA and London: The MIT Press, 1972), pp. 34–69.
30 "Lebenslauf," p. 120; Max von Laue to Leo Szilard, November 27, 1957, Archiv zur Geschichte der Max-Planck-Gesellschaft, Berlin-Dahlem, III. Abt., Rep. 50, Nr. 1971, quoted in Wolff, "Das ungarische Phänomen," p. 234.
31 L. Szilard, "Über die Entropieverminderung in einem thermodynamischen System bei Eingriffen intelligenter Wesen," *Zeitschrift für Physik* 53 (1929), 840–856; reprinted in *Collected Works, op. cit.*, pp. 103–119.

Laue praised it lavishly as "an essential clarification of an old and important question and satisfies more than completely the demands that the faculty expects from a *Habilitationsschrift*."[32] Planck agreed completely, adding that:

> Dr. Szilard has been working for several years in Berlin and often had the opportunity to prove his scientific talent and industry. Also his *Habilitationsschrift* distinguishes itself through the originality of thinking and clarity of presentation. I do not doubt that he would continue to work successfully as a *Dozent*. In time, he hopefully will be able to overcome a certain one-sidedness in the direction of his work.[33]

All of the members of Szilard's *Habilitation* Committee (which included Nobel Laureates Fritz Haber and Walther Nernst, as well as Ernst Bodenstein, Wolfgang Köhler, Richard von Mises, Wilhelm Schlenk, and Arthur Wehnelt) agreed with von Laue and Planck. Szilard thus became a *Privatdozent*, gaining the *venia legendi* [right to lecture] at the University of Berlin.[34] In 1928, he offered courses, mostly in theoretical physics, some jointly with John von Neumann (1903–1957), Hartmut Kallmann (1896–1976), and Fritz London (1900–1954). Beginning in the winter term of 1930-1931, he taught as a member of a group headed by prospective Nobel Laureate Erwin Schrödinger (1887–1961), and in 1931–1932 he offered a joint seminar with Lise Meitner (1878–1968) on "questions of atomic physics and chemistry."[35]

Szilard's work was firmly rooted in the practicalities of technical developments in the 1920s and early 1930s. He was obsessed with practical applications, which took him out of his laboratory and ever more frequently close to the production line. He devised a method of pumping

---

32   Max von Laue in Szilard, *Habilitation* papers, *op. cit.*, pp. 128–129.
33   Max Planck in Szilard, *Habilitation* papers, *op.cit.*, p. 129.
34   Szilard, Biographical Data and List of Publications 1922–1946, Leo Szilard Papers, Box 2, Folder 8.
35   Wolff, "Das ungarische Phänomen," *op. cit.*, p. 235. The courses offered every semester at the University of Berlin (and other universities) were published in the *Physikalische Zeitschrift*.

liquid metal through tubes, which the *Allgemeine Elektrizitäts Gesellschaft* (AEG) [General Electric Company in Germany] wanted to use to develop a pump, and which ultimately found its practical application in nuclear reactors in the United States after World War II. Szilard worked as a consultant to the AEG for three years and patented several of his inventions in Great Britain and the United States.

In the late 1920s, Szilard worked with Einstein on a number of innovative approaches to cooling, making good use and taking some advantage of his celebrated coworker by patenting his inventions under both of their names. These included a refrigerator and an apparatus for transporting liquid metal, especially for concentrating gases and vapors in refrigerators in 1927, an electromagnetic apparatus for producing an oscillatory motion in 1928, a compressor in 1929, and a pump, chiefly for refrigerators in 1930.[36] For some reason, Szilard also patented basically the same inventions a little later under his own name alone, including the refrigerator in 1929 and 1931, the apparatus for transporting liquid metal in 1929, and the compressor as well as a stator for refrigerators in 1931.[37] The principle that Szilard and Einstein conceived promised to lead to a new type of refrigerator that was more efficient and less dangerous to operate than existing ones. One of their main ideas was to produce cooling by causing alcohol to be absorbed by water, but this idea did not prove to be of lasting industrial influence.[38] More important was their invention, which became known as the Einstein-Szilard electromagnetic pump, in which "a traveling electromagnetic field causes a liquid metal

---

36 Reichspatentamt, Patentschrift Nr. 563,403, 561,904, 554,959, 556,535, 562,040, 565,614; Archiv zur Geschichte der Max-Planck-Archiv, Berlin-Dahlem, Va. Abt., Rep. 2, Albert Einstein. Further research is required to determine Einstein's and Szilard's respective contributions to these patents.
37 Reichspatentamt, Patentschrift Nr. 556,536, 564,680 and 548,136, 543,214 and 555,141, 531,581, 581,780, 568,680. Archiv zur Geschichte der Max-Planck-Archiv, Berlin-Dahlem, IX. Abt., Rep. 1, Leo Szilard.
38 Rudolf Plank and Johann Kuprianoff, *Haushalt-Kältemaschinen und kleingewerbliche Kühlanlagen*, second edition (Berlin: Springer, 1934); *Die Kleinkältemaschine*, second edition (Berlin, Göttingen, Heidelberg: Springer, 1960); Rudolf Plank, *Amerikanische Kältetechnik* (Düsseldorf: Deutscher Ingenieur-Verlag, 1950).

to move." The prestigious AEG developed a prototype of their pump for refrigeration purposes.[39]

Although Szilard and Einstein patented their refrigerator in Great Britain, the United States and Hungary, and although Szilard later tried to promote interest in it in the United States,[40] it was never marketed, mainly because of the devastating economic effects of the Great Depression. Einstein also declined to lend his name to advertisements for it. A school friend asked Szilard about this refrigerator shortly before his death. Szilard replied: "Oh that? [...] That went into the atom bomb."[41]

Leo Szilard's Rescue Operations

Two weeks after the Nazi Party's success in the Reichstag elections of September 14, 1930, Szilard assessed its significance in a letter to Einstein: "From week to week I detect new symptoms, if my nose doesn't deceive me, peaceful [political] development in Europe in the next ten years is not to be counted on [...] Indeed, I don't know if it will be possible to build our refrigerator in Europe."[42] Consequently, Szilard left Berlin for Vienna at the end of March 1933.

---

39 Gene Dannen, "The Einstein-Szilard Refrigerators," *Scientific American* 276 (January 1997), 90–95; "Die Einstein-Szilard-Kühlschränke," *Spektrum der Wissenschaft* (June 1997), 94–100. This article also appeared in Arabic, Chinese, French, Japanese, Polish, and Spanish.
40 Szilard's many patents (some with Einstein) in Britain and the United States are given in Szilard, *Collected Works, op. cit.*, p. 543ff. For Hungary, see Magyar Királyi Szabadalmi Bíróság, Szabadalmi leírás, 102079. szám, XVIII/c osztály, published March 2, 1931. For interest in the Einstein-Szilard Refrigerators in the United States, see Szilard to Gano Dunn, September 13, 1939; Leo Szilard Papers, Box 7, Folder 21.
41 Quoted in George Halasz, "Dr. Einstein's Icebox," in Martin Levin, ed., *The Bedside Phoenix Nest* (New York: Ives Washburn, 1965), p. 318.
42 Szilard to Einstein, September 27, 1930; quoted in Michael Grüning, *Ein Haus für Albert Einstein: Erinnerungen, Briefe, Dokumente* (Berlin: Verlag der Nation, 1990), pp. 335–337, and Dannen, "Einstein-Szilard Refrigerators," *op. cit.*, p. 78.

Leo Szilard voluntarily took on the enormous task of contributing to the ensuing rescue operations throughout 1933 and beyond. He was generally recognized as a man of extraordinary abilities and completely unselfish motives, who no doubt was deeply grateful for the help he himself had received from German professors, colleagues and friends throughout the 1920s and early 1930s. Paul Ehrenfest (1880–1933) of the University of Leiden captured Szilard's personality and talents in a letter to Frederick G. Donnan (1870–1956) on August 22, 1933:

> Szilard is a *very rare* example of a man because of his combination of great *purely scientific* acumen, his ability to immerse himself in and solve technical problems, his fascination and fantasy for organizing, and his great sensitivity and compassion for people in need [...] What I find so particularly enviable in him, is that he reacts to any difficulty which may arise with immediate action rather than depression or resignation. For even though this procedure is not always successful, an energetic reaction is still vastly more fruitful than a passive attitude. I feel deeply ashamed when I see how wonderfully energetically he immediately set about doing everything in his power to work for the Jewish-German scholars [...] [He] simply felt that, confronted with this great, wild catastrophe, his first duty was to use his special talents in organizing aid for a specific subgroup of scientists.[43]

Among his fellow Hungarians in Germany, Szilard was well-known as the man who was always ready to help. Philosopher Karl Mannheim (1893–1947), who worked with Szilard in establishing the Academic Assistance Council in 1933, remembered him as someone who "belongs to that rare group of people who never demand something for themselves."[44] Another friend and colleague, physicist Eugene Wigner (1902–1995), also had nothing but lavish praise for Szilard's unselfishness,[45] "rare social

---

43 Paul Ehrenfest (Leiden) to Frederick George Donnan, August 22, 1933, Leo Szilard Papers, Box 7, Folder 22.
44 Karl Mannheim (London) to Max Horkheimer, March 30, 1937, Leo Szilard Papers, Box 12, Folder 14; see also Szilard (Brussels) to unknown, May 14, 1933, *ibid.*, Box 12, Folder 21; Szilard to Neville Laski, May 1933, *ibid.*, Box 11, Folder 18.
45 Wigner (Budapest) to Michael Polanyi, n.d. [July 1933?], Michael Polanyi Papers, Department of Special Collections, University of Chicago Library, Chicago, Box. 2, Folder 12.

abilities" and "unusual social competence," which served him well not only when helping people but also later when mobilizing scientists and politicians in the United States to investigate the nuclear-chain reaction and its consequences.[46]

Perhaps more than anyone else, Szilard was the prime mover behind the founding of the Academic Assistance Council after fleeing Berlin rapidly on the burning of the Reichstag on February 27, 1933. Soon thereafter, he accidentally met Sir William (later Lord) Beveridge in Vienna and persuaded him to form a committee to aid refugee scientists and scholars.[47] "Things in England develop very well," Szilard wrote to the distinguished Austrian chemist Friedrich A. Paneth (1887–1958) from Brussels in mid-May 1933. "Sir William Beveridge, whom I met in Vienna and who has been very active since he came back in London succeeded in getting a very prominent group to make an appeal for raising funds in England. The first contribution will probably be made through voluntary cuts of salaries of University teachers (this is very confidential)."[48]

Szilard functioned like an entire team of people. He had followed Beveridge back to London, where he wrote to Max Delbrück (1906–1981) on May 7, 1933: "What I am concerned with at the present is to co-ordinate the foreign groups which are already in existence, and to stimulate

46   Klaus Fischer, *Changing Landscapes of Nuclear Physics: A Scientometric Study on the Social and Cognitive Position of German-Speaking Emigrants Within the Nuclear Physics Community 1921–1947* (Berlin: Springer Verlag, 1993), p. 203; Wolff, "Das ungarische Phänomen," *op. cit.*, p. 238.

47   Norman Bentwich, *The Rescue and Achievement of Refugee Scholars: The Story of Displaced Scholars and Scientists 1933–1952* (The Hague: Martinus Nijhoff, 1953), p. 11; Fermi, *Illustrious Immigrants, op. cit.*, pp. 63–64; Edward Shils, "Leo Szilard: A Memoir," *Encounter* 23 (December 1964), 38–39; Weiner, "New Site," p. 211; Stefan Wolff, "Frederick Lindemanns Rolle bei der Emigration der aus Deutschland vertriebenen Physiker," in Anthony Grenville, ed., *German-speaking Exiles in Great Britain. The Yearbook of the Research Centre for German and Austrian Exile Studies*, Vol. 2 (Amsterdam and Atlanta: Rodopi, 2000), p. 28.

48   Szilard (Brussels) to Friedrich A. Paneth, May 14, 1933; Nachlass F. A. Paneth, Archiv zur Geschichte der Max-Planck-Gesellschaft, Berlin-Dahlem, Jewish Refugees Committee, 1933, III. Abt. Rep. 45.

the formation of groups in countries where there are no suitable groups as yet."⁴⁹ He then traveled for a month on the Continent. In Belgium, he met the Rectors of all four of the Belgian universities, the physicist Jacques Errera and the philosopher and politician Hendrik de Man of the University of Brussels, who assisted him in mobilizing Belgian colleagues to aid refugee scientists and scholars. In Switzerland, he talked to Gustave Gerard Kullman of the Committee for Intellectual Cooperation of the League of Nations and Walter Kotschnig of the International Student Service.⁵⁰

In London, Szilard met with university leaders and prominent scientists such as Beveridge, Director of the London School of Economics and Political Science, Frederick G. Donnan of University College, London, Gilbert Murray of Oxford, Chairman of the League of Nations Committee for Intellectual Cooperation, Sir John Russell, G.H. Hardy of Cambridge, Nobel Laureate Niels Bohr of Copenhagen, Nobel Laureate Archibald V. Hill of the Royal Society and University College, London, Henry Mond, the Second Lord Melchett, Chairman of the Jewish Agency, and Jewish leaders such as Neville Laski, Claude Joseph Goldsmid Montefiore, Sir Philip Hartog, Chairman of the Committee of the Jewish Board of Deputies and the Anglo-Jewish Association, and Chaim Weizmann, the future President of Israel. Living as always in a hotel, and working from his office at the Academic Assistance Council headquartered at the Royal Society, Szilard apparently contacted all the agencies in London that were formed to help European Jewish scientists in trouble, including the Central Jewish Consultative Committee at 1 Finsbury Square and the Jews' Temporary Shelter at 63 Mansell Street.⁵¹ He put Friedrich Paneth in touch with the Jewish Refugees Committee's Hospitality Committee

---

49 Szilard (London) to Max Delbrück, May 7, 1933, Leo Szilard Papers, Box 7, Folder 9.
50 Jacques Errera (Bruxelles) to Szilard, June 5, 1933 (in French), Leo Szilard Papers, Box 7, Folder 2; Szilard (Brussels) to unknown, May 14, 1933, *ibid.*, Box 12, Folder 21; [Leo Szilard], "Report," May 23, 1933, *ibid.*, Box 4, Folder 30.
51 Szilard (London) to Delbrück, May 7, 1933, Leo Szilard Papers, Box 7, Folder 9; Szilard (Strand Palace Hotel, London) to Friedrich A. Paneth, November 26, 1934 and Szilard (Brussels) to Friedrich A. Paneth, May 14, 1933 (handwritten notes),

at Woburn House in June 1933; soon thereafter, Paneth was appointed as a consultant for the Imperial Chemical Industries (ICI) and later taught at Imperial College, London, and the University of Durham from 1939 to 1953.[52] Szilard also considered mobilizing Nobel Laureates to aid refugee scientists and scholars, but this plan failed to receive general approval and was soon dropped.[53]

The Academic Assistance Council helped several Hungarian scholars, including the economic historian Karl Polanyi (1886–1964), get to England; his younger brother Michael Polanyi (1891–1976), securely on his way to England, also tried to help some of his gifted students remaining in Germany to obtain scholarships in Great Britain.[54] Other Hungarian scientists as well, many of whom have been hitherto unidentified, were rescued by jobs in Great Britain, often serving as a stepping stone to employment in the United States. A case in point was the nutrition expert Paul György (1893–1976), who was dismissed from his position at the University of Heidelberg in 1934 after thirteen years there: he was offered a research fellowship at the University of Cambridge during 1934–1935, then was appointed to a professorship at Western Reserve University in Cleveland (1935–1944) before becoming Professor of Clinical Pediatrics and of Nutrition in Pediatrics at the University of Pennsylvania in Philadelphia.[55]

Nachlass F. A. Paneth, Jewish Refugees Committee, 1933, III. Abt. Rep. 45; Szilard (London) to Wigner, August 17, 1933, Michael Polanyi Papers, Box 2, Folder 12.

52 I. Zinn, Secretary of the Jewish Refugee Committee, to F. A. Paneth, June 7, 1933, Nachlass F. A. Paneth, Jewish Refugees Committee, 1933, III. Abt. Rep. 45; R[alph] E. Oesper, "Fritz A. Paneth (1887–)", *Journal of Chemical Education* 16 (July 1939), 301; J. Mattauch, "Friedrich A. Paneth," *Verbandsausgabe der Physikalischen Verhandlungen*, 8. Lieferung (1958), 165–169.

53 Szilard (London) to Maxwell Garnett, May 9, 1934, Leo Szilard Papers, Box 8, Folder 23; Julian Huxley (London) to Szilard, May 3, 1934, *ibid.*, Box 9, Folder 12.

54 Karl Polanyi (London) to Michael Polanyi, October 31, 1934 (in Hungarian), Michael Polanyi Papers, Box 17, Folder 5; [Lawrence] Bragg (Manchester) to Michael Polanyi, July 10, 1933, *ibid.*, Box 2, Folder 12.

55 Paul György, Biographies, Paul György Papers, American Philosophical Society Library, Philadelphia, Penn.; Fritz Zilliken, "Paul György 7.4.1893–1.3.1976," *MPI*

Szilard realized that an AAC fellowship often would not lead to a permanent position in Great Britain. Thus, as he wrote to Charles S. Gibson in June 1933:

> It is therefore important to take up every case as soon as possible with America and other countries in order to get a more uniform distribution as far as permanent appointments are concerned. A certain number of American scientists and scholars should in view of this problem be asked to act as correspondent members of the Academic Assistance Council... .[56]

The relief efforts met with a great deal of support in the United States, where the academic community was "terribly concerned about the situation in Germany." "I have a letter this morning from an old friend," wrote Abraham Flexner (1866–1959), Director of the Institute for Advanced Study in Princeton on March 30, 1933, to John von Neumann who was traveling in Europe,

> telling me unspeakable things about the way in which Hitler is ruining the German Educational Ministry and other cultural activities. The whole thing seems to me the act of mad men. I cannot believe that it will endure.[57]

Five weeks later he added: "The whole American nation is a unit as respects the crazy performances of the German Government. Göttingen has been absolutely ruined and the University students must all be mad.

Berichte und Mitteilungen, Sonderheft (1977), 15–17; Paul György Papers, Archiv zur Geschichte der Max-Planck-Gesellschaft, Berlin-Dahlem, IX. Abt. Rep. 1. György received an honorary doctorate from the Ruprecht-Karl-University of Heidelberg in 1960 and the U.S. National Medal of Science from President Gerald R. Ford in 1976.

56 Szilard (London) to C. S. Gibson, June 13, 1933, Leo Szilard Papers, Box 8, Folder 23.

57 Abraham Flexner (New York) to John von Neumann, March 30, 1933, John von Neumann Papers, Box 7, The Library of Congress, Rare Book and Special Collections, Washington, DC.

Nothing crazier has happened in human history since the days of the French Terror."[58]

Acting through Benjamin Liebowitz, Szilard was instrumental in securing contributions from Franz Boas of Columbia University, who played a leading role in marshaling support for the refugee cause.[59] Boas invited philosopher John Dewey, economist Frank William Taussig, zoologist Raymond Pearl, physiologist Walter Cannon, poet Ezra Pound, and others to serve on a board to coordinate the efforts of the AAC with those of American universities and scientists.[60]

Besides Szilard, other Hungarians, including von Neumann and Theodore von Kármán (1881–1963), played active roles in the relief efforts. Oswald Veblen (1880–1960), Professor of Mathematics in the Institute for Advanced Study, wrote to his colleague von Neumann, who again was traveling in Europe in May 1933, that "It would be a good idea to write me whatever you know in detail about the mathematicians and physicists who are in difficulties."[61] Veblen reported that "there are a number of attempts being made to raise money to provide relief in this country for the Jews and Liberals who are being dispossessed in Germany." Von Neumann supplied both money and information for the relief efforts to the Emergency Society of German (later Foreign) Scientists Abroad.[62] The Emergency Committee in Aid of Displaced Foreign Physicians in New York City also assisted medical doctors who were trying to escape the Nazi threat. The physician Frederick P. Reynolds of the New York Academy of Medicine, however, warned applicants in the fall of 1933 of

---

58   Abraham Flexner (New York) to John von Neumann, May 6, 1933, John von Neumann Papers, Box 7.
59   Benjamin Liebowitz (London) to Ernst P. Boas, May 4, 1933, Leo Szilard Papers, Box 12, Folder 4.
60   Szilard (London) to Gibson, June 13, 1933.
61   Oswald Veblen (New York) to John von Neumann, May 22, 1933, John von Neumann Papers, Box 7.
62   K. Brandt (New York) to John von Neumann, March 19, 1934, John von Neumann Papers.

"the crowding in the medical profession in this country," adding that, "Apparently these conditions are growing worse each year."[63]

Szilard, despite all of the relief work he did for others, was himself in trouble, writing to his friend Eugene Wigner in June 1933: "Last, not least, someone must take care of myself, as I naturally can't do this myself and it would be incompatible with my current activities anyway."[64] Curiously, it seems at the time, Szilard's fellow Hungarian scientists rated him rather poorly as a physicist. As Wigner wrote to Michael Polanyi, he had

> complete appreciation for his [Szilard's] directness and trustworthiness. His unselfishness is almost unparalleled among my acquaintances. He has an imagination that would be of extraordinary use to him and to any institution for which he works. I don't know if a purely scientific job would be the best for him, although this should be also considered.[65]

Wigner mentioned two possible jobs for Szilard, neither of which was in academia. Similarly, von Kármán, when asked for his comments on Szilard as a prospective visiting professor in America in 1934, said that he did "not think that the case of Szilard is a very strong one."[66]

---

[63] George Baehr, M.D., Secretary of the Emergency Committee in Aid of Displaced Foreign Physicians, to Erich Marx, March 14, 1934; Memorandum of The New York Academy of Medicine, September 15, 1933. Haber-Sammlung von Joh. Jaenicke, Archiv zur Geschichte der Max-Planck-Gesellschaft, Berlin-Dahlem, Va Abt., Rep. 5, 1176–1177.

[64] Szilard, quoted in Wigner (Budapest) to Michael Polanyi, n.d. (July 1933?), Michael Polanyi Papers, Box 2, Folder 12.

[65] Wigner (Budapest) to Michael Polanyi, *ibid.*

[66] Theodore von Kármán (Pasadena) to Robert Oppenheimer, March 12, 1934, Theodore von Kármán Papers, California Institute of Technology Archives, Pasadena, File 22.10.

2 The Copernican Turn of Michael Polanyi

For all these Jewish-Hungarians destined for future greatness, their moving to Germany was not only a question of survival in terms of studies, jobs, and promotions: it also meant an opportunity to resume their professional activities or intellectual directions. It was not merely the acquisition of a new address: it led to the reconstruction of spiritual (and often bodily) health, the realization of the self and restoration of the mind.

Similarly to von Kármán, Michael Polanyi was also offered an opportunity to leave Germany before the Nazi takeover. In early 1932, the University of Manchester in Great Britain invited him to become professor of physical chemistry. Polanyi hesitated to leave Germany, "where I am rooted with the greater part of my being."[67] He also felt that it was unfair to leave Germany when it was in such a difficult situation. "I am unwilling to leave a community which is currently in difficulty after sharing the good times earlier," he answered to Professor Lapworth in Manchester. Nevertheless, he started to make inquiries into the situation at the University of Manchester and established a large set of preconditions in case he decided to come. He demanded that a new laboratory consisting of a suite of 8–10 rooms be built for him for the considerable sum of £20–25,000, equipped with apparatus costing £10,000 and complete with 8–10 "personal collaborators" to work with.[68]

The University of Manchester turned to the Rockefeller Foundation to support Polanyi's new physical chemical laboratories, but was determined to go ahead with the plans even before the Foundation responded. Throughout 1932, intensive planning was carried out to prepare the venture and in mid-December, Vice-Chancellor Walter H. Moberly sent a formal invitation to Polanyi to take the Chair of Physical Chemistry at

---

67 Michael Polanyi to Arthur Lapworth, Berlin, March 15, 1932 (German), Michael Polanyi Papers, Box 2, Folder 8.
68 A. J. [?] Allmand to Michael Polanyi, West Hampstead, May 17, 1932, Michael Polanyi Papers, Box 2, Folder 8.

Manchester for an annual stipend of £1500.[69] As late as Christmas 1932, the University was in the midst of planning to erect the new building "as quickly as possible" so that it comply "fully with the requirements of yourself and Professor Lapworth."[70]

By mid-January 1933, Polanyi abruptly changed his mind. Two weeks before Hitler's takeover he declined to accept the invitation to Manchester citing his unwillingness to settle for good in Manchester, as well as the poor climatic conditions of the area as his main reasons.[71] Though he initially believed that his military service during World War I would exempt him from the early anti-Semitic legislation of the Third Reich and leave him secure in his position at the University, within weeks he realized the gravity of his mistake. He indicated to his British friends that he had changed his mind and was now ready "to accept the chair in Manchester on any conditions that are considered fair and reasonable by the University, in consideration of the changes that have occurred since [I refused the position in December] January."[72] It was almost too late: Manchester had in the meantime invited an organic chemist, and though a modest invitation was extended to Polanyi as a third professor, "the University could not give a salary of more than £1250, and as they have in the meantime embarked on other projects as capital expenditure, they would not be able to embark on the proposed new laboratory for at

---

69 F. G. Donnan to Michael Polanyi, London, May 19, 1932; Arthur Lapworth to Michael Polanyi, Manchester, June 3 and November 27, 1932; Walter H. Moberly to Michael Polanyi, Manchester, December 15, 1932; Michael Polanyi Papers, Box 2, Folders 8 and 10.—By comparison, the average professor received £1200 p.a. at the University of Cambridge, according to Nobel Laureate Paul A. M. Dirac (Physics 1933). P. A. M. Dirac to John von Neumann, Cambridge, January 12, 1934, John von Neumann Papers, Box 7, "1933: Some very interesting letters to J. v. N.," Library of Congress, Washington, DC.
70 E. D. Simon to Michael Polanyi, Manchester, December 22, 1932, Michael Polanyi Papers, Box 2, Folder 10.
71 Michael Polanyi to Arthur Lapworth, Berlin, January 13, 1933; Michael Polanyi to F. G. Donnan, Berlin, January 17, 1933, Michael Polanyi Papers, Box 2, Folder 11.
72 Michael Polanyi to F. G. Donnan, [Berlin, n.d.] draft, Michael Polanyi Papers, Box 2, Folder 11.

least two or three years."[73] Another invitation in early May 1933 to take a Research Professorship in Physical Chemistry at the Carnegie Institute of Technology in Pittsburgh, Pennsylvania, also came too late: by then Polanyi, well known in the United States from Princeton to Minnesota, had made his arrangements to go to England.[74] On April 26, 1933 the *Neues Wiener Abendblatt* reported the resignation of Professor Polanyi in Berlin; on July 14 *The Manchester Guardian* announced his invitation to the Chair of Physical Chemistry at the University of Manchester.[75]

It is important to observe Polanyi's hesitation to relocate to Manchester in 1932–33. For people like Polanyi, deeply rooted in the ideas and ideals of 19th century liberalism, with a tolerant vision of the world and of science, it was difficult to accept the reality of the brutal and manipulative forces of interwar totalitarian systems. He belonged to a generation of scientists which, for the first time in human history, had to witness, and were consequently shocked by, the misuse of science for terrifying autocratic purposes. Polanyi first noticed these threats to freedom in the Soviet Union where he had paid several visits in 1930, 1932, and 1935. According to a note in his *Personal Knowledge*, he met with Nikolai Ivanovich Bukharin, who had even personally tried to convince him "that pure science, as distinct from technology, can exist only in a class society."[76] In due course, the director of the Institute of Physical Chemistry in Leningrad, the prospective Nobel Laureate Nikolai N. Semenov, offered a department to Polanyi in his institute, Polanyi declined the job but consented to come to Leningrad for regular consultations (for six weeks twice a year).[77] Around 1932, Michael Polanyi came to accept the

---

73   F. G. Donnan to Michael Polanyi, London, April 7, 1933, Michael Polanyi Papers, Box 2, Folder 11.
74   Thomas S. Baker to Michael Polanyi, May 10 and June 1, 1933, Michael Polanyi Papers, Box 2, Folder 12. Cf. William Foster, "Princeton's New Chemical Laboratory," *Journal of Chemical Education*, Vol. 6, No. 12, December, 1929, pp. 2094–2095.
75   Clippings, Michael Polanyi Papers, Box 45, Folder 3; Box 46, Folder 4.
76   Michael Polanyi, *Personal Knowledge. Towards a Post-Critical Philosophy* (Chicago, IL: The University of Chicago Press, 1958), p. 238.
77   N. Semenoff—M. Polanyi Correspondence, 1930–1932, Michael Polanyi Papers, Box 2. Cf. *The New Encyclopaedia Britannica*, Chicago, 1990, Vol. 10, p. 629.—Other

opinion of his brother who was highly critical of what went on in Stalin's country and, as Karl reported happily to their mother, they reached an understanding as to "our views of the Soviet Union that were dividing us for such a long time [and] now considerably coincide."[78]

It was at this junction that Polanyi was forced to understand the potential threat of a political change in Germany as well. Almost until it was too late, he had believed in the strength and survival of the tolerant and liberal political and social values of Weimar Germany and found a right wing takeover unlikely.

Radical shifts in the German political scene seem to have represented a much more fundamental shock for Polanyi than totalitarian symptoms in the Soviet Union. For liberal, often left-wing émigré intellectuals and professionals from post-War Hungary, it was a painful and threatening experience to realize that the country, which throughout the 1920s had been a lasting shelter, was about to stop serving as a political asylum: Weimar Germany was being rapidly transformed into the terrorizing *Third Reich*. It was almost unfathomable that the access to all of Europe he had experienced as a young man was about to be gone. Recalling the changes in a 1944 review of F. A. Hayek's *The Road to Serfdom*, Polanyi remembered the bygone world of the 19th century with nostalgic longing:

> Hungarians in Berlin also received invitation to work in the Soviet Union: young musician János Kerekes, then in Berlin, was contracted in 1934 by conductor György Sebestyén [Georg Sebastian] who then served as music director of Radio Moscow, though the plan to become his assistant ultimately failed. The contract referred to a "Verpflegung wie für ausländische Spezialisten," suggesting that the invitation of foreign experts was routine (János Kerekes' contract with Radio Moscow, courtesy János Kerekes; taped interview with Budapest Opera conductor János Kerekes, 1988). Indeed, somewhat earlier, in 1928, Hungarian violinist Joseph Szigeti was also invited to the Leningrad Conservatory to be the follower of Hungarian-born violin professor Leopold Auer. A[lexander K]. Glazounow, A. Ossowsky and A[lexander V]. Alexandrow, Conservatoire de Léningrad to Joseph Szigeti, Leningrad, 1928, Boston University, Mugar Memorial Library, Joseph Szigeti Papers, Box 1, Folder 3.

78   Karl Polanyi to Cecil Polányi, September 27, 1932, [German] Michael Polanyi Papers, Box 18, Folder 2.

Some of us still recall that before 1914 you could travel across all the countries of Europe without a passport and settle down in any place you pleased without a permit. The measure of political tolerance which commonly prevailed in those days can be best assessed by remembering local conditions which at the time were considered as exceptionally bad. The domineering and capricious personal régime of Wilhelm II was widely resented, even though it allowed, for example, the popular satirical paper, Simplicissimus, regularly to print the most biting cartoons, jokes and verse directed against the Kaiser. Europe shuddered at the horrors of Tsarist oppression, though under it Tolstoy could continue to attack from his country seat in Yasnaya Polyana with complete impunity the Tsar and the Holy Synod, and persistently preach disobedience against the fundamental laws of the State, while pilgrims from all the corners of the earth could travel unmolested to Yasnaya Polyana to pay tribute to him. After less than a generation, say in 1935, we find that all the freedom and tolerance which only a few years earlier had been so confidently taken for granted, has vanished over the main parts of Europe.[79]

It was the twin experience of Soviet-Russian and Nazi-German totalitarianism, a shock for Polanyi's entire generation,[80] that ultimately forced him to accept asylum in England. Understanding, finally, in 1934 the nature of forces threatening his freedom, and the freedom of science in general, he made a "Copernican turn," changing not only his country of residence but also his language and, somewhat later, his field of research. In this sense, Polanyi chose a very special, complex form of emigration: first he left medicine, then Hungary and the Hungarian language, then he left Germany for Britain, as well as science for philosophy, and chose English rather than German as an exclusive language of publication. Consequently, it was from having undertaken this enormous change that he was able to work repeatedly to refine the social position of knowledge and science. Throughout his long journey from the "peace" of pre-World War I Hungary, through Weimar Germany and into England, Polanyi pursued democracy and a liberal scientific atmosphere, while broaden-

---

79 Michael Polanyi, "The Socialist Error *[The Road to Serfdom*. By F. A. Hayek]," *The Spectator,* March 31, 1944.
80 Laura Fermi, "The Dictators and the Intelligentsia," in *Illustrious Immigrants: The Intellectual Migration from Europe 1930–41* (Chicago & London: University of Chicago Press, 1968), pp. 53.

ing his own intellectual horizon, from a narrower scientific discipline towards a philosophy of knowledge that was to become sensitive both to ethical and political issues.

That Polanyi's philosophical inquiries developed from his scientific investigations as well as from the political drama he witnessed in Germany and the Soviet Union, was indicated in his 1933 correspondence with Eugene Wigner, who reflected on his friend's concerns as to the purpose of science and the scientist: "I must admit," Wigner wrote to Polanyi from Budapest,

> that the difficulties that I felt so acutely in Berlin are somewhat blurred here. It is so difficult to speak of these things—I think we are afraid that we may come to a "false", i.e. unpleasant result. We have all gone through these questions at the age of 18 and had to give them up as insoluble, and then we have forgotten them. At our age when one is no longer geared so very much towards success, it is more difficult to do so. It seems to be an undertaking of ridiculous courage to be willing to question whether or not all that we have lived for, culture, righteousness, science, has a purpose. [...] I know that you have been dealing with these thoughts for a long time [...] Even if the basic problem is insoluble, when the purpose of science is concerned particularly, [...] the answer must contain the basic questions.[81]

Polanyi's combined inquiries as a scientist and a philosopher resulted ultimately in his 1951–52 Gifford Lectures at the University of Aberdeen in Scotland, which served as the basis of his celebrated *Personal Knowledge*.[82] For Polanyi, becoming a philosopher seems to have been his means of moving out of the complex, cumulative deadlock of his scientific career.

---

81   Eugene Wigner to Michael Polanyi, [Budapest,] June 30, 1933, Michael Polanyi Papers, Box 2, Folder 12.
82   Michael Polanyi, *Personal Knowledge. Towards a Post-Critical Philosophy* (Chicago, IL: The University of Chicago Press, 1958).

3 Networking, Cohorting, Bonding: American Patterns

Rusztem Vámbéry repeatedly called attention to the fact that not all who fled their countries should properly be called refugees. He argued that the Hungarian-American community was in fact a mixture of "two emigrant groups," people with very different backgrounds and circumstances being brought together did not make them a community.[83] Yet, bonding, networking, cohorting within and, less often, between various factions of the Hungarian-American community became more intense than ever during the War years, all of which was abundantly documented by their correspondence.

In order to understand the nature of networking it is essential to appreciating the social structure of immigrant groups and their ties to prospective newcomers. Because the bulk of the quota was earmarked by preferences for one sort of immigrant rather than another, and non-quota emigration was greatly dependent upon letters of recommendations, affidavits, and invitations from fellow nationals who had become U.S. citizens, the social composition of the exile community was virtually self-sustained and self-perpetuating.[84] Because of this, there was very little chance to incorporate new elements or groups. Peasant communities absorbed prospective farmers, professionals attracted fellow professionals, Gentiles invited Gentiles, and Jews welcomed Jews. Thus, American immigration policies, especially during the long period between 1924

---

83 Rusztem Vámbéry, "Két emigráció," [Two Emigrations] *Tárogató,* Vol. III, No. 4, October 1940, Rusztem Vambery Papers, Box 4, Archives of the Hoover Institution on War, Revolution and Peace, Stanford, CA.

84 Patterns of networking were occasionally different in Britain, where intellectual organizations occasionally welcomed distinguished Hungarian newcomers such as Karl Mannheim and Michael Polanyi who joined e.g. the progressive circle of "The Moot" between 1937 and 1946. Cf. Éva Gábor, "Michael Polanyi in The Moot," *Polanyiana,* Vol. II (1992), Nos. 1–2, pp. 120–127. See also Lee Congdon's excellent book on Hungarian exiles in Britain, *Seeing Red: Hungarian Intellectuals in Exile and the Challenge of Communism* (DeKalb, IL: Northern Illinois University Press, 2001).

and 1965, contributed to the growth and stable characteristics of existing social patterns in the immigrant communities. Even though we have had access to a limited number and type of sources regarding this information, typically in the private papers of Jewish-Hungarian scientists and other professionals, this observation seems valid. Statistical evidence regarding all U.S. immigrant visas issued, including enclosed personal material, still needs to be discovered. Nonetheless, it may prove enlightening to survey some case studies which have become available.

Jewish-Hungarians were first warned of the increasing Nazi danger by the *Anschluss* of neighboring Austria by Germany. As the small Hungarian quota was entirely filled for years ahead, immigration seemed possible only for people who had received an invitation e.g. to a university or research institute. Thus, many scientists embarked on a desperate struggle to obtain invitations. "I beg you to give me your assistance in this difficult situation," pleaded the eminent Viennese-Hungarian mycologist József Szűcs to potential employers through his mentor, Theodore von Kármán, who was one of the most willing supporters of refugee scientists.[85] Also begging for von Kármán's support was young aeronautical engineer Miklós Hoff from Budapest who did indeed receive his first U.S. job, as an instructor in Brooklyn, through von Kármán.[86] Vilmos Szilasi explained to his cousin Theodore von Kármán that the letter of affidavit should make it very clear that "you know me since our childhood and give the explicit assurance, that my immigration would not be inimical to the interest of the United States" and "that you assume the responsibility of keeping yourself informed of my conduct in the U. St. as well as immediately reporting to the Department of Justice any irregularity in my activities."[87]

An invitation by itself was not enough: appointments to a particular job had to be for at least two years. When Professor Gábor Szegő secured

---

85 Dr. Josef Szűcs to Theodore von Kármán, and Enclosure, Wien, June 29, 1938, Theodore von Kármán Papers, File 29.20.
86 Miklós Hoff to Theodore von Kármán, Budapest, September 19, 1938 and Palo Alto, CA, April 20, 1940, Theodore von Kármán Papers, File 13.20.
87 Wilhelm Szilasi to Theodore von Kármán, Lisboa, May 20, 1941, Theodore von Kármán Papers, File 29.20.

sufficient funds to invite for a year to Stanford his longtime associate and friend, the distinguished mathematician George Pólya (1887–1985) from Switzerland, "the American Consul in Zurich refused to admit him on non-quota basis because of the temporary character of the appointment."[88] In a desperate attempt to get his friend out of Europe, Szegő turned to von Kármán to secure an additional invitation for Pólya from Caltech. "You understand that although Pólya is not in a concentration camp and not yet dismissed, his situation is very dangerous and he tries desperately to get out before it is too late," Szegő wrote to von Kármán.[89] "It is not necessary to stress how urgent the case is. Every day may bring new restrictions and difficulties."[90] The Polyas left Zurich via Portugal for the U.S. in 1940 where Pólya ultimately succeeded in obtaining a two year teaching position at Brown University and Smith College before joining the Stanford Faculty in 1942, to remain there until the end of his very long life.[91]

The noted Budapest lung and T. B. specialist Gyula Holló, a personal physician of Béla Bartók, Dezső Kosztolányi, Frigyes Karinthy and Joseph Szigeti, turned to his former patient John von Neumann to support him

> by drawing the attention of some influential person who could help me to get a job or an invitation or give instructions through the State Department to the Consulate in Budapest so that I get a non-quota place (which is not unprecedented) or, and

---

88 Gábor Szegő to Theodore von Kármán, Stanford, July 24, 1940, Theodore von Kármán Papers, File 23.35.
89 *Ibid.*
90 *Ibid.*
91 G[abor] Szegő to George Pólya, Stanford, June 11, 1940; President Henry M. Wriston to Georg Polya [sic], Brown University, Providence R.I., July 31, 1940; George Polya Papers, SC 337, 86–036, Department of Special Collections and University Archives, Stanford University Libraries, Stanford, *The Life of Mathematician George Pólya, 1887–1985,* Department of Special Collections and University Archives, Cecil H. Green Library, Stanford University Libraries, December 13, 1987–June 1988 (Exhibit Guide).

this seems to be the most realistic idea, prepares the way and helps me if I come as a visitor searching for a job personally.[92]

Dr. Holló succeeded in getting out of Hungary and accepted a position at Goldwater Memorial Hospital and died in New York City in 1973.[93]

As the War came nearer to Hungary, the non-quota contingent became filled for years ahead, partly by pure and applied scientists, medical doctors and mathematicians. Yet, many did not succeed in getting an invitation. The celebrated Budapest surgeon, Professor Lajos Ádám was told that the Mayo Clinic in Rochester, Minnesota, would not extend an invitation although Dr. C. W. Mayo counted him "as one of my very good friends." Ádám's well-known and well-connected Hungarian-American protector, the journalist and author Emil Lengyel (1895–1985) was told that "we are up against conditions here at present which make it impossible for us to guarantee bringing him here as a Professor or to guarantee any salary."[94] Ádám stayed in Budapest but, miraculously, survived the War.

In the meantime, many non-scientists managed to get out. Refugees included many people from the world of film and theater, entertainers, literary people, actors, directors and musicians. In early 1940, von Kármán had the distinct impression that "New York and Los Angeles are full of newcomers from Budapest, but almost exclusively artists, actors, and writers. Certainly more than half of the music and literature is now in the United States," he commented to a friend in Hungary.[95] Much later, in the early 1950s, Michael Polanyi himself sought to move to the University of Chicago, but because of his leftist political entanglement in various international groups including the Galileo Circle of pre-World

---

92 Gyula Holló to John von Neumann, n.d. [1939?], John von Neumann Papers, Box 6.
93 *Magyar Életrajzi Lexikon,* Vol. III (Budapest: Akadémiai Kiadó, 1981), p. 311.
94 Dr. C. W. Mayo to Emil Lengyel, May 19, 1941, Emil Lengyel Collection, Bakhmeteff Archives, Butler Library, Columbia University Library, New York, NY.
95 Theodore von Kármán to Lajos Bencze, February 19, 1940, Theodore von Kármán Papers, File 2.24.

War I Budapest, he was refused entrance to the United States between 1951 and 1953.[96]

For people dependent upon their native language and culture, immigration was merely the lesser of two evils. It may have saved their lives but, in many cases, emigration nonetheless turned out tragically. A lesser known but important case among authors was that of Ignotus (Hugo Veigelsberg, 1869–1949), the famous liberal critic, essayist and journalist in turn-of-the-century Budapest and interwar Vienna. It is worth recalling his case in some detail as it reveals virtually the entire support mechanism which immigrants could expect in the United States.

Ignotus, a prominent Budapest literary figure, was from the perspective of immigration, a pathetic figure with a difficult case. More than 70 years old, with a poor command of English, he was not in a position to rebuild his literary career. Ignotus was one of those who was forced to leave Austria after the *Anschluss,* and after a brief stay in England, went to Lisbon in an effort to secure a U.S. immigration visa, but was stranded there. His old Hungarian-American friends mobilized their best connections: Emil Lengyel, Rusztem Vambery and Sandor Rado, M.D., wrote to the influential Ingrid and Bettina Warburg as well as to Lotta Loeb, all of whom worked for the Emergency Rescue Committee, and he was able to secure their cooperation.[97] Lengyel pointed out how Ignotus had been "fighting Hitlerism in its Hungarian and German varieties," and

---

[96] On Michael Polanyi and the Galileo Circle see John M. Cash, *Guide to the Papers of Michael Polanyi* (The Joseph Regenstein Library, University of Chicago, 1977), p. 8; Michael Polanyi Papers, Box 46, Folder 5; on other, allegedly pro-Soviet involvement see Malcolm D. Rivkin, "Teachers Protest Bar of Anti-Commie Prof," *The Harvard Crimson,* November 14, 1952; Toni Stolper, "Letter to *The New York Times,*" New York, May 10, 1952; William Taussig Scott and Martin X. Moleski, S.J., *Michael Polanyi: Scientist and Philosopher* (Oxford: Oxford University Press, 2005), pp. 222–223.

[97] Emil Lengyel to Ingrid Warburg, New York, October 25, 1940; Sandor Rado to Bettina Warburg, October 28, 1940; Bettina Warburg to Ingrid Warburg, October 28, 1940; Sandor Rado to Ingrid Warburg, November 11, 1940; Rustem Vambery to Lotta Loeb, February 22, 1941; International Rescue Committee, Box 6, Archives of the Hoover Institution on War, Revolution and Peace, Stanford, CA.

that he was "on the blacklist of the Gestapo."[98] Rado and Edith C. Field provided moral sponsorship affidavits for the State Department; Edith C. Field added an affidavit of support as well.[99] Rusztem Vámbéry prepared a detailed biographical sketch and emphasized how the periodical *Nyugat* under Ignotus had advocated "liberal and progressive ideas" and "was for two decades the center of young intellectuals."[100] The Emergency Rescue Committee used Vambery's text to obtain him a visa, though they also solicited the support of Nobel Laureate Thomas Mann.[101] Other sponsors included Professor Oscar Jászi and Count Ferdinand Czernin.

Ignotus was admitted to the United States in early 1941, along with his wife, but the Immigration and Naturalization Service did not provide them with unlimited permission to stay. When they were asked to leave the country in August 1942, Ignotus's friend Oscar Jászi used his personal connections to U.S. Supreme Court Justice Felix Frankfurter,[102] and it was probably Frankfurter's support which secured an extension for the Ignotus couple.

Ignotus, however, had a difficult time in New York. His wife became seriously ill and the long years in exile made him "a very worried and fearful man" who "can get things unintentionally quite confused," as associates of the International Rescue and Relief Committee taking care of him soon

---

98 Emil Lengyel to Ingrid Warburg, New York, October 25, 1940; International Rescue Committee, Box 6, Archives of the Hoover Institution.
99 Sandor Rado, Affidavit, November 18, 1940; Ingrid Warburg to George Warren, January 28, 1941; International Rescue Committee, Box 6, Archives of the Hoover Institution.
100 Rustem Vambery, "Biographical Sketch of Dr. Hugo Ignotus," New York, January 28, 1941, International Rescue Committee, Box 6, Archives of the Hoover Institution.
101 Ingrid Warburg to George Warren, January 28, 1941; Lotta Loeb to Thomas Mann, November 13, 1940, International Rescue Committee, Box 6, Archives of the Hoover Institution.
102 Oscar Jaszi to Felix Frankfurter, August 21, 1942, Felix Frankfurter to Oscar Jaszi, New Milford, Conn., August 27, 1942; Oscar Jaszi Papers, Rare Book and Manuscript Library, Butler Library, Columbia University Library, New York, NY.

found out.[103] The only income to support the couple came from charitable organizations such as the American Committee for Christian Refugees and, subsequently, the Community Service Society. The monthly allowance of $60, which the Community Service sent him, was insufficient. Furthermore, this organization supported refugees only on a temporary basis and refrained as a matter of policy from helping "chronic" cases.[104] The International Rescue and Relief Committee and the Jewish Labor Committee took joint responsibility for additional sponsorship in the amount of another $50 which was extended to Ignotus through 1948.[105] On the recommendation of the Writers' Project, Ignotus received a prize from New York City in May 1944 which came with $1,000.[106] His wife, however, was so sick that a deportation order was pending against her because she was now in a mental institution, which made their permanent settlement plans in the U.S. hopeless.[107] In early 1949, he departed for Hungary via Britain, leaving his wife behind in the care of the American Committee for Foreign Scholars, Writers and Artists (subsequently the American Council for Emigres in the Professions). He also left behind bitter feelings among the various agencies that had supported him. "Mr. Hugo Ignotus has left for England," commented Charles Sternberg of IRRC adding: "I am glad he did."[108] He was 80 then and approaching

103 Excerpts from Letter of Janet Siebold, August 21, 1944, International Rescue Committee, Box 6, Archives of the Hoover Institution.
104 *Ibid.*
105 Sheba Strupsky to Jewish Labor Committee, September 15, 1943; Eva Lewinski (IRRC) to Jewish Labor Committee, January 10, 1946; IRRC Case Department—Hugo Ignotus Correspondence, 1947–1949; International Rescue Committee, Box 6, Archives of the Hoover Institution.
106 Excerpts from Letter of Janet Siebold, August 21, 1944, International Rescue Committee, Box 6, Archives of the Hoover Institution; cf. *Magyar Irodalmi Lexikon,* Vol. I (Budapest: Akadémiai Kiadó, 1963), p. 491.
107 Minutes of a January 8, 1945 meeting at ACCR, International Rescue Committee, Box 6, Archives of the Hoover Institution.
108 Charles Sternberg (IRRC) to Samuel Estrin (Jewish Labor Committee), January 31, 1949, International Rescue Committee, Box 6, Archives of the Hoover Institution. Cf. Endre Sík, *Egy diplomata feljegyzései* [Notes of a Diplomat] (Budapest: Kossuth, 1966), p. 109.

his end. Upon his arrival in Budapest, he was taken immediately to a hospital where he was observed by an old friend as "shriveled, [...] sitting unstoppably trembling. He was half dead."[109]

The poignant case of the great composer and piano virtuoso Béla Bartók (1881–1945) is well known.[110] In one sense, he was less fortunate than Ignotus: after a few years in voluntary exile during the War years, he died in New York City in 1945, before he could complete his wish to return to his native country.

Invited to give a concert at the Library of Congress in 1939, Bartók, of Gentile origin, was eager to leave Hungary by the time the War broke out. He described his anxieties and fears as if he spoke for all intending exiles:

> [...] at the outbreak of the war, I really came into a really desperate state of mind.... We see that small countries are invaded from one day to another quite unexpectedly by the most terrible armies and subjected to tortures of every kind. As for my own country, now, instead of one dangerous neighbour, we have got two of them; nobody knows what will happen next day. It may happen, if I leave the country for America that I can't return, can't even have news from my family - - - - . I hope you will understand my state of spirit - - - .[111]

Bartók decided to leave Hungary for the United States in late 1940 when he received the honorary degree of Doctor of Music from Columbia University.[112] In February 1941, he was employed by Columbia as a Visiting Associate in Music, to work on the late Professor Milman Parry's Yugoslav music collection of nearly 4,000 discs.[113] Bartók enjoyed this work very

109 Oszkár Gellért, *Kortársaim* [My Contemporaries] (Budapest: Művelt Nép, 1954), pp. 179–180.
110 Agatha Fassett, *Béla Bartók: The American Years* (New York: Dover, 1970).
111 Béla Bartók to Harold Spivacke, Budapest, November 9, 1939, Coolidge Collection/ Béla Bartók, Library of Congress, Music Division, Washington, DC.
112 Nicholas Murray Butler to Béla Bartók, April 1, 1940; Frank D. Fackenthal—Béla Bartók Correspondence, November 1940, Rare Book and Manuscript Library, Butler Library, Columbia University Library, New York, NY.
113 Columbia University to Béla Bartók, February 3, 1941; Béla Bartók to Douglas Moore, April 18, 1941 and January 21, 1942; Rare Book and Manuscript Library, Butler Library, Columbia University Library, New York, NY.

much, which lasted until the end of 1942, but he was never really happy in his voluntary exile and always hoped to return to his native Hungary. While he was relatively healthy, he played a political role in the Movement for Independent Hungary, trying to convince the world that the movement represented millions of Hungarians "supporting those who fight for a free and democratic world."[114]

Some of the immigrants' old political connections or affinities survived even World War II. Theodore von Kármán rediscovered after the War his old ties to the influential Hungarian-Soviet economist Eugen Varga, director of the Institute of World Economy and Politics of the Soviet Academy of Sciences while during a visit to Moscow. He used this reestablished contact to help in the case of Susan Meller, the daughter of art historian Simon Meller, who had apparently been captured by the Soviet military police. Varga did contribute to getting Ms. Meller freed. Friendships such as these, dating back to pre-World War I Hungary, often survived profound political changes in the world and profound changes in the lives of the persons involved.[115]

4 Rescue Operations: Institutional

In the late 1930s, Fascism and Nazism spread across the continent of Europe, civil war raged in Spain and General Franco's victory pushed Republicans into exile, while Hitler took over Austria (1938) and Czechoslovakia (1938–39). "[T]he developments in Germany since 1933...," wrote Louis Adamic in a 1939 *Public Affairs Pamphlet*, a publication of the Public Affairs Committee, Inc. in New York City, "reached a climax in 1938 when

---

114 Béla Bartók to Theodore von Kármán, June 27, 1942, Theodore von Kármán Papers, File 2.5.
115 Theodore von Kármán to Eugen Varga, February 11, 1946, E[ugen] Varga to Theodore von Kármán, April 15, 1946, Theodore von Kármán to Eugen Varga, November 4, 1946; Theodore von Kármán Papers, File 31.21.

Naziism [sic] engulfed Austria and Czechoslovakia." The Nazi takeover in Germany in 1933 forced many thousands to leave that country and to appeal once again to American organizations for aid.

It is a generally accepted historical fact that the United States gave too little support to refugees from Germany and other European countries that were overrun by the Nazis. American anti-Semitism has been often quoted as one of the main reasons for this lack of compassion and cooperation.[116] Some of the arguments used to explain this today had already been voiced in the mid-1930s. In an NBC radio broadcast on July 9, 1934, Cecilia Razovsky of the National Council of Jewish Women, admitted that

> the United States [...] is still confronted with the gigantic task of finding employment for some ten million of its own people... Sympathetic as Americans have always been to the distress of refugees, our own grave problems have caused us to forego our traditional historical policy of asylum for the oppressed and the homeless, and our response in this crisis has necessarily been less generous than in the past.[117]

As late as 1935, the High Commission for Refugees of the League of Nations viewed optimistically a largely European "plan for the liquidation of the refugee problem."[118] Carefully prepared by Walter M.

---

116 For a complex analysis of U.S. refugee policy between 1933 and 1945 see Richard Breitman and Alan M. Kraut, *American Refugee Policy and European Jewry, 1933–1945* (Bloomington and Indianapolis: Indiana University Press, 1987). On anti-Semitism in the United States before and during World War II see David S. Wyman, *Paper Walls: America and the Refugee Crisis 1938–1941* (New York: Pantheon Books, 1968, 1985), as well as David S. Wyman, *The Abandonment of the Jews: America and the Holocaust 1941–1945* (New York: Pantheon Books, 1984).
117 Cecilia Razovsky, "The United States and the German Refugees," NBC radio broadcast, New York, July 23, 1934, Columbia University, Rare Book and Manuscript Library, Herbert H. Lehman Suite and Papers, James G. McDonald Papers, National Coordinating Committee, Cecilia Razovsky File, D356 H21.
118 Walter M. Kotschnig to A. Wurfbain, March 5, 1935, Columbia University, Rare Book and Manuscript Library, Herbert H. Lehman Suite and Papers, James G. McDonald Papers, Walter M. Kotschnig File, 1935—April 1936, D356 H20.

Kotschnig, the plan calculated that the refugees from Germany could be absorbed by countries all around the world. At this point Kotschnig suggested that some 25,000 people would go to European countries and an additional 850 to the U.S.—considering that some 5,000 immigrants were already admitted in the first 18 months of the emigration. Today as we have learned the real figures of the German catastrophy, Kotschnig's estimate sounds naïve.

In what was obviously part of a propaganda war to change the prevailing common opinion in the country, immigration expert Louis Adamic surveyed the immigrant situation in the U.S. between 1932 and 1938 and voiced some of the most important and most typical pro-refugee arguments of the day. He noted that the fears of patriotic, yet in many instances, poorly informed citizens prevailed. Anti-foreign feelings were channeled into several hundred organizations and movements. To counterbalance common sentiment, Adamic came to a number of new conclusions. Out of the total allowance of nearly 1,100,000 people for all the quota countries "only 140,000 quota immigrants actually came in, or about 11 per cent of the quota. During the period before June 30, 1938, only 42,494 quota immigrants had been admitted, which is about 28 per cent of the 153,774 permitted under the quota."[119] He included Hungary in the list of countries that did not approach their small quota in the depression years before 1938.[120] Adamic was quick to point out that very few of the refugee-immigrants from Germany under National Socialism "took jobs to the detriment of anyone who had been in the country before their arrival." Adamic's pamphlet emphatically suggested that not all refugees were Jewish, a common fear of contemporary Americans. He also underlined that "Catholics and Protestants have also suffered new persecutions."[121] Suggesting that the admission of Hitler's victims was good for the country, Adamic quoted Bruce Bliven of *The New Republic* whose enthusiastic report "Thank you, Hitler!" attempted to change the

---

119   Louis Adamic, *op. cit.*, p. 10.
120   *Ibid.*, p. 11.
121   *Ibid.*, p. 19.

generally negative attitude of the American public. Almost simultaneously, *This Week*, a supplement to several major Sunday papers, published a similar article entitled "Thank You, Dictators!"[122]

Adamic's pamphlet was part of an overall propaganda war that responded to the arguments of those who fought for retaining American jobs for Americans. A broadsheet entitled "PROTEST to the President, to Congressmen, to U.S. Senators NOW," probably from the end of 1938, urged everybody to "Write, Wire, Telephone Or Personally See Your Elected Servants In Washington. Demand a Square Deal." John Cecil, President of the American Immigration Conference Board, Inc. used the publicity generated by the flyer to alert the American people that while 20 million of them "are now living by public assistance... 3 million American families subsist on WPA checks, 2½ million American workers lost their jobs in the first six months of this year... 10½ million Americans are totally unemployed, [...] (and meanwhile,) 4 million legally and illegally entered aliens are holding American jobs, [...] (and) over a million aliens are on relief [...]"[123] Cecil concluded by calling on Americans to "demand [...] that American jobs and relief shall go first to jobless and distressed American citizens. *Do it now!*"[124]

The refugee question reopened the post-World War I problem of the quotas, and their eventual abolishment became a hotly debated issue once again in the late 1930s. As "professional alien-haters and Jew-baiters," organizations such as the American Coalition formed serious opposition to the elimination of the quotas. Several organizations interested in spreading anti-foreign sentiment were directly connected with the Nazi

---

122 "Thank you, Hitler," *The New Republic*, November 10, 1937, Louis Adamic, *op. cit.*, p. 15.
123 John Cecil, President, "Protest to the President, to Congressmen, to U.S. Senators Now" (flyer), American Immigration Conference Board, Inc., New York, [1938], CEIP, Committee to Aid Czechoslovakia, Box 288, Folder 5, 102536.
124 John Cecil, *op. cit.*

propaganda machinery in Berlin.[125] Adamic was correct in his balanced assessment in 1939 that

> A very large number of American citizens are deeply interested in getting the refugees out of the reach of the Nazis, but many are afraid, too, that a large increase in immigration to this country is apt to help augment the sentiment against the "foreigners" which—partly as a backwash from nationalism and anti-Semitism in Europe, partly on account of our own economic plight—has been stronger of late in several parts of the United States than ever before.[126]

The Nazi takeover in Germany and subsequent events in Europe occurred at a time when the United States was still coping with the aftermath of the great economic and financial crash of the late 1920s and early 1930s. The New Deal was to transform the country but there was still considerable poverty and distress, discouraging many from contributing to foreign aid and offering a large number of jobs to displaced Europeans.

Large sections of American society were reluctant to admit "foreign refugees, which could mean dispossessing Americans qualified to fill the positions."[127] Some Colorado citizens suggested sending European immigrants to Alaska rather than have them in their own state.[128] In his capacity as President of the Carnegie Endowment for International Peace, Nobel Laureate Nicholas Murray Butler, President of Columbia University, received a large number of letters from Nazi-occupied countries in Europe seeking his assistance in coming to the U.S. His secretary could only send discouraging answers explaining that there are "approximately ten million unemployed in this country at the present time and ... thousands of our young men and women are graduating each year

---

125 Report of the Institute for Propaganda Analysis, January 1, 1939, quoted by Louis Adamic, *op. cit.,* p. 22.
126 Louis Adamic, *op. cit.*, p. 23.
127 Henry S. Haskell, Assistant to the Director, Carnegie Endowment for International Peace to Susan Huntington Vernon, New York, March 13, 1939, Columbia University, Rare Book and Manuscript Library, Carnegie Endowment for International Peace, Aid to Refugees, Box 271, Folder 1, 94619.
128 The Alaska Colonization Society for Refugees, n.d. CEIP, Committee to Aid Czechoslovakia, Box 288, Folder 3, 102441.

"*Incipit Hitler:*" *Double Expulsion, Double Trauma* 283

from colleges and universities and are finding great difficulty in obtaining employment [...]"[129] Some Americans refrained from contributing in support of refugees, as they were deeply convinced of their isolationist wisdom, "charity should begin at home."[130] This was a typical, widely-used argument against spending on refugees. Phelan Beale of the firm Bouvier & Beale on Broadway in New York pointed out that

> I can show you in this country right at your doorstep details just as pitiful, if not more so than can be portrayed in Czechoslovakia. I can also show you a greater number of people in the United States who have lost their homes and means of livelihood than the number of deplorable victims in Czechoslovakia, who have suffered a like fate. Means that are at my disposal to unfortunates, I prefer to apply to sufferers in the United States, because it is my sincere belief that we should put our own house in order before we proceed elsewhere.[131]

The same argument was used by C. Ledyard Blair of Wall Street who declared to "have the greatest sympathy not only for those in Czechoslovakia but those in China, Spain, Palestine and the jews [sic] in Germany. We also have, as you know in this country some ten or eleven millions of American unemployed citizens, for whose support we are unnecessarily taxed."[132] Delavan M. Baldwin of New York who had recently returned from Germany, went so far as to put the question to President Butler, Chairman of the American Committee for Relief in Czechoslovakia, "should not Americans give aid to American institutions for Americans in America, in view of the on rush of emigrants now from Germany to the United States?"[133] Louis Adamic warned that "the situation which the refugees and our economic crisis jointly create is so delicate and dangerous,"

---

129 Henry S. Haskell to Jan Mašek, New York, March 27, 1939, CEIP, Aid to Refugees, Box 271, Folder 1, 94625.
130 Phelan Beale to Nicholas Murray Butler, New York, November 29, 1938, CEIP, Committee to Aid Czechoslovakia, Box 286, Folder 4, 100930.
131 *Ibid.*
132 C. Ledyard Blair to Nicholas Murray Butler, New York, November 23, 1938, CEIP, Committee to Aid Czechoslovakia, Box 286, Folder 4, 100931.
133 Delavan M. Baldwin to Nicholas Murray Butler, New York, December 21, 1938, CEIP, Committee to Aid Czechoslovakia, Box 287, Folder 1, 101194.

especially "in an atmosphere in which alien-baiting and anti-Semitism seem to be increasing."[134] People, he concluded, should not "believe that more Jewish refugees are being admitted than can be absorbed by the country."[135]

In May 1938, when the emigration of Austrian scholars came to the agenda, the American Council of Learned Societies sensed only "a suspicion of anti-Semitism"[136] in the air. Yet by 1939, even the Emergency Committee in Aid of Displaced Foreign Scholars declared that there was no more chance to place Jewish refugees in the U.S. The Committee was shocked to receive David Cleghorn Thomson, General Secretary of the British Society for the Protection of Science and Learning (formerly the AAC), who came from London to visit colleges in the Mid-West and the West, to explore possible placements there for refugee academics from Europe. Leading Jewish members of the Executive Committee were troubled by the prospect of raising the level of existing anti-Semitism in the country.

> Imagine a committee meeting in a city 29% Jewish, attended by Jewish leaders who have raised most of the $600,000 during the past five years for the academic placement of (mostly Jewish) exiles, but who in the face of a generally increasing anti-Semitism here are exceedingly sensitive about colleges and universities being asked [...] to accept any more Jewish emigres.[137]

Alan Gregg noted, "[i]t would be easy to exaggerate the dangers of the undercurrent of anti-Semitism now running in this country and its universities, but it would be hard to exaggerate the intensity of the anxiety of American Jews lest English efforts [...] expose [...] all Jews to the very resentments they are powerless to control."[138]

---

134 Louis Adamic, *op. cit.*, pp. 28–29, 30.
135 *Ibid.*, p. 30.
136 Mortimer Graves to Dr. Stevens, May 27, 1938, Rockefeller Archive Center, Rockefeller Foundation Archives, RG 1.1, Series 200, Box 46, Folder 529.
137 Alan Gregg to A. V. Hill, New York, April 13, 1939, Rockefeller Archive Center, Alfred E. Cohn Papers, RG 450 C661-U, Box 4, Folder 29.
138 *Ibid.*

It is natural that the Jewish leaders of the refugee operations were afraid to lose the social and political balance of the country by overdoing rescue operations and suffering the consequences. At the same time, a trip to universities and colleges undertaken by Felix W. Krauth on behalf of the Emergency Committee in Aid of Displaced Foreign Scholars made it clear that there were relatively few schools (Vermont, Mather, Western Reserve, Syracuse, Bates, Dartmouth, New Hampshire) that were racially prejudiced and only a handful of denominational schools (Colby Junior College, DePauw, Texas Christian) were unlikely to accept Jews.[139] Krauth observed that there was "very little evident antagonism and prejudice towards Jews," but there was "in all faculties a fear of numbers."[140]

In 1940, the Quakers noticed that anti-Semitism was particularly prevalent in the South, where anti-German sentiment was also widespread, as anti-Semitism and anti-foreignism often went hand in hand. However, two other partners also appeared here: isolationism and rising nationalism. The High Commissioner for Refugees (Jewish and Other) Coming from Germany, J. G. McDonald quoted Stephen Duggan of the Institute of International Education "that there was some evidence in college circles of resentment at the increase in foreign teachers, even though this has been relatively so slight." In 1934, the American Association of University Professors investigated the problem of foreigners teaching in American higher education and found that the problem was caused by "the large number of foreign teachers of foreign languages in the [American] universities."[141] By 1939, the Association understood "from many sources [...] that American teachers, particularly our younger teachers in colleges and universities, are disturbed and apprehensive about the influx of

---

139 Felix W. Krauth, Report of Trip to Universities and Colleges, October 1939—January 1940, Emergency Committee in Aid of Displaced Foreign Scholars, Rockefeller Archive Center, Alfred E. Cohn Papers, RG 450 C661-U, Box 13, Folder 24.
140 *Ibid.*
141 James G. McDonald, Memo to Walter M. Kotschnig, December 26, 1934, Columbia University, Rare Book and Manuscript Library, Herbert H. Lehman Suite and Papers, James G. McDonald Papers, Walter M. Kotschnig File, March-December 1934, D356 H19.

refugee teachers. We have so many qualified, well trained men and women seeking in vain for college and university teaching positions that the reaction indicated above is to be expected."[142] Yet Members of the Emergency Committee differed from one another in terms of fanning anti-Semitism (Stein and Flexner) or being indifferent to it (Johnson).[143]

Foreigners were not always meant to be refugees: some universities also signaled the efforts of the Nazi German Government, as Washington University Dean Otto Heller suggested, "to bring Nazi scholars to this country."[144]

Emergency and Social Responsibility

In contrast to American response, the international community of scientists and scholars showed a great deal of compassion for their colleagues who were forced to emigrate from Germany after the promulgation of the cynically named *Gesetz zur Wiederherstellung des Berufsbeamtentums* [Law for the Restoration of the Career Civil Service] of April 7, 1933. They established parallel organizational frameworks and provided material assistance, which eventually allowed some 6,000 professionals, mostly Jewish, to leave Germany.[145] The *Notgemeinschaft Deutscher Wissenschaftler im Ausland* [Emergency Society of German Scholars Abroad], headquar-

---

142 Ralph E. Himstead to Dr. Stephen Duggan, April 28, 1939, Rockefeller Archive Center, Alfred E. Cohn Papers, RG 450 C661-U, Box 4, Folder 29.
143 Memorandum of interview with Bernard Flexner, October 8, 1940, Rockefeller Archive Center, Rockefeller Foundation Archives, RG 1.1, Series 200, Box 52, Folder 622.
144 Dean Otto Heller of Washington University, St.Louis, Missouri. Notes on Dr. Kotschnig's visit to the U.S.A., March 23 to April 11 [1936], Rockefeller Archive Center, Rockefeller Foundation Archives, RG 1.1, Series 717, Box 2, Folder 12.
145 Laura Fermi, *Illustrious Immigrants: The Intellectual Migration from Europe 1930–41* (Chicago: University of Chicago Press, 1968), pp. 60–92; Herbert A. Strauss and Werner Röder, ed., *International Biographical Dictionary of Central European Émigrés 1933–1945*, 3 Vols. (München: Saur, 1980–1983).

tered in Zürich, Switzerland, was founded largely through the efforts of a Hungarian-born scientist. As Lord Beveridge wrote:

> Professor Philip Schwartz, Hungarian by birth but holding a Chair of General Pathology and Pathological Anatomy at Frankfurt-am-Main in Germany, was an immediate victim of Hitler's racial persecution and went in March 1933 to Zürich in Switzerland. There he founded at once the *Notgemeinschaft* and directed it for six months. [...]
>
> [For] money it had to depend almost wholly on contributions from displaced scholars whom it had helped to re-establish. But by its personal knowledge of the scholars themselves and by using its contacts with universities everywhere, it rendered invaluable service... .[146]

The Emergency Society provided a list of nearly 1,500 dismissed academics, which was published in 1936 with the assistance of the Rockefeller Foundation.[147] For German scientists in trouble, the idea of a *Notgemeinschaft* was not new: The *Notgemeinschaft der Deutschen Wissenschaft* [Emergency Society of German Science] was founded immediately after World War I to heal the wounds of German science at a time of total military, economic, and psychological collapse. Thoroughly Nazified after 1933, this Emergency Society, of course, had nothing to do with the newly established one to aid émigré scientists.[148] The first major

---

146 Lord Beveridge, *A Defence of Free Learning* (London, New York, Toronto: Oxford University Press, 1959), pp. 128–129; See also Charles Weiner, "A New Site for the Seminar: The Refugees and American Physics in the Thirties," in Donald Fleming and Bernard Bailyn, eds., *The Intellectual Migration: Europe and America, 1930–1960* (Cambridge, MA: The Belknap Press of Harvard University Press, 1969), p. 212.

147 Fermi, *Illustrious Immigrants*, p. 62; *The Rockefeller Foundation: A Review for 1920–28, 1936–40, 1942–51* (New York: Rockefeller Foundation, 1921–1952); Raymond Blaine Fosdick, *The Story of the Rockefeller Foundation* (New York: Harper, 1952); reprinted with a new introduction by Steven C. Wheatley (New Brunswick, N.J.: Transaction Publications, 1989); The Rockefeller Foundation, *Directory of Fellowships and Scholarships, 1917–1971* (New York: Rockefeller Foundation, 1972).

148 Notker Hammerstein, "Die Geschichte der Deutschen Forschungsgemeinschaft im Nationalsozialismus," in Doris Kaufmann, Hg., *Geschichte der Kaiser-Wilhelm-Gesellschaft im Nationalsozialismus*, Vol. 2 (Göttingen: Wallstein Verlag, 2000), pp. 600–609; Lothar Mertens, *"Nur politisch Würdige"*: Die

success of the latter Emergency Society was to secure a promise from the Turkish government to place 33 German professors at the University of Istanbul. Its staff then discussed the possibly of similar arrangements with Australian, Indian, South African, Soviet, and American authorities, as well as with the Committee for Intellectual Cooperation of the League of Nations.

In May 1933, scientists in Great Britain established the Academic Assistance Council (AAC, first conceived as the International Board of Scientists and Scholars) with Nobel Laureate Lord Rutherford of Nelson (1871–1937) as President and Sir William (later Lord) Beveridge (1879–1963) and Professor Charles S. Gibson (1883–1950) as Secretaries.[149] After 1936, the Academic Assistance Council came to be called the Society for the Protection of Science and Learning (SPSL), and continued to support and save scientists and scholars persecuted for their faith, race or politics.

Over the years, the situation seemed less and less manageable. By 1937, the American Emergency Committee voiced its concern about aiding another 1,000 German refugee professors to be displaced because of their Jewish or partly-Jewish wives or non-Nazi political convictions. Members of the Committee found it "simply impossible to consider taking care of any such number."[150] After the German *Anschluß* in 1938, even the European organizations felt hopeless about carrying out their

---

DFG-Forschungsförderung im Dritten Reich 1933–1937 (Berlin: Akademie Verlag, 2004).

149 Beveridge, *Defence*, p. 2; Szilard (London) to Jacques Errera, June 4, 1933 (in German); Leo Szilard Papers, Box 7, Folder 22; Benjamin Liebowitz (London) to Ernst P. Boas (London), May 4, 1933; *ibid.*, Box 12, Folder 4. The Council remained in existence until 1966 as the Society for the Protection of Science and Learning; see also Leo Szilard to unknown, May 14, 1933; *ibid.*, Box 12, Folder 21, and Robin E. Rider, "Alarm and Opportunity: Emigration of Mathematicians and Physicists to Britain and the United States, 1933–1945," *Historical Studies in the Physical Sciences* 15 (1984), 116.

150 Minutes of the Luncheon Meeting in Honor of Dr. F. Demuth, New York, April 21, 1937, Rockefeller Archive Center, Rockefeller Foundation Archives, RG 1.1, Series 717, Box 2, Folder 13.

refugee work and tried to transfer to the U.S. As no German professor was allowed to communicate with the *Notgemeinschaft*, information became scanty and unreliable to the extent that they made crucial mistakes such as including on their lists of displaced persons some German professors still holding their position in Germany. Along with fellow refugee organizations, these European organizations felt helpless, and lacked any real ability to help the ever-growing masses of refugees, and worked instead to outline a plan for an American Committee in Aid of Continental Intellectuals. Their only hope in 1938 seemed to be a new committee, "in the hands of an American [...]"[151]

The High Commission for Refugees

The Nazi takeover in Germany brought about or strengthened an impressive array of other civic organizations aiding refugees and emigrants. There were three kinds of organizations dealing with the situation: the first dealt with academics, i.e., people who previously held academic appointments in Germany, such as professors, lecturers, and assistants; the second took care of professionals, including doctors, lawyers, teachers, and social workers; the third concerned itself with students.[152]

In addition to the *Notgemeinschaft Deutscher Wissenschaftler im Ausland*, Zurich [the Emergency Society for German Scholars in Exile],[153] an enterprise directed by German emigrants themselves, committees

---

151 Thomas B. Appleget to W. E. Tisdale, New York, December 14, 1937; D. P. O'Brien to R. A. Lambert, January 5, 1938; Gerhard Cole to the Emergency Committee, February 1938; Rudolph M. Littauer, Notgemeinschaft, to Wilbur K. Thomas, Carl Schurz Foundation, October 27, 1938, Rockefeller Archive Center, Rockefeller Foundation Archives, RG 1.1, Series 717, Box 2, Folder 13.
152 High Commission for Refugees (Jewish and Other) Coming from Germany, Report of the Second Meeting of the Governing Body, held in London, May 2nd, 3rd and 4th, 1934, Rockefeller Archive Center, Alfred E. Cohn Papers, RG 450 C661-U, Box 5, Folder 12, p. 14.
153 Stephen Duggan to Dr. Alfred E. Cohn, New York, January 31, 1944, Alfred E. Cohn Papers, RG 450 C661-U, Box 2, Folder 20.

were organized in several countries to work for German scholars such as the Academic Assistance Council in London, Emergency Committee in Aid of Displaced German Scholars in New York City, the Comité des Savants in Paris, and the *Academisch Steunfonds* in Amsterdam. In the U.S., the number and varied nature of refugee and relief organizations is almost overwhelming.

Realizing its own responsibility in the international coordination of refugee matters, the Assembly of the League of Nations appointed a High Commissioner for Refugees Coming from Germany, an autonomous organization with a Governing Body, with both Jewish and non-Jewish bodies represented, including the national committees of France and Czechoslovakia. With the American James G. McDonald as the first High Commissioner, the organization was headquartered in Lausanne, Switzerland.[154] Under the auspices of the High Commission, an international Experts Committee was appointed to coordinate academic assistance. By the spring of 1935, it became evident that the European scene was, as Walter M. Kotschnig of the High Commissioner's office pointed out, "shifting rapidly" and measures taken by the High Commission proved inadequate, new plans had to be made and a major refugee conference was planned for September 1935 to coincide with the meeting of the Assembly of the League of Nations.[155] It is worth noting that although Hungary was a member of the League of Nations between 1922 and 1939, Hungary itself refrained from participating in any of the organizations, committees or bodies connected with the refugee issue.

---

154 High Commission for Refugees (Jewish and Other) Coming from Germany, Report of the Second Meeting of the Governing Body, held in London, May 2nd, 3rd and 4th, 1934, Alfred E. Cohn Papers, RG 450 C661-U, Box 5, Folder 12, pp. 14–15.

155 W[alter] K[otschnig], Tentative Proposals for the Establishment of a Central League Organization for Refugees, Geneva, May 17, 1935, Rockefeller Archive Center, Alfred E. Cohn Papers, RG 450 C661-U, Box 4, Folder 8; Preliminary Plan for a Conference of Organizations interested in Refugee Work [1935], Alfred E. Cohn Papers, RG 450 C661-U, Box 4, Folder 8.

"Incipit Hitler:" Double Expulsion, Double Trauma

The committees formed around the world were originally created for the purpose of taking refugees from Germany but later, most of these extended their scope to Austria and Czechoslovakia—countries, which just a few years before, had served the resettlement of refugees from Germany.[156] Representatives of the High Commission for Refugees visiting Austria and Czechoslovakia in 1935 did not (perhaps purposely) want to learn about actual or potential Hungarian and Hungarian-Jewish aspects of the situation. The U.S. Minister to Vienna, George S. Messersmith, noted "strong anti-semitic feelings" in certain sections of the population but he thought "there was little chance of anti-semitic outbursts."[157] The task of coordinating the already-existing private organizations fell on the High Commissioner for Refugees (Jewish and Other) Coming from Germany. This coordination gave the High Commission a machinery that could be used effectively. The lessons of the first year taught the High Commission that the main job of all the various organizations was not relief, but the permanent settlement of intellectual refugees.[158]

The High Commission for Refugees felt it necessary to make a clear distinction between the procedure for placement of professors and that of other intellectuals.

Cases involving professors were handled by the Academic Assistance Council in London. The AAC developed a central file of all displaced scholars, which by early 1935 numbered more than 1,200, of whom some

---

156 Brackett Lewis to R. B. Inch, League of Nations Society, Ottawa, Canada, November 14, 1938, CEIP, Committee to Aid Czechoslovakia, Box 286, Folder 4, 100886; cf. Walter M. Kotschnig to Professor Norman Bentwich, March 25, 1935, Columbia University, Rare Book and Manuscript Library, Herbert H. Lehman Suite and Papers, James G. McDonald Papers, Walter M. Kotschnig File, 1935—April 1936, D356 H20.

157 [Walter M. Kotschnig], Report of Visit to Austria by WMK, February 5 and 6, 1935; [Walter M. Kotschnig], Report of Visit to Czechoslovakia by WK, February 7 and 8, 1935; James G. McDonald Papers, Walter M. Kotschnig File, 1935—April 1936, D356 H20.

158 Walter M. Kotschnig to James G. McDonald, September 6, 1934, James G. McDonald Papers, Walter M. Kotschnig File, March-December, 1934, D356 H19.

600 had already left Germany, with some 230 permanently and 220 others temporarily placed. After a Paris meeting of the representatives of all the academic committees, Dr. Walter M. Kotschnig of the High Commission found it imperative to emphasize "that the work on behalf of displaced German scholars is not being carried out on a charitable basis, but that every care is being taken to propose to universities only such scholars as are likely to make an outstanding contribution towards the development of the universities in which they are placed."[159]

Jewish groups in Europe considered raising funds to establish a *Flüchtlingsuniversität*, a new university somewhere in Europe to be staffed by refugee faculty, an idea conceived by Albert Einstein,[160] but his longtime colleague and friend Szilard convinced him "that this would not be an easy task," and that he should instead "concentrate on one promising effort."[161] Einstein took Szilard's advice and gave his support to the Academic Assistance Council. Szilard also suggested that money be raised for the Palestine University, but owing to the economic hardships of the Great Depression, these projects never materialized. Instead, some forms of relief were provided by several other agencies, such as the Jewish Relief Committee in Amsterdam. Thanks to the outstanding efforts of Alvin Johnson, the University in Exile came to be realized in New York, and then soon became the Graduate Faculty of Political and Social Science under the New School for Social Research.

To coordinate support for the professional group of refugees, the *Comité International pour le Placement des Intellectuels Réfugiés* [International Committee for the Placement of Refugee Intellectuals] was formed in Geneva, offering positions to refugee intellectuals and professionals from Austria, Germany and Italy.[162] The *Comité International*

---

159 Walter M. Kotschnig to Dr. Samuel Guy Inman, February 21, 1935, James G. McDonald Papers, Walter M. Kotschnig File, 1935–April 1936, D356 H20.
160 Einstein (Le Coq-sur-Mer) to Szilard, April 25 and May 1, 1933; Szilard (London) to Einstein, May 4 and 9, 1933 (in German), Leo Szilard Papers, Box 7, Folder 27.
161 Szilard (Brussels) to Beveridge, May 14, 1933, Szilard Papers, Box 11, Folder 18; Szilard (London) to Beveridge, May 4, 1933, *ibid.*, Box 4, Folder 30.
162 Fermi, *Illustrious Immigrants, op. cit.*, pp. 62–63.

was equipped with the files of all "the doctors, lawyers, teachers, engineers, chemists, social workers, etc. who had to leave Germany." Walter M. Kotschnig added: "[W]e are endeavouring to arrive at a distribution of the emigrant intellectuals from Germany all over the world in order to avoid that any particular country should be flooded with German intellectuals. This argument has borne fruit."[163]

Refugee students, the third major group of exiled Germans, were handled by the International Student Service in Geneva, with branch offices in London, Paris and New York.[164]

By the end of 1934, it became evident that not all refugees were Jews. Members of the Board of the National Committee that coordinated the mushrooming relief organizations in the United States, and liaised with the High Commissioner for Refugees (Jewish and Other) coming from Germany, pointed out that "in the applications from German university men, there is an increasing percentage of Christians [...] the percentage of assistance requested by Christians in other professions and trades is also increasing."[165] The discrepancy between figures secured from the U.S. Commissioner of Immigration and Naturalization of the Department of Labor which showed a relatively low number of Jews among the refugees, and those of the State Department, arose from the fact that the visa applications seen by the consuls had birth certificates which noted the religion of the applicant, whereas steamship lists were filled in by the refugees themselves who routinely did not record themselves as "Hebrew" under the heading marked "Race".[166] The differing figures showed not

---

163 Walter M. Kotschnig to Dr. Samuel Guy Inman, February 21, 1935, James G. McDonald Papers, Walter M. Kotschnig File, 1935–April 1936, D356 H20.
164 High Commission for Refugees (Jewish and Other) Coming from Germany, Report of the Second Meeting of the Governing Body, held in London, May 2nd, 3rd and 4th, 1934, Alfred E. Cohn Papers, RG 450 C661-U, Box 5, Folder 12, p. 16.
165 Cecilia Razovsky, Minutes of Meeting of Board of Directors of the National Coordinating Committee, New York, December 31, 1934, James G. McDonald Papers, National Coordinating Committee, Cecilia Razovsky File, D356 H21, p. 4.
166 Cecilia Razovsky Davidson, "Report of Situation of German Refugees in the United States," April 18, 1934, James G. McDonald Papers, National Coordinating Committee, Cecilia Razovsky File, D356 H21.

only an attempt to avoid belonging to a heavily-charged category but also were the result of more than a century of assimilation in Germany and the former Austro-Hungaran Monarchy. Many of these immigrants had been fully assimilated into German society and were often only one-half or one-quarter Jewish, now torn from their complex religious as well as national backgrounds. They now faced not only racial persecution but also separation from their spiritual integrity and their mixed German-Jewish (or Hungarian-Jewish) national (occasionally even German or Hungarian national*ist*) identity, which made integration into the U.S. sometimes unusually complicated.[167]

Throughout the entire work of resettling some 6,000 academic, professional, and student emigrants in the period 1933–34, the key problem was funding.[168] It was particularly difficult to provide money for administrative costs, which jeopardized the build-up of a stable structure for the work of permanent placement.

The High Commission for Refugees approached the problem of finances in many different ways. One ingenious, if somewhat cynical, idea was the compilation, in October 1934, of a "List of Jewish Personalities"[169] from London, Paris, Belgium, Czechoslovakia, The Netherlands, Italy, Romania, Spain, and Switzerland, with the obvious intention of creating a pool of rich and influential resources to tap for the relief efforts. This list of rich and/or well-connected leaders—religious, business, political, and academic—from the sinking world of Europe, was compiled with largely unfounded hopes and a great sense of humor. It considered

---

167 Cecilia Razovsky, "The United States and the German Refugees," NBC radio broadcast, New York, July 23, 1934, James G. McDonald Papers, National Coordinating Committee, Cecilia Razovsky File, D356 H21; Steven Lowenstein, "Foreword," in: Gloria DeVidas Kirchheimer and Manfred Kirchheimer, *We Were So Beloved: An Autobiography of a German Jewish Community* (Pittsburgh: University of Pittsburgh Press, 1997), p. ix.
168 See the Walter M. Kotschnig—James G. McDonald correspondence in 1934, James G. McDonald Papers, Walter M. Kotschnig File, March–December, 1934, D356 H19.
169 List of Jewish Personalities, October 1934, James G. McDonald Papers, Confidential File, July–December 1934, D356 H3.

wealth—both old and new—in addition to energy and negotiating skills, including persons who were Zionists and anti-Zionists, ranging from the Rothschilds through the Chief Rabbis of Rome and Belgium, to the son of Captain Dreyfus and the diamond dealers of Amsterdam. It is conspicuous that Hungarian-Jewish leaders were not listed. As it appears from the papers of the High Commissioner for Refugees, the list may have been a response to his Lausanne proposal of December 1933 to establish a financial corporation to aid refugees from Germany.[170] The High Commission shared the views that "Jewry, under the menace of an age-old problem, has always been more or less organised to meet a contingency of this sort. [...] In a general way, a religious community is always prepared to render assistance in the form of charity."[171] How much these distinguished Jewish leaders actually contributed to the rescue operations is still to be researched.

It is important to note that contemporary as well as subsequent surveys of the refugee problem did not take non-German Jews in Germany into separate consideration. The large number of Hungarians living or working in Germany is, as a rule, never mentioned. A confidential report prepared at the end of 1933 for the High Commissioner for Refugees (probably by Walter M. Kotschnig) regarding "The German Refugee Problem—A Bird's Eye View" has nothing to say about this dimension of the refugee question, even though German academic and cultural life was full of non-German Jews from Hungary, Russia, Poland, and indeed all over Europe.

Nevertheless, the High Commission for Refugees did think of the non-Jewish aspects of the refugee problem from early on. In late 1935, Walter M. Kotschnig of the High Commission prepared a detailed plan for providing help in the Christian World for the non-Jewish refugees, i.e. Non-Aryan Christians, political refugees and Aryan-Christians. An

---

170 "Scheme of Corporation for the Settlement of Refugees from Germany," n.d. [1934?], James G. McDonald Papers, Confidential File, July–December 1934, D356 H3.
171 "The German Refugee Problem—A Bird's Eye View," n.d., James G. McDonald Papers, Confidential File, July–December 1934, D356 H3, p. 5.

international appeal on behalf of non-Jewish refugees "[...] ought to produce some psychological pressure on the German Government"—suggested Kotschnig, somewhat naïvely.[172]

The many different agencies dealing with refugees provided over the years many widely divergent figures regarding the actual number of those who fled Germany and the rest of Nazi-dominated Europe. Some people show up in several lists, others cannot be found on any. The lists show varied numbers of Hungarians among different professions, but invariably without any reference to their original country of origin. Arguably the most numerous national group on the list of "German" refugees, the Hungarians, after careful analysis, appear to have constituted between 1.7–3.5% of the various German listings. The most complete list of refugee academics was the "List of Displaced German Scholars", printed and published by the *Notgemeinschaft Deutscher Wissenschaftler im Ausland* (London, 1936 and 1937). That the refugee listings "swallowed" the distinctly non-German origin of many of the refugees is well documented by this otherwise carefully compiled and widely distributed booklet. From its list of 1678 names, 28 were Hungarians.

Refugee assistance was aided by a variety of American welfare organizations, both national and local, professional and humanitarian. Founded in 1934, the National Coordinating Committee for Aid to Refugees and Emigrants Coming from Germany came to function as a central clearing agency, in fact the largest umbrella organization in the U.S. to deal with refugees from Germany. The National Coordinating Committee coordinated member organizations, large and small, national and vocational, Gentile and Jewish.[173]

---

172 Plan of an International Appeal for Refugees from Germany, attached to Dr. W[alter] Kotschnig to Dr. Alfred E. Cohn, November 28, 1935, Alfred E. Cohn Papers, RG 450 C661-U, Box 2, Folder 13.
173 American Committee for Christian-German Refugees
American Friends Service Committee (Refugee Section)
American Jewish Committee
American Jewish Congress
American Jewish Joint Distribution Committee

The growing number of, mostly non-political, organizations to aid refugees from Europe led to the formation of an Inter-Governmental Committee for Refugees initiated by President Roosevelt in the Spring of 1938, in the wake of the Austrian *Anschluß*. After the invasion of Czechoslovakia, several Czechoslovak relief organizations appeared on the American refugee scene, such as the American Committee for Relief in Czechoslovakia, the Association of Czech Jews, and the Coordinating Council for Czechoslovak Democracy.[174]

Apart from the above, several other organizations dealt with refugee problems on the national scene.[175]

> B'nai B'rith
> Committee for Catholic Refugees from Germany
> Council of Jewish Federations and Welfare Funds
> Emergency Committee in Aid of Displaced Foreign Physicians [Medical Scientists]
> Emergency Committee in Aid of Displaced Foreign Scholars
> Federal Council of Churches of Christ in America
> German-Jewish Children's Aid, Inc.
> Hebrew Sheltering and Immigrant Aid Society of America
> Hospites (American Social Workers Hospitality Group)
> Intercollegiate Committee to Aid Student Refugees
> International Migration Service, Inc. (American Branch)
> International Student Service
> Jewish Agricultural Society of America
> Musicians Emergency Fund, Inc.
> National Council of Jewish Women
> Russian Committee to Aid Czechoslovakia and Carpathian Russia
> Zionist Organization of America
>   Cf. Louis Adamic, *op. cit.*, p. 25.

174 Brackett Lewis to R. B. Inch, League of Nations Society, Ottawa, Canada, November 14, 1938, CEIP, Committee to Aid Czechoslovakia, Box 286, Folder 4, 100886.
175 American Committee to Save Refugees
American Council for the Emigres in the Professions
American Friends of German Freedom
American Friends Service Committee
Community Service Society
Dominican Republic Settlement Association

In 1939, the National Refugee Service came into being and replaced the NCC as a philanthropic agency. By 1943, the NRS became a huge and complex national organization with a Family Service Department, a child care program carried on by the European-Jewish Children's Aid, Inc., with Employment and Retraining Programs, a Program for Physicians, a Central Loan Trust, and a Social Adjustment Program, among others.[176]

> Emergency Rescue Committee
> Episcopal Committee for European Refugees
> Exiled Writers Committee
> Federal Council of Churches of Christ in America
> Hadassab—Youth Aliyah
> International Catholic Office for Refugee Affairs
> International Relief Association
> International Rescue and Relief Committee
> Jewish Labor Committee
> National Federation of Settlements
> National Refugee Service
> National Travelers Aid Association
> New World Resettlement Fund
> President's Advisory Committee on Political Refugees
> Refugee Economic Corporation
> Self-Help of Emigres from Central Europe
> Spanish Refugee Relief Campaign
> Unitarian Service Committee
>> A list of the Unitarian Service Committee in late 1941 included three Hungarian names, the physicist Peter Havas (Columbia University), as well as the authors Nicholas and Piroska Halász (in New York City). Irene O. Hay to Dr. Alexander Makinsky, Boston, December 2, 1941, Rockefeller Archive Center, Rockefeller Foundation Archives, RG 1.1, Series 200, Box 47, Folder 539.
> United States Committee for the Care of European Children
> National Board, Young Women's Christian Association
>> Cf. "National Agencies in the United States Dealing with Refugee Problems," in: People Without a Country, A Challenge to Civilization, *Survey Graphic,* November 1940, pp. 21–22, Rockefeller Archive Center, Rockefeller Foundation Archives, RG 1.1, Series 200, Box 47, Folder 543.

176 Report of National Refugee Service for 1943, Alfred E. Cohn Papers, RG 450 C661-U, Box 13, Folder 41.

Many of the organizations had local committees in major American cities, the American Committee for Relief in Czechoslovakia was established first in Philadelphia, Pittsburgh, and Texas, later also in Boston, Cleveland, Detroit, Chicago, and San Francisco.[177] As always, people who were asked to contribute to the cause of Czechoslovakia included some who were instantly ready in a major way, such as Mrs. Louise W. Carnegie who lavishly sent a check for $1,000. The former cabinet minister Charles Nagel sent just $25, and a U.S. ambassador, only $5. Many sent nothing at all.

Some organizations such as the American Friends Service Committee offered practical help and administrative know-how to refugees from Germany. The American Quakers sent their representatives to Germany in December 1938 "to explore the needs and possibilities for relief to persecuted groups within the borders of the Reich."[178] As Commissioners Rufus Jones, Robert Yarnall and George Walton stated, "Our task is to support and save life and to suffer with those who are suffering."[179] The Quakers provided assistance in terms of affidavits, sheltered employment and orientation in practical matters.

Few of the major American organizations dealt with Hungarians, many of whom did not escape their country until it was almost too late. In most cases, Hungarian Jews were lumped together with the huge German refugee crowd and their presence can only be discovered through the scrutiny of their names. Yet, as many Hungarian Jews had German names, this is a somewhat complicated task for the non-Hungarian who would easily mistake them as Germans. This happened in most émigré listings, including the case of 1,500 German refugee filmmakers (100 of whom were in fact Hungarians), Germans (or "Germans") served by the Emergency

---

177 Brackett Lewis to R. B. Inch, League of Nations Society, Ottawa, Canada, November 14, 1938, CEIP, Committee to Aid Czechoslovakia, Box 286, Folder 4, 100886.
178 Eleanor Slater, "The Work of the American Friends Service Committee with Refugees from Germany," in How Can We Help? Refugee Section, American Friends Service Committee, Philadelphia, Pa, 1939. CEIP, Committee to Aid Czechoslovakia, Box 288, Folder 5, 102517.
179 *Ibid.*

Rescue Committee and the American Council for the Emigres in the Professions, as well as those considered as rescued and indirectly placed by the Rockefeller Foundation.

U.S. Quota, Visa Policy, and Hungary

In regard to the U.S. quota and visa policy concerning Hungary, it must be noted that the quota laws cast a shadow over the entire period. By the end of December 1938, only preference visas under the Hungarian quota were issued relatively quickly, while those on the nonpreference immigrant lists chargeable to the Hungarian quota had no hope of being reached for a very long time.[180] Bottlenecks formed in many U.S. consulates, even though, as John F. Rich suggested in the *Survey Graphic* in 1940, "eligible people, with affidavits and passage guaranteed, awaited visas [...]"[181] At this time, the quota for Hungary was 869.[182] The U.S. Consulate in Budapest was so overcrowded with affidavit material that there was no more office space to file documents of freshly registered cases.[183] On May 22, 1939, the U.S. Minister to Hungary, John F. Montgomery, bitterly complained from Budapest to his friend George Creel in San Francisco,

> The lack of clerks and Secretaries to cope with the enormous increase in work brought about a situation that to me seemed unbearable since it put me in what

---

180 Cecilia Razovsky quoting recent information from the Department of State, New York City, December 28, 1938, Alfred E. Cohn Papers, RG 450 C661-U, Box 13, Folder 36.
181 John F. Rich, "Why, Where, Who—the Refugees?" In: People Without a Country. A Challenge to Civilization, *Survey Graphic*, November 1940, p. 10, Rockefeller Archive Center, Rockefeller Foundation Archives, RG 1.1, Series 200, Box 47, Folder 543.
182 Manual on Immigration, compiled by the National Coordinating Committee for Aid to Refugees and Emigrants Coming from Germany, 1939, Alfred E. Cohn Papers, RG 450 C661-U, Box 13, Folder 36. This Manual is the best source of all legal, administrative, and organizational details of pre-World War II immigration.
183 Cecilia Razovsky to All Cooperating Committees, New York City, May 11, 1939, Alfred E. Cohn Papers, RG 450 C661-U, Box 13, Folder 36.

"Incipit Hitler:" Double Expulsion, Double Trauma

> I consider a very dangerous position. [...] [T]he work of the visa section of the Consulate General has increased a thousand times or more, and that of the Legation about ten-fold. Further, the importance of the post has very much increased. [...] [T]here was tremendous pressure from Members of Congress and from the Department on visa work, and the place was being swamped by applicants...[184]

Speaking in a confidential manner, the U.S. Minister to Budapest made rude remarks about the class background of the majority of Jews trying to get into the U.S. from Hungary. In mid-January 1939, he complained to George Creel that instead of a selection of "high-type Jews in all these countries [...] the quota is filled up with the least desirable type, and when you say that you have said something."[185] Montgomery also quoted the American Consul from Vienna complaining that "he signed over 5,000 visas for America for people whom he felt were a positive menace to the country, and it made him sick to think about it."[186] Chemist Erwin Chargaff (1905–2002) remembered this U.S. consul as "a nazi."[187]

In a few months Montgomery returned to the subject in writing Creel,

> If your friend the Rabbi were over here, I know he would be concerned about the class of his coreligionists who we are sending into America. Accidentally, a high class Jew got a visa for America, and when he came to the Legation to see the people who are being admitted he almost had a fit. He said the Jews in America must be crazy that they permit these people to enter. They are the ones who have caused

---

184 John F. Montgomery to George Creel, Budapest, May 22, 1939, Országos Széchényi Könyvtár [Hungarian National Széchényi Library], John F. Montgomery Collection, Strictly Personal Correspondence 1938–1939, George Creel Correspondence. On John F. Montgomery see Tibor Frank, "A Vermont Yankee in Regent Horthy's Court: The Hungarian World of a U.S. Diplomat," in Tibor Frank, ed., *Discussing Hitler: Advisers of U.S. Diplomacy in Central Europe 1934–1941* (Budapest—New York: CEU Press, 2003), pp. 13–70.
185 John F. Montgomery to George Creel, Budapest, January 18, 1939, John F. Montgomery Collection, Strictly Personal Correspondence 1938–1939, George Creel Correspondence.
186 *Ibid.*
187 István Hargittai, *Candid Science: Conversations with Famous Chemists* (London: Imperial College Press, 2000), Vol. I, p. 22.

trouble here and elsewhere else and they will cause the same trouble in America. I used to think it was only here, but what I hear from Vienna and other places in Germany it is the same there.[188]

It is difficult to decide whether or not the inimical interpretation of this problem came from social class and social behavior or from radical politics.

Made just days after the second anti-Jewish bill was passed by Hungarian Parliament (May 5, 1939),[189] these remarks revealed an unusual measure of insensitivity and lack of compassion that characterized not just Minister Montgomery and his Vienna colleague Vice Consul G. Frederick Reinhardt (later U.S. Ambassador to Vietnam and Italy), but also the attitude of a vocal part of the U.S. diplomatic corps. Breitman and Kraut found that in the State Department "bureaucratic indifference to moral or humanitarian concerns was a more important obstacle to an active refugee policy" than anti-Semitism.[190] The anti-Jewish sentiment of U.S. diplomats was generally directed against the unassimilated elements of European Jewry, which created unending debates on both sides of the Atlantic. Montgomery's remarks were similar to those made even by Jewish members of the Upper House of Hungarian Parliament, including Lajos Láng, who argued for a sharp distinction between assimilated and non-assimilated Jews in Hungarian legislation.[191]

---

[188] John F. Montgomery to George Creel, Budapest, May 9, 1939, John F. Montgomery Collection, Strictly Personal Correspondence 1938–1939, George Creel Correspondence.

[189] Tibor Frank, "Treaty revision and doublespeak: Hungarian neutrality, 1939–1941," in: Neville Wylie, ed., *European Neutrals and Non-Belligerents during the Second World War* (Cambridge: Cambridge University Press, 2002), pp. 158–159.

[190] Richard Breitman and Alan M. Kraut, *op. cit.*, p. 9.

[191] Address of Lajos Láng on April 17, 1939 in the Upper House of Hungarian Parliament. *Az 1935. évi április hó 27ére hirdetett Országgyűlés Felsőházának Naplója*, IV. kötet (Budapest: Athenaeum, 1939), pp. 153–158.

The Emergency Committee in Aid of Displaced Foreign Scholars

The academic community in America was horrified to learn of the events in Germany, yet action was not quick enough, and certainly did not seem quick enough for Jewish American scholars. Felix Frankfurter, then a Harvard law professor, vehemently criticized with "a deep feeling of mortification [...] the tepid response of American intellectual life compared with that of England to what Mr. Justice Holmes aptly characterizes as 'a challenge to civilization.'"[192] The German-American anthropologist Franz Boas (1858–1942) was one of the first to receive a first-hand report from the American physicist and inventor Benjamin Liebowitz (1890–1977), who traveled throughout Europe collecting information and helping to plan relief efforts. "It is impossible to describe the utter despair of all classes of Jews in Germany," he wrote to Boas in early May 1933.

> The thoroughness with which they are being hunted out and stopped short in their careers is appalling. Unless help comes from the outside, there is no outlook for thousands, perhaps hundreds of thousands, except starvation or the sleeping pill. It is a gigantic "cold" pogrom. And it is not only against Jews; Communists, of course, are included, but are not singled out racially; social democrats and liberals generally are coming under the ban, especially if they protest in the least against the Nazi movement. Please note that I am not speaking from hearsay: I *know* people, friends in many classes–scientists, scholars, doctors, lawyers, business men, economists, etc.[193]

A few weeks later, in June 1933, the Emergency Committee in Aid of Displaced German (later Foreign) Scholars was established as the American counterpart of the AAC to provide grants or fellowships to

---

[192] Felix Frankfurter to Dr. Stephen P. (sic) Duggan, Cambridge, MA, June 8, 1933, Otto Szasz File, Emergency Committee in Aid of Displaced Foreign Scholars, New York Public Library, Manuscripts and Archives Division, New York, NY.

[193] Benjamin Liebowitz (London) to Ernst P. Boas, May 4, 1933, Leo Szilard Papers, Box 12, Folder 4.

refugee scientists and scholars.[194] The main financial contributions to the Emergency Committee came from Jewish foundations and individuals.[195] The work of the Emergency Committee was based on two principles: considering the depression in the U.S., no funds were to be directed away from American scholars, and American universities should employ the same selection process among the refugees that they would normally do among American faculty members. Charity in the realm of academia was to be avoided by all means.

The State Department was particularly anxious to exclude Communists from those admitted as European exiles. Some refugees were found to be doing espionage work or making pro-Russian propaganda, and were turned away as unwanted.[196]

Ultimately, some 6,000 displaced scientists and scholars applied for aid to the Emergency Committee in New York, of which 335 were granted assistance.[197] The Emergency Committee, declared its Secretary in 1937, "must not only confine itself to displaced German Scholars but

---

194 The Emergency Committee Records for 1933–45 were deposited in 1946 in the Manuscripts and Archives Division of the New York Public Library. See the Committee's website <www.nypl.org/research/chss/spe/rbk/faids/Emergency>.
195 Beveridge, *Defence*, pp. 15, 126-127; Karl Brandt Circular, New York, February 1, 1934 (in German), John von Neumann Papers, "1933: Some very interesting letters to J. v. N.," Box 7. See also Rider, "Alarm", pp. 116, 139, 144.
196 Adolph A. Berle, Department of State, to Alfred E. Cohn, Washington, DC, August 9, 1940, Alfred E. Cohn Papers, RG 450 C661-U, Box 5, Folder 5.
197 There are 195 boxes of correspondence and papers in the files of the Emergency Committee in Aid of Displaced Foreign Scholars, New York Public Library, Manuscripts and Archives Division, New York, New York; my lists are based on these documents. Robin E. Rider also compiled a list of mathematicians and physicists who emigrated to the United States or Britain; her list includes a few more Hungarians such as physicists Miklós Kürti (1908–1998), Cornelius Lánczos (1893–1974), and Elisabeth (Erzsébet) Róna (1890–1981) as well as mathematicians Paul Erdős (1913–1996), Tibor Radó (1895–1965), and Steven (István) Vajda (1901–1995); see Rider, "Alarm", pp. 172–176. She did not distinguish between Germans and Hungarians, however, and did not discuss the contributions of Leo Szilard or other Hungarians to the establishment of the Academic Assistance Council or the Emergency Committee. I am grateful to Gábor Palló for additional information

only to the ablest and most distinguished among them."[198] This was an important statement as it spoke on behalf of the principle of competition. Enthusiasm for accepting refugees from Germany was never very high in the United States, but by 1935

> universities and various associations of professors, etc. seem to become restive. ... [T]he Emergency Committee has to go very slow, partly because of lack of funds and partly because of definite signs of xenophobia. Thus it is very unlikely that the Emergency Committee will be able to take many more scholars, nor can we count of the fact that those who have been in America already for a year or two, will be permanently absorbed.[199]

Among the Hungarians (Group A) who received grants or fellowships after they left Germany in 1933–1934 (Section I), or after they left Hungary following the introduction of anti-Semitic legislation there in 1938–39 (Section II), were these notable persons:

Group A
Section I

> Melchior (Menyhért) Pályi (1892–1970), economist
> Otto Szász (1884–1952), mathematician
>   (also aided by the Rockefeller Foundation, 1934–35, 1937–39)
> Gabriel (Gábor) Szegő (1895–1985), mathematician
>   (also aided by the Rockefeller Foundation, 1934–36)
> Leo Szilárd (1898–1964), physicist
>   (aid also offered by the Rockefeller Foundation, 1935–36)
> Edward (Ede) Teller (1908–2003), physicist

---

based upon his own research in the files of the Emergency Committee. See also Fermi, *Illustrious Immigrants*, pp. 76–78.
198 Stephen Duggan, Introduction to the 1937 Report, Emergency Committee in Aid of Displaced German Scholars, March 2, 1937, Alfred E. Cohn Papers, RG 450 C661-U, Box 5, Folder 32.
199 Walter Kotschnig to James G. McDonald, Geneva, April 9, 1935, James G. McDonald Papers, D356.

Section II

> George Pólya (1887–1985), mathematician
> Dezső Rapaport (1911–1960), psychologist
> Ladislas (László) Tisza (b. 1907), physicist
> Charles de Tolnay (1899–1981), art historian
> Rusztem Vámbéry (1892–1948), lawyer, diplomat
>   (also aided by the Rockefeller Foundation, 1939–42)[200]
> Egon Wellesz (1885–1974), musicologist, composer

The following (Group B), perhaps equally notable, Hungarians were among those who applied for but did not receive aid from the Emergency Committee, either to start or continue their academic career in the U.S.

Group B
Section I

> Friedrich (Frigyes) Antal (1887–1954), art historian
> Willy (Vilmos, William John) Fellner (1905–1983), economist
> Pál (Paul) György (1893–1976), pediatrician, nutritionist

Section II

> Elemér Balogh (1881–1955), comparative law
> Béla Bartók (1881–1945), composer, musicologist, pianist
> Mihály Erdélyi (1903–), psychologist
> Zoltán Fekete, conductor
> Imre Ferenczi, statistician

---

200 JHW, Memo on Further Grant in Aid Funds for Refugee Scholars, June 16, 1941;Rockefeller grants quoted from The Rockefeller Foundation, Universities aided under Deposed Scholar Program; RF grants 1942, Rockefeller Archive Center, Rockefeller Foundation Archives, RG 1.1, Series 200, Box 47, Folder 537; RG 1.1, Series 717, Box 2, Folder 8; RG 1.1, Series 200, Box 47, Folder 541.

Béla Frank, mechanical engineer
René Fueloep [Fülöp]-Miller (1891–1963), author
Erzsébet (Elizabeth M.) Hajós, art historian
Albert Béla Halasi, economist
Miklós (Nicholas) Halász (1895–1985), journalist, author, novelist
Péter Havas (b. 1916), physicist
Hugo Ignotus (1869–1949), critic, editor
Aurél Thomas Kolnai (1900–1973), author, philosopher
Ferenc (Francis de) Kőrösy (1906–1997), chemist
Jenő (Eugene) Lukács (1906–1987), mathematician, statistician
Pál (Paul) Neményi, hydrologist
Tibor Szalai, economist
Jani Szántó, violinist
Constantin Szeghő, electrical engineer (1905–1995)
Zoltán Szende, historian and international economist
Nelly Szent-Györgyi
Lajos Székely, psychoanalyst (1904–1995)
József Szűcs, biochemist and plant-physiologist
Emery Weiner [?][201]

It must also be remembered that Columbia Professor J. P. Chamberlain of the High Commission for Refugees expected in the Summer of 1939 "a large number of new refugee applicants from Czechoslovakia, Hungary and Italy..."[202]

It must be noted that some of the people who were not supported by the Emergency Committee (Group B) did in many instances still manage to find a solution of some sort in the U.S. (e.g. Bartók, Halasi, Ignotus).

---

201 In several cases there is no biographical information available. — By comparison, science historian Gábor Palló identified 207 scientists and scholars in the files of the Society for the Protection of Science and Learning [earlier: AAC] whom he considered Hungarian. Gábor Palló, "Magyar tudósok migrációja," *Fizikai Szemle*, 1997/3, p. 83.

202 J. P. Chamberlain to Alfred E. Cohn, New York, June 29, 1939, Alfred E. Cohn Papers, RG 450 C661-U, Box 5, Folder 29.

Altogether some 65 Hungarians appear on the lists of the Emergency Committee. Almost all were Hungarian Jews who immigrated, either directly or indirectly, to the United States, generally after the introduction of the Hungarian anti-Semitic legislation in 1938-39, although a sizable group had been in Germany by 1933 and had then immigrated into the U.S. Most were eminent and some came to be internationally recognized in their own field, a few even beyond. All were especially sensitive to the upheaval in Germany because they had a strong sense of *déjà vu*: the rise of anti-Semitism and xenophobia in Germany and the threats they created were strongly reminiscent of the Hungarian ordeal in 1919-1920. That sensitivity impelled some of them to become highly active in rescue operations which saved the lives and careers of thousands of other scientists and scholars.

A survey of some of the successful cases under the auspices of the Emergency Committee demonstrates features of the Jewish-Hungarian intellectual and professional immigration remarkably different from what Minister Montgomery so bitterly criticized. They had strongly assimilated origins, a broader Austro-Hungarian, rather than narrowly Hungarian background, a rich foreign, typically German study and work experience, and yet still experienced difficult entry and reception in the U.S.

The well-known economist Menyhért (Melchior) Pályi represents a distinct case of a Hungarian scholar who was one of those misperceived as a German. Pályi was born in Budapest in 1892, where his father was a newspaper publisher who secured some of the best education for his son in Hungary, Switzerland and Germany.[203] Pályi received his Ph.D. in Munich, in 1915. Between 1918 and 1933 he served on the faculties of four German universities (Munich, Göttingen, Kiel, and Berlin), then became the chief economist for the *Deutsche Bank* and, between 1931-33, an advisor of the *Reichsbank*, the German Central Bank. Fluent in four languages, he taught at the University of Chicago in 1927-28. After Hitler came to power, he became one of the first foreign scholars to leave Germany, in

---

203 Pályi's biography is partly based on the "Foreword" by Donald L. Kemmerer to Melchior Palyi, *The Twilight of Gold 1914–1936: Myths and Realities* (Chicago: Henry Regnery, 1972), pp. xviii–xix.

early March 1933, and went via London to Chicago. James M. Stifler of the Board of Trustees of the University of Chicago turned to the Emergency Committee to get some funding for Pályi who, he emphasized, is "one of the ousted Jewish professors. He is a Hungarian Jew, but a Catholic."[204] For Americans at the time with no knowledge of the measure and depth of the Jewish assimilation that had occurred earlier, this was a strange mix. In Chicago, Pályi gave courses on monetary theory, the European banking systems and business cycles. In the correspondence with Chicago, the Committee referred to Pályi as "a German scholar."[205] Pályi made such a great impression in Chicago that other schools such as Ohio State University immediately attempted to win him over. "He impressed us very greatly with his wide range of scholarship and his ability as a lecturer."[206] Not only was Pályi a gifted economist and an enjoyable lecturer, but he also knew intimately the world of the leading financial personalities of the 1920s and 1930s, such as Montagu Norman, Benjamin Strong and Hjalmar Schacht.[207]

Forced to wait for a definite commitment from Chicago, Pályi was vacillating between a definitive offer from Ohio State and a vague promise from Chicago until April 1934 when he was offered a continuing position by Chicago.[208] It must be noted that Palyi was partially funded by two Chicago banks.[209] In October 1934, Murrow was proud to report to the New York Foundation that the two articles which Melchior Palyi "has

---

204 James M. Stifler to Dr. Stephen Duggan, Chicago, July 6, 1933, Melchior Palyi File, Emergency Committee in Aid of Displaced Foreign Scholars, New York Public Library, Manuscripts and Archives Division, New York, NY.
205 E. R. Murrow to Dean Frederic Woodward, New York, September 20, 1933, Melchior Palyi File, Emergency Committee in Aid of Displaced Foreign Scholars.
206 William McPherson, Dean to E. R. Murrow, February 8, 1934, February 23, 1934, Melchior Palyi File, Emergency Committee in Aid of Displaced Foreign Scholars.
207 Donald. L. Kemmerer, *op. cit.*
208 Melchior Pályi to Dean W. M. McPherson, March 20, 1934; April 5, 1934, Melchior Palyi File, Emergency Committee in Aid of Displaced Foreign Scholars.
209 William McPherson to E. R. Murrow, March 1, 1934, Melchior Palyi File, Emergency Committee in Aid of Displaced Foreign Scholars.

written since his arrival in this country have been the subject of much editorial comment in the leading newspapers in the United States including the New York Times."[210] However, in Spring 1935, when it became obvious that Pályi could be financed by "the financial men downtown,"[211] the Committee discontinued its grant to the university.[212] Yet, in November 1935, his chances of a permanent faculty appointment were considered as "none," indicating the protracted difficulties of securing a permanent job. The Emergency Committee once again refused to renew its grant in November 18, 1936, as by then, Pályi had taken a position as economist to a brokerage house in Chicago.[213] Pályi's later contribution to the understanding of the course of Nazi Germany ranged from his 1941 article "Economic Foundations of the German Totalitarian State"[214] to his last book, *The Twilight of Gold 1914–1936: Myths and Realities*.[215]

The Emergency Committee found the presence of the German (and "German") scholars in American higher education so important (or had simply wanted to document their importance to the scholars' financing agencies or political adversaries) that E. R. Murrow urgently planned a published symposium on U.S. academia by mid-1935. However, his interest in the comments of displaced scholars on the American academic environment and the quality of higher education in the U.S. did not meet

---

210 E. R. Murrow to Dr. Alfred E. Cohn, Memorandum of the Emergency Committee, October 16, 1934, Melchior Palyi File, Emergency Committee in Aid of Displaced Foreign Scholars.
211 James M. Stifler to E. R. Morrow, Chicago, April 25, 1935, E. R. Murrow to Sydnor Walker, New York, May 1, 1935, Melchior Palyi File, Emergency Committee in Aid of Displaced Foreign Scholars.
212 E. R. Murrow to James M. Stifler, May 23, 1935, Melchior Palyi File, Emergency Committee in Aid of Displaced Foreign Scholars.
213 Analysis of Appointments Made with the Assistance of Emergency Committee Grants, November 4, 1935; B. Drury to John Whyte, Memorandum, November 18, 1936; Memorandum from B. Drury, April 28, 1938, Alfred E. Cohn Papers, RG 450 C661-U, Box 2, Folder 6, and Box 4, Folder 14.
214 Melchior Palyi, "Economic Foundations of the German Totalitarian State", *American Journal of Sociology*, January 1941.
215 Chicago: Henry Regnery, 1972.

with equal enthusiasm from the scholars themselves, and by some such as Melchior Pályi, with criticism and caution.[216] Convinced of the value of his project, Murrow took Palyi's thinly veiled refusal as a sign of approval and commented, "the effect of criticism upon the general university world in this country will, I am confident, be good rather than bad."[217] Within two weeks, however, Murrow must have received sharp criticism from the Committee and had to reconsider his, by now, entirely personal project which he postponed "for a year or eighteen months. This delay will provide ... an opportunity for the more permanent absorption of the entire group into the academic life of this country. ... I have now become convinced that it would probably not be in the best interests of the German scholars now in this country to undertake immediate publication."[218] The rise and fall of the symposium project demonstrated the difficulties of academic integration for the refugee scholars from Germany.

The files on Otto Szász document not only a step-migration towards, but also a measure of step-migration within the United States, due to the fact that it often took considerable time and effort to find an institution of suitable standing where a refugee scholar could permanently rebuild his career. A native of Hungary from a family of agriculturists, mathematics professor Ottó Szász studied mathematics, physics and astronomy in Budapest, Paris, Cambridge, Göttingen, and Munich, and received his Ph.D. in 1911 at the University of Budapest. Szász taught in Frankfurt am Main, Germany between 1914 and 1933 when he left for the United States. There he gave extramural lectures arranged for him by the Institute of International Education, under a grant from the Emergency Committee in Aid of Displaced German Scholars, later to become a visiting professor at MIT, at Brown University and, from 1936 to his

---

216 E. R. Murrow to Melchior Palyi, January 21, 1935, Melchior Palyi File, Emergency Committee in Aid of Displaced Foreign Scholars.
217 E. R. Murrow to Melchior Palyi, January 31, 1935, Melchior Palyi File, Emergency Committee in Aid of Displaced Foreign Scholars.
218 E. R. Murrow to Melchior Palyi, February 11, 1935, Melchior Palyi File, Emergency Committee in Aid of Displaced Foreign Scholars.

death in 1952, at the University of Cincinnati.[219] Szász was a citizen both of Hungary and Germany. As usual, when Szász went back to Hungary after his first year in the U.S., he had to go to the American Consulate in Budapest where they reissued him a re-entry permit.[220] The Emergency Committee took the necessary responsibility for enabling Szász to remain in the United States. Because of the difficulties anticipated in Frankfurt for substantiating his claim that he had taught there earlier, the Visa Section of the State Department was asked to comment on the case.[221] In order to become eligible for non-quota classification as a professor under Section 4 (d) of the Immigration Act of 1924, Szász was advised to secure statements from both MIT and Brown University regarding his appointment and salary. This was standard procedure at the time, in order for the U.S. to avoid admitting "persons likely to become a public charge."[222] As the State Department quoted the legal wording of the 1924 Act in an attachment,

> the term "Professor," as used in the section of the Act cited, has been interpreted to mean a person who is qualified to teach, and who, for two years immediately prior to applying for admission to the United States, has taught some recognized subject in an institution of learning which corresponds to a college, academy, seminary, or

---

[219] Otto Szász, "Curriculum Vitae," n.d., Otto Szász File, Emergency Committee in Aid of Displaced Foreign Scholars; Gabor Szegő, "Otto Szász," *Bulletin of the American Mathematical Society*, Vol. 60, No. 3, May 1954, p. 261; Emergency Committee in Aid of Displaced German Scholars, Agenda, September 27, 1935, Rockefeller Archive Center, Alfred E. Cohn Papers, RG 450 C661-U, Box 4, Folder 9; E. R. Murrow to Dr. Alfred E. Cohn, May 23, 1935, Alfred E. Cohn Papers, RG 450 C661-U, Box 4, Folder 8.

[220] B. G. D. Richardson to E. R. Murrow, May 23, 1934, Otto Szász File, Emergency Committee in Aid of Displaced Foreign Scholars.

[221] E. R. Murrow to John Farr Simmons, Chief of the Visa Division, State Department, May 28, 1934, Otto Szász File, Emergency Committee in Aid of Displaced Foreign Scholars.

[222] John Farr Simmons to E. R. Murrow, Washington, DC, June 5, 1934, Otto Szász File, Emergency Committee in Aid of Displaced Foreign Scholars.

university, as these terms are understood in the United States, and who is coming to the United States solely for the purpose of carrying on such vocation here."[223]

On July 2, 1934, the Consul General in Budapest finally issued a non-quota immigration visa under Section 4 (d) for Dr. Szász, who then returned to the United States for good.[224]

In a year, however, the Emergency Committee sought an expression of intention from MIT as to "Professor Szasz' permanent absorption into the faculty." "The Committee feels," Asst. Secretary Murrow explained, "that its first responsibility is towards those of its previous grantees for whom there is the greatest possibility of permanency at the conclusion of the period for which a stipend is sought."[225] In line with other organizations, the Committee thus reinforced its commitment to excellence, not just to charity.

The case of Otto Szász allows us some insight into how American Jews were considered in terms of the relief operations of European Jewish refugees. In May 1935, it became clear that MIT would not select Szász to add to the permanent faculty and regular MIT funds would not be offered to support a permanent position. By November 1935, the chances of his permanency at MIT were "slight or none."[226] Such a position could only be obtained if his friends succeeded in securing outside funds. In order to strengthen Szász's position, Professor Norbert Wiener attempted to secure funding from Jewish circles, including Felix Frankfurter.[227] He

---

223 Attachment to Simmons' letter above.
224 John Farr Simmons to E. R. Murrow, Washington, DC, July 31, 1934, Otto Szász File, Emergency Committee in Aid of Displaced Foreign Scholars.
225 E. R. Murrow to President Karl T. Compton, MIT, May 2, 1935, Otto Szász File, Emergency Committee in Aid of Displaced Foreign Scholars.
226 Karl T. Compton to E. R. Murrow, May 15, 1935, Otto Szász File, Emergency Committee in Aid of Displaced Foreign Scholars, New York Public Library, Manuscripts and Archives Division, New York, NY; cf. Analysis of Appointments Made with the Assistance of Emergency Committee Grants, November 4, 1935, Alfred E. Cohn Papers, RG 450 C661-U.
227 Hannah Szász to Norbert Wiener, Frankfurt am Main, May 5, 1933; Norbert Wiener to Felix Frankfurter, Cambridge, MA, May 18, 1933, Otto Szász File, Emergency Committee in Aid of Displaced Foreign Scholars.

learned "that, in view of several intensive campaigns for Jewish funds, the moment was not propitious to launch a further claim." One avenue that seemed promising was the Rockefeller Foundation, whose policy regarding renewal of grants for refugee scholars was similar to that of the Emergency Committee. Wiener left the matter in the hands of "my friends in Boston," and went to China. Szász subsequently was forced out of MIT, only to give several highly successful extramural lectures at various universities through the Institute of International Education.[228]

Cases parallel to those of Pályi in Chicago and Szász in Boston of private Jewish financing of refugees came up in other universities such as Washington University in St. Louis, Missouri. Dean Isadore Loeb pointed out "that it would certainly be possible to raise additional funds from Jewish sources in St. Louis to endow one or two additional displaced scholars..."[229]

Another mathematician with an even more distinguished American career was Gábor Szegő. Born in rural Hungary, Szegő received his first degree in Vienna (1918) and his *Habilitation* in Berlin (1921) where he became a professor. His most important job in Germany, however, expected him to be in Königsberg (today Kaliningrad, Russia), between 1926 and 1934. Acknowledging the delicately interwoven relationship of Hungarian and German scholars, J. D. Tamarkin called him one of the most brilliant representatives of the "German-Hungarian mathematical school."[230] Tamarkin was apparently asked by the Emergency Committee to help decide whether or not Szegő should come to the U.S. and made an important point about

---

228 Quotations from Norbert Wiener to E. R. Murrow, May 20, 1935, Karl T. Compton to E. R. Murrow, May 15, 1935, E. R. Murrow to Karl T. Compton, May 23, 1935, Otto Szász File, Emergency Committee in Aid of Displaced Foreign Scholars.
229 Notes on Dr. Kotschnig's visit to the U.S.A., March 23 to April 11 [1936], Rockefeller Archive Center, Rockefeller Foundation Archives, RG 1.1, Series 717, Box 2, Folder 12.
230 J. D. Tamarkin, Memorandum on G. Szegő, n.d., Gabor Szegő File, Emergency Committee in Aid of Displaced Foreign Scholars.

his helpful attitude toward his fellow mathematicians. He is a rarely encountered type of great talent who is not self-centered but is much and effectively interested in the work of other mathematicians.[231]

Professor Tamarkin was pushed into action by Szegő's long and detailed letter written from Copenhagen in May 1934 concerning his future in Königsberg, as well as by another letter from George Polya in Zürich, who in early 1934 had become anxious about his one-time coauthor Szegő.[232] Harald Bohr from Copenhagen, the younger brother of Nobel Laureate Niels Bohr, as well as the great German mathematician Richard Courant from Cambridge also wrote to save Szegő.[233] Just like Courant, Szegő was sheltered for some time by the "front-liner clause" of the German *Beamtengesetz* which exempted him, as a World War I officer, from losing his position in Königsberg for a longer period of time than was made available to fellow Hungarian Jews in contemporary Germany.[234] As the Rockefeller Foundation commented, "we are primarily concerned with the preservation of scientific values, and would be prepared, [...] to extend assistance to a man who is deposed in fact, whether or not he is formally deposed."[235] In other words, the Rockefeller Foundation had to

---

231 J. D. Tamarkin, Memorandum,, *op. cit.*, Gabor Szegő File, Emergency Committee in Aid of Displaced Foreign Scholars.
232 Gabor Szegő to J. D. Tamarkin, Copenhagen, May 23, 1934; Excerpt of a letter from George Polya to J. D. Tamarkin, February 14, 1934, Gabor Szegő File, Emergency Committee in Aid of Displaced Foreign Scholars. On his part, as an already established professor at Stanford, Szegő later helped Pólya into the U.S., in 1940.
233 Harald Bohr to R. S. Richardson, May 25, 1934, R. Courant to Elijah W. Bagster-Collins, May 24, 1934, Gabor Szegő File, Emergency Committee in Aid of Displaced Foreign Scholars.
234 R. Courant to Elijah W. Bagster-Collins, May 24, 1934, Gabor Szegő File, Emergency Committee in Aid of Displaced Foreign Scholars.—The Aryan clause did not apply to officials "who fought at the Front for the German Empire or for her allies during the War or whose fathers or sons fell in the War." Quoted by "A Crisis in the University World," Alfred E. Cohn Papers, RG 450 C661-U, Box 5, Folder 12, p. 5.
235 Warren Weaver, The Rockefeller Foundation, to E. R. Murrow, New York, May 28, 1934, Gabor Szegő File, Emergency Committee in Aid of Displaced Foreign Scholars.

judge Szegő's position untenable, so that they could make a contribution. Once the appropriate letters reached the foundation, $4,000 toward Szegő's salary was appropriated and then doubled almost immediately by the New York Foundation, one of the oldest philanthropic organizations in the United States. For the Emergency Committee, Szegő remained "an outstanding German scholar."[236]

The Dean of the Graduate School at Brown University was also most enthusiastic about Szegő as he believed that "both personally and scientifically Szegő will prove the greatest addition to American mathematics of any of the persons brought over under the auspices of your Emergency Committee."[237] Washington University in St. Louis immediately attempted to raise money for Dr. Szegő for two years, and his chances of a permanent job there were judged "good."[238] Nevertheless, on September 1, 1938 Szegő accepted a permanent professorship at Stanford.[239]

The reason for the Emergency Committee's rejection of certain applications is difficult to discern. A few cases of great international reputation should suffice. Born in Budapest, Frederick Antal studied law and art history in Berlin, Freiburg i. Br., Paris and Vienna where he did his doctorate with Professor Max Dvořák. Antal began work for the Museum of Fine Arts in Budapest in 1914 and headed its directorate during the heated months of the Republic of Councils in 1919, before he had to leave. After several years of research in Italy, he settled in Berlin (1923–1933) and became a naturalized German citizen. With recommendations from Kenneth

---

236 Warren Weaver to Chancellor Throop, Saint Louis, June 12, 1934; E. R. Murrow to Felix Warburg, New York, August 21, 1934, Gabor Szegő File, Emergency Committee in Aid of Displaced Foreign Scholars.
237 R.G.D. Richardson to E. R. Murrow, August 3, 1934, Otto Szász File, Emergency Committee in Aid of Displaced Foreign Scholars.
238 George R. Throop to E. R. Murrow, May 4, 1934, Gabor Szegő File, Emergency Committee in Aid of Displaced Foreign Scholars, New York Public Library, Manuscripts and Archives Division, New York, NY, Analysis of Appointments Made with the Assistance of Emergency Committee Grants, November 4, 1935, Alfred E. Cohn Papers, RG 450 C661-U.
239 Gabor Szegő to the Emergency Committee, February 14, 1938, Gabor Szegő File, Emergency Committee in Aid of Displaced Foreign Scholars.

Clark and Herbert Read ("I do not know of any art historian whose work can, in my opinion, be compared in importance to Dr. Antal's"),[240] he had some preliminary success with the Academic Assistance Council in London in 1935 which referred him to the Emergency Committee in New York and to the Carnegie Corporation. His age (43 years) may have excluded him from consideration of a Carnegie Corporation Junior Research Fellowship.[241] The AAC in London also warned the Emergency Committee in New York that "His vigorous personality may make him a difficult colleague for some people"—another word of caution.[242] No further reasons were given for a refusal, but the language damning Antal was common in anti-Semitic negative references for Jewish academics in the U.S. at this point.[243]

Antal did not receive a stipend to the U.S. and ultimately settled in Britain where his most important books were later published (*Florentine Painting* 1947, *Fuseli Studies* 1956, *Hogarth* 1962). That he was considered a Leftist and Marxist did not appear in his Emergency Committee file.

Hungarian, rather than German citizenship, was a key reason why the Emergency Committee did not work to save many of the applicants. Until 1938 when the first anti-Jewish Bill was passed in Budapest, the Hungarians did not seem to be an "endangered species," so to speak, so the Committee focused its efforts on the Germans and German-Hungarians who were in acute trouble. This explains why the Committee (and probably several other organizations) turned towards those Hungarians who were closely associated with Germany, were German citizens, had a German job, and were under actual threat after the advance of Hitler and the Nazi party.

---

240 Kenneth Clark (May 8, 1934) and Herbert Read (November 21, 1934) to the AAC, Frederick Antal File, Emergency Committee in Aid of Displaced Foreign Scholars.
241 Walter M. Kotschnig to Frederick P. Keppel, January 22, 1935, Frederick Antal File, Emergency Committee in Aid of Displaced Foreign Scholars.
242 Walter Adams, AAC to E. R. Murrow, February 5, 1935, Frederick Antal File, Emergency Committee in Aid of Displaced Foreign Scholars.
243 Personal communication from Professor Thomas Bender, May 3, 2008.

The erudite comparative and Roman law specialist Elemér Balogh taught courses at the University of Berlin for over four years but attempted to gain entry in the U.S. as early as 1928. In spite of the fact that some thirty supportive letters were sent to deans of American law schools in 1932–33, only a lecture tour at several U.S. and Canadian universities came from that effort.[244] "The depression was at fault" and it was "doubted whether he could adjust himself to conditions in this country [...] He speaks English very rapidly but not in such a way as to make him a popular lecturer," Stephen Duggan of the Institute of International Education wrote of him in 1933. "I did not feel from my acquaintance with him that he is altogether the type of lecturer that would appeal to an American college or university."[245] These were important warnings, as Stephen Duggan of the IIE and the Emergency Committee explained, "this Committee is very reluctant to make grants in cases where there appears to be no assurance of a permanent faculty appointment for the scholar at the expiration of the term of our grant."[246] However, the Emergency Committee had more important reasons to refuse Elemér Balogh: "he is probably a Hungarian citizen, he was a professor in Lithuania and not Germany, and was not therefore deprived of affiliation with any German university as a result of the political revolution there."[247] Instead of the United States, Balogh went to Johannesburg, South Africa where he received a professorship at Witwaterstrand University.

Hungarian arrivals after the introduction of anti-Jewish legislation in Hungary and the outbreak of World War II were often aided by a series of numerous agencies in the United States. The internationally

244 Elemér Balogh, Curriculum Vitae, [1939?], Elemér Balogh File, Emergency Committee in Aid of Displaced Foreign Scholars.
245 Elemér Balogh to [Stephen Duggan?], December 23, 1934; quotes from Stephen Duggan to Percy Bordwell (November 29, 1935) and to Judge John Bassett Moore (December 5, 1934), Elemér Balogh File, Emergency Committee in Aid of Displaced Foreign Scholars.
246 Stephen Duggan, IIE, to Professor Percy Bordwell, November 29, 1935, Elemér Balogh File, Emergency Committee in Aid of Displaced Foreign Scholars.
247 E. R. Murrow to Cecelia Razovsky, October 17, 1934, Elemér Balogh File, Emergency Committee in Aid of Displaced Foreign Scholars.

acclaimed statistician Imre Ferenczi left Hungary in 1919 and worked for the International Labour Office in Geneva between 1921 and 1930. He immediately became, upon arrival in the U.S. as a quota immigrant in 1940, a frequent lecturer on population problems. His personal efforts to seek financial assistance that would enable him to write a book on *Postwar Migration and Population Problems after World War I* also led him on a tortuous path. He first turned to his American colleague, the economist and investment authority Dr. Leland Rex Robinson, who directed him to the Refugee Scholar Fund, who advised him to turn to Edgar J. Fisher, professor and dean of Robert College in Constantinople, who in turn referred Ferenczi to the Emergency Committee in Aid of Displaced Foreign Scholars.[248] The Committee closely monitored personal meetings with the applicants and any unpleasant experience could contribute to having one's grant application refused. Ferenczi was found "not too pleasant a man, heavy and intolerant [...] one-sided and very dogmatic" by Alvin Johnson, and his application was turned down in the Summer of 1943. Ferenczi, however, soon received an award from the American Committee for Christian Refugees and the Emergency Committee closed his case in October 1943.[249]

Apart from this sizeable group, the Emergency Committee in Aid of Displaced Foreign Scholars supported a large number of Hungarians outside the United States, many of whom seemed German, and after a successful period in Berlin or some other German scientific or cultural center, were trying to find a job in their field. The Hungarian-born László (Ladislaus) Farkas (of the physical chemist Farkas brothers) studied and received his doctorate at the *Technische Hochschule* in Berlin-

---

248 American Committee for Christian Refugees to Refugee Scholar Fund, October 11, 1943, Imre Ferenczi File, Emergency Committee in Aid of Displaced Foreign Scholars.

249 Emergency Committee notes on Imre Ferenczi, 1942–43, Imre Ferenczi File, Emergency Committee in Aid of Displaced Foreign Scholars; Imre Ferenczi, Subcommittee Agenda, Emergency Committee Fellowship and Subcommittee Minutes, both of July 28, 1943, Alfred E. Cohn Papers, RF 450 C661-U, Box 2, Folder 2.

Charlottenburg and worked under the Nobel Laureate Fritz Haber in the *Kaiser Wilhelm Institut für physikalische Chemie* in Berlin, where he was joined by his brother Béla (Adalbert). Haber's institute was a world class chemistry research center, and the Farkas brothers became immersed in great science. Dismissed from Berlin, Ladislaus went as a "displaced German scientist" temporarily to Cambridge and then on to the Hebrew University in Jerusalem. There the Institute of Chemistry had been founded in 1925 by a fellow Hungarian, Professor Andor Fodor, where Ladislaus Farkas brought physical chemistry which he taught until his untimely death in 1949.[250] The Emergency Committee in Aid of Displaced German Scholars made a grant to the Hebrew University for the partial support in the academic years 1937–38 and 1938–39 of 11 scholars including Professor Farkas. By November 1938, the Hebrew University was forced to lean heavily on the Emergency Committee as income from European countries such as Germany, Austria, Czechoslovakia, and Italy had been significantly curtailed "and the anticipated income from England and other European countries will not materialize and the University will find itself with a considerable deficit this year."[251] Adalbert first followed his brother Ladislaus to Cambridge and then to Jerusalem, but in 1941 immigrated to the U.S.[252] The Farkas brothers belonged to the fairly

---

250 Professor Norman Bentwich, February 15–16, 1935; Stephen Duggan to Roger W. Straus, Committee on Grants, American Friends of the Hebrew University, January 5, 1938; Samuel B. Finkel to Stephen Duggan, November 3, 1938; News Bulletin on the Hebrew University, January 1940; c.v. received October 22, 1941, Ladislaus Farkas File, Emergency Committee in Aid of Displaced Foreign Scholars. Cf. Gábor Palló, "A 'magyar jelenség' és a kémia," *Fizikai Szemle* 2002/4. p. 108.

251 Samuel B. Finkel, Director, American Friends of the Hebrew University to Dr. Stephen Duggan, Secretary, Emergency Committee in Aid of Displaced German Scholars, New York, November 3, 1938, Ladislaus Farkas File, Emergency Committee in Aid of Displaced Foreign Scholars.

252 Edward M. M. Warburg to the Emergency Committee, June 13, 1941, Alfred E. Cohn Papers, RG 450 C661-U, Box 5, Folder 6; Ladislas Farkas to K. F. Bonhoeffer, Jerusalem, July 16, 1946, Ladislas Farkas file, Max-Planck-Gesellschaft Archiv, Berlin-Dahlem, III. Abt., Rep.23, 19.5.

large group of Hungarian-Jewish but German-trained scholars and scientistswho are lumped together in the records of German scholars fleeing from Nazi Germany.[253] This opens the question regarding such scholars and scientists whether it is their country of origin or that of their training that determines their national connection.

The Emergency Rescue Committee, Inc.

Patterns of Hungarian immigration can be also studied through the Emergency Rescue Committee, Inc. in New York, an organization that by 1943 was combined with the International Relief Association, Inc. to form the International Rescue & Relief Committee, Inc. at 2 West 43rd Street in the City. The ERC was instrumental in supporting a certain type of refugee Hungarians. Just like the private foundations, the American refugee commissions had to select, and the selection process favored high-quality professionals with good education, an internationally useful work experience, and appropriate social connections in the United States. Quality and professional usefulness reigned supreme. The Hungarian applicants from the early 1940s (many of whom actually never made it to the U.S.) provided many examples of the type the ERC favored ("the kind of person that the Emergency Rescue Committee should be able to help")[254] including the following people:

---

253 Ute Deichmann, "A German Influence on Science in Mandate Palestine and Israel: Chemistry and Biochemistry," *Israel Studies,* Vol. 9, No. 2, Summer 2004, pp. 34–70.
254 Anna Caples, Executive Secretary, American Friends of German Freedom, New York, December 4, 1940, University Libraries, University at Albany, SUNY, M. E. Grenander Department of Special Collections and Archives, Emergency Rescue Committee, Box 2, Folder 45.

Imre Békessy, journalist and newspaper editor
(father of the author Hans Habe, 1911–1977)
Aladár Farkas, author
Alfred Sendrey (originally Aladár Szendrei) (1884–1976),
musicologist, musician
Dr. József Szűcs, biochemist and plant-physiologist
Dr. László Vajna, journalist
József Vágó (1877–1947), architect
Dr. Mihály Veres, newspaper correspondent[255]

Threatened by the Hungarian anti-Semitic laws of 1938, 1939, and 1941, as well as the outbreak of World War II,[256] these relatively late applicants made a last, usually hopeless effort to escape impending peril. Nevertheless, at age 57 upon arrival in the U.S., Alfred Sendrey became an example of success in America, in part due to his versatility and scholarly interest in Jewish music, in part to his many international connections.

After he received his musical education at the Music Academy in Budapest (where he was taught in German by the Bavarian composition professor Hans Koessler), Alfred Sendrey had a distinguished career as a conductor in various, mostly German, cities. In 1933, he accepted a position as the director of the Central German Radio in Berlin, and simultaneously taught at the Klindworth-Scharwenka Conservatory. Soon, however, he had to move to Paris, where he took a position as director of *Radiodiffusion Nationale* (1933–1940). After seven years

---

255 Compiled from the files of the Emergency Rescue Committee. I listed the Hungarian refugees on the basis of the files of the Emergency Rescue Committee and the American Council for Emigres in the Professions, now in the custody of the M. E. Grenander Department of Special Collections and Archives, University Libraries, University at Albany, SUNY. I am profoundly grateful to Professor John Spalek, Sandra H. Hawrylchak, and Mary Y. Osielski for their kind support and assistance while I was working at Albany.

256 Raphael Patai, *The Jews of Hungary: History, Culture, Psychology* (Detroit: Wayne State University Press, 1996), pp. 535–559.

"Incipit Hitler:" Double Expulsion, Double Trauma

in Paris, he and his family emigrated to New York where he was first a client of the National Refugee Service. His early career in the U.S. was difficult: he was an organist in a synagogue for $30, later $20 a month. He gave piano lessons, copied music, taught at the 92nd Street YMCA, and, supported by the Emergency Committee,[257] worked on his great reference work *Bibliography of Jewish Music* (1951). "I was forced to do all this work far below the average wage level, since my employers took advantage of my need and my status as a refugee."[258] He later published two additional major works, *Music in Ancient Israel* (1969), and *The Music of the Jews in the Diaspora (up to 1800)* (1970). Sendrey's last work, *Music in the Social and Religious Life of Antiquity*, was published on his ninetieth birthday (1974).[259]

A number of Hungarians appear on the list of the *Clients du Centre Américain de Sécours* (an organization attached to the Emergency Rescue Committee under Varian Fry). Further research is needed to find out about the fate and whereabouts of these approximately 45 refugees.[260]

The American Council for Emigres in the Professions

Another group of Hungarian applicants or potential applicants was administered by the American Council for Emigres in the Professions (ACEP) and included eminent names such as

---

257 Subcommittee on Applications, Emergency Committee Fellowships, November 4 and 10, 1942, Alfred E. Cohn Papers, RG 450 C661-U, Box 6, Folder 17.
258 Alfred Sendrey, Application for Renewal of Fellowship, Subcommittee Agenda, Emergency Committee, June 15, 1944, Alfred E. Cohn Papers, RG 450 C661-U, Box 2, Folder 3.
259 Thesaurus of Jewish Music, The Hebrew University of Jerusalem, Jewish Music Research Center, http://jewish-music.huji.ac.il/thesaurus
260 Emergency Rescue Committee list, courtesy of Ms. Sheila Eisenberg, author of *A Hero of Our Own: The Story of Varian Fry* (New York: Random House, 2001).

Dr. Elemér Balogh (1881–1955), professor of law
Pál Dienes (1882–1952), mathematician
Dr. Erős, medical doctor
Dr. Károly Eszláry, financial law expert
Jenő (Eugenio) Faludi (1895–1981), architect
Carl Flesch (1873–1944), professor of violin
Tibor Gergely (1900–1978), artist
Dr. László Goldstein, experimental nuclear physicist (coworker of F. Joliot-Curie)
Drs. Géza and Tibor Grünwald, mathematicians
Dr. László Hámori
Pál Katona, lawyer and journalist
Dr. Kálmán Juris, physicist
Dr. László Ledermann, economist
Simon H. Lónyay, economist
Károly (Karl) Mannheim (1893–1947), economist
Dr. Dezső Papp, newspaper editor
Pál Pártos, social scientist
Endre Pikler, economist
Dr. Géza Policer, lawyer
Sándor Radó (1899–1981), geographer and cartographer
László Radványi (1900–1978), historian, social scientist
Dr. Géza Révész (1878–1955), psychologist
László Rostás, economist
István de Somogyi-Schill, professor of philology and diplomat
Dr. Tibor Szalai, economist
Dr. Lajos Székely (1904–1995), psychologist
Dr. Zoltán Szende, historian and international economist
Dr. József Szűcs, biochemist, mycologist
Dr. Pál Turán (1910–1976), mathematician[261]

---

261 Compiled from the files of the American Council for Emigres in the Professions, see footnote 255 above.

"Incipit Hitler:" Double Expulsion, Double Trauma

These Hungarians were, as Mildred Adams of the Emergency Rescue Committee put it, among the "limited number of outstanding refugees who should be in grave danger if apprehended by the Nazis" and thus were entitled "to make application for special visitor's visas to the United States."[262] However, few of them made it to America. The applicants needed "affidavits of support and moral sponsorship and a brief biographical sketch of the individual showing that he is endangered."[263] These documents were not easy to acquire and present, and consequently, many of the files remained incomplete.

The majority of the group were Jewish or at least their background was Jewish. That in mid-1941 a member of this list such as László Ledermann could be a "racial refugee but still Hungarian citizen" was somewhat of a riddle for ACEP officials.[264] There were obvious examples to the contrary such as the Baron Somogyi-Schill and Dr. Pál Dienes who were Protestant. Some of the institutions openly admitted that they would not want more Jewish members, at least not in any given year. President Clarence R. Decker of the University of Kansas City in Kansas City, Missouri stated this clearly and other schools were probably of the same opinion: "Because of the rather large number of Jewish appointments last year, I think it better that we do not add any more for the time being."[265] When Washington University looked for a professor in the German Department, Chancellor George R. Throop made it very clear

---

262 Mildred Adams, Executive Secretary, Emergency Rescue Committee, New York, September 4, 1940, University at Albany, SUNY, M. E. Grenander Department of Special Collections and Archives, Emergency Rescue Committee, Box 3, Folder 22.
263 Ibid.
264 University at Albany, SUNY, M. E. Grenander Department of Special Collections and Archives, American Council for Emigres in the Professions (ACEP) papers, László Ledermann file, Box 4, Folder 140.
265 Clarence R. Decker to Alvin Johnson, June 17, 1939, University Libraries, University at Albany, SUNY, M. E. Grenander Department of Special Collections and Archives, American Council for Emigres in the Professions, Paul Dienes Papers, Box 2, Folder 88.

that "owing to local circumstances, that professor should not be a Jew."[266] Alvin Johnson of the New School sent an equally clear and bitter answer to Kansas City:

> As you must have realized, your specifications are difficult because mathematics in Europe and very generally in this country is heavily peopled with Jews. The really eminent mathematicians from Germany who have been expelled are all Jews. Hitler had no reason to expel Aryan mathematicians because he is not yet able to discriminate between Aryan mathematics and mathematics in general.[267]

This Jewish-Hungarian group was indeed very European. Their Hungarian background was first of all rooted in the Hungary of the Austro-Hungarian Monarchy. Mihály (Michel) Veres in fact referred to his birthplace Temesvár (today Timişoara in Romania) as a city in Austria, using a type of generic geographic name for the Austro-Hungarian Monarchy. Though all were of Hungarian birth, many of the applicants had a strong German (Balogh, Flesch, Mannheim, Partos, Rostás, Székely, Veres), or

---

266 Notes on Dr. Kotschnig's visit to the U.S.A., March 23 to April 11 [1936], Rockefeller Archive Center, Rockefeller Foundation Archives, RG 1.1, Series 717, Box 2, Folder 12.
267 Alvin Johnson to Clarence R. Decker, New York, June 28, 1939, University Libraries, University at Albany, SUNY, M. E. Grenander Department of Special Collections and Archives, American Council for Emigres in the Professions, Paul Dienes Papers, Box 2, Folder 88. – Alvin Johnson was wrong: by that time Professor Ludwig Bieberbach (1886–1982) of the University of Berlin declared that there is a "Jewish mathematics" and a "German mathematics", separated by "an unbridgeable chasm." Bieberbach described "Jewish mathematics" as "willfully abstract, full of intellectual arrogance and of a devilish cleverness; in general, a juggling with concepts and an unmistakable craftiness..." A lecture at the annual meeting of the Verein zur Förderung des Mathematischen und Naturwissenschaftlichen Unterrichts, *Deutsche Zukunft,* April 8, 1934. Translation in the Alfred E. Cohn Papers, RG 450 C661-U, Box 4, Folder 2. Bieberbach lauched a journal entitled *Deutsche Mathematik.* "*German* mathematicians" included Theodor Vahlen, Oswald Teichmüller, Erhard Tornier, Helmut Hasse, Wilhelm Süss, Helmut Wielandt, and Gustav Doetsch. Hauptseminar Mathematiker während der NS-Zeit, Sommersemester 2003, TU München, http://www5.in.tum.de/lehre/seminare/math_nszeit/SS03/vortraege/de-math/

Austrian (Gergely, Papp, Somogyi-Schill) educational or professional background; and at the time of their application to the U.S., most had already lived outside Hungary, including France (Farkas, Goldstein, Juris, Veres), Britain (Dienes, Mannheim, Partos, Rostás), The Netherlands (Flesch, Révész), Italy (Faludi), Switzerland (Hámori, Ledermann, Policer, Radó), Finland (Székely), Czechoslovakia (Lónyay, Szalai) or Canada (Faludi), Morocco (Katona), and South Africa (Balogh). Their scattered geographic distribution throughout the European continent and beyond, demonstrates the thesis of this book: the Austro-Hungarian background combined with a characteristic step-migration and internationalization among interwar Jewish-Hungarian intellectuals.

Most of these persons went from country to country throughout the 1920s and 1930s, and they moved towards the United States when their European opportunities had ceased and they believed, often mistakenly, that the U.S. was still an option. The forced, externally-driven mobility of these typically high-quality professionals was a continuous migration with several stops, rather than a one-time resettlement. Many were born in pre-World War I Hungary and were first forced to resettle after the Paris Peace Treaties, particularly the Treaty of Trianon. When they were ejected again in the wake of the post-1919 anti-Semitic wave in Hungary, they went to different European countries, as the Quota Laws made it almost impossible for them to go to the U.S. When Nazism emerged in Germany, they began fleeing Hitler: first away from Germany and for some, back to Hungary, or into Austria, France, Switzerland, The Netherlands, Britain, whatever option became available for them. Their multiple temporary relocations and varied destinations followed, and indeed, mirrored Hitler's advances through Europe.

It must be noted that from the late 1920s through 1938, Hungary proved a relatively peaceful haven, a quasi-tolerant island in Europe. Ejected from Germany in or soon after 1933, many Jewish-Hungarians went home in the hope that the regime of Regent Horthy would give them shelter, as it did to well over half a million Jews until the anti-Jewish legislation of 1938–39, and particularly of 1941, proved this belief totally futile. So strong was the belief in the tolerance of Adm. Horthy's system that even a Jewish-German doctor escaping from Berlin went to Budapest and tried, in February 1934, to get a visa there to enter the United States.[268]

A few examples of step-migration should suffice. In the post-World War I years, violin professor Carl Flesch held posts twice in Berlin, then in Philadelphia, Britain, and The Hague. Artist Tibor Gergely went to Vienna in 1919, returned to Budapest in 1931, and entered the U.S. in 1939. Nuclear scientist Kálmán Juris worked in Vienna, until the *Anschluß* when he moved to Paris, worked with the Curies and became involved in the *résistance*. Hungarian sociologist (though German citizen) Karl Mannheim came from Heidelberg through Frankfurt to the London School of Economics, but seriously contemplated a position in the New School in New York in 1940. When Hitler came, geographer Sándor Radó moved from Germany to France and then to Switzerland and tried in 1941 to get a position in the U.S. Imre Békessy moved from Budapest to Vienna in 1920, returned to Budapest in 1926, fled to France in 1939, then on to Geneva, before he and his wife attempted to join their son, the author Hans Habe, in the U.S.

Hungarian refugees with a professional background usually spoke several foreign languages but their English was typically the weakest. A few Hungarians such as Géza Policer spoke English moderately well, but in general, the level of spoken and written English among Hungarian refugees was somewhat marginal, usually with a strong and unmistakable Hungarian accent. Michael Curtis' 1942 film *Casablanca*, one of the most popular and most Hungarian of Hollywood films, made unforgettable fun of the typical Hunglish of the day: "What watch?" "Ten watch." "Such much?"—a dialogue of "foreigners" in the film featuring several Hungarian refugee actors, including Peter Lorre and S. Z. Sakall.

For such migrations to occur, affidavits as well as moral and financial sponsorship were essential, and came from many sources: family members, friends and renowned colleagues at U.S. and European universities, and well-known Hungarian-Americans. After 1941, institutional

---

268 Dr. W. Heilbrun to the Bureau for Aid to German Refugees, Geneva, February 4, 1934 (Translation), Columbia University, Rare Book and Manuscript Library, Herbert H. Lehman Suite and Papers, James G. McDonald Papers, D356.

affidavits began being provided, as designed by James H. Case, Jr. of Brown University.[269] Some of the many Americans and Hungarian-Americans who regularly provided affidavits deserve to be remembered here. The list included sociologist Oscar Jászi, author Dr. Emil Lengyel, dermatology professor István (Stephen) Rothman (1894–1963), and aviation pioneer Theodore von Kármán. Professor Jászi of Oberlin College, Ohio was in close and regular contact with Alvin Johnson of the New School to whom he recommended several of his Hungarian and European friends, including Endre Pikler, Gaetano Salvemini and Franz Rapp.[270]

U.S. Consuls abroad preferred to accept affidavits from American relatives rather than mere friends in the U.S. However, affidavits preserved in the files of the various refugee organizations often came from friends. In this case, they had to be more comprehensive: the American had to substantiate his offer of support by attaching documents suggesting that he/she was able, and not just willing, to support a refugee. A letter from the American's employer, a statement from the bank where an account existed, an auditor's statement with regard to the value of the business, and/or copies of deeds of any property were to be included as supplementary evidence. The friend was also to explain how long he had known the refugee and why he was particularly willing to be of help.[271]

The Rockefeller Foundation

The Rockefeller Foundation was probably the largest private organization to provide care for refugee scholars from Europe. The Foundation's Memorandum on Refugee Scholars acknowledged

---

269 James H. Case, Jr. to Thomas B. Appleget, Providence, RI, August 6, 1941, Affidavit of Sponsorship form attached, Rockefeller Archive Center, Rockefeller Foundation Archives, RG 1.1, Series 200, Box 47, Folder 538.
270 Alvin Johnson—Oscar Jászi Correspondence, 1933–1940, Columbia University, Rare Book and Manuscript Library, Oscar Jászi Papers.
271 Cecilia Razovsky to Mary Ormerod, September 21, 1934, James G. McDonald Papers, National Coordinating Committee, Cecilia Razovsky File, D356 H21.

that for the next five, ten or maybe twenty years America is going to be one of the few places in the world where a real mind will have a free chance to work. The present collapse of European civilizations offers an opportunity for enhancing American culture. Because the Foundation believes this, it is willing to bring to America a limited number of really first-class men.[272]

In a different wording, the Foundation declared that it "is not attempting to face up to the whole problem which Europe presents; it is simply trying to save a small part of what it considers to be the most productive and potentially useful section of the population."[273] Apart from salvaging the best of the refugee scholars, the objective of the Rockefeller Foundation was also to make American scholarship "less provincial" [...] "by mixing in some of the best of European scholars." [...] "At no time was the program intended as a relief program, although such considerations have undoubtedly had some weight in particular instances."[274]

From 1933 to the end of 1939, the Rockefeller Foundation appropriated a total of $775,000 as a Special Research Aid Fund for Deposed Scholars. By the end of 1939, approximately $730,000 had been allocated to institutions world wide: $500,000 went to American institutions, the rest to Europe.[275] By the end of the War, the Foundation aided 295 scholars, spending $1,410,000 on relief.[276]

Rockefeller support was of two kinds: a personal grant from John D. Rockefeller, Jr., and support from the Rockefeller Foundation. In 1934,

---

272 Memorandum on Refugee Scholars, July 11, 1940, Rockefeller Archive Center, Rockefeller Foundation Archives, RG 1.1, Series 200, Box 46, Folder 530.
273 RBF, Memorandum on Refugee Scholars [1941], The Refugee Scholars—A Retrospect, Excerpt from [Rockefeller Foundation] Trustees' Confidential Report, October 1, 1955, Rockefeller Archive Center, Rockefeller Foundation Archives, RG 1.1, Series 200, Box 47, Folder 537 and 542.
274 JHW memo on Refugee Scholars, May 11, 1942, Rockefeller Archive Center, Rockefeller Foundation Archives, RG 1.1, Series 200, Box 47, Folder 541.
275 Refugee Scholar Programs. Former Program 1933–1939, n.d. Rockefeller Archive Center, Rockefeller Foundation Archives, RG 1.1, Series 717, Box 1, Folder 7.
276 The Refugee Scholars—A Retrospect, Excerpt from [Rockefeller Foundation] Trustees' Confidential Report, October 1, 1955, Rockefeller Archive Center, Rockefeller Foundation Archives, RG 1.1, Series 200, Box 47, Folder 542.

"Incipit Hitler:" Double Expulsion, Double Trauma

it was rumored that the Rockefellers were not going to extend their personal support for intellectuals beyond this academic year,[277] as "[John D.] Rockefeller, [Jr.] felt that he was not to be the 'Christian martyr' whom alone of all potential Christian givers in this country was making a larger contribution to the refugee work."[278] Refugee experts such as Walter M. Kotschnig believed, as a result, that the matter might only be reopened with Mr. Rockefeller "if four or five large Christian contributions could be secured."[279] The Foundation, along with the Carnegie Corporation, also showed symptoms of reluctance by 1935, and, as Kotschnig observed, were "beginning to tire of the refugee problem."[280]

The Rockefeller Foundation laid strict rules to regulate the appointment of displaced scholars. The Foundation, Associate Director Sydnor H. Walker explained in 1939, "does not take the initiative in recommending a scholar to a University but considers the application upon its merits when it is sent in by an institution." [...] "We are assuming that any further negotiations will be carried on between [the refugee scholar] and the University."[281] A second rule stipulated that, in almost all cases, the Foundation would contribute only one-half of the total amount required.[282] A year later, the Foundation identified three questions as relevant vis-à-vis refugee applicants, brutal as they sounded:

---

277 James G. McDonald, Memo to Walter M. Kotschnig, December 26, 1934, James G. McDonald Papers, Walter M. Kotschnig File, March–December, 1934, D356 H19.
278 Walter M. Kotschnig to James G. McDonald, October 12, 1934, James G. McDonald Papers, Walter M. Kotschnig File, March–December, 1934, D356 H19.
279 Ibid.
280 Walter M. Kotschnig to James G. McDonald, Geneva, April 9, 1935, James G. McDonald Papers, D356.
281 Sydnor H. Walker to Dr. Leopold Heinemann, New York, September 19, 1939, CEIP, Aid to Refugees, Box 271, Folder 1, 94666.
282 The Rockefeller Foundation, Special Research Aid Fund for Deposed Scholars 1933–1939, Rockefeller Archive Center, Rockefeller Foundation Archives, RG 1.1, Series 717, Box 2, Folder 8, p. 2.

(1) Are the men of real distinction so that their extinction would be a genuine loss to the scholarly world?
(2) Are the persons proposed in some potential danger?
(3) Is the man young enough so that his future contribution can be regarded as important.[283]

The resulting toughness is described in a memo entitled "Refugee Scholars" on July 9, 1940: "There would be inevitable confusion between the hardboiled desire to save intellect and the humanitarian desire to save lives."[284]

Refugee organizations and other charitable foundations were well aware both of the enormous measure of unemployment and of the rising anti-Semitic sentiment in the U.S., and thus called for

> a central organization here to push intellectuals. [...] [T]he Emerg[ency] Com[ittee] for Displaced For[eign] Scholars [...] files information, but does not undertake to place men. Merely makes grants in aid when a university requests help on the budget of a man which it is ready to appoint. The initiative has to come from the institution. They seem to fear (or to have experienced) criticism that they are filling positions with foreigners which ought to go to American teachers, and that is the attack used on anyone who pushed very hard to bring even highly qualified people into this country. I doubt how far any Committee would get which placed this too prominently in its program, or how much money could be raised for this distinct purpose."[285]

By 1938, the Rockefeller Foundation believed that

> the saturation point in the reception of these scholars at American Universities was about reached. We were told that the difficulty was not so much because they

---

283 Joseph H. Willits to Isaiah Bowman, November 6, 1940, Rockefeller Archive Center, Rockefeller Foundation Archives, RG 1.1, Series 200, Box 46, Folder 533.
284 Refugee Scholars, July 9, 1940, Rockefeller Archive Center, Rockefeller Foundation Archives, RG 1.1, Series 200, Box 46, Folder 530.
285 Brackett Lewis [?] to Waitstill H. Sharp, New York, August 3, 1939, CEIP, Committee to Aid Czechoslovakia, Box 288, Folder 2, 102347.

"Incipit Hitler:" Double Expulsion, Double Trauma

were Jews as because their appointment at full professorial rank seemed to close the way of promotion for resident scholars of minor rank.[286]

After 1940 and the threatening Nazi victory across the European continent, the Foundation felt they must act quickly and focus on "relocating such of the best of the scientific and scholarly men and women from France, Great Britain and other over-run countries as may be available to leave."[287] The emphasis was increasingly on the word "best", as Joseph H. Willits explained in a June 1940 memo,

> I would suggest these fundamental departures from the refugee policies which have obtained in the past: 1. I would take the initiative and shop for the best. I would do this cold-bloodedly on the assumption that Nazi domination of these countries makes them a poor place for a first-class person to remain in. And on the further assumption that the Foundation could make no finer contribution to our culture than to bring over, say, 100 of the best minds from Great Britain, 75 from France, and smaller numbers from the other countries. We could contribute to much needed distinction of our universities by facilitating such immigration.[288]

This new philosophy appeared in different forms and at different institutions from 1940 onward. As Rockefeller Foundation Vice President Thomas B. Appleget succinctly stated, "With limited funds, we have to make our grants for those who have the possibility of a productive career of a reasonable number of years after their arrival in America."[289] As late as October 1940, however, the Foundation was convinced that the refugee

---

286 D. S. Freeman, The Richmond News Leader to Raymond B. Fosdick, July 18, 1940, Rockefeller Archive Center, Rockefeller Foundation Archives, RG 1.1, Series 200, Box 46, Folder 530.
287 JHW, Memo, June 3, 1940, Rockefeller Archive Center, Rockefeller Foundation Archives, RG 1.1, Series 200, Box 46, Folder 530.
288 JHW, Memo, June 3, 1940; Raymond B. Fosdick to John D. Rockefeller, 3rd, July 17, 1940, Rockefeller Archive Center, Rockefeller Foundation Archives, RG 1.1, Series 200, Box 46, Folder 530.
289 Thomas B. Appleget to Alexander Makinsky, January 20, 1941, Rockefeller Archive Center, Rockefeller Foundation Archives, RG 1.1, Series 200, Box 47, Folder 535.

scholars did not displace American scholars and "supplemented in new ways the resources of American universities."[290]

For refugees of lesser eminence, temporary assignments were increasingly suggested, such as brief lecture courses, seminars, work as temporary teaching substitutes, in temporary research programs and giving assistance to individual scholars. The mid-western, southern and far western areas were especially singled out for desirable refugee work.[291]

Meanwhile, university and college presidents attributed great importance to the personality of the émigré scholar, citing "difficulty or failure in personal or social adjustments" in a number of specific instances where permanent jobs were not found.[292] Other factors limiting continued appointment cited by the Emergency Committee in Aid of Displaced Foreign Scholars were due to

> adjustability and assimilability. A middle course must be steered between the older and recognized scholar, who may be too "set" for ready adjustment, and the younger scholar who may the more easily fit himself into an American organization but be less deeply versed in his subject. [...] There is also the limitation of subject-matter. Foreigners can best fit into the teaching of "universal" subjects, such as mathematics, psychology, physiology, chemistry, physics, biology, philosophy. Their equipment is more critically considered when their candidacy is for subjects requiring American material, such as geology, political science, applied economics, sociology.[293]

---

290 Thomas B. Appleget to Joseph A. Baer, New York, October 9, 1940, Rockefeller Archive Center, Rockefeller Foundation Archives, RG 1.1, Series 200, Box 46, Folder 532.

291 Plans for assignment—refugee scholars receiving grants, November 22, 1940, TBK, Memo, Luncheon of representatives of organizations assisting displaced foreign scholars, April 3, 1941, Rockefeller Archive Center, Rockefeller Foundation Archives, RG 1.1, Series 200, Box 52, Folder 622; Box 47, Folder 526.

292 RTH memo on Deposed Scholars—Letters from University Presidents, November 25, 1939, Rockefeller Archive Center, Rockefeller Foundation Archives, RG 1.1, Series 717, Box 1, Folder 6.

293 Felix W. Krauth, Report of Trip to Universities and Colleges October 1939—January 1940, Alfred E. Cohn Papers, RG 450 C661-U, Box 13, Folder 24.

Some American universities were keenly aware of the unique value these immigrant scholars brought to their institutions:

> American psychology has limited its effectiveness by the exclusion of European thinkers from American faculties. The student learns of European trends and developments only at second hand, or warped through interpretation by a local scholar. Any University which can and will appoint a foreign psychologist, will gain immeasurably in both the depth and the breadth of its presentation of this subject.[294]

The presence of the refugees influenced American academics to a very considerable degree. Cultural historian Carl Schorske reminisced about

> his interaction with refugee historians during his student days at Harvard, notably with Fritz Epstein. Schorske argued that American students of German history came to intellectual history in part because the refugees discussed problems facing Europe within this framework; this helped American students to wake up from their naive positivism. Schorske also argued against the idea that in OSS the émigrés taught and Americans learned; rather, everyone learned.[295]

In a number of cases, new institutions resulted from the presence of the refugees. The disintegration of the Institute of Mathematics at Göttingen University enabled both Brown University and New York University to develop their own institutes of mathematics, employing 16 émigré mathematicians from Göttingen. The NYU Institute of Fine Arts as well as its Musicology Department were built out of and for the exiles. The New School of Social Research was another beneficiary of refugee scholars and built up its Graduate Faculty as a successor to the University of Exile. The mathematical faculties of California, Chicago, Pennsylvania, Stanford and the Institute for Advanced Study in Princeton

---

294 *Ibid.*
295 Catherine Epstein, "Account of the Discussions at the Conference 'German-Speaking Refugee Historians in the United States 1933–1970s' (Washington, DC, December 1–3, 1988)," *Bulletin of the German Historical Institute,* Washington, DC, No. 4, Spring 1989, p. 10.

also benefited from the exodus of German mathematics in and after 1933. The United States received six Nobel Laureates, and six future prize winners also left Germany or German occupied territories, including the Hungarian George de Hevesy, three of whom also ended up in the United States.[296]

Several Hungarian social scientists may serve as examples. Placed without Rockefeller Foundation aid to academic (Angyal and Deák) or other (Havas) positions, these scholars belonged to the Hungarian contingent of refugees saved by U.S. assistance.[297] Out of the 41 grantees in the natural sciences prior to October 1941, the Rockefeller Foundation supported five Hungarians (Ladislaus [László] Farkas, Ottó Szász, Gábor Szegő, George von Hevesy and Leo Szilard), totaling altogether 12.5%. Economic historian Karl [Károly] Polányi, a former Social Science fellow, received a Rockefeller grant in 1941–1942 to teach at Bennington College, sociologist Ernst Manheim (a cousin of Karl Mannheim) went to teach at Kansas City University, 1938–1940, law professor Rusztem Vámbéry was welcomed at the New School for Social Research between 1939–1942.[298] Younger European Fellowship candidates included economist Claire Hédervary in 1942.[299] An earlier list of Rockefeller grantees in The Netherlands includes, without any date, psychologist Dr. Lajos Székely working under the émigré Hungarian psychologist Géza Révész.[300] Another, similarly undated list (arguably from around 1935) showed six

---

296 The Refugee Scholars—A Retrospect, Excerpt from [Rockefeller Foundation] Trustees' Confidential Report, October 1, 1955, Rockefeller Archive Center, Rockefeller Foundation Archives, RG 1.1, Series 200, Box 47, Folder 542.
297 T. B. K. (Tracy B. Kittredge), Grants for European Scholars, November 4, 1940, Appendix B, Rockefeller Archive Center, Rockefeller Foundation Archives, RG 1.1, Series 200, Box 46, Folder 533.
298 RF grantees, 1939, 1942, Rockefeller Archive Center, Rockefeller Foundation Archives, RG 1.1, Series 200, Box 47, Folder 541 and 543.
299 T. B. K. memo on Younger European Fellowship Candidates, February 27, 1942, Rockefeller Archive Center, Rockefeller Foundation Archives, RG 1.1, Series 200, Box 47, Folder 540.
300 Appointments in Holland, n.d., Alfred E. Cohn Papers, RG 450 C661-U, Box 5, Folder 4.

"Incipit Hitler:" Double Expulsion, Double Trauma 337

Hungarian grantees including Ladislaus [László] Farkas, Karl [Károly] Mannheim, Ottó Szász, Gabriel [Gábor] Szegő, Leo Szilard, George de [György] Hevesy.[301]

Some people were explicitly told that they would not be supported. A case in point was dermatologist Tibor Benedek, originally of Budapest, then of Leipzig, whom Robert A. Lambert of the Rockefeller Foundation "had to tell [...] positively that we could not make him a grant for his work here. [...] I reminded B[enedek] that he was really not a deposed scholar, having never held a university appointment. I could not tell him of J. Gardiner Hopkins' (Columbia) very unfavorable comments on his scientific work."[302]

By the summer of 1944, the Emergency Committee realized that American institutions of learning would face a uniquely difficult situation at the end of the War. Scholars and scientists engaged in the war effort would be returning to their colleges and universities, potentially making refugee scholars jobless. The Army Specialized Training Program and other military units were already shut down by this time, leaving many of the refugee scholars unemployed. Different organizations initiated the Program for the Professional Rehabilitation of Exiles and the groups participated in the National War Fund. Relief programs in the U.S. turned to helping refugee scholars "render services in the rehabilitation of their own countries, and here they are prepared to make an unusual contribution because of the very considerable knowledge that they have acquired about the United States and the American way of life. This contribution [...] will have its share also in the maintenance of international good-will following the War."[303] The Emergency Committee was about to use its accumulated experience for peace (and

---

301 Undated list of grantees, Rockefeller Archive Center, Rockefeller Foundation Archives, RG 1.1, Series 717, Box 1, Folder 6.
302 Robert A. Lambert, memo on Deposed Scholars, New York, November 27, 1935, Rockefeller Archive Center, Rockefeller Foundation Archives, RG 1.1, Series 717, Box 1, Folder 5.
303 Stephen Duggan, "Continuance of Grants-in-Aid Program—Assistance of Older Scholars," June 26, 1944, University at Albany, SUNY, M. E. Grenander Department

American influence?) in the post-War world. However, it announced "the termination of its program and the closing of its office" in New York on June 1, 1945.[304]

The New School for Social Research

Though there were very few Hungarians considered for or actually given a job at the New School for Social Research[305] in New York City, the process of selection may provide a key to understanding how American organizations thought of the European refugees and decided whom they wanted to admit into the United States. Closely cooperating with the Rockefeller Foundation right after 1933, Alvin Johnson, head of the New School, was long thought of as the only chance for the rescue of certain valuable scholars. The Foundation increasingly felt, however, that Johnson only put "the scholars in the warehouse" without taking particular care in regard to their placement.[306] While attempting to bring over as many good people from Nazi-occupied Europe as possible, Alvin Johnson knew full well that "[t]he New School must necessarily operate within the limits of the Immigration Law."[307] Yet, he was exceptionally successful in lobbying for his School, increasingly "a major center of modernist

---

of Special Collections and Archives, Committee for Work Relief for Refugees, Box 7, Folder 155.

304 Emergency Committee Circular, Alfred E. Cohn Papers, RG 450 C661-U, Box 2, Folder 4.

305 For the history of the New School see Peter M. Rutkoff and William B. Scott, *New School: A History of the New School for Social Research* (New York: The Free Press; London: Collier Macmillan, 1986).

306 RAL, RF cooperation with New School for Social Research, October 17, 1940, Rockefeller Archive Center, Rockefeller Foundation Archives, RG 1.1, Series 200, Box 52, Folder 622.

307 Alvin Johnson, "Note on New School Plan for Bringing in Refugee Scholars," n.d., University at Albany, SUNY, M. E. Grenander Department of Special Collections and Archives, American Committee for Émigré Scholars, Box 7, Folder 154.

"Incipit Hitler:" Double Expulsion, Double Trauma

experimentation,"[308] and accomplished more individually than did many agencies. "Johnson maintains," argued Walter M. Kotschnig of the High Commission for Refugees,

> that he has been very much more successful in obtaining legal facilities for his refugees then we have been as he has a status with the government which we have not. Besides he has permanent representative in the various centers, who are in a position to intervene officially and regularly with the various government offices.[309]

The Immigration Law stipulated that scholars could only be considered outside the quota system if they were regularly employed as a teacher in some form of higher education in the last two years before applying for a visa. Yet, there were still other difficulties connected with the quota laws, as Johnson indicated in a 1941 letter identifying requirements the New School had established:

> We have been restricted in our selections first of all by a legal factor. We could appoint only scholars eligible for a non-quota visa by virtue of having done sufficient support only for persons young enough so that, during the initial two-year period at the New School, they may hope to win a permanent post in some American institution. The general rule was to appoint nobody over fifty-five.[310]

As additional reasons for ruling out even some excellent people, Johnson added:

---

308 Thomas Bender, *New York Intellect: A History of Intellectual Life in New York City, from 1750 to the Beginnings of Our Own Time* (New York: Alfred A. Knopf, 1987), pp. 331–332.
309 Walter M. Kotschnig to Professor Norman Bentwich, Geneva, March 25, 1935, James G. McDonald Papers, Walter M. Kotschnig File, 1935–April 1936, D356 H20.
310 Alvin Johnson to Henry H. Haskell, New York, July 17, 1941, CEIP, Aid to Refugees, Box 271, Folder 2, 94822.

1. The candidate was reported to be in no particular danger or distress.
2. The candidate could not get permission to leave his country, or a change in circumstances caused a change in his plan to leave.
3. The candidate was a refugee scholar established at an institution whose work was continuing, and which had given hospitality to a group whose status would have been damaged by the premature departure of any one individual.
4. The candidate was in a relatively safe country, e.g., Brazil.
5. Our efforts to gather the necessary data about the candidate were more or less fruitless.
6. The candidate was, in a general way, eligible and available, but proved to be, according to the consensus of opinions of colleagues consulted, not the first choice among the many in his field.[311]

The list places the problem of refusal into a broader perspective showing that the selection process in the New School was carefully executed. In addition, the New School (commonly called the University in Exile) had to operate within the financial limits set by its sponsors, first and foremost of which was the Rockefeller Foundation.

Johnson was firmly convinced that "in scholarship competition is the life of trade,"[312] and turned openly against those who thought refugee scholars would endanger American academe. Nevertheless, even this select group included several Hungarians such as Dr. Albert Halasi, an expert in practical economic policy who was at the New School for two years until he exhausted the funds available and left in 1942. The Hungarian psychiatrist and psychoanalyst Georg (György) Gerő received a grant to work at the New Mexico State College of Agriculture and Mechanic Arts.[313] Alvin Johnson contemplated extending an invitation in 1940 to

---

[311] *Ibid.*, 94822–3.
[312] Alvin Johnson to the Editor of *The New York Times*, New York, November 12, 1940, *The New York Times*, November 17, 1940.
[313] Grants to the New School for Social Research for refugee scholars, October 2, 1940; European Refugee Scholars in the United States, Medical Sciences, October

the Hungarian scholar Karl [Károly] Mannheim to join the faculty of The New School, viewing him as "one of the two or three most brilliant sociologists of the younger German [sic] generation. Although standing close to the socialist movement, his important contributions have been made in connection with a criticism of Marxism. His lecture on general sociology and social theory at the University of Frankfurt have been among the most frequented at the university."[314] Requested to recommend him, Columbia University professor R. M. MacIver went out of his way to praise Mannheim as "one of the most important figures in the line of sociological theory."[315] The controversial German émigré Dr. Kurt Riezler was also asked to comment on Mannheim's invitation and he had much less favorable things to say: "without any doubt a brilliant man—and very eager to appear as brilliant, therefore sometimes dealing in a rather offhand manner with the fact, in case they contradict his thesis. He enjoys debunking, [...] he is destructive rather than constructive—his main interest is debunking [...]."[316] Johnson was not influenced by Riezler's criticism and an invitation was sent to Mannheim, who suffered from the animosity of the head of his department at the London School of Economics, Morris Ginzberg, had problems with teaching in English, and

---

10, 1941, p. 8; Rockefeller Archive Center, Rockefeller Foundation Archives, RG 1.1, Series 200, Box 52, Folder 622; and RG 1.1, Series 200, Box 47, Folder 538.

314 Memorandum on the Proposed Faculty for the University in Exile, n.d., Alfred E. Cohn Papers, RG 450 C661-U, Box 13, Folder 23.

315 R. M. MacIver to Alvin Johnson, August 9, 1940, University at Albany, SUNY, M. E. Grenander Department of Special Collections and Archives, Emergency Rescue Committee, Box 4, Folder 202.

316 Kurt Riezler on Karl Mannheim, 1940. University at Albany, SUNY, M. E. Grenander Department of Special Collections and Archives, Emergency Rescue Committee, Box 4, Folder 202. Riezler, then at the University of Chicago, intrigued with Leo Strauss to prevent the University from offering an appointment to Karl Popper. David Gordon, "Many Words for Hegemony," *The Mises Review*, Vol. 10, No. 2; Summer 2004.

missed the intellectual curiosity among his British students.[317] Mannheim, however, eventually gave up the idea of leaving Britain.

Johnson also had his rare moments of misjudgment. Though the mathematician Pál Turán was recommended by Professor Gábor Szegő of Stanford University, he was unfairly rated by the Director of the New School: "As for Dr. Turan, he might be eligible for a non-quota visa but I am afraid that his record will not stand up in the competition given by many eminent scholars for the few places open in the field of mathematics. We have sent Dr. Turan's name to a foundation, but we are candidly not very hopeful about the reaction."[318] By that time, Turán was in and out of forced labor camps in Hungary.[319] Efforts on his behalf continued and the Rockefeller Foundation gathered further information about him from Professor Oswald Veblen of the Institute for Advanced Study in Princeton.[320] Turán was one of Alvin Johnson's misperceptions: the young Hungarian became one of the top post-War mathematicians of Hungary with a great international reputation.

Along with Turán, a New School list from December 1940 included two other Hungarian mathematicians, Géza Grünwald (1910–1942) and Tibor Grünwald (later Tibor Gallai, 1912–1992) both of Turán's age, (and both also on the list of the American Council for Emigres in the Professions), but a penciled note declared "no NS interest in anyone of

---

317 Jacob Katz, *With My Own Eyes: The Autobiography of an Historian* (Hanover and London: Brandeis University Press/University Press of New England, 1995), pp. 103–104.
318 Alvin Johnson to Gábor Szegő, New York, January 20, 1941, University at Albany, SUNY, M. E. Grenander Department of Special Collections and Archives, American Council for Emigres in the Professions, Géza and Tibor Grünwald Papers, Box 3, Folder 75.
319 V. T. Sós, "Turbulent Years: Erdős in His Correspondence with Turán from 1934 to 1940," In: *Paul Erdős and his Mathematics*, I. Budapest: Bolyai Society Mathematical Studies, 11, 2002, p. 132.
320 HMM to Oswald Veblen, February 11, 1941, Rockefeller Archive Center, Rockefeller Foundation Archives, RG 1.1, Series 200, Box 47, Folder 535.

"Incipit Hitler:" Double Expulsion, Double Trauma 343

these."[321] The New School also gave brief consideration to the Hungarian theoretical physicist Ladislas (László) Tisza and the biochemist Joseph (József) Szűcs (the latter also appears on the list of the Emergency Committee in Aid of Displaced Foreign Scholars).[322] Among refugee Hungarians, "one of the ablest of the younger theoretical economists", Dr. L. Rostás was "held in suspense" in London "until more information is available,"[323] and the New School also continued to consider A. B. Schwarz in Turkey (History) and Elemér Balogh in "British territory" (Law).[324] Rostás was described in unusually detailed and particularly glowing terms as a scholar "who has command of statistical and empirical methods of research" and for whom it would be no difficulty to arrange an academic position in the U. S.[325]

Overwhelmed by applications and financial limitations, Alvin Johnson came to conclude with pessimism that "the refugees of the Revolution of 1848 had nobody to look after them. Doctors, lawyers or professors, they knew there was only one field open – manual work. I fear it is coming to that."[326] Applications with too extensive a list of qualifications did not make the situation any better and even turned benevolent

---

321 Herbert Solow to H. M. Miller, Jr., December 16, 1940, Encl., Rockefeller Archive Center, Rockefeller Foundation Archives, RG 1.1, Series 200, Box 52, Folder 622. On Géza Grünwald see Pál Turán, "Grünwald Géza élete és matematikai munkássága," [The Life and Mathematics of Géza Grünwald], lecture at the Bolyai János Math. Soc., April 1, 1955. http://www.physics.hu/historia/grunwald/grunwald1.html
322 Alvin Johnson to Thomas B. Appleget, December 5, 1940, Encl., Refugee Scholars, Rockefeller Archive Center, Rockefeller Foundation Archives, RG 1.1, Series 200, Box 52, Folder 622.
323 Grants to the New School for Social Research for refugee scholars, October 2, 1940, Rockefeller Archive Center, Rockefeller Foundation Archives, RG 1.1, Series 200, Box 52, Folder 622.
324 Alvin Johnson to Thomas B. Appleget, April 22, 1941, Encl., Under Consideration at the New School, n.d., [December 4, 1940], Rockefeller Archive Center, Rockefeller Foundation Archives, RG 1.1, Series 200, Box 53, Folder 624.
325 Grants for European Scholars, November 25, 1940, p. 5. Rockefeller Archive Center, Rockefeller Foundation Archives, RG 1.1, Series 200, Box 46, Folder 533.
326 Unsigned copy of a letter by Alvin Johnson to Dr. Alfred A. Cohn, New York, December 5, 1938, University at Albany, SUNY, M. E. Grenander Department of

Americans recipients suspicious, particularly if the bibliography of an applicant, such as that of Tibor Szalai, contained an all too self-conscious title, "Hundred New Ideas for America."[327]

Whether from Germany or Hungary, refugee intellectuals and professionals found themselves increasingly engaged in the American war effort. This was to become the only hope for funding. By 1943–44, private sources as well as foundation assistance for refugee scholars started to dry up. Alvin Johnson found it necessary to develop the Refugee Work Relief Associates as a volunteer agency, a Committee to combine those active in refugee relief and employment in some of the major study and research centers in the United States. The purpose of this "non-political, interracial and non-sectarian" organization was funding coordination. The new organization decided to refrain from separate appeals for funds and obtained its funding solely from the National War Fund.[328] The RWRA emphasized that "many of these men and women have contributed a great deal to our War Effort through their research for various Government Agencies on problems pertaining to Europe. They will be invaluable in their future cooperation."[329] The program of the new organization was

> to aid chiefly exiles who intend to return to their native countries or participate in other ways in the democratic reconstruction abroad, outside of the military, governmental and political fields. The aim of this effort is first to develop the final

---

Special Collections and Archives, American Council for Emigres in the Professions, Dr. Erős Papers, Box 2, Folder 133.

327 Eduard Heimann to Dr. Alvin Johnson, September 4, 1940, University at Albany, SUNY, M. E. Grenander Department of Special Collections and Archives, American Council for Emigres in the Professions, Tibor Szalai Papers, Box 7, Folder 21.

328 Refugee Work Relief Associates. Program for the Professional Rehabilitation of Exiles, n.d. University at Albany, SUNY, M. E. Grenander Department of Special Collections and Archives, Committee for Work Relief for Refugees, Box 7, Folder 155.

329 Unmailed letter by Alvin Johnson to Gerard Swope, National War Fund, June 15, 1944, University at Albany, SUNY, M. E. Grenander Department of Special Collections and Archives, Committee for Work Relief for Refugees, Box 7, Folder 155.

stage of their stay in America into a constructive experience, allow them to work in accordance with their vocational aspirations, equip them with an adequate experience of America, overcoming the limited outlook caused by unemployment, professional displacement, non-citizenship, alien status, social isolation and linguistic handicaps; second in other ways to assist them in reestablishing their contacts in their respective countries.[330]

Hans Staudinger, Dean of the Graduate Faculty of Political and Social Science under the New School, lent his support to the application of the Refugee Work Relief Associates in an effort to convince the National War Fund in 1944 of the usefulness of the refugee scholars for America and divided them into three categories. Many of them would want to return to Europe after the War. "They believe it is their mission to contribute to the moral and intellectual reconstruction of their homelands." Other refugees, Johnson argued, "contributed substantially to our war effort" and should be helped to find jobs in their adopted country. A third group would want to combine "a good European scholastic background with a sound knowledge of the American scientific approach" and is needed in the realm of American education.[331]

By mid-1944, those behind the Refugee Work Relief Associates had to realize that employment for the refugees in the training programs of the Armed Forces would soon come to an end. "We find there will be need for funds from sources that are oriented largely toward rehabilitation for work abroad."[332] The 1944 plans of Alvin Johnson, the New School and the Refugee Work Relief Associates all clearly indicated that refugees

---

330 Refugee Work Relief Associates. Program for the Professional Rehabilitation of Exiles, n.d. University at Albany, SUNY, M. E. Grenander Department of Special Collections and Archives, Committee for Work Relief for Refugees, Box 7, Folder 155.
331 Quotes from unmailed letter by Hans Staudinger to Eliot Jensen, National War Fund, June 9, 1944, University at Albany, SUNY, M. E. Grenander Department of Special Collections and Archives, Committee for Work Relief for Refugees, Box 7, Folder 155.
332 Horace L. Friess to Professor Joseph P. Chamberlain, June 17, 1944, University at Albany, SUNY, M. E. Grenander Department of Special Collections and Archives, Committee for Work Relief for Refugees, Box 7, Folder 155.

were increasingly thought of in terms of their future usefulness vis-à-vis Europe. "Many of them will be needed later on when in this country after the war education will have an enormous boom; part of them will be needed for the manifold work of reconstruction in Europe and other lands."[333] Johnson found it imperative to use the services of the refugees "who potentially have great influence on liberated public opinion in European countries, towards the United States in particular. It would be unwise," he suggested weeks before D-Day, "not to give them the opportunity of continuing their work and of preparing for their contribution in the moral and educational reconstruction of Europe."[334] The coordinated budget estimate of the Refugee Work Relief Associates was calculated as $400,000 and included nine organizations.[335]

Towards the end of the War, with much of Jewish scholarship already destroyed in Europe, American expertise and money were once again used to help refugees through a new organization. Established on February 27, 1945, the American Committee for Refugee Scholars, Writers and Artists, Inc. helped numerous refugees, 80% of whom were Jewish and

---

333 Alvin Johnson, Project of the Refugee Work Associates, December 27, 1944, Alfred E. Cohn Papers, RG 450 C661-U, Box 4, Folder 27.
334 Alvin Johnson to Professor Joseph P. Chamberlain, June 21, 1944, University at Albany, SUNY, M. E. Grenander Department of Special Collections and Archives, Committee for Work Relief for Refugees, Box 7, Folder 155.
335 Cambridge Committee
 Harvard University, Radcliffe College and M.I.T.
 Institute for Advanced Study, Princeton
 Refugee Aid Committees
 Universities of Chicago, Stanford University
 Columbia University
 New School for Social Research
 École Libre des Hautes Études
 International Study Center for Democratic Reconstruction
  Summary of Coordinated Budget Estimate, Refugee Work Relief Associates, October 1, 1944 to September 30, 1945, University at Albany, SUNY, M. E. Grenander Department of Special Collections and Archives, Committee for Work Relief for Refugees, Box 7, Folder 155.

many others of Jewish origin.[336] The Committee used some of the funds of the American Christian Committee for Refugees and the National Refugee Service.[337]

The Carnegie Endowment for International Peace

Though engaged in the matter of aiding victims in, and refugees from, Czechoslovakia after the German occupation, the Carnegie Endowment was not active in matters pertaining to Hungarians, even Hungarian Jews, as Hungary was at war with the United States after December 1941 and only technically independent until March 19, 1944. The few Hungarians who contacted the Endowment were invariably given flat refusals. While being assured of "the deepest sympathy with all who, like you three gentlemen, are in distress through no fault of their own," Imre Lemberger, Endre Mauthner (a "motor-car fitter") and Otto Liebermann (a merchant) from a textile company in Győr were advised by Henry S. Haskell, Assistant to the Director of the Endowment, to turn to the International Migration Service in Geneva, or the National Council of Jewish Women in New York. "[...] [I]t is wholly impossible for us to assist individually the literally hundreds of appeals addressed to us," so the standard answer went to Hungary. "The problem is so vast that it can only be solved by well organized and administered Committees for the purpose with the aid of governments inclined to be helpful."[338]

The Carnegie Corporation, like the Rockefeller Foundation, refused to give Junior Fellowships in 1935, even though a large list of applica-

---

336 Else Staudinger to Dr. Alfred E. Cohn, New York, November 20, 1945, Rockefeller Archive Center, Alfred E. Cohn Papers, RG 450 C661-U, Box 3, Folder 17.
337 Financial Report of May 1, 1945, American Committee for Refugee Scholars, Writers & Artists, Rockefeller Archive Center, Alfred E. Cohn Papers, RG 450 C661-U, Box 3, Folder 17.
338 Henry S. Haskell to Imre Lemberger, December 15, 1938, CEIP, Aid to Refugees, Box 271, Folder 1, 94577.

tions was transmitted at the turn of 1934–35 by the Office of the High Commissioner for Refugees.[339]

Even far-reaching international connections proved futile. The renowned Budapest lawyer Dr. Jenő Kerpel enjoyed a wide variety of contacts with Americans in his capacity as the attorney of the American-Hungarian Chamber, and tried to help his brother Edmund, a well-known dentist in Vienna, find a job at Columbia or some other American university. In this aim, he used the good offices of Dr. Hugo Wolf, a fellow attorney in Vienna who fled Austria and settled in the U.S. To gain the personal goodwill of Columbia President Butler, Dr. Jenő Kerpel thanked him for his "speech to the world famous Hungarian composer [sic] Béla Bartók" which, he suggested, "found a deep echo in this country."[340] Nevertheless, all these efforts led nowhere, as the Endowment felt helpless in the matter because "The regulations regarding university posts in dentistry are so rigid."

The seemingly standard reaction of the Carnegie Endowment was widely shared by other agencies which also used the same language. The National Coordinating Committee for Aid to Refugees and Emigrants Coming from Germany increasingly felt that "the whole situation is so desperate as to be almost hopeless. Private organizations can no longer cope with this situation."[341] Henry S. Haskell of the Carnegie Endowment echoed the National Committee urging "well administered organizations

---

339 Walter M. Kotschnig to Professor Norman Bentwich, March 25, 1935, Columbia University, Rare Book and Manuscript Library, Herbert H. Lehman Suite and Papers, James G. McDonald Papers, Walter M. Kotschnig File, 1935–April 1936, D356 H20; Dr. Walter M. Kotschnig to Dr. Alfred E. Cohn, Geneva, December 3, 1934, Alfred E. Cohn Papers, RG 450 C661-U, Box 2, Folder 11.
340 Dr. Eugene Kerpel to Henry S. Haskell, Budapest, January 16, 1941, CEIP, Aid to Refugees, Box 271, Folder 2, 94749; Dr. Hugo Wolf to Henry S. Haskell, New York, February 22, 1941, CEIP, Aid to Refugees, Box 271, Folder 2, 94748; Henry S. Haskell to Dr. Hugo Wolf, New York, February 24, 1941, CEIP, Aid to Refugees, Box 271, Folder 2, 94747.
341 Cecilia Razovsky, Executive Director of the National Coordinating Committee to Henry S. Haskell, New York, March 20, 1939, CEIP, Aid to Refugees, Box 271, Folder 1, 94624.

"Incipit Hitler:" Double Expulsion, Double Trauma

[...], possibly aided by government action" to take care of the refugee problem. He also suggested that the situation was almost hopeless, that it went beyond the possibilities of "special groups" and that it can only be remedied "with coöperation of governments which still preserve some modicum of altruism."[342]

After the overthrow and collapse of Czechoslovakia, the Masaryk Institute in New York City cooperated with the Carnegie Endowment and tried to establish teaching positions for exiled Czechoslovak professors. The response from various U.S. universities and colleges was overwhelmingly negative; enthusiasm for helping was at an ebb. Brackett Lewis, Executive Secretary of the Masaryk Institute in New York bitterly remarked, "The few men whom we shall be able to assist will not adversely affect the employment situation in this country." It was, however, somewhat characteristic of the refugee administration that he sent this letter to Professor B. Shimek at the University of Iowa who had died two years earlier.[343]

---

342 Henry S. Haskell to Susan Huntington Vernon, New York, March 13, 1939, CEIP, Aid to Refugees, Box 271, Folder 1, 94619.
343 Brackett Lewis, Executive Secretary, Masaryk Institute, to Professor Bohumil Shimek, May 18, 1939, with a note by Ella Shimek, Columbia University, Rare Book and Manuscript Library, Carnegie Endowment for International Peace, Aid to Refugees, Box 288, Folder 1, 101865.

VI Problem Solving and the U.S. War Effort

As seemed so natural, several of the émigré Jewish-Hungarians lent their support to the war effort in their newly adopted country, the United States. They brought along their much needed cultural background, their sophisticated knowledge, and their special brand of sensitivity to make them appreciative of the needs of a country engaged in was with Nazi Germany and its allies. The Jewish-Hungarian group was of paramount importance for the U.S. in the War years: they fought against Hitler enthusiastically, embraced American values and became devoted Americans in this effort. The connection between their intellectual background and their American career marks their journey's end through the troubled history of the first half of the 20th century—and beyond.

1 The Heuristic Tradition: George Pólya

In a pioneering inquiry into the nature of problems and the solution of a problem, Michael Polanyi defined one of the most crucial questions of his generation. European mathematicians and scientists were particularly welcome in the United States from the 1920s onwards. "To recognize a problem which can be solved and is worth solving is in fact a discovery in its own right," Polanyi declared the creed of his generation in his 1957 article for *The British Journal for the Philosophy of Science*.[1] Polanyi spoke for, and spoke of, his generation when discussing originality and invention, discovery and heuristic act, investigation and problem solving.

---

1   Michael Polanyi, "Problem Solving," *The British Journal for the Philosophy of Science*, Vol. VIII, No. 30, August 1957, pp. 89–103; quote p. 89.

"How to Solve It"

The origins of problem solving as a way of thinking particularly associated with the American heritage go back to the pioneering spirit of the frontier times. Its value was first recognized as a necessity for the development of tactics and strategies that the American people could use to perform their daily tasks in creating the United States, and their own lives in the new country.

The first serious American psychologist to emphasize learning as the definition of intelligence was Edward L. Thorndike (1874–1949), who in a 1921 symposium defined intelligence as the ability to give good responses to questions.[2] Thorndike was influenced by William James (1842–1910) at Harvard (1895–1897). The concept of learning took on practical characteristics in regard to problem solving as pertaining not only to survival in the harsh circumstances of the frontier, but also to the newly emerging American tradition of self-help and success. This became an ideal upheld by subsequent generations of American social scientists, authors, businessmen throughout the latter half of the 19th century. The doctrine of self-help and success became, indeed, an American myth and this dream "penetrated, in some guise, every major activity of the period: the new immigration, the rise of socialism, the agrarian revolution (and the exodus of country boys and girls to the city), the march of technology, the growth of corporate business and labor unionism, and more."[3]

The interpretative frame of the educated mind is ever ready to meet somewhat novel experiences and to deal with them in a somewhat novel manner. In this sense, all life is endowed with originality and originality of

---

2   R[obert] J. St[ernberg], "Human Intelligence," *The New Encyclopaedia Britannica* (Chicago: Encyclopaedia Britannica, 1990), Vol. 21, p. 710. Cf. Donald O. Hebb, *Textbook of Psychology* (Philadelphia—London—Toronto: W. B. Saunders, 1972).

3   Kermit Vanderbilt, "The Gospel of Self-Help and Success in the Gilded Age", in: Robert Allen Skotheim, Michael McGiffert, eds. *American Social Thought: Sources and Interpretations,* Vol. II: *Since the Civil War* (Reading, MA: Addison-Wesley, 1972), p. 6.

a higher order is but a magnified form of a universal biological adaptivity. But genius makes contact with reality on an exceptionally wide range: by seeing problems and reaching out to hidden possibilities for solving them, far beyond the anticipatory powers of current conceptions. Moreover, by deploying such powers in an exceptional measure—far surpassing our own as onlookers—the work of genius offers us a massive demonstration of a creativity which can never be explained in other terms nor taken unquestioningly for granted.[4]

Hungarian-born mathematician George Pólya (1887–1985) was one of those who channeled the Hungarian and, more broadly speaking, Central European school tradition into American education in a series of books and articles, starting with his 1945 book *How to Solve It*.[5] In 1944, Pólya remembered the time when, at the turn of the century in Hungary,

> he was a student himself, a somewhat ambitious student, eager to understand a little mathematics and physics. He listened to lectures, read books, tried to take in the solutions and facts presented, but there was a question that disturbed him again and again: "Yes, the solution seems to work, it appears to be correct; but how is it possible to invent such a solution? Yes, this experiment seems to work, this appears to be a fact; but how can people discover such facts? And how could I invent or discover such things by myself?"[6]

Pólya came from a distinguished family of academics and professionals. His father, Jakab, an eminent lawyer and economist, provided the best education for his children. They included George's brother, Jenő Pólya, the internationally recognized Hungarian professor of surgery

---

4   Polanyi, "Problem Solving," *op. cit.*, pp. 93–94.
5   G. Pólya, *How to Solve it. A New Aspect of Mathematical Method* (Princeton, N.J.: Princeton University Press, 1945). *How to Solve It* has never been out of print and has sold well over 1 million copies. It has been translated into 17 languages, probably a record for a modern mathematics book. Gerald L. Alexanderson, "Obituary. George Pólya," *Bulletin of the London Mathematical Society*, Vol. 19, 1987, p. 563, 603.
6   G. Pólya, *How to Solve It, op. cit.*, p. vi.

and honorary member of the American College of Surgeons.[7] George Pólya first studied law, later changing to languages and literature, then philosophy and physics, to settle finally on mathematics, in which he received his Ph.D. in 1912. He was a student of Lipót Fejér, whom Pólya considered one of the people who influenced Hungarian mathematics in a definitive way.

Pólya felt that Fejér, the competitive examination in mathematics and the Hungarian mathematical journal *Középiskolai Mathematikai Lapok* (High School Papers on Mathematics) were responsible for the development of a large number of major mathematicians in Hungary.[8]

For emancipated Jews in Hungary who received full rights as citizens in 1867, it was the Hungarian Law 1867:XII that made it possible, among other things, to become teachers in high schools and even professors at universities. This is one of the reasons that lead to the explosion of mathematical talent in Hungary, just as happened in Prussia after the emancipation of Jews in 1812.[9] John Horváth of the University of Maryland was one who pointed out the overwhelming majority of Jewish mathematicians in Hungary in the early part of the 20th century. Pursuing scientific professions, particularly mathematics, secured a much desired social position for sons of Jewish-Hungarian families, who longed not only for emancipation, but for full equality in terms of social status and

---

7   Vilmos Milkó, "Pólya Jenő emlékezete [In memoriam Jenő Pólya]," *Archivum Chirurgicum*, Vol. 1, No. 1, 1948, p.1.
8   G. Pólya, "Leopold Fejér," *Journal of the London Mathematical Society*, Vol. 36., 1961, p. 501.
9   R. Hersch and V. John-Steiner, "A Visit to Hungarian Mathematics," Ms., pp. 35–37. I received a copy of this article from Professor Gerald L. Alexanderson of the Department of Mathematics, Santa Clara University, Santa Clara, CA. John Horváth compared this explosion of Jewish talent after the Jewish emancipation to the surprising number of sons of Protestant ministers entering the mathematical profession in Hungary after World War II, "Those kids would have become Protestant ministers, just as the old ones would have become rabbis [...] mathematics is the kind of occupation where you sit at your desk and read. Instead of reading the Talmud, you read proofs and conjectures. It's really a very similar occupation." R. Hersch and V. John-Steiner, *op. cit.*, p.37.

psychological comfort. Thus, in many middle class Jewish families, at least one of the sons was directed into pursuing a career in academe.

Culture in the second half of the nineteenth century became a matter of high prestige in Hungary, where the tradition of respect for scientific work started to loom large after the *Ausgleich,* the Austro-Hungarian Compromise in 1867 between Austria and Hungary. For sons of aspiring Jewish families, a professorship at a Budapest university or membership in the Hungarian Academy of Sciences promised entry into the Hungarian élite and eventual social acceptance in Hungarian high society, an acknowledged way to respectability. Distinguished scientists such as Manó Beke, Lipót Fejér, Mihály Fekete, Alfréd Haar, Gyula and Dénes Kőnig, Gusztáv Rados, Mór Réthy, Frigyes Riesz, and Lajos Schlesinger belonged to a remarkable group of Jewish-Hungarian mathematical talents, who, after studying at major German universities, typically Göttingen or Heidelberg, became professors in Hungary's growing number of universities before World War I. A few of them, like Gyula Kőnig and Gusztáv Rados, even became university presidents at the Technical University of Budapest. There were several other renowned scientists active in related fields, such as physicist Ferenc Wittmann, engineer Donát Bánki and some others. Mathematicians were also needed outside the academic world: just before the outbreak of World War I, George Pólya was about to join one of Hungary's large banks, at the age of 26, with a Ph.D. in mathematics and a working knowledge of four foreign languages in which he already published important articles.[10]

Despite what we know about the social conditions which nurtured and even forced out the talent of these many extraordinary scientists, how this occurred still remains somewhat mysterious. Stanislaw Ulam recorded an interesting conversation with John von Neumann when describing their 1938 journey to Hungary in his *Adventures of a Mathematician.*

---

10 György Pólya to Baron Gyula Madarassy-Beck, Paris, February 23, 1914. I am grateful to Professor Gerald L. Alexanderson of the University of Santa Clara for showing me this document as well as his collection of Pólya documents that were to be transferred to the George Pólya Papers, Department of Special Collections and University Archives, Stanford University Libraries, Stanford, CA.

I returned to Poland by train from Lillafüred, traveling through the Carpathian foothills [. . .] This whole region on both sides of the Carpathian Mountains, which was part of Hungary, Czechoslovakia, and Poland, was the home of many Jews. Johnny [von Neumann] used to say that all the famous Jewish scientists, artists, and writers who emigrated from Hungary around the time of the first World War came, either directly or indirectly, from these little Carpathian communities, moving up to Budapest as their material conditions improved. The [Nobel Laureate] physicist I[sidor] I[saac] Rabi[11] was born in that region and brought to America as an infant. Johnny used to say that it was a coincidence of some cultural factors which he could not make precise: an external pressure on the whole society of this part of Central Europe, a feeling of extreme insecurity in the individuals, and the necessity to produce the unusual or else face extinction.[12]

An interesting fact about the turn of the century Jewish-Hungarian mathematicians was that several of them could multiply huge numbers in their head. This was true of von Kármán, von Neumann and Edward Teller. Von Neumann, in particular, commanded extraordinary mathematical abilities. Nevertheless, there is no means available to prove that this prodigious biological potential was more present in Hungary at the turn of the century than elsewhere in Europe.[13]

11   Nobel Prize in Physics, 1944.
12   S. M. Ulam, *Adventures of a Mathematician* (New York: Scribner's, 1976), p. 111. Cf. Tibor Fabian, "Carpathians Were a Cradle of Scientists," Princeton, NJ, November 16, 1989, *The New York Times,* December 2, 1989.—George Pólya's nephew John Béla Pólya had an even more surprising, though cautious proposition to make. He suggested that through George Pólya's mother, Anna Deutsch (1853–1939), Pólya was related to Eugene Wigner and Edward Teller, "who are thought to have" ancestry originating from the same region between the towns of Arad and Lugos in Transylvania (then Hungary, today Romania). Though this relationship is not yet documented and should be taken at this point merely as a piece of Pólya family legend, it is nonetheless an interesting reflexion of the strong belief in the productivity of the Jewish community in North-Eastern Hungary and Transsylvania in terms of mathematical talent. John Béla Pólya, "Notes on George Pólya's family," attached to John Béla Pólya to Gerald L. Alexanderson, Greensborough, Australia, July 28, 1986. Personal collection of Professor Gerald L. Alexanderson, Santa Clara, CA.
13   Norman Macrae, *John von Neumann* (New York: Pantheon, 1992), p. 9; J. M. Rosenberg, *Computer Prophets* (New York: Macmillan, 1969), p. 155. ff.; Edward

Similarly, heuristic thinking was also a common tradition that many other Hungarian mathematicians and scientists shared. John von Neumann's brother remembered the mathematician's "heuristic insights" as a specific feature that evolved during his Hungarian childhood and appeared explicitly in the work of the mature scientist.[14] Von Neumann's famous high school director, physics professor Sándor Mikola, had made a special effort to introduce heuristic thinking into the elementary school curriculum in Hungary by the 1900s.[15]

Fejér drew a number of gifted students to his circle, such as Mihály Fekete, Ottó Szász, Gábor Szegő and, later, Paul Erdős. His students remembered Fejér's lectures and seminars as "the center of their formative circle, its ideal and focal point, its very soul." "There was hardly an intelligent, let alone a gifted, student who could exempt himself from the magic of his lectures. They could not resist imitating his stress patterns and gestures, such was his personal impact upon them."[16] George Pólya remembered Fejér's personal charm and personal drive to have been responsible for his great impact: "F[ejér] influenced more than any other single person the development of math[ematic]'s in Hungary...".[17]

In Budapest, Pólya was one of the founders, along with Károly Polányi, of the student society called *Galilei Kör* [Galileo Circle, 1908–1918], where he lectured on Ernst Mach. The Galileo Circle was the meeting place of radical intellectuals, mostly Jewish college students from the up- and-coming Budapest families of a new bourgeoisie. Members of the

---

Teller and Alan Brown, *The Legacy of Hiroshima* (Garden City: Doubleday, 1962), p. 160. Cf. William O. McCagg, *op. cit.*, 211.

14 Nicholas A. Vonneuman, *John Von Neumann as Seen by His Brother* (Meadowbrook, PA, 1987), p. 44.

15 Sándor Mikola, "Die heuristischen Methode im Unterricht der Mathematik der unteren Stufe," in E. Beke und S. Mikola, Hg., *Abhandlungen über die Reform des mathematischen Unterrichts in Ungarn* (Leipzig und Berlin: Teubner, 1911), pp. 57–73.

16 Gábor Szegő, "[Lipót Fejér]," MS. Gábor Szegő Papers, SC 323, Department of Special Collections and University Archives, Stanford University Libraries, Stanford, CA.

17 [Lecture outline, n.d. unpublished MS] George Pólya Papers, SC 337, 87–034, Box 1.

circle became increasingly radical and politicized. Oddly enough, the Communists of 1919 found it far too liberal, while the extremist rightwing régime of Admiral Horthy after 1919 considered it simply Jewish. In a Hungary of varied totalitarian systems, the radical-liberal tradition remained unwanted.[18] Soon, however, Pólya went to Vienna where he spent the academic year of 1911, after receiving his doctorate in mathematics in Budapest. In 1912–13, he went to Göttingen, and later to Paris and Zurich, where he took an appointment at the *Eidgenössische Technische Hochschule Zürich* [Swiss Federal Institute of Technology Zurich]. He became full professor at the ETH in 1928.

A distinguished mathematician, Pólya drew on several decades of teaching mathematics based on new approaches to problem solving, first as a professor in Zurich, Switzerland, and later at Stanford, California. It was in Zurich that Pólya and fellow Hungarian Gábor Szegő started their long collaboration by signing a contract in 1923 to publish their muchacclaimed joint collection of *Aufgaben und Lehrsätze aus der Analysis* [*Problems and theorems in analysis*].[19] Considered a mathematical masterpiece even today, *Aufgaben und Lehrsätze* took several years to complete,

---

18   Zsigmond Kende, *A Galilei Kör megalakulása* [The Foundation of the Galileo Circle] (Budapest: Akadémiai Kiadó, 1974); Márta Tömöry, *Új vizeken járok: A Galilei Kör története* [Walking on New Waters: A History of the Galileo Circle] (Budapest: Gondolat, 1960); György Litván, *Magyar gondolat— szabad gondolat* [Hungarian Thought—Free Thought] (Budapest: Magvető, 1978); György Litván, "Jászi Oszkár, A magyar progresszió és a nemzet," [Oscar Jaszi, Hungarian Progressives and the Nation], in Endre Kiss, Kristóf János Nyíri, eds., *A magyar gondolkodás a századelőn* [Hungarian Philosophy at the Turn of the Century] (Budapest: Kossuth, 1977). Litván pointed out that while similar social science organizations, such as *Társadalomtudományi Társaság* or *Huszadik Század* had a fair number of gentile contributors, the Galileo Circle almost exclusively drew upon progressive Jewish students. Cf. Attila Pók, *A magyarországi radikális demokrata ideológia kialakulása. A "Huszadik Század" társadalomszemlélete (1900–1907)* [The Rise of Democratic Radicalism in Hungary: The Social Concept of *Huszadik Század* (1900–1907)] (Budapest: Akadémiai Kiadó, 1990) p. 152–165.
19   Georg Pólya—Gábor Szegő, *Aufgaben und Lehrsätze aus der Analysis* (Berlin: Springer, 1925, new editions: 1945, 1954, 1964, 1970–71), Vols. I–II; Translations: English, 1972–76; Bulgarian, 1973; Russian, 1978; Hungarian, 1980–81.

Problem Solving and the U.S. War Effort

and it continues to impress mathematicians not only with the range and depth of the problems contained in it, but also with its organization: their grouping of problems, not by subject but by solution method, was a novelty.[20] Pólya's primary concern had always been providing and maintaining "an independence of reasoning during problem solving,"[21] an educational goal he declared to be of paramount importance when addressing the Swiss Association of Professors of Mathematics in 1931. Several of his articles on the subject preceded this lecture, probably the earliest being published in 1919.[22] Pólya had provided a model for problem solving by the time he was in Berne, Switzerland, suggesting "a systematic collection of rules and methodological advices," which he considered "heuristics modernized."[23]

Pólya was active in a number of important fields of mathematics, such as theory probability, complex analysis, combinatorics, analytic number theory, geometry, and mathematical physics. In the United States after 1940, and at Stanford as of 1942, Pólya became the highest authority on the teaching of problem solving in mathematics.

With his arrival at the United States, Pólya started a new career based on his new-found interest in teaching and heuristics.[24] He developed several new courses such as his "Mathematical Methods in Science," which he first offered in the Autumn 1945 quarter at Stanford, introducing general and mathematical methods, deduction and induction, the relationship between mathematics and science, as well as the "use of physical intuition in the solution of mathematical problems."[25] In his popular and often repeated Mathematics 129 course on "How to Solve the Problem?"

---

20 Gerald L. Alexanderson, "Obituary. George Pólya," *op. cit.*, pp. 562.
21 G. Pólya, "Comment chercher la solution d'un problème de mathématiques?" *L'enseignement mathématique*, 30e année, 1931, Nos. 4–5–6.
22 G. Pólya, "Geometrische Darstellung einer Gedankenkette", *Schweizerische Pädagogische Zeitschrift*, 1919.
23 G. Pólya, "Comment chercher," *op. cit.*
24 Gerald L. Alexanderson, "Obituary. George Pólya," *op. cit.*, p. 563; on "Pólya the mathematician and teacher," see pp. 566–570.
25 Paul Kirkpatrick, Acting Dean, School of Physical Sciences, Stanford University, Course outline, September 4, 1945, George Pólya Papers, SC 337, 87–137, Box 2.

Pólya taught mathematical invention and mathematical teaching, quoting English poet and satirist Samuel Butler (1612–80):

> All the inventions that the world contains
> Were not by reason first found out, nor brains
> But pass for theirs, who had the luck to light
> Upon them by mistake or oversight.[26]

He surveyed all aspects of a problem, general and specific, restating it in every possible way and pursuing various courses that might lead to solving it. He studied several ways to prove a hypothesis or modify the plan, always focusing on finding the solution. He compiled a characteristic list of "typical questions for this course," which indeed contained his most important learnings from a long European schooling.[27]

In a course on heuristics, he focused on problems and solutions, using methods from classical logic to heuristic logic. Offering the course alternately as Mathematics 110 and Physical Sciences 115, he sought to attract a variety of students, including those in education, psychology and philosophy.[28] The courses were based on Pólya's widely used textbook *How to Solve It*.

26   G. Pólya, "Elementary Mathematics from Higher Point of View," Mathematics 129, George Pólya Papers, SC 337, 86–036, Box 1, Folder 9. Cf. Samuel Butler, "Miscellaneous Thoughts," in: *The Poems of Samuel Butler*, Vol. II (Chiswick: C. Willingham, 1822), p. 281.
27   G. Pólya, "Elementary Mathematics from a Higher Point of View," Survey of Typical Questions, George Pólya Papers, SC 337, 87–137, Box 3.—Pólya was indeed very well read and liked to show his erudition by quoting Socrates, Descartes, Leibniz, Kant, Herbert Spencer, Thomas Arnold, J. W. von Goethe, Leonhard Euler and his famous colleagues, such as Albert Einstein, and many others. George Pólya Papers, SC 337, 87–034. Box 1&3, 87–137, Box 2, Department of Special Collections and University Archives, Stanford University Libraries, Stanford, CA.
28   Untitled course description, n. d. George Pólya Papers, SC 337, 86–036, Box 1, Folder 3.

In due course, Pólya published several other books on problem solving in mathematics such as the two-volume *Mathematics and Plausible Reasoning* (1954), and *Mathematical Discovery*, in 1965. Both became translated into many languages.[29] Towards the end of his career his "profound influence of mathematical education" was internationally recognized, as suggested by the words of Sir James Lighthill.[30]

Pólya's significance in general methodology seems to have been his proposition for interpreting heuristics as problem solving, more specifically, the search for those elements in a given problem that may help us find the right solution.[31] For Pólya, heuristics (*Erfindungskunst*) equaled an inventive or imaginative power, the ability to invent new stratagems of learning, and it bordered not only on mathematics and philosophy but also on psychology and logic. In this way, a centuries-old European tradition was renewed and transplanted into the United States where Pólya had tremendous influence on subsequent generations of mathematics teachers well into the 1970s. In 1971, the aged mathematician received an honorary degree at the University of Waterloo, where he addressed the Convocation, calling for the use of "heuristic proofs":

---

29 G. Pólya *Mathematics and Plausible Reasoning* (Princeton, N.J.: Princeton University Press, 1954, 2nd ed. 1968), Vols. 1–2. Translations: Bulgarian, 1970; French, 1957–58; German, 1962–63; Japanese, 1959; Romanian, 1962; Russian, 1957, 1975; Spanish, 1966; Turkish, 1966. G. Pólya, *Mathematical Discovery. On Understanding, Learning, and Teaching Problem Solving* (New York—London—Sidney: John Wiley and Sons, 1965, Vols. 1–2; combined paperback ed. 1981), Translations: Bulgarian, 1968; French, 1967; German, 1966, 1967, 1979, 1983; Hungarian, 1969, 1979; Italian, 1970–71, 1979, 1982; Japanese, 1964; Polish, 1975; Romanian, 1971; Russian 1970, 1976. Cf. Gerald L. Alexanderson, "Obituary. George Pólya," *op. cit.*, pp. 604–605.

30 A good example was the Second International Congress on Mathematical Education at the University of Exeter, England. Cf. the invitation sent to Pólya by the Chairman of the Congress, Professor Sir James Lighthill, FRS, June 23, 1971. [Cambridge] George Pólya Papers, SC 337, 87–034, Box 1.

31 G. Pólya, "Die Heuristik. Versuch einer vernünftigen Zielsetzung," *Der Mathematikunterricht*, Heft 1/64 (Stuttgart: Ernst Klett, 1964); cf. "L'Heuristique est-elle un sujet d'étude raisonnable?", *La méthode dans les sciences modernes*, "Travail et Méthode", numéro hors série, pp. 279–285.

In a class for future mathematicians you can do something more sophisticated: You may present first a heuristic proof, and after that a strict proof, the main idea of which was foreshadowed by the heuristic proof. You may so do something important for your students: You may teach them to do research.[32]

"Heuristics should be given a new goal," Pólya argued, "that should in no way belong to the realm of the fantastic and the utopian."[33]

Problem solving for Pólya was seen as "one third mathematics and two thirds common sense."[34] This was a tactic which he emphatically suggested for mathematics teachers in American high schools. If the teaching of mathematics neglects this tactic, he commented, it misses two important goals: "It fails to give the right attitude to future users of mathematics, and it fails to offer an essential ingredient of general education to future non-users of mathematics."[35]

Throughout his career as a teacher, he strongly opposed believing in what authorities profess. Teachers and principals, he argued, "should use their own experience and their own judgment."[36] His matter-of-fact, experience-based reasoning has been repeatedly described in books and articles. He even made two films on the teaching of mathematics (*Let Us Teach Guessing*, an award winner at the American Film Festival in 1968; *Guessing and Proving*, based on an Open University Lecture, Reading, 1962).[37] The most simple and straightforward summary of his ideas on teaching was Pólya's own, presented in the preface of a course that he gave at Stanford and subsequently published in 1967:

---

[32] G. Pólya, "Guessing and Proving." Address delivered at the Convocation of the University of Waterloo, October 29, 1971. George Pólya Papers, SC 337, 87–034, Box 1.

[33] G. Pólya, "Die Heuristik," *op. cit.*, p. 5.

[34] George Pólya, Untitled note, n. d., George Pólya Papers, SC 337, 87–034, Box 1.

[35] G. Pólya, "Formation, Not Only Information," Address at the Mathematical Association of America, George Pólya Papers, SC 337, 87–034, Box 1.

[36] George Pólya to Robert J. Griffin, Stanford, June 12, 1962. George Pólya Papers, SC 337, 87–034, Box 2.

[37] George Pólya to Anthony E. Mellor, Harper and Row, Stanford, March 11, 1974; Stanford University News Service, February 17, 1969. George Pólya Papers, SC 337, 87–034, Box 1.

Start from something that is familiar or useful or challenging: From some connection with the world around us, from the prospect of some application, from an intuitive idea.
Don't be afraid of using colloquial language when it is more suggestive than the conventional, precise terminology. In fact, do not introduce technical terms before the student can see the need for them.
Do not enter too early or too far into the heavy details of a proof. Give first a general idea or just the intuitive germ of the proof.
More generally, realize that the natural way to learn is to learn by stages: First, we want to see an outline of the subject, to perceive some concrete source or some possible use. Then, gradually, as soon as we can see more use and connections and interest, we take more willingly the trouble to fill in the details.[38]

Pólya had lasting influence on a variety of thinkers in and beyond mathematics. The first curriculum recommendation of the [American] National Council of the Teachers of Mathematics suggested that "problem solving be the focus of school mathematics in the 1980s" [in the U.S.]. The 1980 NCTM Yearbook, published as *Problem Solving in School Mathematics,* the Mathematical Association of America's Compendia of Applied Problems and the new editor of the *American Mathematical Monthly,* the Hungarian-American P. R. Halmos, all called for more use of problems in teaching.[39] Pólya was an integral part of the "problem solving movement" that cut a wide swath in the 1980s.[40] Philosopher Imre Lakatos, a fellow-Hungarian who described mathematical heuristics as his main field of interest in 1957, acknowledging his debt to Pólya's influence, and particularly to *How to Solve It,* which he translated into Hungarian.[41]

38 George Pólya, "Preface," MS George Pólya Papers, SC 337, 87–034, Box 1.
39 [Untitled MS, n.d. "The organizers' choice of George Pólya."] George Pólya Papers, SC 337, 87–034, Box 2, —P. R. Halmos, "The Heart of Mathematics," *American Mathematical Monthly,* Vol. 87, 1980, pp. 519–524.
40 Alan H. Schoenfeld, "George Pólya and Mathematic Education," Gerald L. Alexanderson, Lester H. Lange, "Obituary. George Pólya," *op. cit.,* p. 595. Cf. Rudolf Groner, Marina Groner, Walter F. Bischof, eds., *Methods of Heuristics* (Hillsdale, N.J., London: Lawrence R. L. Baum, 1983); Stephen I. Brown—Marion E. Walter, *The Art of Problem Posing* (Philadelphia, PA: The Franklin Institute Press, 1983).
41 Imre Lakatos to Dr. Maier (Rockefeller Foundation), Cambridge, England, May 5, 1957. George Pólya Papers, SC 337, 87–137, Box 1.— In turn, Pólya expressed his

Critics, however, like mathematician Alan H. Schoenfeld, pointed out that while Pólya's influence extended "far beyond the mathematics education community," "the scientific status of Pólya's work on problem solving strategies has been more problematic."[42] Students and instructors often felt that the heuristics-based approach rarely improved the actual problem-solving performance itself. Researchers in artificial intelligence claimed that they were unable to write problem solving programs using Pólya's heuristics. "We suspect the strategies he describes epiphenomenal rather than real."[43] Recent work in cognitive science, however, has provided methods for making Pólya's strategies more accessible for problem solving instruction. New studies have provided clear evidence that students can significantly improve their problem-solving performance through heuristics.[44] As suggested by Alan H. Schoenfeld, "[i]t may be possible to program computer knowledge structures capable of supporting heuristic problem-solving strategies of the type Pólya described."[45]

The Stanford Mathematics Competition

Professors George Pólya and Gábor Szegő initiated the introduction of the Stanford Mathematics Competition for high school students. Modeled after the Eötvös Competition organized in Hungary from 1894 on, the main purpose of the competition was to discover talent and to revive the competitive spirit of the Eötvös Competition, which Szegő himself

---

admiration for Lakatos's "Proofs and Refutations," and recommended him as Professor of Logic at the London School of Economics and Political Science, "with special reference to the Philosophy of Mathematics." George Pólya to Walter Adams (LSE), Stanford, CA, January 13, 1969, George Pólya Papers, SC 337, 87–034, Box 1.

42 Alan H. Schoenfeld, "George Pólya and Mathematic Education," Gerald L. Alexanderson, Lester H. Lange, "Obituary. George Pólya," *op. cit.,* p. 595.
43 *Ibid.*, p. 596.
44 Alan H. Schoenfeld, *Mathematical Problem Solving* (Academic Press, 1985)
45 Alan H. Schoenfeld, "George Pólya and Mathematic Education," Gerald L. Alexanderson, Lester H. Lange, "Obituary. George Pólya," *op. cit.*, p. 596.

won in 1912.[46] This contest was held annually for over 30 years until it was terminated in 1928. Stress was laid on inherent cognitive ability and insight rather than upon memorization and speed. Those who were able to go beyond the question posed were given additional credit. Those cognizant of the preponderance of Hungarian mathematicians have been tempted to speculate upon the relationship between the Eötvös Prize and "the mathematical fertility of Hungary."[47] Winners of the Eötvös Prize have included Lipót Fejér, Theodore von Kármán, Alfréd Haar, George Pólya, Frigyes Riesz, Gábor Szegő, and Tibor Radó.

The Stanford competition was introduced in 1946 and continued until 1965, when the Stanford Department of Mathematics turned more towards graduate training.[48] When first started, the Stanford Examination was administered to 322 participants in 60 California high schools. The last examination was administered to about 1200 participants in over 150 larger schools in seven states from Nevada to Montana. The Stanford University Competitive Examination in Mathematics emphasized "originality and insight rather than routine competence." Typical questions required a high degree of ingenuity and the winning student was asked "to demonstrate research ability."[49]

46 G[eorge] Pólya and J[eremy] Kilpatrick, "The Stanford University Competitive Examination in Mathematics," *American Mathematical Monthly*, Vol. 80, No.6, June-July, 1963, p. 628.
47 T. Radó, "Mathematical Life in Hungary," *American Mathematical Monthly*, Vol. XXXIX, 1932. pp. 85–90; József Kürschák, *Matematikai versenytételek* (Budapest, 1929); József Kürschák, *Hungarian Problem Book: Based on the Eötvös Competitions, 1894–1928* (New York: Random House, 1963); R. Creighton Buck, "A Look at Mathematical Competitions," *American Mathematical Monthly*, Vol. LXVI, No. 3. March 1959, p. 209.
48 Department of Mathematics, Stanford University, "The Stanford University Mathematics Examination," *American Mathematical Monthly*, Vol. LIII, No. 7, August-September, 1946, pp. 406–409. G[eorge] Pólya and J[eremy] Kilpatrick, *op. cit.*, pp. 627–640; cf. the correspondence between Harley Flanders, George Pólya and Jeremy Kilpatrick, 1970–1972, George Pólya Papers, SC 337, 87–034, Box 1.
49 R. Creighton Buck, "A Look at Mathematical Competitions," *American Mathematical Monthly*, Vol. LXVI, No. 3, March 1959, pp. 204–205.

Organizers of the competition thought of mathematics "not necessarily as an end in itself, but as an adjunct necessary to the study of any scientific subject."[50] It was suggested that ability in mathematical reasoning correlated with success in higher education in any field. Also, the discovery of singularly gifted students helped identify the originality of mind displayed by grappling with difficult problems: mathematical ability was regarded as an index of general capacity.[51] Those responsible for the competition were firmly convinced that "an early manifestation of mathematical ability is a definite indication of exceptional intelligence and suitability for intellectual leadership."[52] Several of the winners of the Stanford competition did not go into mathematics but went on to specialize in electrical engineering (1946), physics (1947), biology (1948), or geology (1956).[53]

It is interesting to note that by introducing Pólya's article about the 1953 Stanford Competitive Examination, the California Mathematics Council Bulletin found it important to make a connection between "the best interests of democracy" and the need "that our superior students be challenged by courses of appropriate content, encouraged to progress in accordance with their capacities."[54] The Competitive Examination seems to have been viewed by some as reflecting the mounting international

---

50   H. M. Bacon, "The Stanford University Competitive Examination in Mathematics," Report at the Meeting of the Mathematical Association of America, University of Washington, Seattle, August 20, 1956. George Pólya Papers, SC 337, 86–036, Box 2.
51   *Ibid.*
52   H. M. Bacon, "The Stanford University Competitive Examination in Mathematics," Report at the Meeting of the Mathematical Association of America, University of Washington, Seattle, August 20, 1956. Cf. Gábor Szegő, "The Stanford University Competitive Examination in Mathematics," 16th Summer Meeting, National Council of Teachers of Mathematics, UCLA, August 21, 1956, p. 2. George Pólya Papers, SC 337, 86–036, Box 2.
53   H. M. Bacon, "The Stanford University Competitive Examination in Mathematics," Report at the Meeting of the Mathematical Association of America, University of Washington, Seattle, August 20, 1956. George Pólya Papers, SC 337, 86–036, Box 2.
54   G. Pólya, "The 1953 Stanford Competitive Examination. Problems, Solutions, and Comments," *California Mathematics Council Bulletin,* May 1953.

tensions, somewhat forecasting the era of Sputnik fears yet to come. Speaking at the National Council of Teachers of Mathematics in 1956, Gábor Szegő articulated this opinion when declaring that

> much is said in these days about the pressing need for science and engineering graduates. Our view is that the nation needs just as well good humanists, lawyers, economists, and political scientists in its present struggle. This is a view which can be defended, I think, in very strong terms.[55]

Through its long and distinguished tenure, the Stanford examination proved to be a pioneer in the discovery of mathematical talent not only in California and the West Coast, but throughout the United States.[56] To this day, George Pólya is best remembered in the United States as one who introduced European models of competitive educational methods of problem solving in mathematics. He served as one of the several bridges that linked Central European, and particularly Hungarian, patterns of reasoning to American achievements in problem solving and heuristic thinking.

2 Heuristics Applied: Theodore von Kármán

One of the most successful Hungarians abroad was Theodore von Kármán (1881–1963). Though he started his American career in the late 1920s, von Kármán was one of those whose excellence was nationally recognized by his contributions to the war effort. Indeed, several of the outstanding émigré professionals from Hungary attained their greatest recogni-

---

55 Gábor Szegő, "The Stanford University Competitive Examination in Mathematics," 16th Summer Meeting, National Council of Teachers of Mathematics, UCLA, August 21, 1956, p. 2. George Pólya Papers, SC 337, 86–036, Box 2.
56 David Gilbarg to George Pólya and Gábor Szegő, April 25, 1966. George Pólya Papers, SC 337, 86–036, Box 2.

Figure 18. Theodore von Kármán, aerospace scientist,
on U.S. and Hungarian stamps, 1992.

tion in the U.S. during, and as a consequence of, World War II and the subsequent Cold War period.

Theodore von Kármán, son of the educational pioneer Mór Kármán, came from a distinguished Jewish-Hungarian professional background.[57] Young Theodore, commented historian William O. McCagg, Jr., "grew up in the leading circles of the Budapest late nineteenth-century literati, living in comfortable flats and villas, schooled as a child by private

---

57 Biographical details referring to Theodore von Kármán are based on the Theodore von Kármán Papers at the California Institute of Technology Archives in Pasadena, CA. I made particularly good use of the following biographical sketches, #135.7.-8: Hugh L. Dryden, "The Contributions of Theodore von Kármán: A Review," *Astronautics and Aerospace Engineering*, July, 1963. pp. 12–17; Frank J. Malina, "Theodore von Kármán, 1881–1963," *Revue Française d'Astronautique*, June 17, 1963; Hugh L. Dryden, "Theodore von Kármán, 1881–1963," *American Philosophical Society Yearbook*, 1963; "In Memoriam Theodore von Kármán, Technische Hochschule Aachen, May 28, 1963;" Hugh L. Dryden, "The Contributions of Theodore von Kármán to Applied Mechanics," *Applied Mechanics Reviews*, Vol. 16., No. 8, August 1963, pp. 589–595. Consult also Theodore von Kármán with Lee Edson, *The Wind and Beyond. Theodore von Kármán, Pioneer in Aviation and Path Finder in Space* (Boston: Little, Brown & Co., 1967).

tutors, meeting everyone who counted even in Vienna, having entrée into aristocratic circles."[58] Well before his formal education started, this sophisticated atmosphere exerted a specific influence on his intellectual development. At the age of nine, young Kármán was sent to the school of his father. One of the characteristics of this education was for the students to develop informal social contact with some of Hungary's best teachers as well as an emphasis on learning from experience.

As a high school student, young von Kármán participated in the competition for the Eötvös Loránd Prize, and won it in 1897, a distinction that added to the special care devoted to his initial grounding in science.[59]

He graduated from the Technical University of Budapest in 1902, and spent four years in Hungary upon graduation, teaching as an assistant professor at the Technical University and as a research engineer at Ganz and Co. His father, however, wanted him to continue his education abroad. Von Kármán remembers his father in 1906 as a man who

> had grown tired and bitter. I remember his saying one day that he had devoted his life to Hungary, but was unappreciated, and even tormented by petty university politics. . . He didn't want me to make the same mistake he had made. If I were going to make something of myself as a scientist and an independent thinker, he insisted that I would have a greater chance outside Hungary.[60]

For his graduate studies, Theodore von Kármán went to Göttingen in 1906 and remained strongly connected with Germany for a quarter of a century. Göttingen attracted him in many ways. He could work there with illustrious scientists such as Ludwig Prandtl, a widely recognized expert of fluid mechanics, Felix Klein who applied mathematics to engineering, and David Hilbert, one of the great figures of pure mathematics. It was during his stay in Göttingen that he made the decision to choose

---

58 William O. McCagg, *op. cit.*, p. 209.
59 *Ibid.*, p. 210.
60 Theodore von Kármán with Lee Edson, *The Wind and Beyond*, p. 33, quoted by William O. McCagg, *op. cit.*, p. 211.

aeronautics as his principal field of study.[61] His dissertation was written on the buckling strength of straight columns and in it he developed the Kármán-Engesser double-modulus theory of the behavior of columns under load. He received his Ph.D. from Göttingen in 1908 and stayed there as a *Privat-Dozent* until 1912.

It was in Göttingen that he became seriously interested in fluid mechanics, his most important contribution being the quantitative analysis based on the theory of vortices. Ever since his Göttingen studies, the pattern of alternating eddies which form behind a circular cylinder in fluid flow has been referred to as the "Kármán Vortex Street (trail)."[62] The von Kármán theory of vortex streets was published in three papers in 1911–12. This classic theory of the unsymmetrical vortex arrangement in the wake of a cylinder provided the sound mathematical foundation and formulae on which aircraft designers have depended ever since.[63] His discovery made him an expert not only of air currents, but also a world-class specialist in the diagnosis of aerodynamic factors affecting the stability of bridges.

In 1912, von Kármán accepted the invitation of the Technical University of Aachen, where he became Professor of Aeronautics and Mechanics and the Director of the Institute of Aerodynamics until 1929. In fact, he helped build up the new Institute where he continued his Göttingen research in fluid mechanics. Gradually, a friendly rivalry developed within the Aeronautical Institute at Göttingen.[64] His Aachen subjects included the statistical theory of turbulence, wing theory, the stability of laminar flow, pressure distribution on airship hulls, the theory

---

61   Frank J. Malina, "Theodore von Kármán (1881–1963)," MS for the *Revue Française d'Astronautique*, June 17, 1963. Theodore von Kármán Papers, 135.8.
62   Hugh L. Dryden, "Theodore Von Kármán (1881–1963)," MS for *The American Philosophical Society Yearbook*, September 4, 1963. Theodore von Kármán Papers, 135.8.
63   Hugh L. Dryden, "In Memoriam Theodore Von Kármán," Technische Hochschule Aachen, May 28, 1963, p. 6. Theodore von Kármán Papers, 135.8.
64   Hugh L. Dryden, "The contributions of Theodore von Kármán: A review," *Astronautics and Aerospace Engineering*, July 1963, p. 12. Theodore von Kármán Papers, 135.8.

of lift, the approximate solutions of problems in boundary layer flow and skin friction (the Kármán Integral Relation).[65] He developed the Kármán-Trefftz method of computing potential flow about given wing sections. Von Kármán was instrumental in showing the interrelationship between pure and applied mathematics and in utilizing these concepts in the solution of problems which until then had been viewed as hopeless.[66]

As aeronautical engineer and head of UNESCO's division of scientific research Frank J. Malina wrote of him in his obituary for the *Revue Française d'Astronautique,* during his years in Germany, von Kármán

> already gave a sympathetic hearing to the first estimates that were being made as to the possibility of propelling a device away from the Earth. A rocket enthusiast at a technical meeting in Berlin had suggested that chemical combinations produced sufficient energy to propel a rocket away from the Earth; he was severely taken to task by a well-known German physicist for talking nonsense. Von Kármán defended the young man, for during the discussion he had made a quick, rough estimate and concluded that it was theoretically possible.[67]

"I am not a Fantast,"[68] he stated. "It is just a simple fact that one pound of kerosene has more energy than is necessary to take [...] one pound out of the gravitational field. It is only a question of technology and progress and time."[69]

Von Kármán's immense knowledge of his several fields, his many languages and his great sense of humor attracted large numbers of eminent students to Aachen, which during his years as Director of the Institute

---

65   Hugh L. Dryden, "Theodore Von Kármán (1881–1963)," MS for *The American Philosophical Society Yearbook*, September 4, 1963. Theodore von Kármán Papers, 135.8.
66   "Dr. Theodore von Kármán," Theodore von Kármán Papers, 135.4.
67   Frank J. Malina, "Theodore von Kármán (1881–1963)," MS for the *Revue Française d'Astronautique*, June 17, 1963. Theodore von Kármán Papers, 135.8.
68   *Fantasist* in German.
69   Hugh L. Dryden, "In Memoriam Theodore Von Kármán," Technische Hochschule Aachen, May 28, 1963, p. 6. Theodore von Kármán Papers, 135.8.

became a highly acclaimed German and international center of aeronautics, astronautics, aerodynamics, and applied sciences.

During his years at the University of Aachen, von Kármán also served as a consultant for several large airplane companies in and out of Germany, such as the Junkers Airplane Works (1912–1928), the Luftschiffbau Zeppelin (1924–28), Handley-Page Ltd., England (1926–30), the Guggenheim Aeronautical Laboratories, California Institute of Technology (1926–30), and the Kawanishi Airplane Company, Japan (1927–29). He designed the Kobe Wind Tunnel in Japan in 1927 and helped build the 10-foot Wind Tunnel of the Guggenheim Lab at Caltech (1926–27).[70]

Von Kármán's reputation had become truly international in the post-War era and it was logical that the Daniel Guggenheim Fund for the Promotion of Aeronautics invited him in 1926 to lecture at various U.S. universities and research institutions. He also served as advisor on the design of the Guggenheim Aeronautical Laboratories at the California Institute of Technology. Following his U.S. lecture series, he made a lecture/study tour of China, India, and Japan.

Following his U.S. tour, Professor von Kármán made arrangements in early 1927 with Caltech in Pasadena and the University of Aachen. Dr. Paul S. Epstein was to be received in Aachen and von Kármán to visit Pasadena for an academic quarter in each case.[71]

It was no coincidence that von Kármán became an asset to aeronautical engineering in the United States, and particularly aerodynamic research: his increasingly frequent and extended invitations to Pasadena were exactly when the United States had become passionately involved in developing aviation and turning it into a profitable business. The Guggenheim family alone invested over $3,000,000 between 1926–1929 in promoting aeronautical education, assisting fundamental aeronautical science, the development of commercial aircraft, as well as the application

---

70   Hugh L. Dryden, "In Memoriam," *op. cit.,* pp. 6, 8.
71   Robert A. Millikan to Theodore von Kármán, Pasadena, CA, January 24, 1927 and London, August 26, 1927; Theodore von Kármán Papers, File 20.27.

of aircraft in business and industry.[72] As Harry F. Guggenheim, President of the New York-based Daniel Guggenheim Fund for the Promotion of Aeronautics, observed in September 1929, "aeronautical developments have taken place [since the beginning of 1926] in this country which have even surpassed the hopes and anticipations of men of the greatest vision." "In the past three years," Guggenheim added, "the general public have changed from a state of apathetic indifference to aviation to one of intense enthusiasm."[73]

After several quarters of visiting professorship and apparently several years of hesitation, von Kármán accepted an invitation from Nobel Laureate Robert Andrews Millikan, head of the Norman Bridge Laboratory of Physics at Caltech in 1929 to settle in Pasadena on a permanent basis.[74] What was offered to von Kármán was probably the single most distinguished job that ever went to a Hungarian in the United States as of that date: on April 1, 1930, before he was 50 years old, he took over as Director of the Daniel Guggenheim Graduate School of Aeronautics at the California Institute of Technology for the then outstanding salary of $12,000 per year, with an astronomical annual budget of $50,000 under his control. Von Kármán also had additional responsibility for the Guggenheim Airship Institute at Akron, Ohio.[75] The Graduate School was part of a larger scheme whereby the Guggenheim Fund assisted in the establishment of aeronautical engi-

---

72   Harry F. Guggenheim to Robert A. Millikan, New York, September 7, 1929, Robert Andrews Millikan Collection, File 16.8, California Institute of Technology Archives, Pasadena, CA.
73   Ibid.
74   Theodore von Kármán to Robert A. Millikan, Aachen, September 10 and (Telegram) October 20, 1929, Robert Andrews Millikan Papers, File 16.8.
75   Robert A. Millikan to Theodore von Kármán, Telegram, October 18, 1929; Harry F. Guggenheim, Commander Hunsaker, and Robert A. Millikan to Paul S. Epstein, Telegram, New York, n. d., Theodore von Kármán Papers, File 20.27; Robert A. Millikan to Captain A. T. Church, [Pasadena,] March 4, 1930; Robert Andrews Millikan Papers, File 16.9.

neering schools at five leading universities and added, somewhat later, another at a Southern university as well.[76]

At the invitation of the Guggenheim Fund for the Promotion of Aeronautics and of the California Institute of Technology, von Kármán came to the United States first in 1926, and more regularly after 1928. He settled permanently in California in 1930. At the age of eighty, von Kármán remembered the United States in the 1920s as a country with "very little military aviation," and where, he had thought, he

> would work in civil aeronautics. It is ironic that for the last 25 years I have devoted most of my time to problems connected with military aviation.[77]

Von Kármán left Germany before Hitler came to power. With his Jewish family background, he was not in a position to return there and maintained a sharply critical distance from the Nazi regime from the very beginning. When he was approached from Berlin in the Summer of 1933 "suggesting that [he] take up [his] activities over there in the fall," he commented from CalTech ironically to his longtime Göttingen mentor and friend, Professor Prandtl,

> I do not think I will do this: I find my situation here quite satisfactory. The German academic life has some advantages, for instance a definitely better beer than here, but I think you will agree with me that this is not sufficient reason for me to neglect the disadvantages.[78]

During his 19 years at Caltech, von Kármán published some fifty papers on the problems of high subsonic, transonic and supersonic flow on buckling problems and on applied mathematics for engineers. Von Kármán was instrumental in establishing what was to become the Jet Propulsion Laboratory sponsored jointly by the U.S. Army and the Air

---

76 Harry F. Guggenheim to Robert A. Millikan, New York, October 22, 1929, Robert Andrews Millikan Papers, File 16.8.
77 Vern Haugland, "Von Karman," Associated Press report, Washington, May 12, [1961], Theodore von Kármán Papers, 137.4.
78 Theodore von Kármán to L. Prandtl, August 2, 1933, Theodore von Kármán Papers, 23.44.

Force. Several of his papers dealt with the statistical theory of isotropic turbulence. In 1944, General H. H. ("Hap") Arnold asked him to organize and chair a U.S. Air Force Scientific Advisory Group to study "the use of science in warfare by the European nations and to interpret the significance of the new developments in rockets, guided missiles, and jet propulsion for the future of the Air Force."[79] Von Kármán chaired the group actively until 1954 and was the founder of a similar body for NATO after 1951. Headquartered in Paris, the NATO Advisory Group for Aeronautical Research and Development (AGARD) had substantial impact on NATO countries in Europe through various projects.

After World War II, von Kármán had an active role in reorganizing German science. As head of the U.S. Army Air Force Scientific Advisory Board, he led a task force on a mission to Germany as well as to several other European countries. As Frank L. Wattendorf remembered in 1956, "[d]uring the European tour the name and international reputation of Dr. von Kármán was the 'Open Sesame' to considerable valuable information far beyond that obtained in normal interrogation. This was especially true in Germany where the respected name of von Kármán drew forth an integrated, intelligent picture of the German technical effort."[80] German scientists quickly found out that he was a key to rebuilding science in their country. In June 1945, he was approached, "through channels," by Professor Dr. Werner Osenberg, earlier Head of the Planning Bureau of the Reich's Research Council *(Leiter des Planungsamtes des Reichsforschungsrates)*, who sent his essay on "Vorschläge zur Organisation der deutschen Forschung im Frieden und für Friedenszwecke" [Suggestions for the Organisation of German Research in Peace and for Peace Purposes] to von Kármán and asked for consultations with him on "the problems of

---

79 Hugh L. Dryden, "The Contributions of Theodore von Kármán to Applied Mechanics," *Applied Mechanics Reviews*, Vol. 16, No. 8, August 1963, pp. 14–15.
80 Frank L. Wattendorf, "Theodore von Kármán, International Scientist," *Zeitschrift für Flugwissenschaft*, 4 (1956) Heft 5/6, p. 165. Theodore von Kármán Papers, 135.7.

future direction of research."[81] The new information was assessed "on-the-spot" and channeled back to General Arnold in the U.S. for use in Air Force planning.[82]

Helpful as he proved to be in the practical field, he was reluctant to rejoin post-War German academic life. The Göttingen-based *Akademie der Wissenschaften* tried to win him back among its members in 1947–48.[83] *Abgelehnt [...] mit einer gewissen Schärfe* [toughly refuted] by von Kármán, President Smend of the Göttingen Academy asked fellow member and Nobel Laureate James Franck (Physics, 1925) to use his influence and convince von Kármán that he should rejoin the Academy:

> [...] wir meinen, dass in dem entsetzlichen Trümmerfeld, das die Vergangenheit sittlich und geistig hinterlassen hat, jede Möglichkeit des Wiederaufbaus eines noch so kleinen Stücks geistiger und sittlicher Gemeinschaft von uns so lange auf das sorgfältigste verfolgt werden sollte, als eine solche Verfolgung noch irgend eine Aussicht auf Erfolg bietet.[84]

Franck himself rejoined the Academy, along with such eminent scientists as Rudolf Ladenburg and Lisa Meitner, and added in a letter to von Kármán:

> ... I [myself] rejoined only after great hesitation. In fact, I did so only because I felt that if one does not help the people who want to work for a future Germany

---

81 Werner Osenberg to Theodore von Kármán, June 12, 1945, Theodore von Kármán Papers, 22.18.
82 Frank L. Wattendorf, *op. cit.*
83 R. Smend to James Franck, December 23, 1947, James Franck to Theodore von Kármán, February 11, 1948, both in Theodore von Kármán Papers, 9.36, California Institute of Technology Archives, Pasadena, CA.
84 R. Smend to James Franck, December 23, 1947, Theodore von Kármán Papers, 9.36, California Institute of Technology Archives, Pasadena, CA "[...] we think that in the abominable field of ruins that the past has left behind both morally and spiritually, every opportunity to rebuild the smallest conceivable piece of a moral and spiritual community should be pursued by us most carefully, until only such a course may have some chance to success."

free of nationalism and racism, etc. the chances for such a Germany to develop become practically zero.[85]

Although he never rejoined the Academy, von Kármán accepted from the mid-1950s a series of high German decorations such as the Federal Grand Cross of Merit with Star of the Federal Republic of Germany in 1955, the Ludwig Prandtl Ring Award of the WGL in Göttingen in 1957, as well as the Karl Friedrich Gauss Medal in Braunschweig, Germany, in 1960, both "for scientific accomplishment in fluid mechanics." He was also showered with honorary doctorates at several universities, including German schools such as the Technische Hochschule in Aachen (1953), and the Technische Universität Berlin-Charlottenburg (1953).[86]

It is not readily apparent which result from von Kármán's many years of research should be considered the most significant. As von Kármán had come from the vigorous school initiated by Felix Klein in Germany, which at the beginning of the century had sought to modernize engineering science by relating it to basic sciences and mathematics, von Kármán viewed his main task and accomplishment that of bridging the gap between basic science and practical aeronautical engineering.[87]

Several of his scientific papers were the results of consulting contracts with many firms, to which von Kármán contributed numerous engineering reports. Some of his work on the aerodynamics of airships rose most probably from his work for Luftschiffbau Zeppelin, in 1924–28. His interest in rocketry also dates back to the 1920s during his time as head of the Aachen Aeronautic Institute. He continued his rocket experiments in the 1930s, with his California Institute of Technology students in the area now known as the Rose Bowl. Von Kármán was considered the only scientist of stature with the foresight to believe in the devel-

---

85 James Franck to Theodore von Kármán, February 11, 1948, Theodore von Kármán Papers, 9.36.
86 Hugh L. Dryden, "In Memoriam Theodore Von Kármán," *op. cit*
87 Frank J. Malina, "Theodore von Kármán, 1861–1963," *op. cit.*, pp. 3–4. Theodore von Kármán Papers, 135.8.— From the great figures of modern engineering L. Prandtl, G. I. Taylor, S. Timoshenko, N. E. Joukowski, G. Eiffel and G. A. Crocco belonged to Felix Klein's school in Germany.

opment of rocketry at a time when most leading scientific figures were skeptical of its potential.[88] When General H. H. Arnold, then Chief of the Army Air Force, asked him to investigate the application of rockets to lift heavy bombers off short runways, this led to the development of the JATO (Jet Assisted Take-Off) rockets, one of the first products of the Jet Propulsion Laboratory.[89]

As a member of the special committee appointed by the U.S. Navy, he investigated the Akron and Macon Dirigible disasters in 1933–37.[90] In 1942, he examined the collapse of Tacoma Narrows Bridge in Washington State, which enabled him to put his long-familiar subject, the "Kármán Vortex Trail," to a practical test.[91] As consultant to the Ballistic Research Laboratory of the U.S. Army at Aberdeen Proving Ground in Maryland between 1938 and 1952, he promoted the early construction of supersonic wind tunnels in the U.S. Wind tunnels he had built earlier in Japan, China, and Italy, helped him study the flow of air across fighters and bombers and led to the development of giant jet airliners, such as the 707 and the DC8, which could cross the United States in five hours.[92]

Well before World War II, the U.S. Army Air Corps commissioned the National Academy of Sciences in Washington, DC to investigate the feasibility of assisting the take-off of heavily loaded aircraft with some form of auxiliary power. A member of the special academy committee appointed in 1938, von Kármán started to investigate at Caltech the possibility of using rockets. He was 57 when he first started working in the

---

88 "Memo to News Editors," May 8, 1961. News from the Institute of Aerospace Sciences, New York, N. Y., Theodore von Kármán Papers, 137.4.
89 "Von Karman Busy at 80," *The Sun,* Baltimore, May 7, 1961.
90 The Akron blew up in 1933, and Mason crashed in 1935. Marie D. Roddenbery to "June," April 14, 1961. Theodore von Kármán Papers, 135.9.
91 "A Tribute to Dr. von Karman," *NATO Letter,* July-August, 1963, p. 23. Cf. Judith Sz. Hódy, "Mindig tanítani akartam. Utolsó beszélgetés Kármán Tódorral," *Irodalmi Újság,* May 15, 1963, p. 3.
92 Ralph Dighton, "Expert on Wind Called Father Of Supersonic Age," *Columbus Dispatch,* May 16, 1961.

field of jet propulsion and rocket flight, which he continued until his death at 82.[93]

Many of his other contributions are still to be discovered once the files of the companies he worked for are declassified and available. A serious biography of von Kármán, still missing at this point, will reveal the role he played in transforming the results of basic research into applied aerodynamics, of which he was an uncontested pioneer.

It was for his contributions "to improve and speed the defenses of this Nation and of the Atlantic Community" that the U.S. Senate expressed its gratitude to Dr von Kármán. When presenting Senate Resolution 133 honoring Dr von Kármán on his 80th birthday, Senator Henry M. Jackson expressed "the admiration and gratitude for the great contributions which Theodore von Karman has made to our country, and indeed, the entire world," recalling the significant share of Hungarian scientists who built up modern science in the U.S.

> The vigor of science in the United States today is due in large part to the contributions of brilliant and dedicated men who came to our shores from Europe [...] It is an interesting bit of history that five of the greatest of these men should have been born, and spent their childhood, in the same district of one city, Budapest, Hungary. I am, of course, thinking of Dr. Leo Szilard, Dr. John von Neumann, Dr. Edward Teller, Dr. Eugene Wigner, and finally, Dr. Theodore von Karman.[94]

Senate Resolution 133 made it clear that Congress acknowledged particularly the work done by von Kármán citing "the cause of strengthening the military defenses of our country and our free world partners."[95] The Hungarian-born scientist was cited as "one of the most influential and respected advisers at the highest level of our Defense Establishment."[96] Senator Jackson emphasized the leading role von Kármán played "in speeding and strengthening aeronautical and space research in the NATO

---

93   Frank J. Malina, *op. cit.*, p.3.
94   *Congressional Record*, Senate, May 3, 1961, pp. 6587–8.
95   *Ibid.*.
96   *Ibid.*

community."[97] The NATO countries indeed valued von Kármán's work which led to the mobilization of the Western scientific effort.[98]

President Kennedy, as well, cited von Kármán's "outstanding [...] counsel and assistance to the United States Air Force and to the NATO Advisory Group for Aeronautical Research and Development," when selecting von Kármán as the first recipient of the National Medal of Science in 1963.[99] The White House's announcement regarding his being awarded the medal, stated that his "distinguished counsel to the Armed Services" came second only to his "leadership in the science and engineering basic to aeronautics."[100] Presenting the nation's highest scientific award, President Kennedy said, "I know of no one else who more completely represents all of the areas with which this award is appropriately concerned—science, engineering and education."[101]

Part of the appreciation von Kármán earned was through his willingness to comment on political questions. His word had weight in a time of superpower confrontations. However, he refrained from commenting on issues such as America's lag in space and whether NASA should launch an effort to beat the Russians in the "Space Race," though many newsmen were confidentially invited to the Institute of the Aerospace Sciences to hear him talk on this particular subject.[102] Von Kármán was willing, however, to address issues such as the U.S. future in manned

---

97　*Congressional Record,* Senate, May 3, 1961, p. 6587.
98　"A Tribute to Dr. von Karman," *NATO Letter,* July-August, 1963, p. 23.
99　John F. Kennedy to Theodore von Karman, The White House, Washington, DC, February 8, 1963, Theodore von Kármán Papers, 135.4.
100　White House Announcement for Palm Beach, Florida, relative to the award of The National Medal of Science to Dr von Karman, December 31, 1962. Theodore von Kármán Papers, 135.4.
101　"President J. F. Kennedy Presents U.S. Science Medal to Dr. von Karman," *The Aerojet Booster,* Vol. II, No. 13., No. 1., March 1, 1963.
102　"For Release: Memo to News Editors," May 8, 1961. News from the Institute of Aerospace Sciences, New York, N. Y., Theodore von Kármán Papers, 137.4; John G. Norris, "Air-Breathing Orbital Planes Urged By Expert as Cheaper Than Rockets," *Washington Post & Times Herald,* May 10, 1961.

flights and missiles, the feasibility of an ideal retaliatory system and new approaches to missile defense.[103]

Nonetheless, von Kármán did not think of himself as a political figure, nor did he consider it appropriate for fellow scientists to play a political role. At a press conference on the eve of his 80th birthday, von Kármán made it clear that he believed scientists were "not necessarily learned in statesmanship and politics," and therefore should refrain from pontificating on television and elsewhere on the state of the world. He jabbed gently at fellow scientists Edward Teller and Leo Szilard, commenting that he had watched them on TV programs talking about the future of the nation: "I don't think that a man such as Edward Teller can say what is the good of the nation—I don't think this is a scientific question," he commented.[104]

Von Kármán was asked at the press conference how it is that so many of America's top scientists are former Hungarians. Smiling, he said, they are not originally from Hungary, but from Mars. "We decided to infiltrate the U.S., and were sent to Hungary—where some queer people live anyway—for conditioning for human life. There are many of us here from Hungary who are not quite earth people, like Zsa Zsa Gabor."[105] More germanely, von Kármán summed up the secret of the Hungarian success, which he attributed both to the "Hungarian fundamental educational method and the U.S. liberal climate," which did the rest, he added, according to an article in the *Washington Post & Times Herald*.[106]

At the subsequent banquet honoring von Kármán's 80th birthday attended by more than 700 leading figures in the world of aerospace science and technology, Air Force Undersecretary Joseph V. Charyk used the example of the octogenarian, equipped with all the experiences

---

103 Ibid.
104 "Von Karman," Associated Press, May 9, 1961. Theodore von Kármán Papers, 137.4.
105 Walter Wingo, "'Supersonic flight will do most...'" *Washington News,* May 10, 1961.
106 John G. Norris, "Air-Breathing Orbital Planes Urged By Expert as Cheaper Than Rockets," *Washington Post & Times Herald,* May 10, 1961.

of two World Wars, to note that technology has become inextricably linked with today's politics, economics, military affairs and international relations." Undersecretary Charyk warned scientists that they should no longer escape to ivory towers and evade responsibility to humanity. "Fear, timidity, compromise and shirking of responsibility are the antithesis of the things that built this great country," Charyk said. The Air Force Undersecretary reminded the distinguished gathering of the time in 1945, when von Kármán had first presented to General "Hap" Arnold his report entitled "Toward New Horizons," which had laid the foundations of research and development programming for several decades. Air Force research development funds had gradually increased to the level urged by von Kármán in that report of 15 years ago, Charyk pointed out.[107]

During a perhaps symbolic, last visit to Aachen, Germany, von Kármán died of a heart attack at the age of eighty-one.[108]

3 Faith in Progress: John von Neumann

Perhaps the finest example of an experimental mind emanating from Hungary is that of John von Neumann (1903–1957). Like many of his compatriots, von Neumann's career in the United States was strongly involved in defense issues, primarily in World War II and during the early years of the Cold War. He came to the U.S. well before the War, but the war effort radically changed his interest and his thinking, and ultimately, the direction of his career, turning him from a pure into an applied mathematician.

The son of a rich and upwardly mobile Budapest banker who was a protégé of Prime Minister Kálmán Széll, von Neumann was very much "a Budapest type," a "good Budapester of his time and social class," as

---

[107] "For Release," May 12, 1961. News from the Institute of Aerospace Sciences, New York, NY, Theodore von Kármán Papers, 137.4.
[108] Hugh L. Dryden, "In Memoriam Theodore Von Kármán," *op. cit.*, p. 6.

his longtime friend and fellow Hungarian, economist William Fellner noted.[109] Though of Jewish origin, the great mathematician had little to fear, even in Horthy's Hungary after 1919–1920. His upper-middle class, well-connected family fled to Austria during the Soviet-type Republic of Councils of the Spring and Summer of 1919. Unlike most fellow Jewish-Hungarians, he was not impacted by the *numerus clausus* quota system set up by the incoming Horthy administration and was accepted at the University of Budapest in 1921. Yet, almost immediately, he left for Berlin, Göttingen and later, Zürich where he became a student of those prestigious universities and their professors, including Albert Einstein and David Hilbert. Though he spoke and wrote excellent Hungarian throughout his life, early in his formative years he became a polyglot European. Mathematician Gábor Szegő remembered the fifteen-year-old to have been "quite good in German and French conversation," "with incredibly fast reactions not only in Mathematics but in many other fields."[110] His daughter Marina von Neumann Whitman remembered her father as "a rather cosmopolitan person" with a household where many of the characteristics "were European, rather than American." His specific Hungarian impact on her life was "very little actually," she recalled in 1982.[111]

Von Neumann's was another important example illuminating the Hungarian situation after 1919–20. Not only were Communists, Leftists, Radicals, and Jews victimized by the consequences of the dissolution of the Austro-Hungarian Monarchy, the revolutions of 1918 and 1919, and the Peace Treaty of Trianon (1920), the devastating aftershocks of World

109 Steve J. Heims, *John von Neumann and Norbert Wiener. From Mathematics to the Technologies of Life and Death* (Cambridge, MA—London: MIT Press, 1980), pp. 26–27.
110 Untitled memoirs by Gábor Szegő, n.d., Gabor Szegő Papers, SC 323, Boxes 85–036, Department of Special Collections and University Archives, Stanford University Libraries, Stanford, CA. Gábor Szegő tutored young Johnny von Neumann in 1918–19, cf. their correspondence between 1919 and 1941, Princeton University Library, Princeton, NJ.
111 Marina von Neumann Whitman interviewed by Mrs Rose Stein, New York, NY, October 8, 1982. Oral History Collection, Butler Library, Columbia University Libraries, New York, NY.

War I left little or no opportunity for major creative talents to develop their abilities and forced them to leave the country.[112] Hungary, and to a lesser extent Austria, ceased to provide the shelter where genius had been produced, nurtured, and educated over the previous several decades. Modernization was no longer possible, and it was not even really wanted. Economic development came to a stop, there was no money available, and in the ensuing spirit of neo-conservatism, the prevailing political and social forces pushed out many of the people who had the capacity to introduce new ideas. After Trianon, progress was no longer the creed and cry of the post-War generation, which was influenced by the various shades of conservative thought of Gyula Szekfű, Bálint Hóman, Gyula Kornis, Kuno Klebelsberg, Ottokár Prohászka, László Ravasz, Ferenc Herczeg and Cecile Tormay.[113]

First invited to Princeton in his late twenties, John von Neumann was one of those who, in the words of his friend and first biographer Stanislaw Ulam, desired "to blaze new trails and to create new syntheses."[114] Ulam distinguished this group of mathematicians from those who had wanted to contribute "to the edifice of existing work" and added: "It was only toward the end of his life that he [von Neumann] felt sure enough of himself to engage freely and yet painstakingly in the creating of a possible new mathematical discipline," namely the theory of self-reproducing automata, as Ulam put it.[115]

Stanislaw Ulam may have been right from a purely mathematical point of view, though he should have noted von Neumann's pioneering studies on the theory of games and economic behavior, and his last efforts on mathematical modeling and the interpretation of the brain. The

---

112 Cf. Tibor Frank, "Double Divorce: The Case of Mariette and John von Neumann," *Nevada Historical Society Quarterly*, Vol. 34, No. 2, Summer 1991, pp. 360–363.
113 Cf. Tibor Frank, "Editing as Politics: József Balogh and *The Hungarian Quarterly*," *The Hungarian Quarterly*, Vol. XXXIV, No. 129, Spring 1993, pp. 5–13.
114 Stanislaw Ulam, *Adventures of a Mathematician* (New York: Scribner's, 1976), pp. 78–79; quoted by Steve J. Heims, *op. cit.*, pp. 117–118.
115 Steve J. Heims, *op. cit.*, p. 118.

"modernism" of von Neumann is an all-embracing feature of his entire work and *Weltanschauung*.

When first arriving in the United States in 1930, von Neumann did not consider himself a refugee scientist.[116] He brought his (and his family's) optimism and faith in technology and modernization which came out of Hungary's great years of economic development.[117] He thought of new technology as something basically beneficial: developments in technology captivated him to such an extent that "he could barely find the time to work out his highly innovative mathematical ideas."[118] Von Neumann's optimism, his belief in "progress," was rooted in a 19th century European tradition which in turn was based on the philosophy of the French Enlightenment, as well as the thinking of Charles Darwin and Herbert Spencer, and which was transmitted continuously by the best Hungarian high schools. Sándor Mikola, the dominating physics teacher of von Neumann's Budapest *Gimnázium*, based his entire textbook *A fizika gondolatvilága* [The Mind of Physics, 1933] on the underlying philosophy that "starting from some basic qualities, human spirit is in constant progress."[119]

Von Neumann's friend and colleague the Nobel Laureate Eugene Wigner described the way von Neumann pictured the development of his own ideas. In an interview recorded years after von Neumann's death, Wigner recalled von Neumann speaking about his way of thinking

---

116   John von Neumann to Maurice R. Davis, Princeton, May 3, 1946, John von Neumann Papers, Box 8, Letters Personal 1938–1946, Rare Book and Special Collections, The Library of Congress, Washington, DC. Von Neumann's statement was made in response to a question from the Committee for the Study of Recent Immigration from Europe at Yale University, of which M. R. Davis was the Director. I found no references to the papers or the achievements of this project though their report was said to have been published by Davis's letter to Von Neumann dated April 24, 1946.
117   Norman Macrae, *John von Neumann* (New York: Pantheon, 1992), pp. 31–59.
118   *Ibid.*, pp. 127, 409, quote p. 122.
119   Sándor Mikola, *A fizika gondolatvilága* [The Mind of Physics] (Budapest: [Published by the Author], 1933), p. 5.

as if you see a fog over a landscape, and then the fog slowly lifts and you see through a chain of mountains, and then the fog lifts more and you see houses on the mountains, and you see the landscape slowly. But I think the relevant part of it is that you don't see the road of the mountain, but you see the mountain. Going up the mountain would be the logical path. Seeing the picture, if the logic is inherent to it, is what really happens (it rarely happens). When you articulate your conclusions you can't describe but by a one-dimensional set, because speaking or reading is one-dimensional, and probably the upper consciousness [...] is one-dimensional, but apparently the subconscious is not that way. When one sees a picture, the logic is of course in it, but the picture is much beyond the logic. The logic is something like the color of something.[120]

When and why did von Neumann turn from pure mathematics toward artificial and natural automata, "computing machines" and the brain? Some time during the early 1940s, he realized that the safety of a system is not so much dependent upon the nature of its constituent elements, but rather on its organizational principles, its complexity, and the quality and quantity of the information processed by it. His movement toward the theories of control and information was influenced by regular contact with his mentor and friend Rudolf Ortvay (1885–1945), professor of physics at the University of Budapest. Some of the ideas that came to captivate von Neumann's mind in the 1940s and 1950s originated in his long correspondence with Professor Ortvay, who considered it his special duty to support and encourage young, talented people both in and out of his physics seminar. The extent of Ortvay's influence is a chapter of von Neumann's biography yet to be fully written.

In his 1939 letters from Budapest, Ortvay pushed his young Princeton friend into dealing with complex issues such as the axiomatic method, the theory of games, computing machines, and particularly, brain research.[121]

---

120 Eugene Wigner quoting John von Neumann in an interview with Harriet A. Zuckerman, New York, NY, November 1, 1964. Oral History Project, Butler Library, Columbia University Libraries, New York, NY — I am indebted to Professor Harriet A. Zuckerman of Columbia University for allowing me to make use of her interviews with Nobel Laureates.
121 Ferenc Nagy, ed., *Neumann János és a "magyar titok" a dokumentumok tükrében* [John von Neumann and the "Hungarian Secret" as Shown by Documents]

Ortvay's influence proved to be profound and lasting, especially for two reasons: it was pertinent to the philosophical foundations of von Neumann's future work, and it came just on the eve of World War II, which gave von Neumann's interest an entirely new focus.

Von Neumann's turn to pioneering subjects in the late 1930s was at least partly the result of several profound changes in his personal life which included his divorce and second marriage, the losing of his Hungarian citizenship, and his final settlement in the U.S.[122] It was, however, the outbreak of World War II in Europe and the entry of the U.S. into the War in 1941 that directed von Neumann's work toward a series of new problems related to defense, the struggle against Nazi Germany, and finally, the Cold War. The War years put him on an unending trail of government connections, starting in 1940 with his membership in the Scientific Advisory Committee of the Ballistic Research Laboratories, his consultancy with the Navy Bureau of Ordnance, as well as with the Los Alamos Scientific Laboratory. By the time he became one of the Atomic Energy Commissioners in 1955, he was invited to serve on some 20 other defense-related boards and committees working on practical issues for the U.S. Armed Forces, particularly the Air Force and Navy. This impressive number of government commissions resulted in a wide array of pioneering tasks of a highly technical and practical nature where his experimental mind and engineering abilities were at their best. The list included the National Security Agency, the Central Intelligence Agency, the Weapons Systems Evaluation Group, the RAND Corporation, as well as nuclear research centers such as Oak Ridge, Livermore Laboratories and the Sandia Corporation.[123] Toward the end of his life, von Neumann became one of the nation's top defense experts involved in dozens of

---

(Budapest: Országos Műszaki Információs Központ és Könyvtár, 1987), pp. 74–77, 128–156.
122 Tibor Frank, "Double Divorce: The Case of Mariette and John von Neumann," *op. cit.,* pp. 360–363.
123 J. Von Neumann Government Connections as of February 1955. Library of Congress, John Von Neumann Papers, "Personal," Box 6, Rare Book and Special Collections, The Library of Congress, Washington, DC.

highly innovative and experimental projects. When the newly established Enrico Fermi Award was conferred on him in 1956, he was applauded primarily for his contributions "to the art and science of the design and application of fast electronic calculating machines," and was cited as "teacher, inspirer and original contributor to the profound problems of the logic of programming for the most effective use of these expensive and elaborate devices."[124]

It is justified to consider the computer a product of the war effort and the Cold War atmosphere. It became central to von Neumann's thinking during World War II, which was a great turning point in von Neumann's career. After Pearl Harbor, he became involved in defense research and worked for the Army Ordnance Department in the Ballistics Research Laboratory in Aberdeen, Maryland, after he had become a naturalized U.S. citizen. In 1941–42, he worked for the National Defense Research Council, mainly on the theory and physical effects of detonation. In 1942–43, he worked for the Navy Bureau of Ordnance in its Mine Warfare Section, which also took him to England. [125] It was during his visit to England in 1943 that von Neumann became involved in "computational techniques":

> I have also developed an obscene interest in computational techniques. I am looking forward to discussing these matters with you. I really feel like proselytizing— even if I am going to tell you only things which you have known much longer than I did.[126]

A little later, in 1943, he was enlisted by Robert Oppenheimer to go to Los Alamos to do research on detonation. His knowledge of hydrodynamics made von Neumann well-prepared for the study of implosions and explosions, but the equations had to be treated numerically by employees known as "computers," who were responsible for the extensive calculations

---

124 U.S. Atomic Energy Commission: First Enrico Fermi Award, p. 3. Library of Congress: J. Von Neumann Papers, "Personal," Box 6.
125 William Aspray, *John Von Neumann and the Origins of Modern Computing* (Cambridge, MA—London: The MIT Press, 1990), pp. 25–7.
126 *Ibid.*, p. 27.

for the scientist. As late as the Fall of 1943, a hand-computing group of twenty people satisfied the computing demands of the Los Alamos laboratory.[127] In late 1943, IBM punch-card equipment was set up, and soon electromechanical IBM accounting equipment was acquired for the large calculations needed for the design of the Bomb. The problems with the availability of computing equipment made von Neumann acutely aware of the missing high speed computation techniques that the Los Alamos project so badly needed in 1944–45. At this point, von Neumann developed a deep understanding of high speed digital computation, which he amassed in a very short time.[128]

There has been considerable controversy about von Neumann's contributions to the design of EDVAC, one of the very first large computers. His "first draft of a report on the EDVAC," written in Spring 1945, clearly showed his expertise in regard to the stored-program computer. It was there that he introduced a comparative terminology from studies of the human nervous system, describing the computer units in terms of the associative sensory and motor neurons. Von Neumann was very much stimulated by the McCulloch-Pitts theory comparing computer functions with the functioning of the human mind which was put forward in a 1943 article.[129] He used those ideas throughout the post-War period, including his early work on digital computers, automata theory, reliability and the brain-computer analogy and in his study on *The Computer and the Brain*.[130] His 1945 report gave a logical framework for the new machine, but several of his colleagues who originally helped construct EDVAC attacked him for merely "translating" some of their ideas "into

127 Ibid., pp. 27–29.
128 Ibid., pp. 30–34.
129 Warren S. McCulloch and W. Pitts, "A Logical Calculus of the Ideas Immanent in Nervous Activity," *Bulletin of Mathematical Biophysics*, Vol. 5, 1943, pp. 115–133.
130 For an account of the McCulloch-Pitts theory, a description of von Neumann's contributions, as well as subsequent developments in the theory of neuro networks, see: Jack D. Cowan, "Von Neumann and Neuro Networks," in James Glimm, John Impagliazzo and Isadore Singer, eds., *The Legacy of John Von Neumann* (Providence, RI: American Mathematical Society, 1990).

a sort of semi-mathematical logical notation of his own."[131] In the ensuing and increasingly bitter dispute over scientific credits, John Mauchly charged von Neumann with having merely substituted neurological terms (taken from McCulloch and Pitts) and "rephrasing our logic."[132] This became a difficult issue by 1946–47, when von Neumann found himself in the middle of a protracted patent dispute, wherein he was required to preserve the interests of the government and the scientific public versus John Mauchly and J. Presper Eckert, Jr. who sought commercial rights for themselves.[133]

His correspondence seems to suggest that a new approach to understand the organization of the brain was first suggested to von Neumann by Professor Rudolf Ortvay from Budapest in early 1941.

> Today's computing machines, automatic telephone exchanges, high-voltage equipment like cascade transformers as well as radio transmitter and receiver equipment, but also an industrial plant or an office are all technical examples of such organizations. I think there is a common element in all these which is capable of being axiomatized. I don't know if there has been an attempt in this direction. I am interested in knowing this because I believe that if it is possible to sharply accentuate the essential elements relevant to the organization, as such, this would give an overview of the alternatives and would facilitate the understanding of such systems as, for instance, the brain.[134]

It was also Ortvay who, repeatedly from 1939 through 1941, hinted at the importance of brain research and the mechanism of the nervous system as a whole, providing a number of useful starting points for an

---

131 William Aspray, *John Von Neumann and the Origins of Modern Computing* (Cambridge, MA—London: The MIT Press, 1990), p. 42.
132 *Ibid.*
133 *Ibid.*, pp. 41–46.
134 Rudolf Ortvay to John von Neumann, February 16, 1941. Published by Ferenc Nagy, ed., *op. cit.*, pp. 177–178. For an English translation see William Aspray, "The Origins of John Von Neumann's Theory of Automata," William Aspray, *John Von Neumann and the Origins of Modern Computing* (Cambridge, MA— London: The MIT Press, 1990), p. 297.

Problem Solving and the U.S. War Effort

elaborate research project.[135] "I looked into your paper on [the theory of] games again [...]," Ortvay wrote to von Neumann in January 1941. "I liked it at the time very much as it gave me the hope that if I succeeded in directing your attention toward the connection of the brain-cells, you might be able to expose this problem."[136] Ortvay also made the comparison between the brain and the electronic calculating machine:

> Of course I don't think that the mechanism of the brain is very similar to a computing equipment consisting of electronic valves but I do believe it is a complicated and very specialized equipment, which may be very simple in terms of basic properties! [...] I am ready to believe that a less detailed treatment, that with the mechanism for the brain, whereby the cell would be the unit and some idea for the interconnection, is perhaps even now timely.[137]

Though war-related issues certainly contributed to von Neumann's development of large computing machines, such as ENIAC, EDVAC, and, chiefly, JONIAC, it seems possible that Ortvay's encouragement and ideas had a share in alerting him to the links between complicated automata and the human nervous system. Even though his first major article in this field, "The General and Logical Theory of Automata," wasn't read as a lecture until after the War at the Hixon Symposium in September 1948, the roots of his experimental interest in automata and brain theory go back to the pre-War years. Thus, his celebrated though tragically undelivered Silliman Lectures at Yale University, published as a booklet after his death in 1958, were partly built on the ideas of Ortvay's in their cor-

---

135 Rudolf Ortvay—John von Neumann Correspondence, Budapest, 1939–1941, *passim,* MTA Akadémiai Könyvtár, Budapest, published by Ferenc Nagy, ed., *op. cit.,* pp. 136–137, 140, 155–156, 159, 162–163, 167–168, 176, 177–178.
136 Rudolf Ortvay to John von Neumann, January 29, 1941, published by Ferenc Nagy, ed., *op. cit.,* p. 176. For a different English translation of the full passage, see William Aspray, *John Von Neumann and the Origins of Modern Computing* (Cambridge, MA—London: The MIT Press, 1990), pp. 296–297.
137 Rudolf Ortvay to John von Neumann, March 30, 1940, published by Ferenc Nagy, p. 159, quoted by William Aspray, *John Von Neumann and the Origins of Modern Computing* (Cambridge, MA—London: The MIT Press, 1990), p. 295–296.

respondence of almost 20 years before,[138] although no credit was given to Ortvay in the booklet, or, indeed, by Arthur W. Burks in the edited text of von Neumann's *Theory of Self-Reproducing Automata*.[139]

Von Neumann began to develop his theory of automata in the late 1940s. He envisaged a theory to embrace both natural and artificial automata, including the human nervous system, as well as analog and digital computers. Von Neumann concentrated on the issues of reliability and self-reproduction, problems closely related to the construction of large computers. At his death, his research in automata theory was unfinished but he left behind in manuscripts most of his thoughts on the subject. "There is one compensation in this:" commented the editor of his work on automata theory, "one can see von Neumann's powerful mind at work."[140]

Von Neumann came to computing during the War, when he had to provide answers to new problems, such as nuclear technology, and they became his main interest after the War when he developed a general method for using computers that was applicable to a whole range of problems in many fields of mathematics. He pioneered the employment of computers in solving problems numerically and in using the results "as a heuristic guide to theorizing [...] It is of the essence of this procedure that computer solutions are not sought for their own sake but as an aid to discovering useful concepts, broad principles and general theories [...]"[141]

The heuristic use of computers was directly related to the deductive tradition of science, based on hypotheses and experimentally tested variables leading to new hypotheses on the basis of new findings. In using a computer heuristically, computation replaces and augments experimen-

---

138 John Von Neumann, *The Computer and the Brain* (New Haven: Yale UP, 1958).
139 John Von Neumann, *Theory of Self-Reproducing Automata*, ed. Arthur W. Burks (Urbana and London: University of Illinois Press, 1966).
140 Arthur W. Burks, "Preface," in John Von Neumann, *Theory of Self-Reproducing Automata, op. cit.*, p. xvi.
141 Arthur W. Burks, Editor's Introduction, in John Von Neumann, *Theory of Self-Reproducing Automata, op.cit.*, p. 3.

tation. In both cases the cycle is reiterated indefinitely. Von Neumann suggested that powerful computers may provide the mathematician "with those heuristic hints which are needed in all parts of mathematics for genuine progress."[142] He thought that pure mathematics should be inspired by the natural sciences and recognized computers as a source of new ideas and problems in mathematics. When von Neumann spoke of the heuristic use of computers, it was the human being and not the machine who was the source of new suggestions, hypotheses and ideas. As Arthur W. Burks, a frequent collaborator of von Neumann noted,

> Von Neumann wished to make the machine as intelligent as possible, but he recognized that human powers of intuition, spatial imagery, originality, etc., are far superior to those of present or immediately foreseeable machines. He wished to augment the ability of a skilled, informed, creative human by the use of a digital computer as a tool.[143]

Once he recognized the importance of computers, he contributed to all aspects of the subject: he developed new methods, wrote programs, provided problem solving techniques and worked on the design and the theory of computers as well.

Von Neumann started to work on his "new electronic calculating machine" in January 1946 at the Institute for Advanced Study in Princeton, N.J. From the beginning, he had problem solving as a major goal. In a letter to Julian Huxley, then Executive Secretary of UNESCO's Preparatory Commission, von Neumann emphasized in late March 1946

> that we intend to use this machine as a research tool, and not as a production facility. In other words, we want to use it to study new methods which are appropriate in high speed computing, and suitably chosen prototypes of problems which can

---

142 John Von Neumann, "The Mathematician," in Collected Works, ed. A. H. Taub (New York: Macmillan, 1961–63), Vol. I, p. 2, quoted by Arthur W. Burks, Editor's Introduction, in John Von Neumann, *Theory of Self-Reproducing Automata, op.cit.*, p. 4.

143 Arthur W. Burks, Editor's Introduction, in John Von Neumann, *Theory of Self-Reproducing Automata, op.cit.*, p. 5.

be solved with such methods (but which cannot be solved without them—i.e. not analytically, and not with less fast computing methods).[144]

Von Neumann proposed using the machine for mathematicians, mathematical physicists, as well as in the field of dynamic meteorology, the theory of statistical prediction, and also certain forms of logic and combinatorics. "Among the first problems I'd like to approach in this way as soon as possible, are those of the turbulent forms of three dimensional motion, both in general fluid dynamics and more specifically in theoretical meteorology."[145] "I feel sure[...]," von Neumann concluded, "that the human tasks of formulating and coding the setup of the problem for the machine, the human sensing of the results, their interpreting, etc. will, if intelligently handled, 'keep up' with the pace of the machine. I know, of course," he added, "that this is in conflict with a good deal of current opinion, but I am satisfied that our thinking on this subject was sufficiently detailed and careful to justify the above assertions."[146]

Von Neumann's success with the computer quickly translated into a practical product. It took only six months in 1951 for Neumann's electronic computer group at Princeton, as well as for his associates at IBM, the National Bureau of Standards, the Remington Rand Company and Los Alamos to complete all the computing necessary for the H-bomb. The "Von Neumann machine" did so many of the H-bomb calculations that *The New York Times* credited him with being largely responsible for the success of the thermonuclear program of the U.S. Atomic Energy Commission in 1954.[147] Though von Neumann disapproved of the embarrassing flattery that gave "me considerably more credit than I deserve,"[148]

---

144 John von Neumann to Julian Huxley, March 28, 1946, John Von Neumann Papers, "Personal Correspondence, 1938–46," Box 3.
145 *Ibid.*
146 *Ibid.*
147 *The New York Times,* July 4, 1954, cf. *Town Topics,* Princeton, July 11–17, 1954.
148 John von Neumann to William Laurence, July 7, 1954, John Von Neumann Papers.

his leading role in solving the mathematical problems of the H-bomb was generally recognized by contemporaries.[149]

Von Neumann also became involved in a number of issues related to defense policy. At the Oppenheimer hearings, conducted under the auspices of the U.S. Atomic Energy Commission, he testified strongly in favor of Oppenheimer. Von Neumann was very anti-Soviet, yet he had no sympathy for any form of McCarthyism. He favored an acceleration of the arms race because he thought that the price was worth paying for the U.S., and supported nuclear tests for the same reason.[150] While Leo Szilard worked feverishly on disarmament, fellow Hungarian von Neumann voted for superiority in arms. Not only was he interested in the design of bombs, but he took an early interest in the development of missiles. In May 1953, he became chairman of the Nuclear Weapons Panel of the Scientific Advisory Board of the U.S. Air Force, then under the chairmanship of Theodore von Kármán. In 1954, Admiral Lewis Strauss offered him the position of Atomic Energy Commissioner, which was the highest official position available for scientists in the U.S. Government. He knew his government position would be ill-received by the liberal scientists who did not like Admiral Strauss or Edward Teller. Yet, he described himself at the Congressional confirmation hearings in March 1955 as "violently anti-Communist, and a good deal more militaristic than most," and later as "violently opposed to Marxism, ever since I can remember."[151]

His anti-Communist sentiments, just like those of Edward Teller, had some of their roots in his early years in Hungary. His family was forced to flee the country during the brief Communist interval in the spring and summer of 1919. John's father, Miksa von Neumann, was a banker, and as such was in constant danger during the "red months" of Hungary, and fled to neighboring Austria. This episode was recalled by John von

---

149 Robert Oppenheimer to John von Neumann, Princeton, N.J., July 15, 1954, John Von Neumann Papers.
150 Steve J. Heims, *John Von Neumann and Norbert Wiener. From Mathematics to the Technologies for Life and Death* (Cambridge, MA—London: The MIT Press, 1981), pp. 261–265.
151 *Ibid.*, pp. 275–278, quote 277–278.

Neumann at the Atomic Energy Commission Personnel Security Board hearings concerning J. Robert Oppenheimer in April, 1954.[152] Throughout his life, von Neumann viewed Communism and the Soviet Union as enemies. This helped him secure a great deal of credibility during the witch-hunting security hearings that declared Oppenheimer unfit to have access to military secrets. The hearings immediately preceded von Neumann's nomination to the Atomic Energy Commission in 1954. Most papers agreed that von Neumann's unanimous nomination was "a sound appointment."[153]

It speaks highly of von Neumann's integrity and independence that he was able to become Atomic Energy Commissioner *despite* his support provided to J. Robert Oppenheimer. At the Oppenheimer security clearance hearings, von Neumann testified that he had "no doubts" about Dr. Oppenheimer's loyalty and integrity. He was able to keep a certain balance between defending Dr. Oppenheimer and denying that he had been a security risk, but reiterated his "strong opposition to communism and Marxism."[154]

The New York Times suggested that "by appointing an Oppenheimer supporter, President Eisenhower appears to have made a useful gesture of conciliation toward the large group of scientists who have been unhappy about the Oppenheimer verdict and who have been concerned about the future penalties, if any, to be exacted of scientists who were or are friendly to the former head of the Los Alamos project."[155] In a characteristic response, von Neumann declared how grateful he was for the interpretation of his nomination "from the point of view of the scientific community."[156] He also found it necessary to point out that he was in

---

152 *Ibid.*, pp. 45–48.
153 *The New York Times*, October 25, 1954.
154 *The New York Times*, March 8, 1955.
155 *The New York Times*, October 25, 1954. *The Washington Post* called him an "Oppenheimer Friend" on the title page. The Washington Post, October 24, 1954.
156 John Von Neumann to *The New York Times*, October 27, 1954, *The New York Times*, October 29, 1954.

agreement with the program of the AEC in "the field of defense, as well as the numerous fields of the peaceful uses of atomic energy [...]"[157]

It was from his pioneering work on computers that his relationship with IBM grew during his last years. In the Fall of 1951, he became a consultant with International Business Machines Corporation for "the mathematical and logical planning of computing machines, the uses of computing machines, the mathematical formulation of problems for machine solution and the mathematical and logical planning of setting up and coding problems for computing machines, and activities related thereto."[158] In October 1954, IBM renewed the agreement, requesting that von Neumann assign rights to IBM to all his inventions "relating to machines, systems or processes pertaining to problems referred to you by IBM or to IBM's research or development activities disclosed to you."[159]

The logical design that von Neumann worked out for EDVAC,[160] which was one of the very first electronic computers and one that he helped produce, included several important new features, such as the comparison of the machine to the human nervous system. Apart from his defense-related innovations, this promised to be a pioneering approach to the structure and mechanism of the human mind, and was evidence of his humanistic approach to science. His approach made possible a comparison and contrast between computer elements and neurons, observing that there was an analogy between the associative, sensory and motor neurons of the human nervous system on the one hand, and the input as well as the output of the computer on the other. The comparison between natural and artificial systems became one of the themes of von Neumann's theory, translating a particular characteristic of human thinking into the workings

---

157 *Ibid.*
158 John C. McPherson (IBM) to John von Neumann, New York, October, 1951, John Von Neumann Papers, Box 3.
159 G. B. Briggs (IBM) to John von Neumann, New York, October 21, 1954, John Von Neumann Papers, Box 3.
160 Electronic Discrete Variable Automatic Computer.

of an artificial intelligence.[161] Thus von Neumann became instrumental in transmitting the legacy of rational thought and the heuristic approach to computing machines, and ultimately contributed to making this tradition into a commonly accepted pattern of the computer age.

Von Neumann was aware of the heuristic advantages in comparing computers with natural organisms, and proposed a systematic theory of automata, describing "the structure and organization of both natural and artificial systems, the role of language and information in such systems, and the programming and control of such systems."[162] Von Neumann's untimely death prevented him from developing his automata theory fully, yet he outlined some of its problems and applications, began a comparative study of natural and artificial automata and identified some of the basic questions on reliability and self-reproduction, and developed a logical design of a self-reproducing automaton that provided a link between natural organisms and digital computers. The mathematics of his automata theory was common to both natural and artificial systems, and in that sense was similar to his theory of games, where the mathematics was common to games, as well as to economic systems. He compared the components in natural and artificial automata, similarly to Norbert Wiener in his *Cybernetics*.[163] Utilizing mathematical logic, von Neumann thought that the mathematics of automata should develop toward analysis, probability theory and thermodynamics. He suggested that the human nervous system should be approached as an automaton of great complexity, wherein the language of mathematical reasoning is analogous to the primary language of a computer. "I suspect that a deeper mathematical study of the nervous system [...] will affect our understanding of the aspects of mathematics itself that are involved. In fact, it may alter the

---

161 Arthur W. Burks, Editor's Introduction, in John Von Neumann, *Theory of Self-Reproducing Automata*, op. cit., p. 10.
162 *Ibid.*, p. 18.
163 *Ibid.*, pp. 21–22. Cf. Norbert Wiener, *Cybernetics, or Control and Communication in the Animal and the Machine* (New York: John Wiley and Sons, 1948, 2nd ed. 1961); see Von Neumann's review in *Physics Today*, Vol. 2, 1949, pp. 33–34.

way in which we look on mathematics and logics proper."[164] It is a sad fact that von Neumann did not live long enough to present a complete theory of automata.

Von Neumann's long-standing experimental interest in automata and the nervous system, a pioneering contribution to modern science, had its origins in the immediate pre-War years and in his continued links to Budapest colleagues such as Rudolf Ortvay. It is evident that the potential to deal with these issues was already there in his younger years and in his very first papers on the theory of games. The genuinely innovative character of his research and inquiry was deepened and accentuated by World War II, rather than being a by-product of it, and his long stay in the United States which, as in so many other cases, helped to bring out the best inherent qualities of the immigrant European mind. Von Neumann's spiritually liberating, yet intellectually reinforcing, two-way effect of having left conservative Hungary and entering the U.S. can be considered a typical experience of Hungarian-American intellectual migrations.

"Commentators on American traits delight in quoting De Crevecoeur's classic remark that 'the American is a new man who acts on new principles,'" author and educator Max Lerner stated.[165] To the many aspects of American exceptionalism and uniqueness one may add an often neglected, though basic secret of success of the innovative immigrant in 20th century U.S.: the genuinely heartfelt reception given to the pioneering spirit, inconceivable in any European country at the time, and the sheer sensation caused by the profoundly hospitable welcome to new ideas, novel approaches, fresh methods, and unexplored dimensions of the human mind. Productive abilities were incomparably more readily welcomed, eagerly appreciated, and carefully accommodated, indeed, institutionalized, in the U.S. than in the threatening atmosphere of totalitarian and dictatorial systems prevailing all across Europe.

164 John Von Neumann, *The Computer and the Brain* (New Haven: Yale University Press, 1958), p. 2.
165 Max Lerner, *America as a Civilization* (New York: Simon and Schuster, 1957; 8th paperback printing 1967), Vol. I, p. 61.

Figure 19. John von Neumann, mathematician, on Hungarian stamp (1992).

Though often overlooked, the uniquely appreciative American welcome was one of the very special forces which drew a large number of creative people to the U.S. in the long period of time from the 1930s until the 1980s. It was this supportive welcome, not the material benefits, which liberated the innovative spirit and experimental eagerness for fresh inquiry from European scientists, scholars, and artists. For non-conventional minds such as von Neumann's and others from Hungary, this provided features and stimuli they had badly missed in their homeland. Increasingly, the U.S. represented the exhilarating experience once offered by turn-of-the-century Paris to the earlier generation Hungarian poet Endre Ady, who felt "noble, fair, and great" not "beside the Danube [where] a demon army jibes and screams," but "beside the Seine" only.[166] Now that experience was to be had in America.

---

166 Endre Ady, "Beside the Seine," in *Poems of Endre Ady,* translated by Anton N. Nyerges (Buffalo, NY: Hungarian Cultural Foundation, 1969), p. 83.

4 The Manhattan Project and Leo Szilard

Nuclear Physics

Budapest-born and educated Leo Szilard turned his attention to nuclear physics in Berlin in 1932, and then moved to England following the Nazi takeover.[167] As a newcomer to this field, it is not surprising that he was not invited to attend the seventh Solvay Conference in Brussels in October 1933, which was devoted to nuclear physics.[168] Within a few years, however, he rose to prominence in this field.

Szilard began experimental work in nuclear physics in the Radium Department of St. Bartholomew's Hospital in London in the summer of 1934.[169] Earlier that year he had patented his invention of what became known as a cyclotron and had recognized the possibility of a chain reaction,[170] achievements that he later cited with pride although he was careful to not take "credit from others to whom credit is due."[171]

At St. Bartholomew's Hospital, Szilard and T. A. Chalmers systematically investigated key features of radioactivity. They devised a technique for separating radioactive nuclei produced by neutron bombardment from their normal isotopic environment (the "Szilard-Chalmers reaction"); they recognized the first case of isomerism among artificially radioactive

---

167 Szilard, "Biographical Data."
168 Roger H. Stuewer, "The Seventh Solvay Conference: Nuclear Physics at the Crossroads," in A.J. Kox and Daniel M. Siegel, eds., *No Truth Except in the Details: Essays in Honor of Martin J. Klein* (Dordrecht: Kluwer, 1995), pp. 333–362.
169 Szilard (Brussels) to Friedrich A. Paneth, August 28, 1934, Nachlass F. A. Paneth, Jewish Refugees Committee, 1933, III. Abt. Rep. 45.
170 Leo Szilard, "Asynchronous and Synchronous Transformers for Particles," British Application 5730/34, filed February 21, 1934; "Transmutation of chemical elements," British Application 7840/34; filed March 12, 1934; issued as Patent No. 440,023; reproduced in Szilard, *Collected Works*, pp. 564–604; 605–622.
171 Szilard to Richard Gehman, April 8, 1952, Leo Szilard Papers, Box 8, Folder 27; see also Szilard-Samuel Glasstone correspondence, 1956-57, *ibid.*, Box 8, Folder 23; Memorandum by E. P. Wigner, April 16. 1941, *ibid.*, Box 3, Folder 23.

elements; and they discovered and made pioneering investigations on the photoemission of slow neutrons from beryllium, which ultimately led to a means of distinguishing the emission of slow neutrons from fast ones in nuclear fission, a critically important problem in a chain reaction.[172] These and other experiments brought Szilard an ICI[173] grant and an invitation to the Clarendon Laboratory in Oxford.[174] There, beginning in 1935, he joined J.H.E. Griffiths in studying the emission of gamma rays when slow neutrons are absorbed by elements of odd atomic number.[175] He also was able to supply Friedrich Paneth with enough radon and other substances from the Clarendon Laboratory for his own experiments.[176] In 1941, Wigner commented about Szilard's work during this period:

> I first heard the possibility of nuclear power seriously discussed in the Spring of 1934, when I saw Szilard during a visit to London. The efficiency of collisions between neutrons and nuclei was realized by Szilard simultaneously with and independently from Fermi. He visualized the possibility of chain reactions involving neutrons even at this time [...] Szilard showed me copies of some of the patent applications which he made in 1934 and 1935 [...] One of his applications contains the following passage:
> (a) Pure neutron chains, in which the links of the chain are formed by neutrons of the mass number 1 alone. Such chains are only possible in the presence of a metastable element. A metastable element is an element the mass of which (packing

---

172 Leo Szilard and T.A. Chalmers, "Chemical Separation of the Radioactive Element from its Bombarded Isotope in the Fermi Effect," *Nature* 134 (1934), pp. 462–463; "Detection of Neutrons Liberated from Beryllium by Gamma Rays: A New Technique for Inducing Radioactivity," *ibid.*, pp. 494–495; "Radioactivity Induced by Neutrons," *ibid.*, 135 (1935), p. 98; reprinted in Szilard, *Collected Works*, pp. 143–144; 145–146; 149. See also Leo Szilard, "Biographical Notes," n.d. (completed after Szilard's death), Leo Szilard Papers, Box 2, Folder 9.
173 Imperial Chemical Industries Ltd.
174 The Earl of Birkenhead, *The Professor and the Prime Minister* (Cambridge: Riverside Press and Boston: Houghton Mifflin, 1962), p. 108; Wolff, "Frederick Lindemanns Rolle," p. 42.
175 J.H.E. Griffiths and Leo Szilard, "Gamma Rays excited by Capture of Neutrons," *Nature* 139 (1937), pp. 323–324; reprinted in Szilard, *Collected Works*, p. 153.
176 Friedrich A. Paneth to Leo Szilard, July 26, 1935, Nachlass F. A. Paneth, Jewish Refugees Committee, 1933, III. Abt. Rep. 45.

fraction) is sufficiently high to allow its disintegration into parts under liberation of energy. Elements like uranium and thorium are such metastable elements; these two elements reveal their metastable nature by emitting alpha particles. Other elements may be metastable without revealing their nature in this way.[177]

Wigner added that, "[t]hese were certainly almost prophetic words in 1934 or 1935." By 1941, Wigner clearly had reevaluated his earlier unenthusiastic view of Szilard as a physicist.

In the spring of 1934, Szilard filed a British patent that included the concept of a chain reaction that was accepted in 1935, but he then assigned that part under seal to the British Admiralty.[178] Thus, in his own way, he began to wage war against Hitler, attempting to translate his theoretical concepts into practical results, becoming increasingly convinced of the vast potential of theoretical physics for industrial applications. As he wrote to Sir Hugo (later Lord) Hirst (1863–1943), founder of the British General Electric Company, in February 1934:

> I do not yet know for certain if we have got immediate important application for fast electrons, but I do believe that a Company like the General Electric Company would be justified in keeping in close touch with the probably very quick development in this new field.[179]

The following month he commented to Sir Hugo on H.G. Wells's book of 1914, *The World Set Free*, adopting Rutherford's term "moonshine" but speculating that Rutherford's pessimism may be off the mark:

> Of course, all this is moonshine. But I have reason to believe that in so far as the industrial applications of the present discoveries in physics are concerned, the forecast of the writers may prove to be more accurate than the forecast of the scientists. The physicists have conclusive arguments as to why we cannot create at

---

177 Eugene P. Wigner, "Memorandum," April 16, 1941, Leo Szilard Papers, Box 3, Folder 23. The quotation is from Szilard, "Transmutation of chemical elements," p. 615.
178 Szilard, "Transmutation of chemical elements;" Samuel Glasstone to Szilard, November 28, 1956; Szilard to Glasstone, January 15, 1957; Glasstone to Szilard, January 17, 1957; Leo Szilard Papers, Box 8, Folder 23.
179 Szilard (London) to Sir Hugo Hirst, February 21, 1934, Leo Szilard Papers, Box 9, Folder 34.

present new sources of energy for industrial purposes; I am not so sure whether they do not miss the point.[180]

Szilard filed one patent application after another in a wide variety of fields, including ones on a new means for reproducing books (which essentially was the forerunner of microfilm and microfiche),[181] the production of fast protons (including by means of an accelerator), and the production of radioactive elements by bombarding nuclei with fast protons, alpha particles, and neutrons, the last one being "based on a process which recently has been discovered by Fermi."[182]

Szilard also sought financial support to carry out experiments that promised "a good chance of highly significant industrial applications,"[183] including, as he wrote to Enrico Fermi on March 13, 1936, those involving "the practical application of modern nuclear physics, though I am by no means certain that such practical applications of importance at present really exist."[184] He did not wish to "consider these patents as [his] private property and that if they are of any importance, they should be controlled with a view of public policy." Any income derived from them should not be used for private purposes, but for further research or, if the income

---

180 Szilard (London) to Sir Hugo Hirst, March 17, 1934, Leo Szilard Papers, Box 9, Folder 34; published in Spencer R. Weart and Gertrud Weiss Szilard, eds., *Leo Szilard: His Version of the Facts. Selected Recollections and Correspondence* (Cambridge, MA and London: The MIT Press, 1978), p. 38; see also Robert C. Williams and Philip L. Cantelon, eds., *The American Atom. A Documentary History of Nuclear Policies from the Discovery of Fission to the Present 1939–1984* (Philadelphia: University of Pennsylvania Press, 1984), p. 7; H. G. Wells, *The World Set Free* (New York: Dutton, 1914).
181 Szilard to Electric & Musical Industries Limited, 1934–1935, Leo Szilard Papers, Box 7, Folder 30.
182 Szilard (Oxford) to Enrico Fermi, March 13, 1936, Leo Szilard Papers, Box 8, Folder 6.
183 Leo Szilard, "Memorandum of Possible Industrial Applications Arising out of a New Branch of Physics," in Weart and Weiss, eds., *Szilard: His Version*, pp. 39–40; quote on p. 40; see also Williams and Cantelon, *American Atom*, pp. 8–9.
184 Szilard (Oxford) to Enrico Fermi, March 13, 1936, Leo Szilard Papers, Box 8, Folder 6.

was large, for other constructive purposes. He was optimistic that "certain applications of very great importance might materialise in a not too distant future," so he suggested to Fermi that the income should be used to create a fund for paying the salaries of young physicists, for acquiring radium, for further experiments, and for travel expenses to facilitate visits of physicists to different laboratories.

In 1938, around the time of the Munich crisis, Szilard foresaw a general war within two years. In 1960, he recalled that he had told British authorities "that if he could work on war work, he would stay in England. If not, he would emigrate to the U.S." He continued:

> The British wouldn't let any foreigner work on war work, but since uranium was not useful and since non-useful things were not secret, refugees could work on uranium studies. He [I] emphasized that there could not have been a bomb if it hadn't been for British contributions. A memorandum on a subject of a bomb from uranium originating from German refugees in England was brought to the U.S. as part of the British contribution to the Ally [sic] scientific efforts. This is mentioned in the *Smyth Report*. The U.S. has not given due credit to those responsible for this British contribution in its official histories.[185]

When Szilard's fellowship at Oxford ended in 1938, he emigrated to the United States, working without salary at Columbia University in New York beginning in March 1939, "developing certain inventions which are at present considered to be important for national defense."[186]

Politics versus *Science: The Moral Dilemmas of War*

Szilard's relationship with Einstein went back to 1920, his first year in Berlin, or soon thereafter. Einstein had a high opinion of the young Hungarian, whom he considered to be a "fine and clever man who is

---

185 Leo Szilard, "Biographical Information," February 22, 1960, p. 5; University of Chicago, Office of Public Relations.
186 Statement Attached to Selective Service Questionnaire of Leo Szilard Order No. 10322, Local Board No. 36, New York, New York, Leo Szilard Papers, Box 1, Folder 27.

ordinarily not given to illusions. Like many people of that type, he may be inclined to exaggerate the significance of reason in human affairs."[187] In 1931, Szilard asked Einstein for a letter in support of his application for a U.S. visa, drafting a few sentences for Einstein's signature. Einstein changed Szilard's modest wording from "he has been well known to me [*persönlich gut bekannt*] for many years of joint work" to "he is closely associated [*eng verbunden*] with me...," adding that he had "a direct interest" in Szilard's journey to America.[188] In October 1931, Einstein also supported the granting of a nonquota immigrant visa to Szilard.[189]

Szilard thus was in a unique position in 1939 to call on Einstein, the most famous Nobel Laureate in the world, to alert President Franklin D. Roosevelt to recent developments in nuclear physics. The first, undated draft of Einstein's famous letter to Roosevelt of August 2, 1939, pointing out the need for funds to carry out research on the nuclear-chain reaction which could lead to the construction of extremely powerful bombs, mentioned Wigner as the prime mover behind it, but from Szilard's correspondence with Einstein through October 1939 we know that Szilard worked closely with Wigner in this effort.[190] Moreover, since both Eugene Wigner and Edward Teller drove Szilard on subsequent occasions to Einstein's

---

187 Einstein to H. M. Brailsford, April 24, 1930, Leo Szilard Papers, Box 7, Folder 27; translated in Otto Nathan and Heinz Norden, eds., *Einstein on Peace* (New York: Simon and Schuster, 1960), pp. 103–104.
188 Szilard (Berlin) to Einstein, June 30, 1931, Leo Szilard Papers, Box 7, Folder 27.
189 Einstein (Caputh bei Potsdam) to U.S. Consulate General in Berlin, October 24, 1931, Szilard Papers, Box 27, Folder 5.
190 Einstein (Peconic, Long Island) to F. D. Roosevelt, n.d. [1939], Leo Szilard Papers, Box 7, Folder 27; Einstein (Peconic, Long Island) to F. D. Roosevelt, August 2, 1939, Archiv zur Geschichte der Max-Planck-Gesellschaft, Berlin-Dahlem, Va Abt., Rep. 2; published for instance in Morton Grodzins and Eugene Rabinowitch, eds., *The Atomic Age: Scientists in National and World Affairs* (New York and London: Basic Books, 1963), pp. 11–12; Nathan and Norden, eds., *Einstein on Peace*, pp. 294–296; Daniel J. Boorstin, ed., *An American Primer* (New York: Mentor Books, 1968), pp. 882–887; Williams and Cantelon, eds., *American Atom*, pp. 12–14. Szilard is quoted on his drafting of the letter and his trip with Wigner to Einstein on Long Island in Weart and Weiss, eds., *Szilard: His Version*, pp. 82–84; Teller mentions only Szilard as his passenger; see Edward Teller, with Judith L. Shoolery, *Memoirs:*

vacation cottage on Long Island, New York, to secure his signature, this effort was indeed a joint Hungarian initiative.[191] These Hungarian refugees, in fact, proved more effective than recent Italian Nobel Laureate Enrico Fermi, who had approached the U.S. Navy Department in March 1939 for funds but was dismissed as a "crazy wop."[192] The Hungarians may have learned from Fermi's failure and saw Einstein as the only possible scientist who could gain the ear of the president. Even so, it took two and a half months before the economist Alexander Sachs, who was known to have close ties to Roosevelt, felt free to deliver Einstein's letter by hand to him,[193] a telling example of the status and image of scientists in America at this time. Refugees from Hitler's Germany, however, knew full well that the Nazis would use every means at their disposal to further their war aims, and these three Hungarian refugee scientists in particular, with their experiences during World War I, the Hungarian revolutions and counter-revolution of 1918–1920, and the Weimar period in Germany, had ample reasons for concern. They also were politically astute, finding and exploiting effective channels of power in the United States.

Two weeks after Einstein signed the letter to Roosevelt, Szilard wrote to the famous American aviator Charles Lindbergh, attaching a letter of support from Einstein,[194] trying to enlist Lindbergh's aid in securing governmental funds for purchasing the tons—not pounds—of uranium needed to sustain a nuclear-chain reaction. In the middle of September 1939, Szilard was feverishly working on plans for experiments "on an

---

A Twentieth-Century Journey in Science and Politics (Cambridge, MA: Perseus Publishing, 2001), pp. 145–147.

[191] István Hargittai, *The Martians of Science: Five Physicists Who Changed the Twentieth Century* (Oxford: Oxford University Press, 2006), pp. 98–99.

[192] Quoted in Donald Fleming, "Albert Einstein's Letter to Franklin D. Roosevelt, 1939," in Boorstin, ed., *American Primer*, p. 884.

[193] Szilard reports this in a letter to Einstein, October 17, 1939, Leo Szilard Papers, Box 7, Folder 27; published and translated in Weart and Weiss, eds., *Szilard: His Version*, pp. 107–109.

[194] Szilard to Charles Lindbergh, August 16, 1939, Leo Szilard Papers, Box 12, Folder 5; published in Weart and Weiss, eds., *Szilard: His Version*, pp. 99–100; Einstein's letter is not published here.

almost industrial scale [...]"[195] He also used the cyclotron at the University of Rochester to continue earlier studies on indium, which led to his and his colleagues' discovery of radioactivity induced by nuclear excitation.[196] Then, working with Walter Zinn at Columbia University, he joined the increasing number of scientists studying the emission of neutrons in nuclear fission to determine if "a chain reaction can in fact be sustained in a system containing uranium."[197] In July 1939, he had concluded that it probably would be self-sustaining in a graphite-uranium system, a conclusion he reported in a paper to the *Physical Review* on February 14, 1940.[198] Since, however, this was vital information that could be used by physicists in Nazi Germany, he "spent six months of hard work getting the Government to ask him to withhold his paper which [...] he wanted to withhold." Publication, in fact, was deferred indefinitely "at the request of the U.S. Government."[199]

In late 1940, Szilard worked with the National Defense Research Committee at Columbia University, and in February 1942, Arthur H. Compton (1892–1962), who was in charge of work on the chain reaction at the University of Chicago and organized the Metallurgical Laboratory (Met Lab) there, placed Szilard in charge of the supply of materials as a member of Fermi's group.[200] Just as Szilard was convinced that he should not publish his research on the chain reaction, he was deeply reluctant to

---

195   Szilard to Gano Dunn, September 13, 1939, Leo Szilard Papers, Box 7, Folder 21.
196   M. Goldhaber, R. D. Hill, and Leo Szilard, "Radioactivity Induced by Nuclear Excitation. I. Excitation by Neutrons," *Physical Review* 55 (1939), 47–49; reprinted in *Collected Works*, pp. 155–157.
197   Szilard "Biographical Data," p. 6.
198   Leo Szilard, "Divergent Chain Reactions in Systems Composed of Uranium and Carbon" reprinted in *Collected Works*, pp. 216–256.
199   Szilard to John T. Tate, February 6 and 14, 1940; John T. Tate to Leo Szilard, February 14, 1940; Madeline M. Mitchell to Leo Szilard, February 14, 1940, Leo Szilard Papers, Box 7, Folder 21.
200   Leo Szilard, "Biographical Information;" see also Richard G. Hewlett and Oscar E. Anderson, Jr., *A History of the United States Atomic Energy Commission*. Vol. I. *The New World, 1939/1946* (University Park: Pennsylvania State University Press, 1962), p. 56.

Problem Solving and the U.S. War Effort

make money from patents related to a new weapon of mass destruction to be used against Germany and Japan. His reluctance vanished only after he concluded at the end of 1942, during the course of the battle of Stalingrad, "that we may win the war by ordinary methods within a couple of years." The new weapon probably would not be ready before the end of the War, mainly "due to the diffusion of responsibility [for its development] [...] and perhaps to a lesser extent, also to the general attitude [of the military] towards the creative scientist."[201] In early 1943, therefore, he decided to file patent applications on his basic inventions.

The resulting negotiations with the government compelled him not to file patent applications on the inventions he had made prior to November 1940, when he was first employed at Columbia University. Ultimately, in August 1943, he was given the choice either of losing his job at Chicago or of assigning to the government "any and all inventions, discoveries, methods and ideas relating to nuclear fission, which are not covered by issued patents or abandoned patent applications."[202] He chose to retain his job and to sign an agreement conferring to the U.S. Government the rights to all of his inventions in the field of nuclear fission. That was a decision of conscience. As he had explained to General Leslie R. Groves on December 3, 1943, and eight days later reported to Compton: [we were,] "rightly or wrongly, convinced that the Germans have caught up with us in this work, and that in this situation I do not wish to leave the project."[203] On December 19, 1944, Szilard and Fermi then filed a patent on the chain reaction in uranium, which had first been achieved at Chicago on December 2, 1942; they assigned it to the U.S. Atomic Energy Commission in 1955.[204]

---

201 Szilard to A.H. Compton, December 3, 1942, Leo Szilard Papers, Box 6, Folder 29.
202 Szilard to Arthur H. Compton, August 9, 1943; see also December 29, 1942, January 13, 1943, April 20, 1943, May 7, 1943, July 20, 1943, August 4, 5, 6, 7, 19, 1943; November 19, 20, 1943, December 11, 15, 1943, n.d. [1943]; Compton to Szilard, August 4, 1943, March 26, 1943, Leo Szilard Papers, Box 6, Folders 29–30.
203 Szilard to A. H. Compton, December 11, 1943, Leo Szilard Papers, Box 6, Folder 29.
204 Enrico Fermi and Leo Szilard, "Neutronic Reactor," U.S. Patent 2,708,656; published in Szilard, *Collected Works*, pp. 691–696. See also Szilard, "Biographical Data,"

Figure 20. Leo Szilard, nuclear scientist, 1960s (HNM).

Admiral Harold G. Bowen, Director of the Naval Research Laboratory in Washington, DC, suggested during a meeting at the U.S. National Bureau of Standards on April 27, 1940, that scientists should withhold information on uranium fission voluntarily but that the government would do nothing to force them to do so.[205] The German invasion of the Netherlands, Belgium and Luxemburg two weeks later, on May 10, 1940, however, brought about "a noticeable change in attitude" on this issue, as was manifest in letters that Szilard received from colleagues. He was committed to finding "a satisfactory substitute in the form of some private publication," but at the same time he also was committed to the intellectual openness characteristic of "the great democracies."[206]

Nonetheless, from the outset, Szilard played an important role in persuading his colleagues and the U.S. Government of the importance of maintaining secrecy about work on the chain reaction. As early as March 1939, he had tried unsuccessfully to persuade Fermi to withhold publication of their observations on the number of neutrons emitted in the fissioning of uranium, and he tried to convince Frédéric Joliot-Curie (1900–1958) at the Collège de France in Paris to do the same. Victor Weisskopf (1908–2002) made a similar plea to Patrick Blackett (1897–1974) in Manchester, and Wigner wrote to Paul Dirac (1902–1984) in Cambridge urging him to support Blackett in not publishing his work on fission. The British reaction was positive, but Joliot-Curie refused to cooperate and in April 1939 published his and his team's results on the number of neutrons emitted in the fissioning of uranium. After the German invasion of Poland on September 1, 1939, however, Joliot-Curie

pp. 6–7, and Henry DeWolf Smyth, *Atomic Energy for Military Purposes* (Princeton: Princeton University Press, 1945), p. 34.
205 Spencer R. Weart, "Scientists with a secret," *Physics Today* 29 (February 1976), 29; Szilard (New York) to Admiral Bowen, May 30, 1940, Leo Szilard Papers, Box 4, Folder 20.
206 Szilard (New York) to Gregory Breit, July 3, 1940, Leo Szilard Papers, Box 5, Folder 6; Leo Szilard, "Attempts at Secrecy from March 1939 to June 1940," November 4, 1942, Szilard Papers, Box 6, Folder 30. For a full account, see Weart, "Scientists," pp. 23–30.

became convinced of the necessity of withholding publications and in late October deposited a sealed envelope with the Académie des Sciences containing an explanation of the principle of nuclear reactors. In the United States, after further efforts by Szilard and others, Gregory Breit (1899–1981) of the University of Wisconsin played a leading role in June 1940 in formulating a general policy on self-censorship of publications about nuclear fission.

Szilard's plea for secrecy backfired: he became a victim of his own initiatives and in the eyes of General Groves, a liability to the Manhattan Project because he, like many other scientists, opposed Groves's policy of "compartmentalization of information." Szilard recalled a telling example of the negative effects of that policy following a conversation with his Hungarian friend Edward Teller (1908–2003) in the summer of 1942:

> Upon Teller's return from the summer conference in Berkeley, I went to see him and asked him whether this point had been considered and whether, in view of this fact, it would not be wise to put more emphasis in autocatalytic methods of explosion which I had discussed with him in the past. Teller replied that he personally is placing considerable emphasis on the autocatalytic method, but that the group did not consider it as important. Teller, as you know, is an old friend of mine and I found him occasionally embarrassed when I tried to discuss with him things which he did not feel free to discuss with me. For this reason I interpreted his reply as meaning that the situation was well in hand, and that there was no need for us to discuss it. Consequently, I changed the subject of our conversation and did nothing further in the matter. Teller, on the other hand, as it now turns out, interpreted my changing of the subject as meaning that I was going to look into this question, and that it was not necessary for him to do anything about it.[207]

Szilard felt that compartmentalization had, "in fact, crippled this work from its very beginning," declaring that:

> we have compartmentalization of information, like in secret societies, but unlike as in secret societies, we do not have a group in the center who knows everything, but rather a group who knows very little. Consequently, we have no sound mechanism

---

207 Szilard to A. H. Compton, November 25, 1942, Leo Szilard Papers, Box 6, Folder 30; published in Weart and Weiss Szilard, eds., *Szilard: His Version*, pp. 160–161.

Figure 21. Edward Teller visiting the Lutheran *Gimnázium*, 1991 (School History Collection, Lutheran *Gimnázium* in the *Fasor*, Budapest).

for reaching decisions and decisions are taken which most of us know to be wrong and which frequently lead to a loss of from four to eight months.[208]

Even "Professor [Harold C.] Urey [1893–1980] is pushed around by General Groves' office," which ironically and nonsensically cut him off from reports relating to his own discovery of heavy water, and which Szilard saw as "part of the general [military] attitude towards the creative scientists." He voiced his concern repeatedly and emphatically to Vannevar Bush (1890–1974), Director of the Office of Scientific Research and Development,[209] arguing that compartmentalization generated mistrust and impeded progress in producing the bomb. Like other leading scientists who worked on the Manhattan Project, Szilard erred in thinking that he, and scientists in general, could control the military and political uses of their work.

Another of Szilard's concerns was that intelligence should be gathered on nuclear research being carried out in Germany. Having lived in Germany for over a decade, he believed he knew German psychology sufficiently well to predict that after the German defeat at Stalingrad in the winter of 1942–1943, they might try to win the War by other means. In a characteristic blend of science, politics, and confidence in his ability to influence events, he sent a letter, with the permission of the U.S. Government, on August 18, 1944, to Lord Cherwell (Frederick A. Lindemann), Prime Minister Winston S. Churchill's Scientific Advisor, whom he knew from his Oxford days, suggesting that German industrial installations capable of producing a nuclear bomb should be identified and

---

208 Szilard to Vannevar Bush, n.d.; Szilard to Vannevar Bush, August 11, 1943, Leo Szilard Papers, Box 5, Folder 21.
209 Szilard to Vannevar Bush, January 10, 1943, n.d., August 11, 1943, December 13, 1943, January 14, 1944; Szilard Papers, Box 5, Folder 21; last letter published in Weart and Weiss Szilard, eds., *Szilard: His Version*, pp. 161–163. See also L. Szilard, "Rough Draft of Proposed Conversation with Dr Bush," February 28, 1944, Leo Szilard Papers, Box 5, Folder 21; published in Weart and Weiss Szilard, eds., *Szilard: His Version*, pp. 164–179.

destroyed.[210] Fully aware of Cherwell's long-standing close association with Churchill, Szilard drew Cherwell's attention to private communications he had received from Switzerland in 1942 indicating that the Germans knew how to produce a chain reaction, concluding that "they must have gone *full scale* into this work soon after Stalingrad at the latest." He argued that British Military Intelligence should augment the routine methods of its agents for gathering information by equipping them with questions devised by physicists "with great care and circumspection." For this purpose, a small group of physicists should be organized under Churchill or Cherwell who would liaise with British Military Intelligence. Through Cherwell, Szilard also alerted the British War Cabinet to the potential detonation of "a small atomic bomb" on a German city should nuclear materials be found to be manufactured there. With chilling precision, he went into detail estimating the radii of destruction of atomic bombs, depending on their sizes and efficiencies, and urging that some first-class British theoretical physicist should be consulted on these questions. "My writing to you may be a breach of etiquette from the official point of view," Szilard concluded, "but as I see it, something more important than etiquette is at present involved." Though well-informed as usual, Szilard could not know that he had overestimated the progress of German nuclear research at this time.[211]

---

210 Szilard (Chicago) to Lord Cherwell, August 18, 1944, Leo Szilard Papers, Box 5, Folder 22; published in Weart and Weiss Szilard, *Szilard: His Version*, pp. 192–196.
211 On German nuclear research, see, for example, Mark Walker, *German National Socialism and the quest for nuclear power 1939–1949* (Cambridge: Cambridge University Press, 1989); Mark Walker, *Nazi Science: Myth, Truth, and the German Atomic Bomb* (New York and London: Plenum Press, 1995); Geoffrey Brooks, *Hitler's Nuclear Weapons: The Development and Attempted Deployment of Radiological Armaments by Nazi Germany* (London: Leo Cooper, 1992); Thomas Powers, *Heisenberg's War* (New York: Alfred Knopf, 1993); Dieter Hoffmann, Hg., *Operation Epsilon: Die Farm-Hall-Protokolle oder die Angst der Alliierten vor der deutschen Atombombe* (Berlin: Rowohlt, 1993).

Science versus Politics: The Moral Dilemmas of Peace

By the spring of 1945, Szilard had convinced himself that the bomb should not be used. He knew that the defeat of Germany was imminent, which obviated the original motivation for creating the Manhattan Project, and that the use of the bomb on Japan would harm the peace process. Ever eager for a cause, he thus decided to alert President Roosevelt in a memorandum to the dangers of a nuclear-arms race, and again asked Einstein for a letter of support for it, which Einstein promptly provided, writing to Roosevelt on March 25, 1945, that Szilard was "greatly concerned about the lack of adequate contact between scientists who are doing this work and those members of your Cabinet who are responsible for formulating policy."[212] In his memorandum, Szilard called for the establishment of an international system of controls to avoid an arms race. He apparently gained an appointment with Roosevelt for April 12, the very day on which Roosevelt died. Szilard then modified his memorandum and sent it along with Einstein's letter to President Harry S. Truman on May 25, 1945, who in turn passed it on to his future Secretary of State James F. Byrnes. Together with Urey, Szilard visited Byrnes at his home in South Carolina on May 28, 1945.

Szilard and Urey tried to persuade Byrnes that an arms race between the United States and the Soviet Union could only be averted if post-War control of atomic energy were not maintained as a U.S. monopoly but rather vested in an international organization. In his memorandum, Szilard warned prophetically that the "competition between the United States and Russia [...] would lead to a rapid accumulation of vast quantities of atomic bombs in both countries," and he noted "the possibility of the outbreak of *a preventive war* ... [that] might be the outcome of the fear that the other country might strike first and no amount of good will

---

[212] Einstein (Princeton) to Roosevelt, March 25, 1945; Leo Szilard, "Enclosure to Mr. Albert Einstein's Letter of March 25, 1945 to the President of the United States," Leo Szilard Papers, Box 7, Folder 27; published in Weart and Weiss Szilard, eds., *Szilard: His Version*, pp. 205–207. See also Szilard to Truman, May 25, 1945, published in *ibid.*, p. 208.

Problem Solving and the U.S. War Effort 417

on the part of both nations might be sufficient to prevent. [...]"[213] Szilard thus suggested the establishment of "a tight control on the atomic power development by a reciprocal agreement with Great Britain and Russia and extended to all territories of the world. [...]"

Byrnes rejected Szilard's arguments completely. He believed that the Soviet Union had no uranium deposits and hence would require many years to make a bomb, enough time for the United States to create its own world order. Byrnes and the Truman Administration believed that American military power, rather than American diplomacy, would keep the Soviets in check.[214] Szilard's failure to convince Byrnes of his arguments was both a tremendous disappointment for him and a cause for alarm. He sensed, for the first time, that control of the bomb was slipping away from the scientists who had created it. Geochemist Harrison S. Brown (1917–1986) commented gravely: "If he [Szilard] had been taken as seriously by Mr. Byrnes as he had been taken seriously by Mr. Roosevelt more than five years previously, the whole course of history might have been altered."[215]

In June 1945, Szilard became one of only seven signers of the Franck Report,[216] and in July he circulated a draft of a petition to President Truman urging him:

> that before this weapon be used, without restriction in the present conflict, its powers should be adequately described and demonstrated, and the Japanese nation should be given the opportunity to consider the further refusal to surrender. We

---

213 Szilard, "Atomic Bombs and the Post-War Position of the United States in the World," Leo Szilard Papers, Box 10, Folder 9.
214 Nicholas and Robert Halász, "The Reluctant Father of the Atom Bomb," *The New Hungarian Quarterly* 15 (1974), 167–168.
215 Quoted in Robert Jungk, *Brighter than a Thousand Suns. A Personal History of the Atomic Scientists* (San Diego, New York, London: Harcourt Brace Jovanovich, 1958), p. 180.
216 James Franck, Donald J. Hughes, J. J. Nickson, Eugene Rabinowitch, Glenn T. Seaborg, Joyce C. Stearns, and Leo Szilard, "A Report to the Secretary of War," in Grodzins and Rabinowitch, eds., *Atomic Age*, pp. 19–27.

feel that this course of action will heighten the effectiveness of the weapon in this war and will be a tremendous effect in the prevention of future wars.[217]

Szilard garnered the signatures of 67 Chicago scientists in support of his petition and on July 19 transmitted it to Arthur H. Compton, asking him to forward it to Truman through the War Department, which Compton did on July 24.[218] In his cover letter to Compton, Szilard commented that:

> Some of those who signed the petition undoubtedly fear that the use of atomic bombs at this time would precipitate an armament race with Russia [...] Others are more inclined to think that if we withhold such a demonstration we will cause distrust on the part of other nations and are, therefore, in favor of an early demonstration.[219]

Compton, in turn, in his letter of transmittal, said that Szilard had modified his position and now approved of the "use of the weapons after giving suitable warning and opportunity for surrender under known conditions." Compton also noted that he had asked chemist Farrington Daniels (1889–1972), Director of the Met Lab, to conduct an opinion poll on Szilard's petition, which Daniels had done on July 12 and had received replies from 150 members of the Met Lab who were asked to choose among the following five options:

---

217 Szilard, "To the President of the United States," n.d. [July 1945], Leo Szilard Papers, Box 6, Folder 29; the final version, dated July 17, 1945, is published in Weart and Weiss Szilard, eds., *Szilard: His Version*, pp. 211–212.
218 Szilard to Compton, July 19, 1945; Compton to Colonel K. D. Nichols, July 24, 1945, Szilard Papers, Box 6, Folder 29; Compton to Colonel K. D. Nichols, July 24, 1945; published in Weart and Weiss Szilard, eds., *Szilard: His Version*, pp. 214–215; Farrington Daniels (Chicago) to A. H. Compton, July 13, 1945, *ibid.*, Leo Szilard Papers, Box 7, Folder 5; see also Arthur Holly Compton, *Atomic Quest: A Personal Narrative* (New York: Oxford University Press, 1956), pp. 242–244.
219 Szilard to Compton, July 19, 1945, in Weart and Weiss Szilard, eds., *Szilard: His Version*, p. 214.

(1) Use the weapons in the manner that is from the military point of view most effective in bringing about prompt Japanese surrender at minimum human cost to our armed forces.
(2) Give a military demonstration in Japan, to be followed by a renewed opportunity for surrender before full use of the weapons is employed.
(3) Give an experimental demonstration in this country, with representatives of Japan present; followed by a new opportunity for surrender before full use of the weapons is employed.
(4) Withhold military use of the weapons, but make public experimental demonstration of their effectiveness.
(5) Maintain as secret as possible all developments of our new weapons, and refrain from using them in this war.[220]

The result was that 46% of the respondents chose the second option. By then, however, the Scientific Panel of the Secretary of War's Interim Advisory Committee already had expressed its opinion "that military use of such weapons should be made in the Japanese War."[221]

Szilard's action became so well known in the United States that he appeared under the pseudonym "Szigny" in Nobel Laureate Pearl S. Buck's novel of 1959, *Command the Morning*, as the scientist who organized the protest against dropping the bomb and embodied the moral dilemma of a scientist who had irretrievably released the genie from its bottle.[222] "Szigny"—pursuing a lost cause—thought that Japan was "already on her knees" and that "we need not to use the bomb."

Farrington Daniels reported at the end of January 1946 that Szilard stated that his "mind [was] so occupied with the social and political implications of the bomb and with the affairs in Washington that he has

---

220 Farrington Daniels (Chicago) to A. H. Compton, July 13, 1945, Leo Szilard Papers, Box 7, Folder 5; see also Compton, *Atomic Quest*, pp. 242–244.
221 Compton to Nichols, July 24, 1945, in Weart and Weiss Szilard, eds., *Szilard: His Version*, p. 215.
222 Pearl S. Buck, *Command the Morning* (New York: John Day Co., 1959), pp. 272–281; quote on p. 281.

found it difficult to give his proper attention to the scientific work of the Metallurgical Laboratory."[223] By then, Szilard was fully confronted with the burden of conflict between his success as a scientist and his failure as a world citizen. As a scientist, he had worked for years on a project that had caused devastation on an unprecedented scale; as a citizen, he had done everything in his power to prevent this tragedy. He now had to live with the greatest problem in his life: to seek redemption and battle the weapon he had helped to create. He spent the rest of his life doing so.

Immediately after the War, Szilard became a leader in the scientists' movement to wrest control of nuclear energy from the military and place it into the hands of a civilian authority.[224] This, and his earlier opposition to the use of the bomb, incurred the wrath of General Groves, who reportedly said:

> You know he wouldn't be allowed to serve in the project if the pending legislation [the May-Johnson Bill] goes through. In the last war he served in the German Army—or rather in the Austrian Army. Anyway after the war he studied—didn't teach, or so to speak ever earn his way. Just a kind of [...] "research assistant." Went to Germany. Did some more studying there—always with people, kind of an assistant you know. He left Germany in 1933. I don't think because he was Jewish, they hadn't really done anything against the Jews yet. In this country he was at Columbia, here and there, never teaching, never did anything really you might say but learn. Everywhere he went from what I hear he was hard to work with. The

---

223 Farrington Daniels to Wayne W. Johnson, January 31, 1946, Leo Szilard Papers, Box 7, Folder 5.
224 Alice K. Smith, *A Peril and a Hope: The Scientist's Movement in America, 1945–1947* (Chicago: University of Chicago Press, 1968); see also Robert Gilpin, *American Scientists and Nuclear Policy* (Princeton: Princeton University Press, 1962); Barton J. Bernstein, "Four Physicists and the Bomb: The Early Years, 1945–1950," *Historical Studies in the Physical and Biological Sciences* 18 (1988), pp. 231–263; Lawrence Badash, *Scientists and the Development of Nuclear Weapons: From Fission to the Limited Test Ban Treaty 1939–1963* (New York: Humanities Press, 1995); and Mary Jo Nye, "A Physicist in the Corridors of Power: P. M. S. Blackett's Opposition to Atomic Weapons Following the War," *Physics in Perspective* 1 (1999), pp. 136–156.

kind of man that any employer would have fired as a troublemaker—in the days before the Wagner Act [the National Labor Relations Act of 1935].[225]

Groves even criticized Szilard's role in convincing Einstein to sign his famous letter to Roosevelt in 1939: "Only a man with his brass would have pushed through to the President. Take Wigner or Fermi—they're not Jewish—they are quiet, shy, modest, just interested in learning."[226] Then, concerned that he might appear anti-Semitic, Groves added: "I don't like certain Jews and I don't like certain well-known characteristics but I'm not prejudiced."[227]

Still, Groves evidently hated Szilard, who to him was an uncontrollable civilian who exhibited a repulsive intellectual superiority, even though he acknowledged his resourcefulness in a backhanded way by admitting,

> of course, most of his ideas are bad, but he has so many [...] You know no firm wants him for a consultant. Why he's the kind of guy that advises a company one way and they're half way through that, says, "No, let's try this way." Of course, *he* isn't paying the bills![228]

Leonard Lyons reported in *The New York Post* on May 7, 1946, that:

---

225 Frances Henderson to Don Bermingham, March 8, 1946, Leo Szilard Papers, Box 9, Folder 11. The Wagner Act, sponsored by Robert F. Wagner (Democrat-New York) and officially called the National Labor Relations Act of 1935, was enacted by Congress to forbid employers to interfere with the organization of labor unions.
226 Quoted in *ibid*. See also Lanouette, *Genius*, pp. 237–242, 248–249, 253–255, 262–269, 271, 273–275, 305–313. For Groves's relationship to scientists see Stanley Goldberg, "Der Endspurt: Zu den Hintergründen der Entscheidung für den Bombenabwurf auf Hiroshima und Nagasaki," *Physikalische Blätter* 51 (September 1995), 828–830.
227 The prejudiced nature of Groves's attitude towards Szilard by presenting Wigner as a non-Jew is pointed out in Palló, "A kívülálló: Leó Szilárd," p. 338.
228 Quoted in Henderson to Bermingham, March 8, 1946, Leo Szilard Papers, Box 9, Folder 11.

Maj. Gen. Groves, head of the Atomic Bomb project, in his private discussions of the Army-sponsored bill and of the opposition to it by the scientists, makes no secret of his dislike for Dr. Szilard, who first alerted Roosevelt to the potential impact of the bomb. If the Army bill passes, Szilard—because he was born in Hungary, and served in the German Army in the first World War—wouldn't be allowed to work on the project. [...][229]

Groves's dislike of Szilard was largely responsible for Szilard's inability to continue as an atomic scientist after 1945. Thus, Farrington Daniels reported to Szilard that the U.S. Army Corps of Engineers had asked Daniels "not to offer you a position in the new Laboratory."[230] Daniels, however, clearly did not share Groves's low opinion of Szilard, since he went on to praise him for his "very valuable contributions to its success." Daniels continued, in words that almost seem like a citation for a national award:

> Your foresight and initiative were largely responsible for obtaining support for the original atomic energy program, and your work on piles and your vision for new types of piles have been important in the development of the research program of the Laboratory. You have made important contributions to the patent structure of the Manhattan District, and you have been vigorous in pointing out the political and social implications of the atomic bomb.[231]

Daniels's subsequent correspondence with Szilard makes clear that he dismissed Szilard from the Met Lab in mid-1946 with uneasiness and a bad conscience.

Szilard had jeopardized his position at the Met Lab by attempting a few weeks after Hiroshima to secure the declassification of his petition with its 67 signatories.[232] Groves had opposed Szilard's attempt, assert-

---

229 Quoted in Szilard (Chicago) to Farrington Daniels, May 9, 1946, Leo Szilard Papers, Box 7, Folder 5.
230 Farrington Daniels to Szilard, May 10, 1946, Leo Szilard Papers, Box 7, Folder 5.
231 *Ibid.*; see also Farrington Daniels to Szilard, May 10 and 15, 1946; Farrington Daniels and Wayne W. Johnson to Szilard, June 1, 1946, Leo Szilard Papers, Box 7, Folder 5.
232 James S. Murray to Szilard, August 27, 1945; August 28, 1945; Szilard to Robert M. Hutchins, August 30, 1945; published in Weart and Weiss Szilard, eds., *Szilard:*

ing that declassification without the approval of the Manhattan District would violate the contract that Szilard had signed on his employment. Szilard thus publicized his opposition to the bomb by other means after his dismissal from the Met Lab. In 1947, he called for a crusade in the *Bulletin of the Atomic Scientists* to support "a bold and constructive solution" to the threat of nuclear weapons.[233] That fall, he realized that such a solution would require the cooperation of the Soviet Union, so he drafted a "Letter to Stalin" in which he expressed deep concern about "the steady deterioration of Russian-American relations," and on October 25, 1947, in accordance with the Logan Act of 1799,[234] requested the permission of the U.S. Government through the Attorney General to send it. He soon lost hope of receiving a favorable reply, so instead of sending his letter to Stalin, he submitted it to the *Bulletin* on November 10 for publication.[235]

Characteristically, Szilard began his letter by identifying the problem to be solved—the lack of an international agreement on nuclear weapons and the concomitant threat of a new and devastating war. Recalling his own experiences during the Great War, he compared the potential confrontation of the two emerging superpowers to the confrontation of two enemy patrols, and suggested that to avoid it, Stalin should speak directly to the American people every month, just as the American president should address the Soviet people directly every month. He invited

---

His Version, pp. 216–222; for the original of the last letter, see Leo Szilard Papers, Box 10, Folder 9.

233 Leo Szilard, "Calling for a Crusade," *Bull. Atom. Sci.* 3 (April–May 1947), pp. 102–106, 125; reprinted in Hawkins, Greb, and Weiss Szilard, eds., *Livable World*, pp. 7–20.

234 The Logan Act forbid American citizens to communicate with foreign governments without the permission of the U.S. Government "with an intent to influence the measures or conduct of any foreign government or of any officer or agent thereof, in relation to any disputes or controversies with the United States..." See Criminal Code, Section 5, amended, R.S. §5335 from Act January 30, 1799, c. 1, 1 Stat. 613.

235 Szilard to the Attorney General, October 25, 1947; Szilard, "A Letter to Stalin," Manuscript, November 10, 1947; Szilard to Robert M. Hutchins, November 11, 1947, Leo Szilard Papers, Box 10, Folder 9; Szilard, "Letter," pp. 26–32.

Stalin to discuss "the framework of a post-War reconstruction of the world," and to convince the American people that "private enterprise and the Russian economic system and also mixed forms of economic organization can flourish side by side; that Russia and the United States can be part of the same world; that 'one world' need not necessarily be a uniform world." He was convinced that unless the American people and the Soviet people understood this clearly, the world was headed toward war. He tried to convince Stalin that by overcoming the difficulties of communications, a people's diplomacy might be initiated, and he offered to form a group of American citizens who could freely discuss "the issues which face the world today."[236]

Szilard's naïve initiative was inevitably doomed to failure, but that did not discourage him. He continued to believe that conditions could be created under which the Soviet Union would have strong incentives to cooperate with the United States to alleviate the nuclear threat in Western Europe. Thus, in April 1948, he proposed that an international body be established to monitor Soviet-American relations, and suggested that the American government could make "many concessions to Russia along the lines of general disarmament, which would alleviate Russia's fears of being attacked. [...]"[237] In that election year of 1948, he went on to criticize the Truman Administration, which

> instead of showing concern for the welfare of Russia, approached Russia as a potential enemy. If the new Administration were to approach Russia in different spirit, if it were to approach her as a potential friend [...] showing willingness to create a situation in which Russia would have an important stake in the economic reconstruction of Europe, indicating the determination to build up an organized world community of which Russia would be an important part, then the new approach might have some chance meeting with a favorable Russian response, and of leading to a stable peace.[238]

---

236 Szilard, "Letter," pp. 29, 32.
237 Szilard to Robert M. Hutchins, April 19, 1948, Leo Szilard Papers, Box 10, Folder 9.
238 *Ibid.*

Throughout the rest of his life, Szilard continued to advocate that the best way to prevent another World War was through direct communication with the Russians. In September 1949, Szilard warned that "we should stop underestimating the Russians."[239]

Toward an Atomic Stalemate

Throughout the 1950s and early 1960s, Szilard became involved in an impressive number of political organizations at the national and international levels. His efforts to achieve civilian control of atomic energy grew into a more general commitment to abolish war by creating a lasting peace. He played an active role in a wide variety of movements, such as the Scientists for Survival, the Emergency Committee of Atomic Scientists, the Council of Inquiry into the Conditions of Peace, the Movement for Abolishing War, the Campaign for World Government, and the Alliance for Progress.

These numerous activities revealed Szilard at his best. To him, the problem of world security was the major problem he felt compelled to tackle in the post-War era and, as always, he appealed to his friend Einstein for letters of support, which Einstein provided to the end of his life.[240] Szilard continued to try to bridge the gap between the United States and the Soviet Union as a self-appointed ambassador-at-large, tirelessly attending meetings to discuss the international political implications of the bomb. He attended, for instance, almost all of the Pugwash Conferences,[241] sponsored by the Cleveland industrialist Cyrus Eaton (1883–1979), and took their inspiration from a speech that Lord Bertrand Russell (1872–1970) delivered in the House of Lords on November 28, 1945, less than

---

239 Szilard, "Biographical Information."
240 Einstein to Jawaharlal Nehru, April 6, 1955, Leo Szilard Papers, Box 7, Folder 27.
241 Joseph Rotblat, *Pugwash—the First Ten Years: History of the Conferences of Science and World Affairs* (New York: Humanities Press, 1968); Joseph Rotblat, *Scientists in the Quest for Peace: A History of the Pugwash Conferences* (Cambridge, MA and London: The MIT Press, 1972).

two months after Hiroshima and Nagasaki. During the second Pugwash Conference at Lac Beauport, Quebec, Canada, from March 31 to April 11, 1958,[242] the American participants raised the problem of international security posed by the bomb and drafted a memorandum that was sent to Alexander Vasilevich Topchiev (1907–1962), Vice President (as of 1958) of the Soviet Academy of Sciences. They urged Soviet scientists to discuss this issue with American scientists,

> who are familiar with the technology of modern weapons and who, by virtue of their relationship to the United States government, are in a position to communicate their own thinking to the government, but who are not, themselves, officials of the United States government.[243]

This described Szilard's position precisely and the role he hoped to play in it.

By that time Szilard had come to believe that the major problem the two superpowers faced was not nuclear disarmament but rather the maintenance of a stalemate between their strategic bombing forces; it seemed impossible to him that a disarmament agreement could be reached in the foreseeable future that would eliminate atomic bombs, bombers and long-range rockets. "Once we have an Atomic Stalemate," he wrote to Congressman Chester Bowles (Democrat-Connecticut) in 1955,

> a full scale atomic war, no matter who gets in the first blow, would end with the devastation of both Russia and the United States to the point where the continued existence of either of them as a nation would be in serious jeopardy. [...] As the Atomic Stalemate draws nearer it becomes much more important to avoid a full scale atomic war. The real issue is, of course, how to get a political settlement that will eliminate the danger of war, make disarmament possible and permit us to eliminate the strategic airforces and their bombs. [...].[244]

---

242 Joseph Rotblat, *Pugwash*, pp. 18–20; Joseph Rotblat, *Scientists*, pp. 37–38.
243 Szilard to Warren C. Johnson, "Memorandum, Confidential," July 2, 1958; n.d.; Leo Szilard Papers, Box 10, Folder 22, pp. 2–3.
244 Szilard to Chester Bowles, "Memo," May 24, 1955; see also Chester Bowles to Szilard, May 15, 1955, Leo Szilard Papers, Box 4, Folder 36.

To alert both the U.S. Government and the general public that America was "headed for an all-out war," Szilard launched a new crusade by founding the Council to Abolish War (later the Council for a Livable World), reinforcing his message through numerous talks, articles and personal contacts. He was one of the first to urge publicly, in the mid-1950s, the ending of the Cold War, and some of his letters, such as the one he published in *The New York Times* in 1955,[245] were highly appreciated in liberal circles.

Szilard, probably through Bowles, also gained the ear of Senator John F. Kennedy in early 1960, who acknowledged "the great responsibility and imagination you have brought to the problem of securing peace."[246] That fall, Szilard briefed Kennedy on "the mood and substance" of private conversations he had had with the Soviet Premier Nikita S. Khrushchev on October 5, 1960, in New York City.[247] Szilard had begun writing to Khrushchev a year earlier on the controversial issues involved in an atomic stalemate—that Szilard initiated this correspondence is all the more surprising because of the shock he must have experienced when the Soviet army brutally suppressed the Hungarian Revolution of 1956. Yet, distressed as he was by the subsequent execution of Prime Minister Imre Nagy and his associates in 1958, Szilard nonetheless was ready to fly to Moscow soon thereafter, and he also corresponded amicably with the Chinese Embassy in London in regard to a pending visit to China. Khrushchev encouraged Szilard's idea of holding informal meetings between scientists from both countries.[248]

---

245 Leo Szilard, "Letter to the Editor," *The New York Times* (February 6, 1955); reprinted in Hawkins, Greb, and Weiss Szilard, eds., *Livable World*, pp. 132–134.
246 John F. Kennedy (Washington, DC) to Szilard, May 27, 1960, Leo Szilard Papers, Box 11, Folder 5.
247 Szilard, "Conversation with K on October 5, 1960," in Hawkins, Greb, and Weiss Szilard, eds., *Livable World*, pp. 279–287.
248 Khrushchev to Szilard, August 30, 1960, in Hawkins, Greb, and Weiss Szilard, eds., *Livable World*, p. 269.

Szilard kept the incoming Kennedy Administration informed about his scientific diplomacy,[249] making clear that nuclear disarmament could be accomplished faster if, he told Bowles, "we are able to communicate with the Russians," which "seems to me that we are not doing ... at present."[250] He continued to act in his self-appointed role as confidential negotiator between Kennedy and Khrushchev, even going into such technical details as those associated with the presence of American troops in West Berlin. In general, Szilard refused to remain silent about his concerns on any subject, expressing his strong views on the Cuban Missile Crisis in a letter to Kennedy in June 1961, blaming the Kennedy Administration for what he perceived to be the neglect of U.S. obligations under the U.N. Charter.[251] In his last letter to Kennedy, just before Kennedy's assassination, Szilard half-ironically revealed that he considered himself to be a one-man Shadow State Department.[252] He saw himself as acting as an uninvited adviser on disarmament and proposed to organize a group of Americans and Russians to conduct a nongovernmental study of disarmament measures that their respective governments could undertake.[253]

Towards the end of his life, Leo Szilard wrote a first-rate social satire, *The Voice of the Dolphins*, probably his best-known work, much praised for its "sophistication, authority, and shrewdness," as well as for "sheer literary inventiveness."[254] In a book still in print, the dolphins address

---

249 Szilard to John F. Kennedy, October 16, November 19, 1960, May 10, June 6, 1961, Leo Szilard Papers, Box 11, Folder 5; last two letters published in Hawkins, Greb, and Weiss Szilard, eds., *Livable World*, pp. 341–346.
250 Szilard to Chester Bowles, March 17, 1961, Leo Szilard Papers, Box 4, Folder 36.
251 Szilard to John F. Kennedy, Letter and Memorandum, June 6, 1961, Leo Szilard Papers, Box 11, Folder 5; letter published in Hawkins, Greb, and Weiss Szilard, eds., *Livable World*, p. 346.
252 Szilard to John F. Kennedy, November 14, 1963, Leo Szilard Papers, Box 11, Folder 5.
253 Szilard to John F. Kennedy, Letter and Memorandum, n.d. [1962?], Leo Szilard Papers, Box 11, Folder 5.
254 Leo Szilard, *The Voice of the Dolphins and Other Stories* (New York: Simon and Schuster, 1961, expanded edition Stanford University Press, 1992). Cf. Edward Rosenheim, Jr., "The Voice of the Dolphins and Other Stories," *The University of Chicago Law Review*, Vol. 29, No. 1 (Autumn, 1961), p. 214.

Szilard's unbelievable prophecies, from "the Cold War to German reunification, oil wars, revolution in Iraq, American invasion of the Middle East, economic depression triggered by overconstruction, and the effects of disarmament on the U.S. economy. Overshadowing all these crises is the threat of nuclear war and its potential to annihilate all life on Earth."[255] Leo Szilard survives today not only as a prophet of the nuclear age but as a social critic of great intellectual foresight and a remarkable acumen in truly complex matters—a pioneer in global thinking.

---

255 Carol Van Strum, "The Voice of the Dolphins and Other Stories by Leo Szilard, 1961. Expanded edition, Stanford University Press, 1992." (Washington, DC: The Department of the Planet Earth, 2008).

VII Conclusion

I

In the new political framework of the Austro-Hungarian Monarchy (1867), Hungary witnessed an unprecedented and unrepeated economic expansion, social transformation, and cultural upsurge. Between the unification of Pest, Buda, and Óbuda in 1873 and World War I, the newly established capital city of Budapest became a thriving metropolis. Migrations in and out of the multiethnic, multicultural, and multilingual Habsburg Empire produced a vivid, lively, and flourishing cultural climate in which Germans and Jews made significant contributions to a blossoming urban lifestyle. The rapidly changing social structure, the appearance of daring social ambitions, and the emergence of new classes all contributed to a need for a modern school system, which became largely imported from Germany.

The *gimnázium* was an elitist institution for the burgeoning middle class. It offered academic studies and approaches that were recognized as appropriate tools for training the mind and nurturing talent. Teaching was typically based upon providing factual knowledge with the intention of using inductive reasoning methods. Most of the best high schools were under the direct control of the Roman Catholic, Calvinist, or Lutheran Church, which represented a high level of discipline and strict moral expectations, in addition to having a faculty that included highly educated and very demanding priests. The *Minta* was a state school, experimental in nature, and different from the average *gimnázium* in many ways, and representing a forerunner of modern educational principles.

Mathematics education was particularly emphasized and promoted by professional organizations, journals, and competitions. Competition was strongly supported and advocated. Outstanding students of mathematics enjoyed both acknowledgment and appreciation.

Much of the foundations of this innovative Hungarian school system came from Germany, and is evidence of how valuable knowledge transfer of this sort can be when serving comparable purposes in another culture. German influence had a long tradition in Hungary: German was the language of culture in general, and serving as a *lingua franca* in the Austro-Hungarian Monarchy, it functioned as a bridge between Germany and the Monarchy.

A subsequent step in transferring German educational expertise occurred after 1919–1920, when émigré scholars and scientists took the fruits of their outstanding Hungarian education with them as they left, mostly, for Germany and then on to the United States.

It would be tempting to think that a careful analysis of the nurturing of talent in fin-de-siècle Budapest would lead us to a reliable method for the creation of genius. When discussing the achievement of John von Neumann and his near equals, a cautious distinction has to be made between talent as teachable and genius as born. Furthermore, formal education, whatever its innovative and exemplary methods, exists within the larger social context of the culture and all its many influences on the student mind.

In a pioneering inquiry into the nature of problems and their solution, Michael Polanyi defined one of the most crucial questions of his generation: "To recognize a problem which can be solved and is worth solving is in fact a discovery in its own right." Declaring this as the creed of his generation in an 1957 article for *The British Journal for the Philosophy of Science*,[1] Polanyi spoke for, and spoke of his generation when discussing originality and invention, discovery and heuristic act, investigation and problem solving. "The interpretative frame of the educated mind," he continued, "is ever ready to meet somewhat novel experiences and to deal with them in a somewhat novel manner." Polanyi had his own views of genius, which he described as making contact with reality

> on an exceptionally wide range: by seeing problems and reaching out to hidden possibilities for solving them, far beyond the anticipatory powers of current conceptions. Moreover, by deploying such powers in an exceptional measure—far

---

[1] Michael Polanyi, "Problem solving," *The British Journal for the Philosophy of Science*, Vol. VIII, No. 30, August 1957, pp. 89–103; quote p. 89.

surpassing our own as onlookers—the work of genius offers us a massive demonstration of a creativity which can never be explained in other terms nor taken unquestioningly for granted.[2]

The extraordinary intellects nurtured by the *Minta,* the *Fasor* and other German-influenced schools of fin-de-siècle Hungary, cannot be attributed exclusively to the unique social and cultural characteristics of the period, the innovative educational approaches, or to the characteristics of innate genius, but to an unusual confluence of these three powerful factors, none of which exists in isolation. While we should attempt to discover talent at an early age and continue to cultivate it through personal attention and acknowledgment, creating a competitive spirit, and training minds through problem solving, just by instituting more of these educational practices into today's pedagogy we would still remain unable to recreate the Hungarian geniuses of the past without also stimulating all other economic, social, political, and cultural factors that helped create Hungary's legendary minds.

II

One of the intentions of this book has been to show and document both the transit role of Germany, and particularly Berlin, in the history of Hungarian intellectual migrations and the role of Hungarians in the great exodus from Germany after the Nazi takeover.

Links between the two countries were anything but new: during much of her modern history, Hungary in some way formed a part of, or was strongly influenced by, the greater German cultural realm; indeed it developed on the fringes of the German civilization. The tendency to frequent German cultural and study centers was a natural for the Hungarian upper and upper-middle classes throughout the 18th, 19th and the early 20th centuries. Most Hungarians who went to Germany after World War I were of Jewish

---

2   Polanyi, "Problem solving," *op. cit.,* pp. 93–94.

origin. Many were forced to leave Hungary because they had been politically involved in the Hungarian revolutions of 1918–19 (in most cases the Hungarian Soviet Republic of 1919). Others became innocent victims of the anti-Semitic campaign and legislation that followed the aborted Bolshevik-type coup in 1919–20, the first of its kind in Europe. These groups typically spoke good German, were educated in the German cultural tradition, and had many earlier contacts with Germany and other German-speaking cultural and scientific centers of Central Europe. It seemed natural for them to seek what turned out to be temporary refuge in the intellectually flourishing and politically tolerant atmosphere of Weimar Germany. Though the Hungarian government realized the potential loss the country would suffer from intellectual exile, most émigrés withstood official endeavors to lure them back to Hungary and chose to stay in Germany until Hitler took over as Chancellor in January 1933. Hungarian scientists, scholars, artists, musicians, filmmakers, authors, and other professionals enjoyed high recognition and prestige in pre-Nazi Germany. This "German" reputation helped them rebuild their subsequent career in England and, particularly the United States, where, after 1933, most of these "German" Hungarians were headed.

The rise of anti-Semitism and the Nazi takeover reminded Jewish-Hungarians in Germany of their former experiences in Hungary and this historical *déjà-vu* often alerted them to take action earlier than did many native Germans. Prompted by the lessons of their *double exile*, several Hungarians played important roles in rescuing the victims of Nazi Germany, became active in anti-Nazi movements, and instrumental in promoting the A-bomb and other Allied efforts to beat Germany and Japan in World War II.

Continuing research is needed to provide further statistical evidence about the actual number of immigrants in Weimar Germany, including the number of émigré Hungarians and their social composition. It would be important to learn more about social networking, bonding and inter-group relations among the various émigré groups and individuals, including Hungarians, as well as the relationship between immigrants and the German population. Little is known of the politics of many of the immigrants: their voting patterns, their party affiliations and their political organizations remain to be investigated.

Individual immigrant groups had specific ways of thinking, communicating and arguing. A comparison would well illuminate their cultural differences and their varied contributions to German civilization. A systematic study of the pre-Nazi German periodical literature may reveal even more of the achievement and contribution of Hungarians and other émigré intellectuals in Weimar Germany.

III

Jewish interwar migration had a long pre-history of earlier resettlements as it came in some ways as a continuation of forced, 19th century Jewish migrations from Russia to the Austro-Hungarian Monarchy or Germany.

Many refugee Hungarians were mistaken by American agencies and individuals as German refugees. Born in the last decades of the Austro-Hungarian Monarchy, Jewish-Hungarian professionals often spoke German as a mother tongue, attended some of the best schools of the Monarchy, many studying and receiving their degrees in Germany and becoming employed by German universities and other institutions. The large group of Jewish-Hungarian scholars and scientists with a German training were often invisible to immigration authories due to being lumped together with German and German-Jewish scholars fleeing from Nazi Germany. This opens the question whether in the case of scholars and scientists it is the country of origin or that of training that provides a national connection.

Hungarian, rather than German citizenship was a key reason why the Emergency Committee in the U.S. did not try to save many of the applicants. Up to 1938, when the first anti-Jewish Bill was passed in Budapest, Hungarians did not seem to be an endangered species and the Committee focused its efforts on the Germans and German-Hungarians who were in acute trouble. This explains why the Committee (and probably several other organizations) turned towards those Hungarians who were closely associated with Germany, were German citizens, had German jobs, and were under actual threat after the advance of Hitler and the Nazi party.

Ousted from Germany in or soon after 1933, many Jewish-Hungarian professional and intellectual refugees still could return to Hungary to work or for a visit. In the decade between 1929 and 1938, the year of the first anti-Jewish bill, Hungary provided a modicum of shelter to its Jewish population, increasingly an illusion that proved to be deceptive and ultimately lethal.

The dissolution of the Austro-Hungarian Monarchy and the Peace Treaty of Trianon eliminated much of the geographic and social mobility in the area or made it very difficult. Escaping interwar Hungary was, in fact, not only a form of geographic relocation, but a vehicle of social mobility. Pre-Hitler Germany was one of the great European centers of modernization, science and culture that attracted migrants from all the peripheries of Europe just as the United States that increasingly became such a center from a global perspective. Emigration served the transfer of Hungarian middle class values and possibilities into the much larger and more articulate German and American middle-class. This made the integration of newcomers usually quick, effective, and lasting, and led to professional success. Upon landing in the U.S., immigrants from socially backward Hungary arrived into an incomparably larger, more modern, dynamic, and professional middle-class where talent was appreciated and fostered. American middle class values and institutions made integration relatively easy, both socially and mentally.

Rescue operations in the pre-World War II period were made extremely difficult by the restrictionist 1924 quota law (in effect until 1965), raging unemployment and growing anti-Semitism in the U.S. As only the top people from even the German group were wanted, the agencies carefully skimmed the very best and refused second-class professionals. The growing need of European professionalism and know-how, especially the later demands of the war effort, made it imperative for the U.S. to allow immigration of the top level specialists.

Refugee organizations in the United States were not pursuing charity: they followed their professional motives and interests and served their country and institutions while also saving European lives. Interwar migration did not stop upon arrival into the U.S. but continued from institution to institution until the newcomer found his/her "final" place or destination. Step-migration was to become an almost global phenomenon.

Networking, cohorting, and bonding were strong among the Hungarian refugees and some, like Leo Szilard and Theodore von Kármán, did their best to help fellow refugees. Their own "private" or combined private/institutional rescue operations were part of U.S. relief, often shared by outstanding American scholars, themselves mostly of European origin.

Jews arriving from Hungary seemed to have been more Hungarian than Jewish, though further research is needed to find out more about the exact nature of their religious affiliation. Assimilation in Hungary certainly left a lasting imprint on their faith. Many of the American citizens initiating or participating in the rescue missions were themselves Jewish and were driven by the special sensitivity of shared background and a more keenly felt danger.

Contrary to common belief, not all émigré Hungarians were Jewish in the period between 1919–1945. Though the overwhelming majority of exiles was Jewish, the country was also left behind by a relatively small group of gentile Hungarians, politically liberal, radical, or leftist, and some eventually just hoping for a more rewarding career. Some of these returned to Hungary at a later point.

The lack of a sufficient knowledge of English isolated many of the immigrants and curtailed their social integration into the American community. However, their repeated traumata in interwar Europe led them to become militant anti-Nazis and anti-Communists, who looked upon the United States as a bulwark of freedom and fought against all forms of totalitarianism. Coming from this background, some of the very best and ablest joined the U.S. war effort and contributed to the fall of tyranny in German-dominated Europe and Japan.

The number of notable Hungarian-American refugees in the interwar years is difficult to assess. A list of some 250 eminent Hungarian professionals who immigrated to the U.S. between 1919–1945 was compiled by the present author and is attached as an appendix to this book. Though the list is incomplete, it presents a wide variety of outstanding specialists whose presence in the United States was, and in many cases, continues to be, an important contribution to American science, education and culture. That the bulk of this outstanding group lived a relatively happy and successful life in America is further evidenced by their life span. As documented by our list, a surprisingly large percentage of immigrant Hungarian-Americans became extremely old: approximately 33% lived to 85 years or more, 20% to 90 and 1,5% lived to more than 100 years. In other words, every third member of this group reached an age that was unusual even for Americans as the elderly U.S. population during the period between 1920–2000 represented only 0,2 to 1,5% of the total U.S. population.[3]

The group of Jewish-Hungarian refugees may be considered to have had a group-biography. One can look upon the members of this large and diverse group as living essentially the same life and write their shared, common biography in terms of a *prosopography*. Yet, this prosopography must not fail to transmit the extent to which Hungary's loss of some of its most outstanding talent remains in the national awareness a source of pain and pride, fear and anger. Hungary's fundamental educational contributions to these outstanding minds, in combination with the energizing modernism of Germany and other western European countries, were fertilized again by the nurturing soil of their new homeland in the U.S. This transient generation's step-migrations, tossed and turned as they were by the traumatizing historical-political events of the era, produced a range of contributions that are rightly owned by many countries, and can be seen as foreshadowing in the 21st century the emergence of a global human identity.

---

[3] For the survey of the U.S. Census Bureau see *The World Almanac and Book of Facts 2008* (New York: World Almanac Books, 2008), p. 598.

Appendix

Select List of
Notable Hungarian–American Émigrés
1919–1945

The list is based on a wide variety of sources, not all of which are fully reliable. Immigration dates are particularly prone to errors. The notation G stands for arrival in Germany, and U.S. for landing in the United States. Where a single year is given for Germany or the U.S., it represents the person having remained in Germany until 1933 and/or to the end of his life in the U.S. Original last names before Magyarization are given in *italics*. Please note that this is a representative, but not fully complete list of all Hungarian-American celebrities in the interwar era. If you care to improve the list in any particular way please contact the author at tzsbe@hu.inter.net

Abraham, Paul [Pál Ábrahám] (1892–1960), operetta composer — G. 1932, U.S. 1933
Agay, Denes [Dénes Ágay] (1912–2007), composer, arranger of piano music, author — U.S. 1939
Alexander, Franz [Ferenc Alexander] (1891–1964), psychoanalyst and physician — G. 1919, U.S. 1930
Alpar, Gitta [Gitta Alpár, Regina *Klopfer*] (1903–1991) actress, opera and operetta singer — G. 1926, U.S. 1936
Alton, John [Johann *Altmann*] (1901–1996), cameraman — U.S. 1924
Antalffy-Zsiross, Dezső (1885–1945), organist, composer, conductor — U.S. 1921, 1926
Árvai, Irén (1912–1950), film actress — U.S. 1938
Auer, John (1906–1975), film director, producer, screenwriter — U.S. 1928

Bak, Robert C. [Robert Bak] (1908–1974), psychiatrist and psychoanalyst — U.S. 1941
Balazs, Frigyes [Frigyes Balázs], violinist
Balogh, Erno [Ernő Balogh] (1897–1989), pianist, composer, author — U.S. 1924
Barati, George [György Baráti] (1913–1966), cellist, conductor, composer — U.S. 1938
Bartók, Béla (1881–1945), composer, musicologist, pianist — U.S. 1940
Bator, Victor [Viktor Bátor] (1891–1967), lawyer, business executive — U.S. 1940
Bánky, Vilma [Vilma Konsics] (1898–1991), silent film actress — U.S. 1925
Beck, Paul A., professor of metallurgy
Békássy, István (1907–1995), actor — U.S. 1936? –1982
Békessy, Imre (1887–1951), journalist, author, newspaper editor — U.S. 1939
Békessy, János [Hans Habe] (1911–1977), author, journalist — U.S. 1940–1945
Bela, Miklos (1900–1966), film actor — U.S. after 1928
Benedek, László (1905–1992), film director — U.S. 1937
Benedek, Therese (1892–1977), psychoanalyst — U.S. 1933
Biller, Irén (1897–1967), actress — U.S. 1933
Biro, Lajos [Lajos Bíró, *Lajos Blau*] (1880–1948), novelist, playwright, and screenwriter — U.S. 1925
Bohem, Endre [Endre Böhm, Andrew Gordon Boehm] (1900–1990), screenwriter and producer — U.S. 1920
Borshy Kerekes, György (1892–1971), clergyman — U.S. 1924
Breuer, Marcel (1902–1981), architect, designer — G. 1920, U.S. 1937
Brunauer, Stephen [István Brunauer] (1903–1986), chemist — U.S. 1920s
Bús-Fekete, Leslie [László Bús-Fekete] (1896–1971), playwright, script writer, author, editor — U.S. 1940
Carelli, Gabor [*Gábor Krausz*] (1915–1999), opera singer — U.S. 1939
Corda, Maria [Mária Antónia Farkas] (1898–1976), silent film actress — G. 1926–27, U.S. 1927, 1930

Curtiz, Michael [Mihály Kertész, *Manó Kaminer*) (1886–1962), film director — U.S. 1927
Czinner, Paul [Pál Czinner] (1890–1972), film director, producer — U.S. 1940
Darling, William S. [Vilmos Sándorházi] (1882–) film director — U.S. 1920?
Darvas, Lili (1902–1974) actress — U.S. 1938
Deák, Francis [Ferenc Deák] (1899–1972), historian — U.S. 1925
Deri, Emery [Imre Déri] (1889–1959), journalist — U.S. 1921–1932, 1949–1959
Deri, Otto [Ottó Déri] (1911–1969), cellist
Dienes, André de [Endre Dienes] (1913–1985), photographer — U.S. 1938
Dienes, Louis L. [Lajos László Dienes] (1885–1974), physician, biologist, bacteriologist — U.S. 1922
Dora, Miklos [Miklós Dóra] (b. 1913) restaurateur, wine consultant — U.S. 1932
Doraine, Lucy [Ilona Kovács] (1898–1989), silent film actress — U.S. 1920s
Dorati, Antal [*Antal Deutsch*] (1906–1988) conductor, composer — G. 1928, U.S. 1939
Duna, Steffi [Stephanie Berindey] (1910–1992), actress — U.S. 1934
Eckhardt, Tibor (1888–1972), politician — U.S. 1941
Eggerth, Marta (b. 1912), actress, singer — U.S. 1939
Eördögh, Elmer [Elemér Eördögh] (1875–1955), Catholic priest — U.S. 1921
Erdélyi, Michael [Mihály Erdélyi] (1903–), psychologist
Faludy, György (1910–2006), author, poet, translator — U.S. 1941–1946
Farago, Ladislas [László Faragó] (1906–1980), screenwriter, journalist — U.S. 1937
Farkas, Adalbert (1906–), physical chemist — G. 1920s, U.S. 1941
Farkas, Aladár (1904–), journalist, author
Farkas, George [György Farkas], interior designer

Fejos, Paul [Pál Fejős] (1897–1963), film director, anthropologist — U.S. 1923
Fekete, Zoltán, conductor
Fellegi, Margit, costume designer
Fellner, Willy [Vilmos Fellner, William John Fellner] (1905–1983), economist, statistician — U.S. 1938
Fényes, László (1871–1944), journalist — U.S. 1940
Ferenczi, Imre, statistician — U.S. 1940
Finta, Alexander [Sándor Finta] (1881–1958), sculptor, author — U.S. 1923
Flesch, Paul [Pál Flesch] (1908–1980), physician — U.S. 1938?
Flesch, Peter [Péter Flesch] (1915–1969), research dermatologist — U.S. 1941
Fodor, Nandor [Nándor Fodor] (1895–1964), journalist, psychical researcher, psychoanalyst — U.S. 1921, 1938?
Freund, Jules Thomas [Gyula Freund] (1890–1960), immunologist
Fried, Theodore [Tivadar Fried] (1902–1980), painter — U.S. 1942
Fülöp-Miller, René [René Fueloep-Miller] (1891–1963), author — U.S. 1939
Gaal, Franciska [Franciska Gaál, *Fanny Zilveritch*] (1904–1973), singer, cabaret performer, film actress — U.S. 1937–1940, 1946–1973
Gabor, Arnold [Arnold Gábor] (1880–1950), opera singer (baritone) — U.S. 1923
Gabor, Eva [Éva Gábor] (1919–1995), film actress, socialite — U.S. 1939?
Gabor, Zsa Zsa [Sári Gábor] (b. 1917), actress, socialite — U.S. 1941
Geray, Steve [István Gyergyai] (1898–1973), actor — U.S. 1941
Gergely, Tibor (1900–1978), artist, book illustrator — U.S. 1939
Gero, George [György Gerő] (1901–1993), psychoanalyst — G. 1924, U.S. 1941
Goldmark, Peter Carl [Péter Károly Goldmark] (1906–1977), engineer, inventor — U.S. 1935

Goldstein, Ladislas (László Goldstein) (1906–), experimental nuclear physicist
Goldzieher, Max A. [Maximilan Alexander Goldzieher, Miksa Goldzieher] (1883–1969), endocrinologist — U.S. 1920s
Gombosi, Otto John [Ottó János Gombosi, Otto Johannes Gombosi] (1902–1955), musicologist — G. 1921–1926, 1929–1933, U.S. 1939
Göndör, Ferenc (1885–1954), journalist, editor — U.S. 1926
Gorog, Laszlo [László Görög] (1903–2003), screenwriter, actor — U.S. 1942?
Grancsay, Stephen V. (1897–1980), art historian, curator
Groesse, Paul (1906–1987), film director — U.S. 1937
Gross-Bettelheim, Jolán (1900–1972), painter, graphic artist — G. 1920–1922, U.S. 1925–1956
Grosschmid, Geza B. [Géza Grosschmid], economist
Gyorgy, Andrew [András György] (1917–), political scientist
György, Pál [Paul György] (1893–1976), pediatrician, nutritionist — G. 1920–1931, U.S. 1933
Hajós, Erzsébet [Elizabeth M. Hajós], art historian
Halasi, Béla Albert (1887–1965), economist — U.S. 1939
Halasz, Leslie [László Halász] (1905–2001), conductor, music director
Halász, Miklós [Nicholas Halász] (1895–1985), journalist, author, novelist — U.S. 1941
Halmos, Paul Richard [Pál Halmos] (1916–2006), mathematician
Haraszti, Zoltan [Zoltán Haraszti] (1892–1980), author, librarian — U.S. 1920
Harmati, Sandor [Sándor Harmati] (1892–1936), composer, conductor, violinist
Harsanyi, Charles [Károly Harsányi] (1905–1973), painter
Harsanyi, Miklos [Miklós Harsányi], violist
Hart, Alfred [Alfréd Hart] (1904–?), businessman, philanthropist
Hatvany, Lili (1890–1968), author, critic, playwright – U.S. late 1930s
Havas, Peter [Péter Havas] (1916–2004), physicist
Hellebranth, Berta de (1899–), painter

Hellebranth, Elena [Ilona] Maria de (1897–), painter
Herczeg, Geza [Géza Herczeg] (1888–1954), playwright, story- and screenwriter – U.S. 1937?
Herz, Otto (1894–1976), pianist, accompanist – U.S. 1940
Hoch, Paul H. [Pál Hoch] (1902–1964), research psychiatrist – U.S. 1933
Hoff, Nicholas J. [Miklós Hoff] (1906–1997), aeronautical engineer – U.S. 1939
Hoffman, John (1904–1980), film editor – U.S. 1931?
Holló, Gyula (1890–1973), physician, TB specialist – U.S. 1939
Ignotus, Hugo (1969–1949), critic, editor — U.S.1938–1948
Incze, Sándor (1889–1966), journalist, critic, editor — U.S. 1938
Járay, Hans [János Járay] (1906–1990), actor — U.S. 1938–1948
Jászi, Oscar [Oszkár Jászi] (1875–1957), sociologist, political scientist — U.S. 1925
Juris, Kálmán, physicist
Kálmán, Imre [Emmerich Kálmán] (1882–1953), operetta composer — U.S. 1940–1951
Kardos, Leslie (László Kardos) (1905–1962), film director
Kármán, Theodore von [Tódor Kármán] (1881–1963), engineer, physicist — G. 1906–08, 1913, 1919, U.S. 1930
Katona, George [György Katona] (1901–1981), psychologist, economist — G. 1919, U.S. 1933
Kecskemeti, Paul [Pál Kecskeméti] (1901–1980), sociologist, political scientist — G. 1927, U.S. 1941?
Kelemen, Pál (1894–), art historian — U.S. 1932
Kemeny, John George [János György Kemény] (1926–1992), mathematician, computer scientist — U.S. 1940
Kepes, Gyorgy [György Kepes] (1906–2001), painter, designer — G. 1930, U.S. 1937
Kerekes, Tibor (1893–1969), historian — U.S. 1927
Kéri, Pál (1882–1961), journalist

Kertész, André [Andor Kertész] (1894–1985), photographer — U.S. 1936
Kiss, George [György Kiss], geographer
Klay, Andrew C. [Andor Sziklay] (1912–1996), diplomat, author — U.S. 1930
Klein, Philip, sociologist
Kober, Leo (1876–1931), artist, cartoonist — U.S. 1921
Kolnai, Aurel Thomas [*Aurél Stein*] (1900–1973), author, philosopher — U.S. 1940–1945
Koni, Sir Nicolaus (1911–2000), sculptor — U.S. 1941
Koppanyi, Theodore [Tivadar Koppányi] (1901–1985), pharmacologist U.S. 1923
Korda, Sir Alexander [Sándor Korda, *Sándor László Kellner*] (1893–1956) film director — G. 1923, U.S. 1926–30, 1941–1943
Korda, Zoltan (Zoltán Kellner) (1895–1961), film director — U.S. 1940
Korek, Valéria [Mrs. Willy Fellner] (1906–), author, literary critic — U.S. 1938
Kormendi, Eugene [Jenő Körmendi] (1889–1959), sculptor — U.S. 1939
Korvin, Charles [Géza Kaiser] (1907–1998), actor
Kostolany, André [Endre Bertalan Kosztolányi] (1906–1999), stock market expert, speculator
Kozary, Myron Theodore (1918–1966), petroleum geologist
Lanczos, Cornelius [Kornél Lánczos, *Kornél Löwy*] (1893–1974), physicist, mathematician — G. 1921, U.S. 1932–1954
Lanyi, George Albert [György Lányi] (1913–1981), political scientist — U.S. 1937
Laszlo, Aladar [Aladár László] (1896–1958), screenwriter — U.S. 1938
Laszlo, Alexander [*Sándor Totis*] (1895–1970), pianist, conductor, film and television composer — G. 1924?, U.S. 1938
Laszlo, Ernest [Ernő László] (1898–1984), cinematographer — U.S. 1926
Laszlo, Erno [Ernő László] (1897–1973), dermatologist and cosmetic businessman

Figure 22. Emil Lengyel, America's Role in World Affairs (Hungarian edition, 1947).

Laszlo, Miklos [Miklós Leitner] (1903–1973), playwright — U.S. 1938
Lax, Henrik (1894–1990), physician — U.S. 1941
Lax, Peter (b. 1926), mathematician — U.S. 1941
Ledermann, László (1904–), economist
Léner, Jenő (1894–1948), violinist
Lengyel, Emil (1895–1985), author, journalist, historian, translator — U.S. 1921
Lengyel, Melchior [Menyhért Lengyel] (1880–1974), author, playwright — U.S. 1937–1962
Lesznai, Anna [Amália Moscovitz] (1885–1966), designer, poet, author — U.S. 1939
Lorand, Edith (1898–1960), violinist — G. 1920s, U.S. 1937
Lorand, Sandor [Sándor Loránd] (1893–1987), psychoanalyst — U.S. 1925

Lóránt, Stefan [István Lóránt] (1901–1997), journalist — U.S. 1940
Lorsy, Erno [Ernő Lorsy] (1889–1961), journalist — G. 1923?, U.S. 1940?
Lorre, Peter [*László Löwenstein*] (1904–1964), film actor — G. 1925, U.S. 1935
Lónyay, Simon H., economist
Lucas, Paul [Pál Lukács] (1894?–1971), film actor — U.S. 1927
Lugosi, Bela [Béla Lugosi] (1882–1956), stage and film actor — G. 1919, U.S. 1920
Lukacs, Eugene [Jenő Lukács] (1906–1987), mathematician, statistician — U.S. 1939
Mahler, Margaret [Margit Schönberger] (1897–1985), psychoanalyst — G. 1919–1922, U.S. 1938
Manheim, Ernest [Ernő Manheim] (1900–2002), sociologist, anthropologist — G. 1920s, U.S. 1937
Marton, Endre (1904–1992), film director, producer — U.S. 1923–1929?, G. 1929?–1933, U.S. 1940
Marton, George Nicholas [György Miklós Marton] (1899–1979), literary agent — U.S. 1939
Massey, Lona [Ilona Hajmássy, *Ilona Hagymási*] (1910–1974), film actress, singer — U.S. 1937
Mate, Rudolph [Rudolf Matheh or Mayer] (1898–1964), cinematographer and film director — U.S. 1934
Matulay, Laszlo, designer, illustrator — U.S. 1935
Meduna, Ladislas Joseph [László Meduna] (1896–1964), neurologist — U.S. 1938
Moholy-Nagy, Laszlo [*László Weisz*] (1895–1946), painter, photographer, designer — G. 1920, U.S. 1937
Molnár, Ferenc [*Ferenc Neumann*] (1878–1952), author, playwright — U.S. 1940
Munkacsi, Martin [Márton Munkácsi] (1896–1963), photographer — G. 1927, U.S. 1934
Nadanyi, Paul [Pál Nadányi], journalist, editor
Nagy, Elemer [Elemér Nagy] (1906–1971), stage designer, opera producer

Neményi, Pál [Paul Neményi], hydrologist
Neumann, Gabor [Gábor Neumann] (–1998), businessman, investor
Neumann, John von [János Neumann] (1903–1957), mathematician — G. 1921–23, 1927–29, U.S. 1930
Nyilas, Tibor (1914–1986), saber fencer — U.S. 1939
Ormandy, Eugene [Jenő Ormándy, *Jenő Blau*] (1899–1985), conductor — U.S. 1921
Ormandy, Martin J. [Ormándy, *Blau*] (1901–1996), cellist — U.S. 1921
Pal, George (1908–1980), filmdirector, producer — G. 1931, U.S. 1940
Pályi, Melchior [Menyhért Pályi] (1892–1970), economist — G. 1918, U.S. 1933
Papp, Dezső Károly, newspaper editor — U.S. 1925?
Partos, Frank (1901–1956), screenwriter — U.S. late 1920s
Pasternak, Joseph [József Pasternak] (1901–1991), film director — U.S. 1921–28, G. 1928–35, U.S. 1935–40
Pauker, Edmund [Ödön Pók] (1887–1962), lawyer, journalist — G. 1920, U.S. 1922
Pelenyi, John [János Pelényi], Hungarian minister to the U.S. — U.S. 1940
Pikler, Andrew [Endre Pikler], economist
Pogány, Imre (1893–1975), violinist — G. 1921, U.S. 1927
Pólya, George [György Pólya] (1887–1985), mathematician — U.S. 1940
Possony, Stephen Thomas [István Pozsony] (1913?–1995), political scientist — U.S. 1940
Pressburger, Arnold (1885–1951), film producer — G. 1925–30, U.S. 1940?
Putti, Lya de [Amália Putti] (1896–1931), silent film actress — G. 1920, U.S. 1926
Racz, Andre [Endre Rácz] (1916–1994), painter, sculptor, art professor — U.S. 1939
Rado, Sandor [Sándor Radó] (1890–1972), psychoanalyst and physician — G. 1922, U.S. 1931
Radó, Tibor (1895–1965), mathematician — U.S. 1929
Radványi, László (1900–1978), historian, social scientist

Raisz, Ervin (1893–1968), geographer — U.S. 1923
Rapaport, David [Dezső Rappaport] (1911–1960), psychologist — U.S. 1938
Rapée, Ernő (1891–1945), conductor, composer, arranger, musical director — G. up to 1913, U.S. 1913–20s, G. 1924?–26, U.S. 1926
Rasko, Aurel [Aurél Miksa Reinitz] (1883–1961), painter
Reiner, Fritz [Frigyes Reiner] (1888–1963), conductor — U.S. 1922
Recsei, Andrew Andor [Andor Récsei] (1902–2002), chemist — U.S. 1938
Rejto, Gabor [Gábor Rejtő] (1916–1987), cellist — U.S. 1939
Reves, Emery [Imre Révész] (1904–1981), political scientist, publisher — U.S. 1941
Roheim, Geza [Géza Róheim] (1891–1953), anthropologist, psychoanalyst — U.S. 1938
Rona, Elizabeth [Erzsébet Róna] (1890–1981), chemist, geochemist, nuclear chemist — U.S. 1941
Rostás, László, economist
Roth, Feri [Franz Roth] (1899–1969), violinist, founder of the Roth string quartet, professor of music — G. 1921, U.S. 1928
Rothman, Stephen [István Rothman] (1894–1963), research dermatologist — U.S. 1938
Rózsa, Miklós (1907–1995), composer — G. 1925–31, U.S. 1940
Ruttkay, György (1890–1955), journalist — U.S. 1938
Sakall, S. Z. [Sándor Gärtner, Jenő Gerő, Szőke Szakáll] (1884–1955), film actor — G. 1925, U.S. 1940
Sándor, György (1912–2005), pianist and piano teacher — U.S. 1939
Schick, Béla (1877–1967), pediatrician — U.S. 1923
Schonbauer, Henry [Henrik Schönbauer] (1895–1973), sculptor
Schorr, Frederick [Frigyes or Friedrich Schorr] (1888–1953), opera singer [bass baritone] — G. 1918–1933, U.S. 1933
Schulhof, Andrew [Andor Schulhof] — G. 1920s–1938, U.S. 1938
Schulhof, Belle (1908–) — U.S. 1939
Scitovsky, Tibor de [Tibor Scitovszky] (1910–2002), economist — U.S. 1939

Sebeok, Thomas Albert [Tamás Sebők] (1920-2001), linguist — U.S. 1937

Sekey, Steve [István Székely] (1899-1979), film director, writer — U.S. 1938

Sendrey, Alfred [Aladár Szendrei] (1884-1976), conductor, composer, musicologist, — G. 1918, U.S. 1940

Sepeshy, Zoltan L. [Zoltán Szepesy] (1898-1974), painter — U.S. 1921

Serly, Tibor (1901-1978), violist, violinist and composer — U.S. 1925?

Sichermann, István, business executive

Spitz, René Arpad [René Árpád Spitz] (1887-1974), psychiatrist and psychoanalyst — U.S. 1939

Stein, Marcel (1901-2002), textile engineer, inventor

Suba, Susanne [Zsuzsanna Suba, Mrs. McCracken] (1913-), author, illustrator — U.S. 1919

Sugar, Peter F. [Péter Frigyes Sugár] (1919-1999), historian — U.S. 1939

Szathmáry, Arthur, philosopher

Szántó, Jani, violinist

Szász, Otto (1884-1952), mathematician — G. 1914, U.S. 1933

Szasz, Thomas Stephen [István Tamás Szász] (b. 1920), psychiatrist — U.S. 1938

Szegho, Constantin S. [Konstantin Szeghő] (1905-1995), electrical engineer, television pioneer — G. 1923, U.S. 1940

Szegő, Gabriel [Gábor Szegő] (1895-1985), mathematician — G. 1921, U.S. 1934

Székely, János [John Pen, John S. Toldy] (1901-1958), author — G. 1920s, U.S. 1938

Szell, George [György Széll] (1897-1970), conductor — G. 1924, U.S. 1939

Szende, Zoltán, historian and international economist

Szenes, Piroska (1899-1972), journalist, author — U.S. 1941

Szent-Györgyi, Kornélia [Kornélia (Nelly) Demény] (married to Albert Szent-Györgyi 1917-1941) — U.S. 1938

Szentkiralyi, Joseph [József Szentkirályi, Joseph St. Clair] (1913-2008), linguist, educator — U.S. 1939

Szigeti, Joseph [József Szigeti] (1892–1973), violinist — U.S. 1926–1960
Szilard, Leo [Leó Szilárd] (1898–1964), physicist — G. 1919, U.S. 1938
Szirmai, Albert [Albert Sirmay] (1880–1967), operetta composer, music editor — U.S. 1928
Szűcs, József, biochemist, mycologist and plant-physiologist
Takaro, Geza [Géza Takaró] (1881–1974), clergyman, journalist — U.S. 1922
Telkes, Maria [Mária Telkes] (1900–1995), physicist, inventor — U.S. 1925
Teller, Edward [Ede Teller] (1908–2003), physicist — G. 1926–1934, U.S. 1935
Tihany, Leslie Charles [László Tihanyi] (1911–1997), diplomat, historian — U.S. 1930
Tisza, Ladislas [László Tisza] (b. 1907), physicist — U.S. 1941
Tolnay, Charles de [Károly Tolnay] (1899–1981), art historian — U.S. 1939–1964
Tors, Ivan (1916–1983), playwright, screenwriter, producer — U.S. late 1930s
Toth, André de [Endre Tóth] (1913–2002), film director — U.S. 1943
Vadnai, Laszlo [László Vadnay] (1904–1967), author, screenwriter — U.S. 1938
Vajda, Ernest [Ernő Vajda, Sidney Garrick] (1887?–1954), actor, playwright, novelist, author of screenplays — U.S. 1924
Vámbéry, Rusztem (1872–1948), lawyer, diplomat — U.S. 1938
Varconi, Victor [Mihály Várkonyi] (1891–1976), silent film star — U.S. 1924
Varró, István (1878–1963) author, sociologist, book-binder — U.S. 1940
Varró, Margit (1881–1978), pianist, piano teacher — U.S. 1938
Verebes, Ernst [Ernő Verebes, Ernő Weisz] (1902–1971), screenwriter — U.S. 1937
Vidor, Charles [Károly Vidor] (1900–1959), film director — G. 1920s, U.S. 1924

Wald, Abraham [Ábrahám Wald] (1902–1950), mathematician — U.S. 1938

Wigner, Eugene Paul [Jenő Pál Wigner] (1902–1995), physicist and mathematician, Nobel Prize in Physics (1963) — G. 1921–25, 1926–30, U.S. 1930

Worth, George V. [György Vitéz] (1915–2006), saber fencer

Zador, Eugene [Jenő Zádor] (1894–1977), composer — U.S. 1939

Zechmeister, Laszlo [László Zechmeister] (1889–1972), organic chemist — U.S. 1940

Zeisel, Eva [Éva Stricker] (b. 1906), designer — U.S. 1938

Zilzer, Gyula (1898–1969), illustrator, painter, etcher, engraver, lithographer — U.S. 1932

Figure 23. Eva Zeisel, designer, 2000s (on the cover of Lucie Young's biography, 2003).

Appendix

Sources

Borbándi, Gyula, ed. *Nyugati magyar irodalmi lexikon és bibliográfia*.
 Hága: Mikes International, Budapest: Országos Széchényi Könyvtár,
 2006
Incze, Sándor, ed. *Magyar Album*.
 Elmhurst, IL: American Hungarian Studies Foundation, 1956.
Kenyeres, Ágnes, ed. *Magyar Életrajzi Lexikon*, Vols. I–IV.
 Budapest: Akadémiai Kiadó, 1967, 1969, 1981, 1994.
Kézdi-Kovács, Zsolt, ed. *Hungarians in Film*.
 Budapest: Magyar Filmunió, 1996.
Nagy, Csaba, ed. *A magyar emigráns irodalom lexikona*.
 Budapest: Argumentum–PIM, 2000.
Nagy, Ferenc, ed., *Magyar tudóslexikon A-tól Zs-ig*.
 Better—MTESZ—OMIKK, 1997.
Pléh, Csaba. *Pszichológiatörténet. A modern pszichológia kialakulása*.
 Budapest: Gondolat, 1992.
Wagner, Francis S., *Hungarian Contributions to World Civilization*.
 Alpha Publications, 1977.

Internet sources:

allmusic allmovie allgame
http://www.allmovie.com/

Bundesarchiv – Zentrale Datenbank Nachlässe
http://www.bundesarchiv.de/zdn/

Demeter, Tibor, ed. Bibliographia Hungarica
http://demeter.oszk.hu/

GovtRegistry.com
http://govtregistry.com/

IBDB Internet Broadway Database
http://www.ibdb.com/

Magyar Életrajzi Lexikon 1000-1990
http://mek.oszk.hu/00300/00355/html/toc/09007.html

MiMi.hu
http://en.mimi.hu/index.html

Opentopia Encyclopedia
http://encycl.opentopia.com/

Pléh Csaba, Magyar hozzájárulások a modern pszichológiához
http://www.cogsci.bme.hu/csaba/docs/magyar/torteneti/MAGYPSZ.DOC.

Steven Béla Várdy and Thomas Szendrey, Hungarian Americans
http://www.everyculture.com/multi/Ha-La/Hungarian-Americans.html

Szűk Balázs, Magyar Hollywood
(Adalékok egy hollywoodi magyar filmlexikonhoz)
http://www.licium.hu/images/content_files/File/szuk_balazs__magyar_hollywood_(adalekok_egy_hollywoodi_magyar_filmlexikonhoz).pdf.

Wikipedia, The Free Encyclopedia. List of Hungarian Americans
http://www.answers.com/topic/list-of-hungarian-americans

Personal information completing a few biographical references is gratefully acknowledged to Peter Czipott, Gabor Kalman, Judit Mészáros, Peter Pastor, and Ágnes Széchenyi.

Bibliography

Primary Sources: Archives and Libraries Consulted

The archival sources of this book are scattered all around the world. This comes from the very nature of the subject matter. Many of the key Hungarian figures discussed here became émigrés early on, worked in universities or other institutions primarily in Germany, and typically left their papers to their last work place or other public institutions in the United States. The list of collections consulted is included in my Acknowledgements.

United States

American-Hungarian Library and Historical Society, New York, NY

American Philosophical Society Library, Philadelphia, PA

Boston University, Mugar Memorial Library, Boston, MA
  Joseph Szigeti Papers
  Michael Károlyi Papers

California Institute of Technology, Robert A. Millikan Memorial Library, Institute Archives, Pasadena, CA
  Theodore von Kármán Papers
  Robert Andrews Millikan Papers

Catholic University of America, Washington, DC
    Manuscript Collection

Columbia University Libraries, New York, NY
    Butler Library; Rare Book and Manuscript Library
    Oscar Jászi Papers
    Carnegie Endowment for International Peace (CEIP)
        Aid to Refugees
        Committee to Aid Czechoslovakia
    Herbert H. Lehman Suite and Papers
    James G. McDonald Papers

The Bakhmeteff Archive of Russian and
    East European History and Culture
        Emil Lengyel Collection
    Oral History Collection
    Avery Library

Harvard University Libraries, Cambridge, MA
    The Houghton Library
        Walter Gropius Papers
    The Widener Library
    Harvard Theatre Collection

Huntington Library
    San Marino, CA

Indiana University, Bloomington Library
    Bloomington, IN

Indiana University, Indianapolis Library
    Indianapolis, IN

Bibliography

Library of Congress, Washington, DC
   Rare Book and Special Collections,
      John von Neumann Papers
   The Law Library,
      Unpublished U.S. House of Representatives Committee Hearings, Committee on Immigration and Naturalization
   The Congressional Research Services
   Music Division
      Coolidge Collection/Béla Bartók

Margaret Herrick Library of the Academy of Motion Picture Arts and Sciences and Academy Foundation, Beverly Hills, CA

National Archives and Records Administration, Washington, DC
   Records of the Immigration and Naturalization Service

National Museum of American History, Smithsonian Institution, Washington, DC

New York Public Library, Central Research Library, New York, NY
   Manuscripts and Archives Division
      Emergency Committee in Aid of Displaced Foreign Scholars

Pierpont Morgan Library, New York, NY

Rockefeller Archive Center, Sleepy Hollow, NY
   Emergency Committee in Aid of Displaced Foreign Scholars
   Alfred E. Cohn Papers

Smithsonian Institution, Archives and Libraries, Washington, DC

Stanford University Libraries, Stanford, CA
    Cecil H. Green Library and University Archives
    Department of Special Collections and University Archives,
        George Pólya Papers
        International Rescue Committee
        Gabor Szegő Papers

Stanford University, Hoover Institution on War, Revolution and Peace,
    Library and Archives, Stanford, CA
        Rusztem Vambery Papers
        International Rescue Committee
        Janos Pelenyi Papers

University at Albany, State University of New York, Albany, NY
    M. E. Grenander Department of Special Collections and Archives,
        American Council for Emigres in the Professions
        Committee for Work Relief for Refugees

University of California, Berkeley, Main Library, Berkeley, CA

University of California, Los Angeles (UCLA), Los Angeles, CA
    University Research Library
    Film and Television Archive, Los Angeles, CA

University of California, San Diego, Geisel Library, La Jolla, CA
    Mandeville Department of Special Collections
        Leo Szilard Papers

University of Chicago, Joseph Regenstein Library,
    Department of Special Collections, Chicago, IL
        Michael Polanyi Papers

University of Denver Library, Denver, CO

University of Michigan, Bentley Historical Library, Michigan Historical Collections, Ann Arbor, MI

University of Pennsylvania, University Archives, Philadelphia, PA

University of Pennsylvania, Van Pelt Library, Philadelphia, PA

Woodrow Wilson International Center for Scholars, Washington, DC

Yale School of Music, Oral History Collection, New Haven, CT

Hungary

Eötvös Loránd Tudományegyetem Egyetemi Könyvtár, Kézirattár
 [Eötvös Loránd University Library, MS Collection], Budapest

Magyar Országos Levéltár [Hungarian National Archives]
 Budapest

Magyar Tudományos Akadémia Könyvtára, Kézirattár
 [Library of the Hungarian Academy of Letters and Science, MS Collection] Budapest

Országos Széchényi Könyvtár, Kézirattár [National Széchényi Library, MS Collection] Budapest
 John F. Montgomery Collection

Petőfi Irodalmi Múzeum [Petőfi Museum of Literature] Budapest

Austria

Haus-, Hof- und Staatsarchiv
    Wien

Österreichische Nationalbibliothek
    Wien

Universitätsbibliothek
    Wien

Germany

Bauhaus Archiv, Berlin

Bayerische Staatsbibliothek, München

John F. Kennedy Institute of North American Studies
    Freie Universität, Berlin

Archiv zur Geschichte der Max-Planck-Archiv, Berlin-Dahlem, Germany
    Jewish Refugees Committee
        Nachlass F. A. Paneth
    Paul György Papers
    Haber-Sammlung von Joh. Jaenicke
    Ladislas Farkas file

Humboldt-Universität zu Berlin, Philosophische Fakultät, Universitätsarchiv, Berlin

Politisches Archiv des Auswärtigen Amtes, Berlin

Geheimes Staatsarchiv Preußischer Kulturbesitz, Berlin-Dahlem

Landesarchiv Berlin

Universitätsarchiv der Universität der Künste, Berlin
Ernst von Dohnányi Papers

Printed Sources

Archivalien des Deutschen Exilarchivs 1933–1945. Bestandsübersicht. Leipzig–Frankfurt am Main–Berlin: Die Deutsche Bibliothek, 2005.
Kürschák, Joseph. *Hungarian Problem Book*, I–II. Washington, DC: Mathematical Association of America, 1963.
Mann, Ruth. "The Adjustment of Refugees in the United States in Relation to Their Background." *Jewish Social Service Quarterly*, Vol. 16, No.1 (1939).
Mikola, Sándor. "Die heuristischen Methode im Unterricht der Mathematik der unteren Stufe," in E. Beke und S. Mikola, Hrg., *Abhandlungen über die Reform des mathematischen Unterrichts in Ungarn*. Leipzig und Berlin: Teubner, 1911. pp. 57–73.
Nagy, Ferenc ed. *Neumann János és a "magyar titok" a dokumentumok tükrében* [John von Neumann and the "Hungarian Secret" as shown by documents]. Budapest: Országos Műszaki Információs Központ és Könyvtár, 1987.
Neumann, John Von. *The Computer and the Brain*. New Haven: Yale UP, 1958.
Neumann, John Von. *Theory of Self-Reproducing Automata*. Urbana and London: University of Illinois Press, 1966.

Polanyi, Michael. "Problem solving." *The British Journal for the Philosophy of Science,* Vol. VIII, No. 30, August 1957. pp. 89–103.

Pólya, Georg—Gábor Szegő, *Aufgaben und Lehrsätze aus der Analysis* (Berlin: Springer, 1925, new editions: 1945, 1954, 1964, 1970–71, Vols. I–II; English translation 1972–76)

Pólya, G. *How to Solve it. A New Aspect of Mathematical Method* (Princeton, N.J.: Princeton University Press, 1945)

Pólya, G. *Mathematics and Plausible Reasoning* (Princeton, N.J.: Princeton University Press, 1954, 2nd ed. 1968, Vols. 1–2)

Pólya, G. *Mathematical Discovery. On Understanding, Learning, and Teaching Problem Solving* (New York-London-Sidney: John Wiley and Sons, 1965, Vols. 1–2; combined paperback ed. 1981)

Pólya, George. Methodology or Heuristics, Strategy or Tactics?" *Archives de Philosophie,* Tome 34, Cahier 4, Octobre–Décembre 1971, pp. 623–629.

Pólya, G. "Die Heuristik. Versuch einer vernünftigen Zielsetzung." *Der Mathematikunterricht,* Heft 1/64. Stuttgart: Ernst Klett, 1964. Cf. "L'Heuristique est-elle un sujet d'étude raisonnable?" *La méthode dans les sciences modernes,* "Travail et Méthode", numéro hors série, pp. 279–285.

Pólya, G[eorge] and J[eremy] Kilpatrick. "The Stanford University Competitive Examination in Mathematics," *American Mathematical Monthly,* Vol. 80, No.6, June–July, 1963,

Pólya, G[eorge] and J[eremy] Kilpatrick. *The Stanford Mathematics Problem Book.* New York: Teachers College Press, 1974.

Pólya, G. "Leopold Fejér," *Journal of the London Mathematical Society,* Vol. 36., 1961.

Révész, Géza. "Das frühzeitige Auftreten der Begabung und ihre Erkennung." *Zeitschrift für angewandte Psychologie,* Band 15, Leipzig: Lippert & Co., 1921.

Révész, Géza. *Talent und Genie. Grundzüge einer Begabungspsychologie.* Bern: Francke, 1952.

Saenger, Gerhart. *Today's Refugees, Tomorrow's Citizens: A Story of Americanization.* New York: Harper and Brothers, 1941.

Smith, William Carlson. *Americans in the Making: The Natural History of the Assimilation of Immigrants.* Ann Arbor, Mich.: Edwards Brothers, 1937.

Tartakower, Aryeh. "The Jewish Refugees: A Sociological Survey." *Jewish Social Studies* Vol. 4, No. 4, 1942.

Tartakower, Aryeh and Grossmann, Kurt. *The Jewish Refugee.* New York: Institute of Jewish Affairs, 1944.

Secondary Literature

Alexanderson, Gerald L. "Obituary. George Pólya." *Bulletin of the London Mathematical Society,* Vol. 19, 1987.

Allende-Blin, Juan, Hg. *Musiktradition im Exil. Zurück aus dem Vergessen.* Köln: Bund-Verlag, 1993.

Ambrose, Tom. *Hitler's Loss: What Britain and America Gained from Europe's Cultural Exiles.* London: Peter Owen, 2001.

Anderson, Mark M., ed. *Hitler's Exiles: Personal Stories of the Flight from Nazi Germany to America.* New York: The New Press, 1998.

Árvai Wieschenberg, Ágnes. "Identification and Development of the Mathematically Talented – The Hungarian Experience." Ph.D. Dissertation, The Graduate School of Arts and Sciences, Columbia University, 1984.

Arvai Wieschenberg, Agnes. "A Conversation with George Pólya." *Mathematics Magazine,* Vol. 60, No. 5, December 1987. pp. 265–268.

Arvai Wieschenberg, Agnes. "The Birth of the Eötvös Competition." *The College Mathematics Journal,* Vol. 21, No. 4, September 1990. pp. 286–293.

Ash, Mitchell G. and Alfons Söllner, eds. *Forced Migration and Scientific Change. Emigré German-Speaking Scientists and Scholars after 1933.* Cambridge: Cambridge University Press, 1996.

Aspray, William. *John Von Neumann and the Origins of Modern Computing.* Cambridge, MA—London: The MIT Press, 1990.

Bahr, Ehrhard. *Weimar on the Pacific: German Exile Culture in Los Angeles and the Crisis of Modernism.* Berkeley—Los Angeles—London: University of California Press, 2007.

Balog, M. and J. Rados, Hg. *Abhandlungen über die Reform des mathematischen Unterrichts in Ungarn.* Nach dem ungarischen Original unter Mitwirkung von M. Balog und J. Rados deutsch herausgegeben von E. Beke und S. Mikola. Leipzig: Teubner, 1911.

Barany, George. "'Magyar Jew or Jewish Magyar?' Reflections on the Question of Assimilation." In: Bela Vago and George L. Mosse, eds., *Jews and Non-Jews in Eastern Europe 1918–1945.* Jerusalem: Keter, 1974.

Barron, Stephanie, ed. *Exiles and Émigrés: The Flight of European Artists from Hitler.* Los Angeles: LACMA, 1997.

Bauer, Yehuda. *American Jewry and the Holocaust: The American Jewish Joint Distribution Committee, 1939–1945.* Detroit: Wayne State University Press, 1981.

Bederson, Benjamin. "Fritz Reiche and the Emergency Committee in Aid of Displaced Foreign Scholars." *Physics in Perspective,* Vol. 7, 2005, pp. 453–472.

Benkart, Paula. "Religion, Family, and Community Among Hungarians Migrating to American Cities, 1880–1930." Ph.D. Diss. Johns Hopkins University, 1975.

Bentwich, Norman. *The Rescue and Achievement of Refugee Scholars: The Story of Displaced Scholars and Scientists, 1933–1952.* The Hague, 1953.

Benz, Wolfgang, Hg. *Das Exil der kleinen Leute: Alltagserfahrung deutscher Juden in der Emigration.* Frankfurt a. M.: C. H. Beck, 1991.

Benz, Wolfgang and Marion Neiss, Hg. *Deutsch-jüdisches Exil—das Ende der Assimilation?* Berlin: Metropol, 1994.

Berthold, Werner, Brita Eckert, Frank Wende. *Deutsche Intellektuelle im Exil. Ihre Akademie und die "American Guild for German Cultural Freedom".* Eine Ausstellung des Deutschen Exilarchivs 1933–1945 der Deutschen Bibliothek, Frankfurt am Main. München–New York: Saur, 1993.

Biller, Marita. *Exilstationen. Eine empirische Untersuchung zur Emigration und Remigration deutschsprachiger Journalisten and Publizisten.* Münster–Hamburg: Kit, 1994.

Bowers, David Frederick, ed. *Foreign Influences in American Life. Essays and Critical Bibliographies.* Princeton, N.J.: Princeton University Press, 1944.

Boyers, Robert, ed. *The Legacy of the German Refugee Intellectuals.* New York: Schockem, 1972.

Brecher, Frank W. *Reluctant Ally: United States Foreign Policy toward the Jews from Wilson to Roosevelt.* Westport: Greenwood Press, 1991.

Breitman, Richard and Alan M. Kraut. *American Refugee Policy and European Jewry, 1933–1945.* Bloomington–Indianapolis: Indiana University Press, 1987.

Bródy, David. "American Jewry, the Refugees and Immigration Restriction (1932–1942)," *Publications of the American Jewish Historical Society* 45, June 1956.

Brown, Lawrence Guy. *Immigration, Cultural Conflicts and Social Adjustments.* New York—London—Toronto: Longmans, Green and Co., 1933.

Buchgestaltung im Exil 1933–1950. Eine Ausstellung des Deutschen Exilarchivs 1933–1945 Der Deutschen Bibliothek. Wiesbaden: Harrasowitz Verlag, 2003.

Buck, R. Creighton. "A Look at Mathematical Competitions." *American Mathematical Monthly,* Vol. LXVI, No. 3. March 1959.

Cartledge, Bryan. *The Will to Survive. A History of Hungary.* London: Timewell Press, 2006.

Congdon, Lee. *Exile and Social Thought. Hungarian Intellectuals in Germany and Austria 1919–1933.* Princeton, N.J.: Princeton University Press, 1991.

Congdon, Lee. *Seeing Red: Hungarian Intellectuals in Exile and the Challenge of Communism.* DeKalb, IL: Northern Illinois University Press, 2001.

Corino, Karl, Hg. *Autoren im Exil.* Frankfurt a. M.: Taschenbuch Verlag, 1981.

Coser, Lewis A. *Refugee Scholars in America: Their Impact and Their Experiences.* New Haven and London: Yale University Press, 1984.
Crawford, W. Rex, ed. *The Cultural Migration: The European Scholar in America.* Philadelphia: University of Pennsylvania Press, 1953.
Czeizel, Endre. *Tudósok, gének, tanulságok* [Scientists, genes, lessons]. Budapest: Galenus, 2006. pp. 234–273.
Daniels, Roger. *Guarding the Golden Door: American Immigration Policy and Immigrants Since 1882.* New York: Hill and Wang, 2004.
Davie, Maurice R. and Koenig, Samuel. "The Refugees are now Americans." Public Affairs Pamphlet No. 111. New York: Public Affairs Committee, 1945.
Davie, Maurice R. et al. *Refugees in America. Report of the Committee for the Study of Recent Immigration from Europe.* New York—London: Harper & Brothers, 1947.
Deák, István. *Weimar Germany's Left-Wing Intellectuals. A Political History of the* Weltbühne *and Its Circle.* Berkeley—Los Angeles: University of California Press, 1968.
Die Deutsche Bibliothek. *Inventar zu den Nachlässen emigrierter deutschsprachiger Wissenschaftler in Archiven und Bibliotheken der Bundesrepublik Deutschland.* Bearb. im Deutschen Exilarchiv 1933–1945 der Deutschen Bibliothek, Frankfurt am Main. Red. Bearb. Gabriele von Glasenapp und Barbara Brunn. Vols. 1–2. München: Saur, 1993.
Dinnerstein, Leonard, Roger L. Nichols, and David M. Reimers. *Natives and Strangers: A Multicultural History of Americans.* New York: Oxford University Press, 4th ed. 2003.
Dinnerstein, Leonard. *Uneasy at Home: Antisemitism and the American Jewish Experience.* New York: Columbia University Press, 1987.
Dinnerstein, Leonard. *Antisemitism in America.* New York: Oxford University Press, 1994.
Divine, Robert A. *American Immigration Policy, 1924–1952.* New Haven: Yale University Press, 1957.
Dobos, Krisztina, István Gazda, László Kovács. *Rátz László, Mikola Sándor, Wigner Jenő, Neumann János* [László Rátz, Sándor Mikola, Eugene Wigner, John von Neumann]. Budapest: Országos Pedagógiai Könyvtár és Múzeum, 2002.

Duggan, Stephen and Betty Drury. *The Rescue of Science and Learning: The Story of the Emergency Committee in Aid of Displaced Foreign Scholars.* New York, 1948.
Duncker, Karl. *Zur Psychologie des produktiven Denkens.* Berlin: Julius Springer, 1935.
Durzak, Manfred, Hg. *Die deutsche Exilliteratur 1933–1945.* Stuttgart: Philipp Reclam. Jun., 1973.
Engelmann, Bernt, Hg. *Literatur des Exils.* Eine Dokumentation über die P.E.N.-Jahrestagung in Bremen vom 18. bis 20. September 1980. München: Wilhelm Goldmann Verlag, 1981.
Fairchild, Henry Pratt. *Immigration. A World Movement and Its American Significance.* New York: Macmillan, 1933.
Feilchenfeldt, Konrad. *Deutsche Exilliteratur 1933–1945.* München: Winkler Verlag, 1986.
Feingold, Henry. *Did American Jewry Do Enough During the Holocaust?* Syracuse: Syracuse University, 1985.
Fejős, Zoltán. *A chicagói magyarok két nemzedéke 1890–1940* [Two generations of Chicago Hungarians 1890–1940]. Budapest: Közép-Európa Intézet, 1993.
Fenyo, Mario D. *Literature and Political Change: Budapest, 1908–1918.* Transactions of the American Philosophical Society, Vol. 77, Part 6, 1987.
Fermi, Laura. *Illustrious Immigrants: The Intellectual Migration from Europe 1930–41.* Chicago & London: University of Chicago Press, 1968.
Fields, Harold. *The Refugee in the United States.* New York: Oxford University Press, 1938.
Fischer, Wolfram, Klaus Hierholzer, Michael Hubenstorf, Peter Th. Walther und Rolf Winau, Hg. *Exodus der Wissenschaften aus Berlin. Fragestellungen–Ergebnisse–Desiderate.* Entwicklungen vor und nach 1933 (= Akademie der Wissenschaften zu Berlin, Forschungsbericht 7.) Berlin–New York Walter de Gruyter, 1994.
Fleck, Christian. "Politische Emigration und sozialwissenschaftlicher Wissenstransfer. Am Beispiel Marie Jahodas." In: *Marie Jahoda, Arbeitslose bei der Arbeit. Die Nachfolgeuntersuchung zu "Marienthal" aus dem Jahr 1938.* Frankfurt/ M.–New York: Campus, 1989. pp. i – lxxii.

Fleming, Donald and Bernard Bailyn, eds. *The Intellectual Migration. Europe and America, 1930–1960.* Cambridge, MA: Belknap Press of Harvard University Press, 1969.

Freyermuth, Gundolf S. *Reise in die Verlorengegangenheit. Auf den Spuren deutscher Emigranten (1933–1940).* Hamburg: Rasch und Röhring Verlag, 1990.

Friedman, Saul S. *No Haven for the Oppressed: United States Policy Toward Jewish Refugees, 1938–1945.* Detroit: Wayne State University Press, 1973.

Frühwald, Wolfgang und Wolfgang Schieder, Hg. *Leben im Exil. Probleme der Integration deutscher Flüchtlinge im Ausland 1933–1945.* Hamburg: Hoffmann und Campe, 1981.

Garis, Roy L. *Immigration Restriction.* A Study of the Opposition to and Regulation of Immigration into the United States. New York: Macmillan, 1928.

Gay, Peter. *Freud, Jews and Other Germans. Masters and Victims in Modernist Culture.* Oxford: Oxford University Press, 1979.

Gay, Peter. *Weimar Culture: The Outsider as Insider.* New York: Harper & Row, 1968.

Genizi, Haim. *American Apathy: The Plight of Christian Refugees from Nazism.* Ramat-Gan, Israel: Bar-Ilan University Press, 1983.

Genizi, Haim. "New York is Big–America is Bigger: The Resettlement of Refugees from Nazism, 1936–1945," *Jewish Social Studies,* Vol. 46, No. 1, 1984.

Glimm, James, John Impagliazzo, and Isadore Singer, eds. *The Legacy of John Von Neumann.* Providence, RI: American Mathematical Society, 1990.

Glazer, Nathan. *American Judaism.* Chicago: University of Chicago Press, 1972.

Gluck, Mary. *Georg Lukács and his Generation 1900–1918.* Cambridge, MA and London: Harvard UP, 1985.

Goldner, Franz. *Austrian Emigration 1938 to 1945.* New York: Frederick Ungar Publishing Co., 1979.

Gordon, Charles, and Harry N. Rosenfield. *Immigration Law and Procedure.* Rev. ed. New York: Matthew Bender, 1980. 6 vols.

Gordon, Milton. *Assimilation in American Life: The Role of Race, Religion, and National Origins.* New York: Oxford University Press, 1964.
Gorn, Michael H. *The Universal Man: Theodore von Kármán's Life in Aeronautics.* Washington and London: Smithsonian Institution Press, 1992.
Groth, Michael. *The Road to New York: The Emigration of Berlin Journalists, 1933–1945.* München: Minerva, 1984.
Hadamard, Jacques. *The Psychology of Invention in the Mathematical Field.* New York: Dover Publications, 1954.
Hagemann, Harald und Claus-Dieter Krohn, Hg. (unter Mitarbeit von Hans Ulrich Eßlinger). *Biographisches Handbuch der deutschsprachigen wirtschaftswissenschaftlichen Emigration nach 1933.* Bd 1–2. München: Saur, 1999.
Halmos, P. R. "The Heart of Mathematics." *American Mathematical Monthly,* Vol. 87, 1980, pp. 519–524.
Hamburg 1981: Die jüdische Emigration aus Deutschland 1933–1945. Die Geschichte einer Vertreibung. Eine Ausstellung der Deutschen Bibliothek Frankfurt am Main (=Sonderveröffentlichungen der Deutschen Bibliothek 15), Frankfurt am Main 1985.
Hanák, Péter. *The Garden and the Workshop. Essays on the Cultural History of Vienna and Budapest.* Princeton, NJ: Princeton University Press, 1998.
Hanák, Péter. "Problems of Jewish Assimilation in Austria-Hungary in the Nineteenth and Twentieth Centuries." In: P. Thane et al., eds., *The Power of the Past.* Cambridge: Cambridge University Press, 1984.
Hanák, Péter, ed. *Zsidókérdés, asszimiláció, antiszemitizmus. Tanulmányok a zsidókérdésről a huszadik századi Magyarországon* [Jewish question, assimilation, anti-Semitism. Studies on the Jewish question in twentieth century Hungary]. Budapest: Gondolat, 1984.
Handlin, Oscar. *The Uprooted.* 2nd ed. Boston: Little, Brown and Co., 1973.
Handlin, Oscar. *The Americans.* Boston: Little, Brown and Co., 1963.
Handlin, Oscar, ed. *Immigration as a Factor in American History.* Englewood Cliffs, N.J.: Prentice-Hall, Inc., 1959.

Hansen, Marcus Lee. *The Immigrant in American History*. Schlesinger, Arthur M., ed. Cambridge, MA: Harvard University Press, 1942.

Hargittai, István. *The Martians of Science: Five Physicists Who Changed the Twentieth Century*. New York: Oxford University Press, 2006.

Harper, Elizabeth J. *Immigration Laws of the United States*. 3rd ed. Indianapolis: Bobbs-Merrill Co., Inc., 1975.

Hartmann, Edward George. "The Movement to Americanize the Immigrant." Ph.D. Thesis; New York: Columbia University, 1948.

Heilbut, Anthony. *Exiled in Paradise. German Refugee Artists and Intellectuals in America, from the 1930s to the Present*. New York: Viking Press, 1983.

Heims, Steve J. *John Von Neumann and Norbert Wiener. From Mathematics to the Technologies for Life and Death*. Cambridge, MA—London: The MIT Press, 1981.

Herget, Winfried and Karl Ortseifen, eds. *The Transit of Civilisation from Europe to America*. Essays in Honor of Hans Galinsky. Tübingen: Günter Narr Verlag, 1986.

Hersh, Reuben, and Vera John-Steiner. "A Visit to Hungarian Mathematics." *The Mathematical Intelligencer* 15(2), 1993, pp. 13–26.

Higham, John. *Strangers in the Land: Patterns of American Nativism 1860–1925*. New Brunswick, N.J.: Rutgers University Press, 1955.

Higham, John. *Send These To Me. Jews and Other Immigrants to Urban America*. New York: Athenaeum, 1975.

Hilchenbach, Maria. *Kino im Exil: Die Emigration deutscher Filmkünstler 1933–1945*. München: Saur, 1982.

Hittrich, Ödön. *A Budapesti Ágostai Hitvallású Evangélikus Főgimnázium első száz esztendejének története*. [The Centenary History of the Lutheran High School in Budapest.] Budapest: Kellner ny., 1923.

Hoch, Paul. "The reception of Central European refugee physicists of the 1930s: USSR, UK, USA." *Annals of Science*, Vol. 40, 1983, pp. 206–246.

Hofner-Kulenkamp, Gabriele. *Kunsthistorikerinnen im Exil*, 2 Teile, Magisterarbeit Hamburg 1991, Typescript.

Hoglund, A. William. *Immigrants and Their Children in the United States: A Bibliography of Doctoral Dissertations, 1885–1982*. New York: Garland, 1986.

Horak, Jan-Christopher. *Fluchtpunkt Hollywood. Eine Dokumentation zur Filmemigration nach 1933*. 2., erw. und korrigierte Aufl., unter Mitarbeit von Elisabeth Tape. Münster: MAkS, 1986.
Horváth, Zoltán. *Magyar századforduló. A második reformnemzedék története 1896–1914* [Hungarian Fin-de-siècle. A History of the Second Reform Generation]. 2nd ed. Budapest: Gondolat, 1974.
Hölbling, Walter and Reinhold Wagnleitner, eds. *The European Emigrant Experience in the U.S.A.* Tübingen: Gunter Narr Verlag, 1992.
Hughes, H. Stuart. *Consciousness and Society: The Reorientation of European Social Thought 1890–1930*. New York: Vintage Books, 1958.
Hughes, H. Stuart. *The Sea Change. The Migration of Social Thought, 1930–1965*. New York: Harper & Row, 1975.
Ignotus, Paul. "The Hungary of Michael Polanyi." In: *The Logic of Personal Knowledge*. Essays Presented to Michael Polanyi on His Seventieth Birthday 11 March 1961. Glencoe, IL: The Free Press, 1961. pp. 3–12.
Illyefalvi, Lajos I. *A közoktatásügy Budapesten a világháborut megelőző években* [Public Education in Budapest before the War]. Statisztikai Közlemények 71, 3. Budapest: Székesfővárosi Házinyomda, 1935.
Jackman, Jarrell C. and Carla M. Borden, eds. *The Muses Flee Hitler: Cultural Transfer and Adaptation 1930–1945*. Washington, DC: Smithsonian Institution Press, 1983.
Janik, Allan and Stephen Toulmin. *Wittgenstein's Vienna*. New York: Simon and Schuster, 1973.
Jarmatz, Klaus. *Literatur im Exil*. Berlin: Dietz Verlag, 1966.
Jay, Martin. *The Dialectical Imagination: A History of the Frankfurt School and the Institute of Social Research 1923–1950*. Boston–Toronto: Little, Brown & Co., 1973.
Jay, Martin. *Permanent Exiles: Essays on the Intellectual Migration from Germany to America*. New York: Columbia University Press, 1985.
Jenks, Jeremiah W., and W. Jett Lauck. *The Immigration Problem. A Study of American Immigration Conditions and Needs*. New York and London: Funk & Wagnalls Company, 1926.
Johnston, William M. *The Austrian Mind: An Intellectual and Social History 1848–1938*. Berkeley—Los Angeles—London: University of California Press, 1972.

Die jüdische Emigration aus Deutschland 1933–1941. Die Geschichte einer Austreibung. Eine Ausstellung der Deutschen Bibliothek, Frankfurt am Main, unter Mitwirkung des Leo Baeck Instituts, New York. Frankfurt a. M.: Buchhändler-Vereinigung, 1985.

Kändler, Klaus A. O., Hg. *Berliner Begegnungen. Ausländische Künstler in Berlin 1918 bis 1933.* Berlin: Dietz Verlag, 1987.

Kantorowicz, Alfred. *Politik und Literatur im Exil. Deutschsprachige Schriftsteller im Kampf gegen den Nationalsozialismus.* Hamburg: Christians, 1978.

Karády, Viktor. *Iskolarendszer és felekezeti egyenlőtlenségek Magyarországon (1867–1945). Történeti-szociológiai tanulmányok* [School system and denominational inequalities in Hungary 1867–1945. Historical-sociological studies]. Budapest: Replika Kör, 1997.

Kármán, Theodore von, with Lee Edson. *The Wind and Beyond: Theodore von Kármán, Pioneer in Aviation and Pathfinder in Space.* Boston–Toronto: Little, Brown and Co., 1967.

Kent, Donald Peterson. *The Refugee Intellectual: The Americanization of the Immigrants of 1933–1941.* New York: Columbia University Press, 1953.

Kesten, Hermann, Hg. *Deutsche Literatur im Exil. Briefe europäischer Autoren 1933–1949.* Wien–München–Basel: Verlag Kurt Desch, 1964.

Kettler, David and Gerhard Lauer, eds. *Exile, Science, and Bildung: The Contested Legacies of German Émigré Intellectuals.* New York: Palgrave Macmillan, 2005.

Koestler, Arthur. *Insight and Outlook: An Inquiry into the Common Foundations of Science, Art and Social Ethics.* New York: Macmillan, 1949.

Koestler, Arthur. *The Sleepwalkers: A History of Man's Changing Vision of the Universe.* New York: Grosset & Dunlap, 1959.

Koestler, Arthur. *The Act of Creation.* New York: Macmillan, 1964.

Kovács, Ilona, ed. *The Hungarians in the United States: An Annotated Bibliography.* Kent State University Press, 1975; Budapest: ELTE Folklore Tanszék, 1981.

Kovács, Ilona. *Az amerikai közkönyvtárak magyar gyűjteményeinek szerepe az asszimiláció és az identitás megőrzésének kettős folyamatában 1890–1940* [The role of the Hungarian collections of American public libraries in the double process of assimilation and identity preservation 1890–1940]. Budapest: Országos Széchényi Könyvtár, 1997.

Kontler, László. *A History of Hungary: Millennium in Central Europe.* Palgrave Macmillan, 2003.

Kovács, László. *Mikola Sándor.* Budapest: Országos Pedagógiai Könyvtár és Múzeum, 2nd ed. 1995.

Kovács, Mária M. *Liberal Professions and Illiberal Politics: Hungary from the Habsburgs to the Holocaust.* Washington, DC: Woodrow Wilson Center Press and New York–Oxford: Oxford University Press, 1994.

Kravetz, Nathan, ed. *Displaced German Scholars: A Guide to Academics in Peril in Nazi Germany during the 1930s.* San Bernadino, CA: The Borgo Press, 1993.

Kretschmer, Ernst. *Geniale Menschen.* 2. Aufl. Berlin: Julius Springer, 1931.

Krohn, Claus-Dieter. *Wissenschaft im Exil. Deutsche Sozial- and Wirtschaftswissenschaftler in den USA und die New School for Social Research.* Frankfurt–New York: Campus Verlag, 1987.

Krohn, Claus-Dieter. *Intellectuals in Exile: Refugee Scholars and the New School for Social Research.* Amherst: University of Massachusetts Press, 1993.

Krohn, Claus-Dieter, Patrick von zur Mühlen, Gerhard Paul, Lutz Winckler, Hg. (in Zusammenarbeit mit der Gesellschaft für Exilforschung). *Handbuch der deutschsprachigen Emigration 1933–1945.* Darmstadt: Wissenschaftliche Buchgesellschaft, 1998.

Kröner, Peter, ed., *Vor fünfzig Jahren. Die Emigration deutschsprachiger Wissenschaftler 1933–1939.* Katalog anläßlich des 21. Symposions der Gesellschaft Wissenschaftsgeschichte. Münster: Gesellschaft für Wissenschaftsgeschichte, 1983.

Laqueur, Walter. *Generation Exodus: The Fate of Young Jewish Refugees from Nazi Germany.* Hanover–London: Brandeis University Press/ University Press of New England, 2001.

Lange-Eichbaum, W. *Genie, Irrsinn und Ruhm*. München: Ernst Reinhardt, 1928.
Lange-Eichbaum, W. *Das Genie-Problem*. München: Ernst Reinhardt, 1931.
lászló moholy-nagy: from budapest to berlin 1914–1923. Newark, DE: University Gallery, University of Delaware, 1995.
Lehmann, Hartmut and James J. Sheehan, eds. *An Interrupted Past. German Speaking Refugee Historians in the United States after 1933*. Washington, DC: German Historical Institute, 1991.
Lendvai, Paul. *The Hungarians: A Thousand Years of Victory in Defeat*. Princeton, NJ: Princeton University Press, 2003.
Lepsius, M. Rainer, Hg. *Soziologie in Deutschland und Österreich, 1918–1945: Materialien zur Entwicklung, Emigration und Wirkungsgeschichte*. Opladen: Westdeutscher Verlag, 1981.
Levenstein, Aaron. *Escape to Freedom: The Story of the International Rescue Committee*. Westport CT: Greenwood Press, 1983.
Lipset, Seymour Martin and Earl Raab. *The Politics of Unreason: Right Wing Extremism in America 1790–1970*. New York: Harper and Row, 1970.
Lipstadt, Deborah E. *Beyond Belief: The American Press and the Coming of the Holocaust 1933–1945*. New York: The Free Press, 1986.
Loewy, Ernst, Hg. *Exil. Literarische und politische Texte aus dem deutschen Exil 1933–1945*. Stuttgart: J. B. Metzlersche Verlagsbuchhandlung, 1979.
Luick-Thramsaus, Michael. "Creating 'New Americans': WWII-Era European Refugees' Formation of American Identities." Ph.D. Dissertation, Humboldt-Universität, Berlin, 1997.
Lukacs, John. *Budapest 1900. A Historical Portrait of a City and Its Culture*. New York: Weidenfeld & Nicolson, 1988.
Mach, Ernst. *Erkenntnis und Irrtum. Skizzen zur Psychologie der Forschung*. 2nd ed. Leipzig: Barth, 1906.
Macrae, Norman. *John von Neumann*. New York: Pantheon, 1992.

Maimann, Helene und Heinz Lunzer. *Österreicher im Exil 1934 bis 1945*. Protokoll des internationalen Symposiums zur Erforschung des österreichischen Exils von 1934 bis 1945. Dokumentationsarchiv des österreichischen Widerstandes und Dokumentationsstelle für Neuere Österreichische Literatur. Wien: Österreichischer Bundesverlag für Unterricht, Wissenschaft und Kunst, 1977.
Mann, Miklós. *Trefort Ágoston élete és működése* [The life and work of Ágoston Trefort]. Budapest: Akadémiai Kiadó, 1982.
Marrus, Michael R. *The Unwanted. European Refugees in the Twentieth Century*. New York–Oxford: Oxford University Press, 1985.
Marx, George, ed., in cooperation with Sybil Francis, Burton C. Hacker, Gábor Palló, *The Martians: Hungarian Émigré Scientists and the Technologies of Peace and War 1919–1989*. Proceedings of the workshop organized by the International Committee for the History of Technology. Budapest: Eötvös Loránd University, 1997.
Marx, George. *The Voice of the Martians*. Budapest: Akadémiai Kiadó, 1997.
McCagg, Jr., William O. *Jewish Nobles and Geniuses in Modern Hungary*. Boulder CO: East European Monographs, 1972, repr. 1986.
McCagg, Jr., William O. *A History of Habsburg Jews, 1670–1918*. Bloomington and Indianapolis: Indiana University Press, 1989.
McCagg, Jr., William O. "Jewish Conversion in Hungary." In: Todd Endelmann, ed., *Jewish Apostasy in the Modern World*. New York: Holmes and Meier, 1987.
Medawar, Jean and David Pyke. *Hitler's Gift: Scientists Who Fled Nazi Germany*. London: Richard Cohen Books and EJPS, 2000.
Mészáros, Judit. "Az Önök Bizottsága." Ferenczi Sándor, a budapesti iskola és a pszichoanalitikus emigráció. ["Your Committee:" Sándor Ferenczi, the Budapest School and the Emigration of Psychoanalysts] Budapest: Akadémiai Kiadó, 2008.
Miller, Michael L. "'A numerus clausus száműzöttjei' a berlini felsőoktatási intézetekben 1920 és 1933 között" [Exiles of the *numerus clausus* at Berlin Universities, 1920–1933]. *Múlt és Jövő*, 2006/4, pp. 84–91.

Mitchell, David. *1919 Red Mirage*. New York: Macmillan, 1970.
Möller, Horst, Hg. *Biographisches Handbuch der deutschsprachigen Emigration nach 1933*. Bd. 1-3. München: Institut für Zeitgeschichte, New York: Research Foundation for Jewish Immigration, 1980-1983.
Möller, Horst. "Wissenschaft in der Emigration—Quantitative und geographische Aspekte." Special Issue: Vor fünfzig Jahren: Emigration und Immigration von Wissenschaft. *Berichte zur Wissenschaftsgeschichte*, Vol. 7, 1984.
Möller, Horst. *Exodus der Kultur. Schriftsteller, Wissenschaftler und Künstler in der Emigration nach 1933*. München: C. H. Beck, 1984, engl. 1983.
Némethné Pap, Kornélia. *Rátz László tanár úr* [Professor László Rátz]. Studia Physica Savariensia, XIII. Szombathely: Berzsenyi Dániel Főiskola, 2006.
Nyíri, Kristóf. *A Monarchia szellemi életéről* [The intellectual life of the (Austro-Hungarian) Monarchy]. Budapest: Gondolat, 1980.
Nyíri, J. C. *Am Rande Europas. Studien zur österreichisch-ungarischen Philosophiegeschichte*. Wien: Böhlau, 1988.
Ostwald, Wilhelm. *Grosse Männer*. Leipzig: Akademische Verlagsgesellschaft m.b.H., 1910.
Österreicher im Exil – USA 1938-1945. Eine Dokumentation, Bd. 1-2. Hg. vom Dokumentationsarchiv des österreichischen Widerstandes. Wien: Österreichischer Bundesverlag, 1995.
Palló, G[ábor]. "Scientists' First Step of Emigration: From the Hungarian Periphery to the Centre." *Periodica Polytechnica. Chemical Engineering*, Vol. 34, No. 4, 1990, pp. 319-323.
Palló, G[ábor]. "Scientists' Second Step of Emigration: Toward the New Centers." *Periodica Polytechnica. Chemical Engineering*, Vol. 35, Nos. 1-2, 1991, pp. 77-86.
Palló, Gábor. *Zsenialitás és korszellem. Világhírű magyar tudósok* [Genius and *Zeitgeist*. World famous Hungarian scientists]. Budapest: Áron, 2004.
Palmer, Alan. *The Lands Between: A History of East-Central Europe since the Congress of Vienna*. New York: Macmillan, 1970.

Palmier, Jean-Michel. *Weimar in Exile. The Antifascist Emigration in Europe and America.* London—New York: Verso. 2006.
Passuth, Krisztina. *Moholy-Nagy.* London: Thames and Hudson, 1985.
Pastor, Peter. *Hungary Between Wilson and Lenin: The Hungarian Revolution of 1918–1919 and the Big Three.* Boulder: East European Quarterly, 1976.
Patai, Raphael. *The Jews of Hungary: History, Culture, Psychology.* Detroit: Wayne State University Press, 1996.
Perspectives in American History, Vol. 2: The Intellectual Migration: Europe and America, 1930–1960. Cambridge, MA, 1968.
Pross, Helge. *Die deutsche akademische Emigration nach den Vereinigten Staaten 1933–1941.* Berlin: Duncker & Humblot, 1955.
Radkau, Joachim. *Die deutsche Emigration in die USA: Ihr Einfluß auf die amerikanische Europapolitik, 1933–1945.* Düsseldorf: Bertelsmann, 1971.
Radnai, Gyula, "Az Eötvös-korszak." [The Eötvös-era]. *Fizikai Szemle,* Vol. XLI, No. 10, 1991, pp. 341–380.
Radó, T. "On Mathematical Life in Hungary." *American Mathematical Monthly,* Vol. XXXIX, 1932. pp. 85–90.
Reibmayr, Albert. *Die Entwicklungsgeschichte des Talentes und Genies.* Vols. I–II. München: J. F. Lehmanns, 1908.
Reingold, Nathan. "Refugee mathematicians in the United States, 1933–1941: Reception and reaction." *Annals of Science,* Vol. 38, 1981, pp. 313–338.
Rider, Robin E. "Alarm and opportunity: Emigration of mathematicians and physicists to Britain and the United States, 1933–1945." *Historical Studies in the Physical Sciences,* Vol. 15, No.1, 1984.
Rozenblit, Marsha L. *The Jews of Vienna: Assimilation and Identity, 1867–1914.* Albany: SUNY, 1983.
Schaber, Will, Hg. *Aufbau/Reconstruction.* Dokumente einer Kultur im Exil. New York: The Overlook Press – Köln: Kiepenheuer & Witsch, 1972.
Schoenfeld, Alan H. "George Pólya and Mathematics Education." In: Gerald L. Alexanderson, Lester H. Lange, "Obituary. George Pólya." *Bulletin of the London Mathematical Society,* Vol. 19, 1987.

Smith, William Carlson. *Americans in the Making. The Natural History of the Assimilation of Immigrants.* New York—London: D. Appleton-Century Co. Inc., 1939.
Somlyódy, László and Nóra Somlyódy, eds. *Hungarian Arts and Sciences 1848–2000.* Boulder, CO: Social Science Monographs–Highland Lakes, NJ: Atlantic Research and Publications, Inc., 2003.
Sőtér, István. *Eötvös József.* 2nd ed. Budapest: Akadémiai Kiadó, 1967.
Spalek, John M., Hg. *Deutschsprachige Exilliteratur seit 1933.* Bd. I–VI. Bern–München: Saur, 1976–2008.
Spalek, John M. und Sandra H. Hawrylchak, Hg. *Guide to the Archival Materials of the German-speaking Emigration to the United States after 1933/Verzeichnis der Quellen und Materialien der deutschsprachigen Emigration in den USA seit 1933.* Vols. 1–3. Bern–München: K. G. Saur, 1992–1997.
Spalek, John M. and Robert F. Bell, eds. *Exile: The Writer's Experience.* Chapel Hill, N.C.: The University of North Carolina Press, 1982.
Stadler, Friedrich, Hg. *Vertriebene Vernunft. Emigration und Exil österreichischer Wissenschaft 1930–45.* Bd. 1–2. Wien: Jugend und Volk, 1987–88.
Stephan, Alexander. *Im Visier des FBI: Deutsche Exilschriftsteller in den Akten amerikanischer Geheimdienste.* Berlin: Aufbau, 1998.
Sternfeld, Wihelm and Eva Tiedemann. *Deutsche Exil-Literatur, 1933–1945: Eine Bio-Bibliographie.* Heidelberg: Lambert Schneider, 1962.
Strauss, Herbert A. and Werner Röder, Hg. *Biographisches Handbuch der deutschsprachigen Emigration nach 1933.* Hg. vom Institut für Zeitgeschichte, München, und von der Research Foundation for Jewish Immigration, New York. Bd. I–III. München: K. G. Saur, 1999.
Strauss, Herbert A., Werner Röder (Hg. mit Hannah Caplan, Egon Radvany, Horst Möller, Dieter Marc Schneider). *International Biographical Dictionary of Central European Emigrés 1933–1945.* Munich–New York: Walter De Gruyter, 1983.
Strauss, Herbert A., Tilmann Buddensieg und Kurt Düwell, Hg. *Emigration. Deutsche Wissenschaftler nach 1933–Entlassung und Vertreibung.* (List of Displaced German Scholars 1936. Supplementary List of Displaced German Scholars 1937. The Emergency Committee

in Aid of Displaced Foreign Scholars 1941.) Berlin: Technische Universität Berlin 1987.

Strauss, Herbert A. *Jewish Immigrants of the Nazi Period in the USA.* Vols. 1–7. New York–München–London–Paris: K. G. Saur, 1981–1992.

Strauss, Herbert A., Klaus Fischer, Christhard Hoffmann, Hg. *Die Emigration der Wissenschaften nach 1933: Disziplingeschichtliche Studien.* München: Alfons Sölner, 1991.

Sugar, Peter F., Péter Hanák, Tibor Frank, eds., *A History of Hungary.* Bloomington–Indianapolis: Indiana University Press, 1994.

Surányi, János and Mária Halmos. "The Evolution of Modern Mathematics Education in Hungary." In: Frank J. Swetz, ed., *Socialist Mathematics Education.* Southampton: Burgundy Press, 1978.

Synott, Marcia Graham. *The Half-Opened Door: Discrimination and Admissions at Harvard, Yale, and Princeton, 1900–1970.* Westport, Conn.: Greenwood Press, 1979.

Szénássy, Barna. *History of Mathematics in Hungary until the 20th Century.* Berlin: Springer-Verlag, 1992.

Széplaki, Joseph, ed. *The Hungarians in America, 1583–1974. A Chronology & Fact Book.* Dobbs Ferry, NY: Oceana Publications, Inc., 1975.

Széplaki, Joseph, ed. *Hungarians in the United States and Canada: A Bibliography.* Minneapolis: Immigration History Research Center, University of Minnesota, 1977.

Szirmay-Pulszky, H. von. *Genie und Irrsinn im Ungarischen Geistesleben.* München: Ernst Reinhardt, 1935.

Szy, Tibor, ed. *Hungarians in America. A Biographical Directory of Professionals of Hungarian Origin in the Americas.* New York: The Kossuth Foundation, Inc. 1966.

Tabori, Paul. *An Anatomy of Exile. A Semantic and Historical Study.* London: Harrap, 1972.

Taylor, John Russell. *Strangers in Paradise: The Hollywood Emigres 1933–1950.* London: Faber and Faber, 1983.

Taylor, Philip. *The Distant Magnet: European Immigration to the U.S.A.* London: Eyre & Spottiswoode, 1971.

Thernstrom, Stephan, ed. *Harvard Encyclopedia of American Ethnic Groups.* Cambridge, MA: Harvard University Press, 1980.

Tokes, Rudolf. *Béla Kun and the Hungarian Soviet Republic: The origins and role of the Communist Party of Hungary in the revolutions of 1918–1919.* New York: Published for the Hoover Institution on War, Revolution and Peace, Stanford, California, by F. A. Praeger, 1967.

Trapp, Frithjof, Werner Mittenzwei, Henning Rischbieter, Hansjörg Schneider, Hg. *Handbuch des deutschsprachigen Exiltheaters 1933–1945.* Bd. 1–2. München: Saur, 1999.

Tutas, H. J. *Nationalsozialismus und Exil: Die Politik des Dritten Reiches gegenüber der deutschen politischen Emigration, 1933–1939.* München: Hanser, 1975.

Türck, Hermann. *Der geniale Mensch.* 7. Aufl., Berlin: Dümmlers, 1910.

Ulam, S. "John Von Neumann." *American Mathematical Society Bulletin,* Vol. 64, Part 2, 1958, pp. 1–49.

Ulam, S. M. *Adventures of a Mathematician.* New York: Scribner's, 1976.

Várdy, Stephen Bela. *The Hungarian-Americans.* Boston: Twayne Publishers, 1985.

Várdy, S. B. and Ágnes Huszár Várdy. "Historical, Literary, Linguistic and Ethnographic Research on Hungarian-Americans. A Historiographical Assessment." *Hungarian Studies,* Vol. I, No. 1, 1985, pp. 77–122.

Vonneumann, Nicholas A. *John von Neumann as Seen by his Brother.* Meadowbrook, PA, 1987.

Vörös, Károly, ed. *Budapest története* [The History of Budapest]. Vol. IV. Budapest: Akadémiai Kiadó, 1978. pp. 321–723.

Wagner, Francis S. *Hungarian Contributions to World Civilization.* Center Square, PA: Alpha Publications, 1977.

Wegner, Matthias. *Exil und Literatur: Deutsche Schriftsteller im Ausland 1933–1945.* Frankfurt-am-Main: Athenäum, 1967.

Weibel, Peter und Friedrich Stadler, eds. *The Cultural Exodus from Austria.* 2nd ed. Vienna–New York: Springer Verlag, 1995.

Wendland, Ulrike. *Biographisches Handbuch deutschsprachiger Kunsthistoriker im Exil: Leben und Werk der unter dem Nationalsozialismus verfolgten und vertriebenen Wissenschaftler.* Teil 1–2. München: Saur, 1999.

Werner, Klaus Ulrich. *Exil im Archiv: Das "Deutsche Exilarchiv 1933–1944" der Deutschen Bibliothek.* Herzberg: Bautz, 1992.

Wyman, David S. *Paper Walls. America and the Refugee Crisis 1938–1941.* New York: Pantheon Books, 1968.

Wyman, David S. *The Abandonment of the Jews: America and the Holocaust 1941–1945.* New York: Pantheon Books, 1984.

Zucker, Norman L. and Naomi Flink Zucker. *The Guarded Gate: The Reality of American Refugee Policy.* San Diego: Harcourt Brace Jovanovich, 1987.

zur Mühlen, Patrick von. *Fluchtweg Spanien-Portugal: Die deutsche Emigration und der Exodux aus Europa, 1933–1945.* Bonn: J. H. W. Dietz, 1992.

Gary P. Zola with Jonathan Krasner, eds. American Jewish History: A Selected Bibliography. The Commission for Commemorating 350 Years of American Jewish History. http://www.350th.org/history/bibliography.html

Zühlsdorff, Volkmar. *Deutsche Akademie im Exil: der vergessene Widerstand.* Berlin: EMV, 1999.

Related Articles by the Author

Permission was generously granted by the copyright owners to use parts or versions of some of the following articles in this book:

Frank, Tibor. "Double Divorce: The Case of Mariette and John von Neumann." *Nevada Historical Society Quarterly,* Vol. 34, No. 2, Summer 1991, pp. 360–363.

Frank, Tibor. "Pioneers Welcome: The Escape of Hungarian Modernism to the US, 1919–1945." *Hungarian Studies,* Vol. 8, No. 2, 1993, pp. 237–260.

Frank, Tibor. "Between Red and White: The Mood and Mind of Hungary's Radicals, 1919–1920." *Hungarian Studies,* Vol. 9, No. 1–2, 1994, pp. 105–126.

Frank, Tibor. "Via Berlin to New York: The Human Geography of Hungarian Migrations after World War I." In: Klaus Frantz (ed.), *Human Geography in North America: New Perspectives and Trends in Research.* Innsbruck, Institut für Geographie der Universität Innsbruck, 1996. pp. 169–180. (Innsbrucker Geographische Studien; 26.)

Frank, Tibor. "The Chemistry of Budapest (The Social Construction of Hungarian Genius)." In: George Marx, ed., in cooperation with Sybil Francis, Burton C. Hacker, Gábor Palló, *The Martians: Hungarian Émigré Scientists and the Technologies of Peace and War 1919–1989.* Proceedings of the workshop organized by the International Committee for the History of Technology. Budapest: Eötvös Loránd University, 1997. pp. 22–43.

Frank, Tibor. "Station Berlin: Ungarische Wissenschaftler und Künstler in Deutschland 1919–1933." *IMIS-Beiträge,* Vol. 10, 1999, pp. 7–38.

Frank, Tibor. "Cohorting, Networking, Bonding: Michael Polanyi in Exile." *Polanyiana,* Vol. 10, No. 1–2, 2001, pp. 108–126.

Frank, Tibor. "The Secret of Survival: Problem Solving and Creativity in Hungarian History." In: László Somlyódy, Nóra Somlyódy, eds. *Hungarian Arts and Sciences 1848–2000.* New York: Columbia University Press, 2003. pp. 5–21. (East European Monographs DCXXXV)

Frank, Tibor. "Patterns of Interwar Hungarian Immigration to the United States." *Hungarian Studies Review,* Vol. XXX, No. 1–2, 2003, pp. 3–27.

Frank, Tibor. "Theodore von Kármán: A Global Life." In: János Vad, Tamás Lajos, Rudolf Schilling, eds., *Modelling Fluid Flow. The State of the Art.* Berlin: Springer, 2004, pp. 79–89.

Frank, Tibor, ed. *George Pólya and the Heuristic Tradition.* Berlin: Max Planck Institut für Wissenschaftsgeschichte, 2004. *210 p.*

Frank, Tibor. "George Pólya and the Heuristic Tradition." *Revista Brasileira de História da Matemática,* Vol. 4, No. 7, Abril 2004, pp. 19–36.

Frank, Tibor, ed. *Ever Ready to Go: The Multiple Exiles of Leo Szilard.* Berlin: Max Planck Institut für Wissenschaftsgeschichte, 2004. Vols. 1–3. 447 p.

Frank, Tibor. "Ever Ready to Go. The Multiple Exiles of Leo Szilard." *Physics in Perspective,* Vol. 7, No. 2, June 2005, pp. 204–252.

Frank, Tibor. "Der Kult des Allwissens im Budapest des Fin de Siècle." In: Frank Baron, David Norman Smith, Charles Reitz, eds., *Authority, Culture, and Communication: The Sociology of Ernest Manheim,* Heidelberg: Synchron Verlag, 2005. *pp. 89–116.*

Frank, Tibor. "Berlin Junction: Patterns of Hungarian intellectual migrations, 1919–1933." *Storicamente* (Bologna) 2, 2006.

Frank, Tibor. "The Social Construction of Hungarian Genius (1867–1930)." Background Paper for the Panel Discussion: "Budapest: The Golden Years.," Princeton Institute for International and Regional Studies, Princeton University, Princeton, N.J., October 5, 2007. Supported by a grant from the John Templeton Foundation.

Index

Abraham, Karl 153
Abraham, Paul [Pál Ábrahám] 8, 22, 137, 139, 156, 239, 439
Acél, Pál 134
Achron, Joseph 107
Ádám, Lajos 273
Adamic, Louis 278, 280–283
Adams, Henry 142, 149
Adler, Friedrich 75
Adler, Marianne [Marianne Flesch] 10, 127
Adler-Goldstein, Vilma 52
Ady, Endre 32, 36, 43, 53, 91, 140, 400
Agay, Denes [Dénes Ágay] 439
Ágoston, Péter 49
Albók, John 8, 206
Albók Vitarius, Ilona 8, 206
Alexander, Bernát 93
Alexander, Franz [Ferenc Alexander] 153, 164, 439
Alexanderson, Gerald L. 11
Alpar, Gitta [Gitta Alpár, Regina Klopfer] 137, 149, 156, 165, 439
Alton, John [Johann Altmann] 439
Anday, Rosette [Piroska] 130, 165
Andrássy, Gyula Count 84
Angyal 336
Antal, Frederick 36, 83, 306, 316, 317
Antal, Mrs. Frederick [Ilona Waldbauer] 10, 22
Antalffy-Zsiross, Dezső 130, 232, 439
Appleget, Thomas B. 333
Appel, Marta 204
Arany, Dániel 72
Aranyi [d'Aranyi], Yelly 22

Archipenko, Aleksandr Porfirevich 117, 154
Arendt, Hannah 208
Arnold, H. H. ["Hap"] 375, 376, 378
Árvai, Irén 439
Astair, Fred 147
Auer, John 439

Babits, Mihály 53
Bach, Johann Sebastian 106, 108, 123
Bailyn, Bernard 11, 17
Bak, Robert C. [Robert Bak] 440
Baker, Josephine 147
Balassa, József 87
Balázs, Béla 22, 53, 83, 103, 127
Balazs, Frigyes [Frigyes Balázs] 440
Baldwin, Delavan M. 283
Balint, Michael [Mihály Bálint] 136, 153
Bálint, Rezső 92
Balogh, Elemér 306, 318, 324, 326, 327, 343
Balogh, Erno [Ernő Balogh] 232, 440
Balogh, Thomas, Lord Balogh of Hampstead 59
Bandholtz, Harry Hill 88
Bang-Kaup, Willy 138
Bánki, Donát 355
Bánki, Veronika 12
Bánky, Vilma [Vilma Konsics] 130, 231, 440
Bányai, Tibor 133
Barany, George 11
Barati, George [György Baráti] 440
Barker, Howard 187
Baron, Frank 11

Báron, Gyula 208
Báron, Sándor 92
Barr, Alfred H., Jr. 119
Barraud, Henri 108
Bársony, János 92
Bársony, Rózsi 137, 156
Bartók, Béla 8, 22, 36, 52–54, 107, 109–111, 124, 130, 135, 208, 209, 272, 277, 306, 307, 348, 440
Bászel, Aurél 66
Bator, Victor [Viktor Bátor] 440
Back, Sir Arnold 107
Beach, Sylvia 223
Beale, Phelan 283
Beck, Paul A. 440
Becker, Karl Heinrich 137–138
Beethoven, Ludwig van 31, 54, 108, 122, 123
Békássy, István 440
Beke, Manó 93, 355
Békésy, Georg von 22
Békessy, Imre 322, 328, 440
Békessy, János [Hans Habe] 322, 328, 440
Békessy, Mrs. Imre 328
Bela, Miklos 440
Bender, Thomas 12, 220–222
Benedek, László 440
Benedek, Therese 440
Benedek, Tibor 337
Berény, Róbert 53, 154,
Berg, Alban 147
Berkeley, George 76
Berkovici, Konrad 227, 228
Bernáth, Aurél 130, 154
Bernhardt, Sarah 46
Bernstein, Henry 46
Berwald, Astrid 127
Berwald, Franz 127
Bessenyei, Gabor de 230
Bethlen, István, Count 103

Beveridge, Sir William [later Lord Beveridge] 258, 259, 287, 288
Biele, Harry D. 219
Biller, Irén 440
Billikopf, Jacob 214, 215
Binet, Alfred 74
Biro, Lajos [Lajos Bíró, Lajos Blau] 85–87, 89–91, 94, 230, 440
Bismarck, Otto von, Prinz 251
Blacket, Patrick 411
Blair, C. Ledyard 283
Bliven, Bruce 280
Bloch, Ernest 107, 109, 147
Boas, Franz 262, 303
Bobertag, Otto 74
Bodenheimer, Anne 11
Bodenstein, Ernst 254
Bogdanov, Alexander Alexandrovich 75
Bohem, Endre [Endre Böhm, Andrew Gordon Boehm] 440
Bőhm, Károly 66
Bohr, Harald 315
Bohr, Niels 102, 164, 259, 315
Bois-Reymond, Emil du 145, 168
Bókay, Árpád 92
Bokros Birman, Dezső 154
Bollobás, Enikő 12
Boltzmann, Ludwig 75
Bolzano, Bernard 78
Born, Max 137, 140
Borshy Kerekes, György 440
Bortnyik, Sándor 23, 130, 154
Boulanger, Nadia 223
Bowen, Harold G. 411
Bowles, Chester 426, 427, 428
Brahm, Otto [Otto Abrahamson, Abramsohn] 44
Brahms, Johannes 31, 51, 52, 105, 106, 123–125
Brassaï [Halász, Gyula] 22, 155
Braun, Marcus 226

Index

Braun, Miklós 154
Braun, Soma 93
Bredig, Georg 132
Brehm, Alfred Edmund 31
Breit, Gregory 412
Breitman, Richard 302
Brentano, Franz 75
Bresslau, Harry 46
Breuer, Marcel 111, 440, 154
Brod, Max 46
Bródy, Imre 136, 137, 155, 156
Bródy, Sándor 39
Brown, Harrison S. 417
Brown, J. J. 190
Bruch, Rüdiger vom 12
Brunauer, Stephen 440
Buck, Pearl S. 419
Bühler, Karl 152
Bukharin, Nikolai Ivanovich 266
Burks, Arthur W. 392, 393
Bús-Fekete, Leslie [László Bús-Fekete] 440
Busch, Fritz 137
Bush, Vannevar 414
Busoni, Ferruccio 106, 107, 149
Butler, Nicholas Murray 282, 283, 348
Butler, Samuel 360
Butzer, Heinrich 152
Byrnes, James F. 416, 417

Cadman, Charles 107
Cannon, Walter 262
Capa, Robert 22, 155
Carelli, Gabor [Gábor Krausz] 440
Carnegie, Louise W. 299
Casals, Pablo 51
Case, James H., Jr. 329
Casella, Alfredo 107
Cecil, John 281
Celli, Gianna 12
Chadwick, Mary 153

Chalmers, T. A. 401
Chamberlain, Joseph Perkins 214, 307
Chargaff, Erwin 301
Charyk, Joseph V. 381, 382
Cherwell, Lord [Frederick A. Lindemann] 414, 415
Cholnoky, Tibor de 230
Churchill, Winston S. 414, 415
Clark, Kenneth 317
Compton, Arthur H. 408, 409, 418
Congdon, Lee 19
Coolidge, Elizabeth Sprauge 109
Copland, Aaron 223
Corda, Maria [Mária Antónia Farkas] 44
Courant, Richard 315
Cowell, Henry 107
Cowley, Malcolm 221
Creel, George 300, 301
Crèvecoeur, J. Hector St. John de 399
Csécsy, Imre 10
Csika 92
Csokor, Franz Theodor 247
Czóbel, Béla 53, 154
Curtis, Sylvia 11
Curtiz, Michael [Mihály Kertész, Manó Kaminer) 22, 103, 138, 328, 441
Czakó, Ambró 86, 87
Czernin, Ferdinand, Count 275
Czinner, Paul [Pál Czinner] 441

D'Abernon, Edgar Vincent, 1st Viscount 145–6
d'Albert, Eugen 106
Daniels, Farrington 418, 419, 422
Dános, Mrs. Árpád 10
Darling, William S. [Vilmos Sándorházi] 441
Darvas, Lili 441
Darwin, Charles 385
Davis, James J. 174, 179, 184

Deák, Francis [Ferenc Deák] 230, 441
Deák, István 12, 121, 148, 149
Deák 336
Decker, Clarence R. 325
Dehn, Paul 145
Delbrück, Max 258
Demuth, Charles 219
Dénes, Oszkár, 137
Deri, Emery [Imre Déri] 441
Deri, Otto [Ottó Déri] 441
Descartes, René 78
Deutsch, Helene 153
Dewey, John 262
Diamond, David 107
Dienes, André de [Endre Dienes] 441
Dienes, Louis L. [Lajos László Dienes] 93, 441
Dienes, Pál 324, 325, 327
Dieterle, Wilhelm 207
Dietze, Sándor 66
Dillingham, William P. 173
Dirac, Paul 411
Disraeli, Benjamin 46
Divine, Robert A. 189, 196
Dohnányi, Ernő [Ernst von] 22, 52, 107, 111, 126
Donnan, Frederick G. 257, 259
Dora, Miklos [Miklós Dóra] 441
Doraine, Lucy [Ilona Kovács] 441
Dos Passos, John 211
Dorati, Antal [Antal Deutsch] 22, 54, 441
Dreyfus, Alfred 295
Dreisziger, Nandor 12
Duczynska, Ilona 95
Duggan, Stephan 285, 318
Duna, Steffi [Stephanie Berindey] 231, 441
Duncan, Isadora 105
Duncker, Karl 74
Dushkin, David 117

Dutka, Ákos 10
Dvořák, Antonín 52
Dvořák, Max 316

Eaton, Cyrus 425
Eckermann, Otto 106
Eckart, Carl 117
Eckert, J. Presper, Jr. 390
Eckhardt, Tibor 194, 195, 441
Eddy, Nelson 147
Eggerth, Marta 441
Ehrenfels, Christian von 75
Ehrenfest, Paul 257
Einstein, Albert 76, 100, 137, 138, 243, 252, 253, 255, 256, 292, 383, 405–407, 416, 421, 425
Eisenhower, Dwight D. 396
Eitingen, Max 153
Elgar, Sir Edward 107
Éltes, Mátyás 74
Engel, Károly 92, 93
Engesser, F. 370
Eördögh, Elmer [Elemér Eördögh] 441
Eötvös, József, Baron 55, 56, 66, 70, 122
Eötvös, Loránd, Baron 66, 69, 70, 71
Epstein, Paul S. 155, 372
Erdélyi, Michael [Mihály Erdélyi] 306, 441
Erdős, Paul 250, 357
Erős 324
Errera, Jacques 259
Eszláry, Károly 324
Euclid 78

Fajans, Kazimierz 132
Faludy, György 441
Faludi, Jenő [Eugenio] 324, 327
Farago Ladislas [László Faragó] 337, 441
Farkas, Adalbert [Béla] 320, 441
Farkas, Aladár 322, 327, 441
Farkas, George [György] 441

Index

Farkas, Ladislaus [László] 319–320, 336
Fehér, Pál 137
Fejér, Andrew 163
Fejér, Lipót 69, 70, 93, 127, 131, 134, 140, 151, 156, 249, 354, 355, 357, 365
Fejos, Paul [Pál Fejős] 442
Fekete, Mihály 355, 357
Fekete, Zoltán 306, 442
Feleky, Charles 230
Fellegi, Margit 442
Fellner, Willy [Vilmos Fellner, William John Fellner] 306, 383, 442
Fényes, László 442
Ferenczi, Imre 306, 319, 442
Ferenczy, Béni 130
Ferenczy, Noémi 130, 154
Fermi, Enrico 402, 404, 405, 407–409, 411, 421
Fermi, Laura 17, 18
Field, Edith C. 275
Field, Marshall 116
Finta, Alexander [Sándor Finta] 231, 442
Fisher, Edgar J. 319
Fleming, Donald 17
Flesch, Karl 324, 326–328
Flesch, Marianne see Adler, Marianne
Flesch, Paul [Pál Flesch] 442
Flesch, Peter [Péter Flesch] 8, 208, 210, 442
Flexner, Abraham 261
Flexner, Bernard 286
Fodor, Andor 320
Fodor, Nandor [Nándor Fodor] 442
Forbes-Martin, Susan 11
Ford, Henry 146
Ford, James L. 211
Forgó, László 102
Foss, Lukas 55
Foster, George, H. 199
Franck, James 100, 137, 376, 417

Franco, Francisco 278
Frank, Béla 307
Frank, Bruno 207
Frank, Ladislas 199, 200
Frankfurter, Felix 275, 303, 313
Franz Joseph I 32, 81
Freud, Sigmund 32, 40, 41, 250
Freund, Jules Thomas [Gyula Freund] 442 12q
Fricsay, Ferenc 22
Fried, Theodore [Tivadar Fried] 442
Fröhlich, Róbert 66
Fry, Varian 323
Fülep, Lajos 36
Fülöp-Miller, René [René Fueloep-Miller] 307, 442
Furtwängler, Wilhelm 147
Füst, Milán 106

Gaal, Franciska [Franciska Gaál, Fanny Zilveritch] 442
Gabo, Naum 154
Gabor, Arnold [Arnold Gábor] 232, 442
Gabor, Dennis 76
Gabor, Eva [Éva Gábor] 442
Gabor, Zsa Zsa [Sári Gábor] 381, 442
Gabrilowitsch, Ossip 191
Garbo, Greta 147
Gauss, Carl Friedrich 31
Gay, Peter 44, 46
Geyer, Stefi 22
Geray, Steve [István Gyergyai] 442
Gergely, Tibor 324, 327, 328, 442
Gero, George [György Gerő] 340, 442
Gershwin, George 52
Gibson, Charles S. 261, 288
Giesswein, Sándor 85
Ginsberg, Morris 341
Girard, Ralph W. 117
Glick, Randi 11

Godowsky, Leopold 105
Goethe, Johann Wolfgang 31, 122
Goldmark, Karl 52
Goldmark, Peter Carl [Péter Károly Goldmark] 442
Goldstein, Ladislas (László Goldstein) 324, 327, 443
Goldziher, Károly 10
Goldzieher, Max A. [Maximilan Alexander Goldzieher, Miksa Goldzieher] 92, 93, 443
Gömbös, Gyula 160
Gombosi, Otto John [Ottó János Gombosi, Otto Johannes Gombosi] 22, 443
Göndör, Ferenc 443
Goodman, Benny 109
Goodstein, Judith R. 11
Gorog, Laszlo [László Görög] 443
Grancsay, Stephen V. 443
Gregg, Alan 284
Griffiths, J. H. E. 402
Grillparzer, Franz 122
Groesse, Paul 443
Gropius, Ise 118,
Gropius, Walter 111–113, 115–119, 154
Gross-Bettelheim, Jolán 8, 235, 443
Grósz, Emil 92
Grosschmid, Geza B. [Géza Grosschmid] 443
Groves, Leslie R. 409, 412, 414, 420–422
Grünwald, Géza 324, 342
Grünwald [Gallai], Tibor 324, 342
Guggenheim, Harry F. 373
Guggenheims 372
Gutenberg, Johannes 114
Gyenge, Anna [Anne Roselle] 130, 232
Gyorgy, Andrew [András György] 443
György, Pál [Paul György] 260, 306, 443
Gyula Paál see Julius Paal

Haar, Alfréd 355, 365
Habe, Hans see Békessy, János [Hans]
Haber, Fritz 100, 254, 320
Haeckel, Ernst 31
Hajmássy, Ilona 130
Hajós, Erzsébet [Elizabeth M. Hajós] 307, 443
Halasi, Béla Albert 307, 340, 443
Halasz, Leslie [László Halász] 443
Halász, Miklós [Nicholas Halász] 307, 443
Hall, Granwille Stanley 168
Halmai, Tibor 137
Halmos, Paul Richard [Pál Halmos] 363, 443
Hámori, László 324, 327
Händel, Georg Friedrich 123
Hansen, Marcus 187
Haraszti, Zoltan [Zoltán Haraszti] 443
Hardy, Godfrey Harold 259
Hargittai István 12, 19
Harmati, Sandor [Sándor Harmati] 232, 443
Harris, Roy 223
Harsányi, Alexander 232
Harsanyi, Charles [Károly Harsányi] 443
Harsányi, János 22
Harsanyi, Miklos [Miklós Harsányi] 443
Hart, Alfred [Alfréd Hart] 443
Hartog, Sir Philip 259
Harty, Sir Hamilton 107
Haskell, Henry S. 347, 348
Hatvany, Lajos, Baron 129
Hatvany, Lili, Baroness 443
Hauser, Arnold 23, 36, 83, 87
Havas, Peter [Péter Havas] 307, 443
Havas 336
Haydn, Joseph 123
Hayek, Friedrich August von 267
Héderváry, Claire 336

Index

Heine, Heinrich 46, 92, 122
Hellebranth, Berta de 443
Hellebranth, Elena [Ilona] Maria de 444
Heller, László 162
Heller, Otto 286
Helmholtz, Hermann Ludwig Ferdinand von 168
Herczeg, Ferenc 38, 39, 384
Herczeg, Geza [Géza Herczeg] 444
Hernadi, Paul 11
Herz, Otto 444
Herzfeld, Victor, Ritter von 124
Hevesy, George de 22, 101, 102, 132, 164, 336, 337
Heymann, Karl 165
Hilbert, David 369, 383
Hill, Archibald V. 259
Hill, Joseph A. 187
Hindemith, Paul 54, 55, 147
Hirst, Sir Hugo [Lord Hirst] 403
Hitler, Adolf 16, 23, 24, 29, 129, 138, 147, 157–160, 192, 199, 216, 243, 251, 261, 265, 278, 280, 287, 308, 317, 326–328, 403, 407, 436
Hoch, Paul H. [Pál Hoch] 444
Hoddis, Jakob van [Hans Davidsohn] 44
Hoff, Nicholas J. [Miklós Hoff] 271, 444
Hoffmann, Dieter 12
Hoffman, John 444
Hoffman, Magda 199
Hoffman, Tibor 199
Hofstadter, Richard 170
Holló, Gyula 272, 273, 444
Holmes, Oliver Wendell, Jr. 303
Hóman, Bálint 384
Hoover, Herbert 185, 187, 189
Hopkins, J. Gardiner 337
Horowitz, Vladimir 150

Horthy, Miklós, 22, 27, 82, 86, 93, 99, 103, 136, 153, 160, 194, 229, 327, 358, 383
Horváth, Ádám 8, 237
Horváth, John 354
Howell, Patricia F. 12
Hubay, Jenő 22, 51, 52, 105, 106, 111, 124
Huber, Jenő 124 *see* Hubay, Jenő
Hughes, H. Stuart 17
Hurwitz, Paula 11
Husband, W. W. 173
Huszár, Vilmos 154
Huxley, Julian 116, 119, 393

Ignotus, Hugo [Hugo Veigelsberg] 88, 165, 274, 275, 276, 307, 444
Illyés Gyula 88, 130
Incze, Sándor 444
Isherwood, Christopher 157
Istók, Kálmán Z. 162

Jackson, Henry M. 379
Jackson, Kenneth T. 220
Jacques-Dalcrose, Émile 95
Jaederholm, Gustav Axel 74
James, W. Frank 180, 181
James, William 352
Janáček, Leoš 55
Járay, Hans [János Járay] 444
Jászi, Oscar [Oszkár Jászi] 76, 82–88, 93, 94, 96, 275, 329, 444
Jendrassik, Ernő 92
Jette, Eric R. 133
Joachim, Joseph 46
Johann, Zita 231
Johnson, Alvin 286, 319, 326, 329, 338–346
Johnson, Albert 28, 173
Johnson, Edwin C. 420
Joliot-Curie, Frédéric 324, 411
Jones, Rufus 299

Joseph II 44
Joyce, James 223
Juhász, Gyula (historian) 12
Juhász, Gyula (poet) 53
Juris, Kálmán 324, 327, 328, 444

Kabalevsky, Dimitri Borisovich 54
Kádár, Béla 23, 154
Kadosa, Pál 107
Kaffka, Margit 53
Kafka, Franz 32
Kaldor, Nicholas, Lord Kaldor of Newnham 59
Kállai, Ernő 23
Kallmann, Hartmut 254
Kalman, Gabor 11
Kálmán, Imre [Emmerich Kálmán] 52, 444
Kálmán, Oszkár 137
Kant, Immanuel 31
Karinthy, Frigyes 53
Kardos, Ludwig [Lajos] 152
Kardos, Leslie (László Kardos) 444
Karinthy Frigyes 272
Kármán, Elemér von 165
Kármán, Theodore von [Tódor Kármán] 6, 8, 22, 31, 36, 42, 45, 55, 56, 59, 60, 76, 99–101, 131–134, 140, 152, 159, 163, 262–264, 271–273, 278, 329, 356, 365, 367–382, 395, 437, 444
Kármán, Mór 42, 55–57, 59, 63, 100, 123, 368
Károlyi, Mihály, Count 22, 79, 80, 83, 92, 94, 195
Kassák, Lajos 23, 114, 130
Katona, George [György Katona] 444
Katona, Pál 324, 327
Kaulbach, Wilhelm von 31, 122
Kazemi, Marion 12
Kecskemeti, Paul [Pál Kecskeméti] 444
Kelemen, Pál 444

Kemeny, John George [János György Kemény] 22, 444
Kennedy, John F. 380, 427, 428
Kepes, Gyorgy [György Kepes] 117, 155, 444
Kerecsényi, Dezső 66
Kerekes, János 12
Kerekes, Tibor 444
Keresztury, Dezső 135
Kéri, Pál 444
Kernstok, Károly 53, 86, 93, 130, 154
Kerpel, Edmund 348
Kerpel, Jenő 348
Kertész, André [Andor Kertész] 22, 155, 445
Kertész, István 22
Kertész, Mihály see Curtiz, Michael
Khachaturian, Aram 107
Khrushchev, Nikita S. 427, 428
Kilenyi, Julio 231
Kisch, Egon Erwin 149
Kiss, George [György Kiss] 445
Klay, Andrew C. [Andor Sziklay] 11, 110, 445
Klebelsberg, Kuno, Count 140–142, 384
Kleiber, Erich 147
Klein, Felix 369, 377
Klein, Melanie 153
Klein, Philip 445
Klemperer, Otto 147
Kober, Leo 445
Kóbor, Tamás 39
Kodály, Zoltán 36, 52–55, 124
Koessler, Hans 52, 125, 322
Koestler, Arthur 22, 77, 110
Kőhalmi, Béla 93
Köhler, Wolfgang 254
Kölcsey, Ferenc 30
Kolnai, Aurel Thomas [Aurél Stein] 307, 445
Koni, Sir Nicolaus 445

Index

Kőnig, Dénes 355
Kőnig, Gyula 355
Konti, Isidore 231
Koppanyi, Theodore [Tivadar Koppányi] 445
Korányi, Sándor, Baron 92
Korda, Sir Alexander [Sándor Korda, Sándor Kellner] 22, 89, 114, 445
Korda, Zoltan (Zoltán Kellner) 445
Korek, Valéria [Mrs. Willy Fellner] 445
Kormendi, Eugene [Jenő Körmendi] 445
Kornis, Gyula 384
Kőrösy, Ferenc [Francis de Kőrösy] 138, 307
Korvin, Charles [Géza Kaiser] 445
Kostolany, André [Endre Bertalan Kosztolányi] 445
Kosztolányi, Dezső 53, 272
Kossuth, Lajos 22, 32, 84, 232, 233
Kotschnig, Walter 259, 279, 280, 290, 292, 293, 295, 296, 331, 339
Kovács, Alajos 45
Kovacs, Arpad 230
Kovács, Ilona 226
Kozary, Myron Theodore 445
Kramer, Charles 199
Kraut, Alan M. 302
Krauth, Felix W. 285
Kretschmer, Ernst 73
Kubelik, Rafael 105
Kullman, Gustave Gerard 259
Kun, Béla, 22, 80, 82, 94, 99
Kun, Ladislas 232

Ladenburg, Rudolf 376
Lagarde, Paul de 143
LaGuardia, Fiorello 222
Lakatos, Imre 363
Lambert, Robert A. 337

Lanczos, Cornelius [Kornél Lánczos, Kornél Löwy] 445
Landau, Edmund Georg Hermann 131
Láng, Lajos 302
Langbehn, Julius 143
Lange-Eichbaum, Wilhelm 73
Lanouette, William 99
Lanyi, George Albert [György Lányi] 445
Lapworth, Arthur 264
Laski, Neville 259
Laszlo, Aladar [Aladár László] 445
Laszlo, Alexander [Sándor Totis] 445
Laszlo, Ernest [Ernő László] 445
Laszlo, Erno, [Ernő László] 445
Laszlo, Miklos [Miklós Leitner] 446
Laue, Max von 100, 133, 243, 252–254
Laughlin, Harry Hamilton 173
Lax, Henrik 446
Lax, Peter 446
Lazar, Filip 107
Ledermann, László 324, 325, 327, 446
Leibniz, Gottfried Wilhelm 78
Lemberger, Imre 347
Lenau, Nikolaus 122
Léner, Jenő 446
Lengyel, Emil 8, 273, 274, 329, 446
Lengyel, Melchior [Menyhért Lengyel] 230, 446
Lenin, Vladimir Ilych 27, 75, 80
Lerner, Max 399
Lesznai, Anna [Amália Moscovitz] 84, 446
Levold, Erwin 11
Lewis, Bracket 349
Lewis, Sinclair 220
Liebermann, Leo 92
Liebermann, Otto 347
Liebermann, Pál 92, 93
Liebowitz, Benjamin 262, 303
Lighthill, Sir James 361

Lindbergh, Charles 407
Lindemann, Albert S. 11
Lindemann, Barbara 11
Lindemann, Frederick A. see Cherwell, Lord
Lissitzky, El 154
Liszt, Franz 22, 27, 51, 52, 108, 123
Lóczy, Lajos 93
Lodge, Sir Oliver 75
Loeb, Isadore 314
Loeb, Lotta 274
Loisch, János 66
Lombroso, Cesare 73
London, Fritz 254
Lónyay, Simon H. 324, 327
Lorand, Edith 446
Lorand, Sandor [Sándor Loránd] 446
Lóránt, Stefan [István Lóránt] 447
Lorenz, Richard 133
Lorsy, Erno [Ernő Lorsy] 447
Lorre, Peter [László Löwenstein] 138, 328, 447
Lónyay, Simon H. 447
Lovecky, Georgene B. 11
Lukas, Paul [Pál Lukács] 138, 231, 447
Ludwig, Carl 168
Lugosi, Bela [Béla Lugosi] 103, 130, 138, 231, 447
Lukacs, Eugene [Jenő Lukács] 307, 447
Lukács, Georg [von] 22, 36, 83, 103, 149
Luth, Helen F. 194
Lyons, Leonard 421

Mach, Ernst 75, 76, 357
MacDonald, James G. 285, 290
MacDonald, Jeanette 147
MacIver, R. M. 341
Madách, Imre 245
Madzsar, József 85, 86, 88, 89, 92, 93, 96
Madzsar, Mrs. József [Alice Jászi] 88, 89, 92, 93, 96

Magaloff, Nikita, Prince 107
Magris, Claudio 41
Mahler, Gustav 54, 55, 105, 125
Mahler, Margaret [Margit Schönberger] 447
Makkai, Endre 10
Malevich, Kazimir 154
Malina, Frank J. 371
Malipiero, Gian Francesco 108
Mályusz, Elemér 165
Man, Hendrik de 259
Manheim, Ernst [Ernő Manheim] 336, 447
Mann, Thomas 147, 207, 275
Mannheim, Karl 36, 77, 83, 138, 257, 324, 326–328, 336, 337, 341, 342
Manowill, Alfred 129
Márai, Sándor 130
Marton, Endre 447
Marton, George Nicholas [György Miklós Marton] 447
Marx, George 19
Marx, Karl 46, 47
Masaryk, Tomáš G. 85
Massey, Lona [Ilona Hajmássy, Ilona Hagymási] 231, 447
Mate, Rudolph [Rudolf Matheh or Mayer] 447
Mattis-Teutsch, János 154
Matulay, Laszlo 447
Matzenauer, Margaret 232
Mauchly, John 390
Mautner, Endre 347
May, Andrew 420
Mayo, C. W. 273
McCagg, Jr., William O. 45, 48, 368
McCulloch, Warren S. 389, 390
Meduna, Ladislas Joseph [László Meduna] 447
Meitner, Lise 254, 376
Meller, Simon 278

Index

Meller, Susan 278
Mendelsohn, Erich 205, 219, 220
Mendelssohn-Bartholdy, Felix 46, 123
Mero, Yolanda 232
Messersmith, George S. 291
Mezey, Ferenc 49
Mikola, Sándor 66, 68, 69, 357, 385
Milhaud, Darius 107
Millikan, Robert Andrews 137, 373
Mises, Richard von 156, 254
Moberly, Walter H. 264
Moeller van den Bruck, Arthur 143
Moholy-Nagy, Laszlo [László Weisz] 22, 105, 111–119, 154, 447
Moholy-Nagy, Sybill 118, 119
Molnár, Antal 10, 107, 125
Molnar, Charles 202
Molnár, Ferenc [Ferenc Neumann] 8, 39, 47, 165, 230, 237, 238, 447
Mommsen, Theodor 66
Mond, Henry [Lord Melchett] 259
Montefiore, Claude Joseph Goldschmid 259
Montgomery, John F. 300, 301, 308
Moore, John 11
Móricz, Zsigmond 53
Morris, Charles W. 117
Moscovitz de Zemplén, Geyza 84
Moses, Robert 220
Mozart, Wolfgang Amadeus 108, 123
Mueller [Müller], Georg Elias 42
Munkacsi, Martin [Márton Munkácsi] 447
Murray, Gilbert 259
Murrow, Edward Roscoe 309–311, 313
Musil, Robert 32

Nadanyi, Paul [Pál Nadányi] 447
Nagel, Charles 299
Nagy, Dénes 86
Nagy, Elemer [Elemér Nagy] 447
Nagy, Imre 427
Nathorff, Hertha 205, 207
Návay 92
Neményi, Pál [Paul Neményi] 307, 448
Nemes-Lampérth, József 154
Németh, Mária 137, 165
Nemeth, Otto Rudolf 201
Nernst, Walther 100, 254
Neumann, Alfred 207
Neumann, Gabor [Gábor Neumann] 448
Neumann, John von [János Neumann] 6, 8, 22, 31, 36, 45, 50, 57, 64, 68, 72, 76, 134, 140, 159, 254, 261, 262, 272, 355–357, 379, 382–400, 432, 448
Neumann, Miksa 395
Neumann Whitman, Marina von 383
Newman, Katherine 12
Nicholas II 268
Nikisch, Arthur 105, 125
Nordau, Max 46
Norman, Montagu 309
Nyilas, Tibor 448
Nyiregyházi, Ervin 127

O'Brian, Howard Vincent 117
Oláh, György 22
Onodi, Adolf 92
Oppenheimer, J. Robert 388, 395, 396
Ormandy, Eugene [Jenő Ormándy, Jenő Blau] 22, 53, 54, 231, 448
Ormandy, Martin J. [Ormándy, Blau] 448
Ortvay, Rudolf 386, 387, 390–392, 399
Osenberg, Werner 375
Ostendorf, Berndt 12
Ostwald, Wilhelm 73

Paal, Julius [Gyula Paál] 200, 201
Pal, George 448
Palló, Gábor 12

Palmer, Alan 21
Pályi, Melchior [Menyhért Pályi] 305, 308–311, 314, 448
Paneth, Friedrich A. 258–260, 402
Pap, Sándor 97
Papp, Dezső Károly 324, 327, 448
Pappus 78
Parikian, Manoug 108
Parry, Milman 277
Partos, Frank 448
Pártos, Imre 152
Pártos, Pál 324, 326, 327
Pasternak, Joseph [Joe, József Pasternak] 22, 138, 448
Pataky, Koloman von [Kálmán] 130, 137, 165
Patai, Raphael 38
Pauker, Edmund [Ödön Pók] 448
Pauler, Tivadar 56
Pearl, Raymond 262
Pearson, Karl 75
Pecz, Gedeon 66
Pecz, Samu 64
Pelenyi, John [János Pelényi] 194, 448
Péri, László 154, 155
Perlman, Louis 202, 203
Perry, Lewis 221
Pesce, Pasquale 12
Pestalozzi, Johann Heinrich 64
Peter the Great 149
Péterfi, Tibor 92, 93
Pfeiffer, Ignác 155
Pikler, Andrew [Endre Pikler] 448
Pikler, Blanka 93
Pikler, Endre 324, 329
Pilat, Oliver 245
Piloty, Karl Theodor von 31, 124
Pink, Louis H. 226, 230
Piston, Walter 223
Pitts, Walter 389, 390
Pizzetti, Ildebrando 107

Planck, Max 100, 138, 252, 254
Pogány, Imre 448
Pogány, William Andrew ["Willy"] 231
Polányi, Cecilia 95, 123
Polányi family, the Polányis 94–97
Polanyi, John C. 95, 123
Polanyi, Karl [Károly Polányi] 22, 42, 83, 95, 96, 99, 123, 162, 260, 266, 336, 357
Polanyi, Michael [Mihály Polányi] 6, 22, 42, 45, 48, 76, 77, 83, 95, 97, 99, 100, 101, 123, 131–134, 136, 137, 140, 141, 151, 155, 158, 162, 164, 260, 263–269, 273, 351, 432
Policer, Géza 324, 327, 328
Pollacsek, Mihály 42
Pólya, George [György Pólya] 6, 22, 48, 70, 77, 140, 163, 272, 306, 315, 351, 353–355, 357–367, 448
Pólya, Jakab 353
Pólya, Jenő 92, 93, 353
Popp, Richard 11
Popper, David 51, 52, 124
Possony, Stephen Thomas [István Pozsony] 448
Pound, Ezra 262
Prandtl, Ludwig 369, 374
Pressburger, Arnold 448
Prilisauer, Adolf 72
Primes, Agnes 227
Proclus 78
Prohászka, Ottokár 384
Prokofiev, Sergei 55, 107, 109
Puni (Pougny), Ivan 154
Putti, Lya de [Amália Putti] 130, 231, 448

Rabi, Isidor Isaac 356
Rabinowitch, Eugene 244
Racz, Andre [Endre Rácz] 448
Radkau, Joachim 251

Index

Rado, Sandor [psychoanalyst] 152, 274, 275, 448
Radó, Sándor [geographer] 324, 327, 328
Radó, Tibor 365, 448
Rados, Gusztáv 245, 355
Rados, Ignácz 245
Radványi, László 324, 448
Raisz, Ervin 449
Rákóczi, Ferenc II 22
Rákosi, Mátyás 22, 29
Ranke, Leopold von 46
Rapaport, David [Dezső Rappaport] 306, 449
Rapée, Ernő 231, 449
Rapp, Franz 329
Rasko, Aurel [Aurél Miksa Reinitz] 449
Rátz, László 7, 67, 68, 69, 72
Ravasz, László 384
Ravel, Maurice 109
Rawsthorne, Alan 107
Razovsky, Cecilia 214, 279
Read, Herbert 317
Recsei, Andrew Andor [Andor Récsei] 11, 449
Reed, David A. 28, 173
Reibmayer, Albert 73
Reiner, Fritz [Frigyes Reiner] 8, 22, 54, 107, 142, 144, 449
Reinhardt, G. Frederick 302
Reinhardt, Max [Goldmann] 44, 149
Reis, Alfred 151
Rejto, Gabor [Gábor Rejtő] 449
Renn, Jürgen 12
Renner, János 66, 69
Réthy, Mór 355
Reves, Emery [Imre Révész] 449
Révész, Géza 41, 42, 74, 93, 164, 324, 327, 336,
Reynolds, Frederick P. 262
Rich, John F. 300

Richter, Hans 105, 125
Riesz, Frigyes 355, 365
Riesz, Marcel 165
Riezler, Kurt 341
Robinson, Leland Rex 319
Rockefeller, John D., Jr. 330, 331
Rogenberg, Julius [Julius Leví] 44
Roheim, Geza [Géza Róheim] 449
Rona, Elizabeth [Erzsébet Róna] 449
Roosevelt, Franklin Delano 171, 192, 193, 222, 297, 406, 407, 416, 417, 421, 422
Roselle, Anne see Gyenge, Anna
Rostás, László 324, 326, 327, 343, 449
Roth, Feri [Franz Roth] 449
Rothauser, Adolf 41
Rothman, Stephen [István Rothman] 208, 329, 449
Rothschilds 295
Roussel, Albert 107, 109
Rózsa, Miklós 449
Russell, Bertrand, Lord 425
Russell, Sir John 259
Rutherford of Nelson, Lord Ernest 288, 403
Ruttkay, György 449
Rutkoff, Peter M. 219

Sachs, Alexander 407
Sakall, S. Z. [Sándor Gärtner, Jenő Gerő, Szőke Szakáll] 138, 328, 449
Salvemini, Gaetano 329
Sándor, Árpád 137
Sándor, György 449
Sarasate, Pablo de 106
Sárkány, Sándor 66
Saul, Mark 12
Schacht, Hjalmar 309
Schedius, Lajos 64
Scheiber, Hugo 23, 154
Schick, Béla 449

Schiller, Friedrich 31, 122
Schlenk, Wilhelm 254
Schlesinger, Lajos 355
Schnitzler, Arthur 46, 122
Schoenberg, Arnold 147
Schoenfeld, Alan H. 364
Schonbauer, Henry [Henrik Schönbauer] 449
Schopenhauer, Arthur 31
Schorr, Frederick [Frigyes or Friedrich Schorr] 232, 449
Schorske, Carl E. 335
Schrödinger, Erwin 100, 254
Schrott, Robert 11
Schulhof, Andrew [Andor Schulhof] 449
Schulhof, Belle 231, 234, 449
Schultz, Ágoston 66
Schubert, Franz 123
Schuman, William 54
Schumann, Robert 123
Schwarz, Andreas Bertholan 343
Schwarz, Hermann Amandus 127
Schwartz, Philip 287
Scitovsky, Tibor de [Tibor Scitovszky] 449
Scott, William B. 219
Sebastian, Georges 22
Sebeok, Thomas Albert [Tamás Sebők] 450
Seelye, Laurens H. 217
Sekey, Andrew 11
Sekey, Steve [István Székely] 450
Semenov, Nikolai N. 266
Sendrey, Alfred [Aladár Szendrei] 322, 323, 450
Sepeshy, Zoltan L. [Zoltán Szepesy] 450
Serly, Tibor 450
Seton-Watson, Hugh 82
Shepperson, Wilbur 11
Shimek, Bohumil 349

Shostakovich, Dimitri 54
Sibelius, Jean 55
Sichermann, István 208, 450
Siebreich 125
Silard, Béla 246, 249
Simanowskí, Karol 107
Simmel, Ernst 153
Simmel, Georg 127
Simon, Théophile 74
Sklarek, Leo 149
Sklarek, Willy 149
Smelser, Neil 11
Smend, Carl Friedrich Rudolf 376
Smyth, Henry DeWolf 405
Sollors, Werner 12
Solti, Sir Georg 22
Somogyi, Béla 86
Somogyi, József 74
Somogyi-Schill, István de 324, 325, 327
Spalek, John M. 11
Spencer, Herbert 83, 385
Speranza, Gino 173
Spiré, André 46
Spitz, René Arpad [René Árpád Spitz] 450
Stahl, Friedrich Julius 47
Stahle, Norma K. 118
Stalin, Josip Vissarionovich 247, 267, 423, 424
Stark, Marcel 201
Starker, János 110
Staudinger, Hans 345
Stefániai, Imre 127
Stein, Gertrude 223
Stein, Marcel 11, 82, 102, 162, 450
Stein, Fred M. 286
Sternberg, Charles 275
Stieglitz, Alfred 219
Stifler, James M. 309
Stokowsky, Leopold 108, 109
Strauss, Lewis 395

Index

Strauss, Richard 54, 147, 149
Stravinsky, Igor 54, 107, 119, 147, 223
Strong, Benjamin 309
Strong, George Templeton 107
Strong, Josiah 143
Stuewer, Roger H. 12
Stürgkh, Karl von, Count 75
Suba, Susanne [Zsuzsanna Suba, Mrs. McCracken] 450
Sugar, Peter F. [Péter Frigyes Sugár] 11, 450
Suk, Josef 52
Sulzberger, David 214
Szabó, Xavér Ferenc 125
Szalai, Tibor 307, 324, 327, 344
Szántó, Jani 307, 450
Szász, Otto 138, 305, 311–314, 336, 337, 357, 450
Szasz, Thomas Stephen [István Tamás Szász] 450
Szathmáry, Arthur 450
Szegho, Constantin S. [Konstantin Szeghő] 307, 450
Szegő, Gabor [Gabriel, Gábor Szegő] 127, 131, 134, 138, 140, 151, 156, 163, 271, 272, 305, 314, 315, 316, 336, 337, 342, 357, 358, 364, 365, 367, 383, 450
Szegő, Nusi [Mrs. Gabor Szegő] 140
Székely, János [John Pen, John S. Toldy] 450
Székely, Lajos 307, 324, 326, 327, 336
Szekfű, Gyula 165, 384
Szell, George [György Széll] 22, 54, 450, 108
Széll, Kálmán 141, 382
Szemere, Bertalan 123
Szende, Zoltán 307, 324, 450
Szenes, Piroska 450
Szenkár, Eugen 22, 135
Szent-Györgyi, Albert 22, 110, 130, 142

Szent-Györgyi, Kornélia [Kornélia (Nelly) Demény, Mrs. Albert Szent-Györgyi] 307, 450
Szentkiralyi, Joseph [József Szentkirályi, Joseph St. Clair] 450
Szigeti, Joseph [József Szigeti] 22, 105–111, 115, 232, 272, 451
Szilard, Leo [Leó Szilárd] 6, 8, 22, 36, 45, 99, 133, 141, 243, 244, 246–263, 292, 305, 336, 337, 379, 381, 395, 401–412, 414– 425, 427–429, 437, 451
Szilasi, Vilmos 271
Szirmai, Albert [Albert Sirmay] 22, 52, 451
Szirmay-Pulszky, Henriette von 74, 165
Szivessy, Tibor 152
Szőllősy, Mrs. Lajos 10
Szűcs, József 271, 307, 322, 324, 343, 451

Takaro, Geza [Géza Takaró] 451
Tamarkin, Jacob David 314, 315
Tammann, Gustav 140
Tansman, Alexander 107
Tatlin, Vladimir 154
Taussig, Frank William 262
Taylor, Frederick Winslow 146
Telkes, Maria [Mária Telkes] 451
Teller, Edward [Ede Teller] 8, 22, 31, 36, 41, 60, 76, 305, 356, 379, 381, 395, 406, 412, 413, 451
Teller, Max 41
Telmányi, Emil 22
Terman, Luis M. 74
Thomas, Barbara 11
Thomson, David Cleghorn 284
Thomson, Virgil 223
Thorndike, Edward L. 352
Throop, George, R. 325
Tihany, Leslie Charles [László Tihanyi] 451

Tihanyi, Lajos 154
Tisza, István, Count 94
Tisza, Ladislas [László Tisza] 306, 343, 451
Toklas, Alice B. 223
Tolnay, Charles de [Károly Tolnay] 22, 36, 83, 306, 451
Tolstoy, Lev Nikolaevich, Count 268
Topchiev, Alexander Vassilevich 426
Tormay, Cécile 384
Tors, Ivan 451
Toth, André de [Endre Tóth] 451
Tóth, Árpád 53
Trefort, Ágoston 70
Trefftz, Erich 371
Trilling, Lionel 221
Truman, Harry S. 416, 417, 418, 424
Turán, Pál 324, 342
Türck, Hermann 73
Twardowsky, Kasimir 75

Ujvári, Péter 46
Ulam, Stanislaw 355, 384
Ungar, Ernest 198
Urey, Harold C. 414, 416

Vadnai, Laszlo [László Vadnay] 451
Vágó, József 322
Vajda, Ernest [Ernő Vajda, Sidney Garrick] 230, 451
Vajna, László 322
Vámbéry, Rusztem 196, 270, 274, 275, 306, 336, 451
Varconi, Victor [Mihály Várkonyi] 138, 451
Varga, Eugen 278
Várkonyi, Zsuzsa F. 12
Varró, István 451
Varró, Margit 451
Vásáry, Tamás 110
Veblen, Oswald 262, 342

Vecsey, Ferenc [Franz von] 22, 105
Venzente, Gary 12
Verdi, Giuseppe 137
Verebes, Ernst [Ernő Verebes, Ernő Weisz] 451
Veres, Mihály [Michel Veres] 322, 326, 327
Vidor, Charles [Károly Vidor] 138, 451
Völgyesi, Mrs. Ferenc 234, 236
Vonneuman, Nicholas A. 50, 357

Wagner, Richard 31, 52
Wagner, Robert F. 180, 196, 421
Wald, Abraham [Ábrahám Wald] 452
Waldbauer, Ilona see Mrs. Frederick Antal
Waldbauer, József 124
Walden, Herwarth 154
Walker, Sydnor H. 331
Walter, Bruno 147, 150
Walton, George 299
Walton, Sir William 55
Warburg, Bettina 274
Warburg, Ingrid 274
Wattendorf, Frank L. 375
Weber, Rudolf 66
Wehnelt, Arthur 254
Weidler, Charlotte 147
Weill, Kurt 147
Weiner, Emery 307
Weiner, Leo 52, 54, 107
Weisskopf, Victor 411
Weizmann, Chaim 259
Wellesz, Egon 306
Wells, Herbert George 114, 403
Werfel, Franz 207
Wharton, Edith 205
Whyte, William H. 222
Wiebe, Robert H. 168
Wiener, Norbert 313, 314, 398

Wigner, Eugene Paul [Jenő Pál Wigner]
    22, 31, 36, 57, 64, 67, 72, 141, 244,
    257, 263, 269, 379, 385, 402, 403,
    406, 411, 421, 452
Wilamowitz-Moellendorff, Ulrich von
    129
Wilhelm II 168, 268
Williams, William Carlos 223
Willits, Joseph H. 333
Wilson, Eric R. 192
Wilson, Woodrow 168–170, 176
Winans, C. S. 177, 178
Wittmann, Ferenc 355
Wolf, Hugo 348
Wolf, Robert J. 119
Worth, George V. [György Vitéz] 452
Wundt, Wilhelm 168

Yarnall, Robert 299
Young, Lucie 8
Ysaÿe, Eugène 51, 106

Zador, Eugene [Jenő Zádor] 452
Zalai, Béla 76, 77
Zathureczky, Ede 22
Zechmeister, Laszlo [László Zechmeister]
    452
Zeisel, Eva [Éva Stricker] 8, 452
Ziller, Tuiscon 55, 123
Zilzer, Gyula 452
Zimmermann, Robert 78
Zinn, Walter 408
Zsoldos, Géza 239, 240
Zuckerman, Harriet A. 12
Zuckmeyer, Carl 150
Zweig, Stefan 104, 151

Reihenverzeichnis Exil-Studien

Vol. 1 Sonja Maria Hedgepeth, «Überall blicke ich nach einem heimatlichen Boden aus»: Exil im Werk Else Lasker-Schülers.
254 pp. 1994.
US-ISBN 0-8204-2219-3.

Vol. 2 Elfe Vallaster, «Ein Zimmer in der Luft»: Liebe, Exil, Rückkehr und Wort-Vertrauen.
278 pp. 1994.
US-ISBN 0-8204-2225-8.

Vol. 3 Waltraud Strickhausen, Die Erzählerin Hilde Spiel oder «Der weite Wurf in die Finsternis».
500 pp. 1996.
US-ISBN 0-8204-2623-7.

Vol. 4 Renata von Hanffstengel, Mexiko im Werk von Bodo Uhse: Das nie verlassene Exil.
251 pp. 1996.
US-ISBN 0-8204-2683-0.

Vol. 5 Harald Reil, Siegfried Kracauers Jacques Offenbach: Biographie, Geschichte, Zeitgeschichte.
159 pp. 2003.
US-ISBN 0-8204-3742-5.

Vol. 6 J. M. Ritchie, German Exiles: British Perspectives.
344 pp. 1997.
US-ISBN 0-8204-3743-3.

Vol. 7 Tibor Frank, Double Exile: Migrations of Jewish-Hungarian Professionals through Germany to the United States, 1919–1945.
501 pp. 2009.
ISBN 978-3-03911-331-6.

Vol. 8 Nicole Brunnhuber, The Faces of Janus:
English-language Fiction by German-speaking Exiles in Great
Britain, 1933–45.
240 pp. 2005.
ISBN 3-03910-180-3 / US-ISBN 0-8204-6989-0.

Vol. 9 · Lee Kyung-Boon, Musik und Literatur im Exil: Hanns Eislers
dodekaphone Exilkantaten.
306 pp. 2001.
US-ISBN 0-8204-4938-5.

Vol. 10 Regina U. Hahn, The Democratic Dream: Stefan Heym in
America.
150 pp. 2002.
ISBN 3-906768-53-8 / US-ISBN 0-8204-5865-1.

Vol. 11 Alexander Stephan (ed.), Exile and Otherness:
New Approaches to the Experience of
the Nazi Refugees.
308 pp. 2005.
ISBN 3-03910-561-2 / US-ISBN 0-8204-7588-2.

Vol. 12 Andrea Hammel, Everyday Life as Alternative Space
in Exile Writing: The novels of Anna Gmeyner, Selma Kahn,
Hilde Spiel, Martina Wied and Hermynia Zur Mühlen.
264 pp. 2007.
ISBN 978-3-03910-524-3.